Lecture Notes in Computer Science 2588

Edited by G. Goos, J. Hartmanis, and J. van Leeuwen

Springer

Berlin
Heidelberg
New York
Barcelona
Hong Kong
London
Milan
Paris
Tokyo

Alexander Gelbukh (Ed.)

Computational Linguistics and Intelligent Text Processing

4th International Conference, CICLing 2003
Mexico City, Mexico, February 16-22, 2003
Proceedings

 Springer

Series Editors

Gerhard Goos, Karlsruhe University, Germany
Juris Hartmanis, Cornell University, NY, USA
Jan van Leeuwen, Utrecht University, The Netherlands

Volume Editor

Alexander Gelbukh
Instituto Politécnico Nacional (IPN)
Centro de Investigación en Computación (CIC)
Col. Zacatenco, CP 07738, Mexico D.F., Mexico
E-mail: gelbukh@cic.ipn.mx

Cataloging-in-Publication Data applied for

A catalog record for this book is available from the Library of Congress

Bibliographic information published by Die Deutsche Bibliothek
Die Deutsche Bibliothek lists this publication in the Deutsche Nationalbibliographie;
detailed bibliographic data is available in the Internet at <http://dnb.ddb.de>.

CR Subject Classification (1998): H.3, I.2.7, I.7, I.2, F.4.3

ISSN 0302-9743
ISBN 3-540-00532-3 Springer-Verlag Berlin Heidelberg New York

Springer-Verlag Berlin Heidelberg New York
a member of BertelsmannSpringer Science+Business Media GmbH

http://www.springer.de

© Springer-Verlag Berlin Heidelberg 2003
Printed in Germany

Typesetting: Camera-ready by author, data conversion by PTP-Berlin, Stefan Sossna e.K.
Printed on acid-free paper   SPIN: 10872459   06/3142   5 4 3 2 1 0

Preface

CICLing 2003 (www.CICLing.org) was the 4th annual Conference on Intelligent Text Processing and Computational Linguistics. It was intended to provide a balanced view of the cutting-edge developments in both the theoretical foundations of computational linguistics and the practice of natural language text processing with its numerous applications. A feature of CICLing conferences is their wide scope that covers nearly all areas of computational linguistics and all aspects of natural language processing applications. The conference is a forum for dialogue between the specialists working in these two areas.

This year we were honored by the presence of our keynote speakers *Eric Brill* (Microsoft Research, USA), *Aravind Joshi* (U. Pennsylvania, USA), *Adam Kilgarriff* (Brighton U., UK), and *Ted Pedersen* (U. Minnesota, USA), who delivered excellent extended lectures and organized vivid discussions.

Of 92 submissions received, after careful reviewing 67 were selected for presentation; 43 as full papers and 24 as short papers, by 150 authors from 23 countries: Spain (23 authors), China (20), USA (16), Mexico (13), Japan (12), UK (11), Czech Republic (8), Korea and Sweden (7 each), Canada and Ireland (5 each), Hungary (4), Brazil (3), Belgium, Germany, Italy, Romania, Russia and Tunisia (2 each), Cuba, Denmark, Finland and France (1 each).

In addition to the high scientific level, one of the success factors of CICLing conferences is their excellent cultural program. CICLing 2003 was held in Mexico, a wonderful country very rich in culture, history, and nature. The participants of the conference—in their souls active explorers of the world—had a chance to see the solemn 2000-year-old pyramids of the legendary Teotihuacanas, a monarch butterfly wintering site where the old pines are covered with millions of butterflies as if they were leaves, a great cave with 85-meter halls and a river flowing from it, Aztec warriors dancing in the street in their colorful plumages, and the largest anthropological museum in the world; see photos at www.CICLing.org.

A conference is the result of the work of many people. First of all I would like to thank the members of the Program Committee for the time and effort they devoted to the reviewing of the submitted articles and to the selection process. Especially helpful were Ted Pedersen and Grigori Sidorov, as well as many others—a complete list would be too long.

Obviously I thank the authors for their patience in the preparation of the papers, not to mention the very development of their scientific results that form the basis for this book. I also express my most cordial thanks to the members of the local Organizing Committee for their considerable contribution to making this conference become a reality. Last, but not least, I thank our sponsoring organization—the Center for Computing Research (CIC, www.cic.ipn.mx) of the National Polytechnic Institute (IPN), Mexico, for hosting the conference for the fourth time.

December 2002   Alexander Gelbukh

Program Committee

1. Barbu, Cătălina (U. Wolverhampton, UK)
2. Boitet, Christian (CLIPS-IMAG, France)
3. Bolshakov, Igor (CIC-IPN, Mexico)
4. Bontcheva, Kalina (U. Sheffield, UK)
5. Brusilovsky, Peter (U. Pittsburgh, USA)
6. Calzolari, Nicoletta (ILC-CNR, Italy)
7. Carroll, John, (U. Sussex, UK)
8. Cassidy, Patrick (MICRA Inc., USA)
9. Cristea, Dan (U. Iasi, Romania)
10. Gelbukh, Alexander (**Chair**, CIC-IPN, Mexico)
11. Hasida, Kôiti (Electrotechnical Laboratory, AIST, Japan)
12. Harada, Yasunari (Waseda U., Japan)
13. Hirst, Graeme (U. Toronto, Canada)
14. Johnson, Frances (Manchester Metropolitan U., UK)
15. Kharrat, Alma (Microsoft Research, USA)
16. Kittredge, Richard (CoGenTex Inc., USA / Canada)
17. Knudsen, Line (U. Copenhagen, Denmark)
18. Koch, Gregers (U. Copenhagen, Denmark)
19. Kübler, Sandra (U. Tübingen, Germany)
20. Lappin, Shalom (King's College, UK)
21. Laufer, Natalia (Russian Institute of Artificial Intelligence, Russia)
22. López López, Aurelio (INAOE, Mexico)
23. Loukanova, Roussanka (Uppsala U., Sweden)
24. Lüdeling, Anke (U. Stuttgart, Germany)
25. Maegard, Bente (Centre for Language Technology, Denmark)
26. Martín-Vide, Carlos (U. Rovira i Virgili, Spain)
27. Mel'čuk, Igor (U. Montreal, Canada)
28. Metais, Elisabeth (U. Versailles, France)
29. Mikheev, Andrei (U. Edinburgh, UK)
30. Mitkov, Ruslan (U. Wolverhampton, UK)
31. Murata, Masaki (KARC-CRL, Japan)
32. Narin'yani, Alexander (Russian Institute of Artificial Intelligence, Russia)
33. Nevzorova, Olga (Kazan State U., Russia)
34. Nirenburg, Sergei (New Mexico U., USA)
35. Palomar, Manuel (U. Alicante, USA / Spain)
36. Pedersen, Ted (U. Minnesota, Duluth, USA)
37. Pineda Cortes, Luis Alberto (UNAM, Mexico)
38. Piperidis, Stelios (Institute for Language and Speech Processing, Greece)
39. Ren, Fuji (U. Tokushima, Japan)
40. Sag, Ivan (Stanford U., USA)
41. Sharoff, Serge (Russian Institute of Artificial Intelligence, Russia)
42. Sidorov, Grigori (CIC-IPN, Mexico)
43. Sun Maosong (Tsinghua U., China)
44. Tait, John (U. Sunderland, UK)
45. Trujillo, Arturo (Canon Research Centre Europe, UK)

46. T'sou Ka-yin, Benjamin (City U. Hong Kong, Hong Kong)
47. Van Guilder, Linda (MITRE Corp., USA)
48. Verspoor, Karin (Applied Semantics, Inc., USA / The Netherlands)
49. Vilares Ferro, Manuel (U. Vigo, Spain)
50. Wilks, Yorick (U. Sheffield, UK)

Additional Reviewers

1. Bassi, Alejandro (U. Chile, Chile)
2. Ferrández, Antonio (U. Alicante, Spain)
3. Hu Jiawei (Canon Research Centre Europe, UK)
4. Inkpen, Diana (U. Toronto, Canada)
5. Koeling, Rob (U. Sussex, UK)
6. Liepert, Martina (U. Tübingen, Germany)
7. Loukachevitch, Natalia (Moscow State University, Russia)
8. Martinez-Barco, Patricio (U. Alicante, Spain)
9. McCarthy, Diana (U. Sussex, UK)
10. McLauchlan, Mark (U. Sussex, UK)
11. Montoyo, Andrés (U. Alicante, Spain)
12. Morris, Jane (U. Toronto, Canada)
13. Müller, Frank Henrik (U. Tübingen, Germany)
14. Muñoz, Rafael (U. Alicante, Spain)
15. Paun, Gheorghe (Romanian Academy, Romania)
16. Pazos Rangel, Rodolfo (CENIDET, Mexico)
17. Roessler, Marc (GMU Duisburg, Germany)
18. Saiz Noeda, Maximiliano (U. Alicante, Spain)
19. Stokoe, Christopher (U. Sunderland, UK)
20. Streiter, Oliver (European Academy, Italy)
21. Suárez, Armando (U. Alicante, Spain)
22. Ule, Tylman (U. Tübingen, Germany)
23. Zong Chengqing (Inst. of Automation, China)

Local Organizing Committee

Baranda, Elda
Gelbukh, Alexander (**Chair**)
Hernández Lara, Luis
Salcedo Camarena, Teresa
Sandoval Reyes, Alejandro
Torres Frausto, Raquel
Vargas Garcia, Soila

Organization. Website and Contact

The conference was organized by the Natural Language and Text Processing Laboratory (www.cic.ipn.mx/Investigacion/ltexto.html) of the Center for Computing Research (CIC, Centro de Investigación en Computación, www.cic.ipn.mx) of the National Polytechnic Institute (IPN, Instituto Politécnico Nacional, www.ipn.mx), Mexico City, Mexico.

The website of the CICLing conferences is www.CICLing.org (mirrored at www.cic.ipn.mx/cicling). Contact: gelbukh@CICLing.org; also gelbukh@cic.ipn.mx, gelbukh@gelbukh.com; see also www.gelbukh.com.

Table of Contents

Syntax and POS Tagging

Parsing Techniques

Morphology

Word Sense Disambiguation

Dictionary, Lexicon, Ontology

Corpus and Language Statistics

Machine Translation and Bilingual Corpora

Text Generation

Natural Language Interfaces

Speech Processing

Intelligent Text Processing

Information Retrieval and Information Extraction

Text Categorization and Clustering

Summarization

Starting with Complex Primitives Pays Off*

Aravind K. Joshi

University of Pennsylvania, Philadelphia, PA 19104, USA
joshi@linc.cis.upenn.edu

Abstract. For the specification of formal systems for a grammar formalism, conventional mathematical wisdom dictates that we start with primitives (basic primitive structures or building blocks) as simple as possible and then introduce various operations for constructing more complex structures. Alternatively, we can start with complex (more complicated) primitives that directly capture crucial linguistic properties and then introduce some general operations (language independent operations) for composing them. This latter approach has led to the so-called strongly lexicalized grammars, providing some new insights into syntactic description, semantic composition, discourse structure, language generation, psycholinguistic and statistical processing, all with computational implications. In this paper, we will illustrate some of these insights in the context of the lexicalized tree-adjoining grammar (LTAG).

1 Introduction

How complex are the primitives of a formal system for characterizing various properties of language? Conventional mathematical approach is to start with primitives (basic primitive structures or building blocks) as simple as possible and then introduce various operations for composition of more complex structures. There is another perspective we can take. We can start with complex (more complicated) primitive structures that directly capture crucial linguistic properties and then introduce some general, language independent operations, for composing these complex structures. This latter approach allows the possibility of localizing almost all complexity (in the form of a range of dependencies of various kinds) in the set of primitives, thereby pushing apparently non-local dependencies to become local, i.e., they are instantiated in the primitive structures to start with. This approach has led to some new insights into syntactic description, semantic composition, discourse structure, language generation, psycholinguistic and statistical processing– all of these are, of course, directly related to computational properties of the system. We will illustrate some of these insights in the context of the framework of the lexicalized tree-adjoining grammar (LTAG).

The complexity of the primitives specifies a domain of locality, i.e., a domain over which various dependencies (syntactic and semantic) can be specified. In

---

* This work was partially supported by NSF grant NSF-STC SBR 8920230

a context-free grammar (CFG) the domain of locality is the one level tree corresponding to a rule in a CFG (Fig. 1). It is easily seen that the arguments of a predicate (for example, the two arguments of likes) are not in the same local domain

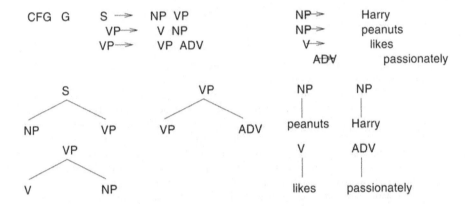

Fig. 1. Domain of locality of a context-free grammar

The two arguments are distributed over the two rules (two domains of locality)– $S \rightarrow NP\, VP$ and $VP \rightarrow V\, NP$. They can be brought together by introducing a rule $S \rightarrow NP\, V\, VP$. However, then the structure provided by the VP node is lost. We should also note here that not every rule (domain) in the CFG in (Fig. 1) is lexicalized. The four rules on the right are lexicalized, i.e., they have a lexical anchor. The rules on the left are not lexicalized. The second and the third rules on the left are almost lexicalized, in the sense that they each have a preterminal category (V in the second rule and ADV in the third rule), i.e., by replacing V by likes and ADV by passionately these two rules will become lexicalized. However, the first rule on the left ($S \rightarrow NP\, VP$) cannot be lexicalized. Can a CFG be lexicalized, i.e., given a CFG, G, can we construct another CFG, G', such that every rule in G' is lexicalized and $T(G)$, the set of (sentential) trees (i.e., the tree language of G) is the same as the tree language $T(G')$ of G'? It can be shown that this is not the case (Joshi and Schabes [2]). This follows from the fact that the domain of locality of CFG is a one level tree corresponding to a rule in the grammar.

It can be shown that CFGs can be lexicalized (Joshi and Schabes [2]), provided we extend the domain of locality, i.e., make the primitives more complex. This is achieved by making the primitives larger than just the one level trees as in a CFG. Further, we introduce two composition operations: (1) substitution (Fig. 2) and (2) adjoining (Fig. 3). Adjoining involves splicing (inserting) one tree into another. More specifically, a tree β as shown in Fig. 3 is inserted (adjoined) into the tree α at the node X resulting in the tree γ.

The tree β, called an auxiliary tree, has a special form. The root node is labelled with a nonterminal, say X and on the frontier there is also a node

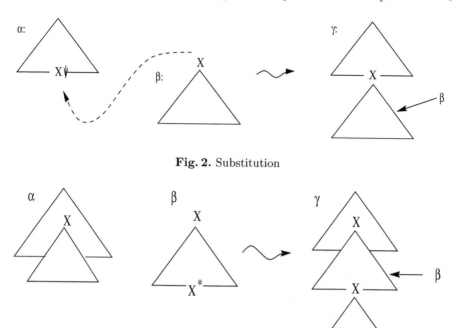

Fig. 2. Substitution

Fig. 3. Adjoining

labeled X called the foot node (marked with *). There could be other nodes (terminal or nonterminal) nodes on the frontier of β, the nonterminal nodes will be marked as substitution sites (with a vertical arrow). Thus if there is another occurrence of X (other than the foot node marked with *) on the frontier of β it will be marked with the vertical arrow and that will be a substitution site. Given this specification, adjoining β to α at the node X in α is uniquely defined. If in a tree grammar with these two composition operations, each elementary (primitive) tree is lexicalized, i.e., there is a lexical item associated with one of the preterminal nodes (we call this lexical item as the lexical anchor of the tree), it is called a lexicalized tree-adjoining grammar (LTAG). In short, LTAG consists of a finite set of elementary trees, each lexicalized with at least one lexical anchor. The elementary trees are either initial or auxiliary trees. Auxiliary trees have been defined already. Initial trees are those for which all nonterminal nodes on the frontier are substitution nodes.

1.1   Lexicalized Tree-Adjoining Grammar

Rather than giving formal definitions for LTAG and derivations in LTAG we will give a simple example to illustrate some key aspects of LTAG. We show some elementary trees of a toy LTAG grammar of English. Fig. 4 shows two elementary trees for a verb such as likes. The tree α_1 is anchored on likes and encapsulates the two arguments of the verb. The tree α_2 corresponds to the object extraction

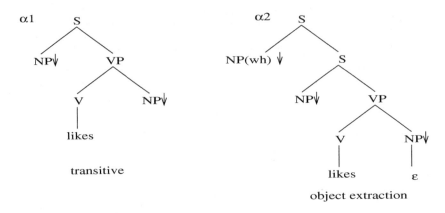

Fig. 4. LTAG: Elementary trees for *likes*

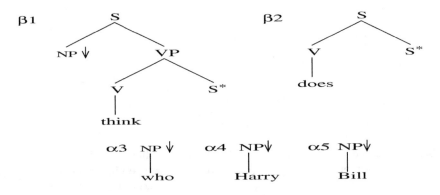

Fig. 5. LTAG: Sample elementary trees

construction. Since we need to encapsulate all the arguments of the verb in each elementary tree for likes, for the object extraction construction, for example, we need to make the elementary tree associated with likes large enough so that the extracted argument is in the same elementary domain. Thus, in principle, for each 'minimal' construction in which likes can appear (for example, subject extraction, topicalization, subject relative, object relative, passive, etc.) there will be an elementary tree associated with that construction. By 'minimal' we mean when all recursion has been factored away. This factoring of recursion away from the domain over which the dependencies have to be specified is a crucial aspect of LTAGs as they are used in linguistic descriptions. This factoring allows all dependencies to be localized in the elementary domains. In this sense, there will, therefore, be no long distance dependencies as such. They will all be local and will become long distance on account of the composition operations, especially adjoining.

Fig. 5 shows some additional trees. Trees α_3, α_4, and α_5 are initial trees and trees β_1 and β_2 are auxiliary trees with foot nodes marked with *. A derivation

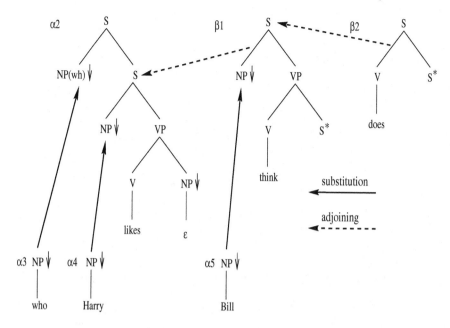

Fig. 6. LTAG derivation for *who does Bill think Harry likes*

using the trees in Fig. 4 and Fig. 5 is shown in Fig. 6. The trees for who and Harry are substituted in the tree for likes at the respective NP nodes, the tree for Bill is substituted in the tree for think at the NP node, the tree for does is adjoined to the root node of the tree for think tree (adjoining at the root node is a special case of adjoining), and finally the derived auxiliary tree (after adjoining β_2 to β_1) is adjoined to the indicated interior S node of the tree α_2. This derivation results in the derived tree for who does Bill think Harry likes as shown in Fig. 7. Note that the dependency between who and the complement NP in α_2 (local to that tree) has been stretched in the derived tree in Fig. 7. This tree is the conventional tree associated with the sentence.

However, in LTAG there is also a derivation tree, the tree that records the history of composition of the elementary trees associated with the lexical items in the sentence. This derivation tree is shown in Fig. 8. The nodes of the tree are labeled by the tree labels such as α_2 together with the lexical anchor.[1] The derivation tree is the crucial derivation structure for LTAG. We can obviously build the derived tree from the derivation tree. For semantic computation the derivation tree (and not the derived tree) is the crucial object. Compositional semantics is defined on the derivation tree. The idea is that for each elementary tree there is a semantic representation associated with it and these representations are composed using the derivation tree. Since the semantic representation

---

[1] The derivation trees of LTAG have a close relationship to the dependency trees, although there are some crucial differences; however, the semantic dependencies are the same.

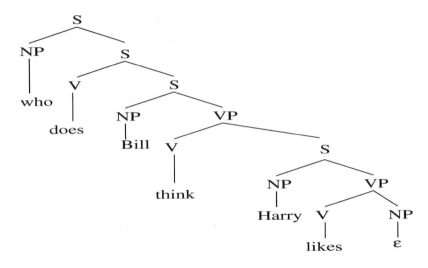

Fig. 7. LTAG derived tree for *who does Bill think Harry likes*

for each elementary tree is directly associated with the tree there is no need to reproduce necessarily the internal hierarchy in the elementary tree in the semantic representation(Joshi and Vijay-Shanker [3] and Kallmeyer and Joshi [4]). This allows the so-called 'flat' semantic representation as well as helps in dealing with some non-compositional aspects as in the case of rigid and flexible idioms[2].

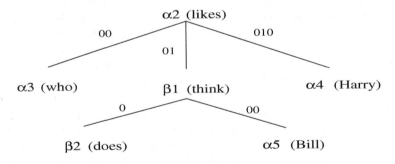

Fig. 8. LTAG derivation tree

2   An Alternate Perspective on Adjoining

In adjoining we insert an auxiliary tree, say with root and foot nodes labeled with X in a tree at a node with label X. In Fig. 9 and Fig. 10 we present an

---

[2] For details of the LTAG grammar for English and the associated parser, the XTAG system, go to http://www/cis.upenn.edu/xtag

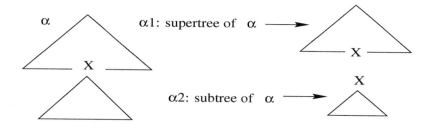

Fig. 9. Adjoining as Wrapping 1

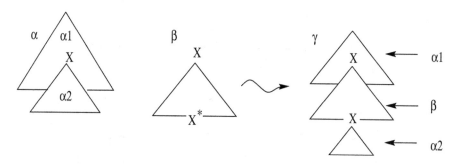

Fig. 10. Adjoining as Wrapping 2

alternate perspective on adjoining. The tree α which receives adjunction at X can be viewed as made up of two trees, the supertree at X and the subtree at X as shown in Fig.9. Now, instead of the auxiliary tree β adjoined to the tree α at X we can view this composition as a wrapping operation–the supertree of α and the subtree of α are wrapped around the auxiliary tree β as shown in Fig. 10. The resulting tree γ is the same as before. Wrapping of the supertree at the root node of β is like adjoining at the root (a special case of adjoining) and the wrapping of the subtree at the foot note of β is like substitution. Hence, this wrapping operation can be described in terms of substitution and adjoining. This is clearly seen in the linguistic example in Fig. 11 and Fig. 12. The auxiliary tree β can be adjoined to the tree α at the indicated node in α as shown in Fig. 11. Alternatively, we can view this composition as adjoining the supertree α_1 (the wh tree) at the root node of β and substitution of the subtree α_2 (the likes tree) at the foot node of β as shown in Fig. 12. The two ways of composing α and β are semantically coherent.

The wrapping perspective can be formalized in terms of the so-called multi-component LTAGs (MC-LTAGs). They are called multi-component because the elementary objects can be sets of trees, in our examples, we have two components (in which α was split). When we deal with multi-components we can violate the locality of the composition very quickly because the different components may be 'attached' (by adjoining or substitution) to different nodes of a tree and these nodes may or not be part of an elementary tree depending on

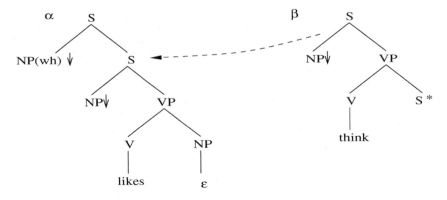

Fig. 11. Wrapping as substitution and adjunction 1

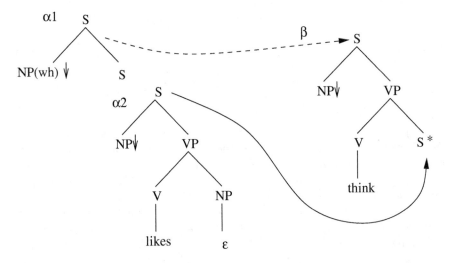

Fig. 12. Wrapping as substitution and adjunction 2

whether the tree receiving the multi-component attachments is an elementary or a derived tree. We obtain what are known as tree-local MC-LTAGs if we put the constraint that the tree receiving multi-component attachments must be an elementary tree. It is known that tree-local MC-TAGs are weakly equivalent to LTAGs, however they can give rise to structural descriptions not obtainable by LTAGs, i.e., they are more powerful than LTAG in the sense of strong generative capacity (Weir [7]),Thus the alternate perspective leads to greater strong generative capacity without increasing the weak generative capacity. MC-LTAG also allow the possibility of defining flexible composition[3]. Given two structures, X and Y, elementary or derived, we can compose them in any order, i.e., X with Y or Y with X subject to the following requirement– the structure which is being composed into must be an elementary structure. This requirement assures locality of composition, in the sense that the different nodes in the tree being composed into are all part of the same elementary tree. It can be shown that MC-LTAG can correctly describe (syntactically and semantically) all possible word orders within and across clauses up to two levels of embedding (i.e, a matrix clause, embedding another clause, which in turn embeds yet another clause). Beyond two levels of embedding, although the relevant strings can be generated but certain compositions of the MC-LTAG trees may not be semantically coherent. Note that this a formal result. Here we have a case where a formal result leads to a result which is traditionally described as a performance result, i.e., a psycholinguistic result (Joshi, Becker, and Rambow [1]).

So far we have illustrated how s system such as LTAG (with complex primitives) has led to some novel insights for syntactic description, semantic composition, and psycholinguistic processing. In the next section, we will describe some insights of this perspective for discourse structure.

2.1   Discourse Structure

At the discourse level, one can take discourse connectives as predicates (lexical anchors) for elementary trees with argument positions to be filled in by the appropriate clauses, some of which may be in the same sentence in which the connective appears, and others in preceding sentences in the discourse. Thus we have dependencies here which are analogous to the dependencies encoded in the LTAG trees at the sentence level (Webber et al. [5]). These dependencies can be stretched also as in the discourse D(1) below.

D1:(a) One the one hand, Fred likes beans. (b) Not only does he eat them for dinner (c) but he also eats them for breakfast and snacks. (d) On the other hand, he is allergic to them.
on the one hand and on the other hand is a paired connective , multiply anchoring the same discourse LTAG tree. The dependencies between the arguments of this tree have been stretched by the adjoining of the elementary tree corresponding to the connective but

Arguments of a discourse connective may be structural (i.e., clauses encoded in the parse trees) or they may be anaphoric (much like pronouns and definite NPs) as in the discourse D(2) below.

D2: (a) John loves Barolo. (b) So he ordered three cases of the '97. (c) But he had to cancel the order (d) because then he discovered he was broke.
The connective then gets its right argument from (d) and its left argument from (b) and must cross the structural connection between (c) and (d) associated with because. Treating the left argument of then as anaphoric avoids crossing. There

---

[3] Flexible composition is also possible in the standard LTAG. However, in this case, flexible composition does not give any increased strong generative power.

are, of course, other reasons for treating the left argument as anaphoric (see, for example, Webber et al. [6]).

3 Summary

We have shown that by starting with complex primitives and localizing dependencies within the domain of the elementary (primitive) structures, in contrast to starting with simple primitives, leads to some novel insights into syntactic description, semantic composition, discourse structure, and some psycholinguistic issues, all relevant to computational properties.

References

1. Joshi, A. K., Becker, T., Rambow, O.: Complexity of Scrambling: A New Twist to the Competence-Performance Distinction. A. Abeille and O. Rambow (editors), *Tree-Adjoining Grammar*, CSLI, Stanford (2000) 167–182
2. Joshi, A. K., Schabes, Y.: Tree-Adjoining Grammars. G. Rosenberg and A. Salomaa, editors, *Handbook of Formal Languages*, Springer, Berlin (1997) 69–123
3. Joshi, A. K., Vijay-Shanker, K.: Compositional Semantics with Lexicalized Tree-adjoining Grammar (LTAG): How Much Underspecification is Necessary? H.C. Bunt and E.G.C. Thijsse, editors, *Proceedings of the Third International Workshop on Computational Semantics (IWCS-3)*, Tilburg. (1999) 131–145
4. Kallmeyer, L., Joshi, A. K.: Factoring Predicate Argument and Scope Semantics: Underspecified Semantics with LTAG. *Proc. of the Twelfth Amsterdam Colloquium*, University of Amsterdam, Amsterdam (1999) 169–174
5. Webber, B., Joshi, A. K., Knott, A., Stone, M.: What are Little Texts Made of? A Structural and Presuppositional Account Using Lexicalized TAG. *Proceedings of the International Workshop on Levels of Representation in Discourse (LORID '99)*, Edinburgh (1999) 151–156
6. Webber, B., Joshi, A. K., Knott, A., Stone, M.: Anaphora and Discourse Structure. To appear in *Computational Linguistics* (2003)
7. Weir, D.: *Characterizing Mildly Context-Sensitive Grammar Formalisms*. Ph.D. Dissertation, University of Pennsylvania, Philadelphia (1988)

Things Are Not Always Equal

Ronald M. Kaplan and Annie Zaenen

Palo Alto Research Center,
3333, Coyote Hill Road, Palo Alto, CA 94304
{Kaplan|Zaenen}@parc.com

Abstract. In this paper we discuss the use of subsumption as device to model linguistic generalizations. Constraint-based linguistic frameworks make ample use of equality relations but, although equality is nothing but two-way subsumption, subsumption itself has not been used much, except as a meta-grammatical device in the HPSG type hierarchy. Here we investigate two cases where subsumption is a useful device to model syntactic phenomena.

1 Introduction

Current constraint-based approaches to natural language modeling use equality relations to assemble information that belongs to one informational unit at an abstract level of representation even though it belongs to more than one unit in the surface representation. This reliance on equality comes a bit as a surprise when one looks back at earlier or current transformational approaches that tend to stress the asymmetry or even the anti-symmetry of linguistic phenomena. For instance, it has often been observed that elements higher-up in a treelike representation control those lower down. This is formalized through c-command constraints on these elements.

Constraint-based approaches tend to retain the spirit of the main device used in transformational approaches by modeling such command relations through tree-structured configurations (e.g. by limiting the association of infinitivals to VP's). In this paper we propose another mechanism to manage such relations, subsumption, and illustrate its use in two cases where the tree configuration solution leads to problems that do not arise in our proposal, namely Partial Fronting in German and Subject Inversion in French.

Subsumption is a familiar relation within several constraint-based formalisms (see e.g. discussions in [3] and [11]). It is used as a meta-grammatical device to characterize the type hierarchy in HSPG, and in LFG the f-structure assigned to a sentence is defined to be the subsumption-minimal model for the set of constraints associated with the sentence. In LFG the subsumption relation is also implicit in the definition of the restriction operator proposed in [5], and in the generalization operator used in [6]'s, treatment of coordination. However, explicit subsumption constraints have not been used directly in accounts of any syntactic phenomena.

A. Gelbukh (Ed.): CICLing 2003, LNCS 2588, pp. 11–21, 2003.
© Springer-Verlag Berlin Heidelberg 2003

2 Subsumption and Linguistic Phenomena

Informally, subsumption establishes an ordering relation between two units of information stating that the one subsuming the other contains less information than the one that is subsumed. The formal definition of subsumption used in this paper is given in Figure 1. and, for comparison the definition of equality is given in Figure 2.

Subsumption: $f \sqsubseteq g$ **iff**

f and g are the same symbol or semantic form, or
f and g are both f-structures, $\mathrm{Dom}(f) \subseteq \mathrm{Dom}(g)$, and $(f\, a) \sqsubseteq (g\, a)$ for all $a \in \mathrm{Dom}(f)$,
or f and g are both sets, and every element of f $\sqsubseteq$ some element of g

$$f = \begin{bmatrix} A & \begin{bmatrix} C & + \end{bmatrix} \end{bmatrix} \sqsubseteq \begin{bmatrix} A & \begin{bmatrix} C & + \\ D & - \end{bmatrix} \\ B & E,, \end{bmatrix} = g$$

Fig. 1.

Equality: $f = g$ **iff**

f and g are the same symbol or semantic form, or
f and g are both f-structures, $\mathrm{Dom}(f) = \mathrm{Dom}(g)$, and $(f\, a) = (g\, a)$ for all $a \in \mathrm{Dom}(f)$,
or
f and g are both sets, and every element of g = some element of f

$$f = \begin{bmatrix} A & \begin{bmatrix} C & + \\ D & - \end{bmatrix} \\ B & E,, \end{bmatrix} = \begin{bmatrix} A & \begin{bmatrix} C & + \\ D & - \end{bmatrix} \\ B & E,, \end{bmatrix} = g$$

Fig. 2.

A linguistic phenomenon that one might consider modeling with subsumption is the relation between an equi controlling subject and the understood subject in an embedded clause in a sentence such as 1

1.   John tries to work hard.

As has often been observed, in English sentence 2 is ungrammatical as is any other version in which the shared subject shows up in the embedded position.

2. * Tries to John work hard.

Note, however, that an equality approach to equi via functional control such as found in LFG, does not rule out (2), as was first discussed in [13], in the context of some Dutch facts. LFG grammars of English handle the ungrammaticality of 2 with a VP phrase-structure rule that does not provide a subject NP position in infinitival clauses.

A different approach to the phenomenon would be to propose that the relation between the matrix subject and the embedded subjects is one of subsumption rather than of equality. Under that assumption the information would flow from the matrix position to the embedded position and not vice versa, as diagrammed in Figure 3. If the NP showed up in an embedded position, its information would not flow up to the matrix and the f-structure would be incomplete.

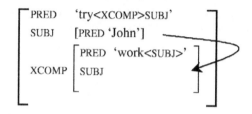

Fig. 3.

For English this seems an unnecessary innovation as the PSR solution is adequate. In other languages, however, it is not so clear that the PSR solution is the simplest and most straightforward one available. In what follows we look at two phenomena, Partial Verb Phrase Fronting (henceforward, PVPF) in German and Stylistic Inversion (Henceforward, SI) in French and show how a subsumption based analysis accounts of a wide range of facts.

3 Partial VP Fronting in German

As has been discussed extensively in the literature (see e.g. [12], [10], [9]), sentences such as the following are grammatical in German[1].

3. a. Das Buch zu geben schien Hans dem Mädchen.
    The book to given seemed Hans the girl.

  b. Dem Mädchen zu geben schien Hans das Buch.
    The girl to give seemed Hans the book.

    'Hans seemed to give the girl the book.'

4. a. Ein Fehler unterlaufen ist ihr noch nie.
    An error happened-to is her still Never
    'Until now she has never made a mistake.'

---

[1] With other researchers we assume that discourse structure constraints account for the degree of acceptability of various examples and concentrate on the structural characteristics of PVPF.

b. Ein Aussenseiter gewonnen hat   hier   noch nie.
   An   outsider   won   has   here   still never.
   'Until now no outsider has won here.'

In the sentences in 3 various pieces of what is in general assumed to be a VP have been topicalized (there are more possibilities); in 4, some kind of infinitival clause is topicalized that has the particularity of containing a subject (the nominative NP). For traditional transformational accounts these sentences present problems because the topicalized elements do not correspond to units that are available in the Mittelfeld from where they are hypothesized to be moved. Non-transformational theories can also have problems depending on their devices for subcategorization.

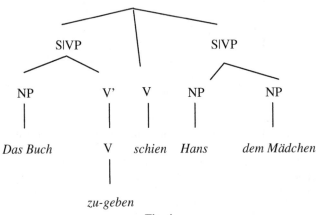

Fig. 4.

In LFG, there are rather less problems than in other theories because the framework allows very supple PSR in which most if not all constituents are optional. Subcategorization constraints are enforced at the level of the f-structure, where the Completeness and Coherence principles need to be satisfied[2]. In traditional LFG a sentence like 3a will have the c-structure and f-structure representation in Fig. 4 and 5 respectively.

These structures are licensed by the following set of rules and lexical entry.

5. S' →   XP   V   (S|VP)
             ($\uparrow$ TENSE) $\uparrow$=$\downarrow$

     where XP = {   NP | S|VP | ...}
                    ($\uparrow$ TOP) =$\downarrow$ ($\uparrow$ TOP) =$\downarrow$
                ($\uparrow$ COMPS* NGF) = $\downarrow$ ($\uparrow$ COMPS* XCOMP) = $\downarrow$

6. a. S|VP →   NP*   (V')   (S|VP)

---

[2] Note that Completeness and Coherence are also rather simple notions in LFG: they hold over complete f-structures: there is no cancellation procedure or the like. Subjects are treated like any other arguments and the obliqueness hierarchy holds only as a metaprinciple.

$$(\uparrow \text{COMPS* NGF}) = \downarrow \quad \uparrow = \downarrow \quad (\uparrow \text{XCOMP* COMPS}) = \downarrow$$

b.   V' →   (V')   V

$$(\uparrow \text{XCOMP}) = \downarrow \qquad\qquad \uparrow = \downarrow$$

$$(\uparrow \text{XCOMP}^{+} \text{NGF}) \neg\prec_{\text{f}} (\uparrow \text{NGF})$$

7.   scheinen   V $(\uparrow \text{PRED}) = \text{'seem} < (\uparrow \text{XCOMP}) > (\uparrow \text{SUBJ})\text{'}$
                     $(\uparrow \text{SUBJ}) = (\uparrow \text{XCOMP SUBJ})$

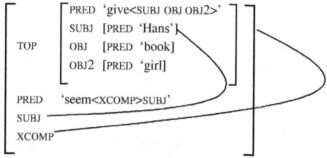

Fig. 5.

These rules are adapted from [17]. COMPS ranges over XCOMP and COMP[3]. NGF ranges over all nominal functions. The functional uncertainty equations (indicated by the Kleene star) define the functional paths that relate NP's in the Mittelfeld or the topicalized material to their embedded functions (see [7] for more information). The functional precedence constraints impose the appropriate ordering on the NP arguments of all the verbs in an XCOMP cluster (see [17] for discussion). Given that all the constraints are equality relations, it does not matter in which of the positions licensed by the PSR the equated entities show up in the c-structure. We do not distinguish between S and VP (and write the conflated category as S|VP). In this way, we allow the same elements in infinitival clauses and in tensed clauses except for the requirement that there be a tensed verb in second position.

While this allows for all the sentences in 3 and 4, it overgenerates. It will, for instance, allow two arguments to be fronted without the verb they depend on. Moreover this account does not allow us to determine from the f-structure what is topicalized and what is not[4].

---

[3] This is an overgeneralization for the dialects of German that allow only fronting out of XCOMPS. This type of variation is ignored in this paper.

[4] Whether this is important or not depends on one's view of the interaction between the f-structure and other modules of linguistic information: for argument structure and purely syntactic wellformedness conditions, this information is not important. But if we assume that there is a discourse-structural difference between the various versions of 3. and that the discourse structure is read off the f-structure without separate input from the c-structure (and even without covert c-structure information via f-precedence relations), the account given is clearly inadequate.

The use of subsumption will allow us to solve these two problems. Under that hypothesis, the relevant part of the rule given in 5 will be replaced by the following:

8. S' →   S|VP   V   S|VP
                          (↑TOP) = ↓   ↑ = ↓   ↑ = ↓
                   ↓ ⊑ (↑ COMPS* XCOMP)

Now the information flows only in one direction, from the topic to the embedded XCOMP, as diagrammed in Fig.6. The information in TOP is just what is fronted in the sentence.

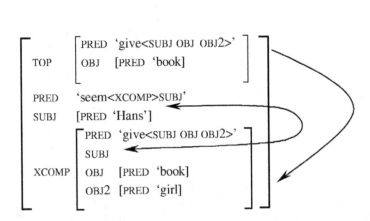

Fig. 6.

We can now also solve the problem with structures such as 9. where two dependents are topicalized without the verb they are dependent on: this becomes a case of incoherence.

9. * Ihr   ein   Märchen   wird   er   erzählen.
      Her   a   story   will   he   tell
    'He will tell her a story.'

But we need an adapted version of completeness because in grammatical sentences the topicalized elements will typically contain predicates that are locally not saturated. The following extension of the definition of Completeness in [4] will take care of this:

10.   An f-structure g is complete iff each of its subsidiary f-structures is
      either locally complete *or subsumes a subsidiary f-structure of g*
      that is locally complete.

This approach to PVPF in German allows us to model in a very simple way the interactions with raising and equi discussed in [9]. In the case of raising the subsumption analysis of fronting interacts with the equality analysis of raising to describe the fact that in sentences like those in 4. we have raising in the f-structure without c-structure raising. Simple equality allows for this as we pointed out above in our discussion of 2. If we assume that in equi the matrix subject subsumes the XCOMP subject we can account for the fact that, as observed by Meurers and De Kuthy, sentences like the following are ungrammatical:

11. * Ein   Aussenseiter zu   gewinnen   versuchte   hier   noch   nie.
        An   outsider   to   win   tried   here   still   never
        'An outsider never tried to win here.'

This is diagrammed as in Fig. 7

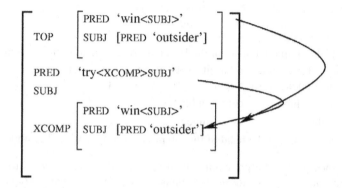

Fig. 7.

To summarize our proposal: the topic f-structure in PVPF always subsumes the XCOMP f-structure. The difference between raising and equi is that in raising there is an equality relation between the matrix and the embedded subject, whereas in equi the matrix subject subsumes the embedded one. The interaction of subsumption and equality thus provides a simple account of the syntax of VP fronting in German. For a more detailed discussion of these facts, see [18].

But new linguistic devices, however simple, are always suspect when they seem to solve only one problem. In the remainder of the paper we summarize another case in which subsumption plays a role in a simple account of another rather complex phenomenon, Stylistic Inversion in French.

4 Stylistic Inversion in French

A phenomenon discussed as much in recent French syntax, starting with [8], as PVPF has been discussed in German, is Stylistic Inversion (henceforth SI), illustrated in sentences such as 12.

12. Voici le texte qu' a écrit Paul.
    See-here the text that has written Paul
    'Here is the text that Paul wrote.'

A first question that arises with respect to these sentences is what the grammatical function is of the post-verbal NP. We follow here the analysis given in [2], who argue that it is a subject.

The observations in [2], that are most relevant to the discussion at hand concern the position of the post-verbal subject in sentences with equi and raising complements. They show that there are two possibilities. The one that interests us here is exemplified in 13[5].

13. a. le   livre que semblait recommander le patron
       the   book that seemed   recommend   the head
       du   labo à   cet étudiant
       of the lab   to this student
       'the book that the head of the lab could recommend to his student...'

    b. le   livre que pourrait recommander le patron
       the   book that might   recommend   the head
       du   labo à   cet étudiant
       of-the lab   to this student
       'the book that the head of the lab might recommend to this student...'

The presence of the oblique complement of the verb *recommander* (to recommend), shows that the subject of the matrix clause is within the lower VP (again see [2] for arguments to that effect, especially for arguments excluding the possibility that there might be free raising of any complement to a higher clause). The situation, then, is similar to that found in German: we have an argument of a higher verb realized as a constituent of a lower infinitival constituent. The difference between German and French is that here we have a case of raising (with *sembler*, to seem) and a case of equi control (with *pouvoir*, be able). Both allow the subject to show up in an embedded position, whereas in German this is only possible with raising verbs as discussed above. If we assume that in French, subject equi and subject raising are both equality relations, the facts are accounted for. This becomes clear when we look at the following lexical entries and partial phrase structure rules[6].

14. sembler   V $(\uparrow \text{PRED}) = \text{'sembler} \langle (\uparrow \text{XCOMP}) \rangle (\uparrow \text{SUBJ})\text{'}$
                    $(\uparrow \text{SUBJ}) = (\uparrow \text{XCOMP SUBJ})$

15. pouvoir   V $(\uparrow \text{PRED}) = \text{'pouvoir} \langle (\uparrow \text{SUBJ}), (\uparrow \text{XCOMP}) \rangle \text{'}$
                    $(\uparrow \text{SUBJ}) = (\uparrow \text{XCOMP SUBJ})$

16. S   →   NP   VP   NP
                $(\uparrow \text{SUBJ}) = \downarrow$ $\uparrow = \downarrow$ $(\uparrow \text{SUBJ}) = \downarrow$

---

[5] For a discussion of how an LFG analysis handles both possibilities, see [18].

[6] Several details about the phrase structure of French have not been worked out in detail, so the rules given in the text can only be indicative.

$$VP \rightarrow V \quad (NP) \quad PP^* \quad \ldots$$
$$\uparrow = \downarrow \quad (\uparrow\{SUBJ|OBJ\}) = \downarrow \quad (\uparrow OBL) = \downarrow$$

The rules in 16 allow a SUBJ within the VP and the equations in 14 and 15 insure that this subject is also interpreted as the subject of the matrix verb.

Let us now turn to object equi verbs and object raising. If we assume that object equi and object raising are also instances of an equality relation, we would expect SI to be possible in their complements too. But this is not what we find, as can be seen from the following examples.

17. * le   livre que le libraire   a   convaincu d' offrir Jean
     the book that the bookseller has convinced to offer Jean
     à   ma fille
     to my daughter
     'the book that the bookseller convinced Jean to offer to my daughter...'

This is an example of an equi construction. It is not completely clear whether there are object raising verbs in French but the perception verbs are plausible candidates (see [1]). Attempting to combine SI with them also gives ungrammatical results as illustrated in 18[7].

18. * La pierre que j' ai   vu   lancer ce   sale gamin contre
     the stone that I have seen throw this nasty kid   against
     Le   gendarme
     the policeman
     'the stone that I saw this nasty kid throw against the policeman.'

These problems can be solved by modeling object raising and object equi with subsumption rather than with the usual equality. So the traditional entries for *convaincre*, to convince, and *voir*, to see, given in 19 become the ones given in 20:

19. convaincre V $(\uparrow PRED) = $ 'convaincre$\langle(\uparrow SUBJ), (\uparrow OBJ), (\uparrow XCOMP)\rangle$'
                      $(\uparrow OBJ) = (\uparrow XCOMP\ SUBJ)$
    voir   V $(\uparrow PRED) = $ 'voir$\langle(\uparrow OBJ), (\uparrow XCOMP)\rangle$' $(\uparrow SUBJ)$
                      $(\uparrow OBJ) = (\uparrow XCOMP\ SUBJ)$

20. convaincre V $(\uparrow PRED) = $ 'convaincre$\langle(\uparrow SUBJ), (\uparrow OBJ), (\uparrow XCOMP)\rangle$'
                      $(\uparrow OBJ) \sqsubseteq (\uparrow XCOMP\ SUBJ)$
    voir   V $(\uparrow PRED) = $ 'voir$\langle(\uparrow OBJ), (\uparrow XCOMP)\rangle$' $(\uparrow SUBJ)$
                      $(\uparrow OBJ) \sqsubseteq (\uparrow XCOMP\ SUBJ)$

This change will force the OBJ to appear in the matrix clause and not in a lower position, allowing only for the versions in 21 and 22

---

[7] The source for this relative clause is:
(i)   J'ai   vu   ce sale gamin lancer une pierre contre le   gendarme.
       I have seen this nasty kid   throw a   stone against the policeman

21. le   livre   que le   libraire   a   convaincu Jean de offrir
    the   book   that the   bookseller   has   convinced Jean to offer
    à   ma   fille
    to   my   daughter
    'the book that the bookseller convinced Jean to offer to my daughter…'

22. la   pierre que j'   ai   vu   ce   sale   gamin lancer contre
    the   stone   that I   have   seen   this nasty kid   throw   against
    le   gendarme
    the   policeman
    'the stone that I saw this nasty kid throw against the policeman…'

5 Discussion

Traditionally in constraint-based grammar formalisms, word order is determined by
PSR. Here we have looked at two cases in which the word order approach is not
obvious. We have proposed a solution in which ordering relations on the f-structure
and subcategorization requirements constrain the c-structure realization of elements
even though they are optional in the c-structure.

The use of subsumption is a natural addition to the devices used in grammatical
formalisms as equality is simply two-directional subsumption. It raises, however,
questions about the nature of information flow in syntax. Most transformational
theories promote an asymmetric or even anti-symmetric view, where equi or raising
are associated with the appearance of the shared (through equi or raising) argument in
a commanding position in the surface structure. Constraint-based formalisms have
more stressed the non-directionality of the information flow and have in general left
non-symmetrical phenomena to be managed through PSR. Here we have presented two
cases in which some equi or raising controllers are not associated with a commanding
position in the c-structure. They illustrate that the non-symmetric intuitions are not
always correct. Subsumption, however, allows us to model the cases where a non-
symmetric relation holds. The interaction of equality and subsumption gives a simple
account of these differences in the behavior between symmetric and non-symmetric
cases whereas a pure PS plus equality account requires the development of less natural
devices (see e.g. [2] and [9]).

From the perspective of linguistic generalizations, it is interesting to observe that
the use of equality versus subsumption does not coincide with the difference between
equi and raising: on the basis of the German facts alone one might be tempted to look
for a semantically based explanation: the argument sharing in raising is purely
syntactical, whereas in equi, it is basically the referential index that is shared. But the
French facts show that this type of distinction does not coincide with the distinction
between the requirement that the shared argument be realized in the c-commanding
position or be allowed to show up in the c-commanded position. In French the
distinction is between subject-subject sharing and object-subject sharing.

References

[1]   Abeillé, A., 1997, Fonction ou position Objet? *Le gré des langues* 12, pp. 8–33.

[2]   Bonami, O., D. Godard & J.-M. Marandin, 1999, Constituency and Word Order in French Subject Inversion. In G. Bouma, E. Hinrichs, G.-J. Kruijff & R. Oehrle (eds.) *Constraints and Resources in Natural Language Syntax and Semantics*, pp. 21–40. Stanford, CSLI Publications.

[3]   Carpenter, B., 1992, *The Logic of Feature Structures*, Cambridge, Cambridge University Press

[4]   Kaplan, R. M. & J. Bresnan, 1982, Lexical Functional Grammar: A Formal System for Grammatical Representation. In J. Bresnan (ed.), *The Mental Representation of Grammatical Relations*, pp. 173–281. Cambridge, The MIT Press.

[5]   Kaplan, R. M. & J. Wedekind, 1993, Restriction and Correspondence-Based Translation. *Proceedings of the 6th Conference of the Association for Computational Linguistics European Chapter*, pp. 193–202, Utrecht University.

[6]   Kaplan, R. M. & J. Maxwell III, 1988, Constituent Coordination in Lexical-Functional Grammar, *Proceedings of COLING-88* vol 1. pp. 303–305, Budapest.

[7]   Kaplan, R. M. and A. Zaenen, 1989, Long-distance Dependencies, Constituent Structures, and Functional Uncertainty. In M. Baltin and A. Kroch (eds.) *Alternative Conceptions of Phrase Structure*, pp. 17–42, Chicago, The University of Chicago Press.

[8]   Kayne, R., 1972, Subject Inversion in French Interrogatives. In J.Casagrande & B. Saciuk (eds.) *Generative Studies in Romance Languages,* pp. 70–126. Rowley, MA, Newbury House.

[9]   Meurers, D. & K. De Kuthy, 2001, Case Assignment in Partially Fronted Constituents. In Chr. Rohrer, A. Rossdeutscher, and H. Kamp, *Linguistic Form and its Computation*, pp. 29–64, Stanford, CSLI Publications.

[10]   Nerbonne, J., 1995, Partial Verb Phrases and Spurious Ambiguities. In J. Nerbonne, K. Netter and C. Pollard, eds., *German in Head-Driven Phrase Structure Grammar*, pp. 109–150, Stanford, CSLI Publications.

[11]   Shieber, S. M., 1989, *Parsing and Type Inference for Natural and Computer Languages*, SRI International Technical Note 460, Menlo Park

[12]   Uszkoreit, H., 1987, Complex Fronting in German. In G. J. Huck and A. Ojeda, eds., *Discontinuous Constituency*, Syntax and Semantics, vol. 20, pp. 405–425, New York, Academic Press.

[13]   Zaenen, A. 1989, *The Place of Bevallen (please) in the Syntax of Dutch.* SSL-89-17, System Sciences Laboratory, PARC, Palo Alto.

[16]   Zaenen, Annie and Ronald M. Kaplan, 1985, Formal Devices for Linguistic Generalization: West Germanic Word Order in LFG. In M. Dalrymple, M. R. Kaplan, J. Maxwell III, and A. Zaenen (eds.) *Formal Issues in Lexical-Functional Grammar*, pp. 215–239, Stanford, CSLI Publications.

[17]   Zaenen, Annie & Ronald M. Kaplan, 2002, Subject Inversion in French: Equality and Inequality in LFG. In C. Beyssade, O. Bonami, P. Cabredo-Hofherr and F. Corblin, eds., *CSSP 2001,* Paris, Presses Universitaires de la Sorbonne.

[18]   Zaenen, Annie & Ronald M. Kaplan, 2002, Subsumption and Equality: German Partial Fronting in LFG. In M. Butt and T. King, eds. *Proceedings of the LFG02 Conference,* Stanford, CSLI on-line publications. http://csli-publications.stanford.edu

GIGs: Restricted Context-Sensitive Descriptive Power in Bounded Polynomial-Time

José M. Castaño

Computer Science Department
Brandeis University
Waltham, MA 02454, U.S.A.
jcastano@cs.brandeis.edu

Abstract. We present Global Index Grammars, a grammar formalism that uses a stack of indices associated to its productions. This formalism has restricted context-sensitive descriptive power. The recognition problem for this class of grammars is polynomial: the time complexity of the algorithm presented here is $O(n^6)$.

1 Introduction

There is increasing consensus on the necessity of formalisms more powerful than CFGs to account for certain phenomena that are characteristic of Natural Languages (NLs).[1] Typical natural language constructions that require context-sensitive power can be exemplified as [10]: reduplication, leading to languages of the form $\{ww \mid w \in \Sigma^*\}$, multiple agreements (or counting dependencies), corresponding to languages of the form $\{a^n b^n c^n \mid n \geq 1\}$, $\{a^n b^n c^n d^n \mid n \geq 1\}$, etc. and crossed agreements, as modeled by $\{a^n b^m c^n d^m \mid n, m \geq 1\}$.

Mildly context-sensitive grammars (MCSGs) [15] have been proposed as capable of modeling the above mentioned phenomena.[2] It has been claimed that a NL model must have the following properties:[3] a) constant growth property (or the stronger semilinearity property); b) polynomial parsability; c) limited cross-serial dependencies.

Mildly Context-sensitive Languages (MCSLs) have been characterized by a geometric hierarchy of levels[4] (level-k control grammars and the corresponding languages) [27]. A level-2 MCSL is able to capture up to 4 counting dependencies (includes $L_4 = \{a^n b^n c^n d^n \mid n \geq 1\}$ but not $L_5 = \{a^n b^n c^n d^n e^n \mid n \geq 1\}$). They were proven to have recognition algorithms with time complexity $O(n^6)$ [19,18]. In general for a level-k control grammar the recognition problem is in $O(n^{3 \cdot 2^{k-1}})$, and the descriptive power regarding counting dependencies is bound to 2^k [26, 27]. Recently, Range Concatenation Grammars (RCGs)[4] were shown capable

---

[1] See for example [21], [8] , [12], [10], among others.
[2] There are many other equivalent or similar formalisms such as, *range concatenation grammars, multiple context-free grammars*[20], *minimalist grammars*[22].
[3] See for example, [16], [26], [17].
[4] Similar hierarchies: multiple CFGs [20], multi-push down automata [6].

A. Gelbukh (Ed.): CICLing 2003, LNCS 2588, pp. 22–35, 2003.

of recognizing the three phenomena mentioned above in $O(n^3)$ exploiting the possibility of computing intersection and negation of languages directly.[5]

Here we present Global Index Grammars (GIGs) - and GILs the corresponding languages - as an alternative grammar formalism that has a restricted context-sensitive power but more powerful than level-2 MCSGs (e.g. LIGs). The class of GILs contains the languages L_4 and L_5 (above). We show that GIGs have enough descriptive power to capture the three phenomena mentioned above (reduplication, multiple agreements, crossed agreements) in their generalized forms. Recognition of the language generated by a GIG is in polynomial time: the time complexity of the algorithm presented here is $O(n^6)$ (section 4). We present a Chomsky-Schützenberger representation of GILs (section 3). These are initial results, there are many interesting characteristics of this formalism and its relations to MCSGs and related formalisms that will be addressed in future research.

2 Global Index Grammars

2.1 Indexed Grammars and Linear Indexed Grammars

Indexed grammars, (IGs) [1], and Linear Index Grammars, (LIGs;LILs) [12], have the capability to associate stacks of indices with symbols in the grammar rules. IGs are not semilinear (the class of ILs contains the language $\{a^{2^n} \mid n \geq 0\}$). LIGs are Indexed Grammars with an additional constraint in the form of the productions: the stack of indices can be "transmitted" only to one non-terminal. As a consequence they are semilinear and belong to the class of MCSGs. The class of LILs contains L_4 but not L_5 (see above).

A **Linear Indexed Grammar** is a 5-tuple (V, T, I, P, S), where V is the set of variables, T the set of terminals, I the set of *indices*, S in V is the start symbol, and P is a finite set of productions of the form, where $A, B \in V$, $\alpha, \gamma \in (V \cup T)^*$, $i \in I$:

    a. $A[..] \rightarrow \alpha B[..]\gamma$ b. $A[i..] \rightarrow \alpha B[..]\gamma$ c. $A[..] \rightarrow \alpha B[i..]\gamma$

Example 1. $L(G_1) = \{a^n b^n c^n d^n \mid n \geq 0\}$
   $G_1 = (\{S, B\}, \{a, b, c, d\}, \{i\}, P, S)$, where P is:
   $S[..] \rightarrow aS[i..]d, \quad S[..] \rightarrow B[..], \quad B[i..] \rightarrow bB[..]c, \quad B[\,] \rightarrow \epsilon$

2.2 Global Indexed Grammars

In the LIG case, the stack of indices is associated with variables. It is a grammar that controls the derivation through the variables of a CFG. The proposal we present here, uses the stack of indices as a unique designated global control structure, independent of local points in the derivation. In this sense these grammars provide a global but restricted context that can be updated at any local point in the derivation. GIGs are a kind of regulated rewriting mechanisms [9]

---

[5] RCGs are closed under intersection and complementation.

with global context and history of the derivation (or ordered derivation) as the main characteristics of its regulating device. The introduction of indices in the derivation is restricted to rules that have terminals in the right-hand side. This feature makes the use of indices dependent to lexical information, in a linguistic sense, and allows the kind of algorithm we propose in section 5. An additional constraint that is imposed on GIGs is strict leftmost derivation whenever indices are introduced or removed by the derivation.

Definition 1. A GIG is a 6-tuple $G = (N, T, I, S, \#, P)$ where N, T, I are finite pairwise disjoint sets and 1) N is the set of nonterminals 2) T the set of terminals 3) I a set of stack indices 4) $S \in N$ is the start symbol 5) $\#$ is the start stack symbol (not in I, N, T) and 6) P is a finite set of productions, having the following form,[6] where $x \in I$, $y \in \{I \cup \#\}$, $A \in N$, $\alpha, \beta \in (N \cup T)^*$ and $a \in T$.

a.1 $A \underset{\epsilon}{\rightarrow} \alpha$ or $A \rightarrow \alpha$ (epsilon or context-free rules)

a.2 $A \underset{[y]}{\rightarrow} \alpha$ or $[y..]A \rightarrow [y..]\alpha$ (epsilon rules with constraints)

b. $A \underset{x}{\rightarrow} a\ \beta$ or $[..]A \rightarrow [x..]a\ \beta$ (push rules)

c. $A \underset{\bar{x}}{\rightarrow} \alpha\ a\ \beta$ or $[x..]A \rightarrow [..]\alpha$ (pop rules)

Note the difference between push (type b) and pop rules (type c): push rules require the right-hand side of the rule to contain a terminal in the first position. Pop rules do not require a terminal at all. That constraint on push rules is a crucial property of GIGs, without that constraint GIGs could be equivalent to a Turing Machine.[7]

Derivations in a GIG are similar to those in a CFG except that it is possible to modify a string of indices. This string of indices are not associated with variables, so we can consider them global. We define the derives relation $\Rightarrow$ on sentential forms, which are strings in $I^*\#(N \cup T)^*$ as follows. Let β and γ be in $(N \cup T)^*$, δ be in I^*, x in I, w be in T^* and X_i in $(N \cup T)$.

1. If $A \underset{\mu}{\rightarrow} X_1...X_k$ is a production of type (a.) (i.e. $\mu = \epsilon$ or $\mu = [x]$, $x \in I$) then:

   $\delta\#\beta A\gamma \underset{\epsilon}{\Rightarrow} \delta\#\beta X_1...X_k\gamma$ (production type a.1 or context-free) or

   $x\delta\#\beta A\gamma \underset{[x]}{\Rightarrow} x\delta\#\beta X_1...X_k\gamma)$ (production type a.2)

   This is equivalent to a CFG derives relation, in the sense that it does not affect the stack of indices (push and pop rules).

---

[6] The notation in the rules at the left makes explicit that operation on the stack is associated to the production and neither to terminals nor to non-terminals. It also makes explicit that the operations are associated to the computation of a Dyck language (using such notation as used in e.g. [14]). The notation of the rules in the right is intended to be more similar to the notation used in IGs and LIGs.

[7] In forthcoming work[5] we show that GIGs are equivalent to a PDA with a **constrained** auxiliary stack. It is well known that a PDA with two stacks is equivalent to a TM. However there is an extensive tradition of increasing the power of PDA adding (additional) stacks with constraints on their operation mode (e.g. [13], [24], [3], including generalized models of multistacks: [2], [6], [25]).

2. If $A \rightarrow aX_1...X_n$ is a production of type (b.) or push, $\mu = x, x \in I$, then:
   $$\delta\#wA\gamma \underset{x}{\Rightarrow} x\delta\#waX_1...X_n\gamma$$

3. If $A \rightarrow X_1...X_n$ is a production of type (c.) or pop, $\mu = \bar{x}, x \in I$, then:
   $$x\delta\#wA\gamma \underset{\bar{x}}{\Rightarrow} \delta\#wX_1...X_n\gamma$$

The reflexive and transitive closure of $\Rightarrow$ is denoted, as usual by $\overset{*}{\Rightarrow}$. We define the language of a GIG, G, $L(G)$ to be: $\{w|\#S \overset{*}{\Rightarrow} \#w$ and w is in $T^*\}$.

It can be observed that the main difference between, IGs, LIGs and GIGs, corresponds to the interpretation of the derives relation relative to the behavior of the stack of indices. In IGs the stacks of indices are distributed over the nonterminals of the right-hand side of the rule. In LIGs, indices are associated with only one nonterminal at the right-hand side of the rule. This produces the effect that there is only one stack affected at each derivation step, with the consequence of the semilinearity property of LILs. GIGs share this uniqueness of the stack with LIGs, but brought to an extreme. There is only one stack to be considered. Unlike LIGs and IGs the stack of indices is independent of nonterminals in the GIG case. GIGs can have rules where the right-hand side of the rule is composed only of terminals and affect the stack of indices. Indeed push rules (type b) are constrained to start the right-hand side with a terminal as specified in (6.b) in the GIG definition.

The derives definition requires a leftmost derivation for those rules (push and pop rules) that affect the stack of indices.

Examples using trGIGS. We call trGIGs a subtype of GIGs where the pop rules (type c.) are constrained to start with a terminal in a similar way as push (type b.) rules in GIGs are. In other words, pop rules must be: $A \underset{\bar{x}}{\rightarrow} a\,\beta$.

Example 2 (agreements).
$L(G_5) = \{a^nb^nc^nd^ne^n|\ n \geq 1\}$,
$G_5 = (\{S, A, C, D^1, D, E\}, \{a, b, c, d, e\}, \{a', g'\}, S, \#, P)$ and P is:

$$S \rightarrow ACE \qquad A \underset{i}{\rightarrow} aAb \qquad A \underset{i}{\rightarrow} ab \qquad C \underset{i}{\rightarrow} cD^1 \qquad D^1 \rightarrow CD$$

$$C \underset{\bar{i}}{\rightarrow} cD \qquad D \underset{j}{\rightarrow} d \qquad E \underset{\bar{j}}{\rightarrow} eE \qquad E \underset{\bar{j}}{\rightarrow} e$$

The derivation of $w = aabbccddee$:

$\#S \quad \Rightarrow \quad \#ACE \quad \Rightarrow \quad i\#aAbCE \quad \Rightarrow \quad ii\#aabbCE \quad \Rightarrow \quad i\#aabbcD^1E \quad \Rightarrow$
$i\#aabbcCDE \quad \Rightarrow \quad \#aabbccDDE \quad \Rightarrow \quad j\#aabbccdDE \quad \Rightarrow \quad jj\#aabbccddE \quad \Rightarrow$
$j\#aabbccddeE \Rightarrow \#aabbccddee$

Now we generalize the example 2 and show how to construct a trGIG that recognizes any finite number of dependencies:

Claim. The language $L_m = \{a_1^na_2^n...a_k^n \parallel n \geq 1, k \geq 4\}$ is in trGIL

Proof. Construct the GIG grammar
$G_k = (\{S, E_2, O_3, ..., A_k\}, \{a_1, ..., a_k\}, \{a'_2, a'_4, ..., a'_j\}, S, \#, P)$ such that $k \geq 4$ and $j = k$ if k is even or $j = k - 1$ if k is odd, and P is composed by:

1. $S \to a_1\, S\, E_2$ 2. $S \to a_1\, E_2$

and for every E_i and O_i such that i is odd in O_i and i is even in E_i add the following rules:

3a. $E_i \xrightarrow[a_i]{} a_i\, E_i$ 4a. $E_i \xrightarrow[a_i]{} a_i\, O_{i+1}$ 5a. $O_i \xrightarrow[\bar{a}_{i-1}]{} a_i\, O_i\, E_{i+1}$

6a. $O_i \xrightarrow[\bar{a}_{i-1}]{} a_i\, E_{i+1}$

If k is even add: 3b. $A_k \to a_k\, A_k$ 4b. $A_k \to a_k$

If k is odd add: 5b. $A_k \xrightarrow[\bar{a}_{k-1}]{} a_k\, A_k$ 6b. $O_k \xrightarrow[\bar{a}_{k-1}]{} a_k$

$L(G_n) = \{a_1^n a_2^n ... a_k^n \mid n \geq 1, 4 \leq k\}$

GIG examples. The following languages can be defined with a GIG and we conjecture they cannot be defined using a trGIG. We mentioned the difference between push and pop rules in GIG. This difference enables to use left recursive pop rules so that the order of the derivation is a mirror image of the left-right order of the input string. This is not possible in the trGIG case because pop rules cannot be left recursive according to the additional constraint imposed on trGIGs.

Example 3 (copy language).

$L(G_{ww}) = \{ww \mid w \in \{a,b\}^*\}$, $G_{ww} = (\{S,R\}, \{a,b\}, \{i,j\}, S, \#, P)$ and P is:

$S \xrightarrow{i} aS$ $S \xrightarrow{j} bS$ $S \to R$ $R \xrightarrow{\bar{i}} Ra \parallel a$ $R \xrightarrow{\bar{j}} Rb \parallel b$

The derivation of abbabb

$\#S \Rightarrow i\#aS \Rightarrow ji\#abS \Rightarrow jji\#abbS \Rightarrow ji\#abbRb \Rightarrow i\#abbRbb \Rightarrow \#abbRabb \Rightarrow \#abbabb$

The following example is the generalization of the previous one.

Example 4 (multiple copies language).

$L(G_{wwn}) = \{w_1 w_2 ... w_n \mid w \in \{a,b\}^*, n \geq 2\}$

$G_{wwn} = (\{S,R,A,B\}, \{a,b\}, \{i,j\}, S, \#, P)$ and $P =$

$S \to AS \parallel BS \parallel RS \parallel R$ $A \xrightarrow{i} a$ $B \xrightarrow{j} b$ $A \to a$

$B \to b$ 6. $R \xrightarrow{\bar{i}} RA \parallel A$ $R \xrightarrow{\bar{j}} RB \parallel B$ $R \xrightarrow{\bar{i}} a$ $R \xrightarrow{\bar{j}} b$

The derivation of ababab

$\#S \Rightarrow \#AS \Rightarrow i\#aS \Rightarrow i\#aBS \Rightarrow ji\#abS \Rightarrow ji\#abRS \Rightarrow i\#abRBS \Rightarrow \#abABS \Rightarrow i\#abaBS \Rightarrow ji\#ababS \Rightarrow ji\#ababR \Rightarrow i\#ababRB \Rightarrow \#ababAB \Rightarrow \#ababaB \Rightarrow \#ababab$

In the next example we can see that using the same mechanism (left recursion) a language with a higher number of crossing dependencies than using a trGIG, can be generated. It is easy to see that generalizing the same mechanism any finite number of crossing dependencies can be generated.

Example 5. $G_{cr3} = (\{S, F, L, B, C, D, E\}, \{a, b, c, d, e, f\}, \{i, j, k\}, S, \#, P)$, P:

$$S \to FL \qquad F \underset{i}{\to} aF \parallel aB \qquad B \underset{j}{\to} bB \parallel bC \qquad C \underset{k}{\to} cC \parallel c$$

$$L \underset{\bar{k}}{\to} Lf \parallel Ef \qquad E \underset{\bar{j}}{\to} Ee \parallel De \qquad D \underset{\bar{i}}{\to} Dd \parallel d$$

$$L(G_{cr3}) = \{a^n b^m c^l d^n e^m f^l\}$$

3 GILs and Dyck Languages

We argue in this section that GILs correspond to the result of the "combination" of a CFG with a Dyck language. The well-known Chomsky-Schützenberger theorem [7] shows that any CFG is the result of the "combination" of a Regular Language with a Dyck Language. The analogy in the automaton model is the combination of a Finite State Automata with a stack, which results in a PDA. Push and pop moves of the stack have the power to compute a Dyck language using the stack symbols. This "combination" is formally defined in the CFG case as follows: each context-free language L is of the form $L = \phi(D_r \cap R)$, where D is a semi-Dyck set, R is a regular set and ϕ is a homomorphism (Cf. [14]) .

Dyck languages can also characterize GILs. A GIG is the "combination" of a CFG with a Dyck language: GIGs are CFG-like productions that may have an associated stack of indices. This stack of indices, as we said, has the power to compute the Dyck language of the vocabulary of indices relative to their derivation order. As we have seen above, GIGs include languages that are not context-free. GILs can be characterized using a natural extension of Chomsky-Schützenberger theorem (we will follow the notation used in [14]).

Theorem 1 (Chomsky-Schützenberger for GILs). For each GIL L, there is an integer r, a CFL L1 and a homomorphism ϕ such that $L = \phi(D_r \cap L1)$.

Proof. Let $L = L(G)$, where $G = (NT, T, I, S, \#, P)$.
T and I are pairwise disjoint and $\|T \cup I\| = r$
The alphabet for the semi-Dick set will be $\Sigma_0 = (T \cup I) \cup (\bar{T} \cup \bar{I})$. Let D_r be the semi-Dyck set over Σ_0.
Define ϕ as the homomorphism from $\Sigma_0{}^*$ into T^* determined by
$\phi(a) = a$, $\phi(\bar{a}) = \epsilon$ if $a \in T$.
$\phi(i) = \epsilon$, $\phi(\bar{i}) = \epsilon$ if $i \in I$.

Define a CFG grammar $G1 = (N, \Sigma_0, S_1, P1)$ such that P1 is given according to the following conditions. For every production $p \in P$ where $a \in T$, $i \in I$, and α, $\beta \in (N \cup T)^*$ create a new production $p_1 \in P1$, such that α_1 and $\beta_1 \in (N \cup T\bar{T})^*$ as follows:[8]

1. **if** $p = A \to \alpha a \beta$ **then** $p_1 = A_1 \to \alpha_1 a \bar{a} \beta_1$
2. **if** $p = A \underset{i}{\to} \alpha$ **then** $p_1 = A_1 \to i\alpha_1$

---

[8] We use a subscript "1" to make clear that either productions and nonterminals with such subscript belong to the CFG $G1$ and not to the source GIG.

3. **if** $p = A \underset{i}{\rightarrow} \alpha$ **then** $p_1 = A_1 \rightarrow \bar{i}\alpha_1$

4. **if** $p = A \underset{[i]}{\rightarrow} \alpha$ **then** $p_1 = A_1 \rightarrow \bar{i}i\alpha_1$

It can be seen that L(G1) is a CFL, so we have defined D_r, ϕ and the corresponding CFL. We have to show that $L = \phi(D_r \cap L(G1))$. The proof is an induction on the length of the computation sequence.

First direction $L \subseteq \phi(D_r \cap L(G1))$. Suppose $w \in L$.

Basis

a) $w = \epsilon$ then $\#S \Rightarrow \#\epsilon$ and $S_1 \Rightarrow \epsilon$

b) $\|w\| = 1$ then $\#S \Rightarrow \#a$ and $S_1 \Rightarrow a\bar{a}$

Both ϵ and $a\bar{a}$ are in $D_r \cap L(G1)$

The induction hypothesis exploits the fact that any computation starting at a given configuration of the index stack and returning to that initial configuration, is computing a Dyck language.

Induction Hypothesis. Suppose that if there is a GIL derivation $\delta\#uA \overset{k}{\Rightarrow} \delta\#uyB$ (where $u, y \in T^*$) implies there is a L(G1) derivation $u'A \overset{k}{\Rightarrow} u'zB$ (where $u', z \in (T\bar{T} \cup I \cup \bar{I})^*$) such that $z \in D_r$ and $\phi(z) = y$ for every $k < n, n > 1$ then:

Case (A) If:

$\#S \overset{n-1}{\Rightarrow} \#yB \Rightarrow \#ya$ so by Induction Hypothesis and (1)

$S_1 \overset{n-1}{\Rightarrow} zA_1 \Rightarrow za\bar{a}$

It is clear that if $z \in D_r$, so is $za\bar{a}$. And if $\phi(z) = y$ then $\phi(za\bar{a}) = ya$.

Case (B) If:

$\#S \overset{k}{\Rightarrow} \#uA \underset{i}{\Rightarrow} i\#uaB \overset{n-1}{\Rightarrow} i\#uayC \overset{n}{\underset{i}{\Rightarrow}} \#uaya$

by Induction Hypothesis, (2) and (3):

$S \overset{k}{\Rightarrow} u'A_1 \Rightarrow u'ia\bar{a}B_1 \overset{n-1}{\Rightarrow} u'ia\bar{a}zC_1 \overset{n}{\Rightarrow} u'ia\bar{a}\bar{z}ia\bar{a}$

If $u', z \in D_r$, so is $u'ia\bar{a}\bar{z}ia\bar{a}$. And if $\phi(z) = y$ and $\phi(u') = u$ then $\phi(u'ia\bar{a}\bar{z}ia\bar{a}) = uaza$.

The **reverse direction** $\phi(D_r \cap L(G1)) \subseteq L$. Suppose $w \in \phi(D_r \cap L(G1))$.

Basis:

a) $w = \epsilon$ then $S_1 \Rightarrow \epsilon$ and $\#S \Rightarrow \#\epsilon$

b) $\|w\| = 1$ then $S_1 \Rightarrow a\bar{a}$ and $\#S \Rightarrow \#a$ and $\phi(a\bar{a}) = a$

Induction Hypothesis. Suppose that if there is a derivation $uA \overset{k}{\Rightarrow} uzB$ in L(G1) and $z \in D_r$ then there is a GIL derivation $\delta\#u' \overset{k}{\Rightarrow} \delta\#u'yA$ such that $\phi(z) = y$.

Case (A) If:

$S_1 \overset{n-1}{\Rightarrow} zA_1 \Rightarrow za\bar{a}$ then

$\#S \overset{n-1}{\Rightarrow} \#yA \Rightarrow \#ya$

If $z \in D_r$ so is $za\bar{a}a\bar{a}$ and if $\phi(z) = y$ then $\phi(za\bar{a}a\bar{a}) = yaa$.

Case (B) If:

$S_1 \overset{k}{\Rightarrow} u'A_1 \Rightarrow u'ia\bar{a}B_1 \overset{n-1}{\Rightarrow} u'ia\bar{a}zC_1 \Rightarrow u'ia\bar{a}\bar{z}ia\bar{a}$ then

$$\#S \stackrel{k}{\Rightarrow} \#yA \underset{i}{\Rightarrow} i\#yaB \stackrel{n-1}{\Rightarrow} i\#uayC \underset{i}{\Rightarrow} \#uaya$$

If $u', z \in D_r$ so is $u'ia\bar{a}z\bar{i}a\bar{a}$ and if $\phi(z) = y$ and $\phi(u') = u$ then $\phi(u'ia\bar{a}z\bar{i}a\bar{a}) = uaza$.

If other (possible) derivation were applied to $u'ia\bar{a}zC$ then the corresponding string would not be in D_r.   □

4   Recognition of GILs

4.1   Graph-Structured Stacks

We will use a graph-structured stack [23] to compute the operations correspond-ing to the index operations in a GIG. It is a device for efficient handling of nondeterminism in the stack operations. If all the possible stack configurations in a GIG derivation were to be represented, the number of possible configura-tions might grow exponentially with the length of the input. Each node of the graph-structured stack will represent a unique index and a unique length of the stack. Each node at length n can have an edge only to a node at length $n - 1$. This is a departure from Tomita's graph-structured stack. Although the number of possible nodes increases, however the number of edges connecting a node to others is limited. The set of nodes that represents the top of the stack will be called active nodes (following Tomita's terminology).

For instance in figure 1, active nodes are represented by circles and the inac-tive ones are represented by squares. The numbers indicate the length.

Fig. 1. Two graph-structured stacks

The graph-structured stack at the left represents the following possible stack configurations: iii#, iji#, ijj#, jjj#, jij#, jii#. The one at the right is equivalent to the maximal combination of stack configurations for indices i, j with maximum length of stack 3. (i.e.) #, i#, j#, ii#, ij#, ji#, jj#, iii#, etc.

The following operations are possible on the graph-structured stack:

Push(newnode,oldnode). Creates a newnode if it is not in the graph and creates an edge from newnode to oldnode if necessary.

Pop(curretnode). Retrieves all the nodes that are connected by an edge from the currentnode. Given we use nodes of unambiguous length, currentnode can connect only to nodes of current length-1. Therefore the number of edges con-necting a node to a preceding one is bound by the size of the indexing vocabulary.

4.2   GILs Recognition Using Earley Algorithm

Earley Algorithm. Earley's parsing algorithm [11] computes a leftmost derivation using a combination of top-down prediction and bottom-up recognition.
Earley main data structures are states or "items", which are composed of a
"dotted" rule and a starting position: $[A \rightarrow \alpha \bullet \beta, p_j]$. These items are used to
represent intermediate steps in the recognition process. Earley items are inserted
in sets of states. There are as many sets as positions in the input string. Therefore, given a string $w = a_1 a_2 ... a_n$ with $n \geq 0$ any integer i such that $0 \leq i \leq n$
is a position in w. An item $[A \rightarrow \alpha \bullet \beta, p_j]$ is inserted in the set of states S_i if α
corresponds to the recognition of the substring $a_j ... a_i$.

Algorithm 1 (Earley Recognition for GFGs) Let $G = (N, T, S, P)$ be a
CFG. Let $w = a_1 a_2 \cdots a_n$ be an input string, $n \geq 0$, and $a_i \in T$ for $1 \leq i \leq n$.
Create the Sets S_i:
1 $S_0 = [S' \rightarrow \bullet S\$, 0]$
2 For $0 \leq i \leq n$ do:
  Process each item $s \in S1_i$ in order performing one of the following:
    a) **Predictor**: (top-down prediction closure)
      If $[B \rightarrow \alpha \bullet A\beta, j] \in S_i$ and $(A \rightarrow \gamma) \in P$:
        add $[A \rightarrow \bullet\gamma, i]$ to S_i
    b) **Completer**: (bottom-up recognition)
      If $[B \rightarrow \gamma\bullet, j] \in S_i$:
        for $[A \rightarrow \alpha \bullet B\beta, k] \in S_j$:
          add $[A \rightarrow \alpha B \bullet \beta, k]$ to $S1_i$
    c) **Scanner**: equivalent to shift in a shift-reduce parser.
      If $[A \rightarrow \alpha \bullet a\beta, j] \in S_i$ and $w_i + 1 = a$:
        add $[A \rightarrow \alpha a \bullet \beta, j]$ to $S_i + 1$
3 **If** S_{i+1} is empty, **Reject.**
4 **If** $i = n$ and $S_{n+1} = \{[S' \rightarrow S\$\bullet, 0]\}$ then **accept**

Earley Algorithm for GIGs. We use the graph-structured stack and we
represent the stack nodes as pairs of indices and counters (the purpose of the
counters is to keep track of the length of the stack for expository and debugging
purposes).

  We modify Earley items adding two parameters: $[\Delta, O, A \rightarrow \alpha \bullet \beta, p_j]$ where
Δ, is a pointer to an active node in the graph-structured stack, and O used to
record the ordering of the rules affecting the stack, such that $O \leq n$ where n is
the length of the input.[9]

Algorithm 2 (Earley Recognition for GIGs) Let $G = (N, T, I, \#, S, P)$
be a GIG. Let $w = a_1 a_2 \cdots a_n$ be an input string, $n \geq 0$, and $a_i \in T$ for
$1 \leq i \leq n$.

---

[9] Indeed $O \leq 2n$, if *pop* rules "erase" symbols from the stack. An example of such
 case would be the following grammar: $G_d = (\{S\}, \{a,b\}, \{i\}, \{\#\}, \{S\}, \{P\})$ with P:
 $S \underset{i}{\rightarrow} aS \mid bS$ $S \underset{i}{\rightarrow} S \mid \epsilon$

Initialize the graph-structured stack with the node $(\#, 0)$.

Create the Sets S_i:

1 $S_0 = [(\#, \mathbf{0}), 0, S' \to \bullet S\$, 0]$

2 For $0 \leq i \leq n$ do:

    Process each item $s \in S_i$ in order

    performing one of the following:

        a) Predictor

        b) Completer

        c) Scanner

3   If S_{i+1} is empty, **Reject.**

4   If $i = n$ and $S_{n+1} = \{[(\#, 0), 0, S' \to S\$\bullet, 0]\}$ then **accept**

It can be seen that the structure of the main loop of Earley's algorithm remains unchanged except for the requirement that the initial item at S_0 (line 1) and the accepting item at $S_n + 1$ (line 4) point to the empty stacknode $(\#, 0)$, and have the corresponding initial order in the derivation.

The operations **predictor, scanner, completer** used in the **For** loop in **2** are modified as follows, to perform the corresponding operations on the graph-structured stack. As we said, we represent nodes in the graph-structured stack with pairs (δ, C) such that $C \leq n$.

1. Predictor

    If $[(\delta_1, C_1), O_1, B \underset{\mu}{\to} \alpha \bullet A\beta, j] \in S_i$ and $(A \underset{\delta}{\to} \gamma) \in P$:

1.2   add every $[(\delta_2, C_2), O_2, A \underset{\delta}{\to} \bullet\gamma, i]$ to S_i

    such that:

        if $\delta \in I$ then $\delta_2 = \delta$, $O_2 = O_1 + 1$ and

          push($(\delta_2, C_2), (\delta_1, C_1)$) s.t. $C_2 = C_1 + 1$

        if $\delta = \bar{i}$ and $i = \delta_1$ then $O_2 = O_1 + 1$ and

          $(\delta_2, C_2) \in$ **pop**$((\delta_1, C_1))$ s.t. $C_2 = C_1 - 1$

        if $\delta = \epsilon$ then $(\delta_1, C_1) = (\delta_2, C_2)$ and $O_1 = O_2$ (ϵ **move**)

        if $\delta = [\delta_1]$ then $(\delta_1, C_1) = (\delta_2, C_2)$ and $O_1 = O_2$

2. Scanner

    If $[\Delta, O, A \underset{\mu}{\to} \alpha \bullet a\beta, j] \in S_i$ and $w_i + 1 = a$:

      add $[\Delta, O, A \underset{\mu}{\to} \alpha a \bullet \beta, j]$ to $S_i + 1$

3. Completer A

    If $[\Delta_1, O, B \underset{\mu}{\to} \gamma\bullet, j] \in S_i$:

      for $[\delta_2, C_2, O - 1, A \underset{\delta}{\to} \alpha \bullet B\beta, k] \in S_j$ where $\delta_2 = i$ if $\mu = \bar{i}$

        add $[\Delta_1, O - 1, A \underset{\delta}{\to} \alpha B \bullet \beta, k]$ to S_i

3. Completer B

    If $[\Delta_1, O, B \underset{\mu}{\to} \gamma\bullet, j] \in S_i$ where $\mu = \epsilon$ or $\mu = [i]$:

      for $[\delta_2, C_2, O, A \underset{\delta}{\to} \alpha \bullet B\beta, k] \in S_j$ where $\delta_2 = i$ if $\mu = [i]$

        add $[\Delta_1, O, A \underset{\delta}{\to} \alpha B \bullet \beta, k]$ to S_i

The following example shows why the Order parameter is required in the Earley items. Consider the language $L_{ww} = \{ww \mid w \in \{a, b\}^*\}$, the productions of the grammar G_{ww} repeated here and the string aaba.

1. $S \underset{i}{\rightarrow} aS$ 2. $S \underset{j}{\rightarrow} bS$ 3. $S \rightarrow R$ 4. $R \underset{i}{\rightarrow} Ra \parallel a$ 5. $R \underset{j}{\rightarrow} Rb \parallel b$

The following derivation is not possible (in particular step 4). The pairs in parenthesis represent the nodes of the graph-structured stack:

(#,0) S $\underset{i}{\overset{1}{\Rightarrow}}$ (i,1) aS $\underset{i}{\overset{2}{\Rightarrow}}$ (i,2) aaS $\Rightarrow$(i,2) aaR$\underset{i}{\overset{3}{\Rightarrow}}$ (i,1), aaRa $\underset{i}{\overset{4}{\Rightarrow}}$ (?,?) aaba

However the following sequences can be generated using Earley's Algorithm if no ordering constraint is enforced at the Completer Operation. In the following example the square brackets represent substrings to be recognized.

(#,0) S $\underset{i}{\overset{1}{\Rightarrow}}$ (i,1) aS $\underset{i}{\overset{2}{\Rightarrow}}$ (i,2) aaS $\underset{j}{\overset{3}{\Rightarrow}}$ (j ,3) aabS $\Rightarrow$(j ,3) aabR$\underset{j}{\overset{4}{\Rightarrow}}$(i,2) aabR[b]$\underset{i}{\overset{5}{\Rightarrow}}$

(i,1) aabR[a][b]$\underset{i}{\overset{6}{\Rightarrow}}$(#,0) aaba[a][b]

In the completer operation the just recognized substring jumps up two steps and completes the "R" introduced after step 3, instead of the one introduced at step 5. In other words, the following complete operation would be performed:

Given $[(\#, 0), 6, R \underset{j}{\rightarrow} a \bullet, 3] \in S_4$ **and** $[(j, 3), 3, S \rightarrow \bullet R, 3] \in S_3$:

add $[(\#, 0), 3, S \rightarrow R \bullet, 3]$ *to* S_4

Then the following items are sequentially added to S_4:

a) $[(\#, 0), 3, S \underset{j}{\rightarrow} bS \bullet, 2]$

b) $[(\#, 0), 2, S \underset{i}{\rightarrow} aS \bullet, 1]$

c) $[(\#, 0), 1, S \underset{i}{\rightarrow} aS \bullet, 0]$

Complexity Analysis. The algorithm presented above has one sequential iteration (a for loop). It has a maximum of n iterations where n is the length of the input. Each item in S_i has the form:

$[(\delta, C), O, A \rightarrow \alpha \bullet B\beta, j]$ where: $0 \leq j, C, O, \leq i$

Thus there might be at most $O(i^3)$ items in each S_i. Scanner and Predictor operations on an item each require constant time. The Completer operation (3) can combine an item from S_i with at most all the items from S_j $(i \neq j)$ where O_j is $O_i - 1$: so it may require up to $O(i^2)$ time for each processed item. The required time for each iteration (S_i) is thus $O(i^5)$. There are S_n iterations then the time bound on the entire 1-4 steps of the algorithm is $O(n^6)$. The computation of the operations on the graph-structured stack of indices are performed at a constant time where the constant is determined by the size of the index vocabulary I.

It can be observed that this algorithm keeps a CFG $(O(n^3))$ complexity if the values of C and O are dependant of i, i.e., if for each item:

$[(i, C_i), O_i, A \rightarrow \alpha \bullet B\beta, p_j]$, where $0 \leq j \leq i$

there is only one value for C_i and O_i for each i.

In such cases the number of items in each set S_i is proportional to i, i.e., $O(i)$ and the complexity of the algorithm is $O(n^3)$. This is true even for some ambiguous grammars such as the following:

$G_{amb} = (\{S, B, C, D, E\}, \{a, b, c, d\}, \{i, \}, \#, S, P)$ where P is

$$S \underset{i}{\rightarrow} aSd \quad S \rightarrow BC \quad B \underset{i}{\rightarrow} bB \quad B \underset{i}{\rightarrow} b \quad C \rightarrow cC \quad C \rightarrow c$$

$$S \rightarrow DE \quad D \rightarrow bD \quad D \rightarrow b \quad E \underset{i}{\rightarrow} cE \quad E \underset{i}{\rightarrow} c$$

$$L(G_{amb}) = \{a^n b^m c^n d^n \| n, m \geq 1\} \cup \{a^n b^n c^m d^n \| n, m \geq 1\}$$

In this case, somehow the ambiguity resides in the CFG backbone, while the indexing is so to speak, deterministic. Once the CF backbone chooses either the "BC" path or the "DE" path of the derivation, only one indexing alternative can apply at each step in the derivation.

The properties of Earley's algorithm for CFGs remain unchanged, so the following results hold:

$O(n^6)$ is the worst case; $O(n^3)$ holds for grammars with unambiguous indexing[10]; $O(n^2)$ holds for unambiguous context-free back-bone grammars with unambiguous indexing and $O(n)$ for bounded-state[11] and $LR(0)$ context-free back-bone grammars with unambiguous indexing. These results seem consistent with those from [4] mentioned in the introduction.

About Correctness of the Algorithm. The correctness of Earley's algorithm for CFGs follows from the following two invariants (top down prediction and bottom-up recognition) respectively:

Proposition 1. An item $[A \rightarrow \alpha \bullet \beta, i]$ is inserted in the set S_j if and only if the following holds:

1. $S \overset{*}{\Rightarrow} a_1...a_i A\gamma$
2. $\alpha \overset{*}{\Rightarrow} a_{i+1}...a_j$

The corresponding invariants of the Earley's algorithm for GIGs are:

Claim. An item $[(y, n), k, A \underset{\mu}{\rightarrow} \alpha \bullet \beta, i]$ is inserted in the Set S_j if and only if the following holds (where k indicates that k moves on the GIG stack have been performed, according to the ordering parameter):

1. $\#S \overset{k}{\Rightarrow} x...\#a_1...a_i A\gamma$
2. $x...\#\alpha \overset{*}{\Rightarrow} y...\#a_{i+1}...a_j$
   such that the length of $y...\#$ is n.

The CFG backbone remains the same, the only changes in the invariants and the introduced item correspond to the configuration of the index stack. What needs to be proven then is the correctness of the operations in the graph-structured stack. This can be done using the same strategy we used to prove Theorem 1.

---

[10] Unambiguous indexing should be understood as those grammars that produce for each string in the language a unique indexing derivation.

[11] Context-free grammars where the set of items in each state set is bounded by a constant.

5 Conclusions

We have made a very succinct presentation of GIGs and GILs and what we consider their most important properties. We showed a Chomsky-Schützenberger representation of GILs, the main result in this paper. We showed the descriptive power of GIGs regarding the three phenomena concerning natural language context-sensitivity: reduplication, multiple agreements and crossed agreements. We introduced a more restricted subset of GIGs (trGIGs): we conjectured they are not able to capture the reduplication phenomena, and that they are more limited regarding crossed agreements. An algorithm for the recognition problem of GILs was presented with a bounded polynomial time result. This algorithm must be analyzed in much greater detail, including an account of grammar-size, time-complexity and space complexity properties, and complete analysis of the ambiguity impact when originated from the indexing mechanism. The proof of correctness of this algorithm is still due, although we sketched how to construct it. We conjecture that GILs are semilinear therefore GILs might share mildly context-sensitive properties. The similarity between GIGs and LIGs, suggests that LILs might be included in GILs. However that might not be the case and turn out to be incomparable. The possible relations between GILs and MCSLs in general will be considered in future work. The equivalent automaton class for GIGs is provided in [5].

Acknowledgments. Thanks to J. Pustejovsky for his continuous support and encouragement on this project and to R. Saurí for her comments on previous versions. Many thanks also to an anonymous reviewer who provided many detailed and helpful comments to improve this version and fix some errors.

References

1. A. V. Aho. Indexed grammars - an extension of context-free grammars. *Journal of the Association for Computing Machinery*, 15(4):647–671, 1968.
2. T. Becker. *HyTAG: a new type of Tree Adjoining Grammars for Hybrid Syntactic Representation of Free Order Languages*. PhD thesis, University of Saarbruecken, 1993.
3. R. Book. Confluent and other types of thue systems. *J. Assoc. Comput. Mach.*, 29:171–182, 1982.
4. P. Boullier. A cubic time extension of context-free grammars. Research Report RR-3611, INRIA, Rocquencourt, France, January 1999. 28 pages.
5. J. Castaño. Lr-2pda and global index grammars. Ms., Computer Science Dept. Brandeis University, available at http://www.cs.brandeis.edu/~jcastano/GIGs.ps, 2002.
6. A. Cherubini, L. Breveglieri, C. Citrini, and S. Reghizzi. Multipushdown languages and grammars. *International Journal of Foundations of Computer Science*, 7(3):253–292, 1996.
7. N. Chomsky and M.-P. Schützenberger. The algebraic theory of context-free languages. In P. Braffort and D. Hirschberg, editors, *Computer Programming and Formal Systems*, pages 118–161. North-Holland, Amsterdam, The Netherlands, 1963.

8. C. Culy. The complexity of the vocabulary of bambara. *Linguistics and Philosophy*, 8:345–351, 1985.

9. J. Dassow and G. Păun. *Regulated Rewriting in Formal Language Theory*. Springer, Berlin, Heidelberg, New York, 1989.

10. J. Dassow, G. Păun, and A. Salomaa. Grammars with controlled derivations. In G. Rozenberg and A. Salomaa, editors, *Handbook of Formal Languages, Vol. 2*. Springer, Berlin, 1997.

11. J. Earley. An Efficient Context-free Parsing Algorithm. *Communications of the ACM*, 13:94–102, 1970.

12. G. Gazdar. Applicability of indexed grammars to natural languages. In U. Reyle and C. Rohrer, editors, *Natural Language Parsing and Linguistic Theories*, pages 69–94. D. Reidel, Dordrecht, 1988.

13. S. Ginsburg and M. Harrison. One-way nondeterministic real-time list-storage. *Journal of the Association for Computing Machinery*, 15, No. 3:428–446, 1968.

14. M. H. Harrison. *Introduction to Formal Language Theory*. Addison-Wesley Publishing Company, Inc., Reading, MA, 1978.

15. A. Joshi. Tree adjoining grammars: How much context-sensitivity is required to provide reasonable structural description? In D. Dowty, L. Karttunen, and A. Zwicky, editors, *Natural language processing: psycholinguistic, computational and theoretical perspectives*, pages 206–250. Chicago University Press, New York, 1985.

16. A. Joshi, K. Vijay-Shanker, and D. Weir. The convergence of mildly context-sensitive grammatical formalisms. In Peter Sells, Stuart Shieber, and Thomas Wasow, editors, *Foundational issues in natural language processing*, pages 31–81. MIT Press, Cambridge, MA, 1991.

17. J. Michaelis and M. Kracht. Semilinearity as a syntactic invariant. In Christian Retoré, editor, *LACL'96: First International Conference on Logical Aspects of Computational Linguistics*, pages 329–345. Springer-Verlag, Berlin, 1997.

18. S. Rajasekaran. Tree-adjoining language parsing in $o(n^6)$ time. *SIAM J. of Computation*, 25, 1996.

19. G. Satta. Tree-adjoining grammar parsing and boolean matrix multiplication. *Computational linguistics*, 20, No. 2, 1994.

20. H. Seki, T. Matsumura, M. Fujii, and T. Kasami. On multiple context-free grammars; theor, 1991.

21. S.M. Shieber. Evidence against the context-freeness of natural language. *Linguistics and Philosophy*, 8:333–343, 1985.

22. E. P. Stabler. Derivational minimalism. *Lecture notes in computer science*, 1328, 1997.

23. M. Tomita. An efficiente augmented-context-free parsing algorithm. *Computational linguistics*, 13:31–46, 1987.

24. Daniel A. Walters. Deterministic context-sensitive languages: Part ii. *Information and Control*, 17:41–61, 1970.

25. C. Wartena. Grammars with composite storages. In *Proceedings of the Conference on Logical Aspects of Computational Linguistics (LACL '98)*, pages 11–14, Grenoble, 1998.

26. D. Weir. *Characterizing mildly context-sensitive grammar formalisms*. PhD thesis, University of Pennsylvania, 1988.

27. D. J. Weir. A geometric hierarchy beyond context-free languages. *Theoretical Computer Science*, 104(2):235–261, 1992.

Total Lexicalism and GASGrammars: A Direct Way to Semantics

Gábor Alberti, Katalin Balogh, Judit Kleiber, and Anita Viszket

University of Pécs – Department of Linguistics
gelexi@btk.pte.hu

Abstract. A new sort of generative grammar is demonstrated to be more radically "lexicalist" than any earlier one. It is a modified Unification Categorial Grammar from which even the principal syntactic "weapon" of CGs, Function Application, has been omitted. What has remained is lexical sign and the mere technique of unification as the engine of combining signs. The computation thus requires no usual linguistic technique (e.g. Move, Merge, traces, Function Application); which promises a straightforward implementation of GASG in Prolog. Our parser decides whether a Hungarian sentence is grammatical and creates its (practically English) DRS.

1 DRT, UCG, and Total Lexicalism

A "totally lexicalist" generative grammar will be demonstrated in this paper. The first motivation of the enterprise was the stubborn problem of compositionality in DRT (Discourse Representation Theory; e.g. [7], [4])[1].

The failure of elaborating a properly compositional solution to the language → DRS transition arises from the fundamental incompatibility of the strictly hierarchically organized generative syntactic phrase structures (PS; e.g. [9], [5]) with the basically unordered DRSs. Nowadays [2], [4] some kind of Categorial Grammar (CG) is held to promise the best chance for capturing the language → DRS transition in a properly compositional manner. The reason lies in the fact that, in a CG system, language-specific information (about how words can combine to form constituents, and then sentences), stored in PS rules in the transformational generative theory, is stored in the Lexicon; the reduced syntax only "concatenates": it permits the words with compatible lexical information to combine (this operation of concatenation is referred to as Function Application).

---

[1] DRT is a successful attempt to extend the sentence-level Montagovian model-theoretic semantics to the discourse level. Its crucial proposal is that a level of discourse representation *must* be inserted in between the language to be interpreted and the world model serving as the context of interpretation. The insertion of this level, however, has given rise to a double problem of *compositionality* (language → DRS, DRS → world model), at least according to the very strict sense of the Fregean principle of compositionality introduced by Montague [8]. As for the DRS → world model transition Zeevat [2] has provided a compositional solution, which could successfully be built in the new version of DRT [4].

A. Gelbukh (Ed.): CICLing 2003, LNCS 2588, pp. 36–47, 2003.

The problem with Classical CG is that it has only a context free generative capacity, which is held to be insufficient for the description of human languages. There seem to be two ways to increase the generative capacity of CCG: to let in, in opposition to the original goals, a few combinatorial means or to introduce the technique of unification, applied e.g. in Prolog (UCG). It is straightforward in the spirit of what has been said so far that DRT is (more) compatible with UCG insisting on a reduced syntax.

UCG is a monostratal grammar, which is based on the formalized notion of the Saussurean sign: a structure that collects a number of levels of linguistic description and expresses relations between the levels by sharing variables in the description of the level information [3 : p145]. The set of well-formed expressions is defined by specifying a number of such signs in the lexicon and by closing them under rule applications (i.e. the selected lexical signs can be combined to form sentences via a finite number of rule applications). In monostratal grammars the syntactic and semantic operations are just aspects of the same operation. A prime example of such grammars, besides UCG, is HPSG.

The basic problem with UCG, which has amounted to the starting-point of GASG, lies in the fact that syntax, deprived of the information concerning sentence cohesion in favor of the unification mechanism and reduced to the primitive task of combining adjacent words, will produce linguistically irrelevant constituents. According to Karttunen's [1 : p19] remark on UCG trees: they look like PS trees but they are only "analysis trees"; and he adds "all that matters is the resulting [morphological] feature set." Let us take this latter remark on trees and feature sets seriously: adjacency of words is to be registered in the course of analysis exclusively and precisely in the linguistically significant cases. The corresponding technique is to be based on an approach where adjacency and order among words are treated by, instead of the usual categorial apparatus, the same technique of unification as morphological cohesion. And what will be then the "engine" combining words to form sentences (since in CGs the lexical features of words only serve as filters to avoid inappropriate combinations)?

There is no need for a separate engine at all! The engine must be unification itself, which is capable of running Prolog programs properly. The rich description of a lexical sign serves a double purpose: it characterizes the potential environment of the given sign in possible grammatical sentences in order for the sign to find the morphologically (or in other ways) compatible elements and to avoid the incompatible ones in the course of forming a sentence, and the lexical description characterizes the sign itself in order for other words to find (or not to find) it, on the basis of similar "environmental descriptions" belonging to the lexical characterizations of these other words. And while the selected words are finding each other on the basis of their formal features suitable for unification, their semantic features are also being unified simultaneously; so by the end of a successful building it will have been verified that a particular sequence of fully inflected words constitutes a grammatical sentence, and its semantic representation, a DRS, will also have been at our disposal.

Section 2 provides the system of definitions of generative argument structure grammars (whose superiority over PS grammars will be argued for in footnote 3), and in the last section our parser is sketched.

2 Definition System of GASGrammars

First of all, we provide the abstract definition of language, which is similar to the one in [6]. Different alphabets (e.g. that of sounds and intonational symbols) can be considered, however, depending on the task, and the definition of phonological model is ambitious: it is the (morpho-) phonologist's task to collect both the relevant set of morpheme segments and the relations among them.

[**Def1:** 1.1. Let A be a finite set: the alphabet. Let $\#$ and "." are special symbols which are no members of A: the space symbol and the full stop. Suppose that, together with other symbols, they constitute a set Y, that of auxiliary symbols. A member s of $(A \cup Y)^*$ is called a sentence if at least one of its members is an element of A, $(s)_1 \neq \#, (s)_1^R = .$, there are no further full stops in the list, and $(s)_i = \# = (s)_{i+1}$ for no i.
1.2. An element of A^* is the i-th word of a sentence s if it is the affix of s between the $i-1$-th and the i-th symbol $\#$; the first word is the prefix of s before the first $\#$, and if the last $\#$ is the j-th, the suffix of s after it (and before the full stop) is the $j+1$-th, or last, word.
1.3. We call a subset L of $(A \cup Y)^*$ a language (over alphabet A) if all of its members are sentences.
1.4. We call Phon $= \langle$Mors, Rel$\rangle$ a phonological model (over alphabet A) if Mors is a subset of A^*, called a set of morpheme segments, and Rel is a set of relations in Mors.]

Numbering will prove to be a crucial question because corresponding elements of intricately related huge representations should be referred to.

[**Def2:** 2.1. Let s be a sentence of a language L over an alphabet A. We call an element n of $(\mathbf{N}^3)^*$ a (three-dimensional) numbering if $(n)_1 = \langle 1, 1, 1 \rangle$, [if $(n)_m = \langle i, j, k \rangle$, either the first projection of $(n)_{m+1}$ is i or $(n)_{m+1} = \langle i+1, 1, 1 \rangle$], and [for each number i in the first projection, the set of second elements consists of natural numbers from 1 to a maximal value p, and for each pair $\langle i, j \rangle$ there are exactly the following three members in the numbering: $\langle i, j, 1 \rangle, \langle i, j, 2 \rangle$ and $\langle i, j, 3 \rangle$, necessarily in this order (but not necessarily next to each other)].
2.2. An element mos of $(\mathbf{N}^3 \times A^*)^*$ is a morphological segmentation of s if [the $[1, 2, 3]$-projection of mos is a numbering (the numbering of mos)], [it is excluded in the case of each pair $\langle i, j \rangle$ that all three fourth members belonging to the triples $\langle i, j, 1 \rangle, \langle i, j, 2 \rangle$ and $\langle i, j, 3 \rangle$ in mos are empty lists], and [for each number u of the domain of the first projection of mos, the u-th word of s coincides with the concatenation of the fourth projection of the element of mos of the form $\langle u, 1, 1, \_ \rangle$ with the fourth projections of all the following elements with number u as its first projection, just in the order in mos].
2.3. If $\langle i, j, k, a \rangle$ is an element of mos, we say that a is the $\langle i, j, k \rangle$-th morph segment of the given morphological segmentation; we can also say that the triple

consisting of the $\langle i, j, 1\rangle$-st, $\langle i, j, 2\rangle$-nd and $\langle i, j, 3\rangle$-rd morph segments, respectively, is the $\langle i, j\rangle$-th morph of mos.]

Thus each morpheme is divided into exactly three segments, $\langle i, j, 1\rangle$, $\langle i, j, 2\rangle$ and $\langle i, j, 3\rangle$ (out of which at most two are allowed to be empty). Why? In Semitic languages certain stems are discontinuous units consisting of three segments between which other morphemes are to be inserted in. It is allowed in GASG that the cohesion between a morpheme and a particular segment of another morpheme is stronger that the cohesion between the three segments of the latter.

In Hungarian, segments of the same morpheme can never be separated from each other. It is useful, however, to refer to a certain segment of a morpheme — in cases where another morpheme determines just the segment in question[2]. Segmentation into just three parts is proposed as a language universal.

Important numbering techniques are defined below again.

[**Def3:** 3.1. We call an element m of $(\mathbf{N}^2)^*$ a strict (two-dimensional) numbering if $(m)_1 = \langle 1, 1\rangle$, and [if $(m)_k = \langle i, j\rangle$, then $(m)_{k+1} = \langle i, j+1\rangle$ or $\langle i+1, 1\rangle$].
3.2. A two-dimensional numbering m is a homomorphic correspondent of a three-dimensional numbering n if there is a function hom such that for each triple $\langle i, j, k\rangle (k = 1, 2, 3)$ occurring in n, hom$(\langle i, j, k\rangle) = \langle i, j\rangle$; which can be said as follows: member $\langle i, j, k\rangle$ of the three-dimensional numbering is the k-th segment of member $\langle i, j\rangle$ of the two-dimensional numbering.]

Despite their great length, Def4-6 are worth commenting together because the intricate construction of gasg's described in Def4 can be evaluated through understanding its functioning: generation (acceptance) of sentences.

[**Def4:** 4.1. A sextuple $G = \langle A, Phon, B, int, X, R\rangle$ is a generative argument structure grammar (gasg) belonging to the phonological model Phon $= \langle$Mors, Rel$\rangle$ over alphabet A (see def1.4.) if [X is a list of lexical items [def4.3.] whose members are elements of Lex(Term)], and [R is a ranked rule system [def4.4.] also over term set B [def4.2.].
4.2. B, the set of basic terms, is the sequence of the following sets:

Con$(j) = \bigcup Con(j)_i$, for $j = 1, 2, 31, 32$, and $i = 0, 1, 2, \ldots$: finite sets of constants of arity i,
Icon$(j) = \bigcup Icon(j)_i$, for $j = 1, 2$, and $i = 1, 2,$: finite sets of interpretable constants of arity i; int can be defined here as a total function int: Icon$(j) \to$ Rel,
Numb: a set of numbers that necessarily includes all natural numbers,
VAR$_0$: variables that can substitute for elements of Con$(2)_0$ and Numb,
Rank $= \{r_1, \ldots, r_K\}$ (K=7).

4.3. A lexical item is a triple li $= \langle$ownc, frmc, pdrs$\rangle$ where [1–3]:

---

[2] In this footnote Hungarian morphs are demonstrated with stable first and third segments but altering middle ones: *al-hat* 'sleep-can,' *szúr-hat* 'prick-can,' *kér-het* 'ask-can,' *űz-het* 'chase-can.' Besides this frontness harmony, other morphemes are sensitive to roundness as well.

1. Set ownc, own word conditions, is a subset of the following set Form(1) of well-formed fomulas:
   a) For an arbitrary $p \in Icon(1)_k, k = 1or2$, the expression $p(t_1, \ldots, t_k) \in Form(1)$ where an argument t_i is a term, $i = 1, 2, \ldots, k$.
   b) Triples of numbers, precisely, elements of $Numb^2 \times \{1, 2, 3\}$ are terms; and lists of terms are also terms.
   c) Formula $p \vee q$ is an element of Form(1) if p and q are its elements.
2. Set frmc, formal conditions, is a subset of the following set Form(2) of well-formed fomulas:
   a) For an arbitrary $p \in Con(2)_k, k = 2, 3, \ldots$, the expression $p(t_1, \ldots, t_k) \in Form(2)$ where argument t_i is a term for $i = 2, \ldots, k$, but $t_i \notin Rank$ for these values of i, whereas $t_1 \in Rank$. We call the formulas defined in this step ranked formulas. We also say that out of these ranked formulas those which are members of set frmc belong to the given lexical item li.
   b) For an arbitrary $p \in Con(2)_k$ or $p \in Icon(2)_k, k = 1, 2, \ldots$, the expression $p(t_1, \ldots, t_k) \in Form(2)$ where argument $t)i$ is a term for $i = 1, 2, \ldots, k$, but $t_i \notin Rank$ for these values of i.
   c) Elements of $\bigcup Con(2)_i$, for $i = 0, 1, 2, \ldots$, are terms;
      elements of $\bigcup Icon(2)_i$, for $i = 0, 1, 2, \ldots$, are terms;
      elements of Numb and VAR_0 are terms;
      lists of terms are also terms;
      elements of Form(2) which are not ranked formulas are all terms too.
   d) Formula $p \vee q$ is an element of Form(2) if p and q are its elements.
   e) Formula $p \wedge q$ is an element of Form(2) if p and q are its elements.
3. Set pdrs, the proto-DRS provided by the given lexical item is a pair $\langle$ bdrs, embc $\rangle$ where bdrs (the basic DRS) is a subset of the following set Form(31) of well-formed fomulas, and embc (the embedding conditions) is a subset of set Form(32) of well-formed fomulas defined after that:

   a) For an arbitrary $p \in Con(31)_k$, the expression $p(t_1, \ldots, t_k) \in Form(31)$ where an argument t_i is a term. If the given formula is an element of subset bdrs, the terms occupying its argment positions are called referents belonging to bdrs.
   b) Elements of $\{ref\} \times (Numb\,VAR_0)^3$ are terms where ref is a distinguished element of $Con(31)_3$.
   c) The expression $p(t_1, \ldots, t_k) \in Form(32)$ where argument t_i is a term for $i = 1, 2, \ldots, k$, and $p \in \{oldref, newref\} = Con(32)_1$ or $p \in \{fixpoint, \langle, \leq, \neq, \sim\} = Con(32)_2$.
   d) Elements of $\{ref\} \times (Numb \cup VAR_0)^3$ are terms where ref is a distinguished element of $Con(32)_3$, and it is also a
      restriction that a quadruple $ref(i, j, k)$ can be considered here a term if it is a referent belonging to set bdrs.

4.4. The ranked rule system denoted by R is defined as an arbitrary subset of the set rr(Form(2)) of ranked rules over set Form(2) of formulas (defined in def4.3.2.): all formulas of the form $p \leftarrow q$ is an element of rr(Form(2)) if p is a ranked formula, and [q is a conjunction of elements of Form(2): $q = q_1 \wedge q_2 \wedge \ldots \wedge q_d$ for some d].]

[**Def5:** 5.1. An element num of $(\mathbf{N}^2 \times X)^*$ is called a numeration (over a gasg G) if [the [1,2]-projection of the list is a strict two-dimensional numbering], and [members of the third projection are lexical items (coming from the fifth component of G)].
5.2. If $\langle i, j, li \rangle$ is an element of num, we can say that the given lexical item li is the $\langle i, j \rangle$-th element of the numeration.]

[**Def6:** 6.1. A sentence s – a member of $(A \cup Y)^*$ in Def1, is grammatical according to a gasg $G = \langle A, \text{Phon}, B, \text{int}, X, R \rangle$ if

there is a numeration num of $(\mathbf{N}^2 \times X)^*$,
there is a (cohesion) function coh: $\text{VAR}_0 \to \text{Con}(2)_0 \cup \text{Numb}$ (def4.2.!),
and sentence s has a morphological segmentation mos of $(\mathbf{N}^3 \times A^*)^*$ (Def2.2.)
such that the numbering of numeration num is a homomorphic correspondent of the numbering of segmentation mos
and the $\langle \text{coh}, \text{int} \rangle$ pair satisfies [def6.2.] numeration num according to rule system R.

6.2. Pair $\langle \text{coh}, \text{int} \rangle$ satisfies (def6.2.) numeration num according to rule system R if for each possible $\langle i, j \rangle$, the lexical item li which is the $\langle i, j \rangle$-th member of the numeration is satisfied. This lexical item li = $\langle \text{ownc}, \text{frmc}, \text{pdrs} \rangle$ is satisfied if its all three components are satisfied.

1. Formula set ownc is satisfied if,
   [in the case of 4.3.1.a., $\langle \text{int}'(t_1), \ldots, \text{int}'(t_k) \rangle \in \text{int}(p) \in \text{Rel}$, where (Rel is the set of relations in the phonological model Phon belonging to gasg G, and) function int' is an extension of int that assigns a number triple $\langle i, j, k \rangle$ the $\langle i, j, k \rangle$-th morph segment of the morphological segmentation mos, and a number pair $\langle i, j \rangle$ the $\langle i, j, 1 \rangle$-st morph of mos];
   [in the case of 4.3.1.c., p is satisfied or q is satisfied].
2. Formula set frmc is satisfied if one of the cases discussed below is satisfied. First of all, however, coh'(p) is to defined for elements of formulas of Form(2) and Form(3): it is a formula whose only difference relative to p is that each occurrences of variable v (elements of VAR_0) has been replaced with coh(v). In the case of 4.3.2.a., a ranked formula $p(t_1, \ldots, t_k)$ is satisfied if there is a formula $p(t'_1, \ldots, t'_k) \leftarrow q'$ in rule system R such that
   coh($p(t'_1, \ldots, t'_k)$) = $p(t_1, \ldots, t_k)$, there is a formula q such that coh(q) = coh(q'), and q belongs to the $\langle i', j' \rangle$-th lexical item in numeration num for an arbitrary pair $\langle i', j' \rangle$, and coh(q') is satisfied.
   In the case of 4.3.2.b., a formula $p(t_1, \ldots, t_k)$ is satisfied if
   EITHER there is a formula $p(t'_1, \ldots, t'_k) \leftarrow q'$ in rule system R such that
   coh($p(t'_1, \ldots, t'_k)$) =coh($p(t_1, \ldots, t_k)$), there is a formula q such that coh(q) = coh(q'), and q belongs to the $\langle i', j' \rangle$-th lexical item in numeration num for an arbitrary pair $\langle i', j' \rangle$, and coh(q') is satisfied (indirect satisfaction),

OR $coh(p(t'_1, \ldots, t'_k))$ belongs to the $\langle i', j' \rangle$-th lexical item in numeration num for an arbitrary pair $\langle i', j' \rangle$ (direct satisfaction),

OR $\langle \text{int}'(coh(t_1)), \ldots, \text{int}'(coh(t_k)) \rangle \in \text{int}(p) \in \text{Rel}$ (int' has been defined in def6.2.1. (direct satisfaction).

In the case of 4.3.2.d., $p \vee q$ is satisfied if p is satisfied or q is satisfied.

In the case of 4.3.2.e., $p \wedge q$ is satisfied if p is satisfied and q is satisfied.

3. Formula sets bdrs and embc are satisfied if each formula p that can be found in one of them is satisfied. This arbitrary formula p is satisfied without conditions.

6.3. Let us denote sem the set consisting of the $\langle coh(\text{bdrs}), coh(\text{embc}) \rangle$ for all lexical items in the numeration. We can call it the discourse-semantic representation of sentence s.]

In harmony with our "total lexicalism," lexical item is the crucial means of a gasg (def4.3.). Its first component out of the three (def4.3.1.) consists of conditions on the ⌷own word⌷ deciding whether a morpheme in a (potential) sentence can be considered to be a realization of the given lexical item (see def6.2.1. and the last footnote on allomorphs). It is our new proposal [12] that, instead of fully inflected words (located in a multiple inheritance network), li's are assigned to morphemes – realizing a "totally lexicalist morphology"

The component of formal conditions (def4.3.2.) is responsible for selecting the other li's with which the li in question can stand in certain grammatical relations (def6.2.2.). It imposes requirements on them and exhibits its own properties to them. As for the range of grammatical relations in a universal perspective [10], there are unidirectional relations, e.g. an adjective "seeks" its noun, where the "seeking" li may show certain properties (number, gender, case, definiteness) of the "sought" one, and bidirectional relations, e.g. an object and its regent (in whose argument structure the former is) "seek" each other, where the argument may have a case-marking depending on the regent, and the regent may show certain properties (number, person, gender, definiteness) of the argument. The rule system in the sixth component of gasg's (def4.4.), among others, makes it possible to store the above listed language-specific factors outside li's so $frmc$ (def4.3.2.) is to contain only references to the relations themselves.

It is ranked implication rules (def4.3.2., def6.2.2.) that we consider to be peculiar to GASG. In addition to satisfying a requirement described in a li directly by proving that either some property of another li is appropriate or the morphemes / words in the segmented sentence stand in a suitable configuration, the requirement in question can be satisfied indirectly by proving that there is a lexical item which has a competitive requirement ranked higher. This optimalistic technique enables us to dispense with phrase structure rules: the essence (precise details in [13,14]) is that, if word (morpheme) w_1 stands in a certain relation with w_2, w_1 is required to be adjacent to w_2, which can be satisfied, of course, by putting them next to each other in a sentence, but we can have recourse to an indirect way of satisfaction by inserting other words between them whose adjacency requirements (concerning either w_1 or w_2) are ranked higher (and these intervening words, in a language-specific way, may be allowed to "bring" their dependents)[3]. In def4.2. seven ranks are proposed as a universal concerning the complexity of human languages.

The discourse-semantic component of li's (def4.3.3.) is practically intended to check nothing[4] (def6.2.3.) but their "sum" coming from the whole numeration (def6.3.) provides a "proto-" DRS in the case of sentences that have proved to be grammatical. Our proto-DRSs seem to have a very simple structure in comparison to DRSs with the multiply embedded box constructions demonstrated in [11]. Nevertheless, they store the same information due to the conditions of a special status defined in def4.3.3.2. Moreover, several cases of ambiguities can simply be traced back to an underspecified state of these special conditions. Let us consider an illustration of these facilities.

(1) Most widowers court a blonde.

(2)

$most(e_0; e_1, e_2)$	$fixpoint(e_0)$, $e_0 < e_1$, $e_1 < e_2$, $newref(e_0)$
$widower(e_1; r_2)$	$newref(e_1)$, $newref(e_2)$
$court(e_2; r_2, r_3)$	$newref(r_2)$, $e_1 \approx r_2$
$blonde(r_3)$	$newref(r_3)$, $r_3 \approx \ ???$

(3) $e_2 \approx r_3$: 'It is often true that if someone is a widower he courts a blonde.'
    $e_0 \approx r_3$: 'There is a blonde whom most widowers court.'

The basic proposition (whose eventuality referent is e_0) is that a situation [e_1: somebody is a widower] often implies another situation [e_2: he courts somebody]; symbols '<' refer to these situations' not being facts but their and some of their characters' belonging to fictive worlds [15]. The widower necessarily belongs to the fictive world of our thinking about an abstract situation ($e_1 \approx r_2$). But which world does the blonde belong to? Referent r_3 is looking for its place... And it can find its place in different worlds (3) – without assuming different syntactic structures behind the two readings[5].

Let us finish the section with the definition of a language generated by a gasg:

---

[3] We regard [14] the phenomenon of free-word-order languages sketched below as a clear advantage (of (the ranked rule system) of GASG over PS grammars: the word-order version '*I gave yesterday Mary in the library a paper.' of the correct sentence 'Yesterday I gave Mary a book in the library.' is also acceptable in Hungarian (with no difference in meaning), but not in English. Thus certain free adverbs ('yesterday,' 'in the library') can be inserted between the finite verb and its arguments quite freely (in the case of idioms as well, as if 'Peter kicked yesterday the bucket.' were correct in English); which can be accounted for in GASG easily - by choosing the same rank parameter, namely 7, for both the regent-argument adjacency requirement and that between free adverbs and the finite element of sentences - in the case of Hungarian. In English, however, the regent-argument adjacency requirement is to be qualified as stronger. Whilst in a PS grammar a regent and its arguments are to constitute a phrase so the case of Hungarian (with intervening free adverbs) is hard to explain.

[4] Semantic restrictions (e.g. on the [+human] status of an argument) can be put in the set of formal conditions (def4.3.2.) among morphologic and syntactic ones.

[5] The freedom in finding the appropriate world has language-dependent restrictions depending also on the argument status and other grammatical relations of the li of the indefinite article in question, of course.

[**Def7:** In the circumstances defined above in def6, we can say that gasg G generates sentence s through segmentation mos and numeration num, and G assigns the given sentence DRS sem as its discourse-semantic representation. It can also be said in this situation that gasg G has generated reading $\langle s, mos, num, sem \rangle$. $L(G) \subset (A \cup Y)^*$ is called the language defined by gasg G if $L(G)$ consists of the sentences generated by G.]

3 Implementation in Prolog

Our work is permanently developed, and the version which is available now can parse uncompound neutral Hungarian sentences. In our parser we insist on the theoretically clear principles of GASG, but naturally we have to make some technical changes according to the special features of programming in Prolog. Hence, parts of the lexical items in GASG are stored in different places in the program. The **database** section contains the lexical items which are morphemes and consist of the ownword, phonological features and some inherent syntactic conditions (e.g. the argument structure). Other environmental conditions and properties of morphemes that a lexical item searches are put down in the **synrelations** predicate. This part means the syntactic parsing together with a checking that contains the **immprec** predicate. The third part of a GASG lexical item – which is semantics – is represented in the **semantics** predicates.

The parsing starts with the main predicate **gramm**, which, after a successful phonological and morphosyntactic parsing, gives semantic representation formulated as a DRS:

```
gramm(SENTENCE):-
    words(SENTENCE,WL1), corr(WL1,WL), morphwl(WL, MLABL),
    numberlist(1,MLABL,NMLABL), phon(NMLABL,WL), immprec(NMLABL),
    synrel(NMLABL, SYNRELLIST, MIXEDLIST),
    semantics(MIXEDLIST, DRS, SYNRELLIST, MIXEDLIST),
    write(S), writeline(NMLABL), writeln2(SYNRELLIST), writeln3(DRS).
```

The first six predicates provide for the morphophonological cheking. The input is a simple string e.g.: "A fiú beül a székbe." 'the boy in-sit the chair-INESS' (The boy sits into the chair.). The **words** and the **corr** predicates find the words in the string and give us a list: ["a", "fiú", "beül", "a", "székbe"], and after this the **morphwl** predicate searches the morphemes in the sentence according to the lexical items in the database section. Before the linguistic parsing there is a technical but quite important step: to give serial numbers to the morphemes. It is necessary because of the unambiguous identification of the morphemes in the sentence. The morphemes get double numbers that shows in which word is which morpheme. For example in the sentence Péter be-ül-tet-i a lány-t a szék-be 'Peter in-sit-cause-3sg.defobj the girl-ACC the chair-INESS' (Peter sits the girl into the chair.) the morpheme -tet gets the numbers (2,3). In this way we can always refer squarely to the morphemes.

The **database** section contains such lexical items as it is shown below:
```
lexi(m("","ül",""),labstem("sit",phonfst(1,1,1,2),2,[["NOM","LOC"]])).
lexi(m("t","A","t"),labder("cause",phonfsu(2,2,0.2,2),2,ac(-1,0,1))).
```

All lexical items contain the ownword of the morpheme (m("","fiú","")), and a "label" with the English "translation", the phonological features (phonfst), the category (1=noun/suffix for nouns, 2=verb/suffix for verbs, 3=determiners, 4=adjunct) and the syntactic conditions.

In this phase of the programme we can already account for such phonological phenomena as vowel-harmony, lowering, V~ ⊘ alternation, linking vowels, lengthening, shortening etc. Phonologically two kinds of requirements are needed. The first one accounts for the choice of the possible realizations of the given morpheme (lexical item), these possible realizations are technically variables in the own words. E.g. in the case of bokor ('bush') the own word is bokOr, and the phonological realization depends on the following suffix: bokor-ban 'bush-INESS' but bokr-ot 'bush-ACC'. Or in the case of the suffix -ban/-ben ('in') the own word is -bAn, and the frontness of the vowel depends on the frontness of the stem: bokor-ban 'bush-INESS' but szék-ben 'chair-INESS'. The other kind of requirements says how the lexical items effect on the phonological realizations of other lexical items in the same word (e.g. lowering stems or suffixes, or again vowel-harmony).

The most simple example of indirect satisfaction (def6.2.2) is the calculation of order of morphemes within words. Every suffix would like to be adjacent to the stem, but these requirements are not equally strong. According to the definition, if a requirement cannot be satisfied directly (there are more than one suffix in a word), it could be satisfied indirectly. If a suffix A wants to be adjacent to the stem on rank α, and a suffix B wants to be adjacent to the stem on rank β, and $\alpha < \beta$ then the acceptable morpheme order is: stem, A, B.

The checking/parsing demonstrated above gives us a list that calls the synrel predicate, which provides the syntactic parsing accordig to the morphemes in the words of the sentence. The synrel predicate calls the synrelations predicates, namely the morphemes call their own syntactic requirements. In this way the programme creates a new list, where next to the morphemes there is always another list, which contains the grammatical relations that the given morpheme can establish in the given sentence. The representation of a grammatical relation is an ordered septuple: gr[X,Z,Y, N,M, K,L]. In the expression the first three elements are the determiners of the relation: the first string is the name of the element that calls the relation, the second string is the environmental element that the first one searches and the third one is the type of the relation. The other four elements in the representation are the two numberpairs of the morphemes that have the relations.

In our system finite verbs look for the two pillars of their arguments – the arguments are defined in the lexical item. For example a non-transitive verb searches the noun pillar and the determiner pillar of its nominativ argument (relations: gr("regent", "noun", "subj", X, Y, N, M) and gr("regent", "det", "subj", X, Y, K, L) and a transitive verb searches four elements: the noun and determiner pillar of its nominative argument (the same as before) and looks for the determiner pillar and an accusative suffix as the representative of the noun pillar of its accusative argument. Determiners look for a noun stem for relation gr("det", "noun", "free", X, Y, K, L) and the stem of the finite verb for relation gr("det", "regent", "_", X, Y, K, L). The common nouns search the finite verb for a subject relation if they do not have a case marking suffix. In the case when the noun has a case marking suffix, it looks for the environmental morpheme. And finally the affixes search the stem for gr("pref/suff", "stem", "free", X, Y, N, M) and an environmental morpheme for a grammatical relation. For example the prefix be- 'in' searches a case marking suffix, which is the -bAn 'INESS'.

At this point the programme executes a "local search" – in the sense that every morpheme is to find environmental morphemes satisfying the appropriate grammatical relations. But this is far from enough becuse in this way sentence A Ɉµ a ļɲny ɪ̂ 'The boy the girl is sitting' could be accepted as a grammatical one. That is why some mutual search is required, which means that members of a pair of morphemes in a grammatical relation must find each other but no further morphemes can be found for the same relation. The mutual search is satisfied if every relation gr(A,B,REL,X,_,Z,_) finds the relation gr(B,A,REL,Z,_,X,_).

If all predicates above are satisfied, the sentence is grammatical "according to" morphosyntax, and the program gives us a right morphosyntactic output, which calls the predicate semantics.

If a sentence has a right morphosyntactic output, predicate semantics carries out semantic selection, and if it is also successful, it can provide the semantic representation: a DRS.

According to DRT, determiners (and proper names) provide referents, common nouns predicate something of them, and finite verbs provide a situation referent besides predicating something (of other predicates). In our new conception determiners tell in which world they provide the given referent [15]. The output of our semantic representation is shown in (4-5). The referents contain three numbers that refer to the morpheme that has provided it (e.g. r(3,1,1)=the first provided referent by the first morpheme of the third word). The ordering between the worlds they belong to (see (2-3)) is also represented by the following relations: ∼, <or=, <.

(4) A fiú be-ül-tet-het-i a büszke medvé-jé-t a szék-em-be.
the boy in-sit-cause-can-sg3.objdef the proud bear-poss.3sg-ACC the chair-poss.1sg-INESS
'The boy can sit his/her proud bear in my chair.'

(5) semantic output for sentence (4):
```
provref("old",[r(1,1,1)])
provref("<or=",[r(1,1,1),(e(4,4,1)])
pred("clever",[r(1,1,1)])
pred("boy",[r(1,1,1)])
provref("new",[e(4,2,1)])
provref("∼",[(e(4,3,1),e(4,2,1)])
pred("sit_into",[e(4,2,1),r(5,1,1),r(8,1,1)])
provref("new",[e(4,3,1)])
provref("<",[(e(4,4,1),e(4,3,1)])
pred("cause",[e(4,3,1),r(1,1,1),e(4,2,1)])
```

```
provref("fixpoint",[e(4,4,1)])
pred("may",[e(4,4,1),r(1,1,1),e(4,3,1)])
provref("old",[r(5,1,1)])
provref("<or=",[r(5,1,1),(e(4,4,1)])
pred("proud",[r(5,1,1)])
pred("bear",[r(5,1,1)])
pred("owns",[r(0,1,3),r(5,1,1)])
provref("old",[r(8,1,1)])
provref("<or=",[r(8,1,1),(e(4,4,1)])
pred("chair",[r(8,1,1)])
pred("owns",[r(0,1,1),r(8,1,1)])
yes
```

References

1. Karttunen, L.: Radical Lexicalism. Report No. CSLI 86 68. Stanford (1986).
2. Zeevat, H.: A Compositional Version of Discourse Representation Theory. Linguistics and Philosophy 12 (1991) 95–131.
3. Zeevat, H.: Aspects of Discourse Semantics and Unif. Gr. Ph.D., U. Amsterdam (1991).
4. van Eijck, J., H. Kamp: Representing discourse in context. In: van Benthem, J., A. ter Meulen (eds.): Handbook of Logic and Language. Elsevier, Amst. & MIT Press, Cambridge, Mass. (1997).
5. Chomsky, N.: The Minimalist Program. MIT Press, Cambridge, Mass. (1995).
6. Partee, B. H., G. B. ter Meulen, R. P. Wall: Mathematical Methods in Linguistics. Kluwer Academic Publ (1990).
7. Kamp, H.: A theory of truth and semantic representation. In: Groenendijk, J., T. Janssen, M. Stokhof (eds.): Formal methods in the study of language. Amsterdam, Math. Centre.
8. Groenendijk, J., M. Stokhof: Dynamic Predicate Logic. Linguistics and Philosophy 14 (1991) 39–100.
9. Chomsky, N.: Syntactic Structures. The Hague, Mouton (1957).
10. Lehmann, Ch.: On the Function of Agreement. In Barlow, M., Ch.A. Ferguson (eds): Agreement in Natural Languages. Approaches, Theories, Descriptions. CSLI Stanford (1988) 55–65.
11. Kamp, H., U. Reyle: From Discourse to Logic. Kluwer Academic Publ. (1993).
12. Alberti, G., K. Balogh, J. Kleiber, A. Viszket: Totally Lexicalist Morphology. Talk at the Sixth International Conference on the Structure of Hungarian. Düsseldorf (2002).
13. Alberti, G.: Indo-Germanic Word Order Phenomena in a Totally Lexicalist Grammar. In Sprachteorie und germanistische Linguistik 11.2. Univ. of Debrecen, Hungary (2001) 135–193.
14. Alberti, G., K. Balogh, J. Kleiber: GeLexi Project: Prolog Implementation of a Totally Lexicalist Grammar. In de Jongh, H. Zeevat, Nilsenova (eds.): Proceedings of the Third and Fourth Tbilisi Symposium on Language, Logic and Computation. ILLC, Amsterdam, and Univ. of Tbilisi.
15. Alberti, G.: Lifelong Discourse Representation Structure. In Poesio, M., D. Traum (eds.): Gothenburgh Papers in Computational Linguistics 00-5 (2000) 13–20.

Pseudo Context-Sensitive Models for Parsing Isolating Languages: Classical Chinese – A Case Study

Liang Huang[1], Yinan Peng[1], Zhenyu Wu[1], Zhihao Yuan[1], Huan Wang[2], and Hui Liu[1]

[1] Department of Computer Science and Engineering, Shanghai Jiao Tong University
1954 Huashan Road, Shanghai 200030, P.R. CHINA
{lhuang, ynpeng, neochinese, yuanzhihao, lh_Charles}@sjtu.edu.cn
[2] Department of Chinese Literature and Linguistics, East China Normal University
No. 3663 North Zhongshan Road, Shanghai, P.R. China 200062

Abstract. In this paper, we compare the performance of three probabilistic pseudo context-sensitive models on parsing isolating languages. These models are all based on the conventional probabilistic context-free grammar (PCFG). The first one is well known for statistical parsing of English, while the other two are novel models conditioning the siblings of an expanding nonterminal. We experiment these models on Classical Chinese, a typical isolating language. And it is quite surprising to see that through only a little more conditioning, the new models significantly outperform the first model. To this end, our work shows the impact of typological distinction on parsing and provides two simple-yet-effective conditioning models for isolating languages.

1 Introduction

The traditional Probabilistic Context-Free Grammar (PCFG) is widely used for parsing natural languages, but generally the results are far from satisfactory, due to the wrong context-freeness assumptions. There are various approaches to go beyond PCFG, such as Constraint-based grammar (like HPSG), and Mildly Context Sensitive Grammar (like TAG). But the simplest method is to maintain the PCFG backbone and condition on some history or lexical information. Typical instances include history-based parsing [7] and data-oriented parsing. Some state-of-the-art statistical parsers [4,5,6] are also in this approach, conditioning on lexical heads. In fact, this approach refines the nonterminal set with additional features that represent contextual and lexical information. But theoretically it still remains context-free. So these models are generally called pseudo context sensitive models, as in [3].

Ideally it is obvious that conditioning on more history results in better predictions. But practically as the sparse-data problem occurs, it is really a matter of experimentation to decide what features to condition. In addition, typological and genetic classifications suggest different methods of conditioning. Unfortunately however, in recent years, the majority of statistical parsers have been for

A. Gelbukh (Ed.): CICLing 2003, LNCS 2588, pp. 48–51, 2003.

English and other inflecting languages. Then it should be really interesting to do some pioneering study of conditioning for isolating languages. In these latter languages such as Chinese and Vietnamese, all the words are morphologically unanalyzable, and grammatical functions are expressed mostly by word order. Intuitively one should condition more on contextual information for isolating languages. And in the following sections, we will present and study three such models on a typical isolating language – Classical Chinese.

2   The Three Models

Most state-of-the-art statistical parsers [4,5,6] make heavy use of conditioning on lexical headwords. But in our work, as there are no large treebank for isolating languages, we do not use lexicalization. Instead, all the three models in this paper condition on parent and/or contextual nonterminals/terminals. All the parameters are learned from a treebank, using the naïve Maximum Likelihood Estimation, and without smoothing.

Model 1: The Old Model. Model 1 is essentially an abstraction and simplification of well-known conditioning models in the parsing literature. It is based on pure PCFG and conditions on the parent nonterminal only. Given a rule $N \rightarrow N_1, N_2, \ldots, N_m$, we use the conditional probability

$$P(N \rightarrow N_1, N_2, \ldots, N_m \mid parent(N)) \tag{1}$$

in training and parsing. It is almost the same model used in [3], except that their estimations are made from unsupervised iterations. Some later models like [4] still use this as backbone.

Model 2: Parent-Rule Model. In comparison, Model 2 is a novel model, but with only a small difference: it further conditions on the parent-rule, i.e., the rewriting rule used by the parent to generate the expanding nonterminal. So we condition the probability as

$$P(N_i \rightarrow N_{i,1}, N_{i,2}, \ldots, N_{i,n} \mid N \rightarrow N_1, N_2, \ldots, N_i, \ldots, N_m) \tag{2}$$

As the parent-rule already implies the parent nonterminal, Model 1 is properly contained in this model. And intuitively this model is appealing for isolating languages, because different parent-rule implies different siblings, thus different context symbols (nonterminals or terminals).

Model 3: The Left-Right Model. Model 3 is a brand new model, also motivated for context distinction. It conditions explicitly on the direct left/right context symbols. Here we use a simplified approach, defining the left/right symbol to be the nearest symbol to the left/right on the path to the root. Consider, for instance, a rule $N \rightarrow N_1, N_2, \ldots, N_m$, we have:

$$Left(N_i) = N_{i-1}(1 < i \leq m), \quad Left(N_1) = Left(N) \tag{3}$$

$$Right(N_i) = N_{i+1}(1 \leq i < m), \quad Right(N_m) = Right(N) \tag{4}$$

To complete the recursive Left/Right definition, we intentionally add a rule $TOP \to LEFT\ \ S\ \ RIGHT$ to the grammar, where S is the original start nonterminal. And the probability of a rule is conditioned as

$$P(N \to N_1, N_2, \ldots, N_m \mid Left(N),\ Right(N)) \tag{5}$$

In some sense, this model considers more information than Model 2, as some recursive backtracking symbols are lost there. Illustrations of the three models are shown in Figure. 1.

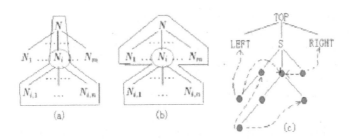

Fig. 1. Illustrations of the three models. (a) Model 1. the siblings of the expanding nonterminal are ignored. (b) Model 2. the siblings (contexts) are considered. (c) Model 3. Examples: dashed lines point to the Left/Right symbols.

3   Results

To test the performances of these models, we conducted a very preliminary experiment based on [1,2] for Classical Chinese, a typical isolating language. All the three models are implemented by CKY-style dynamic programming. The POS tags [1] incorporate some syntactic distinctions, and the forward-backward tagger outputs for each word possible POS tags with probabilities. And there are 1100 sentences in the treebank [2], where 5% (randomly chosen) is used as testset, and the others as trainset. The average sentence length is only 5.376 words, since generally Classical Chinese is extremely succinct. And the grammar rules [2] are binary or unary. To make a better comparison, we experimented the three models against the baseline pure PCFG model (with a little variation [2] inherited by the three conditioning models). We use the standard PARSEVAL measures to compare the performance, and the results are shown in Table. 1.

All the results are generally much better than the state-of-the-art results for Penn Treebank, mainly because the extremely short sentence length in Classical Chinese. It is quite promising to find that with only a little more conditioning on nonterminal history, the two new models substantially outperform Model 1. This is partly because contextual distinction is very crucial in isolating languages. And new models capture this distinction either by indirectly considering the

Table 1. Results of different models. We use the same notation as in [4,5,6]

MODEL	LR	LP	CBs	0 CBs	≤ 2 CBs
pure PCFG	86.9	85.7	0.31	72.5	92.4
Model 1	89.5	90.2	0.28	89.1	94.8
Model 2	96.1	96.1	0.10	96.5	97.8
Model 3	94.0	93.3	0.14	94.4	96.9

parent-rule or by directly conditioning the Left/Right symbol. In comparison, such distinction for inflecting languages may be marginal, as evidenced by the success of Model 1 in [3]. We also see that Model 3 is slightly below Model 2, possibly due to data sparseness. Furthermore, it does not distinguish which side (Left/Right) is closer to the expanding nonterminal, which is partially captured by Model 2.

4   Conclusion

In this paper, we have proposed three pseudo context-sensitive models for parsing isolating languages. The two novel models, simple as they are, make promising improvements against the old model that is successful for English. Our work advocates different conditioning models for different families of languages and suggested two working methods of context distinction.

Acknowledgements. We are grateful to Prof. Ruzhan Lu, Dr. John Chen, Prof. Dan Jurafsky, and the two anonymous reviewers for their helpful advices and comments.

References

1. Huang, L., Peng, Y., Wang, H., Wu, Z.: Statistical Part-of-Speech Tagging for Classical Chinese, In: Proceedings of TSD'02, LNAI 2448, pp. 115–122.
2. Huang, L., Peng, Y., Wang, H., Wu, Z.: PCFG Parsing for Restricted Classical Chinese, In: Proc. of the 1st SIGHAN workshop (at COLING 2002), pp. 19–24.
3. Charniak, E.: Context-Sensitive Statistics for Improved Grammatical Language Models Programs. In Proceedings of AAAI'94, pp. 728–733.
4. Charniak, E.: Statistical Parsing with a Context-free Grammar and Word Statistics, In Proceedings of AAAI'97.
5. Magerman, D.: Statisitical decision-tree models for parsing. In Proceedings of ACL'95, pp. 276–283.
6. Collins, M.: Three generative, lexicalized models for statistical parsing. In Proceedings of ACL'97, pp. 16–23.
7. Black, E., Jelinek, F., Lafferty, J., Magerman, D., Mercer, R., Roukos, S.: Towards history-based grammars: using richer models for probabilistic parsing, In Proceedings of DARPA Speech and Natural Language Workshop, 1992

Imperatives as Obligatory and Permitted Actions

Miguel Pérez-Ramírez and Chris Fox

Computer Science Department
University of Essex
Wivenhoe Park, Colchester CO4 3SQ,
United Kingdom
{mperez, foxcj}@essex.ac.uk

Abstract. We present a dynamic deontic model for the interpretation of imperative sentences in terms of Obligation (O) and Permission (P). Under the view that imperatives prescribe actions and unlike the so-called "standard solution" (Huntley [10]) these operators act over actions rather that over statements. By distinguishing obligatory from non-obligatory actions we tackle the paradox of Free Choice Permission (FCP).

1 Introduction

The aim of this paper is to provide a model for the interpretation of direct imperative sentences in terms of Obligation and Permission. The model possesses properties that corresponds with our intuitions about the use of obligatory imperatives and is not affected by inferential problems such as the paradox of Free Choice Permission (FCP) (von Wright [34, 35, 36]; Wieringa and Meyer [39], Kamp [13]), which in non-deontic approaches is known as Ross's counterexample (Ross [28]; von Wright [34]).

In general, imperatives are conceived as sentences used to issue orders or commands (Radford [26]; Lyons [15]; Nodine [21]; Megginson [19]; MacFadyen [16]). Sentences involving requests, threats, exhortations, permissions, concessions, warnings, advices, etc. can also be taken to be imperatives (see Huntley [11]; Sperber and Wilson [30] and Hamblin [7] for an extensive classification of imperatives). This is a broad characterisation, which may include other types of sentences. For simplicity of exposition, we will adopt a syntactic view of *direct imperatives*, since this view locates appropriate sentences[1] in a language and allows us intuitively to distinguish them from statements and questions. We shall adopt the following definition.

Definition: *Imperatives are sentences used to ask someone to do or not to do something and that do not denote truth-values.*

---

[1] Imperatives are a type of sentence. Levinson says "it seems that the three basic sentence types, *interrogative*, *imperative*, and *declarative* are universals, all languages appear to have at least two and mostly three of these" Levinson [14] p. 242).

A. Gelbukh (Ed.): CICLing 2003, LNCS 2588, pp. 52–64, 2003.
© Springer-Verlag Berlin Heidelberg 2003

This 'something' we shall call *requirement*. Examples are *Come here!* and *Stop!* They have no truth conditions as such.

Arguably, Jorgensen [12] began the modern debate about the modelling of imperatives. His main concern was to account for the inferential role of imperatives under apparent contradiction that they cannot be *true* or *false*. Having the imperative a) *Love your neighbours as yourself!* and the premise b) *Alison is your neighbour* it seems reasonable to infer c) *Love Alison as yourself* even thought a) and c) cannot be *true* or *false* (this pattern is called Jorgensen's dilemma, see Ross [28]; Walter [37]). Since 1937 there have been different ways of approaching imperatives (Weinberger [38]). In particular the *standard solution* (Huntley [10]) describes a common feature in different approaches. Its key characteristic is the assumption that the core meaning of imperatives is propositional: something that can be *true* or *false*. Typical of this approach is to split imperatives into two parts: a descriptive or propositional and a prescriptive part[2]. Jorgensen's offers a typical approach akin to the 'standard solution' where, for instance, *Post the letter!* is translated into *!The letter has to be posted*, using the symbol '!' and a statement. In this way classical logic is used to account for practical inference[3] leading to the derivation of unintuitive conclusions (see description in Pérez-Ramírez [22, 23]).

Deontic logic focuses on imperatives by using deontic concepts such as *obligation* and *permission* (von Wright [34] p. 14). It is one of the most prolific branches devoted to the study of imperatives (norms: sentences conveying obligation or permission) by using the operators Op and Pp, where usually p is a statement.

von Wright [34] presents a standard deontic logic which is akin to the standard solution. This logic validates the counterintuitive expression $Op \rightarrow O(p \vee q)$ which means that if 'it is obligatory that p' then 'it is obligatory that $p \vee q$'. For instance, "If one ought to mail a letter, one also ought either to mail or to burn it" (von Wright, 1968: p. 20). If $O(p \vee q)$ means that it is obligatory that $p \vee q$, a hearer may choose to perform q.

In more recent approaches the operator P acts over actions. However Dignum et al. [5] say that event thought dynamic logic solve some paradoxes in standard deontic logic, the paradox of FCP still remains under the form $P(\alpha) \rightarrow P(\alpha + \beta)$ where α and β are actions and + is the choice operator. They illustrate with the example $P(Talk$ to the $president) \rightarrow P(Talk$ to the $president + Shoot$ the $president)$. They propose a logic in which P operates on actions and they distinguish strong (P_s) and weak permission (P_w) (when applied to statements these operators satisfy $P_w(p \vee q) \equiv P_w p \vee P_w q$ and $P_s(p \vee q) \equiv P_s p \wedge P_s q$). However, they face new problems, for instance their logic validates the expression $P_s(\alpha) \rightarrow P_s(\alpha \& \beta)$. They explain, "if α is permitted, it is (also) permitted in any combination with other actions". So the logic validates the example $P(fire$ a $gun) \rightarrow P(fire$ a gun $\&$ aim at the $president)$. They propose a solution to these new problems by making reference to context.

---

[2] Hare [8] used the terms *phrastic* and *neustic* respectively to refers these two components.

[3] The term *practical inference* usually refers inferences in which imperatives take part as premises.

There have been different proposals to solve the paradox of FCP but according to von Wright [36], even though a huge literature on the topic has grown up, a universally accepted solution to these difficulties has not yet been found.

The paradox of FCP is an inferential problem initially caused by the scope of the classical logic connectives when used with non-propositional objects. Given a statement we can introduce any other statement to form a disjunction. Also, given a conjunction of statements we can eliminate one of the components. These properties are not desirable when modelling imperatives. Approaches in which O and P operate over actions try to restrict the scope of dynamic operators by introducing new operators and sometimes also new problems. Thus, either we should restrict the application of classical logic rules when operating on statements in the scope of O and P, or else we can consider O and P to be applied to something other than statements, and consider the rules that are appropriate for the operations on such expressions. It is the latter option that we take here.

Thus, to this end, we follow the intuition that imperatives prescribe actions. Thus, a dynamic deontic logic (L_{DL}) is developed here in which the operators for Obligation O(-) and permission P(-) operate over actions rather that over statements. The intended meaning of the operators O(-) is "*It is obligatory to –*" and for P(-) is "*It is permitted to –*" where "–" is the place for the requested action. The multimodal operator '[-]' is used to model actions behaviour [9] and Hoare's triple ($Pre \rightarrow [\alpha]Pos$ where α is an action, *Pre* are pre-conditions and *Pos* are post-condition) is used to verify correctness of actions. We use the dynamic operators composition ';' and choice '+' to model the conjunction and disjunction of requirement respectively. One of the key ideas introduced in the model is the intuition of encapsulating what is obligatory in order to distinguish what is obligatory from what is not. This solves some of the paradoxes mentioned above. Actually, it will be shown that the distinction between obligatory actions and simple actions solves the problem of FCP and the model behaves according to our intuitions about the use of imperatives.

In particular, if an action is obligatory two things are assumed a) it belongs to a set where all the obligatory actions are kept and b) it is satisfiable (the action can be performed). The second assumption is analogous to Chellas's axiom where 'ought' implies 'can' (Chellas [4] p. 125).

The remainder of the paper is organised as follows: Section 2 analyses properties of imperatives and their relation with the paradox of FCP. Section 3 presents the model that involves the main features observed in Section 2. Section 4 illustrates the use of the model to solve inferential problems. Section 5 includes the main conclusions.

2   Analysis

It is not appropriate to use classical logical connectives between imperatives [22, 23]. Imperatives can be seen to prescribe actions. For this reason, it is more appropriate to model imperatives in terms of actions and operations between them (as in Dynamic Logic [9]). In turn, we will argue that obligation and permission (O and P) should operate over imperatives, not statements. Modelling imperatives in terms of actions help to solve some counterintuitive results such as the lack of truth–values. Further, by 'encapsulating' what is obligatory, we can solve the FCP in a fairly simple way. This mirrors a proposal for the treatment of certain issues in the interpretation of imperatives and imperative inference.

2.1   Physical Action and Imperatives

We have said that imperatives convey requirements. Requirements are requests for action or prescriptions of actions. This view is shared by other authors (Ross [28], von Wright [34], Hamblin [7] p. 45 and Segerberg [29] among others). For instance Segerberg [29] takes imperatives to be prescriptions for actions. For Ross ([28] p. 54), an imperative is a sentence that expresses an immediate demand for action but that does not describe a fact: an imperative is satisfied if we have the result of an agent's action.

Hamblin suggests that the core meaning of an imperative is an action. "We can analyse, as it were, the kernel or content of the imperative -*the action* (though the word is not sufficiently general) that the imperative enjoins- without worrying about the way in which it enjoins it ..." (Hamblin [7] p. 45, emphasis added).

An imperative might be used to indirectly change the world through the hearer or to prevent an action, by conveying a requirement. Some examples of prescriptions of actions are, *Write a letter!* that prescribes the action of writing and *Come here!* that prescribes the action of approaching. Examples of imperatives requiring that a state of affairs remains unchanged by forbidding or preventing actions are *Don't close the door!* and *Don't turn the lights off!* Thus prescribing and forbidding actions are included in our definition of imperative and requirements. In our model, imperatives will prescribe obligatory or permitted actions. The following expressions illustrate schemas of obligatory imperatives in which dynamic operators model the operators between requirements.

- $O(a)$	*It is obligatory to* a
- $O(\alpha_1 ; \alpha_2)$	*It is obligatory to* α_1 AND α_2
- $O(\alpha_1 + \alpha_2)$	*It is obligatory to* α_1 AND α_2
- $O(\phi \Rightarrow \alpha)$	*It is obligatory to* α if ϕ
- $O((\phi \Rightarrow \alpha_1) + (\neg \phi \Rightarrow \alpha_2))$	*It is obligatory to* (α_1 if ϕ else α_2)

An action is not *true* or *false*. The operator ';' describes a sequencing suitable to model the property of dependence. As with conjunctions of imperatives, this operator is not commutative. We will see that there is no rule to eliminate an action from a conjunction of actions. The operator '+' describes a disjunction of actions.

2.2   Obligation and Permission

One of the first intuitions about obligatory and permitted actions is that if the action is obligatory, then it is permitted. That is, if we assume a fixed state of affairs, the set of all obligatory actions in that state is contained in the set of permitted actions in that state. See Fig. 1 below, where *PAct* is the set of all permitted actions, *OAct* is the set of all obligatory actions, and *CAct* is the complement set between permitted and obligatory actions.

Usually it is assumed that O and P are interdefinable, as follows $O(\alpha) = \neg P(\alpha')$ and $P(\alpha) = \neg O(\alpha')$, where α is an action and α' is the negation of the action α. That is, if an action α produces the result Q, then α' produces the result $\neg Q$. We can define the negation of composed actions as follows.

- If a is an atomic action then a' is the negation of a
- The negation of $(\alpha_1 ; \alpha_2)$ is $(\alpha'_1 + \alpha'_2)$
- The negation of $(\alpha_1 + \alpha_2)$ is $(\alpha'_1 ; \alpha'_2)$
- The negation of $(\phi \Rightarrow \alpha)$ is $((\neg\phi)? + \alpha')$

Example: α=*Come here* α'=*Don't (Come here)*

Negation of composed actions does not necessarily correspond with common use of sentences in language but logically actions behave according to the formulation above. von Wright [35] p. 17 seems to hesitate about the idea of considering that O and P are interdefinable. Weinberger argues, "If we understand normative systems as control systems we cannot chose permission as the basic operator, because a system embracing only permission cannot function as a control system, since permission does not exclude any possible state" (Weinberger [38] p. 289).

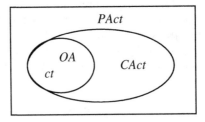

Fig. 1. Relation between Obligatory (OAct) and Permitted (PAct) actions

2.3   Obligation in a Context

Intuitively, *context* refers to the situational information or state of affairs where imperatives and other type of sentences are uttered. Context might involve a variety of different factors such as situation, agents (speaker and hearer) and their roles, amongst others. Whatever precise nature, it appears to play a crucial role in the interpretation of imperatives. Depending on the conditions provided by a context, an imperative can be obligatory in that context. For instance, in a military environment a soldier is not usually in position to give orders to a general.

Authors such as Sperber and Wilson [30], Bunt [2], Manara and De Roeck [17] agree that context is related to people's view or perception of the world or a particular situation rather than the world or the situation themselves. These authors conceive context in terms of what people have in their minds. That is, the concept of context includes the broad band of beliefs, knowledge and intentions. All of them can be represented as propositions. Following these authors, we subscribe to the view that:

Definition: *A context is a consistent collection of propositions that reflects a relevant subset of agents' beliefs.*

Nevertheless, the view of context as a set of propositions (see Buvac [3]) will not commit us here to an ontology or classification of components or to the use of operators such as **B** for beliefs and **K** for knowledge (see Ramsay [27]; Turner [32]). We simply assume that all that which constitutes a context can be represented in terms of propositions so the context is viewed as a consistent set of propositions. We agree with Chellas [4] that an imperative can be obligatory in some contexts but not in others.

A context can be conceived of as a collection of beliefs. As with any logic of beliefs, there may be constraints upon what can be inferred. For example, if we believe P, it need not mean that we can infer that we also believe $(P \vee Q)$. Similarly, if we believe that we are under an obligation to *Post a letter*, we do not necessarily believe that we are obliged to *Post the letter or burn it.*

3   Model for Imperatives in Terms of Obligation and Permission

The model we present here goes along the lines of First-order dynamic logic, similar to the logic provided by Harel [9], in which the operators for obligation and permission are introduced in the language L_{DL}. Once the set of action is defined we encapsulate the actions that are obligatory or permitted. Thus the obligation or permission of actions is given in terms of their membership in these sets.

3.1   Syntax of L_{DL}

3.1.1   Definition of Sets
We define the following sets. Let $C = \{c, c_1, c_2, ...\}$ be a set of constant symbols; let $V = \{x, y, z, ...\}$ be a set of variable symbols; let $F = \{f, g, h, ...\}$ be a set of function symbols; let $AtAct = \{a, a_1, a_2, ...\}$ be a set of atomic actions; and let $AtPred = \{p, q, r,...\}$ be a set of atomic predicate symbols.

3.1.2   Definition of Terms

$$t ::= c|v|f(t_1, t_2, ..., t_n)$$

The recursive definition of terms is as follows: a term is a constant (c), a regular variable (v), or a function $(f(t_1, t_2, ..., t_n))$ of arity n (n arguments), where f is a function and $t_1, t_2, ..., t_n$ are terms.

3.1.3   Syntax of L$_{DL}$

It is assumed here that *Pred* contains all formulae of L$_{DL}$. Thus, if $p \in$ *AtPred*, t_1, t_2, ..., t_n are terms, $x \in V$, and $\alpha \in$ *Act* (the set of actions, defined below), then all possible wffs in L$_{DL}$ are defined as follows:

$$\phi ::= p(t_1, t_2, ..., t_n) \mid t_1 = t_2 \mid \neg\phi \mid \phi_1 \wedge \phi_2 \mid \exists x\phi \mid O(\alpha) \mid P(\alpha) \mid [\alpha]\phi$$

where $p(t_1, t_2, ..., t_n)$ is an atomic formula (predicate), with arity n. $t_1 = t_2$ is the equal-ity predicate (=). $\neg\phi$ is the negation of ϕ. $\phi_1 \wedge \phi_2$ is the conjunction of formulae ϕ and ψ. $\exists x\phi$ is the existential quantifier. $O(\alpha)$ indicates that α is obligatory. $P(\alpha)$ indicates that α is permitted. $[\alpha]\phi$ is a modal expression indicating that ϕ holds after the action α is performed. We assume the usual classical definitions for $\vee, \rightarrow, \bullet, \forall$, together with $[\alpha]\phi = \neg<\alpha>\neg\phi$.

Note that both O and P are introduced in L$_{DL}$ and both of them operate over actions. If α is an action, $O(\alpha)$ stands for *it is obligatory to* α and $P(\alpha)$ stands for *it is permit-ted to* α.

3.1.4   Category of Actions

We define here the set *Act* of actions as follows.

$$\alpha ::= a(t_1, t_2, ..., t_n) \mid \phi? \mid \alpha_1 \; ; \; \alpha_2 \mid \alpha_1 + \alpha_2$$

where $a(t_1, t_2, ..., t_n)$ is the atomic action. $\alpha_1; \alpha_2$ is the sequential composition of ac-tions used to represent conjunction of requirements. $\alpha_1 + \alpha_2$ is the disjunction of ac-tions and is used to represent disjunction of requirements. $\phi?$ is a test and it just veri-fies whether ϕ holds or not and is used to represent conditional requirements ($\phi?; \alpha) = (\phi \Rightarrow \alpha)$.

3.2   Axioms

A0) T any tautology
A1) $O(\phi \Rightarrow \alpha)$ • $\phi \rightarrow O(\alpha)$
A2) $P(\phi \Rightarrow \alpha)$ • $\phi \rightarrow P(\alpha)$
A3) $[\phi?]\psi$ • $\phi \rightarrow \psi$
A4) $[\alpha_1; \alpha_2]\phi$ • $[\alpha_1]([\alpha_2])\phi$
A5) $[\alpha_1 + \alpha_2]\phi$ • $[\alpha_1]\phi \wedge [\alpha_2]\phi$
A6) $[\alpha](\phi \rightarrow \psi)$ $\rightarrow$ $[\alpha]\phi \rightarrow [\alpha]\psi$
A7) $\forall x\phi(x)$ $\rightarrow$ $\phi(t)$ Universal instantiation. t is free in $\phi(x)$.
A8) $\forall x(\phi \rightarrow \psi)$ $\rightarrow$ $\phi \rightarrow \forall x\psi$ provided that x is not free in ϕ
OPA) $O(\alpha)$ $\rightarrow$ $P(\alpha)$

3.3   Inference Rules

a) Modus Ponens   **(MP)** : If ϕ and $\phi \rightarrow \psi$ then ψ
b) Necessitation rule for actions   **(Nec)** : If ϕ then $[\alpha]\phi$
c) Universal generalization   **(UG)** : If ϕ then $\forall x\phi$ provided x is not free in ϕ

The following are derived rules, which operate between actions, obligatory or not. *Pre* usually indicates pre-conditions and *Pos* post-conditions. Hoare's triple ($Pre\{\alpha\}Pos$) will be represented by the expression $Pre \rightarrow [\alpha]Pos$ in L_{DL} (see Harel [9]; Gries [6]; Hoare [10]). The expression (Hoare's triple) $Pre \rightarrow [\alpha]Pos$ means that "If the assertion *Pre* is *true* before initiation of the action α, then the assertion *Pos* will be *true* on its completion" (Hoare [10] p. 577). We assume that $Pre\{\alpha\}Pos= Pre \rightarrow [\alpha]Pos$ and that the equality restricts both sides to hold in the same context.

(I;):	If $\vdash Pre \rightarrow [\alpha_1]Pos'$	and $\vdash Pos' \rightarrow [\alpha_2]Pos$	then $\vdash Pre \rightarrow [\alpha_1;\alpha_2]Pos$
(I+):	If $\vdash Pre \rightarrow [\alpha_1]Pos$	and $\vdash Pre \rightarrow [\alpha_2]Pos$	then $\vdash Pre \rightarrow [\alpha_1+\alpha_2]Pos$
(I⇒):	If $\vdash (Pre \wedge \phi) \rightarrow [\alpha]Pos$	and $\vdash (Pre \wedge \neg\phi) \rightarrow Pos$	then $\vdash Pre \rightarrow [\phi?;\alpha]Pos$
(WP):	If $\vdash Pre \rightarrow [\alpha]Pos$	and $\vdash Pos \rightarrow \gamma$	then $\vdash Pre \rightarrow [\alpha]\gamma$
CDR 1:	If $\vdash Pre \rightarrow [\alpha]Pos$	and $\vdash P' \rightarrow [\alpha]Q'$	then $\vdash (Pre \wedge P') \rightarrow [\alpha](Pos \wedge Q')$
CDR 2:	If $\vdash Pre \rightarrow [\alpha]Pos$	and $\vdash P' \rightarrow [\alpha]Q'$	then $\vdash (Pre \vee P') \rightarrow [\alpha](Pos \vee Q')$

3.4   Interpretation

The interpretation for L_{DL} and its soundness follows Harel's (1979) semantics for first order dynamic logic. A model for L_{DL} is presented elsewhere [23]. Due to the lack of space, we do not repeat the details here. The model uses a possible worlds semantics in which actions define sets of pairs of states (w, w') such that the performing of an action starting in state w reaches state w'. If a state w satisfies a formula ϕ we use the notation $w \vDash \neg\phi$.

3.5   Correctness of Actions

An action α is *partially correct* with respect to a state w iff $w \vDash Pre \rightarrow [\alpha]Pos$. α is *totally correct* with respect to a state w iff $w \vDash Pre \rightarrow <\alpha>Pos$. Here 'correctness' corresponds to the term used by Hoare [10] for programs and that we adopt here for actions. When an action is totally correct it means that it is possible to perform that action: it is not an impossible action. In L_{DL}, the assumption that an obligatory action is satisfiable can be expressed as $O(\alpha) \rightarrow <\alpha>true$.

3.6   Encapsulation

In Dynamic Logic [9], if α is an action, α is correct iff $[\alpha]\psi$ holds in some state. Given the correctness of an action $[\alpha_1]Pos_1$ it is possible to infer the correctness of a disjunction of actions $[\alpha_1 + \alpha_2]Pos$. If we do not make explicit which actions are obligatory and which are not, we would derive the wrong conclusions. We can encapsulate within a sequence all those actions which are obligatory or permitted. In this way we can have expression such as $O(\alpha_1) \wedge [\alpha_1 + \alpha_2]Pos$ which says that α_1 is obligatory and that the disjunction of the obligatory action α_1 with α_2 ($[\alpha_1 + \alpha_2]Pos$) is *correct*, but not that $\alpha_1 + \alpha_2$ is *obligatory*.

3.7   Defining Sets of Obligatory Actions

Here we give some of the formal details of the idea of encapsulating what is obligatory and permitted by defining subsets of *Act* as follows. A similar distinction can be found in Segerberg [29] and Piwek [24, 25].

Definition: *Permitted and Obligatory requirements*
Let *Pact* and *OAct* be the sets of permitted and obligatory actions, respectively, such that $OAct \subseteq PAct \subseteq Act$.

The sets of permitted and obligatory actions at a world can be defined as follows.

Definition: *Permitted actions at a world w*
Let $PAct_w$ be $\{\alpha | \alpha \in PAct$ and α is permitted in $w\}$

Definition: *Obligatory actions at a world*
Let $OAct_w$ be $\{\alpha | \alpha \in OAct$ and α is obligatory in $w\}$

OAct can be expressed as the union of all obligatory actions at each world w in W $[OAct = \cup_{w \in W} OAct_w]$. Analogously *PAct* can be expressed as the union of all permitted actions at each world $w \in W$, $PAct = \cup_{w \in W} PAct_w$. The following conditions apply on the sets $OAct_w$ and $PAct_w$ respectively.

C1) If $\alpha_1 \in OAct_w$ and $\alpha_2 \in OAct_w$ then $\alpha_1; \alpha_2 \in OAct_w$ or $\alpha_2; \alpha_1 \in OAct_w$
C2) If $\alpha_1 \in PAct_w$ and $\alpha_2 \in PAct_w$ then $\alpha_1; \alpha_2 \in PAct_w$ or $\alpha_2; \alpha_1 \in PAct_w$

C1 indicates that if α_1 and α_2 are obligatory then both are obligatory. $\alpha_1; \alpha_2$ and $\alpha_2; \alpha_1$ simply cover the case of dependent actions.

The validity of obligatory and permitted actions can be expressed in terms of their membership of the sets in which they are characterised

$$w \vDash O(\alpha) \text{ iff } \alpha \in OAct_w$$
$$w \vDash P(\alpha) \text{ iff } \alpha \in PAct_w$$

4   Obligation/Permission and Inference

4.1   Jorgensen's Dilemma

As we can see L_{DL} combines obligatory actions and propositions in inference. The analogous of Jorgensen's dilemma would be as follows. If $p(x) = x$ *is your neighbour* and $\alpha(x) = Love\ x\ as\ yourself$, then we can write the deontic version of the dilemma as follows.

> $\forall x\ O(p(x) \Rightarrow \alpha(x)) = It\ is\ obligatory\ to\ love\ your\ neighbour\ as\ yourself$
> $p(Alison) = Alison\ is\ your\ neighbour$

1) $k \vDash \forall x\ O(p(x) \Rightarrow \alpha(x))$	assumption
2) $k \vDash \forall x\ p(x) \to O(\alpha(x))$	1), axiom A1)
3) $k \vDash p(Alison)$	assumption
4) $k \vDash p(Alison) \to O(\alpha(Alison))$	2), Univ. Inst.
5) $k \vDash O(\alpha(Alison)) = It\ is\ obligatory\ to\ love\ Alison\ as\ yourself$	3), 4) and MP

This shows that L_{DL} mixes obligatory action with statements and allows making inference without being affected by inferential problems.

4.2   Paradox of Free Choice Permission-FCP

There is no rule to infer the membership of a disjunction of actions from the membership of one action in the set of obligatory or permitted actions. This is reinforced by the condition C1). That is, from $O(\alpha_1)$ is not possible to infer $O(\alpha_1+\alpha_2)$, for some other action α_2 and from $P(\alpha_1)$ is not possible to infer $P(\alpha_1+\alpha_2)$. Thus, L_{DL} does not validate the following inferences.

> $O(Post\ the\ letter) \to O(Post\ the\ letter + Burn\ the\ letter)$
> $P(Talk\ to\ the\ president) \to P(Talk\ to\ the\ president + Shoot\ the\ president)$

Therefore, the model is not affected by the paradox of FCP and also it does not introduce new problems.

4.3   Conjunction Elimination and Obligations

It is not possible to eliminate an action from a conjunction of either obligatory or permitted actions. That is, from $O(\alpha_1;\alpha_2)$ is not possible to infer either $O(\alpha_1)$ or $O(\alpha_2)$ and from $P(\alpha_1;\alpha_2)$ is not possible to infer either $P(\alpha_1)$ or $P(\alpha_2)$. This solves the problem of incomplete satisfaction derived in some approaches akin to the standard solution. For instance, if we represent the obligation of the imperative *Buy oranges and apples!*, as $O(Buy\ oranges\ ;\ Buy\ apples)$, the model validates neither

$$O(Buy\ oranges\ ;\ Buy\ apples) \rightarrow O(Buy\ oranges)\ \text{nor}$$
$$O(Buy\ oranges\ ;\ Buy\ apples) \rightarrow O(Buy\ apples)$$

We can observe that the model describes properties of imperatives such as the lack of truth-values and dependence. For instance the model may validate O(*Write a letter*; *send the letter to your family*) but not O(*send the letter to your family*; *Write the letter*). Examples using the operator for permission are analogous.

5   Feasibility of Implementation and Applications of the Model

Implementation of the model involves first a syntactic analysis as presented in [23] where actions prescribed are associated with imperatives by identifying verbs in imperative mood. The analysis provides the Hoare´s triple representation of the imperative in a formal language, which introduces Generalized quantifiers into dynamic logic. Once we have a logical representation for imperatives, a theorem   prover could be applied to reason with these representations, incorporating the notion of encapsulation.

Regarding applications for a model for imperatives and deontic concepts, Meyden [20], mentions that the deontic modalities are becoming increasingly of wide interest in computer science, with proposed applications including intelligent legal information systems, computer security, software engineering, database integrity constraints and agent oriented programming. Martino [18] provides more examples of applications related to information retrieval, databases and legal information systems. In a more ambitious plan, he proposes that the public administration might be automated on the basis of verification and application of regulations. Recently agents have become quite popular. For instance Piwek [24, 25] models imperatives within a framework for communicating agents. Vere and Bickmore [33] report the constructions of a basic agent. They affirm that a person can make statements to the agent, ask it questions, and give it commands. Thus, a robot receiving an order might be able to assess the order before making decisions towards the satisfaction of the order. Such autonomous behaviour requires a system of reasoning which does not derive inappropriate obligations.

6   Conclusions

L_{DL} is given under first order dynamic logic, the operators for obligation and permission operate over actions rather that over statements. L_{DL} models the deontic concepts of obligation and permission not what it is uttered but what it is obligatory and permitted. Obligation can be verified with respect to context.

L_{DL} associates actions with imperatives; therefore it is not committed to assign truth-values to these sentences. Rather, it evaluates the membership of the action in turn in the set of obligatory actions. L_{DL} combines obligatory actions and propositions in inference. The model deals satisfactorily with the deontic version of Jorgensen's dilemma. It is not possible the elimination of an action from a conjunction of either obligatory or permitted actions. There is not rule to infer the membership of a disjunction of actions from the membership of one action in the set of obligatory or permitted actions. This avoids the paradox of FCP. Both Segerberg [29] and Piwek [24,25] model actions in terms of their descriptions, which are governed by classical logic. We, instead, use a logic of actions. Because operations between actions are not governed by classical logic, this avoids some counterintuitive conclusions.

Acknowledgements. The first author would like to thank CONACYT-IIE.

References

1. Alchourrón Carlos, Martino Antonio, 1990. *"Logic Without Truth."* Ratio Juris. March 1990. 46–67.
2. Bunt, Harry. 2000. *"Dialogue pragmatics and context specification"* in *"Abduction, Belief and Context in Dialogue;"* Studies in Computational Pragmatics, Amsterdam: Benjamins, Natural Language. Processing Series No. 1, 2000. P. 81–150.
3. Buvac, Sasa. 1995. *"Resolving Lexical Ambiguity Using a Formal Theory of Context."* Visited in October 1998. in http://www-formal.Stanford.EDU/buvac/
4. Chellas, B., 1971. *"Imperatives."* Theoria. Vol 37, 114–129. 1971
5. Dignum F., Meyer J.-J.Ch., and Wieringa R.J., 1996. *"Free choice and contextually permitted actions."* Studia Logica, 57:193–220, 1996.
6. Gries, David, 1983. *"The Science of programming."* Department of Computer Science. Cornell University. Upson Hall Ithaca, NY. 1983.
7. Hamblin, C. L, 1987. *"Imperatives."* Basil Blackwell. USA. 1987
8. Hare R. M., 1961. *"The Language of Morals."* Oxford at the Clarendon Press. Reprinted in 1961.
9. Harel David, 1979. *"First-Order Dynamic Logic."* Lecture Notes in Computer Science. Edited by Goos and Hartmanis. 68. Springer-Verlag.Yorktown Heights, NY. 1979.
10. Hoare. C. A. R., 1969. *"An Axiomatic Basis for Computer Programming."* Communications of the ACM, Vol. 12, No 10. October 1969. pp. 576–580, 583.
11. Huntley Martin, 1984. *"The Semantics of English Imperatives."* Linguistics and Philosophy. Vol 7. 1984. 103–133.
12. Jorgensen Jorgen, 1937. *"Imperatives and logic."* Erkenntnis. Vol. 7, (1937-1938), pp. 288–296.
13. Kamp, H., 1973. *"Free-Choice Permission."* Chicago: University of Chicago Press. Kamp, H. 1973. Proc. of the Aristotelian Society, N.S. 74: 57–74.
14. Levinson Stephen C., 1983. *"Pragmatics."* Cambridge textbooks in linguistics. Cambridge University Press. 1983.
15. Lyons John, 1968. *"Introduction to Theoretical Linguistics."* Cambridge at the University Press. 1968.
16. MacFadyen Heather, 1996. *"Using Verb Moods."* HyperGrammar. University of Ottawa. 1996.
17. Manara and De Roeck, 1997. *"Context as Partial Beliefs, and the Pragmatic Modelling of Presuppositions."* Context 97. Brazil. 66–74.
18. Martino A. Antonio, 1981. *"Deontic logic, Computational linguistics and legal information systems."* Proceedings of the first international conference on logic, informatics, law. Vol. 2. Florence, Apr. 6–10. 1981.
    http://www.idg.fi.cnr.it/pubblicazioni/monografie/lid1bint.htm
19. Megginson David, 1996. *"The Purpose of a Sentence."* HyperGrammar. University of Ottawa. 1996.

20. Meyden R. van der, 1996. *"The Dynamic Logic of Permission."* Journal of Logic and Computation, Vol 6, No. 3 pp. 465–479, 1996. A version of this paper appeared at the IEEE Symposium on Logic in Computer Science, Philadelphia, 1990.
21. Nodine Mark H., 1996. *"Glossary of Grammatical Terms."* A Welsh Course. 1996. http://www.cs.brown.edu/fun/welsh/Glossary_main.html#I
22. Pérez-Ramírez, M., 2000. *"Imperatives, state of the art."* CLUK 3. University of Brighton. UK. April, 2000.
23. Pérez-Ramírez, M., 2002. *"Formal pragmatic model for imperatives interpretation"* University of Essex. UK. (draft thesis).
24. Piwek, P., 2000. *"Imperatives, Commitment and Action: Towards a Constraint-based Model."* In: LDV Forum: Journal for Computational Linguistics and Language Technology, Special Issue on Communicating Agents, 2000.
25. Piwek, P., 2001. *"Relating Imperatives to Action."* In: Bunt, H. and R.J. Beun, Cooperative Multimodal Communication, Lecture Notes in Artificial Intelligence Series 2155, Springer, Berlin/Heidelberg. 2001.
26. Radford Andrew, 1997. *"Syntactic theory and the structure of English. A minimalist approach."* Cambridge University Press. 1997.
27. Ramsay, A. 2000. *"Speech act theory and epistemic planning"* in *"Abduction, Belief and Context in Dialogue;"* Studies in Computational Pragmatics, Amsterdam: Benjamins, Natural Language. Harry Bunt, Bill Black (eds). Processing Series No. 1, 2000. P. 293–310.
28. Ross A., 1941. *"Imperatives and Logic."* Theoria (journal). Vol. 7. 53–71. 1941.
29. Segerberg Krister, 1990. *"Validity and Satisfaction in Imperative Logic."* Notre Dame Journal of Formal Logic Volume 31, Number 2, Spring 1990. 203–221.
30. Sperber Dan and Wilson Deirdre, 1986. *"Relevance."* Communication and Cognition. Great Britain London. 1986.
31. Stirling, Colin. 1992. *"Modal and temporal logics."* Handbook of Logic in Computer Science, vol. 2. Edit. S. Abramsky and D. Gabbay and T. Maibaum. Publisher, Oxford University Press. 477–563. 1992.
32. Turner Raymond. 1992. *"Properties, Propositions and Semantic Theory. In Computational Linguistics and Formal Semantics."* Edited by Michael Rosner and Roderick Johnson.Cambridge University Press. Cambridge. 159–180. 1992.
33. Vere, Steven and Bickmore, Timothy, 1990. *"A Basic Agent."* Computational Intelligence, Vol. 6.
34. von Wright George Henrik, 1968. *"An Essay in Deontic Logic and The General Theory of Action."* North Holland Publishing Company-Amsterdam. 1968.
35. von Wright, Henrik Georg. 1991. *"Is There a Logic of Norms?"* Ratio Juris. 1991. 67–79. 1991.
36. von Wright, Henrik Georg. 1999. *"Deontic Logic: A personal View"* Ratio Juris. 1999. 26–38. 1999.
37. Walter Robert, 1996. *"Jorgensen's Dilemma and How to Face It."* Ratio Juris. Vol 9. No. 2 June 1996. 168–71.
38. Weinberger Ota, 1991. *"The Logic of Norms Founded on Descriptive Language."* Ratio Juris. 1991. 284–307.
39. Wieringa R.J. and Meyer J.-J.Ch.. 1993. *"Applications of deontic logic in computer science: A concise overview."* In J.-J.Ch. Meyer and R.J. Wieringa, editors, Deontic Logic in Computer Science: Normative System Specification. Wiley, 1993. 17–40.

Formal Representation and Semantics of Modern Chinese Interrogative Sentences

Jia-ju Mao, Qiu-lin Chen, and Ru-zhan Lu

Department of Computer Science and Engineering, Shanghai JiaoTong University
Shanghai, People's Republic of China, 200030
{mao-jj, lu-rz}@cs.sjtu.edu.cn, qiulinchen@hotmail.com

Abstract. In modern Chinese, interrogative sentences are transformed from indicative sentences. At first, this paper gives the classification of modern Chinese interrogative sentences and their transformation from indicative sentences. Then we analyze the querying focus and point out that the querying focus is an abstract of a component of an indicative sentence and so an interrogative sentence is formed. Adopting the idea of the structured meaning approach, we present the semantics of modern Chinese interrogative sentences and their formal representations basing on the functor. All kinds of Chinese interrogative sentences including "NP+ne" and "VP+ne" are analyzed. Why we start from QF to study interrogative sentences is also discussed.

1 Introduction

As a kind of expressions, interrogative sentences play important roles in people's communication. In question-answering systems [1] and human-computer spoken dialogue systems [2], the using of interrogative sentences is also indispensable. One uses interrogative sentences to express doubts and put forward doubts [3].

Research on the interrogative sentence is continuous. With the development of computational linguistics, the semantics of the interrogative sentence is investigated from a formal view. A number of theoretical frameworks have been proposed [4], [5]. The two general approaches are proposition set approach and structured meaning approach [6]. People always use these approaches to study English. As to Chinese, the study has lagged behind. Almost all researchers study Chinese by focusing on segmentation, tagging and parsing [7]. Only linguists study Chinese interrogative sentences, but they rarely study them from the formal view.

Unlike English, Chinese has no morphology [8]. It is an open language. Its expression is very flexible and full of ellipses. So the Chinese interrogative sentence is. And there is no Wh-movement in Chinese. In addition, some Chinese interrogative sentences have no corresponding format in English. Thus, theories that study English cannot be applied to Chinese directly. They cannot present a reasonable interpretation of Chinese sometimes.

A. Gelbukh (Ed.): CICLing 2003, LNCS 2588, pp. 65–74, 2003.

In this paper, we adopt the idea of structured meaning approach, present a formal representation of Chinese interrogative sentences and give an interpretation to their semantics. The paper is structured as follows. First, we describe the representation and interpretation of Chinese semantics (in Section 2). In section 3, we give the classification and querying focus of modern Chinese interrogative sentences. In section 4, the formal representation and semantics of modern Chinese interrogative sentences are described in detail. Then we give a discussion about why we start from QF to study interrogative sentences. And the last part is a conclusion.

2   Representation and Interpretation of Chinese Semantics

As discussed above, Chinese is an open language and its word order is flexible. We can not get its logical form for computation as easily as we get it from English. The method for representing Chinese is a gradual process as follows [9].

Natural language sentence
↓
Functor or expanded functor with all arguments
↓
High order predicate formula
↓
Logical form
↓
The interpretation of semantics

Here we use *functor* as the media between a Chinese sentence and its logical form, which makes it possible to get the logical form automatically. The functor has features of both verbs and predicates. So it can be used to analyze and interpret semantics [10].

Functor needs all arguments. Although Chinese allows ellipses, in logic we must figure out all its necessary components. Thus a functor is a whole high order predicate. Here is an example of a Chinese sentence and its functor.

(1)   *Xin shu xuesheng mai le yiben.*
      New book student buy le one
      The student has bought a new book.

The functor of (1) is : V_{MAI} (XUESHENG, YIBEN, XINSHU).
And we can get the logical form of the sentence:

$$\exists x \,\exists y(\text{XUESHENG}\,(x) \wedge \text{XINSHU}\,(y) \wedge V_{MAI}(x, y))$$

We will interpret our sentences under the Chinese intentional language model with possible world W [11].

3   Classification and Querying Focus of Interrogative Sentences

It is not until 1980's that linguists began to study Chinese interrogative sentences. The structure, character and grammatical meaning etc. are their emphasis. Basing on their achievements, we describe the classification of Chinese interrogative sentences and how they are transformed from indicative sentences. Then we analyze the concept of querying focus.

3.1 Classification

An interrogative sentence[1] is transformed from its corresponding indicative sentence [12]. In Chinese, the word order of an interrogative sentence is the same as that of the indicative sentence. And there are no Wh-movement and no helping verb. Interrogative sentences exist in four kinds. They are Yes/No (Y/N) interrogative sentence, Wh-interrogative sentence, alternative interrogative sentence (A or B) and Positive/Negative (P/N) interrogative sentence (A not A).

Y/N Interrogative Sentence. We can get a Y/N interrogative sentence by changing the intonation from the indicative particle to the interrogative particle. Particle words "a, ba, ma" can be attached to a Y/N interrogative sentence. For example:

(2)   *Jintian shi xingqisan. ⇒ Jintian shi xingqisan ma?*
       Today is Wednesday. ⇒ Today is Wednesday ma?
       Today is Wednesday. ⇒ Is today Wednesday?

Wh-interrogative Sentence. We can get a Wh-interrogative sentence by changing the intonation to the interrogative particle and substituting words in the indicative sentence with corresponding interrogative pronouns without changing the word order. Particle words "a, ne" can be attached to a Wh-interrogative sentence. For example:

(3)   *Zhangsan qu Beijing le. ⇒ Zhangsan qu na'er le?*
       Zhangsan go Beijing le. ⇒ Zhangsan go where le?
       Zhangsan has gone to Beijing. ⇒ Where has Zhangsan gone?

Alternative Interrogative Sentence (A or B). We can get an alternative interrogative sentence by juxtaposing several items of an indicative sentence and changing the intonation to the interrogative particle. Particle words "a, ne" can be attached to an alternative interrogative sentence. For example:

(4)   *Xiaohong chi pingguo. ⇒ Xiaohong chi pingguo haishi chi li?*
       Xiaohong eat apple. ⇒ Xiaohong eat apple or pear?
       Xiaohong eat apple. ⇒ Does Xiaohong eat an apple or a pear?

P/N Interrogative Sentence (A not A). Actually, the P/N interrogative sentence is a special kind of alternative interrogative sentences. We can get it by placing the

---

[1]   Denoting the modern Chinese interrogative sentence in the following except for illustrating clearly.

positive and negative formats of the predicate together. So the P/N interrogative sentence has a format of A-not-A. For example:

(5) *Xiaohong chi pingguo.* ⇒ *Xiaohong chi bu chi pingguo?*
     Xiaohong eat *apple.* ⇒ *Xiaohong eat not eat apple?*
     Xiaohong eat apple. ⇒ *Does Xiaohong eat an apple or not?*

3.2 Querying Focus

Querying focus (QF) is the information focus of an interrogative sentence and the object that the interrogator wants to know [13]. No QF, no interrogative sentence [14]. This is the essence of an interrogative sentence.

In Y/N interrogative sentences, QF is the proposition. Sometimes it can be centralized on a point. This point can be noted by accent when talking or stress when writing[15]. In Wh-interrogative sentences, QF is interrogative pronouns. In alternative interrogative sentences (A or B), QF is the difference between A and B. For example, the QF of (4) is "apple or pear". In P/N interrogative sentences (A not A) , A-not-A embodies the interrogative information. So it is the QF[16]. In Chinese a word or a phrase aiming at QF is enough to answer the question that an interrogative sentence brings out. One needn't to use a full sentence.

4   Representation and Semantics of Interrogative Sentences

4.1 Proposition Set Approach and Structured Meaning Approach

In computational linguistics, there are two general approaches proposed for the meanings of interrogative sentences. They are the proposition set approach and the structured meaning approach.

Proposition Set Approach. The proposition set approach dates back to Hamblin [17], [18] and was further developed and refined by Karttunen [19] and Groenendijk & Stokhof [20]. Its essential idea is that the meaning of an interrogative sentence is the set of its possible full answers, that is, a set of propositions. For example

(6) Q: *Did Mary like roses?*   {LIKE(R)(M), ¬LIKE(R)(M)}
     A: *No.*   [No]=¬[Antecedent of]{LIKE(R)(M),¬LIKE(R)(M)}

Structured Meaning Approach. The structured meaning approach goes back to Ajdukiewicz [21], as noticed in Hiz [22]. It was developed by Hull [23], Tichy [24] , Hausser & Zaefferer [25], von Stechow [26] and Ginzburg [27]. Generalizing over a number of important differences between the theories that follow this approach, the basic idea is that the meaning of an interrogative is a function that, when applied to the meaning of the answer, yields a proposition. For example:

(7) Q: *Did Mary like roses?* λf [f(LIKE(R)(M))]
     A: *No.* λp [¬p]
     Question applied to answer: λf [f(LIKE(R)(M))](λp[¬p]) = ¬LIKE(R)(M)

Manfred Krifka [28] pointed out that the proposition set approach runs into three problems. These problems also occur in Chinese. So we adopt the idea of structured meaning approach to analyze the representation and semantics of Chinese interrogative sentences. We formalize the sentence based on the functor. To keep notation simple, we will suppress the reference to possible world and presume that correct parsing tree is available.

4.2 Representation and Semantics of Chinese Interrogative Sentences

As we have known, an interrogative sentence comes from its corresponding indicative sentence and QF is the unknown object. According to the formation of interrogative sentences discussed above, we can conclude that QF is an abstract of a component of an indicative sentence. Thus we define the semantics of interrogative sentences as the result of abstracting indicative sentences. The representation of an interrogative sentence is expressed as follows.

(8) $<\lambda x[\mu(x)], R>$

μ is the formal expression of its corresponding indicative sentence; x is the QF and R is the restriction that restricts the domain of x.
Basing on this definition, we will discuss specific semantics of all kinds of interrogative sentences respectively.

Y/N Interrogative Sentence. The QF of this kind is the whole sentence. According to (8), we can get the formal expression as follows.

(9) $<\lambda f[f(\mu)], \{\lambda p[p], \lambda p[\neg p]\}>$

The truth-value operators λp [p] and λp [$\neg$p] form the restriction, which enable to answer *yes* and *no*. For example, the formal expression of (2) is

$<\lambda f[f (V_{SHI}(JINTIAN, XINGQISAN))], \{\lambda p[p], \lambda p[\neg p]\}>$

We have mentioned above that sometimes QF can be centralized on a point, not the whole sentence. For example:

(10) Q:*Xiaohong chi pingguo ma?*   A: *chi/bu chi*
     Q:*Xiaohong eat apple ma?*   A: *Eat/not eat*
     Q:*Does Xiaohong eat an apple?*   A: *Yes/No*

Here QF is "chi". This phenomenon is caused by the ellipsis of Chinese. The interrogative sentence of (10) has the same meaning as (5). The answer to this kind of question depends on the hearer's understanding. It can be looked as a Y/N interrogative sentence or an ellipsis of a P/N interrogative sentence.

Wh-interrogative Sentence. The QF of this kind is the interrogative pronouns. According to (8), we can get the formal expression as follows

(11) $<\lambda x [\mu(x)], \{D\}>$

Here D is the domain that can be PERSON, TIME or PLACE etc. For example, the formal expression of (3) is

$$<\lambda x \ [V_{QU}(ZHANGSAN, x) \bullet O_{LE}], PLACE>$$

O_{LE} is the temporal operator.

Alternative Interrogative Sentence (A or B). The QF of this kind is the difference between alternative items. According to (8), we can get the expression as follows.

(12) $<\lambda x \ [\mu(x)], \{A, B\}>$

For example, the formal expression of (4) is

$$<\lambda x \ [V_{CHI}(XIAOHONG, x)], \{PINGGUO, LI\}>$$

P/N Interrogative Sentence (A-not-A). This kind exists only in Chinese. The QF is "A-not-A". According to (8), we can get the expression as follows.

(13) $<<\lambda x[V_x(a_1,...)],\{ A, \neg A \}>$

For example, the formal expression of (5) is

$$<<\lambda x[V_x (XIAOHONG, PINGGUO)], \{CHI, \neg CHI>$$

The format of A-not-A also occurs as an attaching interrogative sentence. Then the sentence is like "non-interrogative sentence, A-not-A? ". According to (8), the formal expression of this kind of questions is as follows.

(14) $<\lambda x[V_x(p)],\{ A, \neg A \}>$

Here, p is the formal expression of a non-interrogative sentence. For example

(15) *Xiaohong chi pingguo, xin bu xin?*
Xiaohong eat apple, believe not believe?
Xiaohong eats an apple, do you believe it or not?

The formal expression of (15) is

$$<\lambda x[V_x (HEARER, V_{CHI}(XIAOHONG, PINGGUO))], \{XIN, \neg XIN\}>$$

In Chinese, the rule to distinguish that "A-not-A" serves as an attaching interrogative sentence is that "A-not-A" can be canceled without destroying the integrity of the whole sentence.

"A-not-A" as an attaching interrogative sentence in Chinese is not the same as it in English. The positive or negative of English attaching interrogative sentence is determined by its former indicative sentence. In Chinese, there is no such limitation. A in "A-not-A" can be verb, adjective etc. But in English, the attaching interrogative sentence can only be a positive or negative auxil.v. plus a pronoun of the subject.

4.3 "W+ne" Interrogative Sentence

"W+ne" is a special phenomenon of Chinese interrogative sentences. It is an abbreviated version of an interrogative sentence. W stands for a sentence of non-interrogative format. "W+ne" includes "NP+ne" and "VP+ne". We will describe their meanings and representations respectively.

"NP+ne". Almost all linguists think that "NP+ne" has two meanings [29].

(16)   Meaning A: Querying the location of a person or thing, which equals to an interrogative sentence "Where is NP?"
Meaning B: Querying other information except the location, which equals to an interrogative sentence "How is NP?"

Correspondingly, we get formal expressions of "NP+ne" as follows.

(17) A $<\lambda x[V_{zai}(NP,x)], PLACE>$
B $<\lambda Q[Q(NP)], R>$

How to determine the domain R depends on the context and situation.

"NP+ne" is sensible to the context and situation very much. It is often used in spoken language. So to determine its concrete meaning is very difficult. Generally, we think that meaning A is used as a beginning question and meaning B can only be used as a continuing question. For example:

(18) Q: *Xiaohong ne?*   A: *Zai wuli.*
Q: *Xiaohong ne?*   A: *In room.*
Q: *Where is Xiaohong?* A: *In the room.*

(19) Q: *Xiaohong hen congming, Xiaozhang ne?*   A: *Geng congming.*
Q: *Xiaohong very clever, Xiaozhang ne?*   A: *More clever.*
Q: *Xiaohong is very clever, how about Xiaozhang?* A: *He is cleverer than Xiaohong.*

In (18), *"Xiaohong ne?"* chooses meaning A, whereas *"Xiaozhang ne?"* in (19) chooses meaning B.

"VP+ne". Here VP can be a verb structure, an adjective structure or a subject-predicate structure. The general meaning of "VP+ne" is that "If VP, what should be done or happened or other condition" [30]. So the formal expression of "VP+ne" is

(20) $<\lambda f[\text{Logic Form}(VP) \rightarrow f], R>$

There are two cases in which "VP+ne" has no presumption. The first case is that the subject is the second person and that the predicate limits to cognitive verb such as "kan, shuo, xiang, yiwei, xiwang etc.". So, the meaning of "VP+ne" is that "what is your opinion?". The goal is to know the opinion of the other side. The second case is that "VP+ne" has such a structure as "NP1 dui NP2 ne?". The word between the two NPs can be "dui, bi, wei, ba etc.". The meaning of it is that "How is NP1 to NP2? ".

5 Discussion

In this section, we discuss the reason that we start from QF to study interrogative sentences.

In past researches, the formal expression of interrogative sentences including English was defined according to that of indicative sentences [31]. However, the obtaining process of its formal expression is not pointed out clearly. This paper describes how it is obtained by using the concept of QF. This approach also suits English. More over, in Chinese, the answer to a question just needs to aim at the QF. One can say a verb or its negative to answer a question, but this is not permitted in English. So the λ-expression in this paper is more suitable for interpreting Chinese question and answer. For example:

(21) Q: *Xiaohong chi bu chi pingguo?*   A: *Chi.*
     Q: *Xiaohong eat not eat apple?*   A: *Eat.*
     Q: *Does XiaoHong eat apple or doesn't she?*   A: *She eats an apple.*

In (21), the first line is a Chinese question and its answer. We use our method to interpret as follows:

Question: $<\lambda x[V_x(XIAOHONG,PINGGUO)], \{CHI,\neg CHI\}>$
Answer: CHI
Question applied to answer: $<\lambda x [V_x(XIAOHONG,PINGGUO)], \{CHI,\neg CHI\} >$
                            (CHI)
                            $=V_{CHI}(XIAOHONG, PINGGUO)$

This is a correct interpretation.

In (21), the third line is its corresponding English question and answer. We use Ginzburg's method to interpret as follows.

Question: $<\lambda f [f], \{EAT(XIAOHONG,APPLE), \neg EAT(XIAOHONG, APPLE)\}>$
Answer: EAT(XIAOHONG, APPLE)
Question applied to answer: $<\lambda f [f], \{EAT(XIAOHONG,APPLE),$
                            $\neg EAT(XIAOHONG, APPLE)\}>$
                            $(EAT(XIAOHONG, APPLE))$
                            $= EAT(XIAOHONG, APPLE)$

Using Ginzburg's method to interpret its corresponding English question and answer, we also get a correct result. But if we apply Ginzburg's method to Chinese (the first line), we have no way to get a satisfying result. Because some of the phenomena in Chinese are not permitted in English, we can not use Ginzburg's method to interpret them.

6 Conclusion

Unlike English, Chinese is an open language. Its expression is flexible and full of ellipses. It has many special features in its interrogative sentences. By adopting the idea of the structured meaning approach, this paper studied Chinese interrogative sentences from a view of themselves.

In modern Chinese, interrogative sentences are transformed from their corresponding indicative sentences. At first, we gave the classification of modern Chinese interrogative sentences and their transformation. Then we analyzed the QF and pointed out that the QF is an abstract of a component of an indicative sentence and so an interrogative sentence is formed.

We also presented the semantics of modern Chinese interrogative sentences and their formal representations basing on the representation and interpretation of Chinese semantics. All kinds of Chinese interrogative sentences including "NP+ne" and "VP+ne" were analyzed. And we gave a discussion about why we started from the QF to study interrogative sentences.

References

1. Prager, etc. Question-answering by predictive annotation. Proceedings of SIGIR (2000)
2. Zdravko Kacic. Advances in spoken dialogue system development. IEEE ISIE'99 Bled, Slovenia (1999)
3. Jingmin Shao. Research on modern Chinese interrogative sentence. East China Normal University Press. (1996) 73–83
4. Ginzburg, Jonathan. Interrogatives: Questions, facts and dialogue. In S. Lappin (Ed.), The handbook of contemporary semantic theory. Oxford: Blackwell. (1995) 385–422.
5. Groenendijk, Jeroen, & Stokhof, Martin. Questions. In J. van Bentham & A. Ter Meulen (Eds.). Handbook of logic and language. Amsterdam: Elsevier (1997) 1055–1124
6. Manfred Krifka. Workshop on spoken and written texts. Austin (1999)
7. Jiaju Mao etc.. Formal interpretation of Chinese "na" in situations. JSCL'2001 (2001)
8. Tongqiang Xu. Language theory. North East Normal University press (1997)
9. Guangjin Jin, Ruzhan Lu. A method for extracting logical form from ellipsis sentences. Journal of software. Vol.9 No.6 (1998)
10. Ruzhan Lu etc. The representation, interpretation and computation of Chinese semantics. Proceedings of ICCLC Chicago (2000) 97–101
11. Guangjin Jin. The computational theory of modern Chinese Verb. Beijing University press (2001)
12. Dexi Zhu. The corpus of Dexi Zhu. Commerce press vol.1 (1999) 228–231
13. Shuxiang Lü. Chinese grammar summary. Commerce press. (1982) 281–287
14. Mingcen Lü. Searching grammar. Central China Normal university press (1989)
15. Shuxiang Lü. Interrogative, Negative, Positive. China Chinese. No. 4 (1985)
16. Yuwen Lin. Interrogative sentence. China Chinese. No.2 1985
17. Hamblinn,C.L. Questions. The Australian Journal of Philosophy, (1958) 36,159–168
18. Hamblin, C.L Questions in Montague grammar. Foundations of Language, (1973) 10, 41–53
19. Karttunen, Lauri. Syntax and semantics of questions. Linguistics and Philosophy. (1977) 1,3–44.
20. Groenendijk, Jeroen, & Stokhof, Martin. Studies on the semantics of questions and the pragmatics of answers. Doctoral Dissertation. University of Amsterdam. (1984)
21. Ajdukiewcz,Kazimierz. The logical foundation of teaching (1928)
22. Hiz, Henry. Introduction. In H. Hiz (Ed.), Questions (pp. IX–XVII). Dordrecht:Reidel. (1978).

23. Hull, R. A semantics for superficial and embedded questions in natural language. In E. Keenan (Ed.), Formal semantics of natural language. Cambridge University Press. (1975).
24. Tichy, Pavel. Questions, answers, and logic. American Philosophical Quarterly, 15, (1978).275–284.
25. Hausser, Roland, & Zaefferer, Dietmar. Questions and answers in a context-dependent Montague grammar. In F. Guenthner & S. J. Schmidt (Eds.), Formal semantics and pragmatics for natural languages. Dordrecht: Reidel. (1979) (339–358)
26. Von Stechow, Arnim. Focusing and backgrounding operators. In W. Abraham (Ed.),Discourse particles Amsterdam: John Benjamins. (1990). (37-84).
27. Ginzburg, Jonathan. Interrogatives: Questions, facts and dialogue. In S. Lappin (Ed.), The handbook of contemporary semantic theory. Oxford: Blackwell (1995) 385–422.
28. Manfred Krifka. For a structured meaning account of question and answers. Workshop on Spoken and Written Texts. Austin (1999)
29. Mingyu Li. "NP+ne"understanding. Chinese study No. 3 (1989)
30. Jianming Lu. Interrogative sentence caused by "non-interrogative format + Ne". Chinese No.6 (1982)
31. Ginzburg Jonathan and Ivan A. Sag. Interrogatives Investigations. CLSI publications (2001)

Analyzing *V+Adj* in Situation Semantics

Jia-ju Mao, Qiu-lin Chen, and Ru-zhan Lu

Department of Computer Science and Engineering, Shanghai JiaoTong University
Shanghai, People's Republic of China, 200030
{mao-jj, lu-rz}@cs.sjtu.edu.cn, qiulinchen@hotmail.com

Abstract. Sentences with V+Adj format (VA-statements) have the same syntax structure, whereas their semantic structures are always different owing to the semantic pointer of the adjective of V+Adj. In this paper we separate the verb and the adjective and start from the semantics of a VA-statement. The VA-statement can be decomposed into two statements, one formed from the verb (V-statement), and the other formed from the adjective (A-statement). We also point out the difference between the V-statement and A-statement and present a formal semantic representation using a fine-grained analysis of propositions in situation semantics. Then we propose that the verb and the adjective of V+Adj correspond to two kinds of predicates – relation and type, and give a formal model of the semantic pointer. An automatic analysis of the meaning of VA-statement is also presented. During the analysis, ambiguities that exist in VA-statements can be distinguished.

1 Introduction

Verb complement phrases have been the focus of discussion among Chinese grammarians because of their complexity. Since 1990s, many people, such as Peter Ke [1], Qingzhu Ma [2] and Wangxi Zhang [3], have been trying to reconstruct the Chinese verb complement system. The main notion about the verb complement is that it belongs to syntax and consists of a verb followed by a complement [4]. As a kind of verb complements, a "V+Adj " phrase is composed of a verb and an adjective as the complement. For example:

(1)a. Zhangsan he zui le jiu.
    Zhangsan drink drunk le wine.
    Zhang drank wine and Zhangsan was drunk.

(1)b. Zhangsan kan dun le dao.
    Zhangsan cut blunt le reamer.
    Zhangsan cut something and the reamer is blunt.

(1)c. Zhangsan chi wan le fan.
    Zhangsan eat done/none le rice.
    Zhangsan have eaten the rice. Or Zhangsan ate up the rice.

he zui , *kan dun* and *chi wan* in (1) are V+Adj phrases. They have the same syntax structure, but their semantic structures are thoroughly different. This is a difficulty in Chinese computational linguistics. Here we call a sentence with "V+Adj" format a

A. Gelbukh (Ed.): CICLing 2003, LNCS 2588, pp. 75–84, 2003.

VA-statement. The VA-statement has a more complex semantic relation than a general subject-predicate sentence. This is because of the complex relation between the agent of complementary adjective and the things related to the verb. In (1)a, adjective *zui* is used to describe the status of *Zhangsan*, but adjective *dun* in (1)b illustrates the property of the *reamer*. In (1)c, *wan* can modify either *chi* or *rice*. Thus, it is difficult to give the agent of the adjective according to the syntax structure of V+Adj. Shuxiang Lü [5] called the relation between the agent of complementary adjective and the things related to the verb as an expression. Now, this relation is characterized by semantic pointer of the complement [6].

In Chinese computational linguistics, one of the difficulties is how to analyze the meaning of a VA-statement automatically. Jiangsheng Yu [7] looked a V+Adj phrase as a predicate. His method can solve this problem to some extent, but it also carries other problems. In Chinese, there are lots of verbs and adjectives that can be combined together randomly. So it is difficult to enumerate each V+Adj. It is also difficult to express its arguments in a general form. As a result, he put the difficulty into the representation of the predicate. However, the propositional content of a VA-statement is looked as a composite proposition in Chinese logic theory [8]. In other words, we should not look a V+Adj phrase as a single predicate. So it is necessary to process the verb and the adjective of a V+Adj phrase separately.

This paper separates the verb and the adjective of a V+Adj phrase. We start from the semantics of VA-statements. A VA-statement can be decomposed into two statements [8], one formed from the verb that is noted as the V-statement, and the other formed from the adjective as the A-statement. So the propositional content of a VA-statement can be acquired from that of its V-statement and A-statement. In this paper we point out the difference between the V-statement and the A-statement. A V-statement corresponds to a thetic statement or a categorical statement [9], but A-statements can only correspond to a categorical statement. We present a formal semantic representation of the V-statement and the A-statement using a fine-grained analysis of propositions in situation semantics [10]. We also give the propositional content of a VA-statement. Then we present a method to process the V+Adj phrase basing on the semantics of the VA-statement. We propose that the verb and the adjective in a V+Adj phrase correspond to two kinds of predicates — relation and type. Then we can process the VA-statement from its syntax structure. We give a formal model of the semantic pointer that connects the agent of the adjective and the things related to the verb. An automatic analysis of the meaning of a VA-statement is also presented. During the analysis, ambiguities that exist in VA-statements can be distinguished. Finally, we give a conclusion.

2   Difference between V-Statement and A-Statement

We first give the V-statement and the A-statement of (1)a in (2):

(2)a. Zhangsan he jiu. (V-statement)
     Zhangsan drink wine.
     Zhang drank wine.

(2)b. Zhangsan zui le. (A-statement)
    Zhangsan drunk le.
    Zhangsan was drunk.

We compare (2)a and (2)b according to whether they have a sentence topic. The result is related to an interesting distinction identified by [9], namely the distinction between categorical and thetic statements, which has received attention in the linguistics literature [11], [12], [13], [14].

The two statements in (3), from Schmerling [15], exemplify a categorical statement and a thetic statement, respectively. In English, different intonation patterns are used for the two types of statements. A thetic statement is made by placing primary stress on the subject, whereas a categorical statement is made by placing stress on the predicate as well as the subject. (4) illustrates how a different intonation type, hence a different type of the statement, is chosen depending on the context.

(3)a. TRUman's DIED. (categorical)
(3)b. JOHNson's died. (thetic)

Both (3)a and (3)b describe an event of death of some individual, but they are uttered in different ways to make different packaging of information possible. We could characterize the different contexts for (3)a and (3)b using different salient questions in (4)a and (4)b, respectively.

(4)a. What happened to Truman?
(4)b. What is new?

As these questions show, in (3)b the information of Johnson's death is significant as a whole. Both parts, the event and the individual involved, are of equal communicative values. In (3)a, the question is put in such a way as to require information about Truman. Hence, it is assumed that Truman and the event of his death are of different communicative values.

In sum, categorical statements name an individual and an event, ascribing a property to and thereby adding information about an independently established individual, which is denoted by the "predication base" or "sentence topic". On the other hand, thetic statements simply posit a state of affairs and no entity involved is picked out as a predication base; all are presented simply as a part of the event [16].

Now let's consider the difference between (2)a and (2)b. Using the distinction between thetic and categorical statements relating to the sentence topic, we can say that the V-statement is a thetic statement[1] and the A-statement is a categorical statement with *Zhangsan* as the sentence topic for the VA-statement of (1)a, the V-statement is the main component that describes the state of an affair, whereas the A-statement is the complementary component that shows the property of *Zhangsan*. We could characterize the different contexts for (2)a and (2)b by using different questions in (5).

(5)a. What's new?
(5)b. What about Zhangsan?

---

[1] A V-statement can be a categorical statement sometimes, but it doesn't matter when analyzing the semantic pointer in a VA-statement.

Thus, (2)a describes the situation and no part is singled out as a predication base. The information of *Zhang drank wine* is significant as a whole. Both the state and the individual involved are of equal communicative value. On the other hand, (2)b is used to characterize *Zhangsan*. The word *Zhangsan* and its characteristics are of different communicative values.

We can analyze (1)b and (1)c similarly, and we can also get that the V-statement is a thetic statement and the A-statement is a categorical statement.

3 Formalizing VA-Statements in Situation Semantics

We have shown that the V-statement and the A-statement in a VA statement indicate different information articulation. We need a more fine-grained tool than those provided by the classical view of propositions as sets of possible world to incorporate such distinction in a formal analysis. In situation semantics, a fine-grained classification of information is achieved by adopting a structured universe of situation theoretic objects, in which various things such as individuals, properties, relations, types, situations, propositions and units of information are objects in their own rights.

We base our account on the distinction between two kinds of propositions — Russellian propositions and Austinian propositions [17]. We use Extended Kamp Notation (EKN) of Barwise and Cooper [18] which represents situation theoretic objects using a graphical notation similar to DRT(Discourse Representation Theory)[19]. Propositions in EKN include objects of the form (6).

(6)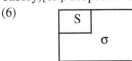

(6) is the proposition that a situation S supports the infon σ. A proposition like this is called an Austinian proposition. A second kind of situation theoretic propositions is a predication that some arguments are of a certain type, as represented in (7).

(7)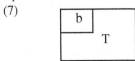

T is a type term and individual b is a proper assignment to the argument roles of T. A proposition like this one is called a Russellian proposition.

A parameter term[2] instead of a constant term can be used in any situation-theoretic objects. For example, when a parameter X occupies the argument position of a type as in (8), we call such a proposition a parametric proposition.

(8)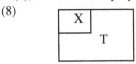

---

[2] A parameter is comparable to a variable in other formal languages, but a parameter is not only a syntactic term but also a semantic object, unlike a variable.

Operations between propositions include conjunction, disjunction, negation and so on. Here we give the notation of the propositional conjunction as in (9).

(9)

$$\boxed{\begin{array}{l} P_1 \\ P_2 \end{array}}$$

where P_1 and P_2 are propositions.

According to Kim Yookyung [16], situation semantics can readily accommodate different information articulations of a statement and the propositional content of a sentence should reflect its information articulation. Therefore, a sentence may have two different propositional contents depending on the information articulation: the propositional content of a thetic statement is an Austinian proposition about a certain situation, whereas that of a categorical statement is a Russellian one about an individual denoted by the sentence topic. A similar distinction was also exploited by Glasbey[20] to account for the existential reading and the generic reading of bare plurals[21]. So we can get that the propositional content of a V-statement is an Austinian proposition and the propositional content of an A-statement is a Russellian proposition.

Now, we consider (2) again. The V-statement in (2)a and the A-statement in (2)b are analyzed formally as an Austinian proposition and a Russellian proposition in (10)a and (10)b respectively.

(10)a.

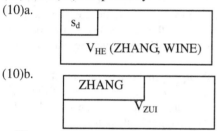

(10)b.

How to compound (10) to form the propositional content of the VA-statement in (1)a depends on the logic relation between the verb *he* and the adjective *zui*. In Chinese, there are two kinds of logic relations between the verbs and the adjectives of VA-statements. They are $p \wedge q$ and $p \wedge q \wedge (p \rightarrow q)$ where p and q are propositions. For simpleness, we just consider the case of conjunction of $p \wedge q$.

Then we get the propositional content of (1)a as (11)

(11)

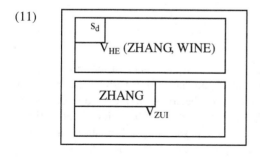

4   Analyzing VA-Statements

In section 3, we present the formal expression of a VA-statement from its meaning. In this section, we will present a method to get the formal expression from its syntax structure. As we have shown the propositional content of a V-statement is an Austinian proposition and that of a A-statement is a Russellian proposition. So we propose that the verb and the adjective in a V+Adj phrase correspond to two kinds of predicates–relation that can form an Austinian proposition and a Russellian proposition and type that can only form an Austinian proposition.

In the automatic analysis of a VA-statement, the difficulty is how to determine the agent of the adjective, which is also a difficulty in Chinese computational linguistics. VA-statements have the same syntax structure, but their semantic structures are different. Here we need the concept of *semantic pointer* that directly posits the semantic relation between components of a sentence.

4.1   Formal Model of Semantic Pointer

In a sentence, the semantics of a component A is directly related to that of another component B. Then B is the semantic pointer of A. The process to determine a semantic pointer is called semantic pointer analysis.

Jianming Lu [22] pointed out that there are six kinds of semantic pointers of the adjectives of VA-statements. They are the behavior of verb itself, the agent of the verb predicate, the patient of the verb predicate, the tool of the verb behavior, the location of the verb behavior and the goal of the verb behavior. We can conclude that they are all related to the verb in the VA-statement.

Now we can get that the semantic pointer of *zui* in (1)a is the agent of verb predicate *Zhangsan*, while the semantic pointer of *dun* in (1)b is the tool of the verb behavior *dao*. *wan* in (1)c has an ambiguity, its semantic pointer can be either the behavior of the verb itself *chi* or the patient of the verb predicate *fan*.

As mentioned above, the adjective in a V+Adj phrase corresponds to the predicate type in situation semantics, whereas the verb corresponds to the relation. We assume that we have a denotation function D that assigns a denotation to the basic constants and parameter symbols. For instance, if R is a verb, then D(R) is a relation. The predicate type of an Adjective can be represented as D(Adj). We note (12) as a parametric Austinian proposition formed by type D (adj).

(12)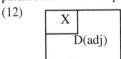

As to the possible scope of the semantic pointer, we can get that the scope is a set composed of the objects appropriate for the arguments of the verb relation and the behavior of the verb itself. Here we define the behavior of the verb itself as an argument of the verb relation. So a verb relation has roles of behavior, agent, patient, tool, location, goal and so on. In our automatic analysis, the verb relation must have roles necessary for determining the semantic pointer except that the verb relation does not have certain arguments in nature. For example the relation D(walk) has no patient. The relation can be represented as (13) in the format of Keith Devlin [23].

(13) < D(V)| Behavior, Agent, Patient, Tool, Goal, Location, Time, ... >

Assuming $a_1, a_2 ..., a_n$ are objects appropriate for the roles of D(V). Then parameter X in (12) can be anchored to one of the objects.

Now we can define the formal model of a semantic pointer of the adjective of a VA-statement.

Definition. The semantic pointer of an adjective of a VA-statement is the object to which the parameter X in (12) is anchored. In other words, any condition such as $X = a_i$ indicates a semantic pointing from the adjective to a_i, where X is a parameter and a_i is an object appropriate for a role of D(V). The process is called the semantic pointer analysis.

4.2   Automatic Analysis

In this section, we give an automatic analysis of a VA-statement from its syntax structure. Here we presume that correct parsing trees of relevant sentences are available. There are three steps:

Step1. Determining the roles of the verb relation.
Step2. Analyzing the semantic pointer.
Step3. Acquiring the propositional content.

According to these steps, let's look at sentences in (1). To consider VA-statement in (1)b[3], we rewrite (1)b as (14).

(14) Zhangsan kan dun le dao.
      Zhangsan cut blunt le reamer.
      Zhangsan cut something and the reamer is blunt.

Step1. Determining the roles of the verb relation. The *kan* relation V_{KAN} is represented as in (15)

(15) < V_{KAN} | *Behavior*: KAN, *Agent*: ZHANG, *Patient*: DEFAULT, *Tool*: DAO, *Goal*: DEFAULT, *Location*: DEFAULT, *Time*: DEFAULT >

We express it in the propositional format as (16)[4].

(16)
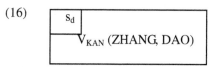

Step2. Analyzing the semantic pointer. The parametric Austinian proposition formed by type D (*dun*) is expressed in (17).

---

[3] The automatic analyses of VA-statements in (1)a and (1)b are similar. The difference lies in the semantics pointing from adjectives in V+Adj to different roles in Verb relations.
[4] We ignore roles whose values are DEFAULT.

(17)

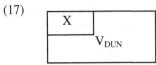

The role in (15) that satisfies (17) is *Tool*. Then X can be anchored to the object DAO. So we get (18).

(18) X= DAO

Step3. Acquiring the propositional content. The propositional content of (14) can be acquired from (16), (17) and (18). We represent it in (19)

(19)

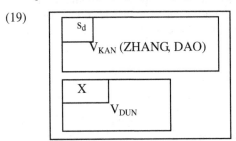

The VA-statement in (20)(=(1)c) is a little different from that in (1)a and (1)b in that there is an ambiguity.

(20) Zhangsan chi wan le fan.
    Zhangsan eat done/none le rice.
    Zhangsan have eaten the rice. Or Zhangsan ate up the rice.

Here the semantic pointer of *wan* can be the behavior of *eating* that is done or the rice that has been eaten up. Now we analyze the VA-statement in (20) using our method.

Step1. Determining the roles of the verb relation. The *chi* relation V_{CHI} is represented as in (21)

(21) < V_{CHI} | *Behavior*: CHI, *Agent*: ZHANG, *Patient*: RICE, *Tool*: DEFAULT, *Goal*: DEFAULT, *Location*: DEFAULT, *Time*: DEFAULT >

We express it in the propositional format as (22).

(22)

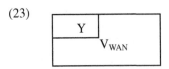

Step2. Analyzing the semantic pointer. The parametric Austinian proposition formed by type D (adj) is expressed in (23).

(23)

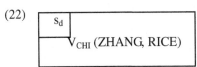

Either *Behavior* or *Patient* in (21) satisfies (23). Then Y can be anchored to the object CHI or RICE. So we get (24).

(24)a.   Y= CHI or
(24)b.   Y= RICE

Here we get an ambiguity. In other words, our method can distinguish the ambiguity in a VA-statement[5], which is an important step in an ambiguity resolution. The resolution of this ambiguity can only be achieved in the context of certain situations. Here we do not plan to discuss it further. We just give all possible results.

Step3. Acquiring the propositional content. The propositional content of (20) can be acquired from (22), (23) and (24). We represent it in (25).

(25)a.   (25)b.

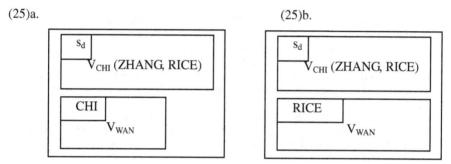

5   Conclusion

The understanding of VA-statements is a difficulty in Chinese computational linguistics for their semantic complexity. All VA-statements have the same syntax structure, whereas their semantic structures are always different owing to the difference between semantic pointers of the adjectives. Jiangsheng Yu looked a V+Adj phrase as a predicate. He put the difficulty into the representation of the predicate. In this paper we separated the verb and the adjective of a V+Adj phrase according to Chinese logic theory. We started from the semantics of VA-statements. A VA-statement can be decomposed into two statements: a V-statement, and an A-statement. So the propositional content of a VA-statement can be acquired from that of its V-statement and A-statement. Then we pointed out the difference between the V-statement and the A-statement. A formal semantic representation of the V-statement and the A-statement using a fine-grained analysis of propositions in situation semantics was also presented. We gave the formal representation of VA-statements. Then we proposed that the verb and the adjective of a V+Adj phrase correspond to two kinds of predicates–relation and type, and gave a formal model of

---

[5] There are many kinds of ambiguities in Chinese. But the ambiguity in (20) is difficult to distinguish with classical methods such as methods of hierarchy, syntax or sentence style because from the views of hierarchy, syntax or sentence style, the VA-statement in (20) is the same. So semantic pointer is an efficient method to distinguish this kind ambiguity.

semantic pointers. We also presented an automatic analysis of the meaning of a VA-statement. During the analysis, we can distinguish the ambiguity that can't be discerned with classical methods.

References

1. Peter Ke: Questions in Chinese Grammatical system. Proceeding of the 3rd International Conference on Chinese Linguistics. Beijing Language and Culture University Press (1990)
2. Qingzhu Ma and Hongqi Wang: Reflection on the some grammatical questions. Proceeding of the 1st International Conference on Chinese Linguistics (1998)
3. Wangxi Zhang: Research on the Semantics of Chinese Special Syntax. Beijing Language and Culture University Press (1998)
4. Wenhua Lü: Verb Complement System. World Chinese Teaching No. 3 Vol. 57. (2001)
5. Shuxiang Lü: Semantic Relation of Verb Complement Sentence. The collection of Chinese Grammatical Papers. Commerce Press (1984)
6. Jianming Lu: About the Semantic Pointer Analysis. Modern Linguistics No. 1. (1996)
7. Jiangsheng Yu: A Formal Model of Semantic Pointer. Natural Language Understanding and Machine Translation. Ed. Changning Huang and Pu Zhang. Tsinghua University Press (2001)
8. Zongming Chen: Chinese Logic Theory. People Press (1993)
9. Brentano, Franz: Psychology from an Empirical Standpoint. Translated by Antos C. Rancurello, D. B. Terrell, and Linda L. Mcalister, Psychologie vom empirischen Standpunkt (1874) (1973)
10. Barwise Jon, and John Perry: Situation and Attitudes. Cambridge, MA: Mit press (1983)
11. Kuroda, S.- Y.: Japanese Syntax and Semantics. Dordrecht: Kluwer (1992)
12. Sasse, Hans Jurgen: The Thetic/Categorical Distinction Revisited. Linguistics Vol. 25. (1987) 511–580.
13. Ladusaw, William: Thetic and Categorical, Stage and Individual, Weak and Strong. In Proceedings of SALT IV, 220–229. Ithaca, NY. Cornell University (1994)
14. McNally, Louise: Stativity and Theticity. In proceedings of Bar-Ilan Conference on Event and Grammar (1995)
15. Schmerling, Susan F.: Aspects of English Sentence Stress. Austin: University of Texas Press (1976)
16. Kim, Yookyung: Information Articulation and Truth Conditions of Existential Sentences. Language and Information 1.1. (1998)
17. Barwise, Jon, and John Etchemendy: The Liar: An Essay on Truth and Circularity. New York: Oxford University Press (1987)
18. Barwise Jon, and Robin Cooper: Extended Kamp Notation: A Graphical Notation for Situation Theory. In Situation Theory and its Application, ed. P. Aczel, D. Israel, Y. Katagari, and S. Peters. 29–54. Stanford: CSLI. (1993)
19. Kamp, Hans and Uwe Relye: From Discourse to Logic. Dordrecht: Kluwer (1993)
20. Glasbey Sheila: Bare Plurals, Situation and Discourse Content Logic, language and computation. Vol. 2, edited by Lawrence S. Moss, Jonathan Ginzburg and Maarten de Rijke. CSLI publications (1999)
21. Carlson, Gregory N.: Reference to Kinds in English. Bloomington: Indiana University Linguistics Club (1977)
22. Jianming Lu: Complexity of Verb Complement Structure. Language Teaching and Study No. 1. (1990)
23. Keith Devlin: Logic and Information. Cambridge University Press (1991)

Diagnostics for Determining Compatibility in English Support-Verb-Nominalization Pairs

Leslie Barrett[1] and Anthony R. Davis[2]

[1] Transclick, Inc., 250 W. 57th street, New York, NY 10107
leslie@transclick.com

[2] StreamSage, Inc., 1202 Delafield Pl. N.W., Washington DC 20008
tony.davis@streamsage.com

Abstract. This paper describes the results of a study on the semantics of so-called support-verb-nominalization (SVN) pairs in English. These constructions consist of a semantically impoverished verb and a complement nominalization sharing an unexpressed role with the verb. The study builds on the results of Davis and Barrett (2001), where it was argued that the semantic roles of the support-verb have a compatibility constraint with respect to the roles present in the nominalization. The results of the present study point to additional constraints based upon the Aktionsart category of both the support-verb and the verb from which the nominalization is derived.

1 Background and Problem

The English support-verb-nominalization (SVN) construction consists of a semantically impoverished verb and an associated nominalization. Such constructions have been analyzed previously by creators of the NOMLEX nominalization dictionary (Macleod et al 1997, 1998), and by Danlos (1992), Krenn and Erbach (1994), and Mel'cuk (1996), as well as work on light verbs in various languages by many other scholars. Each entry of the approximately 850 in NOMLEX contains the verb associated with the nominalization and encodes the relationship between the nominal arguments and the predicate argument structure of the verb. Some examples appear in (1):

(1)   a. *Microsoft launched a takeover of Intel.*
       b. *Intel suffered a setback.*
       c. *The negotiators reached an agreement.*
       d. *Mary took a walk.*

The relationships between arguments encoded in NOMLEX entries express the associations between the support-verb subject and arguments in the nominalization. Thus in (1a) above, the subject "Microsoft" is the subject of the support verb *and* the nominalization of the verb "take over". In other words, the construction in (1a) has a

A. Gelbukh (Ed.): CICLing 2003, LNCS 2588, pp. 85–90, 2003.

paraphrase "Microsoft took over Intel"[1]. In (1b), however, notice that the subject of the support-verb "suffer" is the *object* of "setback". The theoretical basis for the encoding of these relationships is derived from classes discussed in Mel'čuk (1996).

Davis and Barrett (2001) explored a semantic explanation for the associations between arguments found in English nominalizations and encoded by NOMLEX. In particular, to predict, and eventually extract, all support-verb nominalization paraphrases of a particular sentence, a combinatory diagnostic would have to be derived from principles based upon data like (1). Thus, for example, are there any constraints on SVN constructions that would rule out (2c) and (2d) as paraphrases of (2a), while allowing the attested (2b)?

(2)   a. *Mary bathed yesterday.*
       b. *Mary took a bath yesterday.*
       c. **Mary made a bath yesterday.*
       d. *??Mary did a bath yesterday.*

Simple encoding of associations, while helpful for certain information extraction tasks, is not enough to predict grammatical support-verb-nominalization combinations, or to rule out unattested and ungrammatical ones. While idiosyncrasies and blocking effects of individual SVN constructions may make the goal of complete prediction impossible, we believe that it is possible to find constraints on attested SVNs that rule out many combinations of support verb and nominalization. At least two types of constraints are operative: compatibility of semantic roles and Aktionsart relationships, which are the focus of this paper.

1.1   Semantic-Role Constraints as a Predictive Model

Grefenstette and Teufel (1995) used nominalizations as a seed to find examples of support verbs. Their algorithm was successful in finding lists of grammatical verbs matching a given nominalization, and is a useful source for finding good support-verb examples. It is not, however, a robust methodology for finding paraphrases, due to its lack of extensibility to new data. Here we will compare two methodologies based on the underlying assumption that support-verbs are a type of "light" verb and constitute a limited class. First, without obtaining extensive corpus data, we aim to find good associations between support-verbs and nominalizations by semantic algorithms alone.

Davis and Barrett (2001) proposed that a set of constraints on semantic role associations could successfully account for many of the ungrammatical combinations of support verbs and nouns. Using an inheritance hierarchy of semantic roles, we argued that the "controlling" argument of a support verb must bear a role that is the same as or more general than the role of its complement nominalization that it merges with. The following examples illustrate this point:

(3)   a. **Kim made a drop (of the book)*
       b. *The Army made an airdrop (of supplies)*

---

[1] There is an inchoative component added here as well

In (3b), the nominalization and support-verb share a Volitional Actor subject, but in (3a) the nominalization denotes a possibly unintentional action. This idea is based upon relationships of inclusion in a hierarchy of semantic roles; Volitional Actor is a more specific role than (possibly non-volitional) Actor. We assume that semantic roles can be arranged by specificity in a partially-order hierarchy, and that two roles are compatible if they are the same or one is a subrole of the other.

While semantic role compatibility seems to be helpful in ruling out some ill-formed SVN combinations, there are many others it does not prohibit. The examples in (4) are illustrative:

(4)   a. *Kim made a walk/ride/bath.
       b. *Sandy took a belief/claim that the stock was more valuable than Beanie Baby futures.

There are sufficient numbers of such ill-formed combinations that we are led to seek additional constraints to rule them out. In the remainder of this paper we examine the influence of Aktionsart on the grammaticality of SVN constructions.

The analysis we present here suggests a more robust predictor of support-verb-nominalization compatibility not plagued by exceptions like those in (4). We suggest that Aktionsart classes of support verbs and the verb roots of complement nominalizations fall into certain patterns, which we discuss in the following section.

2   Aktionsart Classes and SVN Combinations

In this paper, we employ the standard four-way classification of predicators into stative, activities, accomplishments, and achievements (Vendler 1967, Dowty 1979), while acknowledging that determining the Aktionsart of a verb or nominalization in isolation, without regard to its complements, can be difficult.

Our first observation is that the Aktionsart of the SVN construction as a whole is generally determined by the Aktionsart of the nominalization. This differs somewhat from Krenn and Erbach's (1994) observations about German support-verb constructions; they claim that the support verb is the primary source of the Aktionsart in a support verb construction. Most of their examples, however, differ from ours in that the complement of the support verb is not an event nominalization, and the semantics of the support verb determines not just Aktionsart of the construction but also its causal structure (for example, *ins Schwitzen kommen*, 'to break out into a sweat', vs. *zum Schwitzen bringen*, 'to make somebody sweat').

In our data, we find that the complement nominalization does generally determine the Aktionsart of an SVN construction. For instance, although 'make' in its non-support-verb uses is not typically an achievement, the SVNs 'make a bet', 'make a gift', 'make a claim', 'make an attempt', and so on are all achievement-like in their behavior. 'Take a walk', 'take a bath', 'give a ride', and 'give a performance' are all activities or accomplishments, though the verbs are typically achievements in their non-support-verb uses.

With the exception of stative support verbs and stative nominalizations, which do tend to combine (as we will see in the following section), attested SVN constructions frequently involve support verbs and nominalizations with different Aktionsarten. But the pattern is not random, and suggests that some features of the support verb's Aktionsart must be compatible with those of its complement nominalization.

2.1   First Sample and Results

We began by compiling lists of support verbs and nominalizations in each of the four Aktionsart categories. The main sources for the examples were Van Valin and La Polla (1997), Dowty (1979) and Levin (1993). We then used the lists as input to a LISP program that produced all the possible combinations of verbs and nominalizations. The output of the program yielded 3,049 SVN pairs. We went through the new list by hand to determine the grammaticality of each combination. The "good" and "bad" examples were then automatically extracted and reclassified. We noted that the percentages of "good" examples varied with the category. The data is shown in Table 1:

Table 1. Grammatical Pairs

Category	%"good"	% of corpus
st/st	0.088968	0.267
act/act	0.044248	0.111
accm/accm	0.17126	0.166
Ach/ach	0.086093	0.445

Taking a correlation statistic where Cov(R) is given by:

$$\mathbf{R} = \frac{1}{n} \sum_{j=1}^{n} \left(x_j - \mu_x \right)\left(y_j - \mu_y \right) \text{ and } -1 \leq \mathbf{R} \geq 1 \qquad (1)$$

We found R= -.049, showing an extremely weak negative correlation between the percentage of a category's "good" examples, and the percentage of the overall corpus represented by the category.

When we separated and reclassified the "good" examples together, however, generalizations emerged, falling into two categories. First, we noticed that like-categories were most common. That is, among "good" samples, a support verb of a given Aktionsart category was most likely to be found with a nominalization of the same category. The exception to this was in the category *Accomplishment*; support-verbs in this category combined most commonly with *Achievement* nominalizations. The second generalization is that *Achievement* and *Accomplishment* support-verbs combine commonly with either category. We attributed this initially to a certain amount of ambiguity in the classification metrics causing overlap. However, the relationship between support-verb Aktionsart category and nominalization Aktionsart category was strong. For the data in Table 2 below, $\chi^2 = {>}45.0$, showing significance at $<.0000001$ with 9 degrees of freedom.

Having observed these tendencies in the preliminary test sample, we conducted another test on newspaper-corpus data to compare real-world data against this sample.

Table 2. Selected Pairs

	StV	*accV*	*AchV*	*actV*
stN	64	5	13	0
accN	2	31	37	1
achN	0	46	45	3
actN	9	5	22	11

2.2   Testing on Corpus Data

We used the tools created by Dekang Lin (see Lin 1998) to find nominal objects for each of the support-verbs in our original corpus. In particular, we utilized the tool, which finds dependencies between a verb and following nominal object (see http://www.cs.ualberta.ca/~lindek/). We took all the resulting combinations of support-verbs and nominalizations and classified each nominalization according to its Aktionsart category. There were 231 combinations in total. Achievements were the most common category, followed by accomplishments and activities. Statives were least common. Achievement support-verbs and Achievement nominalizations were the most prevalent combination. No examples were found in the corpus of Stative-Activity or Stative-Accomplishment. In general, support verbs combined most often either with a nominalization in the same category, or an Achievement nominalization. The evidence of interaction between the Aktionsart category of the support-verb and the Aktionsart category of the nominalization is strong; a chi-squared test showed significance at <.0000001 with 9 degrees of freedom. Table 3 below shows the actual data.

Table 3. Observed Pairs

	StateN	*accN*	*achN*	*actN*
StateV	20	0	3	0
AccV	3	11	21	18
AchV	2	27	64	9
ActV	11	6	20	16

We attribute at least some of the outlying data in both the first and second samples to a degree of semantic overlap between Aktionsart classes. In fact, Van Valin and La Polla (1997) recognize a fifth class (in a departure from the original four classes proposed in Vendler 1967) of "active" accomplishments. The logical form proposed for this class is as follows:

$$\textbf{do'}(x,[\textbf{predicate1'}(x,(y))])\&BECOME\ \textbf{predicate2'}\ (z,x)\ or\ (y) \qquad (2)$$

We did not include a fifth Aktionsart class for this study, nor did we have sufficient context in every case to make judgments clear-cut. Without the surrounding context of the examples, which we did not obtain from the corpus, the culmination of an event could not always be determined. Such contextual ambiguity could be a cause of mislabeling particularly between the Achievement and Accomplishment categories. A pairwise correlation test between matching categories in the two samples discussed so far was positive at **R**=.66.

3 Summary and Conclusion

Despite possible ambiguities in categorization metrics, which may have accounted for category overlap, the generalizations that can be derived from the analysis of both samples fall into two categories. First, the most likely candidate nominalization following a support verb is that which is of the same Aktionsart category. Second, the most likely candidate nominalization following a support verb, other than a nominalization of its own type, is a nominalization in the Achievement class. Such generalizations, although not perfect estimators of all and only good English SVN combinations, can be used to create an estimation algorithm to choose the n-best candidate combinations in a corpus. This is a significant improvement over previous combinatory diagnostics for these constructions.

References

1. Danlos, L.: Support Verb Constructions: Linguistic Properties, Representation, Translation. *French Language Studies* 2: 1–32.
2. Davis, A.R., Barrett, L.: Support Verbs, Nominalizations and Participant Roles. In: Proceedings of the First International Workshop on Generative Approaches to the Lexicon. University of Geneva, Geneva (2001).
3. Dowty, D.: *Word Meaning and Montague Grammar..* Reidel, Dordrecht (1979).
4. Dowty, D.: Thematic proto-roles and argument selection. *Language* (1991) 67(3):547–615.
5. Grefenstette, G., Teufel, S.: A corpus-based method for Automatic Identification of Support Verbs for Nominalisations. In: *Proceedings of EACL 1995.* University College Dublin, Dublin (1995).
6. Krenn, B., Erbach, G.: Idioms and Support Verb Constructions. In: J. Nerbonne, K. Netter, C. Pollard (eds.): *German in Head-Driven Phrase Structure Grammar.* CSLI Publications, Stanford, CA (1994).
7. Levin, B.: *English Verb Classes and Alternations: A Preliminary Investigation.* University of Chicago Press, Chicago, IL (1993).
8. Lin, D.: Automatic Retrieval and clustering of Similar Words. In: *Proceedings of COLING-ACL-98,* Montreal, Canada (1998).
9. Macleod, C., Grishman, R., Meyers, A., Barrett, L. Reeves, R.: NOMLEX: A Lexicon of Nominalizations. In: Proceedings of EURALEX '98, Liege, Belgium (1998)
10. Macleod, C, Meyers, M., Grishman, R., Barrett, L., Reeves, R.: Designing a Dictionary of Derived Nominals. In: *Proceedings of Recent Advances in Natural Language Processing,* Tzigov Chark, Bulgaria (1997).
11. Mel'cuk, I. Lexical Functions: A Tool for the Description of Lexical Relations in the Lexicon. In: L. Wanner (ed.): *Lexical Functions in Lexicography and Natural Language Processing.* Benjamins, Amsterdam Philadelphia (1996) 37–102.
12. Van Valin, R., and R. La Polla, R. *Syntax: Structure, Meaning and Function.* Cambridge University Press, Cambridge, (1997).
13. Vendler, Z.: *Linguistics and Philosophy.* Cornell University Press, Ithaca (1967).

A Maximum Entropy Approach for Spoken Chinese Understanding

Guodong Xie, Chengqing Zong, and Bo Xu

National Laboratory of Pattern Recognition, Institute of Automation
Chinese Academy of Sciences, Beijing, 100080
{gdxie,cqzong,xubo}@nlpr.ia.ac.cn tel:(010)82614468

Abstract. In this paper, we present a spoken language understanding method based on the maximum entropy model. We first extract certain features from the corpus, and then train the maximum entropy model with an annotated corpus. We use this model to analyze spoken Chinese into semantic frames. Experiments show that the model can work effectively.

1 Introduction

Spoken Language understanding, the focus of this paper, is an important subsystem of both human-machine dialog systems and machine translation systems (Figure 1) – the subsystem in which the users' voice input is processed by an Automatic Speech Recognition (ASR) module and then sent to a Language Understanding module, which can analyze a sentence in order to obtain its semantic representation. (Thereafter, the semantic representation is sent to a Natural Language Generation (NLG) module or Dialog Management module, according to the task.)

The task of spoken language understanding is to extract the semantic meaning from a sentence. In spoken language, sentences are seldom grammatical – there are many repetitions, omissions, reversals, etc. [3] – so it is difficult to analyze sentences with purely rule-based methods. It is true that some systems have obtained better results by adapting and improving rule-based methods, for example Alon Lavie's [4] and Yan Pengju's [5]; but all of these systems have been specialized for certain limited domains. When they are applied to other domains, much time and work is necessary for adaptation.

Recently, statistical approaches have shown several advantages over rule-based approaches for natural language processing. One advantage of the statistical approach is that a statistical model can be easily ported to a new domain. Since a statistical model is trained with an annotated corpus, if it needs to be transplanted to a new domain, one need only annotate the corpus of the new domain, and then use this annotated corpus to train the model.

For example, [1,3,8] presented a statistical method for understanding natural language in which the semantic analyzer is an HMM (Hidden Markov Model) [11]. In the HMM, the words of a sentence are treated as observations and the semantic meaning of the sentence is treated as states.

A. Gelbukh (Ed.): CICLing 2003, LNCS 2588, pp. 91–100, 2003.

One shortcoming of HMMs is that they can use only the adjacent few words to predict the semantic meaning of the current word [10]. Our goal here is to make greater use of grammars and word information to analyze sentences, in order to obtain better results. For this purpose, we will employ the maximum entropy (ME) model [12], which can indeed combine various features of grammars or words into a probability model for sentence analysis. These features may be dependent upon, or independent of, each other.

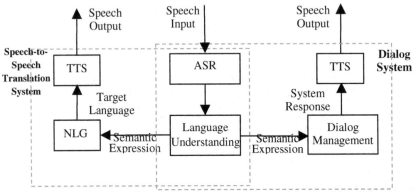

Fig. 1. Spoken Language Translation System and Human-Machine Dialog System

The ME model is a powerful mathematic tool which has been applied to many NLP studies. In [14], the author adopted the ME model to perform natural language ambiguity resolution, including sentence boundary detection, part-of-speech identification, parsing, and prepositional phrase attachment. In [6], the author built a language model based on the ME model; and in [12], the ME model was used to select the proper words in statistical machine translation. All of these studies obtained good results. Natural language understanding is an important part of NLP, and many statistical models have been applied to it, but apparently the ME model has seldom been chosen. In this paper, however, we will attempt to apply this model to perform spoken Chinese understanding. We first extract features for every word of an annotated corpus, and then train the ME model on that corpus, based on these features. We apply this model to extract the semantic meaning of spoken Chinese, and obtain good experimental results.

For this work, we have used a corpus taken from the hotel reservation domain, and have manually annotated 2500 sentences to train the ME model.

This paper is organized as follows: Section 2 discusses semantic representation and semantic symbols; Section 3 describes the maximum entropy analysis method; Section 4 discusses our experiments and analyzes our results; and Section 5 presents our conclusions.

2   Semantic Representation and Semantic Symbol

There are many methods for representing the semantic meanings of sentences, e.g. first-order logic, semantic networks, etc. All these methods have some advantages when applied to different domains. For now, rather than concentrate on the choice of method, we will first consider sentence annotation.

The first step when building a model is to annotate the relevant corpus. We do this by converting the semantic representation into symbol sequences and then assigning these symbols to every word in every sentence. But this process is not arbitrary. The result of our analysis will be precisely such a symbol sequence, so we must ensure that symbol sequences can be converted into the semantic representation correctly and easily. Thus the symbols must include information about their original position in the semantic structure. We will call these symbols *annotated symbols* or *semantic symbols*. If the semantic representation is structurally complex, the position information in our semantic symbols will also be complicated; and as the number of semantic symbols increases, the difficulty of the semantic analysis will also increase accordingly. For this reason, we want the semantic representation to be as simple as possible in structure. Fortunately, one characteristic of spoken language is that sentences are short and simple, the average sentence length being 7.8 words [3]. This relative brevity ensures that a sentence's semantic meaning can in fact be represented with a simple semantic structure.

IF (Interchange Format) is an artificial semantic representation or interlingua based on medium-level semantic relations [15]. It has been adopted by C-STAR (the Consortium for Speech Translation Advanced Research)[16], which aims to build speech-to-speech translation systems. The IF semantic representation is now quite mature, following many years' development and improvement. An IF structure is composed of speech-acts, concepts, arguments, and relations between them [15]. IF structures can express the meanings of most dialogues in the travel planning domain. We originally hoped to adopt the IF as our semantic representation. However, an IF structure for a sentence normally has two or more levels in depth. For example, the IF structure for the sentence *I want to reserve a single room* has four levels, as shown in Figure 2(a). And unfortunately this sort of structure is too complex to meet the simplicity constraint for our semantic symbols, as described above.

Thus we choose to define our own semantic representation, derived from the IF representation. We call it the Semantic Frame representation. It is composed of frames and their slots. A frame represents the main idea of a sentence, while slots and their fillers can be words which convey the sentence's semantic details. Most frames and slots are similar or equal to the concepts or arguments of the IF format. For example, the semantic frame *reserve_room*, which expresses the concept of reserving a room, is derived from *reserve* and *room*, which are IF concepts. The slots of *reserve_room* include *who, for_whom, room_spec, quantity* etc, which are the same as the corresponding IF arguments: *who* represents the person or people who want to reserve a room, *for_whom* represent the people for whom the room is reserved, *room_spec* represents the room type to be reserved, and *quantity* represents the number of rooms to be reserved. Our Semantic Frame format can thus be thought of as a subset of the IF format, except that we restrict the Semantic Frame to two levels in structure – the frame and its slots, with the frame at the top level and the slot level below it. (All slots are at the same level.) IF expressions which have three or more structural levels will be converted to two levels in the Semantic Frame representation. For example, the IF in Figure 2(a) has been converted to the structure shown in Figure 2(b), in which the concepts *reserve* and *room* are merged into the frame name *reserve_room*, and the argument *quantity* has been upgraded.

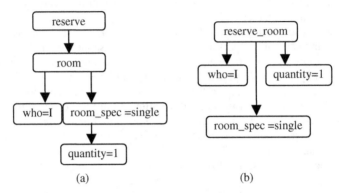

Fig. 2. (a) IF structure. (b) Semantic frame structure

A Semantic Frame has only two levels, so we need only two kinds of semantic symbol: the frame name, marked with *f:* as its prefix; and the slot name, marked with *c:* as its prefix. We add braces to all semantic symbols for programming convenience. For example, the Semantic Frame {f:reserve_room} is a frame name, and {c:room} is a slot name. Those words that we can't assign semantic symbols are simply assigned a pair of empty braces {}, which will be omitted when mapping the semantic symbol sequence into the Semantic Frame. Following is an example of a sentence and its corresponding semantic symbols. C is Chinese, E is English and S is the semantic symbols.

C: 我　　　想　　　预定　　　　　一　　　　　　　个　单人间
E: I　　　want　reserve　　　　　one　　　　　　single room
S: {c:who} {}　{f:reserve_room} {c:quantity} {}　　{c:room_spec}

After studying the corpus, we defined 166 different Semantic Frames, with 297 slots in total.

3 The Maximum Entropy Analysis Method

3.1 The Maximum Entropy Model

Most natural language processing tasks can be reformulated as statistical classification problems, in which the task is to estimate the probability of class A occurring in context B [13]. For semantic analysis, we can conceptualize this process as a search for the *s* that will maximize the conditional probability $p(s|c)$. Here, *s* is a semantic symbol and *c* is a word's context. In practice, training data is often sparse, so it is impossible to get all statistics (s,c) in order to calculate $p(s|c)$; thus the key problem is to find a good method for estimating $p(s|c)$ with sparse data.

The ME model gives a feasible way of solving this problem. It can convert different kinds of context to features and at the same time assign every feature a weight. Then it uses these features and weights to estimate the $p(s|c)$. In this paper the ME model is a probability model defined over C*S, where C is the set of word contexts and S is the set of semantic symbols.

Given a context c and a semantic symbol s, their joint probability can be expressed as follows in the ME frame:

$$p(s,c) = \frac{1}{Z(c)} \prod_{j=1}^{k} \alpha_j^{f_j(s,c)}, \qquad (1)$$

where k is the number of features, $Z(c)$ is a normalization factor, and $\{a_1, a_2,..... a_k\}$ are the parameters of the ME model. $\{f_1, f_2,.....f_k\}$ are features, where $f_j \in \{0,1\}$. Each parameter a_j corresponds to a feature f_j, which can be thought of as the weight of this feature. c is the context, and s is the semantic symbol. The parameters can be obtained by training on an annotated corpus. Indeed, the point of the training process is to assign a_j the right value under certain constraints so that the entropy of the probability distribution $p(s,c)$ is maximized. The constraints are supplied by the training corpus.

The entropy of the probability distribution is defined as follows:

$$H(p) = - \sum_{c \in C, s \in S} p(s,c) \log p(s,c)$$

The constraints are given by

$$Ef_j = \tilde{E}f_j \qquad 1 \le j \le k$$

where the model's feature probability is

$$Ef_j = \sum_{c \in C, s \in S} p(s,c) f_j(s,c)$$

and the observed feature probability is

$$\tilde{E}f_j = \sum_{c \in C, s \in S} \tilde{p}(s,c) f_j(s,c)$$

and where $\tilde{p}(s,c)$ denotes the observed probability of a certain (s,c) in the training data. Thus the constraints force the model to match its feature probabilities with those observed in the training data. In practice, since C is often very large and it is impossible to compute $\tilde{E}f_j$ directly, one often uses following approximation [6]

$$Ef_j \approx \sum_{c \in C, s \in S} \tilde{p}(c) p(s \mid c) f_j(s,c)$$

where $\tilde{p}(c)$ is the observed probability of the context c in the training data.

3.2 Features for ME Analysis Model

Features are relative to words. They show which semantic symbol should be assigned to a word in a certain context. In the ME semantic analysis model, the features normally take certain words in context as constraints. If these constraints are satisfied, the feature value will be 1; otherwise, it will be 0. For example, consider

$$f(w) = \begin{cases} 1 & w_0(v) = \text{reserve} \,\&\, w_{right1}(n) = \text{room} \,\&\, s_0 = \{f : \text{reserve\_room}\} \\ 0 & \text{otherwise} \end{cases}$$

in which w_0 is the current word with the given POS condition; s_0 is the semantic symbol corresponding to the current word; w_{right1} is the first word to the right of the current word (but not including it) with the given POS condition. The POS condition is inside the bracket directly following w_*., where the star * represents a subscript like *right1*. This feature's meaning is that if the current word is *reserve* and its POS is verb, and the first noun word to the right of the current word is *room*, and the current semantic symbol is {f:reserve_room}, then the feature value is 1; otherwise it is 0.

The features play important parts in the ME analysis model: their plausibility will directly affect the analysis results. In theory, we could define features for every word by hand in order to obtain reasonable feature distributions, but this is impossible in practice. So we actually extract features for every word from the training corpus automatically. We begin by defining a number of feature templates. The program can then try to match these feature templates with every word and its context in the training corpus. If a template matches with a word and its context, the program will generate a feature for the word according to the template.

Some of the feature templates are shown in Table 1, in which w_{left1} is the first word with the given POS to the left of the current word (not including the current word); w_{left} is the first word to the left with the given POS; and w_{right} is the first word to the right with the given POS. As mentioned, the POS condition is inside the bracket following w_*. Feature templates give some constraints concerning words which must be matched, including POS and position. Given a word in a sentence and a feature template, if all words specified in the template can be found in the sentence, they will be extracted from the context as the feature constraints, and we can generate a new feature with these constraints.

Table 1. Feature Templates

Features Templates							
1	$w_0(v)$, $w_{right1}(n)$			5	$w_0(n)$, $w_{right}(q)$,$w_{right1}(l)$		
2	$w_0(v)$, $w_{left1}(n)$		s_0	6	$w_0(p)$, $w_{right1}(v)$		s_0
3	$w_0(n)$, $w_{right1}(v)$			7	$w_0(q)$, $w_{right}(l)$,$w_{left1}(v)$		
4	$w_0(n)$, $w_{left1}(v)$			8	$w_0(q)$, $w_{right}(l)$,$w_{right1}(n)$		

Let's take the first template in the table as an example. This template requires that two words be matched, $w_0(v)$ (the current word with the verb POS), and $w_{right1}(n)$ (the first noun to the right of the current word). In other words, given any word, if it is a verb and there exists one or more nouns to its right, then the template is matched, and we can take the word and the first noun to its right as constraints of new features.

We now display a sample sentence and its features, generated from the templates of Table 1. As shown in Table 2, C indicates Chinese, E indicates English, P indicates POS and S indicates semantic symbols.

```
C:我        想          预定                     一        个      单人间
E:I         want to     reserve                 one               single room
P:p         va          v                        q          l      n
S:{c:who} {}    {f:reserve_room} {c:quantity} {} {c:room_spec}
```

Table 2. Features

Word	Features	Template NO.
我(I)	$w_0(p)$=我(I) && $w_{right1}(v)$=预定(reserve) && s_0={c:who}	6
预定(res erve)	$w_0(v)$=预定(reserve) && $w_{right1}(n)$=单人间(single room) && s_0={f:reserve_room}	1
两(tow)	$w_0(q)$=两(two) && w_{right} (l)=个, $w_{right1}(n)$=单人间 (single room) && s_0={c:quantity}	8
单人间(single room)	$w_0(n)$=单人间(single room) && $w_{left1}(v)$= 预定 (reserve)&& s_0={c:room_spec}	4

The feature templates are defined according to the characteristics of natural language as seen in the training corpus. For example, in natural language, the semantic meaning of simple sentences is often decided by the verb and its object. Thus we can define a template to generate features which show the verb-object relation. However, in natural spoken language, there are also many extra-grammatical phenomena, as mentioned. Therefore we must design some feature templates to capture these phenomena as well.

After generating features according to the feature templates, we will obtain a complete feature set. Most of the features will appear many times. Certain authors [9] believe that features which appear only a few times can't embody significant language phenomena; accordingly, these authors simply filter out features with low hit counts. In our case, however, the current training corpus is very limited, so even the rare features are often reasonable. If we filter them, many reasonable features will be lost; so in our model, we filter the features in the following way. As a first alternative, as in [9], we use a threshold value for hit counts, and retain features whose counts pass this threshold. Our second alternative method proceeds as follows: (1) if the current feature is the only feature that contains a word as w_0 (the current word) in its constraints, it can't be filtered. (If it were filtered, the relevant word would never satisfy any feature's constraints no matter what its context might be, so the ME model would be unable to analyze the word's semantic meaning correctly.) (2) If there are two or more features containing the same w_0 and s_0 in their constraints, and all of them appear only once, we merge them into a new feature and then filter them out. (Merging involves taking the common or shared constraints of the merged features as constraints of a new feature.) Section 4 gives the number of features filtered using these two alternative methods.

3.3 Parameter Estimation and Semantic Analysis

The parameter of the ME model can be trained with the Generalized Iterative Scaling (GIS) algorithm [7] which must be calculated repeatedly. Normally, it is a good "rule of thumb" to carry out 100 iterations [14]. More iterations would not increase the accuracy of the parameters.

The semantic analysis can be expressed as following:

$$s = \arg\max_{s \in S} p(s \mid c) = \arg\max_{s \in S} \frac{p(s,c)}{p(c)}, \qquad (2)$$

where S is the set of all semantic symbols, s is a semantic symbol corresponding to the current word, and c is the context of the current word (including the current word). Combining (2) and (1) yields the following expression:

$$s = \arg\max_{s \in S} p(s \mid c) = \arg\max_{s \in S} \frac{1}{p(c)} * \frac{1}{Z(c)} \prod_{j=1}^{k} \alpha_j^{f_j(s,c)} = \arg\max_{s \in S} \prod_{j=1}^{k} \alpha_j^{f_j(s,c)}$$

To find the s, one needs only a simple search algorithm. However, in a practical system, k and s are very large, so the algorithm is time-consuming. One way to reduce the time is to limit the scope of the s to be searched. Thus we limit our calculation to s elements which correspond to the current word in the training corpus. That is, we traverse the training corpus to construct a list containing the s for every word; and then, when analyzing the semantic symbol of a word, we calculate s only for members of this list. This technique improves the analysis speed dramatically.

4   Experiments and Results Analysis

We used 2500 annotated sentences to train our ME model. The training originally yielded 2930 features. We filtered these features with (1) the simple threshold value method and (2) our alternative method, as described above. The resulting number of features was 980 and 1168, respectively. We then tested our analysis model with 300 sentences taken from the training corpus and 300 sentences from outside of the training corpus. The analysis accuracy figures and model training times are shown in Table 3.

Table 3 shows that the best test results are obtained when 1167 features are used. Either increasing or decreasing the number of features degrades the results. This is because, when we increase the number of features, certain unreasonable features are added to the feature set; and conversely, when we decrease the number, certain reasonable features are discarded. The analysis results are affected accordingly.

Table 3. Training time and Test results

Features amount	Training time	Closed test	Open test
2930	4 hours	87%	72%
1167	2 hours	92%	83%
980	1.5 hours	90%	73%

Analysis of the results indicates that the errors are caused mostly by:

(1) Long sentences. Sometimes in spoken language people say several sentences without clearly pausing between them. The ASR (automatic speech recognition) result is then one sentence. In such cases, the ME model can't detect sentence

boundaries, so the words in earlier sentences may be treated as words in later sentences, and analysis errors result.

(2) Implausible features and parameters. Even though we have filtered features, some implausible features remain in some feature sets. Further, certain parameters can't be estimated correctly using only our sparse training corpus. These shortcomings directly cause errors.

In the future, we hope to increase the size of the training corpus in order to obtain more reasonable feature distributions and parameters. We also hope to add sentence boundary detection to our model. It is hoped that these improvements will yield improved ME analysis models.

5 Conclusion

In this paper we employ maximum entropy models to analyze spoken Chinese. The analysis result is represented as a Semantic Frame, a format derived from the IF interlingua representation. We define a set of feature templates for generating word-based semantic features; then these features are filtered to obtain reasonable feature sets. Finally, we train ME models based on these features. Experiments demonstrate that the ME analysis model can effectively analyze spoken Chinese.

Acknowledgements. The authors are grateful to Dr. Mark Seligman for his helpful work. The authors also would like to say a very big thank to the anonymous reviewers for their beneficial comments.

The research work described in this paper is supported by the National Natural Science Foundation of China under grant number 60175012.

References

1. W.Minker, S.Bennacef& J.Gauvain. A stochastic Case Approach for Natural Language Understanding. Proc.of ICSLP1996. Vol.2. 569–573
2. Yunbin Deng, Bo Xu. Chinese Spoken Language Understanding Across Domain. Proc. ICSLP2000. Vol1.1.230–233.
3. Chengqing Zong, Hua Wu. Analysis on Characteristics of Chinese Spoken Language, Proc. of 5th Natural Language Processing Pacific Rim Symposium, (1999). 358–362.
4. Alon Lavie. GLR*:A Robust Grammar-Focused parser for Spontaneously Spoken Language. PhD. Thesis. Carnegie Mellon University. Pittsburge, PA, (May 1996)
5. Yan Pengju,Zheng Fang. Robust Parsing in Spoken Dialogue Systems. Proc. of 7th European Conference on Speech Communication and Technology. Aalborg, Denmark, Vol3. 2149–2152. (2001)
6. Ray Lau, Ronald Rosenfeld & Salim Roukos. Adaptive Language Modeling Using The Maximum Entorpy Principle. Proc. of the Human Language Technology Workshop.(1993) 108–113. ARPA
7. J.N.Darroch and D. Ratcliff.. Generalized Iterative Scaling for Log-Linear Models. The Annals of Mathematical statistics, (1972) ,34(5) 1470–1480

8.   Guodong Xie, Chengqing Zong & Bo Xu. Chinese Spoken Language Analyzing Based On Combination of Statistical and Rule Method. Proc. of ICSLP2002. 613–616
9.   Adwait Ratnaparkhi. A Maximum Entropy Model for Part-Of-Speech Tagging. Proc. EMNLP. New Brunswick New Jersey: Association for Computational Linguistics. 133–141. (1996)
10. McCallum, A., Freitag, D. & Pereira, F. Maximum Entropy Markov Models for Information Extraction and Segmentation. Proc.17th ICML. (2000).591–598
11. Weng Fu-Liang, Wang Ye-Yi. Introduction to Computational Linguistics(in Chinese), China Social Science Publisher.(1996)
12. Adam L.Berger, Stephen A.Della Pietra,&Vincent J.Della Pietra. A Maximum Entropy Approach to Natural Language Processing. Computational Linguistics Vol22, NO.1.39-71. (1996)
13. Adwait Ratnaparkhi. A Simple Introduction to Maximum Entorpy Models for Natural Language Processing. IRCS Report 97-8 (May 1997)
14. Adait Ratnaparkhi. Maximum Entropy Models for Natural Language Ambiguity Resolution. Ph.D thesis. University of Pennsylvania. 1998
15. Hua Wu, Taiyi Huang. Interlingua-Based Response Generation. Proc. JSCL-99
16. Jun Park, Jae-Woo Yang. ETRI Speech Translation System. C-STAR Workshop. Schwetzingen, 1999

A Study to Improve the Efficiency
of a Discourse Parsing System

Huong T. Le and Geetha Abeysinghe

School of Computing Science, Middlesex University,
The Burroughs, London NW4 4BT, UK.
{H.Le, G.Abeysinghe}@mdx.ac.uk

Abstract. This paper presents a study of the implementation of a discourse parsing system, where only significant features are considered. Rhetorical relations are recognized based on three types of cue phrases (the normal cue phrases, Noun-Phrase cues and Verb-Phrase cues), and different textual coherence devices. The parsing algorithm and its rule set are developed in order to create a system with high accuracy and low complexity. The data used in this system are taken from the RST Discourse Treebank of the Linguistic Data Consortium (LDC).

1 Introduction

Rhetorical Structure Theory (RST) (Mann and Thompson, 1988) is a method of structured description of text. It provides a general way to describe the relations among clauses in a text, whether or not they are grammatically or lexically signaled. RST can be applied in many fields, such as automatic text summarization, text generation and text indexing.

Recognizing textual rhetorical structures still remains a hard problem because discourse is complex and vague. Literature shows that a considerable amount of work has been carried out in this area. However, only a few algorithms for implementing rhetorical structures have been proposed so far.

One of the pioneering works has been proposed by Marcu (1997). His advanced discourse parser is based on cue phrases, and therefore faces problems when cue phrases are not present in the text. Corston-Oliver (1998a) improved Marcu's system by integrating cue phrases with anaphora, deixis and referential continuity. Webber (2001) started from a different approach by implementing a discourse parsing system for a Lexicalized Tree Adjoining Grammar (LTAG). Webber developed a grammar that uses discourse cue as an anchor to connect textual trees. Like Marcu's system, Webber's parser too cannot recognize relations when there is no cue phrase present in the text.

Another trend in discourse analysis is learning-based, such as the decision-based approach i(Marcu, 1999) and the unsupervised one (Marcu and Echihabi, 2002). This approach produces an impressive result but requires a large enough corpus for training purpose to be available. Such a sufficient discourse corpus is difficult to find[1].

---

[1] The biggest discourse corpus nowadays is the RST Discourse Treebank from LDC, with 385 Wall Street Journal articles.

A. Gelbukh (Ed.): CICLing 2003, LNCS 2588, pp. 101–114, 2003.

We take the approach proposed by Marcu (1997) and extended by Corston-Oliver (1998a), and concentrate on improving the efficiency of the discourse parser. We proposed to do this by several ways: improving the correctness of dividing text into elementary discourse units (edus)[2] by combining syntactic-based method with cue-phrase-based method; using cohesive devices as relation's predictors; refining rules for the discourse parser; and improving Corston-Oliver's parser to reduce its complexity. The data used in the experiment are the discourse documents from The RST Discourse Treebank.

Our discourse analysis involves the following three computational steps. Firstly, we split text into elementary discourse units. Secondly, after defining edus, all potential rhetorical relations between these units are discovered. Finally, based on this relation set, all rhetorical structures will be produced using a discourse parser to combine small texts into larger ones. The basic framework for our discourse analysis system is depicted in Figure 1.

The way of dividing text into elementary discourse units is discussed in Section 2. Section 3 analyzes different factors that can be used in deciding rhetorical relations among discourse units. The relation set and the method for recognizing relations are described in Section 4. The discourse parser and its rule set are discussed in Section 5. We present our conclusions in Section 6.

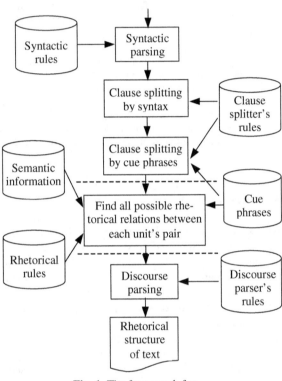

Fig. 1. The framework for a Discourse Analyzing System

2 Identifying Elementary Discourse Units

According to Mann and Thompson (1988), each discourse unit should have an independent functional integrity. Thus, a discourse unit can be a clause in a sentence or a single sentence. Marcu (1997) identifies edus based on regular expressions of cue phrases. If all edus contain cue phrases, this method is simple and very efficient since only a shallow parsing is required. However, Redeker (1990) has found that only 50%

---

[2] For further information on "edus", see (Marcu, 1997).

of clauses contain cue phrases. Marcu has not provided any solution to deal with the non-cue phrase cases, and his system fails in this situation. In addition, the use of cue phrases in Marcu's system does not guarantee to produce correct edus. Cue phrases do not provide any syntactic information; hence the edus generated by his system might not have an independent functional integrity.

Instead of using cue phrases, Corston-Oliver (1998a) implemented a syntactic parser and then used syntactic information to identify edus. This method suffers from high complexity, but can solve the problems faced by Marcu's system (Marcu, 1997). Corston-Oliver's parser did not process correctly the case where strong cue phrases make noun phrases become a separate edu. Two edus shown below in example (1) are considered as one edu in Corston-Oliver's parser:

(1) [*According to a Kidder World story about Mr. Megargel,*] [all the firm has to do is "position ourselves more in the deal flow."]

To deal with this problem, we divide the task of identifying edus into two processes. First, the system uses syntactic information to split text. In order to get the syntactic information, a syntactic parser is integrated to the system. Then, the system seeks strong cue phrases from the splitted text to make a further splitting when cue phrases are found, as in example (1). Due to lack of space, a detail description of this process is not presented in this paper.

3 Factors Used for Recognizing Relations

3.1 Text Cohesion as Relation's Predictors

Syntax provides us with information about how words combine to form sentences. What it does not show is how sentences combine to form an understandable and informative text. This is the role of text and discourse analysis. Cohesion can fill up this gap. They seek linguistic features and analyze their occurrence. Text can therefore be evaluated according to how cohesive they are. Cohesive devices are not the unique factor to make text coherence. However, they are chosen here because of their efficiency and simplicity. Salkie (1995) presented different types of cohesive devices. We have considered a few of them to be implemented in our system. They are synonyms, superordinates/hyponyms, opposite words, ellipsis, reference words and connectives. These cohesive devices are categorized into four groups: reiterative devices, reference words, ellipsis and cue phrases.

The Reiterative devices include synonyms (employer/boss), superordinates/hyponyms (country/Mexico), co-hyponyms (United Kingdom/Mexico), and antonyms (simple/complex). They are important features to define relations. For example, co-hyponyms (or multiple opposites), binary opposites (male/female) and antonyms often express a CONTRAST relation.

The Reference words include personal pronouns (I, you, he, she, it, we, they), their object forms (me, him, etc.) and their possessive forms (my, mine, your, yours, etc.), demonstratives (this, that, these, those) or comparative constructions (the same thing, a different person, etc.). Reference words need help from their environment to determine their full meaning. Thus, they create links between texts.

Another important cohesive device is ellipsis. This is a special form of substitution, where only a part of a sentence is omitted. Ellipsis can be found by analyzing syntax of the sentence. The ellipsis situation often occurs in question/answer sequences. Therefore, ellipsis can be used to recognize the SOLUTIONHOOD relation (see Section 4).

In order to recognize the reiteration and reference words from text, a lexical database is required. We have chosen WordNet for this purpose. It is a machine-readable thesaurus and semantic network developed and maintained by the Cognitive Science Laboratory at Princeton University. Two kinds of relations are represented in this database: lexical and semantic. Lexical relations hold between word forms, whereas semantic relations hold between word meanings. These relations include hypernymy/hyponymy, antonymy, entailment, and meronymy/holonymy.

3.2 Cue Phrases

Cue phrases (e.g., however, as a result), sometime called connectives or conjunctions, are used to indicate a specific connection between different parts of a text. This is the strongest cohesive device due to two reasons. Firstly, most cue phrases have a rhetorical meaning. If two text spans are connected by a cue phrase, their relation will be determined by the cue phrase's rhetorical meaning. Secondly, identifying cue phrases is quite simple because it is essentially based on pattern matching. Syntactic information is needed in order to explore other text devices such as synonyms and antonyms. Because of its strength and simplicity, there are many approaches which use cue phrases to recognize rhetorical relations (Knott and Dale, 1995; Marcu, 1997). However, these approaches have problems when no cue phrase is found.

One solution to this problem is to further expand the cue phrase's definition. We propose three kinds of cue phrases:

1. Normal cue phrase (called cue phrase) ;
2. Special words or phrases in a main noun phrase of a sentence (called Noun-Phrase cue or NP cue);
3. Special words or phrases in a verb phrase of a sentence (called Verb-Phrase cue or VP cue).

Cue phrases must match exactly, whereas noun phrases and verb phrases are simplified or stemmed before being compared with NP/VP cue. Examples of NP and VP cues are shown in (2) and (3), respectively, below.

(2) [New York style pizza meets California ingredients,] [and the *result* is the pizza from this Church Street pizzeria.]

(3) [By the end of this year, 63-year-old Chairman Silas Cathcart retires to his Lake Forest, Ill., home, possibly to build a shopping mall on some land he owns. "I've done what I came to do" at Kidder, he says.] [And that *means* 42-year-old Michael Carpenter, president and chief executive since January, will for the first time take complete control of Kidder and try to make good on some grandiose plans. Mr. Carpenter says he will return Kidder to prominence as a great investment bank.]

The noun "*result*" indicates a RESULT relation in example (2); meanwhile the VP cue "*means*" determines an INTERPRETATION relation in example (3).

A word/phrase can be a cue word/phrase in some cases, but this may not be in the others. For example, the word "*and*" is a cue word in example (4), but not so in example (5) as shown below.

(4) [Mary borrowed that book from our library last Monday,] [*and* she returned it this morning.]

SEQUENCE

(5) Mary has a cat *and* a dog.

In contrast, some phrases (e.g., "*in spite of*") have a discourse meaning in all of their occurrences. Thus, each cue phrase has a different effect in deciding rhetorical relations. To control their strength, scores are assigned to different cue phrases.

If a word/phrase always has a discourse meaning and represents only one rhetorical relation, it will get the highest score, 1. If a word/phrase always has a discourse meaning and represents N relations (e.g., cue phrase "*although*" can express an ANTITHESIS relation or a CONCESSION relation), the score of that cue phrase for each type of relation will be 1/N. If a cue phrase only has a discourse meaning in some cases (e.g., "*and*"), its maximum score will be lower than 1.

Examples (4) and (5) show that the word's position is also important in deciding the word's discourse role. Therefore, if a word or a phrase has a discourse meaning in only some special positions inside a sentence, the information about its position will be given to the word/phrase. If a word/phrase has a discourse role irrespective of its position in the sentence, no information will be provided about its position.

For example, the word "*second*" only has a discourse meaning when it stands at the beginning of a clause/sentence (indicated by the letter "B"). It has 50% certainty to be a LIST relation (hence given a score of 0.5). Then it will be stored in the cue phrases' set for the LIST relation as "*second*(B, 0.5)".

Similarly, NP cues and VP cues also have scores depending on their strength in deciding rhetorical relations.

4 Relation Set and Relation Recognition

To generate a rhetorical structure from text, we need to decide which rhetorical relations,[3] and how many relations are enough. If we define just a few relations, the rhetorical trees will be easy to construct; but they will not be very informative. On the other hand, if we have a large relation set, the trees will be very informative; but they will be difficult to construct.

The RST discourse corpus consists of 78 rhetorical relation types. It is difficult to automatically construct RST trees based on such a large relation set. Therefore, we define a smaller set but sufficient to characterize relations by grouping similar relations into one. Based on the rhetorical relations that have been proposed in the litera-

---

[3] A rhetorical relation involves two or more text spans (typically clauses or larger linguistic units) related such that one of them has a specific role relative to the other. For further information on "rhetorical relation", see (Mann and Thompson, 1988).

ture, e.g., (Mann and Thompson, 1988), and (Hovy, 1990), the following set of 22 relations has been chosen to be used in our system:

LIST, SEQUENCE, CONDITION, OTHERWISE, HYPOTHETICAL, ANTITHESIS, CONTRAST, CONCESSION, CAUSE, RESULT, CAUSE-RESULT, PURPOSE, SOLU-TIONHOOD, CIRCUMSTANCE, MANNER, MEANS, INTERPRETATION, EVALUA-TION, SUMMARY, ELABORATION, EXPLANATION, and JOINT.

4.1 Relation Recognition

Similar to Corston-Oliver (1998a), we divide the features, which help us to recognize a rhetorical relation, into two parts:

(1) the conditions that two text spans must satisfy in order to *accept* a specific re-lation between them;
(2) and, the tokens used for *predicting* a relation.

We call the features in part (1) as the necessary conditions and the features in part (2) as the Cue set. A Cue set consists of heuristic rules which involve cue phrases, NP cues, VP cues and cohesive devices. The necessary conditions ensure that the two text spans has no conflict with the concept of the relation being tested. The necessary conditions may not consist of any token to realize a specific relation. The system can only recognize a rhetorical relation between two units if all necessary conditions and at least one cue are satisfied.

Corston-Oliver tests the Cue set after the necessary conditions are satisfied. Thus, all rhetorical relations have to be checked sequentially one by one (thirteen relations are checked in his system).

The system that we propose detects relations in a different order. It first extracts cues from the two edus. When several relations are suggested by cues, the necessary conditions of these relations are checked in order to find the appropriate one. Since each cue represents one or two rhetorical relations in average, there are much less relations that need to be checked by our system. The definition of LIST relation dis-cussed in Section 4.3 will further illustrate this idea.

4.2 Scoring Heuristic Rules

Cue phrases, NP cues, VP cues and cohesive devices have different effects in decid-ing rhetorical relations. Therefore, it is necessary to assign a score to each heuristic rule. The cue phrase's rule has the highest score of 1, as cue phrases are the strongest signal. NP cues and VP cues are the extension cases of cue phrases. They are also strong cues, but weaker than normal cue phrases. Thus, the heuristic rules involving NP cues and VP cues have the score of 0.9. The cohesive devices have lower scores than NP cues and VP cues. Depending on their certainty, the heuristic rules corre-sponding to these devices receive the scores of 0.2 to 0.8. It is of interest to notice that each score can be understood as the percentage of cases in which the cue recognizes a correct rhetorical relation.

Heuristic scores can be trained by evaluating the output of the discourse parser with RST trees in an existing discourse corpus. Unfortunately, no discourse corpus large enough for training purposes currently exists. For this reason, scores are first assigned to heuristic rules according to human linguistic intuitions. After building the whole system, different sets of scores will be tested in order to find the optimal scores for the system.

As mentioned is Section 3.2, each cue phrase, NP cue or VP cue has its own score. It follows that the actual score for those cues is:

Actual Score = Score(heuristic rule) * Score(cue phrase, or NP cue, or VP cue).

The final score of a relation is equal to the sum of all heuristic rules contributing to that relation. The system will test the necessary conditions of that relation if its final score is more than or equal to a threshold θ. [4]

In the following section, we analyze the LIST relation to illustrate the usage of necessary conditions, Cue set and scores in recognizing rhetorical relations between two edus.

4.3 LIST Relation

A LIST is a multinuclear relation whose elements can be listed, but not in a CON-TRAST or other stronger type of multinuclear relation. A LIST exhibits some sort of parallel structure between the units involved in the relation (Carlson and Marcu, 2001). A LIST relation is often considered as a SEQUENCE relation if there is an explicit indication of temporal sequence.

The necessary conditions for a LIST relation between two units, $Unit_1$ and $Unit_2$, are shown below:

1. Two units are syntactically co-ordinates.
2. If both units have subjects and do not follow the reported style, then these subjects need to meet the following requirement: they must either be identical or be synonym, co-hyponym, or superordinate/hyponym; or the subject of $Unit_2$ is a pronoun or a noun phrase that can replace the subject of $Unit_1$.
3. There is no explicit indication that the event expressed by $Unit_1$ temporally precedes the event expressed by $Unit_2$.
4. The CONTRAST relation is not satisfied.

The first condition is based on syntactic information to guarantee that the two units are syntactically independent. The second condition checks the linkage between the two units by using reiterative and co-reference devices. Syntactic and semantic information are used to determine these units' subjects and their relations. The third condition distinguishes a LIST relation from a SEQUENCE relation. The last condition ensures that the stronger relation, CONTRAST, is not present in that context. In order to check this condition, the CONTRAST relation is always examined before the LIST relation.

The cue set of the LIST relation is shown below:

---

[4] Threshold θ is selected as 0.5.

1. Unit$_2$ contains a LIST cue phrase.   Score: 1
2. Both units contain enumeration conjunctions (*first, second, third...*). Score: 1
3. Both subjects of Unit$_1$ and Unit$_2$ contain NP cues.   Score: 0.9
4. If both units are reported sentences, they mention the same object.   Score: 0.8
5. If the subjects of two units are co-hyponyms, then the verb phrase of Unit$_2$ must be the same as the verb phrase of Unit$_1$, or Unit$_2$ should have the structure "*so + auxiliary + sbj*".   Score: 0.8
6. Both units are clauses in which verb phrases agree in tense (e.g., past, present).
                                                                              Score: 0.5
7. Both units are sentences in which verb phrases agree in tense (e.g., past, present).
                                                                              Score: 0.2

For example, the cue word "*also*" in the sentence "He *also* improved the firm's compliance procedures for trading" suggests a LIST relation between two discourse units (6.1) and (6.2) in the following case [5]:

(6) [Mr. Cathcart is credited with bringing some basic budgeting to traditionally free-wheeling Kidder.[6.1]] [He *also* improved the firm's compliance procedures for trading.[6.2]]

Since only cue 1 is satisfied in this case, the final score is:

Final score = Actual score(cue 1) = Score(cue 1) * Score("*also*"). The cue word "*also*" has the score of 1 for the LIST relation, so the final score is $1 * 1 = 1 > \theta$. Therefore, the necessary conditions of the LIST relation are checked. Text spans (6.1) and (6.2) are two sentences, thus they are syntactically coordinate (condition 1). In addition, the subject of text span (6.2), "*he*", is a pronoun, which replaces for the subject of text span (6.1), "Mr. Cathcart" (condition 2). There is no evidence of an increasingly temporal sequence (condition 3), and also no signal of a CONTRAST relation (condition 4). Therefore, a LIST relation is recognized between text spans (6.1) and (6.2).

The cue word "*and*" is found in example (7):

(7) [But the Reagan administration thought otherwise,[7.1]] [*and* so may the Bush administration.[7.2]]

"*And*" is considered as a cue word because it stands at the beginning of clause (7.2) (cue 1). The subjects of two text span, "the Reagan administration" and "the Bush administration", are co-hyponyms. In addition, clause (7.2) has the structure "*so + auxiliary + sbj*". With the score of 0.3 for the cue word "*and*" in the LIST relation, and with the satisfaction of cue 5, the final score is:

Final score = Score(cue 1) * Score("*and*") + Score(cue 5) = $1 * 0.3 + 0.8 = 1.1 > \theta$.

As in the previous example, the necessary conditions of the LIST relation are checked and then a LIST relation is recognized between clause (7.1) and clause (7.2).

---

[5] The superscripts such as 6.1 and 6.2 are used to distinguish different discourse units focussed on in each example.

5 Rhetorical Parser

5.1 Rules for the Rhetorical Parser

Rhetorical rules are constraints of text spans in a RST tree. They are used in a discourse parser to find rhetorical relations between non-elementary discourse units. To formalize these rules, the following definitions are applied:

- $<T>$ is a text span that can be presented by a RST tree, a RST subtree, or a leaf.
- $<T_i T_j>$ is a text span in which a rhetorical relation exists between two adjacent text spans $<T_i>$ and $<T_j>$. The possible roles of $<T_i>$ and $<T_j>$ in a rhetorical relation are Nucleus – Nucleus, Nucleus – Satellite, and Satellite – Nucleus. These cases are coded as $<T_i T_j \mid NN>$, $<T_i T_j \mid NS>$, and $<T_i T_j \mid SN>$, respectively.
- rhet_rels($<T_i>$,$<T_j>$) is the rhetorical relations between two adjacent text spans $<T_i>$ and $<T_j>$, each of which has a corresponding RST tree.

The paradigm rules in our proposed system are shown below:

Rule 1:
rhet_rels($<T_1 T_2 \mid NN>$, $<T>$) $\equiv$ rhet_rels($<T_1>$, $<T>$) $\cap$ rhet_rels($<T_2>$, $<T>$).

If: there is a relation between two text spans $<T_1>$ and $<T_2>$, in which both of them play the nucleus roles,

Then: the rhetorical relations between the text span $<T_1 T_2>$ and its right-adjacent text span T hold only when they hold between $<T_1>$ and $<T>$, and between $<T_2>$ and $<T>$.

Rule 2: rhet_rels($<T_1 T_2 \mid NS>$, $<T>$) $\equiv$ rhet_rels($<T_1>$, $<T>$).
Rule 3: rhet_rels($<T_1 T_2 \mid SN>$, $<T>$) $\equiv$ rhet_rels($<T_2>$, $<T>$).
Rule 4: rhet_rels($<T>$, $<T_1 T_2 \mid NS>$) $\equiv$ rhet_rels($<T>$, $<T_1>$).

Rules 1-4 are based on the proposal of Marcu (1997) which states, "*If a rhetorical relation R holds between two text spans of the tree structure of a text, that relation also holds between the most important units of the constituent spans*". From this point of view, Marcu (1997) and Corston-Oliver (1998a) analyzed relations between two text spans by considering only their nuclei.

However, the rule with the left side rhet_rels($<T>$, $<T_1 T_2 \mid SN>$), is not formalized in the same way as rules 1-4. This is a special case which has not been solved in (Marcu, 1997) and (Corston-Oliver, 1998a). This case is illustrated by example (8) below:

(8) [With investment banking as Kidder's "lead business," where do Kidder's 42-branch brokerage network and its 1,400 brokers fit in? Mr. Carpenter this month sold off Kidder's eight brokerage offices in Florida and Puerto Rico to Merrill Lynch & Co., refueling speculation that Kidder is getting out of the brokerage business entirely. Mr. Carpenter denies the speculation.[8.1]] [[*To answer the brokerage question,*[8.2]] [Kidder, in typical fashion, completed a task-force study....[8.3]]]

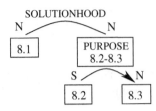

Fig. 2. The discourse tree of text (8)

The cue *"To (+Verb)"* in text span (8.2) indicates a PURPOSE relation between two text spans (8.2) and (8.3), while the VP cue *"answer"* in text span (8.2) indicates a SO-LUTIONHOOD relation between two larger text spans (8.1) and (8.2-8.3).

Example (8) shows that although the content of the satellite does not determine rhetorical relations of its parent text span, special cue phrases inside the satellite are still a valuable source. We apply a different treatment in this situation than the rules proposed by Marcu (1997), as shown below.

To recognize the relations rhet_rels(<T>, <T_1 T_2 | SN>), we firstly find all cue phrases *restCPs* in text span <T_1> which have not been used to create the relation between <T_1> and <T_2>, then check rhet_rels(<T>, <T_1>) by using *restCPs*. If a relation is found, it is assigned to rhet_rels(<T>, <T_1 T_2| SN>). Otherwise, rhet_rels(<T>, <T_1 T_2 | SN>) ≡ rhet_rels(<T> <T_2>).

Applying this rule to example (8) with two text spans (8.1) and (8.2-8.3), we have *restCPs* = *"answer"* since the cue *"To"* is used for the relation between (8.2) and (8.3). The relation between (8.1) and (8.2-8.3) is recognized as SOLUTIONHOOD by using the cue *"answer"* in *restCPs*. In contrast, if we use the Marcu's rules, rhet_rels((8.1), (8.2 8.3 | SN)) = rhet_rels((8.1), (8.3)). That means the cue *"answer"* is not considered in this case.

5.2 Algorithm for Rhetorical Parser

The idea for this algorithm was first introduced by Marcu (1996) and then further developed by Corston-Oliver (1998a). Marcu proposed a shallow, cue-phrase-based approach to discourse parsing. Marcu's system splits text into edus and hypothesizes theirs rhetorical relations based on the appearance of cue phrases. Then, all the RST trees compatible with the hypothesized relations are generated. Although Marcu's discourse parser was considerably advanced at that time, it still had weaknesses. When the number of hypothesized relations increases, the number of possible RST trees increase exponentially. Marcu's parser creates all possible pairs of text spans by permutation operations without considering of their usefulness. As a result, a huge amount of ill-formed trees are created.

The improved algorithm in RASTA, proposed by Corston-Oliver (1998a), solves this problem by using a recursive, backtracking algorithm that produces only well-formed trees. If RASTA finds a combination of two text spans leading to an ill-formed tree, it will backtrack and go to another direction, thus reducing the search space. By applying the higher score hypotheses before the lower ones, RASTA tend to produce the most reliable RST trees first. Thus, RASTA can stop after a number of RST trees are built.

Although a lot of improvement had been made, RASTA's search space is still not optimal. Given the set of edus, RASTA checks each pair of edus to determine rhetorical relations. With N edus {U_1, U_2, ..., U_N}, N(N-1) pairs of edus {(U_1,U_2),

$(U_1,U_3),\ldots,(U_1,U_N),(U_2,U_3),\ldots,(U_{N-1},U_N)\}$ are examined. Then, all possible relations are tested in order to build RST trees.

The search space in our system is much less than that in RASTA. Since only two adjacent text spans can be combined to a larger text span, only N-1 pairs of edus (U_1,U_2), (U_2,U_3), ..., (U_{N-1},U_N) are selected. Instead of checking every pair of edus as in RASTA, only N-1 pairs of adjacent edus are examined by our system. The relations recognized by this examination are called hypothesis relations (or hypotheses). They are stored in a hypothesis set. Relations in this set will be called from the highest score to the lowest score ones.

To illustrate this idea, we consider a text with four edus U_1, U_2, U_3, U_4, and the hypothesis set H of these edus, H= $\{(U_1,U_2), (U_1,U_3), (U_2,U_3), (U_3,U_4)\}$. The set H consists of all possible relations between every pair of edus. (U_i,U_j) refers to the hypotheses that involve two edus U_i and U_j. Since two edus U_1 and U_3 are not adjacent, the hypothesis (U_1,U_3) is not selected by our proposed parser. Figure 3 shown below displays the search space for the set H. In this figure, each edu U_i is replaced by the corresponding number i.

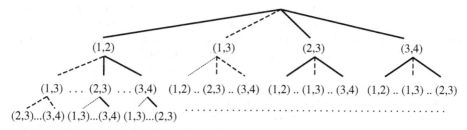

Fig. 3. The search spaces for the hypothesis set $\{(U_1,U_2), (U_1,U_3), (U_2,U_3), (U_3,U_4)\}$. RASTA visits all branches in the tree. The branches drawn by dotted lines are pruned by our proposed parser [6]

Another problem with RASTA is that one RST tree can be created twice by grouping the same text spans in different orders. If derived hypotheses of the set H contain $\{(U_1,U_2),(U_3,U_4)\}$, RASTA will generate two different combinations which create the same tree as shown below:

Join U_1 and U_2 -> Join U_3 and U_4 -> Join (U_1,U_2) and (U_3,U_4).
Join U_3 and U_4 -> Join U_1 and U_2 -> Join (U_1,U_2) and (U_3,U_4).

To deal with this redundancy problem faced by RASTA, our algorithm uses a tracing method. The hypothesis set is updated every time a new branch on the search tree is visited. When the parser visits a new branch, all nodes previously visited in the same level as that branch are removed from the hypothesis set. This action ensures that the algorithm does not recreate the same RST tree again.

Let's assume that both RASTA and our proposed parser start from the search space drawn by solid lines in Figure 3. Our proposed tracing method is explained in more detailed using Figure 4 below.

---

[6] Due to lack of space, all nodes of this tree cannot be presented together in this figure.

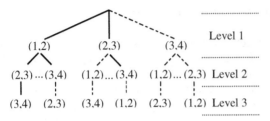

Level 1

Level 2

Level 3

Fig. 4. Routes visit by the two parsers. RASTA visits all branches in the tree. The branches drawn by dotted lines are pruned by our proposed parser, which uses the tracing method

Our proposed parser first visits the branches which start with node (1,2) in level 1. After visiting these branches, the parser continues to the branches which start with node (2,3) in level 1. Since all RST trees or subtrees involving the node (1,2) are already visited, this node does not need to be revisited in the future. The branch that connects node (2,3) in level 1 with node (1,2) in level 2 is pruned from the search tree. As a result, the route (2,3) → (1,2) → (3,4) is not visited by our algorithm.

The discourse parser for our system is explained below.

A set called *Subtrees* is used in our parser to store the temporal subtrees created during the process. This set is initiated with all edus {U_1, U_2, ..., U_N}.

All possible relations that can be used to construct bigger trees at a time t form a hypothesis set *PotentialH*. If a hypothesis involving two text spans <T_i, T_j> is used, the new subtree, created by joining <T_i> and <T_j>, is added to the set *Subtrees*. The two small trees corresponding to the two text spans <T_i> and <T_j> are removed from *Subtrees*. Thus, all members of the set *Subtrees* are disjoined and their combination covers the entire text.

Each time the *Subtrees* changes, the hypothesis set *PotentialH* becomes obsolete. The hypotheses in the *PotentialH* relating to the subtrees that are removed in the previous step cannot be used. For that reason, the hypotheses, which do not fit with the new *Subtrees*, are removed from the *PotentialH*. Although some hypotheses are not considered as candidates to construct RST trees at one round of the parser, they may be needed later when the parser follows a different searching branch. All hypotheses computed by the discourse parsing system are stored in a hypothesis set called *StoredH*.

The *PotentialH* has not got any hypothesis to process the new subtree after the *Subtrees* changes. These relations will be added to the *PotentialH* after the relations between the new subtree and its adjacent trees are checked by using rules of the rule set.

When checking for a relation, the parser searches for that relation in the set of all hypotheses *StoredH*. If it is not found, the new hypothesis will be created by applying rules shown in Section 5.1. The hypotheses involving two unadjacent edus may be created during this process when the algorithm tries to create a rhetorical relation between two larger-adjacent text spans containing these edus.

The following algorithm briefly describes the steps in our discourse parser.

```
Function PARSER(Subtrees, PotentialH, <T₁,T₂>) {
/* <T₁,T₂> is created in the previous step by the two text spans
    T₁ and T₂ */
    If the number of final RST trees reaches a required limit,
    Exit.
```

```
If Subtrees has only one tree, store it in the set of final
RST trees and Return.
If <T₁,T₂> = null (this is the first call to PARSER),
    NewH = all rhetorical relations between pairs of adjacent
    edus.
Else, NewH = all rhetorical relations between <T₁,T₂> with its
    left adjacent text span LT and its right adjacent text
    span RT.
Add all members of NewH to PotentialH.
Remove all obsolete hypotheses from PotentialH.
While PotentialH is not empty {
   - AppliedH = the highest score hypothesis in PotentialH.
   - Remove AppliedH from PotentialH.
   - Find two subtrees ST₁ and ST₂ in Subtrees satisfying Ap-
     pliedH. The text spans corresponding to ST₁ and ST₂ are
     <T₁> and <T₂>, respectively.
   - Remove ST₁ and ST₂ from Subtrees.
   - Add the new subtree created by ST₁ and ST₂ to Subtrees.
   - Call PARSER(Subtrees, PotentialH, <T₁,T₂>).
}
Return
}
```

6 Conclusion

In this paper, we have presented a discourse parsing system, in which syntactic information, cue phrases and other cohesive devices are investigated in order to define elementary discourse units and hypothesize relations.

To determine relations between texts, we explored all variants of cue phrases, combining with other feasible cohesive devices. It was shown that the position of cue phrases in a sentence, Noun-Phrase cues, and Verb-Phrase cues are good predictors for discovering rhetorical relations. In the case where cue phrases are not available, other text cohesive devices (e.g., synonyms, and antonyms) can be a reasonable substitution.

The construction of a discourse parser from the set of elementary discourse units was further analyzed. We have proved that the satellite in a rhetorical relation sometimes can provide good relation indications. This notation is implemented in creating the rule set for the parser. Based on the adjacency constraint of discourse analysis adapted from (Mann and Thompson, 1988), several improvements have been made to reduce the algorithm's complexity and at the same time improve its efficiency.

References

1. Bouchachia, A., Mittermeir, R., Pozewaunig, H.: Document Identification by Shallow Semantic Analysis. NLDB (2000) 190–202
2. Carlson, L. and Marcu, D.: Discourse Tagging Manual. ISI Tech Report, ISI-TR-545 (2001)

3. Corston-Oliver, S.: Computing Representations of the Structure of Written Discourse. PhD Thesis. University of California, Santa Barbara, CA, U.S.A (1998a)
4. Corston-Oliver, S.: Beyond string matching and cue phrases: Improving efficiency and coverage in discourse analysis. In: Eduard Hovy and Dragomir Radev: The Spring Symposium. AAAI Technical Report SS-98-06, AAAI Press (1998b) 9–15
5. Gundel, J., Hegarty, M., Borthen, K.: Information structure and pronominal reference to clausally introduced entities. In: ESSLLI Workshop on Information Structure: Discourse Structure and Discourse Semantics. Helsinki (2001)
6. Hobbs, J.: On the Coherence and Structure of Discourse. Technical Report CSLI-85-37, Center for the Study of Language and Information (1985)
7. Hovy, E. H.: Parsimonious and profligate approaches to the question of discourse structure relation. In: Proceedings of the 5th International Workshop on Natural Language Generation. Pittsburgh (1990) 128–136
8. Knott, A., Dale, R.: Using linguistic phenomena to motivate a set of coherence relations. Discourse Processes 18 (1995) 35–62
9. Komagata, N.: Entangled Information Structure: Analysis of Complex Sentence Structures. In: ESSLLI 2001 Workshop on Information Structure, Discourse Structure and Discourse Semantics. Helsinki (2001) 53–66
10. Mann, W. C. and Thompson, S. A.: Rhetorical Structure Theory: Toward a Functional Theory of Text Organization. Text, vol. 8 (1988) 243–281
11. Marcu, D.: Building Up Rhetorical Structure Trees. In: Proceedings of the Thirteenth National Conference on Artificial Intelligence (AAAI), volume 2 (1996) 1069–1074
12. Marcu, D.: The Rhetorical Parsing, Summarization, and Generation of Natural Language Texts. PhD Thesis, Department of Computer Science, University of Toronto (1997)
13. Marcu, D.: A decision-based approach to rhetorical parsing. The 37th Annual Meeting of the Association for Computational Linguistics (ACL). Maryland (1999) 365–372
14. Marcu, D., Echihabi, A.: An Unsupervised Approach to Recognizing Discourse Relations. In: Proceedings of the 40th Annual Meeting of the Association for Computational Linguistics (ACL). Philadelphia, PA (2002)
15. Polanyi, L.: The Linguistic Structure of Discourse (1995)
16. Poesio, M., Di Eugenio, D.: Discourse Structure and Anaphoric Accessibility. In: ESSLLI Workshop on Information Structure, Discourse Structure and Discourse Semantics. Helsinki (2001)
17. Redeker, G.: Ideational and pragmatic markers of discourse structure. Journal of Pragmatics (1990) 367–381
18. RST Discourse Treebank - http://www.ldc.upenn.edu/Catalog/LDC2002T07.html
19. Salkie, R.: Text and discourse analysis. London, Routledge (1995)
20. Webber, B. et al.: D-LTAG System – Discourse Parsing with a Lexicalized Tree Adjoining Grammar. In: ESSLLI Workshop on Information structure, Discourse structure and Discourse Semantics (2001)
21. Webber, B., Knott, A., Stone, M., Joshi, A.: Discourse Relations: A Structural and Presuppositional Account Using Lexicalised TAG. Meeting of the Association for Computational Linguistics, College Park MD (1999)
22. WordNet, http://www.cogsci.princeton.edu/~wn/index.shtml

Conversion of Japanese Passive/Causative Sentences into Active Sentences Using Machine Learning

Masaki Murata and Hitoshi Isahara

Communications Research Laboratory,
2-2-2 Hikaridai, Seika-cho, Soraku-gun, Kyoto, 619-0289, Japan,
{murata,isahara}@crl.go.jp,
http://www.crl.go.jp/khn/nlp/members/murata/index.html

Abstract. We developed a new method of machine learning for converting Japanese case-marking particles when converting Japanese passive/causative sentences into active sentences. Our method has an accuracy rate of 89.06% for normal supervised learning. We also developed a new method of using the results of unsupervised learning as features for supervised learning and obtained a slightly higher accuracy rate (89.55%). We confirmed by using a statistical test that this improvement is significant.

1 Introduction

This paper describes how to automatically convert Japanese passive/causative sentences into active sentences. We show some examples of Japanese passive/caus- ative sentences in Figures 1 and 2. The sentence in Figure 1 uses the passive voice. The Japanese suffix reta functions as an auxiliary verb indicating the passive voice. The sentence in Figure 2 uses the causative voice. The Japanese suffix seta functions as an auxiliary verb indicating the causative voice. The corresponding active-voice sentences are shown in Figure 3. When the sentence in Figure 1 is converted into an active sentence, (i) ni (by), which is a case-marking particle with the meaning of "by", is changed into ga, which is a case-marking particle indicating the subject case, and (ii) ga (subject), which is a case-marking particle indicating the subject case, is changed into wo (object), which is a case-marking particle indicating the object case. When the sentence in Figure 2 is converted into an active sentence, (i) kare ga (he subject) is eliminated, (ii) ni (indirect object), which is a case-marking particle indicating an indirect object, is changed into ga, which is a case-marking particle indicating the subject case, while (iii) wo (object), which is a case-marking particle indicating the object case, is not changed. In this paper, we convert Japanese case-marking particles (i.e. ni → ga) and eliminate unnecessary parts (kare ga in Figure 2) by using machine learning.[1] (In this paper, the word "conversion" includes the idea of elimination.)

---

[1] In this study, we do not handle the conversion of the expression of the auxiliary verb because auxiliary verbs can be converted based on the Japanese grammar.

A. Gelbukh (Ed.): CICLing 2003, LNCS 2588, pp. 115–125, 2003.

inu   ni   watashi ga   kama- reta.
(dog) (by) (I)   *subject-case-marking particle* (bite) passive voice
(I was bitten by a dog.)

Fig. 1. Passive sentences

kare ga   kanojo ni   kami   wo   kira- seta
(he) subject (her)   indirect object (hair) direct object (cut) causative voice
(He had her cut his hair.)

Fig. 2. Causative sentences

The conversion of passive/causative sentences into active sentences is useful in many research areas including generation, knowledge extraction from a database written in natural languages, information extraction, and question answering. For example, in question answering, when the answer is in the passive voice and the question is in the active voice, a question-answering system cannot match the answer with the question because the sentence structures are different and it is thus difficult to find the answer to the question. Methods for converting passive/causative sentences into active sentences are important in natural language processing.

The conversion of case-marking particles in the conversion of passive/causative sentences into active sentences is not easy because the choice of particles depends on verbs and their usage. In the conventional approach, the conversion is done by using a case frame dictionary with the rules that describe how to convert case-marking particles. However, it is difficult to write the rules for all the verbs and all their usages. So methods based on a case frame dictionary are not effective. In contrast, we convert case-marking particles based on machine learning using supervised data. We constructed a corpus with tags for case-marking conversion to obtain supervised data. Our method based on machine learning has the following advantages: It enables obtaining higher precision with a bigger corpus of supervised data. It forms the basis for the development of other better methods of machine learning with higher accuracy rates.

2   Tagged Corpus as Supervised Data

We used the Kyoto University corpus [4] to construct a coprus tagged with tags for the conversion of case-marking particles. It has approximately 20,000 sentences (16 editions of the Mainichi Newspaper, from January 1st to 17th, 1995). In the Kyoto University corpus, tags for morphology and syntax had already been added. So we only had to add tags for the conversion of case-marking particles. We extracted the case-marking particles in the passive/causative-voice sentences from the Kyoto University corpus. There were 4,671 particles. We assigned to each case-marking particle a corresponding case-marking particle of the active

inu   ga   watashi wo   kanda.
(dog) subject (I)   object (bite)
(Dog bit me.)

kanojo ga   kami   wo   kitta.
(her)   subject (hair) direct object (cut)
(She cut his hair.)

Fig. 3. Active sentences

inu   ni   watashi ga   kama- reta.
   ga   wo
(dog) (by) (I)   subject-case-marking particle (bite) passive voice
(I was bitten by a dog.)

kare ga   kanojo ni   kami   wo   kira- seta
  other   ga   wo
(he) subject (her)   indirect object (hair) direct object (cut) causative voice
(He had her cut his hair.)

Fig. 4. Examples of corpus

voice. Some examples are shown in Figure 4. The five underlined particles, "ga",
"wo", "other"[2], "ga", and "wo", which are given for "ni", "ga", "ga", "ni", and
"wo", are the tags for the case-marking particles in the active voice. We call the
given case-marking particles of the active voice target case-marking particles,
and the original case-marking particles in the passive/causative-voice sentences
source case-marking particles. We created tags for target case-marking particles
in the corpus. If we can determine the target case-marking particles in a given
sentence, we can convert the case-marking particles in the passive/causative-
voice sentences into the case-marking particles of the active voice. So our goal
is to determine the target case-marking particles.

We show the distribution of the target case-marking particles in the corpus
in Table 1. The number of kinds of target case-marking particles is finite. So
we can determine the target case-marking particles by using classification as
in machine learning methods. In this study, we used the constructed corpus as
supervised data for machine learning. We also used it as a test corpus to evaluate
our method. (We used cross validation for the evaluation.)

---

[2] The tag for "other" indicates that the noun phrase is eliminated when the sentence
is converted into the active voice.

Table 1. Distribution of the target case-marking particles in the tagged corpus

Target case-marking particle	Number
wo	1,348
ni	898
ga	744
to	724
de	702
kara	136
made	45
he	9
yori	3
Other	62
Total	4,671

3   Machine Learning Method (Support Vector Machine)

We used a support vector machine method as the basis for our machine learning method. This is because support vector machine methods are comparatively better than other methods in many research areas [3,8,6]. The main point of our study is to use machine learning methods for conversion of Japanese passive/causative sentences into active sentences. Although we used a support vector machine method for this study, we can also use any other machine learning method for this study. In this section, we describe the support vector machine method we used.

In the support vector machine method, data consisting of two categories are classified by using a hyperplane to divide a space. When the two categories are, for example, positive and negative, enlarging the margin between the positive and negative examples in the training data (see Fig. 5[3]), reduces the possibility of incorrectly choosing categories in open data.[4] The hyperplane which maximizes the margin is thus determined, and classification is carried out using that hyperplane. Although the basics of this method are as described above, in the extended versions of the method the region between the margins through the training data can include a small number of examples, and the linearity of the hyperplane can be changed to a non-linearity by using kernel functions. Classification in the extended versions is equivalent to classification using the following discernment function, and the two categories can be classified on the basis of whether the value output by the function is positive or negative [1,2]:

---

[3] In the figure, the white and black circles respectively indicate positive and negative examples. The solid line indicates the hyperplane which divides the space and the broken lines indicate the planes that indicate the margins.

[4] Open data refers to data which is not used for machine learning, and closed data refers to data which is used for machine learning.

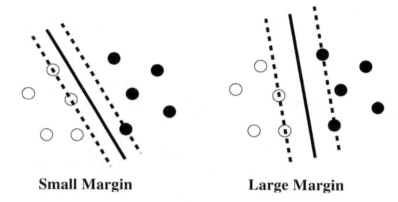

Small Margin   **Large Margin**

Fig. 5. Maximizing the margin

$$f(\mathbf{x}) = sgn\left(\sum_{i=1}^{l} \alpha_i y_i K(\mathbf{x}_i, \mathbf{x}) + b\right) \tag{1}$$

$$b = \frac{max_{i,y_i=-1}b_i + min_{i,y_i=1}b_i}{2}$$

$$b_i = -\sum_{j=1}^{l} \alpha_j y_j K(\mathbf{x}_j, \mathbf{x}_i),$$

where $\mathbf{x}$ is the context (a set of features) of an input example, $\mathbf{x}_i$ indicates the context of a training datum and y_i $(i = 1, ..., l, y_i \in \{1, -1\})$ indicates its category, and the function sgn is:

$$sgn(x) = 1 \ (x \geq 0), \tag{2}$$
$$-1 \ (otherwise).$$

Each α_i $(i = 1, 2...)$ is fixed as the value of α_i that maximizes the value of $L(\alpha)$ in Equation (3) under the conditions set by Equations (4) and (5).

$$L(\alpha) = \sum_{i=1}^{l} \alpha_i - \frac{1}{2} \sum_{i,j=1}^{l} \alpha_i \alpha_j y_i y_j K(\mathbf{x_i}, \mathbf{x_j}) \tag{3}$$

$$0 \leq \alpha_i \leq C \ (i = 1, ..., l) \tag{4}$$

$$\sum_{i=1}^{l} \alpha_i y_i = 0 \tag{5}$$

Although the function K is called a kernel function and various functions are used as kernel functions, we have exclusively used the following polynomial function:

$$K(\mathbf{x}, \mathbf{y}) = (\mathbf{x} \cdot \mathbf{y} + 1)^d \tag{6}$$

C and d are constants set by experimentation. For all experiments reported in this paper, C was fixed as 1 and d was fixed as 2.

A set of $\mathbf{x}_i$ that satisfies $\alpha_i > 0$ is called a support vector (SV_s)[5], and the summation portion of Equation (1) is calculated using only the examples that are support vectors. Equation 1 is expressed as the following by using support vectors.

$$f(\mathbf{x}) = sgn \left(\sum_{i:x_i \in SV_s} \alpha_i y_i K(\mathbf{x}_i, \mathbf{x}) + b \right) \tag{7}$$

$$b = \frac{b_{i:y_i=-1, x_i \in SV_s} + b_{i:y_i=1, x_i \in SV_s}}{2}$$

$$b_i = - \sum_{i:x_i \in SV_s} \alpha_j y_j K(\mathbf{x}_j, \mathbf{x}_i),$$

Support vector machine methods are capable of handling data consisting of two categories. In general, data consisting of more than two categories is handled by using the pair-wise method [3].

In this method, for data consisting of N categories, pairs of two different categories (N(N-1)/2 pairs) are constructed. The better category is determined by using a 2-category classifier (in this paper, a support vector machine[6] is used as the 2-category classifier), and the correct category is finally determined on the basis of the "voting" on the N(N-1)/2 pairs that results from analysis by the 2-category classifier.

The support vector machine method discussed in this paper is in fact a combination of the support vector machine method and the pair-wise method described above.

4   Method of Using the Results of Unsupervised Data as Features

We developed a new method of using the results of unsupervised learning as features.

We first describe our method of unsupervised learning. We can use active-case sentences as supervised data for the conversion of cases. We show an example in Figure 6. In this figure, an active sentence was converted into supervised data. This means that the input passive/causative sentence is "inu (?) watashi

---

[5] In Fig. 5, the circles in the broken lines indicate support vectors.
[6] We used Kudoh's TinySVM software [2] as the support vector machine.

Active sentence:
inu   ga   watashi wo   kanda.
(dog) subject (I)   object (bite)
(Dog bit me.)

⇓

Supervised data:
inu (?) *watashi* (?) *kanda*
ga   wo

Fig. 6. Supervised data construction from active sentences

(?) kanda", source case-marking particles are not given as shown by "(?)", and the target case-marking particles are the two underlined particles, ga and wo. Although we cannot use source case-marking particles, we can use the target case-marking particles in the active sentence, so we use the active sentence as supervised data. In this study, we call this method unsupervised learning and call the supervised data constructed from an active sentence unsupervised data, because active sentences are not the original supervised data, which are passive/causative sentences. We can use both supervised data and unsupervised data simultaneously as instances for learning, because the forms of both types of data are similar. In this study, we call the method using both supervised and unsupervised data supervised/unsupervised learning.

Unsupervised data do not contain source case-marking particles and have less information than supervised data. However we can use many examples as unsupervised data because we have many active sentences and do not need to tag target case-marking particles manually. So unsupervised learning or supervised/unsupervised learning can give a higher accuracy rate than supervised learning.

We developed a new method of using the results of unsupervised learning or/and supervised/unsupervised learning as features for supervised learning. In this method, we add the results obtained by unsupervised learning or/and supervised/unsupervised learning to features and use supervised learning. For example, when certain supervised data have features {a, b, c} and the result of unsupervised learning is "d", features {a, b, c, unsupervised_learning_result=d} are used as new features. This method is called stacking and it is used to combine results obtained by many systems [9]. In this study, we used this method to combine the results of unsupervised and supervised learning. Thus, we can use the advantages of each method of learning.

5   Features (Information Used in Classification)

In our study, we used the following features:

1. the case-marking particle taken by N (source case-marking particle)

2. the part of speech (POS) of P
3. the word of P
4. the auxiliary verb attached to P
   (e.g., reru (an auxiliary verb for the passive voice), saseru (an auxiliary verb for the causative voice))
5. the word of N
6. the first 1, 2, 3, 4, 5, and 7 digits of the category number of N. The category number indicates a semantic class of words.

   A Japanese thesaurus, the Bunrui Goi Hyou [7], was used to determine the category number of each word. This thesaurus is of the 'is-a' hierarchical type, in which each word has a category number. This is a 10-digit number that indicates seven levels of the 'is-a' hierarchy. The top five levels are expressed by the first five digits, the sixth level is expressed by the next two digits, and the seventh level is expressed by the last three digits.
7. the case-marking particles of nominals that have a dependency relationship with P and are other than N,

where N is the noun phrase connected to the case-marking particle being analyzed, and P is the predicate of the noun phrase. The features are made by consulting experimental results in the paper [5]. We did not use semantic classes of words for verbs because we obtained lower precisions when using semantic classes of words for verbs in the paper [5].

The method of unsupervised learning cannot use the first feature since supervised data are sentences in the active voice.

The stacking method described in the previous section uses the results of other systems as features in addition.

6   Experiments

We used the constructed corpus described in Section 2 as supervised data, and we also used it as a test corpus for evaluation. We used 10-fold cross validation to evaluate our method. We used all the case-marking particles in the active-voice sentences of the Kyoto University corpus as unsupervised data. The number of case-marking particles was 53,157. The distribution of the case-marking particles are shown in Table 2.

We conducted experiments for converting case-marking particles by using the following methods:

- The use of supervised learning
- The use of unsupervised learning
- The use of supervised/unsupervised learning
- The use of stacking methods
  - Stacking 1
    The use of the results of unsupervised learning for stacking
  - Stacking 2
    The use of the results of supervised/unsupervised learning for stacking

Table 2. Distribution of the target case-marking particles in the unsupervised data

Target case-marking particle	Number
wo	14,535
ni	13,148
ga	9,792
to	7,849
de	5,654
kara	1,490
made	322
yori	187
he	177
nite	2
yo	1
Total	53,157

Table 3. Experimental results

Method	Accuracy
Supervised	89.06%
Unsupervised	51.15%
Super/Unsuper	87.09%

- Stacking 3

  The use of the results of unsupervised learning and super-vised/unsupervised learning for stacking

The results are shown in Tables 3 and 4.

The following results were obtained:

- The accuracy rate of supervised learning was 89.06%. This means that we can convert Japanese case-marking particles in passive/causative sentences into target case-marking particles at least at this accuracy rate by using machine learning. Because there are no previous studies on case-marking particle conversion using machine learning, these results are valuable.
- The accuracy rate of unsupervised learning was very low. Information about source case-marking particles would thus be critical.
- The accuracy rate of supervised/unsupervised learning was lower than that of supervised learning. Unsupervised data would have characters different from those in supervised data. So a simple adding of unsupervised data would reduce the accuracy rate.
- As in Table 4, all the stacking methods improved the accuracy rate of supervised learning. However, the improvement was not big. So we conducted a statistical test by using a binomial test. The result is that all the stacking

Table 4. Experimental results obtained by using stacking methods

Method	Accuracy
Stacking 1	89.47%
Stacking 2	89.55%
Stacking 3	89.55%

methods had a significant difference in the accuracy rate against supervised learning at a significance level of 0.01. Thus our new methods based on stacking for using the results of unsupervised learning as features in learning are effective.

Unsupervised data would have characters different from those in supervised data. So a simple adding of unsupervised data would be not sufficient. The use of stacking methods to combine the results of unsupervised learning would enable us to use good the advantages of supervised learning and unsupervised learning appropriately.

Another reason for unsupervised data to be ineffective in supervised/unsuper- vised learning and effective in stacking is this. The purpose of this study is to obtain the maximum accuracy rate for the conversion of case-marking particles when converting passive/causative sentences into active-voice sentences. So we must use machine learning to obtain the maximum accuracy rate for the conversion of case-marking particles when converting passive/causative sentences into active-voice sentences. When we use supervised/unsupervised learning, we use both supervised data and unsupervised data. Thus, in supervised/unsupervised learning, learning is performed so as to give the maximum accuracy rate for supervised and unsupervised data. Since unsupervised data are not for the conversion of case-marking particles, supervised/unsupervised learning is not performed to obtain the maximum accuracy rate for the conversion of case-marking particles. In contrast, when we use stacking methods, we use only supervised data as instances for learning. Unsupervised data are only used to extend features. Thus, in stacking methods, learning is performed to give the maximum accuracy rate for supervised data. Thus, stacking methods can perform learning with the maximum accuracy rate for the conversion of case-marking particles.

7   Conclusion

We developed a new method of machine learning for converting Japanese case-marking particles when converting Japanese passive/causative sentences into active sentences. We obtained an accuracy rate of 89.06% by using normal supervised learning. Because there are no studies on the conversion of case-marking particles by using machine learning, our results are valuable. We also developed a new method of using the results of unsupervised learning as features for supervised learning and obtained a slightly higher accuracy rate (89.55%) by using this method. We verified that this improvement is statistically significant. Thus we developed a new effective method for machine learning.

The conversion of passive/causative sentences into active sentences is useful in many research areas including generation, knowledge extraction from a database written in natural languages, information extraction, and question answering. In the future, we intend to use our study for natural language processing.

References

1. Nello Cristianini and John Shawe-Taylor. *An Introduction to Support Vector Machines and Other Kernel-based Learning Methods.* Cambridge University Press, 2000.
2. Taku Kudoh. TinySVM: Support Vector Machines. http://cl.aist-nara.ac.jp/ taku-ku// software/TinySVM/ index.html, 2000.
3. Taku Kudoh and Yuji Matsumoto. Use of support vector learning for chunk identification. *CoNLL-2000*, 2000.
4. Sadao Kurohashi and Makoto Nagao. Kyoto University text corpus project. pages 115–118, 1997. (in Japanese).
5. Masaki Murata. Japanese case analysis based on a machine learning method that uses borrowed supervised data. *IPSJ-WGNL 2001-NL-144*, 2001.
6. Masaki Murata, Kiyotaka Uchimoto, Qing Ma, and Hitoshi Isahara. Using a support-vector machine for Japanese-to-English translation of tense, aspect, and modality. *ACL Workshop on the Data-Driven Machine Translation*, 2001.
7. NLRI. *Bunrui Goi Hyou.* Shuuei Publishing, 1964.
8. Hirotoshi Taira and Masahiko Haruno. Feature selection in svm text categorization. In *Proceedings of AAAI2001*, pages 480–486, 2001.
9. Hans van Halteren, Jakub Zavrel, and Walter Daelemans. Improving accuracy in word class tagging through the combination of machine learning systems. *Computational Linguistics*, 27(2):199–229, 2001.

From Czech Morphology through Partial Parsing to Disambiguation

Eva Mráková and Radek Sedláček

NLP Laboratory, Faculty of Informatics, Masaryk University
Botanická 68, CZ-602 00 Brno, Czech Republic
{glum,rsedlac}@fi.muni.cz

Abstract. This paper deals with a complex system of processing raw Czech texts. Several modules were implemented which perform different levels of processing. These modules can easily be incorporated into many other linguistic applications and some of them are already exploited in this way. The first level of processing raw texts represents a reliable morphological analysis – we give a survey of the effective implementation of the robust morphological analyser for Czech named **ajka**. Texts tagged by **ajka** can be further processed by the partial parser DIS and its extension VADIS which is based on verb valencies. The output of these systems serves for automatic partial disambiguation of input texts. The tools described in this paper are widely used for parsing large corpora and can be employed in the initial phase of semantic analysis.

Keywords: Morphological analysis, partial syntactic parsing, disambiguation, verb valencies

1 Introduction

Czech belongs to a family of highly inflectional free-word order languages. These characteristics demand special treatment during text processing systems of Czech words and sentences.

In analytical languages a simple approach can be taken in morphological analysis: usually it is enough to list all word forms to capture most morphological processes. In English, for example, a regular verb has usually only 4 distinct forms, and irregular ones have at most 8 forms. On the other hand, highly inflected languages like Czech and Turkish [7] present a difficulty for such simple approaches as the expansion of the dictionary is at least an order of magnitude greater; a Czech verb, for instance, can have up to fifty distinct forms.

Chunking in Czech is also more difficult than in English. There are two reasons for this: first, a gap within a verb group may be more complex and it may even be a whole clause. Second, Czech language is a free word-order language which requires a much more complex approach to recognising the verb group structure.

A. Gelbukh (Ed.): CICLing 2003, LNCS 2588, pp. 126–135, 2003.
© Springer-Verlag Berlin Heidelberg 2003

Statistical methods of disambiguation [3] are suitable for analytical languages like English, but the problem of spare learning data arises for languages like Czech with a huge amount of possible morphological tags (compare approximately 1600 tags in `ajka` to 160 tags in the BNC extended tagset). Thus, it turns out that rule-based methods [5] have to be developed and employed to obtain better results.

2 Morphological Analyser `ajka`

We developed a universal morphological analyser which performs the morphological analysis based on dividing all words in Czech texts into their smallest relevant components that we call segments. We define several types of segments – most of them roughly corresponds to the linguistic concept morpheme (e.g. ending) and some of them represents the combinations of two or more morphemes (e.g. stem).

Our morphological analyser consists of three major parts: a formal description of morphological processes via morphological patterns; an assignment of Czech stems to their relevant patterns; and a morphological analysis algorithm.

The description of Czech formal morphology is represented by a system of inflectional patterns with sets of endings and it includes the lists of segments and their proper combinations. The assignment of Czech stems to their patterns is contained in the Czech Machine Dictionary [6]. Finally, the algorithm of morphological analysis using this information splits each word into its appropriate segments.

2.1 Description of Czech Morphology

The main part of the algorithmic description of formal morphology, as it was suggested in [6], is a pattern definition. The basic notion is a morphological paradigm – a set of all forms of the lemma expressing a system of its respective grammatical categories.

As stated in [2], the traditional grammar of Czech suggests a much smaller paradigm system than exists in reality. For this reason we decided to build a large set of paradigm patterns to cover all the variations of Czech from scratch. Fortunately, we were not limited by technical restrictions, which allowed us to follow a straightforward approach to a linguistically adequate and robust solution.

Nouns, adjectives, pronouns and numerals decline for case and number. Verbs conjugate for person and number and have paradigms for different tenses (past, present etc.). For example, the noun blecha (flea) displays the following forms in the singular paradigm: blecha (Nom.), blechy (Gen.), bleše (Dat.), blechu (Acu.), blecho (Voc.), bleše (Loc.), blechou (Ins.) and another seven forms for the plural paradigm.

The corresponding word forms within each paradigm have the same ending and that allows us to divide the given word form into two parts: a stem and an ending. For the word blecha we obtain the following segmentation: blech-{a,y,u,o,ou}, ble ̶l ̶-{e,e}.

We introduced a system of ending sets and distinguish two types:basic and peripheral ending sets. The basic ones (in our example {a,y,u,o,ou}) contain endings that do not influence the form of the stem, while endings from the peripheral ending sets (e.g. {e,e}) cause changes in the stem. These changes occur regularly and represent typical alternations in the last letter (ch- ̶l ̶) or in the final group of the stem.

Every ending carries values of grammatical categories of the relevant word form. These values are encoded in the form of a grammatical tag which is assigned to the respective ending. Thus, ending sets contain pairs of the ending and the appropriate tag.

In the next step, because of possible alternations, we perform further segmentation of stems into a stem base (e.g. ble) and an intersegment (e.g. ch, ̶l ̶). The stem base is the part that is common to all word forms in the paradigm, i.e. it doesn't change, and the intersegment is a final group of the stem whose form changes.

A pattern definition then stores the information about the only possible combinations of a stem base, intersegments and endings (e.g. ble-<ch>-{a,y,u,o,ou}, < ̶l ̶>-{e,e}). From this point of view, our system of declension and conjugation patterns is considered to be a complete and systematic description of all the alternations that can occur in the inflection process. Moreover, this approach allows us not to store all word forms from the paradigm, but only the common stem base assigned to the relevant pattern.

2.2 Implementation of the Analyser

The key to the successful implementation of the analyser is an efficient storage mechanism for lexical items. A trie structure [4] is used for storing stem bases of Czech word forms. One of the main disadvantages of this approach is high memory requirements. We attempted to solve this problem by implementing the trie structure in the form of a minimal finite state automaton. This incremental method of building such an automaton was presented in [1] and is fast enough for our purpose. Moreover, the memory requirements for storing the minimal automaton are significantly lower (see Table 2).

There are two binary files that are essential for the analyser. One of them contains definitions of sets of endings and morphological patterns; its source is a plain text file. The second is a binary image of the Czech Machine Dictionary [6] and contains stem bases and auxiliary data structures. We developed a program abin that can read both of these text files and efficiently store their content into appropriate data structures in destination binary files.

The analyser's first step is loading these binary files. These files are not further processed – they are only loaded into memory. This is mainly to allow as quick a start of the analyser as possible.

The next steps of the analyser are determined by those within the morphological analysis algorithm. The basic principle of the algorithm is based on the segmentation described in Section 2.1. The separated ending then determines values of grammatical categories. More details can be found in [10]. Another feature of the analyser is a possibility to select various forms of the basic word form, the so called lemma.

Finally, the user can have more versions of binary files that contain morphological information and stem bases, and can specify which pair should be used by the analyser. Users can take advantage of this feature to "switch on" an analysis of colloquial Czech, domain-specific texts etc.

Table 1 shows the sentence Já jsem se té přednášky zúčastnila. (I have participated in that lecture.) fully but ambiguously morphologically analysed by ajka. To explain the output, for example, the tag k5eApFnStMmPaP of the word

Table 1. Example of the sentence analysed by ajka.

```
Já          <l>já
            <c>k3xPnSc1p1
            <c>k1gNnSc1 <c>k1gNnSc4
            <c>k1gNnSc5 <c>k1gNnPc2
            <c>k1gNnSc6 <c>k1gNnSc7
            <c>k1gNnSc3 <c>k1gNnSc2
            <c>k1gNnPc6 <c>k1gNnPc3
            <c>k1gNnPc1 <c>k1gNnPc4
            <c>k1gNnPc5 <c>k1gNnPc7
jsem        <l>být
            <c>k5eAp1nStPmIaI
se          <l>sebe
            <c>k3xXnSc4p2 <c>k3xPnSc4p2
            <l>s
            <c>k7c7
té          <l>ten
            <c>k3xDgFnSc2 <c>k3xDgFnSc3
            <c>k3xDgFnSc6
            <l>té
            <c>k1gNnSc1 <c>k1gNnSc4
            <c>k1gNnSc5 <c>k1gNnPc2
            <c>k1gNnSc6 <c>k1gNnSc7
            <c>k1gNnSc3 <c>k1gNnSc2
            <c>k1gNnPc6 <c>k1gNnPc3
            <c>k1gNnPc1 <c>k1gNnPc4
            <c>k1gNnPc5 <c>k1gNnPc7
přednášky   <l>přednáška
            <c>k1gFnSc2 <c>k1gFnPc1
            <c>k1gFnPc4 <c>k1gFnPc5
zúčastnila  <l>zúčastnit
            <c>k5eApNnPtMmPaP
            <c>k5eApFnStMmPaP
```

zúčastnila (participated) means: part of speech (k) is verb (5), negation (e) is affirmative (A), person (p) is feminine (F), number (n) is singular (S), tense (t) is past (M), modus (m) is participium (P) and aspect (a) is perfective (p). Lemmata and possible tags are prefixed by <l>, <c> respectively. This example also depicts both lemma and tag ambiguity of Czech word forms. The first one is for instance represented by the word form se which belongs to two possible lemmata – sebe (reflexive pronoun) and s (preposition); the second one by the word form zúčastnila which has two alternative tags for the same lemma – for neuter plural and feminine singular.

The power of the analyser can be evaluated by two features. The most important is the number of words that can be recognised by the analyser. This number depends on the quality and richness of the dictionary. Our database contains 223,600 stem bases from which ajka is able to analyse and generate 5,678,122 correct Czech word forms. The second feature is the speed of analysis. In the brief mode, ajka can analyse more than 20,000 words per second on PentiumIII processor with a frequency of 800MHz. Some other statistical data, such as number of segments and size of binary files, is shown in the Table 2.

Table 2. Statistical data

#intersegments	779
#endings	643
#sets of endings	2,806
#patterns	1,570
#stem bases	223,600
#generated word forms	5,678,122
#generated tags	1,604
speed of the analysis	20,000 words/s
dictionary	1,930,529 Bytes
morph. information	147,675 Bytes

3   Partial Parser DIS

The partial parser DIS consists of a robust grammar for the main sentence groups in Czech – verb, nominal and prepositional – and the parsing mechanism. As mentioned above, chunking in Czech is quite difficult particularly because of some properties of verb groups.

Thus the main focus is put on the method for obtaining verb rules from an annotated corpus. One of the most important results of our work is a complete and robust algorithmic description of Czech verb groups; an appropriate version of such a description was not elaborated before.

On the other hand, noun and prepositional groups are quite well described in Czech grammars. For the construction of the grammar rules for recognition of such groups we have used existing resources but the rules have been slightly modified according to the corpus data and our requirements (we prefered higher recall to precision). Further details of the rules for noun and prepositional groups in our system can be found in [11].

3.1   Verb Rules

Recognition and analysis of the predicate in a sentence is fundamental to the meaning of the sentence and its further analysis. In more than 50% of Czech sentences, the predicate contains a compound verb group (e.g. the group jsem se zµßastnila in the example presented in the section describing ajka). Moreover, compound verb groups in Czech are often discontinuous and contain so called gaps. In our example the gap is t¢ pßednµßky. Until all parts of a compound verb group are located, it is impossible to continue with any kind of syntactic or semantic analysis. We consider a compound verb group to be a list of verbs and maybe the reflexive pronouns se, si. Such a group is obviously compound of auxiliary and lexical verbs.

We describe here the method that results in definite clause grammar rules – called verb rules – that contain information about all components of a particular verb group and about their respective tags. The algorithm for learning verb rules takes as its input sentences from the annotated and fully disambiguated corpus DESAM [8]. The algorithm is split into three steps: finding verb chunks, generalisation and verb rule synthesis. These three steps are described below.

1. The observed properties of a verb group are the following: their components are either verbs or a reflexive pronoun se (si); the boundary of a verb group cannot extend beyond a sentence boundary; and between two components of the verb group there can be a gap consisting of an arbitrary number of non-verb words or even a whole clause. In the first step, the boundaries of all clauses are found. Then each gap is replaced by the symbolic tag gap. The method exploits only the lemma of each word i.e., the nominative singular for nouns, adjectives, pronouns and numerals, infinitive for verbs, and its tag.
2. The lemmata and the tags are now generalised. Three generalisation operations are employed: the elimination of (some) lemmata, generalisation of grammatical categories and finding grammatical agreement constraints.
   All lemmata apart from forms of the auxiliary verb být (to be) (být, by, aby, kdyby) are rejected. Lemmata of modal verbs and verbs with similar behaviour are replaced by the symbolic tag modal. These verbs have been found in the list of more than 15 000 verb valencies [9].
   Exploiting linguistic knowledge, several grammatical categories are not important for verb group description (very often it is negation or aspect). These categories may be removed.

Another situation appears when two or more values of some category are related. In the simplest case they are the same, but in more complicated cases (e.g. formal modes of address in Czech) are treated through special predicates.

3. Finally the verb rule in DCG formalism in Prolog is constructed by rewriting the result of the generalisation phase. For the verb group jsem se té přednášky zúčastnila, which contains the gap té přednášky, the following rule is constructed:

```
vg(vg(Be,Se,Verb), Gaps) -->
    be(Be,_,P,N,tP,mI,_),
    % jsem
    reflex_pron(Se,xX,_,_),
    % se
    gap([],Gaps),
    % té přednášky
    k5(Verb,_,_,P1,N1,tM,mP,_),
    % zúčastnila
    { check_num(N,N1,Be,Vy) }.
```

The interpretation of non-terminals used in the rule is following: be() represents auxiliary verb být, reflex_pron() stands for reflexive pronoun se (si), gap() is a special predicate for dealing with the gaps, and k5() stands for an arbitrary non-auxiliary verb. The particular values of some arguments of non-terminals represent obligatory properties. Simple cases of grammatical agreement are not present in this example, more complicated situations are solved employing constraints such as the predicate check_num(). In the comments there are mentioned words processed by the particular non-terminal. The method has been implemented in Perl. More than 150 definite clause grammar rules were constructed from the annotated corpus that describe all the verb groups that are frequent in Czech.

3.2 Parsing Mechanism

DIS exploits the standard Prolog DC parsing mechanism extended in two ways. First, the special predicate for processing gaps was designed, implemented and incorporated. Second, it was extended by a procedure which controls the whole parsing, calls the DC mechanism when necessary, and selects the best parses for a particular context. In our example sentence, the partial parser recognises the verb group jsem se zúčastnila and the noun group té přednášky. It assigns to each word involved in one of these groups the correct tag in the context of the whole sentence. More than one analysis of a group can be made and on the partial parsing level it is not possible to choose the correct one. DIS outputs all of these analyses to its extension VADIS which can solve some of these ambiguities.

4   Extension VADIS

Techniques of partial parsing exploited by DIS aim to find syntactic information efficiently and reliably from unrestricted texts by sacrificing completeness and depth of analysis. The main purpose of the extension VADIS is to find more complex syntactic relations from the output of the partial parser. It is based on the processing of verb valencies and possible functions of nominal and prepositional groups in a sentence.

The list of Czech verb valencies [9] was transformed to the dictionary suitable for the effective processing by VADIS. The lexical verb from the verb group found during the preceding partial analysis is searched in this dictionary. There can be several verb valency frames associated with one verb. A verb valency frame consists of one or more parts which express the requirements for their possible participants. If there is at least one potential participant for every part of the verb valency frame in the analysed sentence, this frame is tagged as a contender. Thus we obtain a list of all possible verb frames with all their potential participants. One of these frames is correct in the particular context. Although we are not yet able to determine the correct frame automatically, selecting from possible cases is very useful. Combination with other methods can bring even better results in the future. In addition to processing verb valencies, VADIS searches for all possible arguments of other functions of noun and prepositional groups in a sentence. Thus, all possible functions are assigned to every such a group in the particular clause.

The following results are obtained for our example input sentence: only one possible verb frame (out of four frames in the dictionary) is selected for the full-meaning verb zúčastnit se. The successful frame is zúčastnit se <čeho> (participate <in st>) and its only potential participant is the noun group tе přednašky. The other relation found is Ja as the only possible subject of the sentence.

5   Partial Automatic Disambiguation

The output of both DIS and VADIS can serve for automatic partial disambiguation of input texts. For every word in the analysed sentence, the output contains all tags of the particular word which are involved either in a recognised group containing this word, or the functions which the word can perform in the sentence. One of these groups and roles is correct for the word in the given context. Thus, if we reduce the full set of tags assigned initially to the word by ajka to those tags which occur in the DIS or VADIS output, the only correct tag remains in the new restricted set. This method is used for obtaining partially disambiguated texts. Table 3 shows our example sentence disambiguated according to the output of the VADIS programme.

In this case the sentence is disambiguated fully and every word has been assigned its correct tag in the given context. The recall of our system is 99.03% and the precision of 66.10% which are slightly better results when compared with

Table 3. Disambiguation performed according to the VaDis output.

```
Já          <l>já
            <c>k3xPnSc1p1
jsem        <l>být
            <c>k5eAp1nStPmIaI
se          <l>sebe
            <c>k3xXnSc4p2
té          <l>ten
            <c>k3xDgFnSc2
přednášky   <l>přednáška
            <c>k1gFnSc2
zúčastnila  <l>zúčastnit
            <c>k5eApFnStMmPaP
```

best current Czech rule-based disambiguator [5]. Considerably better precision of disambiguation could be achieved by combining our system with an efficient statistical component which is unfortunately not readily available to us now.

6   Conclusion

We have described our system consisting of modules performing two particular levels of natural language analysis, namely, morphological and syntactic.

The morphological analyser has been tested on large corpora containing approximately 10^8 positions. Based on the test results we consider ajka to be robust enough to analyse any raw Czech text. Nowadays it is being used for lemmatisation and morphological tagging, as well as for generating correct word forms, and also as a spelling checker. Moreover, ajka can be readily adapted to other inflected languages that have to deal with morphological analysis. In general, only the language-specific parts of the system, i.e. definitions of sets of endings and the dictionary, have to be replaced for this purpose.

We have presented a survey of the main features of the partial parser Dis; the main focus has been put on the algorithm for obtaining verb rules for Czech from an annotated corpus. The extension VaDis recognises further syntactic relations in the output of Dis. It is based on the processing of verb valencies and it searches possible arguments of roles of noun and prepositional groups in a sentence.

The results of the partial disambiguation performed by our system are slightly better than results of other comparable rule-based systems for Czech. We achieved a recall of 99.03% and a precision of 66.10%. A combination of our system with an efficient statistical component will bring a considerably higher score of precision.

References

1. Daciuk, J., Watson, R. E. and Watson, B. W. Incremental Construction of Acyclic Finite-State Automata and Transducers. In *Finite State Methods in Natural Language Processing*, Bilkent University, Ankara, Turkey, June–July 1998.
2. Hajič, J. Disambiguation of Rich Inflection (Computational Morphology of Czech). Charles University Press, 1st edition, 2000.
3. Hajič, J. and Hladká, B. Probabilistic and Rule-Based Tagging of an Inflective Language – a Comparsion. In *Proceedings of the 5th Conference on Applied Natural Language Processing*, Washington 1997.
4. Knuth, D. E. *The Art of Computer Programming: Sorting and Searching*, Volume 3, Chapter 6.3. Addison Wesley, 2nd edition, 1973.
5. Oliva, K., Hnátková, M., Petkevič, V. and Květoň, P. The Linguistic Basis of a Rule-Based Tagger of Czech. In *Proceedings of the Third International Workshop TSD 2000*, Springer, Berlin 2000.
6. Osolsobě, K. *Algorithmic Description of Czech Formal Morphology and Czech Machine Dictionary*. Ph.D. Thesis, Faculty of Arts, Masaryk University Brno, 1996. In Czech.
7. Oztaner S. M. A Word Grammar of Turkish with Morphophonemic Rules. Master's Thesis, Middle East Technical University, 1996.
8. Pala, K., Rychlý, P., and Smrž, P. DESAM - Annotated Corpus for Czech. In *Proceedings of SOFSEM'97, LNCS 1338*, Springer, 1997.
9. Pala, K. and Ševeček, P. Valencies of Czech Verbs. Studia Minora Facultatis Philosophicae Universitatis Brunensis, A45, 1997.
10. Sedláček, R. and Smrž, P. Automatic Processing of Czech Inflectional and Derivative Morphology. Technical Report FIMU-RS-2001-03, Faculty of Informatics, Masaryk University Brno, 2001.
11. Žáčková, E. Partial Parsing (of Czech). Ph.D. Thesis, Faculty of Informatics, Masaryk University Brno, 2002. In Czech.

Fast Base NP Chunking with Decision Trees – Experiments on Different POS Tag Settings

Dirk Lüdtke and Satoshi Sato

Kyoto University, Graduate School of Informatics
Yoshida-Honmachi, Sakyo-Ku, 606-8501 Kyoto, Japan
`dludtke@pine.kuee.kyoto-u.ac.jp`, `sato@i.kyoto-u.ac.jp`
`http://pine.kuee.kyoto-u.ac.jp/`

Abstract. We introduce a chunking system based on probability distribution approximation and decision trees. The system was tested on the large standard evaluation set for base noun phrases. While the training time of the system is remarkable short (about 3 hours), results are comparable with the best systems reported so far. We trained our system with different settings of POS tags and show how much chunking results depend on POS tag accuracy.

1 Introduction

Chunking means extracting non-overlapping segments from a stream of data. These segments are called chunks. Chunks can be consecutive but also interposed. There are several applications in text analysis, e.g.:

- sentence segmentation
- core phrase detection
- named entity extraction
- word segmentation (in languages such as Japanese, where words are not separated by spaces)

Other problems unrelated to text processing can also be reduced to chunking tasks, e.g.:

- phoneme extraction from speech data
- finding genes in DNA

A frequent application for chunking is the detection of base noun phrases (noun phrases which do not contain other noun phrases). The expression "core noun phrase" is synonymously used. Most of the syntactic ambiguities in English clauses are above base NP level. The following example shows an ambiguity where a preposition can either attach to a noun (1) or a verb (2).

(1) saw (the man (with the telescope))
(2) saw (the man) (with the telescope)

However, this ambiguity does not exist in base NP chunk representation.

(3) saw [the man] with [the telescope]

A. Gelbukh (Ed.): CICLing 2003, LNCS 2588, pp. 136–147, 2003.

Since many ambiguities of natural language can be left unsolved in base NP chunking, recognition rates are comparatively high (word level accuracy of almost 99%). The basic idea is that employing accurate results of low level analysis could be advantageous for solving more elaborate tasks. For example, Abney [1] proposed chunking as a precursor for full parsing. But, also other low level NLP tasks like POS-tagging could benefit from base NP chunk information.

Several chunking methods have been introduced in the past years, and it seems that limits of result improvement are reached. The system we will introduce in Section 4 is among the best, but has the additional merit that training time is comparatively short.

Ramshaw and Marcus [7] proposed two test environments for base NP chunking. A problem of the larger environment is that POS tags must be added later. This leaves room for using different tags than initially intended, but when different tags are used, comparison with other systems becomes difficult. For understanding what impact other POS-tags have on the chunking results, we trained our system with 4 different POS tag settings. Using this information, it should be possible to estimate how results of other systems change when a different tagset is used.

2   Chunking

A chunking problem can easily be transferred to a tagging task. Ramshaw and Marcus [7] use the IOB tag set, where words are separated in words inside a chunk (I), outside a chunk (O), and at the beginning of a consecutive chunk (B). Other representations operate with chunk ends (IOE) or don't distinguish non-consecutive and consecutive beginnings (IOB2). However, not every possible tag sequence is valid, e.g., in the IOB set B must not follow O. Therefore, care has to be taken that no such wrong sequence be produced.

Muñoz et al. [5] proposed a method where two classifiers are trained to recognize opening and closing brackets (O+C). This seems to be a different approach, but on the other hand, there are at least similarities to a tagging problem with four tags: beginning, end, both and neither.

Lüdtke [4] distinguishes four boolean categories: whether the word is first in a chunk (f), inside a chunk (i), last in a chunk (l) and beginning of a consecutive chunk (c). Each possible combination of these categories (there are 7) can then be used as tag. Since all of the categories are boolean, tags are written as binary 4-tuples: 0000, 0100, 0110, 1100, 1101, 1110 and 1111. We call this representation filc-representation, because of the first letters of the four categories (first, inside, last, consecutive).

The advantage of this representation is that each of these four categories can be learned independently. A combination of only 2 of the categories leads to the tagsets mentioned before, e.g., combining only (i) and (c) is equivalent to IOB, combining (f) and (l) is equivalent to (O+C).

Because the categories are binary, probability estimation is more tractable and hence deviations lower. As an example, the tagging in filc-representation of the sentence beginning of "In [early trading] in [Hong Kong] [Monday] , [Gold] was quoted at [\$ 366.50] [an ounce] ." is shown in Table 1.

Table 1. Example for our tagging system

word	filc tags	explanation
In	0000	outside
early	1100	first and inside
trading	0110	inside and last
in	0000	
Hong	1100	
Kong	0110	
Monday	1111	first in a consecutive
,	0000	
gold	1110	first, inside and last
was	0000	

2.1 Probability Estimation

A typical approach for learning tags from a tagged text corpus is to look at different types of patterns in the text and count how often the patterns appeared (n) and how often it lead to each of the tags (k)[1]. A pattern type could be a 3-gram where the tag of the second word should be guessed.

From this point forward, tagging is a straightforward classification problem: finding the best classification borders in the $(pt, t, \langle n, k \rangle)$ space, where pt is the pattern type, t the tag, and n and k the counts of t in the patterns of type pt.

Though it might be possible to work directly with the n and k counts, there are two reasons not to do so. First, the optimal classification borders in $\langle n, k \rangle$ are usually non-trivial, hence much data is needed to learn them. Second, given a distribution model, it is possible to approximate a probability p for each n and k, without using additional data. Section 4.1 introduces our distribution model and the probability approximations.

2.2 Combination of Pattern Types

The reason to make use of different patterns is, that long patterns like 5-grams tend to give our guesses a high accuracy, but we hardly can use them, since the longer the pattern the higher chance, that we have not seen it before. Short patterns like single words, on the other hand, occur much more frequently, but

---

[1] n and k are used for consistency with the notation of binomial distributions, where usually n denotes the number of trials and k the number of positive outcomes.

accuracy is low. A combination of different pattern types must hence lead to better results.

In our experiments (described in Section 5) we were using 31 pattern types (all patterns in a window of 5) for both the plain words and the POS tags. For this step we used decision trees, which don't return classes, but probability estimates of the classes. This is further explained in Section 4.2.

Other classification methods could be used for this task. Support Vector Machines [3] led to the best results we are aware of so far. The reason we decided to use decision trees is that they are fast (both in training and runtime) and flexible classifiers. Though there are theoretical limitations on accuracy, the low training time allows the training and comparison of different systems, which is one of the aims of this paper.

There also are fundamentally different approaches. Ramshaw and Marcus [7] use Transformation Rules to improve incorrect tag sequences. The approach of Argamon et al. [2] is memory based.

2.3 Combination of Categories

In our approach, probabilities are approximated independently for all four categories of the filc-representation scheme. Combining these categories leads to filc-tags, which then can be used as representation for chunks. This combination is also done by decision trees and described in more detail in Section 4.3.

A similar combination was also performed by other groups: e.g., Erik F. Tjong Kim Sang et al. used weighted voting to combine the output of different chunking systems.

It could be questioned, why the classification is not done in one step by using the $(pt, t, \langle n, k \rangle)$ space described earlier. Surely, a combination of all values in one step is most powerful. But unfortunately this feature space is rather large. In our case 248 probability estimates have to be combined. Our decision tree algorithm could learn a classifier for this number of features even in a reasonable time. But, with the size of training data provided our trees had an average depth of between 10 and 15, so only 10 to 15 features are used for one decision. In a large feature space many of the weaker (but still usable) features would never be used.

3 Test Environments

Ramshaw and Marcus [7] proposed two test environments for noun phrase chunking which have become a quasi standard for the evaluation of chunking algorithms. The first and smaller environment (baseNP-S) uses sections 15-18 of the Wall Street Journal corpus for training and section 20 for evaluation. The second environment (baseNP-L) uses sections 02-21 for training and section 00 for evaluation. Tjong Kim Sang [9] offers a script on his web site for extracting Ramshaw and Marcus style data sets from parsed text in Penn Treebank format. POS-tags were produced by the Brill tagger.

While the baseNP-S dataset can be downloaded[2], baseNP-L must be constructed from the Penn Treebank. Unfortunately, there is a source of confusion: POS-tags are to be produced by the Brill tagger. However, the temptation to use the more or less perfect tags of the treebank or another tagger (more accurate then Brill's or with another more promising tag set) is high, since this can improve the results significantly.

While better results are of course always welcome, it has to be admitted that methods are not comparable when different data is used for evaluation. This paper examines the influence of different POS-taggers. And it is shown that there are significant differences depending on the tags used.

It should also be noted that there is critics on using the Ramshaw and Marcus datasets for evaluating chunking methods:

1. Overfitting in the base NP task: since chunking methods are more and more optimized on solving this special problem, generality concerning other chunking problems gets lost. Therefore, the original intention to compare standard chunking methods can not be maintained.

2. Overfitting in the evaluation set: the evaluation sets are relatively small (there are usually only about 500 chunks which are not found[3]). A combination of different algorithms or parameter settings which already proved to be suitable to this task, could lead to too optimistic results.

3. Usefulness of this chunking scheme: base NP chunking is not the final goal. Because chunking results are to be used in further applications, some thoughts should be made about whether the chunking scheme is really optimal for this. The chunks were automatically derived from treebank parses, which surely limits the room for creative design. But there are some decisions we consider unfortunate:

- Prepositions are outside the chunk. Astonishingly "'s" (between two noun phrases, expressing possession) is usually inside the second chunk. This leads to problems when the second NP is omitted or when it is complex. Despite this, mistakes with other usages of "'s" lead to more chunking errors than necessary.
- Conjunctions of simple noun phrases form only one chunk. This also makes the task more difficult. And it is difficult to motivate why "with [A and B]" and "with [A] and with [B]" should be treated different.

4. Usefulness of the evaluation scheme: evaluation is based on chunk f-score, which equally weights chunk recall and chunk precision. It is questionable whether this represents the demands of the applications for chunking algorithms. A word based evaluation would alleviate the penalty for partial errors (e.g., when only the beginning of a chunk was guessed wrong) and decrease the overfitting described in point 1. and 2. A sentence based evaluation could be useful when full parsing is the application.

---

[2] The address is ftp.cis.upenn.edu/pub/chunker/.
[3] The evaluation part of baseNP-L consists of 46451 words or 12145 baseNP chunks. A chunk recall of 95% leads to 607 chunks not found.

4   Method

Our chunking algorithm consists of three steps:

1. Probability estimation: probabilities of filc-categories are estimated for word and POS patterns by approximating probability distribution functions.
2. Combination of pattern types: probability estimates concerning one filc-category are combined by decision trees.
3. Combination of categories: results of the previous step are combined by a decision tree.

4.1   Probability Estimation

Supposed it should be decided whether the word "total" in the sentence "Today, PC shipments annually total some \$ 38.3 billion world-wide" is inside a noun phrase or not. Since "total" can be used as an adjective, noun or verb, the decision is non-trivial.

Table 2 shows different word patterns, how often they appeared in the training corpus (n) and how often the word at position i (which is "total" in our case) was inside a noun phrase chunk (k).

Table 2. Patterns and their counts (k/n) for deciding whether the word at position i is inside a noun phrase chunk.

pattern type	position			count
	$i-1$	i	$i+1$	k/n
(--w)			some	18/362
(-w-)		total		69/73
(-ww)		total	some	0/0
(w--)	annually			0/22
(w-w)	annually		some	0/0
(ww-)	annually	total		0/0
(www)	annually	total	some	0/0

A common approach to calculate probabilities from (k, n)-pairs is adding one (or Laplace's Law), where 1 is added to each class (in our case $p = (k+1)/(n+2)$). This estimation produces good results for uniform probability distributions, but can lead to high deviations in other cases.

Because of this problems, we chose the Bayesian approach described by Lüdtke [4], where counts of (k,n)-pairs are used to approximate the probability distribution. An example for count counts is given in Table 3. These count counts are for the decision whether a word is inside a noun phrase (filc-category i) given the word itself (pattern type (-w-)).

Table 3. Count counts for category i and pattern type (-w-)

k/n: count count	
0/3:	327
1/3:	89
2/3:	112
3/3:	1132

The count counts in this example suggest a parabolic distribution with high frequencies of events with high and low probability, where naïve approaches like adding one usually fail.

In our approach probability distributions are approximated by segments of linear functions. Approximation is done by optimizing an equation system derived from count count numbers. The probability distribution approximation for category i and pattern type (-w-) is shown in Figure 1.

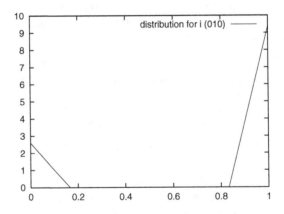

Fig. 1. Approximated probability distribution of category i and pattern type (-w-).

From these distribution functions, the distribution of events given their k and n values is easily computable. The mean of this function is used as probability estimate. In this way errors are minimized.

The probability estimates for the patterns in Table 2 are shown in Table 4.

4.2   Combination of Pattern Types

In the previous section we described how to derive probability estimates for filc-categories using the count count of word patterns. In this step probability estimates for the same filc-category are combined.

Table 4. Patterns and their probability estimates for deciding whether the word at position i is inside a noun phrase chunk.

pattern	position			prob.
type	$i-1$	i	$i+1$	est.
(--w)			some	0.057
(-w-)		total		0.943
(-ww)		total	some	0.632
(w--)	annually			0.039
(w-w)	annually		some	0.586
(ww-)	annually	total		0.555
(www)	annually	total	some	0.588

When looking again to Table 4, we see, that the estimates can differ considerably, e.g., the probability for pattern type (--w) was estimated with 0.057, the probability for pattern type (-w-) with 0.943.

The combination is done by decision trees which don't return classes, but class probabilities. We developed a simple decision tree algorithm for this task, where decisions are based on the information gain inside the training data (which is equivalent to the improvement of entropy). By erasing constants the formula of information gain can be reduced to:

$$-\sum_{b \in B} \sum_{c \in C} freq(b, c) * log(prob(b, c)), \tag{1}$$

where B is the set of subtrees branching from the node in question (2 for binary trees), C the classes, $freq(b, c)$ the frequency of class c in the part of training data which was branched to b, and $prob(b, c)$ the probability of c in b.

The C4.5 decision tree package (Quinlan [6]) is also based on information gain. There, $prob(b, c)$ is approximated by

$$\frac{freq(b, c)}{\sum_{d \in C} freq(b, d)}. \tag{2}$$

Quinlan reports problems when using the pure information gain criterion, because it does not punish very unbalanced decisions, e.g., where 1000 training cases are separated in 2 groups of 1 case and 999 cases. In order to overcome these problems Quinlan combines the information gain with another measure he calls split info.

However, unbalanced splitting is not bad per se. The problem of a split where only one case is separated is, that a probability estimation of 1.0 for the class of this case is usually wrong.

We solved this problem by trying to find a better approximation of $prob(b, c)$. Assuming that the probability of the parent node has an influence on the children nodes, we move the child probability a bit in its direction depending on the size of the child. Our formula of $prob(b, c)$ is:

$$\frac{prob(parent, c) * w + freq(b, c)}{w + \sum_{d \in C} freq(b, d)}. \tag{3}$$

w is a parameter expressing how much weight the probability of the parent node should get. This parameter has an influence on the results and could be object of further tuning. However, we were using a value $w = 2$ in all our experiments.

There is another reading of equation 3. The result is equal to the probability mean of freq(b, c) if the parental distribution is a multinomial distribution with a count of class c $freq(parent, c) = prob(parent, c) * w - 1$ and a count sum $\sum_{d \in C} freq(parent, d) = w - size(C)$. The probability mean for class c in this parental distribution is $prob(parent, c)$.

This method is a generalization of adding one (also known as Laplace's Law). Adding one also assumes a multinomial distribution, though a uniform one. This sets $prob(parent, c) = 1/size(C)$ and $w = size(C)$.

Our trees are pruned by cutting off all nodes where score increase was below a certain threshold. This threshold is the one which performs best in a test on unseen data. Because only one parameter has to be determined, this pruning method does not need much data.

We compared our decision tree algorithm to C4.5 and found out that results of our algorithm were better. C4.5 is a broad coverage system using several optimization strategies like windowing and cross validation, which makes it difficult to compare single system components. But we believe that our probability estimation method of equation 3 largely contributed to the better results.

4.3   Combination of Categories

In the previous section, we explained how probabilities of different pattern types are combined. At this point, we have a probability estimation for each of the 4 filc-categories for every word in the text. Now filc-categories of the word before, the word itself and the word behind (12 features) are combined to filc-tags. This is done by the same decision tree algorithm.

Table 5 shows probability estimations for filc-categories and result tags for the sentence: "Today, PC shipments annually total some $ 38.3 billion worldwide".

When setting a threshold of 0.5, there were two mistakes in the filc-probability values. 1. the word "total" had a probability of 0.855 to be inside a noun phrase chunk and 2. the word "world-wide" had a probability of 0.656 to be inside and 0.838 to be at the end of a chunk. But due to the combination of different values these errors could be removed. The result tags are equivalent to the sentence chunked: "[Today], [PC shipments] annually total [some $ 38.3 billion] world-wide".

5   Experiments

We performed experiments on the large evaluation environment for base NP chunks provided by Ramshaw and Marcus [7]. The evaluation measure in this en-

Table 5. Filc-probabilities and chunking result in IOB-tagset

word	filc-probabilities				result
	first	inside	last	cons	
Today	0.994	0.996	0.583	0.000	1110
,	0.000	0.022	0.000	0.000	0000
PC	0.892	0.988	0.000	0.000	1100
shipments	0.002	0.988	0.989	0.003	0110
annually	0.002	0.000	0.002	0.013	0000
total	0.002	0.855	0.069	0.002	0000
some	0.806	0.997	0.025	0.013	1100
$	0.008	0.996	0.000	0.002	0100
38.3	0.002	0.997	0.000	0.000	0100
billion	0.000	0.997	0.950	0.000	0110
world-wide	0.002	0.656	0.838	0.002	0000
.	0.000	0.000	0.000	0.000	0000

vironment is the f-score of whole chunks where recall and precision are weighted equally ($\alpha = 0.5$ or $\beta = 1$).

In order to see the influence of different POS tags we trained our system with four different settings:

- no_tags: without using POS tags but only lexical data.
- brill_1: tags of the Brill tagger which was only trained on the Brown Corpus.
- brill_2: tags of the Brill tagger which was also trained on the Wall Street Journal Corpus (the original tags of the evaluation environment).
- ptb_tags: tags of the Penn Treebank which were corrected by human experts.

Table 6 shows the results of our experiments. For emphasizing the influence of the tagger, tagging accuracy of the tagger (compared to the treebank tags) are given next to the final results of our system.

Table 6. Results of experiments

setting	POS tag accuracy	chunk f-score
no_tags	—	91.56
brill_1	94.22	93.12
brill_2	96.29	93.90
ptb_tags	100.00	94.99

One training run needs about 3 hours on one 450MHz processor of a sun enterprise machine, while more than half of the time is used for compiling the training data from the Penn Treebank and less than half for actually training the system.

Table 7 shows results reported in other publications[4]. It is not always high-lighted whether brill_2 or ptb_tags was used as tagset. Assuming that brill_2 was used in all other systems as specified in the testset description, our system would be third.

Table 7. Results of other systems

publication	f-score
Ramshaw and Marcus [7]	93.3
Tjong Kim Sang and Veenstra [10]	93.81
Tjong Kim Sang [8]	94.90
Kudo and Matsumoto [3]	95.77

Also training times are not reported frequently. The best system [3] uses Support Vector Machines which need weeks to get trained.

6   Discussion

Our chunking system achieved one of the three best results for base noun phrase chunking. However, the best result was reported by [3] with their support vector machine based system. SVMs can find much better classification borders than decision trees, but since time costs are significantly higher, there are limitations on training data size and number of features which are used for learning. This limits the benefit of a larger corpus or usage of more features (such as capitalization or suffixes). Decision trees don't have these problems.

Experiments show that POS tag accuracy has a considerable influence on chunking results. The result of chunking without POS-tags was more than 3% lower than the result with perfect tags. Under real world conditions results were still more than 1% lower. Though it is rather dangerous to assume that other algorithms will show a similar decrease, it is very probable that chunk f-score generally decreases some points, when doing experiments with a tagger not trained on the test set.

We believe, that it will be difficult to further improve results of baseNP chunking without using significantly larger corpora or exploiting other resources like human made dictionaries or semantics. But even with a chunk f-score of

---

[4] The numbers were taken from
lcg-www.uia.ac.be/erikt/research/np-chunking.html, a web page maintained by Erik F. Tjong Kim Sang.

less than 95%, baseNP chunks contain much information about the syntactic structure of language. Despite this, we are not aware of applications making use of NP chunks.

A topic for future work could be to examine how baseNP chunk information could be used to improve POS tagging or full parsing. It would also be interesting to apply chunking systems to other chunking tasks like named entity extraction or word segmentation in languages like Japanese.

References

1. Steven Abney. Parsing by chunks. In Berwick, Abney, and Tenny, editors, *Principle-Based Parsing*. Kluwer Academic Publishers, 1991.
2. Shlomo Argamon, Ido Dagan, and Yuval Krymolowski. A memory-based approach to learning shallow natural language patterns. *Journal of Experimental and Theoretical AI*, 11(3), 1999.
3. Taku Kudo and Yuji Matsumoto. Chunking with support vector machines. In *2nd Meeting of the North American Chapter of the Association for Computational Linguistics, Proceedings of the Conference*, 2001.
4. Dirk Lüdtke. Chunking with decision trees. In *6th Natural Language Processing Pacific Rim Symposium, Proceedings*, pages 693–699, 2001.
5. Marcia Muñoz, Vasin Punyakanok, Dan Roth, and Dav Zimak. A learning approach to shallow parsing. In *Proceedings of EMNLP-WVLC'99*. Association for Computational Linguistics, 1999.
6. John Ross Quinlan. *C4.5 – Programs for Machine Learning*. Morgan Kaufmann, 1993.
7. Lance A. Ramshaw and Mitchel P. Marcus. Text chunking using transformation-based learning. In *Proceedings of the Third ACL Workshop on Very Large Corpora*. Association for Computational Linguistics, 1995.
8. Erik F. Tjong Kim Sang. Noun phrase representation by system combination. In *Proceedings of ANLP-NAACL 2000*, 2000.
9. Erik F. Tjong Kim Sang et al. Applying system combination to base noun phrase identification. In *The 18th International Conference on Computational Linguistics, Proceedings*, 2000.
10. Erik F. Tjong Kim Sang and Jorn Veenstra. Representing text chunks. In *Proceedings of EACL'99*, 1999.

Guaranteed Pre-tagging for the Brill Tagger

Saif Mohammad and Ted Pedersen

University of Minnesota, Duluth, MN 55812 USA
moha0149@d.umn.edu, tpederse@umn.edu
http://www.d.umn.edu/{~moha0149,~tpederse}

Abstract. This paper describes and evaluates a simple modification to the Brill Part–of–Speech Tagger. In its standard distribution the Brill Tagger allows manual assignment of a part–of–speech tag to a word prior to tagging. However, it may change it to another tag during processing. We suggest a change that guarantees that the *pre–tag* remains unchanged and ensures that it is used throughout the tagging process. Our method of guaranteed pre-tagging is appropriate when the tag of a word is known for certain, and is intended to help improve the accuracy of tagging by providing a reliable anchor or seed around which to tag.

1 Introduction

Part–of–speech tagging is a prerequisite task for many natural language processing applications, among them parsing, word sense disambiguation, machine translation, etc. The Brill Tagger (c.f., [1], [2], [3], [5]) is one of the most widely used tools for assigning parts–of–speech to words. It is a hybrid of machine learning and statistical methods that is based on transformation based learning.

The Brill Tagger has several virtues that we feel recommend it above other taggers. First, the source code is distributed. This is rare, as most other part–of–speech taggers are only distributed in executable format. Second, the simplicity of the transformation based learning approach makes it possible for us to both understand and modify the process to meet our needs. Finally, the tagger is quite accurate, and consistently achieves overall accuracy of at least 95%.

Part–of–speech taggers normally assume that the sentence it is processing is completely untagged. However, if the tags for some of the words in a text are known prior to tagging, then it would be desirable to incorporate that information in such a way that the tagger can use it and hopefully improve its accuracy. The act of manually assigning tags to selected words in a text prior to tagging will be referred to as pre⊔tagging. The affected words are said to be pre⊔tagged and the actual tags assigned to them are known as pre⊔tags.

Pre–tagging is intended to take advantage of the locality of part–of–speech tags. The tag for any word is generally determined by one or two immediate neighbors. Pre–tagging can be thought of as the process of manually priming or seeding the tagging process with reliable prior information. If the part–of–speech of a word can be manually assigned prior to tagging, then the surrounding tags

A. Gelbukh (Ed.): CICLing 2003, LNCS 2588, pp. 148–157, 2003.

may be tagged more accurately as a result of this additional information. Pre–tagging is possible because of this locality property; assigning a tag to a word does not affect the tagging of the entire sentence and can be thought of as introducing a very localized constraint on the tagging process.

We have developed a pre–tagging technique for the Brill Tagger that allows words to be assigned pre–tags, and then guarantees that the pre–tag will remain unchanged throughout tagging and will affect the tagging of its neighbors. Thus, if we are certain that a word should have a particular part–of–speech tag, we can provide that information and be assured that the pre–tag will remain in the final output and will have been used to determine the tags of neighboring words. While the Brill Tagger provides a form of pre–tagging, it gives no assurances that the pre–tag will actually be used in the tagging process. Thus our approach is distinct in that it guarantees that prior information about part–of–speech tags will be incorporated into the tagging process.

This paper continues with a short introduction to the Brill tagger and its existing form of pre–tagging. It goes on to introduce our guaranteed form, and then discusses an evaluation of the impact of this new form of tagging.

2   The Brill Tagger

The Brill Tagger proceeds in two phases. In the first phase, the Initial State Tagger assigns each word its most likely tag based on information it finds in a lexicon. In the second phase, a series of contextual rules are applied by the Final State Tagger to determine which of those initial tags should be transformed into other tags. Our experiments and modifications are based on the August 1994 version of the Brill Tagger, known as RULE_BASED_TAGGER_1.14.

2.1   Initial State Tagger

The first phase of tagging is performed by the Initial State Tagger, which simply assigns the most likely tag to each word it encounters. The most likely tag for a word is given in the lexicon. If the word is not in the lexicon it is considered as an unknown word and is tagged as a proper noun (NNP) if it is capitalized and as a noun (NN) if it is not.

The lexicon (LEXICON.BROWN.AND.WSJ) we use in our experiments is from the standard distribution of the Brill Tagger (1.14) and was derived from the Penn TreeBank tagging of the Wall Street Journal and the Brown Corpus. This lexicon consists of almost 94,000 words and provides their most likely part–of–speech, based on frequency information taken from the aforementioned corpora. It also lists the other parts–of–speech with which each word can be used. Note that there are separate entries for the different morphological and capitalized forms of a word. The lexicon shown in Table 1 follows the standard form of a Brill Tagger lexicon and is referred to in examples throughout this paper.

Table 1. Example Lexicon

Word	Most Frequent Tag	Other Possible Tags	
brown	JJ	NN VB	...(L1)
chair	VB	NN	...(L2)
evening	NN	JJ	...(L3)
in	IN	FW NN	...(L4)
meeting	NN	VB	...(L5)
pretty	RB	JJ	...(L6)
sit	VB	FW VB	...(L7)
the	DT	NNP PDT	...(L8)
this	DT	PDT	...(L9)
time	NN	VB	...(L10)
will	MD	VBP NN	...(L11)

Entry L1 tells us that brown is usually used as an adjective (JJ) but may also be used as a verb (VB) or a noun (NN). L2 shows that chair is most often a verb (VB) but can also be a noun (NN). Note that the order of the other possible tags is not significant, it simply indicates that the word was used in these parts–of–speech in the corpus the lexicon was induced from.

The tags assigned by the Initial State Tagger may be transformed following a set of lexical rules based on suffixes, infixes, and prefixes of the word. The tagger comes with predefined lexical rule files that have been learned from the same corpora used to learn the lexicon. The lexical rules file affects only the unknown words and as such is not directly involved in or affected by pre–tagging, so we will not discuss it any further.

2.2   Final State Tagger

The next stage of tagging determines if any of the tags assigned by the Initial State Tagger should be changed based on a set of contextual rules. These rules specify that the current tag of a word may be transformed into another tag based on its context. This context usually consists of one, two or three words (and their part–of–speech tags) to the left and right of the tagged word.

For our experiments we use a contextual rule file (CONTEXTUALRULE-FILE.WSJ) provided in the standard 1.14 distribution of the Brill Tagger. This consists of 284 rules derived from the Penn TreeBank tagging of the Wall Street Journal. The examples in this paper rely on just a few contextual rules, and those are shown in Table 2.

The rule C1 indicates that if a word is tagged as a noun (NN) then its tag should be changed to verb (VB) if the part–of–speech of the next word is a determiner (DT). Rule C2 says that the tag of a word should be changed from adverb (RB) to adjective (JJ), if the next word is tagged as a noun (NN). Rule C3 says that an adjective (JJ) should be changed to a noun (NN) if the next

Table 2. Example Contextual Rules

Current Tag	New Tag	When	
NN	VB	NEXTTAG DT	...(C1)
RB	JJ	NEXTTAG NN	...(C2)
JJ	NN	NEXTTAG VB	...(C3)
NN	JJ	NEXTWD meeting	...(C4)

word has a verb tag (VB). Finally, rule C4 is lexicalized, and says that a word tagged as a noun (NN) should be changed to an adjective (JJ) if the next word is meeting.

3   Standard Pre-tagging with the Brill Tagger

Pre–tagging is the act of manually assigning a part–of–speech tag to words in a text prior to that text being automatically tagged with the Brill Tagger. The following example will illustrate the general concept of pre–tagging, and show the limitations of pre–tagging as provided in the standard distribution of the Brill Tagger.

Suppose that it is critical to an application to know that chair is being used as a noun (NN) in the following context. We could apply a pre–tag as follows:

$$\texttt{Mona will sit in the pretty chair//NN this time} \qquad (1)$$

The Initial State Tagger will assign the most likely tag to each word, except for chair which is pre–tagged as a noun (NN) and for Mona which is not in the lexicon but is tagged as a proper noun (NNP) since it is capitalized. The results of this initial tagging are as follows:

$$\texttt{Mona/NNP will/MD sit/VB in/IN the/DT}$$

$$\texttt{pretty/RB chair//NN this/DT time/NN} \qquad (2)$$

The Final State Tagger will look for contextual rules to apply, and will transform tags accordingly. It treats a pre–tagged word like any other, so the pre–tag may be changed during the course of tagging. While the standard distribution of the Brill Tagger allows a user to specify a different initial tag for a word via pre–tagging, it does not guarantee that this be used throughout tagging. Given the input above, the Brill Tagger will produce the following tagging:

$$\texttt{Mona/NNP will/MD sit/VB in/IN the/DT}$$

$$\texttt{pretty/RB chair//VB this/DT time/NN} \qquad (3)$$

Note that the tag of chair has been changed to a verb (VB). While chair can be a verb, as in Mona will chair the meeting this time, in this case it is not. In

particular, chair was pre–tagged as a noun (NN) but this was overridden by the
Final State Tagger which mis–tagged it as a verb (VB). This change occurred
due to the contextual rule C1 shown in Table 2. This rule says that a word that
is tagged as a noun (NN) should be changed to a verb (VB) when it is followed
by a determiner (DT). This error is compounded, since pretty was tagged by the
Initial State Tagger as an adverb (RB), due to lexicon entry L6 in Table 1. Since
chair is considered a verb, the initial tagging of pretty as an adverb (RB) will be
allowed to stand.

In this example the erroneous tagging of chair causes the tag of pretty to
remain unchanged. We can observe the opposite behavior with a simple change
in the example. Suppose that Mona is sitting in a brown chair. We could again
pre–tag chair to indicate that it is a noun:

$$\text{Mona will sit in the brown chair//NN this time} \tag{4}$$

The Initial State Tagger will assign the same tags as it did in Sentence 2,
except that brown will be tagged an adjective (JJ) since that is its most likely
tag, as shown in L1 in Table 1.

$$\text{Mona/NNP will/MD sit/VB in/IN the/DT}$$

$$\text{brown/JJ chair//NN this/DT time/NN} \tag{5}$$

From this the Final State Tagger will produce the following:

$$\text{Mona/NNP will/MD sit/VB in/IN the/DT}$$

$$\text{brown/NN chair//VB this/DT time/NN} \tag{6}$$

Here the pre–tag of chair is changed to a verb (VB) due to contextual rule
C1. This triggers a change in the tag of brown due to rule C3, which says that
an adjective (JJ) should be changed to a noun (NN) when it is followed by a
verb (VB). Thus, the improper changing of the pre–tag of chair has resulted in
the incorrect tag being applied to brown as well.

The standard distribution of the Brill Tagger provides relatively weak pre–
tagging that simply overrides the Initial State Tagger. However, those pre–tags
can be altered by the Final State Tagger, and such changes can trigger other
transformations in the tags of neighboring words.

4   Guaranteed Pre-tagging

Our objective is to guarantee that a manually assigned pre–tag be respected (and
left unchanged) by both the Initial State Tagger and the Final State Tagger. We
believe that there are cases when the pre–tag should be considered absolute
and affect the outcome of the tags on surrounding words (and not vice–versa).
If a contextual rule changes a pre–tag from what is known to be correct to
something that is not, then the surrounding words may also be incorrectly tagged

via applications of contextual rules that rely upon the improperly changed pre–tag.

To achieve guaranteed pre–tagging, we have made a simple change to the Brill tagger that prevents it from applying contextual rules that result in changes to a pre–tagged word. However, we still allow contextual rules to change surrounding tags based on the pre–tag. So while a pre–tag may not be changed, the tags of surrounding words may be changed based on that pre–tag.

Let's return to the examples of Sentences 1 and 4. In each a noun (NN) pre–tag was assigned to chair prior to tagging, but it was overridden. As a result chair was improperly tagged as a verb (VB) and this had an impact on the tagging of pretty and brown.

With guaranteed pre–tagging, the final output of the Brill Tagger for Sentence 1 is as follows:

$$\text{Mona/NNP will/MD sit/VB in/IN the/DT}$$

$$\text{pretty/JJ chair//NN this/DT time/NN} \tag{7}$$

Note that the pre–tag of chair remains unchanged. The contextual rule C1 is not applied due to our prohibition against changing pre–tags. Since chair remains a noun, contextual rule C2 changes pretty from having an adverb (RB) tag to having an adjective (JJ) tag.

In the case of Sentence 4, the output of the Brill Tagger is:

$$\text{Mona/NNP will/MD sit/VB in/IN the/DT}$$

$$\text{brown/JJ chair//NN this/DT time/NN} \tag{8}$$

Note that the pre–tag of chair has not been changed, and in fact no contextual rules have been triggered. All of the other words in the sentence retain the tags as assigned by the Initial State Tagger.

These simple examples show how guaranteed pre–tagging can affect the outcome of the Brill Tagger. Next, we describe an extensive experiment that we carried out in assessing the impact of pre–tagging in part–of–speech tagging text to be used in a series of word sense disambiguation experiments.

5   Impact of Guaranteed Pre-tagging on Senseval-2 Data

We evaluated the effect of guaranteed pre–tagging on a large corpus of data that we part–of–speech tagged. It was our experience with this data that actually motivated the development of the guaranteed pre–tagging approach.

5.1   Experiment

The English lexical sample data for the SENSEVAL-2 word sense disambiguation exercise includes 4,328 test instances and 8,611 training instances [4]. Each instance consists of a few sentences where a single target word within each instance is manually assigned a sense–tag that indicates its meaning in that particular context. There are 73 different nouns, verbs, and adjectives that are sense–tagged and serve as target words. This data is typically used for corpus–based supervised learning experiments where a model of disambiguation is learned from the training instances and then evaluated on the test instances.

We part–of–speech tagged this data with the Brill Tagger in preparation for some word sense disambiguation experiments. This tagging was done with the posSenseval package, now available from the authors. The focus of the word sense experiment was on the utility of part–of–speech tags of words near the target word as features for disambiguation, so we were particularly concerned that the tagging be as accurate as possible. Since the crude part–of–speech of the target word is known (noun, verb, or adjective) we decided it would be worthwhile to manually tag all of the target words with their appropriate part–of–speech tag, so as to possibly improve the tagging of nearby words.

5.2   Results

The pre–tagging feature of the original Brill Tagger was used to specify the appropriate pre–tags of the target words. An analysis of the tagging results surprised us. Of the 4,328 target words in the test instances assigned pre–tags, 576 were changed. Of those, 388 were minor changes within a single part–of–speech (e.g., from a past tense verb to a present tense) and 188 tags had been changed to completely different parts–of–speech (e.g., from a verb to a noun). We call the latter radical changes since they pose a greater concern. It seems likely that the surrounding tags have a reasonable chance of being mis–tagged as a result of radical errors. Of the 8,611 target words in the training data that were pre–tagged, 1,020 of those were mis–tagged, with 291 radical errors and 729 minor errors. Since we were certain of the pre–tags we assigned, and since we were quite concerned about the negative impact of radical errors in the tagging of target words, we developed the guaranteed approach to pre–tagging described here.

The guaranteed pre–tagging prevented radical errors and ensured that target words retained their pre–tags. We noted that of the 291 sentences in the training data where radical errors had previously existed, 36 sentences now had a change of a neighboring tag due to the correctly applied pre–tag. In the 188 sentences from the test data where radical errors had occurred, 18 sentences had a change in a neighboring tag due to an erroneous change of a pre–tag.

5.3   Discussion

At first the number of changes in the neighboring tags struck us as rather small. However, upon reflection they appear reasonable, and we shall explain how we arrive at that conclusion.

There are approximately 529,000 tokens in the test data, and of those only 25,000 are changed from their initial state taggings via contextual rules. In the training data there are 1,059,000 tokens, where 48,000 are changed from their initial state taggings via contextual rules. Thus, in both cases only about 5% of the assigned tags are something other than what the initial state tagger decided.

Guaranteed pre–tagging corrected the 188 radical errors in the test data and the 291 radical errors in the training data. Since most contextual rules affect only one word to the left or one word to the right of the target word, we would expect that contextual rules might change the tags of adjacent neighbors of the target words about 5% of the time. Based on this rather loose analysis we would expect that $(188*2)*.05 = 19$ neighboring tags should change in the test data and $(291*2)*.05 = 29$ should change in the training data. It turns out that these estimates are not far off, as the actual number of changes were 18 and 36.

In fact the analysis can be made a bit more precise, by noting that contextual rules can be divided into those that are triggered by content words, e.g., nouns, verbs, adjectives, and adverbs, and those that are triggered by function words. In the test data 14,100 tokens were changed based on transformations triggered by the current tag being a function word, and 10,300 were based on it being a content word. In the training data, 27,800 were triggered by the current tag being a function word and 20,500 were based on it being a content word.

This distinction is relevant since we know that the target words in the SENSEVAL-2 data are content words, and these are the only words that have been pre–tagged. We can estimate the probability that a target word will trigger a contextual rule by determining the overall probability in the test and training data that a contextual rule will be triggered, given that the token under consideration is a content word. The number of content tokens in the test data is 273,000 and the number in the training data is 546,000. Based on the counts of the number of contextual rules triggered by content words already provided, we can determine that the expected probability of a contextual rule triggering when the given token is a content word is about 4%. Thus, the expected number of changes that we computed above can be refined slightly, $(188*2)*.04 = 15$ and $(291*2)*.04 = 23$. These are still reasonably close to the observed number of changes (18 and 36). This suggests that pre–tagging is having an impact on the assignment of tags, and that the rate of change to neighboring tags is consistent with the rates of change of 4% and 5% that we have derived above.

We are uncertain whether we should expect 95% of the tokens to retain their initial state tags in general. We suspect this figure would be lower if the SENSEVAL-2 data were more like the Wall Street Journal and Brown Corpus from which the contextual rule file was learned. However, the SENSEVAL-2 data is from varied sources and is much noisier than the TreeBank and Brown Corpus data.

6   An Anomaly in Lexicalized Contextual Rules

During the testing of guaranteed pre–tagging we noticed somewhat unusual behavior in the Brill Tagger. If a contextual rule is lexicalized with a word that has been pre–tagged, then that rule will not be applied under any circumstances. A lexicalized contextual rule is simply one where a specific word appears as a part of the rule, as in contextual rule C4 in Table 2. Consider the following case, where we pre–tag meeting as a noun (NN):

$$\texttt{Mona will chair the evening meeting//NN} \qquad (9)$$

The Initial State Tagger of the standard distribution will assign the following tags:

$$\texttt{Mona/NNP will/MD chair/VB the/DT evening/NN meeting//NN} \qquad (10)$$

We were surprised that in cases like these the Final State Tagger made no transformations. In particular, it surprised us that it did not apply rule C4, which says that if a noun (NN) precedes the word meeting then it should be tagged as an adjective (JJ). By all accounts this rule should be triggered.

However, after some investigation in the source code we determined that the Brill Tagger internally appends a backslash (/) to a word that has been pre–tagged, which makes it impossible for it to trigger any contextual rule that is lexicalized with that word. Thus in the above case the Brill Tagger viewed the word in the sentence as meeting/, whereas it viewed rule C4 as requiring meeting. But, as these are different the sentence does not trigger the contextual rule. We see no particular reason to avoid this behavior, so we overrode this particular feature and now allow lexicalized contextual rules to be triggered by pre–tagged words as well. With that change in place, the Brill Tagger uses rule C4 and produces the expected output:

$$\texttt{Mona/NNP will/MD chair/VB the/DT evening/JJ meeting//NN} \qquad (11)$$

7 Conclusions

This paper describes an approach which guarantees that the pre–tagged words provided to the Brill Tagger will be unchanged throughout tagging and appear in the final output, and that they will affect the tags of neighboring words. We argue that this is a reasonable way to utilize prior knowledge that may be provided to the Brill Tagger, and showed via an extensive pre–tagging experiment with the SENSEVAL-2 English lexical sample data that pre–tagging has a reasonable impact on the tagging. We also show how the impact is commensurate with what we would expect any change in contextual rule processing to have. The authors have made a patch available to the Brill Tagger from their web sites that will implement guaranteed pre–tagging, and also correct a slight anomaly in handling lexicalized contextual rules.

Acknowledgments. We would like to thank Rada Mihalcea, Grace Ngai, and Radu Florian for useful discussions regarding pre–tagging. Grace Ngai suggested describing pre–tags as anchors or seeds, and we have adopted that terminology. We are grateful to Eric Brill for making the source code to his tagger available, without which this project would not have been possible.

Ted Pedersen is partially supported by a National Science Foundation Faculty Early CAREER Development award (#0092784). Any opinions, findings, conclusions, or recommendations expressed in this publication are those of the authors and do not necessarily reflect the views of the National Science Foundation or the official policies, either express or implied, of the sponsors or of the United States Government.

References

1. E. Brill. A simple rule-based part of speech tagger. In *Proceedings of the Third Conference on Applied Computational Linguistics*, Trento, Italy, 1992.
2. E. Brill. Some advances in rule-based part of speech tagging. In *Proceedings of the 12th National Conference on Artificial Intelligence (AAAI-94)*, Seattle, WA, 1994.
3. E. Brill. Transformation–based error–driven learning and natural language processing: A case study in part of speech tagging. *Computational Linguistics*, 21(4):543–565, 1995.
4. P. Edmonds and S. Cotton, editors. *Proceedings of the Senseval-2 Workshop*. Association for Computational Linguistics, Toulouse, France, 2001.
5. L. Ramshaw and M. Marcus. Exploring the statistical derivation of transformational rule sequences for part-of-speech tagging. In *ACL Balancing Act Workshop*, pages 86–95, 1994.

Performance Analysis of a Part of Speech Tagging Task

Rada Mihalcea

University of North Texas
Computer Science Department
Denton, TX, 76203-1366
rada@cs.unt.edu

Abstract. In this paper, we attempt to make a formal analysis of the performance in automatic part of speech tagging. Lower and upper bounds in tagging precision using existing taggers or their combination are provided. Since we show that with existing taggers, automatic *perfect* tagging is not possible, we offer two solutions for applications requiring very high precision: (1) a solution involving minimum human intervention for a precision of over 98.7%, and (2) a combination of taggers using a memory based learning algorithm that succeeds in reducing the error rate with 11.6% with respect to the best tagger involved.

1 Introduction

Part of speech (POS) tagging is one of the few problems in Natural Language Processing (NLP) that may be considered almost solved, in that several solutions have been proposed so far, and were successfully applied in practice. State-of-the-art systems performing POS tagging achieve accuracies of over 93-94%, which may be satisfactory for many NLP applications. However, there are certain applications that require even higher precision, as for example the construction of annotated corpora where the tagging needs to be accurately performed. Two solutions are possible for this type of sensitive applications: (1) manual tagging, which ensures high accuracy, but is highly expensive; and (2) automatic tagging, which may be performed at virtually no cost, but requires means for controlling the quality of the labeling process performed by machine.

POS tagging is required by almost any text processing task, e.g. word sense disambiguation, parsing, logical forms and others. Being one of the first processing steps in any such application, the accuracy of the POS tagger directly impacts the accuracy of any subsequent text processing steps.

We investigate in this paper the current state-of-the-art in POS tagging, derive theoretical lower and upper bounds for the accuracy of individual systems or combinations of these systems, and show that with existing taggers perfect POS tagging is not possible (where perfect tagging is considered to be 100% accuracy with respect to manually annotated data). Subsequently, we provide two possible solutions for this problem. First, we show that it is possible to design

A. Gelbukh (Ed.): CICLing 2003, LNCS 2588, pp. 158–167, 2003.

a tagging scheme that guarantees a precision of over 98.7% with minimum human intervention. Secondly, we show how individual taggers can be combined into a new tagger, with an error reduction of 11.6% with respect to the best tagger involved.

1.1   Classifiers Combination

Combining classifiers for improved performance is a technique well known in the Machine Learning (ML) community. Previous work in the field has demonstrated that a combined classifier often outperforms all individual systems involved [1].

Classifier combination has been successfully used in several NLP problems, including POS tagging [4,14], word sense disambiguation [6,8], and others. Brill [4] and van Halteren [14] show how several POS taggers can be combined using various approaches: voting schemes (simple or weighted), decision trees, and rules learned using contextual cues. Brill [4] uses four taggers: an unigram tagger, an N-gram tagger, Brill's tagger and the Maximum Entropy tagger, for an error reduction of 10.4% with respect to the best tagger involved. In concurrent work, van Halteren [14] combines again four different taggers and obtains a reduction of 19.1% in error rate using a pairwise voting scheme.

In this paper, we attempt to formalize the combination of various taggers for improved accuracy: we provide lower and upper bounds for POS tagging precision. Since we prove that the performance of existing taggers or their combinations cannot exceed a certain limit, we suggest two possible solutions for applications requiring high tagging accuracy: (1) a solution that involves minimum human intervention for an accuracy of over 98.7%; and (2) a combination of taggers using a memory based learning algorithm that succeeds in reducing the error rate by 11.6% with respect to the best tagger involved.

2   Mathematical Foundations

This section describes a mathematical model for the problem of text tagging, and shows how the level of confidence in tagging precision can be formally estimated. First, given the fact that voting is a widely used scheme in classifier combination, we are interested in finding lower and upper bounds for the tagging precision on the set where two taggers agree. Results pertaining to this problem were previously reported in [11]. Additionally, we want to determine lower and upper bounds for the precision on the entire tagged set (including both agreement and disagreement sets).

2.1   Precision on Agreement Set

It was previously shown [11] that given two classifiers with their estimated precisions, it is possible to determine a minimum and a maximum for the precision achieved on the agreement set, i.e. the set where the two classifiers agree in the tag they independently assign.

The following formulae were derived:

$$minP_{A_{12}} = \frac{P_{T_1} + P_{T_2} - 1 + A_{12}}{2 * A_{12}} \tag{1}$$

$$maxP_{A_{12}} \simeq \frac{P_{T_1} + P_{T_2} - 1 + A_{12} + (1 - P_{T_1})(1 - P_{T_1})}{2 * A_{12}} \tag{2}$$

where P_{T_1} is the precision of the tagger T_1, P_{T_2} is the precision of the tagger T_2, $P_{A_{12}}$ is the precision on the agreement set, A_{12} is the size of the agreement set. Experiments with POS tagging have validated this result, leading to almost identical theoretical and empirical values.

2.2   Lower and Upper Bounds for Overall Precision

The second problem that we address from a theoretical perspective regards the limitations in POS tagging precision. Similar theoretical analyses were previously performed for the problem of word sense disambiguation [7], and recently for the problem of question answering [9].

The simplest approach in POS tagging is the unigram tagger that lexically disambiguates words based on their frequency in a large corpus, and was found to perform very well, with an accuracy of about 93.26% precision [4]. This can be considered as a **lower bound** (i.e. a baseline) for the problem of POS tagging in general.

Finding the upper bound is a process significantly more difficult, since it has to take into account the precision of all individual and combined classifiers. It is however an important issue, since accurate predictions of upper bound would enable a complete analysis of the performance in POS tagging. Moreover, such theoretical evaluations may influence the decision in selecting the best individual / combined tagger for particular applications.

To the end of finding this upper bound, we differentiate the absolute precision of a tagger, as compared to the nominal precision. It is common to report precision in POS tagging by referring to all words in a particular test set. This is the nominal precision. However, a fairly large set of words in any text have only one possible tag. These words are not lexically ambiguous, and therefore they account for a subset with 100% tagging precision towards the overall nominal precision of a tagger. The absolute precision is the precision achieved by the same tagger when applied only to the set of ambiguous words. Measurements performed on a large tagged corpus have shown that about 40% of the words in the corpus are not lexically ambiguous. This is in agreement with the corresponding figures reported in [4].

By denoting with P_{T_i} the nominal precision of a tagger T_i, and with AP_{T_i} the absolute precision of the same tagger, the following equation can be written:

$$P_{T_i} = 0.40 * 1.0 + 0.60 * AP_{T_i} \Rightarrow AP_{T_i} = \frac{(P_{T_i} - 0.40)}{0.60} \tag{3}$$

meaning that the nominal precision of a tagger on any set can be divided in two terms: the precision of 100% achieved on 40% of the set (i.e. the set of non ambiguous words), and the absolute precision achieved on the rest of 60% of the set (i.e. the set of ambiguous words).

On the other hand, given two taggers T_1 and T_2, the overall precision for these two taggers can be written as the precision on the set where the two taggers agree, plus the precision on the set where the two taggers disagree:

$$P = \mathcal{A}_{12} * P_{\mathcal{A}_{12}} + (1 - \mathcal{A}_{12}) * P_{1 - \mathcal{A}_{12}} \tag{4}$$

The maximum overall precision that can be achieved by these two taggers, individually or combined, is determined as the sum of (a) the maximum precision achieved by the two taggers on the agreement set and (b) the maximum absolute precision of the individual classifiers on the disagreement set. This is based on the observation that the words that are not lexically ambiguous are all included in the agreement set, and this is why the maximum accuracy that can be achieved by any individual tagger on the disagreement set is given by its absolute precision.

$$\begin{aligned}
maxP &= \mathcal{A}_{12} * maxP_{\mathcal{A}_{12}} + (1 - \mathcal{A}_{12}) * max(AP_{T_1}, AP_{T_1}) \\
&= \mathcal{A}_{12} * \frac{P_{T_1} + P_{T_2} - 1 + \mathcal{A}_{12} + (1 - P_{T_1})(1 - P_{T_1})}{2 * \mathcal{A}_{12}} \\
&\quad + (1 - \mathcal{A}_{12}) * max(AP_{T_1}, AP_{T_1})
\end{aligned} \tag{5}$$

Using this theoretical model, we are able to derive lower and upper bounds in tagging precision, for individual or combined classifiers. In addition to POS tagging, this model is applicable to the analysis of other NLP labeling tasks, such as word sense disambiguation, prepositional attachment and others.

3   Empirical Results

We provide in this section empirical support for the model derived above. First, we measure the performance of four part of speech taggers on a test set extracted from the Penn Treebank corpus. Next, we show that the values empirically determined in practice are very close to the values found in theory. Finally, we apply the formula derived in the previous section to derive an upper bound for the overall precision that can be achieved with these state-of-the-art taggers.

3.1   State of the Art in POS Tagging

Several methods have been proposed so far for POS tagging, including transformation based systems, taggers based on maximum entropy models, or derived using decision trees. The accuracies achieved by these taggers range from 94 to 96%, depending on the method employed, and/or on the training and testing sets.

Transformation based tagger [T1]. The tagger developed by Brill [3] works by first assigning the most frequent tag to each word; next, rules are applied to change the tag of the word based on the context in which they appear. It is one of the most popular taggers, due to its accuracy and public availability.

Maximum entropy tagger [T2]. Mxpost tagger was developed by Ratnaparkhi [12]; it is a statistical model based on maximum entropy, integrating many contextual features.

TnT tagger [T3]. The TnT (Trigrams'n'Tags) tagger is a statistical part of speech tagger, written by Brants [2]; TnT incorporates several smoothing methods, and is optimized for training on a variety of corpora. The tagger is an implementation of the Viterbi algorithm for second order Markov models.

TreeTagger [T4]. TreeTagger [13] is a probabilistic tagger that attempts to avoid the problems encountered by Markov model taggers: the transition probabilities in TreeTagger are estimated using decision trees.

3.2   Experiments

To evaluate the precision of the individual taggers and to determine the upper bound for overall combined precision, the following experiment was performed: the Penn Treebank corpus [10] was divided in two parts: sections 0-19, used for training the four POS taggers, and sections 20-60, separately tagged with each of the four classifiers. Subsequently, during the experiments reported in section 4.2, this second set was divided into a subset of 1,500,000 words for training the classifier combination model, respectively 298,000 words for testing.

The precision of each individual tagger was measured on this last set of 298,000 words. This set is sufficiently large to provide accurate measures of precision, and at the same time enables a fair comparison with the precision of the combined taggers, which are tested on the same subset.

Table 1 lists the precisions for individual taggers, as found empirically on the test set, and the size of the agreement sets and precision achieved on these sets. Using equations 1 and 2, the theoretical values can be computed. Notice that the values associated with the combination of all four taggers are determined in a recursive manner: taggers T_1 and T_2, respectively T_3 and T_4 are paired and form two "new" taggers, T_{12} and T_{34}, with their associated minimum and maximum precisions. As shown by the results in Table 1, the values determined empirically are tightly close to the figures that can be computed in theory.

Furthermore, with the model described in the previous section, we can induce upper bound values for the precision that may be achieved with various classifiers. Table 2 shows the values determined using equation 5. It follows that the taggers considered in this experiment, individually or combined, cannot exceed the overall precision of 98.43%.

The equation for the maximum precision has an intuitive explanation: it depends on the precision of the individual taggers, and it also depends on the size of their agreement set. Brill [4] has noticed that higher differences among classifiers can lead to higher combined precision. Here, a smaller agreement set (e.g. the agreement set of taggers T_1 and T_2) results in larger overall precision, compared with the smaller overall precision achieved with larger agreement sets (e.g. the agreement set between T_3 and T_4).

4   Solutions for High Precision POS Tagging

In the previous section, we have shown – using theoretical and empirical means – that the precision of current state-of-the-art taggers cannot exceed a certain

Table 1. Values determined empirically on the Penn Treebank corpus

Measure	Notation	Value
Precision of the taggers		
T_1	P_{T_1}	0.9403
T_2	P_{T_2}	0.9598
T_3	P_{T_3}	0.9602
T_4	P_{T_4}	0.9599
Absolute precision of the taggers		
T_1	AP_{T_1}	0.9005
T_2	AP_{T_2}	0.9330
T_3	AP_{T_3}	0.9336
T_4	AP_{T_4}	0.9331
Size of agreement set between taggers		
T_1 and T_2	$\mathcal{A}_{12}$	0.9369
T_3 and T_4	$\mathcal{A}_{34}$	0.9799
T_1, T_2, T_3 and T_4	$\mathcal{A}_{1234}$	0.9155
Precision on agreement set		
T_1 and T_2	$P_{\mathcal{A}_{12}}$	0.9810
T_3 and T_4	$P_{\mathcal{A}_{34}}$	0.9702
T_1, T_2, T_3 and T_4	$P_{\mathcal{A}_{1234}}$	0.9860

Table 2. Maximum overall precisions

Measure	Notation	Value
Maximum overall precision		
T_1 and T_2	$maxP_{12}$	0.9785
T_3 and T_4	$maxP_{34}$	0.9686
Absolute maximum overall precision		
T_1 and T_2	$maxAP_{12}$	0.9641
T_3 and T_4	$maxAP_{34}$	0.9476
Maximum overall precision		
T_1, T_2, T_3 and T_4	$maxP_{1234}$	0.9843

upper limit. In this section, we propose two possible solutions that can be used for sensitive applications where high precision POS tagging is critical.

4.1 Solution 1: Highly Accurate Tagging Using Minimum Human Intervention

One first solution is to use minimum human intervention for an overall higher performance. Given several automatic taggers, we can devise a scheme where a human checks only the part of the corpus where the taggers disagree. Assigning a 100% accuracy to manual tagging, we can determine the minimum overall precision achieved by various combinations of taggers, using a variation of equation

4, which encodes the precision of 100% achieved by a human on the disagreement set:

$$minP_{12h} = \mathcal{A}_{12} * minP_{\mathcal{A}_{12}} + (1 - \mathcal{A}_{12}) * 1 \tag{6}$$

Table 3 shows the minimum values for overall precision for various combinations of taggers, and the size of the set that has to be manually checked.

Table 3. Minimum overall precisions achieved with human intervention

Measure	Notation	Value
Minimum overall precision		
T_1 and T_2	$minP_{12h}$	0.9815
T_3 and T_4	$minP_{34h}$	0.9700
T_2 and T_3	$minP_{23h}$	0.9717
T_1, T_2, T_3 and T_4	$minP_{1234h}$	0.9871
Disagreement set (to be manually checked)		
T_1 and T_2	$1 - \mathcal{A}_{12}$	0.0631
T_3 and T_4	$1 - \mathcal{A}_{34}$	0.0201
T_2 and T_3	$1 - \mathcal{A}_{23}$	0.0349
T_1, T_2, T_3 and T_4	$1 - \mathcal{A}_{1234}$	0.0845

It is debatable what combinations are better from the point of view of precision and recall. A compromise between precision, recall and number of taggers involved is achieved using the first two taggers. It guarantees a minimum precision of 98.15%, significantly larger than the best tagger involved, with 6% of the tags being checked by a human.

4.2   Solution 2: Combining Taggers for Improved Precision

An alternative solution is to combine different classifiers using a machine learning approach. The combination of taggers reported in [4] led to an error reduction of 10.3%; we follow their direction and show that a memory based learner can lead to a slightly higher reduction in error rate, of 11.6%.

The learning system is Timbl [5]. It is a memory based learner that works by storing training examples; new examples are classified by identifying the closest instance in the training data. The similarity among examples is computed using an overlap metric (Manhattan metric), improved with an information gain feature weighting. It provides good results in short time (learning from about 125,000 examples and testing 25,000 examples takes about 9 seconds).

First, we tagged sections 20-60 from Treebank using all four part of speech taggers. Next, we divided this corpus in two sets: a training set, comprising 1,500,000 words and a testing set with 298,000 words. Finally, we eliminated those examples for which all taggers agree. There are two reasons for this decision: first, we have already proved that very high precision (98.6%) can be achieved on the agreement set, and therefore we want to focus only on the remaining "problematic" cases where the taggers disagree. Second, the cases where all taggers agree account for about 91% of the examples. Since we use a learning algorithm that computes the difference between training examples and testing examples, these large number of cases where all taggers agree will favor the majority voting algorithm, which might not always be the best decision.

After eliminating these cases when $T_1 = T_2 = T_3 = T_4$, we are left with a training set of 126,927 examples, and a testing set of 25,248 examples; they both contain only disagreement examples. The precisions of the four taggers on these test examples are 40.19%, 63.24%, 63.70% and 63.44%.

The following sets of features are used for learning:

- **4T**. The tags assigned by the four taggers.
- **4T+TB**. The tags assigned by the four taggers and the tag of the word before the current word (assigned by the best performing tagger, i.e. TnT)
- **4T+TB+TA**. The tags assigned by the four taggers, plus the tag of the word before, plus the tag of the word following the current word.
- **4T+TB+W**. The tags assigned by the four taggers, plus the tag of the word before, plus the word itself.
- **4T+TB+TA+W**. The tags assigned by the four taggers, plus the tag of the word before, plus the tag of the word after, plus the word itself.

Table 4 shows the precision achieved using the memory based learning algorithm on the test set. We also compute the minimum overall precision, using equation 4.

Table 4. Precision for the combination of four taggers, for various sets of features.

Feature set	Precision on test set (disagreement set)	Min.overall precision
4T	70.10%	96.19%
4T+TB	71.06%	96.27%
4T+TB+TA	71.59%	96.31%
4T+TB+W	72.11%	96.36%
4T+TB+TA+W	73.55%	96.48%

Using the last set of features, which includes the tags assigned by the four taggers and contextual clues, the largest reduction in error rate is obtained. On our test set, the reduction in error rate is 27% (73.55% vs. the best tagger precision of 63.70% on the same set). For the overall precision, the reduction in error rate is 11.6% with respect to the best tagger involved.

5   Conclusion

We have addressed in this paper the limitations of existing POS taggers. Even though current state-of-the-art systems provide high accuracies in the range of 94-96%, we have shown that the precision of individual or combined taggers cannot exceed an upper bound of 98.43%. Two solutions have been provided for sensitive applications requiring highly precise tagging. First, we have shown how minimum human intervention can guarantee a minimum overall precision of 98.7%. Second, we have shown that a combination of existing taggers using a memory based learning algorithm succeeds in reducing the error rate with 11.6% with respect to the best tagger involved.

We have also derived a theoretical model for the analysis of lower and upper bounds in POS tagging performance. This theoretical scheme is equally applicable to other NLP labeling tasks such as word sense disambiguation, prepositional attachment and others.

References

1. ALI, K., AND PAZZANI, M. Error reduction through learning multiple descriptions. *Machine Learning 24*, 3 (1996), 173–202.
2. BRANTS, T. Tnt - a statistical part-of-speech tagger. In *Proceedings of the 6th Applied NLP Conference, ANLP-2000* (Seattle, WA, May 2000).
3. BRILL, E. Transformation-based error driven learning and natural language processing: A case study in part-of-speech tagging. *Computational Linguistics 21*, 4 (December 1995), 543–566.
4. BRILL, E., AND WU, J. Classifier combination for improved lexical disambiguation. In *In Proceedings of the Seventeenth International Conference on Computational Linguistics COLING-ACL '98* (Montreal, Canada, 1998).
5. DAELEMANS, W., ZAVREL, J., VAN DER SLOOT, K., AND VAN DEN BOSCH, A. Timbl: Tilburg memory based learner, version 4.0, reference guide. Tech. rep., University of Antwerp, 2001.
6. FLORIAN, R., CUCERZAN, S., SCHAFER, C., AND YAROWSKY, D. Combining classifiers for word sense disambiguation. *JNLE Special Issue on Evaluating Word Sense Disambiguation Systems* (2002). forthcoming.
7. GALE, W., CHURCH, K., AND YAROWSKY, D. Estimating upper and lower bounds on the performance of word-sense disambiguation programs. In *Proceedings of the 30th Annual Meeting of the Association for Computational Linguistics (ACL-92)* (1992).
8. KLEIN, D., TOUTANOVA, K., ILHAN, I., KAMVAR, S., AND MANNING, C. Combining heterogeneous classifiers for word-sense disambiguation. In *Proceedings of the ACL Workshop on "Word Sense Disambiguatuion: Recent Successes and Future Directions* (July 2002), pp. 74–80.
9. LIGHT, M., MANN, G., RILOFF, E., AND BRECK, E. Analyses for elucidating current question answering technology. *Journal of Natural Language Engineering (forthcoming)* (2002).
10. MARCUS, M., SANTORINI, B., AND MARCINKIEWICZ, M. Building a large annotated corpus of english: the Penn Treebank. *Computational Linguistics 19*, 2 (1993), 313–330.

11. MIHALCEA, R., AND BUNESCU, R. Levels of confidence in building a tagged corpus. Technical Report, SMU, 2000.

12. RATNAPARKHI, A. A maximum entropy part-of-speech tagger. In *Proceedings of the Empirical Methods in Natural Language Processing Conference* (Philadelphia, May 1996), pp. 130–142.

13. SCHMID, H. Probabilistic part-of-speech tagging using decision trees. In *International Conference on New Methods in Language Processing* (Manchester, UK, 1994).

14. VAN HALTEREN, H., ZAVREL, J., AND DAELEMANS, W. Improving data driven wordclass tagging by system combination. In *In Proceedings of the Seventeenth International Conference on Computational Linguistics (COLING-ACL '98)* (Montreal, Canada, 1998).

An Efficient Online Parser for Contextual Grammars with at Most Context–Free Selectors

Karin Harbusch

Univ. Koblenz–Landau, Computer Science Dept., `harbusch@uni-koblenz.de`

Abstract. Here we explore an efficient parser for a variant of contextual grammars (CGs) which is available via the internet. Contextual Grammar with context–free selectors allows for a simple representation of many non–context–free phenomena such as the copy language. Up to now, this specific type of selectors has hardly ever been addressed because even for simpler types no efficient parsing algorithms were known. In this paper, we describe a new polynomial parser which is based on the Earley algorithm. Furthermore we illustrate the linguistic relevance of Contextual Grammars with context–free selectors.

1 Introduction

Contextual Grammars (CGs) were originally introduced by Solomon Marcus [Marcus 1969] as "intrinsic grammars" without auxiliary symbols, based only on the fundamental linguistic operation of inserting words into given phrases according to certain contextual dependencies. The definition of CGs is simple and intuitive. Contextual Grammars include contexts, i.e. pairs of words, associated with selectors (sets of words). A context can be adjoined to any associated element in the selector (selector element). In this way, starting from a finite set of words (axioms), the language is generated.

For many variants of CG, a wide variety of properties has been studied. For instance, CGs do not fit into the Chomsky hierarchy (see, e.g., [Ehrenfeucht et al. 1997] for a recent overview of formal properties of CG). Concerning applications, it can be shown that this formalism provides an appropriate description of natural languages (cf. [Marcus et al. 1998]) such as the language $L_1 = \{a^n c b^m c a^n c b^m | n, m \geq 1\}$, which is not a context–free language. L_1 circumscribes phenomena in a dialect spoken around Zurich (Switzerland) [Shieber 1985], which allows constructions of the form $\mathrm{NP}_a^n\ \mathrm{NP}_d^m\ \mathrm{NP}_a^n\ \mathrm{NP}_d^m$.[1] However, a surprising limitation of CGs with maximal global (Mg) use of selectors is discussed in [Marcus et al. 1998]. There exist center–embedded structures that cannot be generated by such a grammar even if regular selectors are imposed (cf. L_3 in Section 3). This limitation has led to the study of the variant of Contextual Grammars with context–free selectors which encompasses this shortcoming. Our claim is that CGs with context–free selectors provide a simple and adequate specification of a wide variety of linguistic phenomena as the selectors

---

[1] Here NP_a stands for an accusative noun phrase and NP_d for a dative one.

A. Gelbukh (Ed.): CICLing 2003, LNCS 2588, pp. 168–179, 2003.

may range from linear to context–free and allow for a concise specification of linguistic pattern.

In order to apply all linguistically relevant classes of CGs for natural language processing an efficient parser has to be provided. In [Harbusch 1999], a polynomial parser for CGs with finite, regular and context–free selectors is outlined. Here we describe how to overcome its shortcoming of dealing with selector sets at run time. We propose to rewrite the selector language by an equivalent context–free grammar. All exponents in the infinite selector set, i.e. the Kleene star as well as up to two corresponding identical numerical ones, are couched into recursive rules. This behaviour reduces the grammar size and accordingly the average runtime. Furthermore, this paper focuses on the description of an online parser for this grammar type.

In the following section, Contextual Grammars are defined. In Section 3, the linguistic relevance of Contextual Grammars with context–free selectors is discussed. In Section 4, the online parser is presented. The paper ends by addressing some open questions and future work.

2   The Formalism of Contextual Grammars

In this section, we introduce the class of grammars we shall investigate in this paper. Here we adopt the terminology of [Marcus et al. 1998][2].

As usual, given an alphabet or vocabulary V, we denote by V^* the set of all words or strings over V, including the empty string which is denoted by the symbol "λ". The set of all non–empty words over V, hence $V^* - \{\lambda\}$, is denoted by V^+. The length of $x \in V^*$ is depicted as $|x|$.

A Contextual Grammar (with choices) is a construct $G = (V, A, \{(S_1, C_1), \dots, (S_n, C_n)\})$, $n \geq 1$, where V is an alphabet, A is a finite language over V, $S_1, \dots, S_n$ are languages over V, and $C_1, \dots, C_n$ are finite subsets $V^* \times V^*$. The elements of A are called axioms or starting words, the sets S_i are called selectors, and the elements $(u, v) \in C_i$ contexts. The pairs (S_i, C_i) define productions or context⎕selector pairs.

For our purposes, the following terminology is added. For all $s_i \in S_i$ and all pairs $(c_{i_k l}, c_{i_k r}) \in C_i$ ($1 \leq k \leq$ cardinality of C_i) and (S_i, C_i) is a production of the CG G, $(s_i, (c_{i_k l}, c_{i_k r}))$ is called a context⎕selector pair⎕element; $c_{i_k l}$ is called a left context and $c_{i_k r}$ a right context of the selector element s_i.

---

[2] The reader is also referred to [Martín–Vide *et al.* 1995], [Ilie 1996], [Ehrenfeucht *et al.* 1997], [Kudlek *et al.* 1997], [Marcus 1997], [Păun 1997], [Ehrenfeucht *et al.* 1998] [Marcus *et al.* 1998], [Martín–Vide 1999], [Niemann & Otto 2002] or [Boullier 2001] for discussions of CG variants and their properties.

The direct derivation relation on V^* is defined as $x \Longrightarrow_{in} y$ iff $x = x_1 x_2 x_3, y = x_1 u x_2 v x_3$, where $x_2 \in S_i$, $(u, v) \in C_i$, for some $i, 1 \leq i \leq n$.[3]
If we denote the reflexive and transitive closure of the relation $\Longrightarrow_{in}$ by $\Longrightarrow_{in}^*$, the language generated by G is $L_{in}(G) = \{z \in V^* | w \Longrightarrow_{in}^* z,$ for some $w \in A\}$.

Two variants of the relation $\Longrightarrow_{in}$ are defined as follows:

- $x \Longrightarrow_{Ml} y$ (maximal local mode) iff $x = x_1 x_2 x_3, y = x_1 u x_2 v x_3, x_2 \in S_i, (u, v) \in C_i$, for some $i, 1 \leq i \leq n$, and there are no $x_1', x_2', x_3' \in V^*$ such that $x = x_1' x_2' x_3', x_2' \in S_i$, and $|x_1'| \leq |x_1|, |x_3'| \leq |x_3|, |x_2'| > |x_2|$;
- $x \Longrightarrow_{Mg} y$ (maximal global mode) is defined the same as Ml but here all selectors are regarded $(x_2' \in S_j, 1 \leq j \leq n$, the number of selectors).

For $\alpha \in \{Mg, Ml\}$ we denote: $L_\alpha(G) = \{z \in V^* | w \Longrightarrow_\alpha^* z,$ for some $w \in A\}$. In the next section, an example illustrating the selection according to the three derivation definitions is outlined.

If in a grammar $G = (V, A, \{(S_1, C_1), \ldots, (S_n, C_n)\})$ all selectors $S_1, \ldots, S_n$ are languages in a given family F, then we say G is a Contextual Grammar with F choice or with F selection. The families of languages $L_\alpha(G)$, for G a Contextual Grammar with F choice, are denoted by $CL_\alpha(F)$, where $\alpha \in \{in, Ml, Mg\}$.

3 Linguistic Relevance of CG with Context-Free Selectors

In [Marcus et al. 1998], the appropriateness of CGs for the description of natural languages is outlined. This property basically results from the fact that the grammar writer is able to straightforwardly describe all the usual restrictions appearing in natural languages. These statements require often more powerful formalisms than Context–Free Grammars (cf. reduplication, crossed dependencies, and multiple agreement).

For instance, the language $L_2 = \{xcx | x \in \{a, b\}^*\}$, which duplicates words of arbitrary length (copy language), allows for the construction of compound words of the form string–of–words–o–string–of–words as in Bambara, a language from the Mande family in Africa [Culy 1985]. Furthermore, the non–context–free language L_1 introduced in the introduction (crossed dependecies) circumscribes phenomena in a dialect spoken around Zurich (Switzerland) [Shieber 1985]. All these languages can be specified, e.g. with CGs with regular selectors under the assumption of Mg (cf. [Marcus et al. 1998])[4].

---

[3] The index in distinguishes the operation from $\Longrightarrow_{ex}$, i.e. the *external derivation* (cf. the original definition by [Marcus 1969]) where the context is adjoined at the ends of the derived words: $x \Longrightarrow_{ex} y$ iff $y = uxv$ for $(u, v) \in C_i, x \in S_i$, for some $i, 1 \leq i \leq n$. We do not investigate $\Longrightarrow_{ex}$ here. [Păun & Nguyen 1980] proposed internal derivations.

[4] $(\{a, b, c\}, \{c\}, (\{c\}\{ab\}^*, \{(a, a), (b, b)\}))$ yields the copy language; $(\{a, b, c, d\}, \{abcd\}, (ab^+c, \{(a, c)\}, (bc^+d, \{b, d\}))$ obtains crossed dependencies. Notice that for both grammars holds that the languages they produce are the same under the assumption of Ml and Mg, respectively.

However, a surprising limitation of Contextual Grammars with maximal global use of selectors was briefly mentioned in the introduction. As stated in [Marcus et al. 1998] some so–called center[]embedded structures such as $L_3 = \{a^n cb^m cb^m ca^n | n, m \geq 1\}$ cannot be generated. Note that L_3 is a linear language in Chomsky's sense and that it belongs to the families $CL_{in}(FIN)$ and $CL_{Ml}(FIN)$. However, L_3 is not in the family $CL_{Mg}(REG)$[5]

In the following we explore the class of contextual languages with context–free selectors. Note here that CGs with context–free selectors yield in fact the full range of finite, regular and context–free selectors. Consequently, they cover all the languages mentioned in the beginning of this section. Furthermore, this adequacy constraint imposed on the process of grammar writing reduces the average runtime of the parser. For reasons of space we only investigate the question here whether Contextual Grammars with context–free selectors are able to capture L_3. The grammar $G_{cf} = (\{a, b, c\}, \{bcb\}, \{((\{a^n cb^* cb^* ca^n | n \geq 0\}, \{(a, a)\}), (\{b^m cb^m | n \geq 0\}, \{(b, b), (ac, ca)\})\})$ generates L_3 under the assumption of Mg. For an illustration how CG essentially works, all accepted input strings of G_{cf} up to the length 11 are outlined here:

The axiom bcb derives $bbcbb$ or $acbcbca$ according to in, Mg, Ml because $b^1 cb^1$ is the only applicable selector. For the two resulting strings the following holds:

- The string $bbcbb$ derives $bbbcbb$ and $acbbcbbca$ according to Ml, Mg (here $x_1 = \lambda, x_2 = b^1 cb^1, x_3 = \lambda$; $x_1' = b, x_2' = b^0 cb^0, x_3' = b$ is suppressed as it would produce the same string; according to in, furthermore $bbacccabb$, $bacbcbccab$ (i.e., $x_1' = bb, x_2' = b^0 cb^0, x_3' = bb, x_1' = b, x_2' = b^1 cb^1, x_3' = b$) would be produced; for reasons of space, we omit their further consideration here).

- The string $acbcbca$ derives $aacbcbcaa$ according to Mg (here $x_1 = \lambda, x_2 = a^1 cb^1 cb^1 ca^1, x_3 = \lambda$; $x_1' = a, x_2' = a^0 cbcbca^0, x_3' = a$ is suppressed as it would produce the same string; according to in, furthermore $acbbcbbca, acbacccabca, acacbcbcaca$ would be produced (i.e., $x_1' = ac, x_2' = b^1 cb^1, x_3' = ca, x_1' = acb, x_2' = b^0 cb^0, x_3' = bca$); again, we omit their further consideration).

So, for the three strings $bbbcbbb$, $acbbcbbca$ and $aacbcbcaa$ the following holds:

- The string $bbbcbbb$ derives $bbbbcbbbb$ and $acbbbcbbbca$ according to Mg with the line of argumentation as before.
- The string $acbbcbbca$ derives $aacbbcbbcaa$ according to Mg (here $x_1 = \lambda, x_2 = a^1 cb^2 cb^2 ca^1, x_3 = \lambda$; e.g., $x_1' = a, x_2' = a^0 cb^2 cb^2 ca^0, x_3' = a$ or $x_1' = aacb, x_2' = b^2 cb^2, x_3' = bcaa$ are suppressed as they would produce

---

[5] Here $CL_\alpha(F)$, $\alpha \in \{in, Mg, Ml\}$, $F \in \{FIN, REG\}$ denotes the contextual language where the selectors belong to the family of regular (REG) or finite (FIN) languages and the recursion definition is unrestricted (in) or selects maximal adjoinings (Ml/Mg, i.e. the longest element of the same selector/all selectors); CF refers to the family of context–free languages. For the formal definitions of FIN, REG, CF see, e.g., [Rozenberg & Salomaa 1997].

the same strings as $acbbacccabbca, acbacbcbcabca, acacbbcbbcaca, acbbbcbbbca$ according to in).

- The string $aacbcbcaa$ derives $aaacbcbcaaa$ according to Mg ($x_1 = \lambda, x_2 = a^2cbcbca^2, x_3 = \lambda$; e.g. $x_1' = a, x_2' = a^1cbcbca^1, x_3' = a, x_1' = aa, x_2' = a^0cbcbca^0, x_3' = aa$ or $x_1' = aac, x_2' = bcb, x_3' = caa$).

Again, the string $bbbbcbbbb$ derives $bbbbbcbbbbb$ and $acbbbbcbbbbca$ under the assumption of Mg according to the line of argumentation as before.

4   An Earley-Based Parser for CGs

CG parsing is addressed, e.g., in [Ilie 1996] or [Boullier 2001]. In [Ilie 1996] External Contextual Grammars (i.e. CGs where the contexts can be added only at the end of the current string) are studied and it has been shown that this variant is basically parsable in polynomial time. In [Boullier 2001] a subclass of CGs is studied which can be translated into RCGs (Range Concatenation Grammars). For the resulting grammar it can be shown that parsing is polynomial. However some linguistically relevant variants cannot be covered by the transformation process. A more general approach is presented in [Harbusch 1999] or [Harbusch 2000]. Here, the basic idea of a polynomial parser for CGs with linear, regular, and context–free selectors is outlined. In the following, we extend this parser with respect to efficiency and describe the features of an online version through the internet.

First, a sketch of the intertwined two–level Earley–based[6] parser is presented for Contextual Grammars with finite, regular or context–free selectors on the basis of the three derivation definitions in, Ml, Mg.

In the following, the online parser becomes essentially extended in comparison to the algorithm described in [Harbusch 1999] or [Harbusch 2000]. Here the transformation of the selectors into a grammar is no more dependent on the length of the input string. From this fact the shortcoming arises that the grammar transformation has to be performed during the run time. Furthermore, the number of rules could grow dramatically because all accepted input strings up to the length of the currently considered input were enumerated. In the variant presented here a Context–Free Grammar is exploited to yield the acceptable selector pairs. We'll show that this is more efficient than the comparison between strings. The online parser provides an automatic transformation of specified languages into a finite Context–Free Grammar lincensing infinite selector languanges. Furthermore this routine is a test whether the grammar is at most context–free. More powerful specifications are rejected. Before we address this transformation we describe the components of the CG parser.

---

[6] The Earley algorithm is adopted here as it basically avoids normal–form transformations such as the elimination of ϵ rules (rules such as $X \longrightarrow \lambda$) which are highly appreciated to state empty selectors and contexts, respectively.

4.1   The Components of the Parser

Our parser consists of two passes. Basically, in the first pass all individual contexts and selectors are identified and stored in items denoting the left and right boundary of these fragments. This task is performed by an ordinary Earley parser called $FRAG$ (compute FRAGments) on the basis of a Context–Free Grammar with rules $(sel_i \longrightarrow s_i)^7$, $(con_{i_k l} \longrightarrow c_{i_k l})$, $(con_{i_k r} \longrightarrow c_{i_k r})$ for all selector elements $s_i \in S_i$ and all its context pairs $(c_{i_k l}, c_{i_k r}) \in C_i$ ($sel_i, con_{i_k l}, con_{i_k r}$ are nonterminals of the according Context–Free Grammar). All these items are used in the second–phase Earley–parser ($PROCO$ — PROduction COmbination) in order to check the only context–free rule–type ($sel_i \longrightarrow con_{i_k l} \; sel_i \; con_{i_k r}$), i.e. the identification of a derivation step of a CG. Notice that both components reuse the same implemented procedures ⟦PREDICT⟧, ⟦SCAN⟧ and ⟦COMPLETE⟧ of the basic Earley algorithm. Any procedure is parametrized by the currently considered grammar and the input string (parameters may differ in the individual reruns which result from the intertwined definition). All item lists are always available for prediction, scanning and completion[8].

In order to become able to identify context–selector pairs after the elimination of contexts in the input string[9] the two phases run intertwined (reruns). Beside continuing the iteration in PROCO, for each successfully applied rule ($sel_i \longrightarrow con_{i_k l} \; sel_i \; con_{i_k r}$), the input string where $con_{i_k l}$ and $con_{i_k r}$ are eliminated is handed back to the CG parser (i.e. FRAG and PROCO). It is important to note that the numbering in the newly build input strings remains the same so that the parsers in both phases can reuse all previously computed results. The strings to be erased are only marked to be empty by the new terminal ϵ. The rules ($q \longrightarrow \epsilon \; q$) and ($q \longrightarrow q \; \epsilon$) eliminate all occurances of ϵ and represents that the selector element covers the eliminated context as well.

In the worst case the space complexity of this acceptor is $O(n^4)$ and the run time is $O(n^6)$ for the ordinary recursion definition in. The computation according to Mg, Ml and parsing according to in, Ml, Mg, i.e. the computation of a condensed representation of all derivations, costs at most $O(n^6)$ space and $O(n^9)$ time units (see, e.g., [Harbusch 1999]).

The online parser provides the selection of predefined grammars beside the possibility of specifying the user's own grammars. As output the transformed

---

[7] Notice that this is exactly the point where the infinite length of selectors lead to the enumeration of accepted input strings or a grammatical representation of these strings. In Section 4.2, a more efficient alternative to circumscribe an infinite set S_i is presented.

[8] As the parser is implemented in JAVA, according to the independence of processing, all these procedures run as individual Threads on possibly different machines. Actually, we use a 14x336 MHz 8–slot Sun Enterprise E4500/E5500 (sun4u) for our testing. However, the online parser runs on the local machine of the user. Accordingly, the performance may vary.

[9] The following context-selector pairs provide an example of this necessity: $(\{bd\}, \{(a, \lambda)\}), (\{d\}, \{(c, e)\})$. A possible derivation is $bd \implies abd \implies abcde$. Here the selector element bd is not a substring of the input string $abcde$. So the proper items which are constructed in the first phase are missing.

Context–Free Grammars, the initial item lists, the final item lists, a list of items causing reruns and the enumeration of all individual parses are presented in individual windows. With the decision of showing individual parses for reasons of readability by a human reader, the online parser could run exponentially in this final routine. If the core components become part of an natural language system this routine is not required. Accordingly the entire system is polynomial.

In Figure 1 the start and result window for the CG similar to Footnote 9 = $(\{a, b, c, d, e\}, \{bd, a, \lambda\}, \{(\{bd, d\}, \{(a, \lambda), (a, b)\}), (\{d\}, \{(c, e)\})\})$ is shown for the input string = $abcde$. The representation of the item lists is omitted here for reasons of space (run the online parser with the provided grammar1 for this information).

4.2   Transformation of Infinite Selector Languages

In the following any given context–free selector w (i.e. the original rule $(S \longrightarrow w)$) is wrapped up in a Context–Free Grammar which gives rise to a more efficient parser. For this endevour the given selector language is inspected for substrings with exponents of the sort $*$, $+$, and n, respectively. These substrings are rewritten by recursive context–free rules. These procedures also allow to identify context–sensitive selectors (e.g., $a^n b^n c^n$) which are rejected as they cannot be parsed by the parser presented here.

First, the procedure KLEENETRANS with the parameters (string s, nonterminal nt), where initially $s = w, nt = S$, explores all substrings w' with exponent "$*$" or "$+$" or a numerical number that only occurs once in w. Its first occurrence is rewritten by a new nonterminal nt_i in the rules $(nt \longrightarrow w)$. The rule $(nt_i \longrightarrow w'$ without the exponent nt_i) is added. In case of exponent "$*$" $(nt_i \longrightarrow \lambda)$ is also deployed. KLEENETRANS is activated for the revised w and the substring w' which may contain nested exponents of the respective sort until no (more) exponents of these three sorts exist.

Second, the resulting rule set (which at least contains the original rule $(S \longrightarrow w)$) is explored. Let us assume each rule has the form $(lhs \longrightarrow rhs)$. If in rhs two times the same exponent occurs, the recursive procedure CFTRANS with the parameters (string w, nonterminal nt) with $w = rhs, nt = lhs$ runs in the following manner:
w is divided into $x_1 x_2^n x_3 x_4^n x_5$ (cf. pumping lemma; see, e.g., [Rozenberg & Salomaa 1997]) where x_1 does not contain any exponent. For the five new nonterminals $nt2_1, \ldots, nt2_5$, the following rules are constructed:

1. $(nt \longrightarrow x_1\ nt2_1\ nt2_2) + \text{CFTRANS}(x_5, nt2_2)$,
2. $(nt2_1 \longrightarrow nt2_3\ nt2_1\ nt2_4) + \text{CFTRANS}(x_2, nt2_3) + \text{CFTRANS}(x_4, nt2_4)$,
3. $(nt2_1 \longrightarrow nt2_5) + \text{CFTRANS}(x_3, nt2_5)$.

If no such exponents exist $(nt \longrightarrow w)$ is returned (end of the recursion).

Basically it is clear that both procedures terminate because always one or two exponents are rewritten. It can formally be shown that any context–free language can be rewritten. For reasons of space, we skip this proof here. As for the

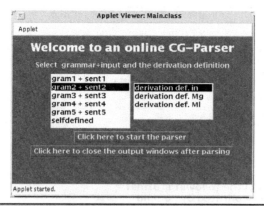

Fig. 1. Start window and result window for a predefined CG

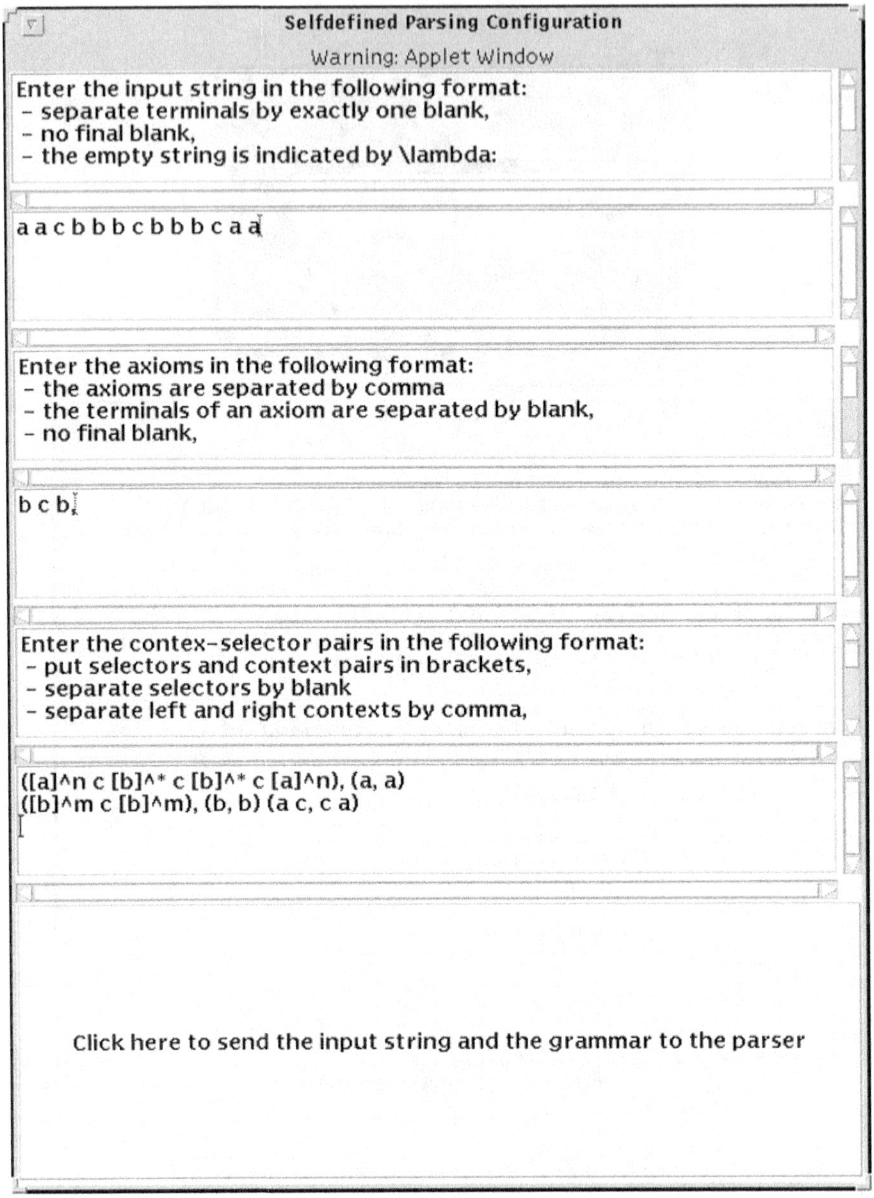

Selfdefined Parsing Configuration

Warning: Applet Window

Enter the input string in the following format:
- separate terminals by exactly one blank,
- no final blank,
- the empty string is indicated by \lambda:

a a c b b b c b b b c a a

Enter the axioms in the following format:
- the axioms are separated by comma
- the terminals of an axiom are separated by blank,
- no final blank,

b c b

Enter the contex–selector pairs in the following format:
- put selectors and context pairs in brackets,
- separate selectors by blank
- separate left and right contexts by comma,

([a]^n c [b]^* c [b]^* c [a]^n), (a, a)
([b]^m c [b]^m), (b, b) (a c, c a)

Click here to send the input string and the grammar to the parser

Fig. 2. Example of a user–defined grammar

constructed rules in KLEENETRANS, it is directly obvious that the input word $w = a_1 x_1^{\{*|+\}} a_2 \ldots a_k x_k^{\{*|+\}} a_{k+1}$ (in a_i no exponents of the form "*" or "+" occur (single numerical exponents are assumed here to be synonymously expressed by "*" or "+", respectively; $1 \le i \le k + 1$); x_j denotes a finite terminal string (1

```
┌─────────────────────────────────────────────────────────────────┐
│  ▽        Context--Free Grammars of FRAG and PROCO According to the CG │
│                      Warning: Applet Window                       │
├─────────────────────────────────────────────────────────────────┤
│ Terminals of the CG which become nonterminals of CFG_FRAG:        │
│                                                                   │
│ !b !a !c                                                          │
│                                                                   │
│ ReadCG.Axioms of the CG:                                          │
│ !b !c !b,                                                         │
│                                                                   │
│ Nonterminals in CFG_FRAG:                                         │
│ CON_L1 CON_R1 CON_L2 CON_R2 SEL_1-1 NTS_151 NTS_149 NTS_150 CON   │
│                                                                   │
│ Rules of CFG_FRAG of the form _(_lhs rhs(+rhs)* _)_:              │
│                                                                   │
│ Gr1[1]= CON_L1 !b                                                 │
│ Gr1[2]= CON_R1 !b                                                 │
│ Gr1[3]= CON_L2 !a !c                                              │
│ Gr1[4]= CON_R2 !c !a                                              │
│ Gr1[5]= SEL_1-1 NTS_151                                           │
│ Gr1[6]= NTS_151 NTS_149 NTS_151 NTS_150+!c                        │
│ Gr1[7]= NTS_149 !b                                                │
│ Gr1[8]= NTS_150 !b                                                │
│ Gr1[9]= CON_L3 !a                                                 │
│ Gr1[10]= CON_R3 !a                                                │
│ Gr1[11]= SEL_2-2 NTS_173                                          │
│ Gr1[12]= NTS_173 NTS_171 NTS_173 NTS_172+NTS_174 NTS_176 NTS_17   │
│ Gr1[13]= NTS_174 !c                                               │
│ Gr1[14]= NTS_176 NTS_175 NTS_176+\lambda                          │
│ Gr1[15]= NTS_175 !b                                               │
│ Gr1[16]= NTS_7 !c                                                 │
│ Gr1[17]= NTS_177 NTS_7 NTS_9 NTS_10                               │
│ Gr1[18]= NTS_9 NTS_8 NTS_9+\lambda                                │
│ Gr1[19]= NTS_8 !b                                                 │
│ Gr1[20]= NTS_10 !c                                                │
│ Gr1[21]= NTS_171 !a                                               │
│ Gr1[22]= NTS_172 !a                                               │
│ Gr1[23]= !b !b*+!b \epsilon+\epsilon !b                           │
│ Gr1[24]= !a !a*+!a \epsilon+\epsilon !a                           │
│ Gr1[25]= !c !c*+!c \epsilon+\epsilon !c                           │
│                                                                   │
│ Terminals in CFG_PROCO;                                           │
│ {}                                                                │
│                                                                   │
│ Nonterminals in CFG_PROCO:                                        │
│ SEL_1-1 SEL_2-2                                                   │
│                                                                   │
│ Rules of CFG_PROCO of the form _(_lhs rhs(+rhs)* _)_:             │
│                                                                   │
│ Gr2[1]= SEL_1-1 CON_L1 SEL_1-1 CON_R1+CON_L2 SEL_1-1 CON_R2       │
│ Gr2[2]= SEL_2-2 CON_L3 SEL_2-2 CON_R3                             │
└─────────────────────────────────────────────────────────────────┘
```

Fig. 3. Context–free transformations of the user–defined grammar in Figure 2

$\leq j \leq k$)) is produced by a rule set consisting of $(S \longrightarrow a_1 nt_1 \ldots a_k nt_k a_{k+1})$ and $(nt_i \longrightarrow x_i nt_i)$ plus rules $(nt_i \longrightarrow \lambda)$ in case of the exponent "*".

Concerning related exponents: with the pumping lemma and Chomsky–Schützenberger's theorem (see, e.g., [Rozenberg & Salomaa 1997]), non–Dyck words are not context–free (e.g. $(\{[\}]))$. Accordingly, CFTRANS identifies recursively the outermost Dyck word $(x_1[x_3]x_5)$. Furthermore it checks whether Dyck words (i.e. nested exponential structures such as $a^m[b^nc^n]^m$) only lay inside a substring or behind the currently considered pair. By this method any construction with crossed brackets and more than two controlled brackets is rejected to be not context–free.

The runtime complexity of this procedure is linear with respect to the number of inspected rules. In general, it can only find finitely many exemplars of exponents in a rule of finite length to be rewritten. Any part without corresponding exponents is transformed into a single (no exponent in the source specification) or two (Kleene star repetition and inititialization rewriting the Kleene star in the source specification) context–free rule(s) which costs $O(1)$. The resulting grammar is much more condensed compared to the original parsing method, e.g., outlined in [Harbusch 1999] and hence impigning this represenation on the online parser reduces the average runtime.

Figure 2 and 3 show the transformation of the grammar G_{cf}. Notice that the online parser currently requires completely bracketed structures if exponents are specified. Furthermore, the variables in any exponent are interpreted as greater or equal to zero. Only for reasons of simplicity the user driven specification of two types of exponents is omitted. In the code both variants are yet tested.

5   Final Discussion

In this paper, we have addressed the linguistic relevance of Contextual Grammars with context–free selectors and described a more efficient version of the polynomial parser for CGs with $CL_\alpha(F)$ ($F \in \{FIN, REG, CF\}$, $\alpha \in \{in, Ml, Mg\}$). The parser is implemented in JAVA and online available under the address:

http://www.uni–koblenz.de/∼harbusch/CG-PARSER/welcome-cg.html

In the future, we'll focus on the following two questions. Since we are especially interested in natural language parsing with CGs, we are going to build a Contextual Grammars with context–free selectors for English and German. Currently we are exploiting how to extract context–selector pairs from corpora. The heads are specified as features for selectors. The patterns, i.e. the contexts are extracted according to the significant examples in the corpus. On the theoretical side the properties of Contextual Grammars with context–free selectors will be studied in more detail.

References

[Boullier 2001] Boullier, P.: From Contextual Grammars to Range Concatenation Grammars. *Electronical Notes in Theoretical Computer Science*, 53 (2001)

[Culy 1985] Culy, C.: The Complexity of the Vocabulary of Bambara. *Linguistics and Philosophy*, 8 (1985) 345–351

[Earley 1970] Earley, J.: An Efficient Context–Free Parsing Algorithm. *Communications of the ACM*, 13(2) (1970) 94–102

[Ehrenfeucht *et al.* 1997] Ehrenfeucht, A., Păun, G., Rozenberg, G.: Contextual Grammars and Natural Languages. In G. Rozenberg and A. Salomaa (eds.) Handbook of Formal Languages, Vol. 2 (Linear Modeling: Background and Application), Springer–Verlag, Berlin Heidelberg, Germany (1997) 237–294

[Ehrenfeucht *et al.* 1998] Ehrenfeucht, A., Păun, G., Rozenberg, G.: On representing recursively enumerable languages by internal contextual languages. *Theoretical Computer Science*, 205 (1998) 61–83

[Harbusch 1999] Harbusch, K.: Parsing Contextual Grammars with Linear, Regular and Context–Free Selectors. Procs. of *"MOL6 - Sixth Meeting on the Mathematics of Language"*, Orlando, Florida/USA (1999) 323–335

[Harbusch 2000] Harbusch, K.: A Polynomial Parser for Contextual Grammars with Linear, Regular and Context–Free Selectors. In C. Martín–Vide and V. Mitrana (eds). Words, Sequences, Grammars, Languages: Where Biology, Computer Science and Mathematics Meet, Springer, London/UK (2000)

[Ilie 1996] Ilie, L.: The computational complexity of Marcus contextual grammars. *Theoretical Computer Science*, 183 (1996) 33–44

[Kudlek *et al.* 1997] Kudlek, M., Marcus, S., Mateescu, A.: Contextual Grammars with Distributed Catenation and Shuffle. TUCS Technical Report No 103, Turku Centre for Computer Science, Finland (1997)

[Marcus *et al.* 1998] Marcus, S., Martín–Vide, C., Păun, G.: Contextual Grammars as Generative Models of Natural Languages. *Computational Linguistics*, 24(2) (1998) 245–274

[Marcus 1969] Marcus, S.: Contextual Grammars. *Revue roumaine des mathématiques pures et appliquées*, 14 (1969) 1525–1534

[Marcus 1997] Marcus, S.: Contextual Grammars and Natural Language. In G. Rozenberg and A. Salomaa (eds.). *Handbook of Formal Languages*, Vol. 2 (Linear Modeling: Background and Application), (1997) 215–235

[Martín–Vide 1999] Martín–Vide, C.: Contextual Automata. Procs. of the Sixth Meeting on Mathematics of Language (1999) 315–321

[Martín–Vide *et al.* 1995] Martín–Vide, C., Mateescu, A., Miquel–Vergés, J., Păun, G.: Internal Contextual Grammmars: Minimal, Maximal and Scattered Use of Selectors. Procs. of the *Fourth A Bar–Ilan Symposium on Foundations of AI* (1995) 132–142

[Niemann & Otto 2002] Niemann, G., Otto, F.: Restarting automata, Church–Rosser languages, and confluent contextual grammars. To appear in C. Martín–Vide and V. Mitrana (eds.), Grammars and Automata for String Processing: from Mathematics and Computer Science to Biology, and Back, Gordon and Breach, London/UK. (2002)

[Păun & Nguyen 1980] Păun, G., Nguyen, X.M.: On the inner contextual grammmars. *Revue roumaine des mathématiques pures et appliquées*, 25 (1980) 641–651

[Păun 1997] Păun, G.: Marcus Contextual Grammmars. Kluwer, Boston, MA/USA, Dortrecht/NL (1997)

[Rozenberg & Salomaa 1997] Rozenberg, G., Salomaa, A. (eds.): Handbook of Formal Languages, Vol. 1 (Word, Language, Grammar), Springer, Berlin/Heidelberg, Germany (1997)

[Shieber 1985] Shieber, S.M.: Evidence against the Context-Freeness of Natural Language. *Linguistics and Philosophy*, 8 (1985) 333–343

Offline Compilation of Chains for Head-Driven Generation with Constraint-Based Grammars

Toni Tuells, German Rigau, and Horacio Rodríguez

Dept. de LSI, Universitat Politècnica de Catalunya
atuells@gcelsa.com, {g.rigau,horacio@lsi.upc.es}

Abstract. In this paper we investigate the possibility of compiling off-line the chains of lexical signs in order to improve on some known limitations of Head-Driven generation with constraint-based grammars. The method allows the detection of problematic constructions off-line and obtains substantial performance improvements over standard head-driven algorithms.

1 Introduction

Constraint-based Grammars that both can be used for parsing and generation are called *reversible grammars*, and their theoretical and practical aspects have been largely acknowledged; see [1],[2] ,[3]. The most widespread control strategy for generation with reversible constraint-based grammars has been the idea of head-driven generation, which is a control strategy almost symmetrical to head-corner parsing. The underlying idea of this approach is that semantic information encoded in logical forms originates mainly from lexical entries. Therefore, in order to generate from a semantic structure, heads should be predicted first using top down information. Then, the elements of the head's subcategorization list should be generated bottom-up using the rules of the grammar, until the generated semantics matches input semantics. Rules that are used in a bottom-up fashion are called *chain rules*; and we define a chain as a sequence of application of chain rules. The Semantic head-driven generation algorithm (SHDG) [4] and the bottom-up generation algorithm (BUG) [1] are some well known instances of algorithms following a head-driven control strategy.

In spite of its natural elegance, head-driven generation suffers from different drawbacks, even when generating from simple logical forms:

- Some linguistically motivated constructions and analysis may lead to *termination or efficiency problems:* empty heads and head movement, markers, raising to object constructions and words with empty semantics.

- During the generation process, variables in the semantic representation may take inappropriate values, causing over and undergeneration problems. As noted by [5], [6],[1], precautions should be taken in order to guarantee that the semantics of the generated string matches the original semantics.

It is well known that some of the problems before mentioned (termination, efficiency, matching) are caused by uninstantiated variables during program execution.

A. Gelbukh (Ed.): CICLing 2003, LNCS 2588, pp. 180–190, 2003.

Therefore, it is an interesting idea to investigate the possibility of using off-line compilation either to adapt grammars prior to processing or to improve the efficiency of the control strategy[1]. In this paper we investigate this possibility by compiling off-line all possible chains corresponding to the lexical signs of the grammar. This off-line compilation technique, along with a grounding analysis, improves the performance of a standard head-driven algorithm and detects problematic constructions prior to generation[2]. We will assume a lexicalist grammar formalism, such as HPSG [7] where lexical categories have considerable internal structure. To assess the utility of our investigation, the methods and generators described in this paper have been applied to the grammar described in [8]. This grammar follows basically HPSG and covers – admittedly, in a simplified manner – among other linguistic phenomena, co-ordination, control and raising verbs, passive constructions, auxiliaries, extraposition and long-distance dependencies. The original grammar uses a flat semantics encoding; to make it suitable for Head-driven generation we have adapted it to a structured semantic encoding.

The structure of rest of the paper is as follows: in section 2 we review the literature on off-line compilation of chains. In section 3 we describe the proper method that computes chains corresponding to lexical signs. In section 4 we present some applications of our method; section 5 describes our experiments with a medium-size lexicalized grammar [8]. Finally, we present our conclusions. Hereafter we will assume some familiarity on the reader's part with Head-Driven Generation.

2   Related Work

The idea of off-line compilation of chains corresponding to lexical signs is not new: [9] describes a method to compile HPSG lexical entries into a set of finite-state automata. The aim of their work is at parsing efficiency: by compiling off-line all possible chains of lexical entries, many failing unifications can be avoided at run-time. [10] Describes a similar method that translates HPSG into lexicalized feature-based TAG. From our perspective, [9], [10] are concerned with the computation of maximal projections of HPSG lexical entries .

[11] Describes an algorithm for head-driven generation. The rules of the grammar are reorganized to reflect the predicate-argument structure rather than the surface string. This is done by compiling off-line chains corresponding to lexical entries. Once the grammar reflects the semantic structure rather than the surface string, LR parsing techniques are applied to obtain an efficient algorithm. His method can be seen as using the same algorithm for parsing and generation, where the grammar for generation is obtained from the grammar for parsing. However, due to the nature of LR Parsing, a grammar with a Context-free Backbone is assumed: this makes his method unsuitable for lexicalist frameworks. Obviously, one could skip the second part of his work (the application of LR parsing techniques) and apply other (parsing) algorithms: this has been done for the AMALIA system [13] , where a bottom-up parsing algorithm is applied. However, to the best of our knowledge, none of them uses a grounding analysis to predict problematic constructions.

---

[1] See [12] for an excellent source of off-line compilation techniques for NLP.

[2] For our purposes, grounding analysis consists in collecting information about how variables states change during program execution.

3   Offline Compilation of Chains

Before we describe the compilation method we make the following assumptions:

- Grammars have productions of the form :
$$X \rightarrow X_1,...,\underline{X_h}...X_n$$
  where the X constituents include complex syntactic and semantic information and the constituent X_h is the *head* of the production.
- Only chain rules are considered.
- The method has to be applied to fully expanded lexical entries; no on-line application of lexical rules is taken into account.
- Lexical entries are of the form $X \rightarrow$ [Phon], where X includes complex syntactic and semantic information. *Phon* is the surface realization of the lexical entry.

For illustration purposes we will use the tiny grammar shown in figures 1a,1b below.

1. s(Sem)→np(SemS), <u>vp(</u>[np(SemS],Sem)
2. s(Sem)→ s(SemO), <u>pp(</u>[SemO],Sem).
3. vp(Scat,Sem)→ <u>v</u>(Scat,Sem).
4. vp([S|R],Sem)→ <u>vp(</u>[S|[Arg|R]],Sem), Arg.
5. np(Sem)→ <u>pn(</u>Sem).
6. np(Sem)→ <u>det</u>(SemNp,Sem), nx(SemNp).
7. nx(Sem)→ <u>n</u>(Sem).
8. nx(Sem)→ nx(X), <u>pp(</u>[X],Sem).
9. pp([X],Sem)→ <u>prep(</u>[X,Y],Sem),np(Y).

Fig. 1.a. Rules of the Grammar

%% Lexical Entries
n(banana) → [banana].
det(X,def(X) → [the].
pn(john)   → [john].
det(X,undef(X)) → [a].
v([np(X),np(Y)],eats(X,Y)) → [eats]. % transitive reading
v([np(X)],eats(X,Y)) → [eats].   % intransitive reading
prep([X,Y],on(X,Y)) → [on].
prep([X,Y],with(X,Y)) → [with].

Fig. 1.b. Lexical Entries of the Grammar.

The head of each production is identified by underlying the syntactic category; for example, the head daughter of rule 1 is the verbal phrase (vp). Note also that Prepositional phrases can be attached at sentence level (rule 2) or at noun level (rule 8). Rule 4 deals with verbal complements. A further remark about this grammar is that we find the transitive and intransitive readings of verb *eat*: we will refer to these entries extensively throughout this paper. Intuitively, a chain of a lexical category is a sequence of rule applications which corresponds to the reflexive and transitive closure of the head relation. We now turn to the inductive definition of the chain of a lexical sign:

Definition 1. A Chain of a lexical sign X_1 is a sequence $\langle X_1...X_N \rangle$ such that :

- $X_1 \rightarrow$ [Phon].
- For every X_i, X_{i+1} in $\langle X_1...X_N \rangle$,

  $1 <= i < N$, there is a production of the form $X_{i+1} \rightarrow Y_1,...,\underline{Y_H}...Y_K$ such that X_i and Y_H unify.

In figure 2 below we show the computation of the chain for the intransitive reading of eat, after aplication of rules 3 and 1.:

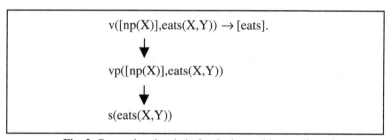

Fig. 2. Computing the chain for the intransitive reading of eat.

Some valid chains derived from the grammar in figure 1 are shown below. For expository purposes, we only show major syntactic categories. Furthermore, we mark with an upper index the rule from the grammar in figure 1 which has been applied to obtain that category:

1. Chain(eats) = $\langle v, vp^3, vp^4, sentence^1 \rangle$. (transitive reading)

2. Chain(eats) = $\langle v, vp^3, sentence^1 \rangle$. (intransitive reading)
3. Chain(banana) = $\langle n, nx^7 \rangle$.
4. Chain(with) = $\{ \langle prep, pp^9, nx^8 \rangle, \langle prep, pp^9, sentence^2 \rangle \}$

Note that *with* has two possible chains which correspond to the *sentence* and *nx* attachment of prepositional phrases. We provide the following simple iterative algorithm which computes all chains of a lexical entry:

$Chains = \{\langle X \rangle\}.$

Repeat .

$NewChains = \{\}.$

1 For every sequence $\langle X_1 ... X_N \rangle$ in *Chains,* do the following:
    1.1For   every   production   of   the   form
$X_M \rightarrow Y_1,...,\underline{Y_H}...Y_K$ such that Y_H and X_N unify ,do the following:

    add $\langle X_1...X_N X_M \rangle$ to *NewChains.*

2. *if NewChains not = {} Chains = NewChains.*

Until *NewChains =* $\{\}.$

Several things are noteworthy about the process just outlined:

- Chains are computed using syntactic and semantic information.
- There may be more than one chain for a given lexical entry.
- Our method computes maximal projections of lexical entries.

3.1   Termination Criteria

For the simple grammar in figure 1 termination of the method can be guaranteed since it is off-line parsable. Informally, termination can be guaranteed if for each rule application syntactic and semantic information of the mother node is identical to those of the head-daughter node minus the information used to select the non-head daughter of the rule. For example, in the HPSG head-complement schema, the list-value COMP of the mother node is the list-value COMP of the head-daughter minus the value of the non-head daughter.

In general, however, termination cannot be guaranteed. A good example is the well known head-adjunct schemata in HPSG: the syntactic information of the mother node is selected from the syntactic head-daughter, whereas the semantic information of the mother node is selected from the non-head daughter node (the adjunct). The application of our method to any adjunct would loop for the head-adjunct rule since the syntactic information of the mother node would not be sufficiently constrained. Not surprisingly, the solution to these problems is a restriction technique: a restrictor has to be defined for each rule schema. Similar problems and solutions are described in [9], [10].

3.2 Boundness Situation of Semantic Variables of a Lexical Sign

While computing the chains of lexical entries we maintain two data structures that will track how semantic variables state changes in a chain derivation. Both structure will be used to detect problematic constructions for head-driven generation.

The structure *SemVars* of a lexical sign X is a list of the variables in the semantic dimension of lexical sign X along with his boundness situation. This structure controls the coindexation of semantic variables among the head and non head daughters in a chain derivation. We represent this structure as a tuple:

$$\text{SemVars}(X) = \{(V_1, \uparrow), (V_2, \downarrow), ..., (V_N, \uparrow)\} \tag{1}$$

The flag '$\uparrow$' stands for a connected variable, whereas '$\downarrow$' stands for an unconnected variable. A connected variable is a variable which gets bound after rule aplication in a chain computation with a variable of a non-head daughter.

An example will clarify this definition. Let us look at the transitive reading of *eat* in figure 1, which we repeat here for expository purposes:

$$v([np(X), np(Y)], eats(X, Y)) \rightarrow [eats]. \tag{2}$$

The initial value of SemVars(eats) is $\{(X, \downarrow), (Y, \downarrow)\}$, i.e, initially, all variables in its semantic structure are unconnected. When computing the chain for this lexical entry, we first apply rule 3, obtaining a goal of the form:

$$vp([np(X), np(Y)], eats(X, Y)) \tag{3}$$

Since the variables in SemVars(eats) do not get bound with any variable of a non-head daughter, their status does not change. Then, we apply rule 4, obtaining the following situation:

$$vp([np(X)], eats(X, Y)) \rightarrow \underline{vp}([np(X), np(Y)], eats(\mathbf{X}, \mathbf{Y})), \ np(\mathbf{Y}). \tag{4}$$

We observe that variable Y in SemVars(eats) has been bound with a variable of the non-head daughter of the rule. Therefore, SemVars(eats) is now the following:

$$\{(X, \downarrow), (Y, \uparrow)\} \tag{5}$$

Now it is the turn to apply rule 1; the obtained goal is shown below:

$$s(eats(X, Y)) \rightarrow np(\mathbf{X}), \ \underline{vp}([np(X)], eats(\mathbf{X}, Y)) \tag{6}$$

Here variable X has been bound with a variable of a non-head daughter. Thus, the final situation of the Semvars(eats) structure is: $\{(X,\uparrow),(Y,\uparrow)\}$

Let us now turn to the intransitive reading of eat:

$$v([np(X)],eats(X,Y)) \rightarrow [eats]. \tag{7}$$

Again, its initial SemVars structure is $\{(X,\downarrow),(Y, \downarrow)\}$. When computing the chain for this lexical entry, we first apply rule 3, obtaining a goal of the form:

$$vp([np(X)],eats(X,Y)) \tag{8}$$

Afterwards we can only apply rule 1, since the intransitive reading of eat does not have any complements:

$$s(eats(X,Y)) \rightarrow np(\mathbf{X}),\ \underline{vp}([np(X)],eats(\mathbf{X},Y)). \tag{9}$$

Here variable X has been bound with a variable of a non-head daughter; however, variable Y has not been bound during the computation of the chain. Thus, the final situation of the SemVars(eats) structure is: $\{(X,\uparrow),(Y,\downarrow)\}$.

3.3 Non Instantiated Variables in Non Head Daughters

So far we have seen that structure SemVars indicates whether a variable in the semantic dimension of a lexical sign is going to bound a variable of a non-head daughter during the execution of a chain. Now we will concern us with a different problem, namely, whether during the execution of a chain, a non instantiated variable of a non-head daughter shows up. Consider the following infelicitious lexical entry:

$$v([np(Z),np(Y)],read(X,Y)) \rightarrow [reads]. \tag{10}$$

The chain for this lexical entry would be the same as the chain for the transitive reading of eat. After applying the rule 1, we would end up with a situation like the following:

$$s(eats(X,Y)) \rightarrow np(Z),\ \underline{vp}([np(Z)],eats(X,Y) \tag{11}$$

Note that this situation indicates that the generator would try to generate a non instantiated np. Therefore, we enrich our chains structure with information about the degree of instantiation of non-head daughters variables. As a result, chains look now like the following:

$$\langle (X_1,-),(X_2,+)...(X_N,+) \rangle \tag{12}$$

where '-' indicates non instantiated variables in non head daughters; '+' indicates fully instantiated variables in non head daughters. Of course, one is tempted to derive all the information related to the boundness degree of variables by inspecting lexical signs only. However, caution has to be taken with this approach. It is perfectly possible to have a non bound lexical variable that may get bound after applying a chain rule. A look at a rule for simple NP formation will clarify this point. Assume the following skeletal lexical entries:

(cat: noun, sem: rel: house, sem: def: X) → [house].

(cat:det , sem:def:yes) → [the]. $\tag{13}$

and the following chain rule:

rule NP formation

(cat:np,sem:S)→(cat:noun,sem:S,sem:def:D),(cat:det,sem:def:D). $\tag{14}$

It is clear that by inspecting solely the lexical entry for 'house' one cannot conclude whether a variable is going to be used or not. Variable 'DEF' is not used in the lexical entry for house, but it gets bound after applying the rule on NP formation.

4   Applications

In this section we present some applications of the previously shown method described to some known problems in Head-Driven Generation.

4.1   Preventing Over- and Undergeneration

Overgeneration has been defined as the production of sentences whose semantics is more specific than input semantics, and undergeneration has been defined as the production of sentences whose semantics is less specific than input semantics [5]. Following these definitions, a correct generator produces sentences whose semantics matches exactly with the input semantics. Matching is defined in terms of mutual subsumption between input and output semantics. Of course, an incorrect generator (i.e, a generator that produces sentences whose semantics do not match exactly input semantics) is generating sentences which are simply wrong. As reported in [4], [5] constraint-based generators follow the common practice of using the metalanguage (Prolog, for example) variables for object language variables in the semantic representation, which may lead to unwanted unification of variables taking inappropriate values.

Consider the lexical entries in figure 1 for the transitive and intransitive alternation of verb *eat*, and the following input semantics for *John eats a banana* : eats(john,banana). Both entries would qualify as lexical heads since they unify with input semantics. However, only the transitive one had to. As noted by [4], [5], a simple way to prevent unwanted unifications would be to ground our semantic representations. If the lexical entry for the intransitive entry for *eat* looked like the following:

$$vp([np(X)],eats(X,\mathbf{23})) \tag{15}$$

where **23** has to be understood as a fresh atom, then we would avoid the problem.

Assuming that the grounding process should be done automatically, how can we detect the variables to be ground ? The structure *SemVars* in section 2 provides the source of the necessary information to ground our variables; we refer to the the slogan : 'a variable which is not going to get bound is a good candidate to get ground'. We have seen in section 2 that the *SemVars* structure for the intransitive lexical entry of eat is the following:

$$\{(X,\uparrow),(Y,\downarrow)\} \tag{16}$$

Therefore, we observe that variable Y should be grounded.

4.2   Avoiding Failing Unifications

Unification is the most expensive operation performed in constraint-based frameworks [14]; therefore it is an interesting issue to avoid failing unifications by applying methods cheaper than unification. A crucial step in head-driven generation is the selection of the chain rules that connect lexical entries to the original semantics. The connection is done by selecting the appropriate chain rules, i.e. those rules whose semantic and syntactic features of the head-daughter node unify with the semantics of the lexical entry. Instead of applying each chain rule in turn, a straightforward application of our method consists in applying only those rules that appear in the chain derivation of a lexical entry. The results of this experiment are shown in next section.

5   Evaluation

We have tested two versions of the BUG algorithm with the medium-size lexicalized grammar described in [8]. The first version of the algorithm was the standard (non-deterministic) version. The second (more deterministic) version uses off-line compilation of chains. The grammar follows basically HPSG and covers a wide range of linguistic phenomena, including control and raising verbs, passive constructions, auxiliaries and long-distance dependencies. It contains about 1200 full-fledged lexical entries and 6 rule schemata. We have tested the performance of the two algorithm on 30 sentences; results are given below (average time per sentence):

Generator	Msec / sentence
Standard BUG	467
Deterministic BUG	278

Mean string length was 5.5 words per sentence. On the other hand, the method correctly predicted problematic constructions related to object to raising constructions and transitive/intransitive alternations (like verb to eat).

6   Conclusion

The off-line compilation technique described here treats some well known limitations on Head-driven generation on a uniform basis. It has several advantages for generating with contraint-based grammars:

1. Problems related to uninstantiated variables occurring in run time can predicted off-line. Thus, some adaptations prior to processing can be made.
2. Efficiency is improved compared to the standard BUG algorithm.
3. The method is especially suitable for lexicalist frameworks, where lexical entries have considerable internal structure. Note that in lexicalist frameworks syntactic covariation is expressed in different lexical entries rather than in multiple grammar rules. Thus, there will be one or few chains for each lexical entry.
4. The method is compatible with other techniques designed to improve efficiency (memoization, chart generation,...).

References

1. van Noord, G.: Reversibility in Natural Language Processing , PhD Thesis, University of Utrecht. (1993)
2. Strzalkowski, T. (ed.): Reversible Grammar In Natural Language Processing. Kluwer Academic Publisher, Dordrecht, The Nederlands (1994)
3. Neumann, G.: Interleaving Natural Language Parsing and Generation through Uniform Processing. In Artificial Intelligence(99)1, 121–163 (1998)
4. Shieber, S., van Noord, G., Pereira, F., Moore, R.: Semantic-Head-Driven Generation. In Computational Linguistics, vol 16(1),30–43 (1990)
5. Wedekind, J.: Generation as structure driven derivation. In Proceedings of Coling-88, Budapest, Hungary (1988)
6. Gerdemann, D., Hinrichs, E.: Some Open Problems in Head-Driven Generation. In Linguistics and Computation, CSLI (1996)

7. Pollard ,C., Sag, I.: Head-Driven Phrase Structure Grammar. Chicago University Press, Chicago and CSLI Publications, Stanford (1994)
8. Sag, I., Wasow, T.: Syntactic Theory: A Formal Introduction. CSLI Publications (1999)
9. Torisawa,K., Tsujii, J.: Computing Phrasal-Signs in HPSG prior to Parsing. In Proceedings of Coling-96, Copenhagen, Denmark (1996)
10. Kasper, R., Kiefer, B., Netter, K.: Compilation of HPSG to TAG. In Proceedings of ACL-95 (1995)
11. Samuelsson, C.: An efficient algorithm for surface generation. In Proceedings of the Fourteenth International Joint Conference on Artificial Intelligence, Montreal, Canada (1995)
12. Minnen, G. : Off-line Compilation for Efficient Processing with Constraint-logic Grammars, PhD Thesis, University of Tübingen (1998)
13. Wintner, S., Gabrilovich E., Francez, N.: AMALIA – a unified platform for parsing and generation. In Recent Advances in Natural Language Processing (RANLP-97), Tzigoz Chark, Bulgaria (1997)
14. Kiefer, B., Krieger, H., Carroll, J., Malouf, R.: A Bag of Useful Techniques for Efficient and Robust Parsing. In Proceedings of ACl 1999 (1999)

Generation of Incremental Parsers

Manuel Vilares, Miguel A. Alonso, and Victor M. Darriba

Department of Informatics, Campus As Lagoas s/n, 32004 Orense, Spain
{vilares,darriba}@uvigo.es alonso@udc.es
http://www.grupocole.org

Abstract. An incremental development environment for unrestricted context-free languages is described and tested. Our proposal includes a parse generator, an incremental facility to make the overall parsing efficient in the context of program development; and a graphical interface that provides a complete set of customization and trace facilities. The tool, baptized ICE after Incremental Context-Free Environment, appears to be superior to other general context-free parsing environments and is comparable to deterministic ones, when the context is not ambiguous.

1 Introduction

There are many reasons for the development of incremental parsing in natural language. Initially, interest was shown in it due to the need for efficient handling of arbitrary changes within current input during text composition in language-sensitive editors. Here, incremental parsing can be used to increase the efficiency of the overall parsing process, in a context where several consecutive corrections of the text are usually made. This means that preparing a text requires significantly less effort than developing it from scratch. Another application that can motivate incremental parsing is the growing importance of highly interactive and real-time systems, where the analysis process must be prompted immediately at the onset of new input. Incrementality is also required in systems allowing incomplete parsing, as is the case of speech recognition [4,5], where the input language can only be approximately defined, and individual inputs can vary widely from the norm. Finally, the incremental facility can be of interest in parse systems capable of combining pieces of information from different sources of knowledge. This is the case of systems involving multimodal communication.

In our proposal, parser generation is inspired by BISON [2], which we have extended in order to deal with general context-free grammars (CFGs). Parsing is stated in the context of parallel methods, a variation of Earley's construction [3] proposed by Lang [6] that separates the execution strategy from the implementation of the push-down automaton (PDA).

Finally, incremental parsing within general context-free parsing has been addressed by van den Brand [11] and Rekers [7]. Both authors take the variable covering the modification as a parameter to which the text that is to be parsed should be reduced, to prevent the system from doing unnecessary work during the search for this minimal node, for example, when the input contains an error.

A. Gelbukh (Ed.): CICLing 2003, LNCS 2588, pp. 191–202, 2003.

Instead, we update runs in parallel to the parsing [12], which ensures the earlier detection of errors, thus avoiding any unnecessary work.

2   Parser Generation

Parser construction is an extension from BISON [2] in order to permit the generation of extended LALR(1) PDAs. More explicitly, the generation of tables has been re-implemented in order to deal with both incremental and non-deterministic parsing. We direct our attention to constraining the space bounds for the generation process, which involves to the consideration of default actions as well as array compacting methods in the PDA.

The language representing all possible elementary actions in the PDA allows us to decompose complex actions in terms of simple push and pop transitions, which constitutes the basis for introducing dynamic programming in the parsing process. In order to take care of the trace of pop transitions in reduce actions, possibly in the context of non-deterministic interpretation, the system also provides the facility to go back over the schema in the automata. What follows is a short description of tables and functionalities:

- yytranslate: vector mapping yylex□stokens into user's token numbers. The token translation table is indexed by a token number as returned by the user's yylex routine. It yields the internal token number used by the parser.
- yyr1[r]: symbol that rule r derives.
- yyr2[r]: number of symbols composing the right hand side of rule r.
- yydefact[s]: default rule to reduce within state s, when yytable does not specify something else to do.
- yydefgoto[i]: default state to go to after a reduction that generates variable YYNTBASE + i, except when yytable specifies something else to do.
- yypact[s]: index in yytable of the portion describing state s. The lookahead token type is used to index that portion to find out what to do. If the value in yytable is positive, it indexes the corresponding elementary action on yyautomaton If the value is zero, the default action from yydefact[s] is used. We can avoid the access to yytable in the following cases:
  - If the only action in state s is the default one. This case can be detected in three different forms without accessing to yytable
    * When yypact[s] = YYFLAG.
    * When yypact[s] + lookahead < 0.
    * When yypact[s] + lookahead > YYLAST.
  - If the current action is the default one, we can also avoid the access to yytable when $yycheck[yypact[s] + lookahead] \neq lookahead$, as will be explained below.
- yypgoto[i]: the index in yytable of the portion describing what to do after reducing a rule that derives variable YYNTBASE + i. This portion is indexed by the parser state number as if the text for this non-terminal had been previously read. The value from yytable is the state to go to. We can avoid the access to yytable when the action to apply is the default one:

- When yypgoto[i] + state ≥ 0.
- When yypgoto[i] + state ≤ YYLAST.
- When yycheck[yypact[s] + state] ≠ state.

- yytable vector with portions for different uses, found via yypact and yypgoto
- yycheck vector indexed in parallel with yytable It indicates, in a roundabout way, the bounds of the portion you are trying to examine. Suppose that the portion of yytable starts at index p and the index to be examined within the portion is i. Then if yycheck[p+i] ≠ i, i is outside the bounds of what is actually allocated, and the default from yydefact or yydefgoto should be used. Otherwise, yytable[p+i] should be used.
- yyautomaton vector containing the descriptors for actions in the automaton: block → 0, halt → 1, non-determinism → 2, reduce → 3, shift → 4.
- yystos[s]: the accessing symbol for the state s. In other words, the symbol that represents the last thing accepted to reach that state.
- yyreveaLmap[s]: index in yyreveal of the portion that contains all the states having a transition over the state s.
- yyreveal vector indexed by yyreveaLmap that groups together all the states with a common transition.

where we have considered the following set of constants:

- YYFINAL: the termination state. The only state where a halt is possible.
- YYFLAG: the most negative short integer. Used to flag in yypact.
- YYLAST: the final state, whose accessing symbol is the end of input. It has a only one transition, over YYFINAL. So, we obey the parser's strategy of making all decisions one token ahead of its actions.
- YYNTBASE: the total number of tokens, including the end of input.

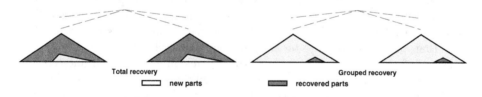

Fig. 1. Practical incremental recovery

3 Standard Parsing

Our aim is to parse a sentence $w_{1...n} = w_1 \ldots w_n$ of length n, according to a CFG $\mathcal{G} = (N, \Sigma, P, S)$, where N is the set of non-terminals, Σ the set of terminal symbols, P the rules and S the start symbol. The empty string will be represented by ε. We generate from $\mathcal{G}$ a PDA having as finite-state control a LALR(1) automaton built as indicated in Sect. 2. The direct execution of PDAs may be exponential with respect to the length of the input string and may even loop. To get polynomial complexity, we must avoid duplicating stack contents when several transitions may be applied to a given configuration. Instead of storing all the information about a configuration, we must determine the information we need to trace in order to retrieve that configuration. This information is stored into a table $\mathcal{I}$ of items:

$$\mathcal{I} = \left\{ [st, X, i, j], \ st \in \mathcal{S}, \ X \in N \cup \Sigma \cup \{\nabla_{r,s}\}, \ 0 \le i \le j \right\}$$

where $\mathcal{S}$ is the set of states in the LALR(1) automaton. Each configuration of the PDA is represented by an item storing the current state st, the element X placed on the top of the stack and the positions i and j indicating the substring $w_{i+1} \ldots w_j$ spanned by X. The symbol $\nabla_{r,s}$ indicates that the final part $A_{r,s+1} \ldots A_{r,n_r}$ of a context-free rule $A_{r,0} \to A_{r,1} \ldots A_{r,n_r}$ has been recognized.

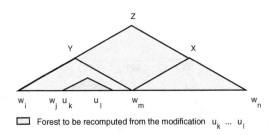

Forest to be recomputed from the modification $u_k \ \cdots \ u_l$

Fig. 2. A pop transition $XY \mapsto Z$ totally recovering a modification

We describe the parser using Parsing Schemata, a framework for high-level description of parsing algorithms [9]. A parsing scheme is a triple $\langle \mathcal{I}, \mathcal{H}, \mathcal{D} \rangle$, with $\mathcal{I}$ a set of items, $\mathcal{H} = \{[a, i, i+1], \ a = w_i\}$ an initial set of special items called hypothesis that encodes the sentence to be parsed[1], and $\mathcal{D}$ a set of deduction steps that allow new items to be derived from already known items. Deduction steps are of the form $\{\eta_1, \ldots, \eta_k \vdash \xi \mid \text{conds}\}$, meaning that if all antecedents η_i of a deduction step are present and the conditions conds are satisfied, then the consequent ξ should be generated by the parser[2]. In the case of the parsing algorithm we propose, the set of deduction steps is the following one

$$\mathcal{D} = \mathcal{D}^{\text{Init}} \cup \mathcal{D}^{\text{Shift}} \cup \mathcal{D}^{\text{Sel}} \cup \mathcal{D}^{\text{Red}} \cup \mathcal{D}^{\text{Head}}$$

where

$$\mathcal{D}^{\text{Init}} = \left\{ \vdash [st_0, -, 0, 0] \right\}$$

---

[1] The empty string, ε, is represented by the empty set of hypothesis, $\emptyset$. An input string $w_{1\ldots n}$, $n \ge 1$ is represented by $\{[w_1, 0, 1], [w_2, 1, 2], \ldots, [w_n, n-1, n]\}$.

[2] Parsing schemata are closely related to *grammatical deduction systems* [8], where items are called *formula schemata*, deduction steps are *inference rules*, hypothesis are *axioms* and final items are *goal formulas*.

$$\mathcal{D}^{\text{Shift}} = \{[q, X, i, j] \vdash [q', a, j, j+1] \; \Big/ \begin{array}{l} \exists \, [a, j, j+1] \in \mathcal{H} \\ \text{shift}_{q'} \in \text{action}(q, a) \end{array} \}$$

$$\mathcal{D}^{\text{Sel}} = \{[st, X, i, j] \vdash [st, \nabla_{r,n_r}, j, j] \; \Big/ \begin{array}{l} \exists \, [a, j, j+1] \in \mathcal{H} \\ \text{reduce}_r \in \text{action}(st, a) \end{array} \}$$

$$\mathcal{D}^{\text{Red}} = \{[st, \nabla_{r,s}, k, j][st, X_{r,s}, i, k] \vdash [st', \nabla_{r,s-1}, i, j], st' \in \text{reveal}(st)\}$$

$$\mathcal{D}^{\text{Head}} = \{ \, [st, \nabla_{r,0}, i, j] \vdash [st', A_{r,0}, i, j], st' \in \text{goto}(st, A_{r,0}) \, \}$$

with $X \in N \cup \Sigma$, st referring to the initial state and action, goto and reveal referring to the tables that encode the behavior of the LALR(1) automaton:

- The action table determines what action should be taken for a given state and lookahead. In the case of shift actions, it determines the resulting new state and in the case of reduce actions, the rule which is to be applied for the reduction.
- The goto table determines what the state will be after performing a reduce action. Each entry is accessed using the current state and the non-terminal, which is the left-hand side of the rule to be applied for reduction.
- The reveal table is used to traverse the finite state control of the automaton backwards: $st^i \in \text{reveal}(st^{i+1})$ is equivalent to $st^{i+1} \in \text{goto}(st^i, X)$ if $X \in N$, and is equivalent to $\text{shift}_{st^{i+1}} \in \text{action}(st^i, X)$ if $X \in \Sigma$.

As is shown in [1], this set of deduction steps is equivalent to the dynamic interpretation of non-deterministic PDAS:

- A deduction step Init is in charge of starting the parsing process.
- A deduction step Shift corresponds to pushing a terminal a onto the top of the stack when the action to be performed is a shift to state st'.
- A step Sel corresponds to pushing the ∇_{r,n_r} symbol onto the top of the stack in order to start the reduction of a rule r.
- The reduction of a rule of length $n_r > 0$ is performed by a set of n_r steps Red, each of them corresponding to a pop transition replacing the two elements $\nabla_{r,s} X_{r,s}$ placed on the top of the stack by the element $\nabla_{r,s-1}$.
- The reduction of a rule r is finished by a step Head corresponding to a swap transition that replaces the top element $\nabla_{r,0}$ by the left-hand side $A_{r,0}$ of that rule and performs the corresponding change of state.

Deduction steps are applied until new items cannot be generated. The splitting of reductions into a set of Red steps allow us to share computations corresponding to partial reductions of rules, attaining a worst case time complexity $\mathcal{O}(n^3)$ and a worst case space complexity $\mathcal{O}(n^2)$ with respect to the length n of the input string. The input string has been successfully recognized if the final item $[st_f, S, 0, n]$, with st_f final state of the PDA, has been generated.

Following [6], we represent the shared parse forest corresponding to the input string by means of an output grammar $\mathcal{G}_o = (N_o, \Sigma_o, P_o, S_o)$, where N_o is the set of all items, Σ_o is the set of terminals in the input string, the start symbol S_o corresponds to the final item generated by the parser, and a rule in P_o is generated each time a deduction step is applied:

- For Shift, a production $[st', a, j, j+1] \rightarrow a$ is generated.
- For Sel, a production $[st, \nabla_{r,n_r}, j, j] \rightarrow \varepsilon$ is generated .
- For Red, a production $[st', \nabla_{r,s-1}, i, j] \rightarrow [st, \nabla_{r,s}, k, j][st, A_{r,s}, i, k]$ is generated.
- For Head, a production $[st', A_{r,0}, i, j] \rightarrow [st, \nabla_{r,0}, i, j]$ is generated.

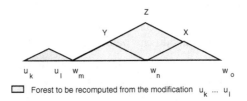

Fig. 3. A pop transition $XY \mapsto Z$ independent of the modification

4   Incremental Parsing

Incremental parsing has been attempted in two senses: firstly, as an extension of left-to-right editing, and secondly, in relation with the full editing capability on the input string. We are interested in the latter, called full incrementality, in the domain of general CFGs, without editing restrictions, guaranteeing the same level of sharing as in standard mode, but without any impact. In practice we have focused on two cases, shown in Fig. 1:

- Total recovery, when recovery is possible on all the syntactic context once the modification has been parsed.
- Grouped recovery, when recovery is possible for all branches on an interval of the input string to be re-parsed.

which allows us to increase the computational efficiency by avoiding the recovery of isolated trees in a forest corresponding to an ambiguous node. We consider a simplified text-editing scenario with a single modification, in order to favor understanding. Let's take a modified input string from a previously parsed initial one. We must update the altered portion of the original shared forest. To do so, it is sufficient to find a condition capable of ensuring that all possible transitions to be applied from a given position in an interval in the input string are independent from the introduced modification. We focus our attention on those transitions dependent on the past of the parsing, that is, on pop transitions. If the portion of the input to be parsed is the same, and the parts of the past to be used in this piece of the process are also the same, the parsing will be also the same in this portion. That corresponds to different scopes in this common past: when this extends to the totality of the structures to be used in the remaining parsing process, we have total recovery, as is shown in Fig. 2. If it only extends to a region after the modification, we have grouped recovery, as is shown in Fig. 3.

To ensure that pop transitions are common between two consecutive parses, in an interval of the unchanged input string, we focus on the set of items which are arguments of potential future pops. This is the case of items resulting from non-empty reductions before a shift. These items can be located in a simple fashion, which guarantees a low impact in standard parsing.

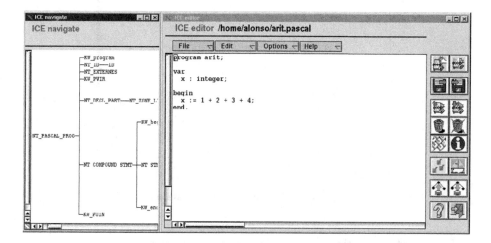

Fig. 4. Analyzing a program

To now find a condition ensuring that all pop transitions from any given transition, taking one of these items as argument, are common in an interval, we use the notion of the back pointer i of items $[st, X, i, j]$. When corresponding items between consecutive parses have equivalent back pointers, incremental recovery is possible. Back pointers are equivalent iff they point to a position of the input string not modified since the previous parsing, or when they are associated to a position corresponding to a token belonging to a modified part of the input string. In the first case, we can ensure total recovery since both parses have returned to a common past. In the second one, we can only ensure grouped recovery since common computations are only possible while there are no pop transitions returning on the scope of the modification, which limits the extension of the interval to be recovered.

5   User Interface

The tool helps the language designer in the task of writing grammars, with a dedicated editor. At any moment the user can request a parse of the grammar, which is done according to the parsing scheme chosen in advance, from an input file written in a BISON-like format. A view of the interface is shown in Fig. 4.

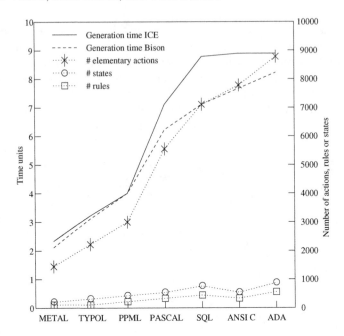

Fig. 5. Results on parser generation

The interface for the programming environment allows the user to choose the parsing mode, standard or incremental, and load a language generated in advance. A set of options allows the user to choose the class of information reported: conflicts that have been detected, statistics about the amount of work generated and so on. Debugging facilities also incorporate information about the recovery process during incremental parsing, and errors are always reported. The interface allows parse forests to be recovered and manipulated. We can also select the language in which the system interacts with us: English, French and Spanish are currently available. A help facility is always available to solve questions about the editors and the incremental facilities.

6   Experimental Results

We have compared ICE with BISON [2], GLR [7] and SDF [10], which are to the best of our knowledge some of the most efficient parsing environments, from two different points of view: parser generation and parsing process. We also show the efficiency of incremental parsing in relation to the standard one, and the capability of ICE to share computations. In order to provide a classical point of reference, we have also included the original Earley's parsing scheme [3] in ICE. All the measurements have been performed using generic time units.

In relation to parser generation, we took several known programming languages and extracted the time used to generate parser tables, comparing BISON

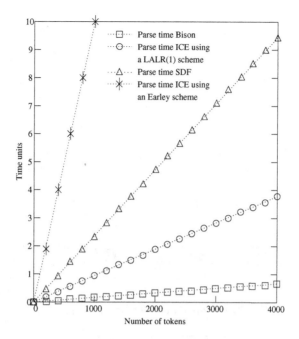

Fig. 6. Results on deterministic parsing

with the generation of LALR(1) schema in ICE[3]. Results are given in relation to different criteria. So, Fig. 5 shows these according to the number of rules in the grammar, and to the number of states associated with the finite state machine generated from them[4]. At this point, it is important to note that the behavior of ANSI-C does not seem to correspond to the rest of the programming languages considered in the same test. In effect, the number of rules in the grammar, and the number of states in the resulting PDA may not be in direct relation with the total amount of work necessary to build it. In order to explain this, we introduce the concept of elementary building action as an action representing one of the following two situations: the introduction of items in the base or in the closure of a state in the PDA, and the generation of transitions between two states.

We use the syntax of complete PASCAL as a guideline for parsing tests. In Fig. 6 comparisons are established between parsers generated by ICE[5], BISON and SDF, when the context is deterministic. We consider ICE, SDF and GLR when the context is non-deterministic, as is shown in Fig. 7. We have considered two versions for PASCAL: deterministic and non-deterministic, the latter including ambiguity for arithmetic expressions. Given that in the case of ICE, SDF and GLR mapping between concrete and abstract syntax is fixed, we have generated in the case of BISON, a simple recognizer. To reduce the impact of lexical time,

---

[3] Earley's algorithm is a grammar oriented method.

[4] BISON and ICE generate LALR(1) machines, SDF LR(0) ones.

[5] Using both, LALR(1) and Earley's schema.

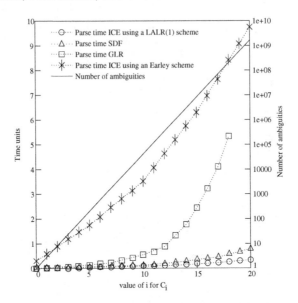

Fig. 7. Results on non-deterministic parsing

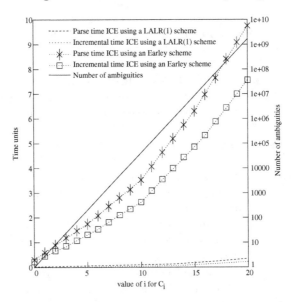

Fig. 8. Results on incremental and standard parsing using ICE

we have considered, in the case of non-deterministic parsing, programs of the form:

$$\textbf{program } P \textbf{ (input, output); var } a, b : \textbf{ integer};$$
$$\textbf{begin} \quad a := b\{+b\}^i \qquad \qquad \textbf{end}.$$

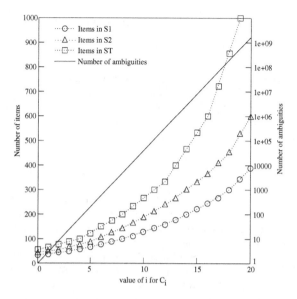

Fig. 9. Items generated using S^1, S^2 and S^T schema.

where i is the number of $+$'s. The grammar contains a rule `Expr ::= Expr + Expr`, therefore these programs have a number of ambiguous parses which grows exponentially with i. This number is:

$$C_0 = C_1 = 1 \quad \text{and} \quad C_i = \binom{2i}{i} \frac{1}{i+1}, \text{ if } i > 1$$

All tests have been performed using the same input programs for each one of the parsers and the time needed to "print" parse trees was not measured. To illustrate incrementality, we analyze the previous programs in which we substitute expressions $b + b$ by b. Results corresponding to incremental and standard parsing are shown in Fig. 8, and those related to sharing in Fig. 9.

7   Conclusions

The ICE system is devoted to simultaneous editing of language definitions and programs, in the domain of unrestricted context-free languages. The modular composition includes a parser generator, standard and incremental parse interpretation and a graphic interface, where customizations can be carried out either interactively, or through an initialization file. In a practical comparison, our algorithm seems to surpass previous proposals.

Although efficient incremental parsing may have seemed a difficult problem, we were able to keep the complexity of the algorithm low. So, practical tests have proved the validity of the approach proposed when the number of ambiguities remains reasonable, as is the case in practice. In addition, ICE is compatible with the standard parser generators in UNIX, which permits a free use of all the input that has been developed for these generators.

Acknowledgments. This work has been partially supported by the European Union, Government of Spain and Autonomous Government of Galicia under projects 1FD97-0047-C04-02, TIC2000-0370-C02-01 and PGIDT99XI10502B, respectively.

References

1. M.A. Alonso, D. Cabrero, and M. Vilares. Construction of efficient generalized LR parsers. In Derick Wood and Sheng Yu, editors, *Automata Implementation*, volume 1436 of *Lecture Notes in Computer Science*, pages 7–24. Springer-Verlag, Berlin-Heidelberg-New York, 1998.
2. Charles Donnelly and Richard Stallman. *Bison: the YACC-compatible Parser Generator, Bison Version 1.28.* Free Software Foundation, 675 Mass Ave, Cambridge, MA 02139, USA, Tel: (617) 876-3296, USA, January 1999.
3. J. Earley. An efficient context-free parsing algorithm. *Communications of the ACM*, 13(2):94–102, 1970.
4. H. Höge and E. Marschall. Statistical analysis of left-to-right parser for word-hypothesing. *NATO ASI Series*, F46:297–303, 1988.
5. M. Kay. Algorithm schemata and data structures in syntactic processing. Technical report, XEROX Palo Alto Research Center, Palo Alto, California, U.S.A., 1980.
6. Bernard Lang. Deterministic techniques for efficient non-deterministic parsers. In J. Loeckx, editor, *Automata, Languages and Programming*, number 14 in Lecture Notes in Computer Science, pages 255–269. Springer, Berlin, DE, 1974.
7. J. Rekers. *Parser Generation for Interactive Environments.* PhD thesis, University of Amsterdam, Amsterdam, The Netherlands, 1992.
8. S.M. Shieber, Y. Schabes, and F.C.N. Pereira. Principles and implementation of deductive parsing. *Journal of Logic Programming*, 1-2:3–36, 1995.
9. K. Sikkel. *Parsing Schemata.* PhD thesis, Univ. of Twente, The Netherlands, 1993.
10. Mark van den Brand, Paul Klint, and Pieter A. Olivier. Compilation and memory management for ASF+SDF. In *93*, page 15. Centrum voor Wiskunde en Informatica (CWI), ISSN 1386-369X, February 28 1999. SEN (Software Engineering (SEN)).
11. M.G.J. van den Brand. *A Generator for Incremental Programming Environments.* PhD thesis, Katholieke Universiteit Nijmegen, Nijmegen, The Netherlands, 1992.
12. M. Vilares. *Efficient Incremental Parsing for Context-Free Languages.* PhD thesis, University of Nice. ISBN 2-7261-0768-0, France, 1992.

Computing with Realizational Morphology

Lauri Karttunen

Palo Alto Research Center,
3333 Coyote Hill Road, Palo Alto, CA 94304
karttunen@parc.com
http://www.parc.xerox.com/istl/members/karttune

Abstract. The theory of realizational morphology presented by Stump in his influential book *Inflectional Morphology* (2001) describes the derivation of inflected surface forms from underlying lexical forms by means of ordered blocks of realization rules. The theory presents a rich formalism for expressing generalizations about phenomena commonly found in the morphological systems of natural languages.

This paper demonstrates that, in spite of the apparent complexity of Stump's formalism, the system as a whole is no more powerful than a collection of regular relations. Consequently, a Stump-style description of the morphology of a particular language such as Lingala or Bulgarian can be compiled into a finite-state transducer that maps the underlying lexical representations directly into the corresponding surface forms or forms, and vice versa, yielding a single lexical transducer.

For illustration we will present an explicit finite-state implementation of an analysis of Lingala based on Stump's description and other sources.

1 Introduction

Morphology is a domain of linguistics that studies the formation of words. It is traditional to distinguish between surface forms and their analyses, called lemmas. The lemma for a surface form such as the English word `bigger` typically consists of the traditional dictionary citation form of the word together with terms that convey the morphological properties of the particular form. For example, the lemma for `bigger` might be represented as `big+Adj+Comp` to indicate that `bigger` is the comparative form of the adjective `big`. Alternatively, the morphological properties might be encoded in terms of attribute-value pairs: `Cat:Adj, Degr:Comp`.

There are two challenges in modeling natural-language morphology:

1. **Morphotactics**
   Words are typically composed of smaller units: stems and affixes that must be combined in a certain order. Most languages build words by concatenation but some languages also exhibit non-concatenative processes such as interdigitation and reduplication [3].
2. **Morphological Alternations**
   The shape of the components that make up the word often depends on their

A. Gelbukh (Ed.): CICLing 2003, LNCS 2588, pp. 203–214, 2003.
© Springer-Verlag Berlin Heidelberg 2003

context. For example, the comparative degree of adjectives in English is expressed sometimes by -er, sometimes by -r, and the stem may also vary, as in bigger.

Computational linguists generally take it for granted that the relation between the surface forms of a language and their corresponding lemmas can be described as a regular relation [4]. If the relation is regular, it can be defined using the metalanguage of regular expressions; and, with a suitable compiler, the regular expression source code can be compiled into a finite-state transducer that implements the relation computationally. In the resulting transducer, each path (= sequence of states and arcs) from the initial state to a final state represents a mapping between a surface form and its lemma, also known as the lexical form.

Comprehensive lexical transducers have been created for a great number of languages including most of the European languages, Turkish, Arabic, Korean, and Japanese. They are commercially available through companies such as **Inxight**.

2   Realizational Morphology

The success of finite-state morphology has so far had very little impact within linguistics as an academic discipline. Practical issues that arise in the context of real-life applications such as completeness of coverage, physical size, and speed of applications are irrelevant from an academic morphologist's point of view. The main purpose of a morphologist writing to an audience of fellow linguists is to be convincing that his theory of word formation provides a more insightful and elegant account of this aspect of the human linguistic endowment than the competing theories and formalisms.

Gregory Stump's work on PARADIGM FUNCTION MORPHOLOGY [17] is a contribution to a theoretical tradition that goes back to Matthews [15], including works by authors such as Zwicky [18] and Anderson [1]. In these INFERENTIAL-REALIZATIONAL theories, as Stump characterizes them, the presence of affixes in the inflected form of a word arises from rules that express some morphological property or a combination of properties that are present in its lexical representation. The paradigm functions that generate all the possible forms of a word from all of its valid lexical representations are defined in terms of REALIZATION RULES, also called RULES OF EXPONENCE. These rules all have the general form shown in Table 1. The subscript n is an index for a particular block of rules; τ

$$RR_{n,\tau,C}(< X,\sigma >) =_{def} < Y',\sigma >$$

Table 1. A Template for Realization Rules

is the set of morphological features that are realized by the application of the rule; C is the lexical category that the rule is concerned with; X is a phonological input string that is either a part of the lexical representation or has been derived by realization rules that have already been applied, σ is a set of morphosyntactic properties (= features), and Y' is the resulting output string. The derivation of Y' may involve several steps. The first output of the rule, Y, is produced by adding some (possibly zero) affix to X and subjecting the result to any number of applicable morphophonological rules. An example of Stump's morphophonological rules is given in Table 2 (Stump p. 48). If no morphophonological rule is

If X=W[vowel$_1$] and Y = [vowel$_2$]Z, then the indicated [vowel$_1$] is absent from Y' and the indicated [vowel$_2$] is stressed in Y' iff [vowel$_1$] is stressed in Y.

Table 2. A Morphophonological Rule

applicable, Y' consists of the input form X possibly with some added phonological material as in Table 3. This rule is in Block B and realizes the present tense of a verb as e' suffixed to the end of the stem.

$$RR_{B,Tns:pres,V}(< X, \sigma >) =_{def} < Xe', \sigma >$$

Table 3. A Simple Realization Rule

The rule blocks are applied in a given order. Within each block the rules are in principle unordered but ranked by PANINI'S PRINCIPLE: If two or more rules could apply, the most specific one takes precedence and the others do not apply.

Realization rules may also be specified in terms of other realization rules. Such rules Stump calls RULES OF REFERRAL. For example, if there is a rule that expresses some set of features by a given affix, another rule can be derived from it by modifying the feature set but retaining the affix. This is an important aspect of Stumps formalism because it gives an account of SYNCRETISM, that is, cases where the same affix appears in several places in a paradigm, possibly associated with different morphological properties. For example, in the case of the Lingala inflected form bababetaki 'they hit them', the same affix ba encodes both subject and object agreement features.

Lexical representations are of the general form $< Stem, Features >$ where Stem is a phonological representation and Features is some collection of attribute-value pairs. For example, the lexical representation of the Lingala inflected form bambetaki 'they hit me' might have a lexical representation shown in Table 4.

$< bet, Sub : [Per : 3, Num : Pl, Gen : 1, 2], Obj : [Per : 1, Num : Sg], Tns : Past : Hist >$

Table 4. A Lexical Form

The underlying stem of the verb is bet and its feature set consists of three attributes Sub, Obj, and Tns whose values encode the subject and object agreement features and tense.

3   Formal and Computational Issues

Formal precision and unambiguous notation are clearly important for Stump but there is no discussion in the book about what the formal power of Realizational Morphology might be. It is obvious that the underlying lexical representations constitute a REGULAR LANGUAGE. Although the features may have set values, there is no recursion. All the examples of realization rules given by Stump seem to represent REGULAR RELATIONS. The same is clearly true of Stump's morphophonological rules that are essentially rewrite rules in the old Chomsky-Halle tradition [5]. As was first shown by Johnson [8] and subsequently by Kaplan and Kay [10], such rules represent regular relations. They can be written as regular expressions and compiled into transducers. If the lexicon itself is regular and if all the realization rules and morphophonological rules are regular, it is possible to compile the lexicon and the rules individually to finite-state automata and to compose them into a single transducer.

The possibility of a finite-state implementation of realizational morphology is not surprising to computational linguists. Lexical transducers have already been constructed for a great number of languages using other finite-state formalisms. However, it is not as evident that this can be done without losing the theoretical advantages of the framework. Notions such as Panini's Principle for resolving competition between competing rules and Stump's rules of referral have no obvious finite-state implementation. In the next section we will show that rules of exponence and rules of referral can be expressed simply and elegantly as regular expressions and compiled with the publicly available PARC/XRCE **xfst** tool [4].

A finite-state implementation of realizational morphology has a fundamental advantage over the implementations in systems such as DATR/KATR proposed by Finkel and Stump [7]. A system of realization rules expressed as a DATR theory can be used to generate an inflected surface form from its lexical description but such a system is not directly usable for recognition. In contrast, finite-state transducers are bidirectional. The same transducer can generate an inflected form from its underlying representation or analyze it into a lexical stem or stems and the associated feature bundles.

4   Application to Lingala

In this section we will show in detail how Realizational Morphology can be expressed in terms of the PARC/XRCE regular expression calculus as defined in Beesley and Karttunen [4]. The regular expressions given in this section constitute a script that can be directly compiled with the **xfst** tool. The data and the analysis of Lingala come from Chapter 5 in Stump's book, from a short monograph on Lingala by Meeuwis [16], and from Michael Gasser's course notes at http://www.indiana.edu/~gasser/L103/hw10.html. Lingala is a Bantu language spoken in Kinshasa and along the Congo river. Like other Bantu languages, Lingala has an elaborate system of noun classes or genders. The verbs contain affixes that mark agreement with the verb's subject's and object's person, number, and gender properties.

4.1   Features

We start with the auxiliary definitions in Table 5. The **xfst** tool interprets the command **define** as the instruction to bind the next symbol to the network compiled from the regular expression that follows. The stems of Lingala are assigned to the variable **Stem**. In this case, the set includes just the stem for the verb meaning 'hit'. The braces around **bet** indicate that the stem consists of a sequence of single-character symbols: b e t. The variable L is defined as the surface alphabet (the union of all lower-case letters). The vertical bar is the UNION operator. Following Stump, we ignore tones here.

```
define Stems {bet} ;
define L [a|b|c|d|e|f|g|h|i|j|k|l|m|n|o|p|q|r|s|t|u|v|w|x|y|z];
```

Table 5. Auxiliary Definitions

The next step consist of defining the feature set. To make comparisons easy, we closely follow Stump's notation altough it makes things more cumbersome than they would need to be otherwise. A feature consists of an attribute, such as **Per** for 'person' and a value such as 1. For the sake of legibility, we separate them with a colon (quoted for technical reasons). The definitions for Person, Number, Gender, and Tense are expressed in Table 6. The value of the variable **Person1** for example, is a sequence consisting of three symbols: Per, :, and 1.

```
define Person1 [Per ":" 1];
define Person2 [Per ":" 2];
define Person3 [Per ":" 3];
define Number  [Num ":" [Sg | Pl] ];
define Gender3 [Gen ":" [1 "." 2 | 1a "." 2 | 3 "." 4 | 5 "." 6 |
                         7 "." 8 | 9a "." 10a | 10 | 11 "." 6 |
                         14 "." 6 | 15]];
define PastTense [Past ":" [Rec|Hist|MoreRem|MostRem]];
define PresTense [Pres ":" [Cont|Hab1|Hab2]];
define FutTense [Fut ":" [Immed|MostRem]];
```

Table 6. Features with Atomic Values

The next set of feature definitions in Table 7 makes reference to features already defined in Table 6. For example, the **Tense** feature consists of words such as Tns:Past:Rec and Tns:Fut:Immed. The definition of **Agreement** includes values such as Per:1 Num:Pl and Per:3 Num:Sg Gen:5.6 . These values are to be interpreted as sets containing a number of features separated a space.

The definition of Agreement feature in Table 8 builds on the definition of the Agreement values in Table 7. There is a minor complication here. Gender 15 is not expressed at all as an object marker. As a subject marker it only exists in the singular. For this reason we have to eliminate some otherwise possible strings by subtraction. The dollar sign in Figure 8 is called the CONTAINS operator.

```
define Tense [Tns ":" [PastTense|PresTense|FutTense]];
define Agreement [[[Person1 | Person2] " " Number] |
                   [Person3 " " Number " " Gender3]];
```

Table 7. Features with Set Values

$15 denotes the language of strings that somewhere contain 15. The & operator represents INTERSECTION. Thus [$P1 & $15] denotes strings that contain both Pl (= plural) and gender 15.

```
define SubjAgr [Sub ":" Agreement]  - [$P1 & $15];
define ObjAgr  [Obj ":" Agreement] - $15 ;
define Agr     [Func ":" Agreement];
```

Table 8. Subject and Object Agreement Features

We now have nearly all the definitions we need to define the lexical forms of Lingala in the style of realizational morphology. The final definitions are in Table 9. The verb lexicon consists of forms such as <bet,Sub:Per:3 Num:Sg Gen:14,6 Obj:Per:2 Num:Sg>, <bet,Sub:Per:3 Num:Pl Gen:5,6 Obj:Per:3 Num:Pl Gen:5,6>, etc.,.in which the stem bet is paired with some valid combination of morphosyntactic features.

```
define Features  [SubjAgr " " ObjAgr " " Tense];
define VerbLex "<" Stems "," Features ">" ;
```

Table 9. Verb Lexicon

4.2   Realization Rules

The rules of exponence can be expressed in PARC/XRCE regular expression notation quite easily using the REPLACE operator ->. We will need two types of rules. Certain rules introduce specific subject or object markers, others introduce markers for both syntactic functions. Table 10 contains the specific rules.

Each rule inserts (= rewrites the empty string as) a particular affix in the beginning of the form derived so far, that is, immediately after the initial < bracket. For example, rule R302 inserts ko to the beginning of the stem if the object agreement features of the stem include second person and singular. Thus the rule will apply to an underlying lexical form such as

<bet,Sub:Per:1 Num:Sg Obj:Per:2 Num:Sg Gen:1.2 Tns:Past:Rec>

changing bet to kobet and leaving everything else unmodified. Note that although the features occur in the underlying lexical form in a certain order, none of the rules refer to the order and would apply even if the order was changed, say, by reversing the subject and object agreement features. The naming of the rules indicates what block each rule belongs to. The rules in Block 1 (R101, R102, etc.) realize subject agreement markers; the rules in Block 3 (R301, R02, etc) mark object agreement. In Lingala verbs, the subject markers precede the object

```
define R101 [[. .] -> {na} || "<" _ [$[SubjAgr & $Person1 & $Sg]]] ;
define R102 [[. .] -> o    || "<" _ [$[SubjAgr & $Person2 & $Sg]]] ;
define R103 [[. .] -> a || "<" _ [$[SubjAgr & $Person3 & $Sg & $2]]];
define R104 [[. .] -> e   || "<" _ [$[SubjAgr & $Person3 & $Sg & $7]]];
define R105 [[. .] -> {ei} || "<" _[$[SubjAgr & $Person3 & $Sg & $15]]];
define R111 [[. .] -> {to} || "<" _ [$[SubjAgr & $Person1 & $Pl]]] ;


define R301 [[. .] -> n || "<" _ [$[ObjAgr & $Person1 & $Sg]]] ;
define R302 [[. .] -> {ko} || "<" _ [$[ObjAgr & $Person2 & $Sg]]] ;
define R303 [[. .] -> {mo} || "<" _ [$[ObjAgr & $Person3 & $Sg & $2]]];
define R304 [[. .] -> {ei}  || "<" _ [$[ObjAgr & $Person3 & $Sg & $7]]];
define R310 [[. .] -> {lo} || "<" _ [$[ObjAgr & $Person1 & $Pl]]] ;
```

Table 10. Specific Subject and Object Agreement Rules

markers, and both come before the stem. Because the rules are designed to build the verb forms "from inside out" starting with the stem, the rules in Block 3 have to apply before the rules in Block 1.

With the rules in Table 10 we can already produce some Lingala stems fully marked with subject and object agreement markers. Table 11 illustrates the process with the **xfst** program. The first command composes the input string <bet,Sub:Per:1 Num:Sg Obj:Per:2 Num:Sg Tns:Past:Rec> with Rule R302 and the result again with Rule R101. Because angle brackets, commas, and colons have a special meaning in regular expressions, we have to put them in double quotes. The separating space symbols, " ", also have to be quoted. The symbol .o. is the COMPOSITION operator. The result of the composition is a single transducer containing one path. The **xfst** command 'print upper-words' shows the original input, the 'print lower-words' shows the resulting output. In the finite-state world, the linguistic notion of "rule application" corresponds to the composition of an input string with one or more rules in a cascade. As we see in Table 11, the effect of the two rules of exponence is to change bet, to nakobet

```
xfst[0]: regex "<" {bet} "," Sub ":" Per ":" 1 " " Num ":" Sg " "
                            Obj ":" Per ":" 2 " " Num ":" Sg " "
                            Tns ":" Past ":" Rec ">"
             .o.
             R302
             .o.
             R101;
1.5 Kb. 34 states, 33 arcs, 1 path.
fst[1]: print upper-words
<bet,Sub:Per:1 Num:Sg Obj:Per:2 Num:Sg Tns:Past:Rec>
fst[1]: print lower-words
<nakobet,Sub:Per:1 Num:Sg Obj:Per:2 Num:Sg Tns:Past:Rec>
```

Table 11. A Cascade of Compositions

This is almost what we want but it is evident that to produce actual surface forms on Lingala, we need to suppress the morphological features on the output side. For that we need the cleanup rule defined in Table 12. It eliminates everything that is not part of the surface alphabet defined in Table 5, that is, brackets, punctuation, spaces, numerals, and the multi-character symbols for attributes and values. The backslash in Table 12 is the TERM COMPLEMENT operator. The zero represents an epsilon. With Cleanup as the last rule of the cascade, the lower-side output string on the single path is reduced to nakobet. The upper-side string of the path still has its original form. That is, we now have a minimal lexical transducer that generates and analyzes the string nakobet.

```
define Cleanup \L -> 0;
```

Table 12. Elimination Rule for Non-Alphabetic Symbols

4.3   Rules of Referral

In addition to specific subject and object markers, Lingala contains many affixes that are used both for subjects and objects. To be faithful to the principles of Realizational Morphology, we will not define them directly but derive them from a common source by a rule of referral. Table 13 contains the common sources. Note that the rules in this table all contain the symbol Agr defined in Table 8. In other words, the rules do not identify themselves as Subject or Object rules. The features are assigned to the place holder attribute Func.

```
define RAgr1 [[. .] -> {mo} || "<" _ [$[Agr & $Person3 & $Sg & $4]]];
define RAgr2 [[. .] -> {li} || "<" _ [$[Agr & $Person3 & $Sg & $5]]];
define RAgr3 [[. .] -> e  || "<" _ [$[Agr & $Person3 & $Sg & $[9a"."10a]]]];
define RAgr4 [[. .] -> {lo} || "<" _ [$[Agr & $Person3 & $Sg & $[10|11]]]];
define RAgr5 [[. .] -> {bo} || "<" _ [$[Agr & $Person3 & $Sg & $14]]];

define RAgr6 [[. .] -> {bo} || "<" _ [$[Agr & $Person2 & $Pl]]] ;
define RAgr7 [[. .] -> {ba} || "<" _ [$[Agr & $Person3 & $Pl & $2]]];
define RAgr8 [[. .] -> {mi} || "<" _ [$[Agr & $Person3 & $Pl & $4]]];
define RAgr9 [[. .] -> {ma} || "<" _ [$[Agr & $Person3 & $Pl & $[5|6]]]];
define RAgr10 [[. .] -> {bi}  || "<" _ [$[Agr & $Person3 & $Pl & $7]]];
define RAgr11 [[. .] -> i  || "<" _ [$[Agr & $Person3 & $Pl & $[9a|10]]]];
```

Table 13. Shared Agreement Rules

The rules of referral in Table 14 all use a construct indicated by ' in the PARC/XRCE regular expression calculus that modifies a given transducer by systematically replacing all occurrences of a given symbol with some other symbol. Rule R106, for example, derives a subject agreement rule from Rule RAgr1 in Table 13. Rule R305 derives an object agreement rule from the same source. Alternatively, we could have chosen either the subject or the object agreement

```
define R106 '[RAgr1, Func, Sub];
define R107 '[RAgr2, Func, Sub];
define R108 '[RAgr3, Func, Sub];
define R109 '[RAgr4, Func, Sub];
define R110 '[RAgr5, Func, Sub];
define R112 '[RAgr6, Func, Sub];
define R113 '[RAgr7, Func, Sub];
define R114 '[RAgr8, Func, Sub];
define R115 '[RAgr9, Func, Sub];
define R116 '[RAgr10, Func, Sub];
define R117 '[RAgr11, Func, Sub];
define R305 '[RAgr1, Func, Obj];
define R306 '[RAgr2, Func, Obj];
define R307 '[RAgr3, Func, Obj];
define R308 '[RAgr4, Func, Obj];
define R309 '[RAgr5, Func, Obj];
define R311 '[RAgr6, Func, Obj];
define R312 '[RAgr7, Func, Obj];
define R313 '[RAgr8, Func, Obj];
define R314 '[RAgr9, Func, Obj];
define R315 '[RAgr10, Func, Obj];
define R316 '[RAgr11, Func, Obj];
```

Table 14. Rules of Referral

rule as the basic one and derived the other by a rule of referral that substitutes the attribute Sub for Obj, or vice versa. Either way, Rule RAgr1 gets used twice, once as an object agreement rule, once as a subject agreement rule. Whatever theoretical insight there is in insisting that it is the same rule that applies in both cases, this insight is faithfully captured by the implementation.

```
define R201 [[. .] -> {ko} || "<" _ [$[Fut":"Immed]]] ;
define R401 [[. .] -> {ak} || _ "," [$[Pres":"[Hab1 | Hab2]|
                                      Past":"[Hist | MostRem]]]];
define R402 [[. .] -> a    || _ "," [$[Pres":"Cont Fut":"Immed]]];
define R501 [[. .] -> i || _ "," [$[Fut":"MostRem Past":"[Rec|Hist]]]];
```

Table 15. Rules of Tense and Aspect Marking

The final set of rules yet to be discussed involves the realization of Tense and Aspect features. The rules are expressed in Figure 15. Unlike the agreement features that come before the stem, most tense features are realized as suffixes after the stem. Consequently, the context specification of the tense rules refer to the comma, the marker that separates the stem from the feature specification as the right context. The one exception is the immediate future tense that is marked both by a prefix and by a suffix.

All that remains to be done now is to define the cascade of compositions that maps each of the lexical forms to its proper surface realization, and vice versa. Figure 16 gives the explicit definition of Lingala verbs in Realizational Morphology. The text following the hash mark is a comment, not part of the definition.

```
define LingalaVerbs [
    VerbLex
    .o.
    R301 .o. R302 .o. R303 .o. R304 .o. R305 .o.    # singular object
    R306 .o. R307 .o. R308 .o. R309
    .o.
    R310 .o. R311 .o. R312 .o. R313 .o. R314 .o.    # plural object
    R315 .o. R316
    .o.
    R201                                             # future
    .o.
    R101 .o. R102 .o. R103 .o. R104 .o. R105 .o.    # singular subject
    R106 .o. R107 .o. R108 .o. R109 .o. R110
    .o.
    R111 .o. R112 .o. R113 .o. R114 .o. R115 .o.    # plural subject
    R116 .o. R117
    .o.
    R401 .o. R402 .o. R501                           # tense
    .o.
    Cleanup ] ;
```

Table 16. Definition of Lingala Verbal Morphology

Some examples to show how the system is working are given in Table 17 where we are exploring the contents of the lexical transducer resulting from the script in Table 16 and the preceding definitions in **xfst**. The command 'print random-upper 5' print five lexical strings at random; the command 'print random-lower 5' prints five random surface strings. The command 'apply up loibeta' prints out all the possible feature bundles associated with the surface form. The last command generates loibeta from one of its lexical interpretations.

5 Conclusion

What we have shown in this paper is that Stump's theory of realizational morphology is yet another incarnation of finite-state morphology, different in notation, but not in substance, from the technology that the successful commercial morphology applications are based on. Moving from Stump's notation to a more standard regular expression calculus does not incur any loss of simplicity or elegance. Rather the opposite.

Computational phonology and morphology have a curious non-relationship with "real" linguistics extending back to more than three decades. Time after

```
fst[1]: print random-upper 5
<bet,Sub:Per:3 Num:Sg Gen:5.6 Obj:Per:3 Num:Sg Gen:14.6 Tns:Pres:Cont>
<bet,Sub:Per:3 Num:Sg Gen:14.6 Obj:Per:3 Num:Pl Gen:11.6 Tns:Pres:Cont>
<bet,Sub:Per:3 Num:Sg Gen:1.2 Obj:Per:3 Num:Sg Gen:5.6 Tns:Pres:Hab1>
<bet,Sub:Per:3 Num:Pl Gen:7.8 Obj:Per:1 Num:Pl Tns:Fut:MostRem>
<bet,Sub:Per:3 Num:Sg Gen:15 Obj:Per:3 Num:Pl Gen:5.6 Tns:Past:MostRem>
xfst[1]: print random-lower 5
mamibeta
loibeta
ikolobeta
mimobetak
ekoeibeta
xfst[1]: apply up loibeta
<bet,Sub:Per:3 Num:Sg Gen:11.6 Obj:Per:3 Num:Pl Gen:9a.10a Tns:Pres:Cont>
<bet,Sub:Per:3 Num:Sg Gen:11.6 Obj:Per:3 Num:Pl Gen:10 Tns:Pres:Cont>
<bet,Sub:Per:3 Num:Sg Gen:10 Obj:Per:3 Num:Pl Gen:9a.10a Tns:Pres:Cont>
<bet,Sub:Per:3 Num:Sg Gen:10 Obj:Per:3 Num:Pl Gen:10 Tns:Pres:Cont>
xfst[1]: apply down
apply down> <bet,Sub:Per:1 Num:Sg Obj:Per:2 Num:Sg Tns:Past:Rec>
nakobeti
apply down> <bet,Sub:Per:3 Num:Pl Gen:7.8 Obj:Per:1 Num:Pl Tns:Fut:MostRem>
bilobeti
```

Table 17. Exploring Lingala Verbal Morphology

time, from Johnson [8] to Eisner [6], including Kaplan and Kay [9,10], Kosken-niemi [14], myself [11,12], Beesley [2], Kiraz [13], and others, the computational knights have presented themselves at the Royal Court of Linguistics, rushed up to the Princess of Phonology and Morphology in great exitement to deliver the same message "Dear Princess. I have wonderful news for you: You are not like some of your NP-complete sisters. You are regular. You are rational. You are finite-state. Please marry me. Together we can do great things." And time after time, the put-down response from the Princess has been the same: "Not interested. You do not understand Theory. Go away you geek."

This constant rejection of the most suitable suitor is puzzling. The Princess must have a vested interest in making simple things appear more complicated than they really are. The good news that the computational knights are trying to deliver is unwelcome. The Princess prefers the pretense that phonology/morphology is a profoundly complicated subject, shrouded by theories.

If that is the right analysis of the situation, computational linguists should adopt a different strategy. Instead of being the eternal rejected suitor at the Royal Court, they should adopt the role of the innocent boy in the street shouting "The Princess has no clothes. The Princess has no clothes..." That is my conclusion.

Acknowledgements. I thank Louisa Sadler for stimulating discussions of Stump's work, and Jason Eisner, Ronald M. Kaplan, Kemal Oflazer and Annie Zaenen for many helpful suggestions and comments.

References

1. Stephen R. Anderson. *A-Morphous Morphology*. Cambridge University Press, Cambridge, England, 1992.
2. Kenneth R. Beesley. Arabic morphology using only finite-state operations. In Michael Rosner, editor, *Computational Approaches to Semitic Languages: Proceedings of the Workshop*, pages 50–57, Montréal, Québec, August 16 1998. Université de Montréal.
3. Kenneth R. Beesley and Lauri Karttunen. Finite-state non-concatenative morphotactics. In *SIGPHON-200. Fifth Workshop of the ACL Special Interest Group in Computational Phonology.*, pages 1–12, Luxembourg, August 5-6 2000. Association for Computational Linguistics.
4. Kenneth R. Beesley and Lauri Karttunen. *Finite State Morphology*. CSLI Publications, Palo Alto, CA, 2003.
5. Noam Chomsky and Morris Halle. *The Sound Pattern of English*. Harper and Row, New York, 1968.
6. Jason Eisner. Phonological comprehension and the compilation of optimality theory. In *Proceedings of the 40th Annual Meeting of the Association for Computational Linguistics*, pages 56–63, Washington, DC, July 2002. Association for Computational Linguistics.
7. Raphael Finkel and Gregory Stump. Generating hebrew verb morphology by default inheritance hierarchies. In *Proceedings of the Workshop on Computational Approaches to Semitic Languages*, pages 9–18, Washington, DC., 2002. Association for Computational Linguistics.
8. C. Douglas Johnson. *Formal Aspects of Phonological Description*. Mouton, The Hague, 1972.
9. Ronald M. Kaplan and Martin Kay. Phonological rules and finite-state transducers. In *Linguistic Society of America Meeting Handbook, Fifty-Sixth Annual Meeting*, New York, December 27-30 1981. Abstract.
10. Ronald M. Kaplan and Martin Kay. Regular models of phonological rule systems. *Computational Linguistics*, 20(3):331–378, 1994.
11. Lauri Karttunen. Finite-state constraints. In John Goldsmith, editor, *The Last Phonological Rule*. University of Chicago Press, Chicago, Illinois., 1993.
12. Lauri Karttunen. The proper treatment of optimality in computational phonology. In *FSMNLP'98. International Workshop on Finite-State Methods in Natural Language Processing*, Bilkent University, Ankara, Turkey, June 29 1998. cmp-lg/9804002.
13. George Anton Kiraz. Multi-tiered nonlinear morphology using multitape finite automata: A case study on Syriac and Arabic. *Computational Linguistics*, 26(1):77–105, 2000.
14. Kimmo Koskenniemi. Two-level morphology: A general computational model for word-form recognition and production. Publication 11, University of Helsinki, Department of General Linguistics, Helsinki, 1983.
15. P. H. Matthews. *Inflectional Morphology: a Theoretical Study Based on Aspects of Latin Verb Conjugation*. Cambridge University Press, Cambridge, England, 1972.
16. Michael Meeuwis. *Lingala*. Lincom Europa, München, Germany, 1998.
17. Gregory T. Stump. *Inflectional Morphology. A Theory of Paradigm Structure*. Cambridge University Press, Cambridge, England, 2001.
18. Arnold Zwicky. How to describe inflection. In *Proceedings of the Eleventh Anual Meeting of the Berkeley Linguistic Society*, pages 372–86, Berkeley, CA, 1985. Berkeley Linguistic Society.

Approach to Construction of Automatic Morphological Analysis Systems for Inflective Languages with Little Effort*

Alexander Gelbukh and Grigori Sidorov

Center for Computing Research (CIC),
National Polytechnic Institute (IPN),
Av. Juan de Dios Bátiz, esq. Miguel Othón de Mendizábal,
Mexico D. F., Zacatenco, CP 07738, Mexico
{gelbukh, sidorov}@cic.ipn.mx, www.gelbukh.com

Abstract. Development of morphological analysis systems for inflective languages is a tedious and laborious task. We suggest an approach for development of such systems that permits to spend less time and effort. It is based on static processing of stem allomorphs and the method of analysis known as "analysis through generation." These features allow for using the morphological models oriented to generation, instead of developing special analysis models. Normally, generation models are presented in traditional grammars and correspond very well to the intuition of speakers. Systems based on this approach were developed for Russian and Spanish.

1 Introduction

Languages can have poor morphology (so called analytic languages, in which the grammar categories normally are expressed by standalone functional words), e.g, English or Chinese, or rich morphology (so called synthetic languages, in which the grammar categories normally are expressed inside the word), e.g., Finnish or Russian. Synthetic languages can use one of the following two ways of morphological arrangement:

- *Agglutination* (a tendency to use a separate morpheme for each grammatical category; there are no stem alternations or these alternations are predictable), e.g., Finnish or Turk languages;
- *Fusion* (a tendency to express all grammatical categories by one flexion; often implies complex non-predictable stem alternations), e.g., Russian, Czech, and other Slavic languages, Spanish, Portuguese; such languages are called **inflective**.

In this paper, we discuss an approach that allows for rapid development with little effort (in comparison with other approaches) of systems for automatic morphological analysis/generation for *inflective* languages.

---

* Work was done under partial support of Mexican Government (CONACyT, SNI), IPN, Mexico (CGEPI, COFAA, PIFI), and RITOS-2.

A. Gelbukh (Ed.): CICLing 2003, LNCS 2588, pp. 215–220, 2003.

Morphological systems of inflective languages are finite (usually about 2-3 million grammatical word forms for a dictionary of about 100,000 words), so in fact any method leads to the same result. Still, there are differences in time and effort required to apply different methods. In addition, there is a difference in similarity of the used models to the models described in traditional grammars. In our opinion, the more similar these two kinds of models the better the system, because computational models based on traditional grammars are much clearer intuitively and it is much easier to apply them in the system's development.

Note that our point in this paper is not to discuss the formalism (different formalisms can be used with our method) but the approach to the treatment of stem allomorphs, which does not depend on formalism.

2   Some Considerations on Inflective Languages

The main problem in automatic morphological analysis of inflective languages is the treatment of non-predictable stem alternations. Indeed, if there are no such stem alternations then the algorithm of morphological analysis is very straightforward: (1) Beforehand, we assign a morphological class to each stem that uniquely defines a set of flexions; it is enough to store only one stem in the dictionary for each word because there are simple rules to build all its allomorphs. (2) During the morphological analysis of a given wordform, we find the flexion in the wordform and after this, the stem (the rest of the wordform; it may be modified according to the rules) is looked up in the dictionary. (3) If the flexion is compatible with the stem, then the analysis is finished. This is the case of agglutinative languages, like Finnish or Turk.

The case of non-predictable stem alternations is more complicated. There are two important points to discuss:

- Method of processing of stem allomorphs (static versus dynamic), and
- Morphological models used ("artificial" models for the direct analysis approach versus "natural" models for the "analysis through generation" approach).

2.1   Static vs. Dynamic Methods

There are two methods of processing of stem allomorphs (sometimes, the terms "allomorphs vs. morpheme" is used [2]): static and dynamic. Static method means that all stem allomorphs are stored in the dictionary (normally there are 2–4 allomorphs, so the dictionary size is not significantly affected; note that normally the majority of words—say, in Russian more than 70%—does not have any stem alternations). The allomorphs are generated beforehand, which is not difficult because the information about each stem is available.

Dynamic method means that the allomorphs are constructed dynamically basing on only one dictionary record. In inflective languages, the corresponding rules cannot be standardized, so the number of such rules is very large (more than 1000 rules are mentioned in [4]). Besides, they do not have any intuitive correspondence in common knowledge of the language. For example, in order to generate the dictionary stem for Russian *okon-* (*window*), it is necessary to delete *-o-*: *okn-*. The corresponding example for English can be (in English, there are much fewer such words): for *took* it is necessary to change *-oo-* to *-a-* and add *-e* to obtain *take*. It is difficult, because we do not have any beforehand information about the possible type of stem, so it is necessary to develop and apply many unintuitive rules. This method is of high computational complexity (NP-complete) [2, p.255].

Therefore, the static method is more reasonable and easy to implement than the dynamic one for inflective languages. On the contrary, for agglutinative languages it is easy to use the dynamic method, because the rules are rather simple and intuitive. For example, the dynamic method was applied in the well-known two-level morphology [3] that was initially developed for Finnish. Indeed, the idea of the two-level morphology is to create the correspondence between the abstract level of morphemes and the level of their realizations, i.e., the allomorphs (these are the two levels). It is dynamic processing of stem alternations that is used the two-level model for implementation of rules of correspondence between the two levels. As we have mentioned before, for inflective languages it *is* possible to use this kind of processing, however, this requires development of much greater number of rules, which are less intuitive in these languages.

2.2 Morphological Models

Another choice deals with the kind of morphological models. The obvious direct way for developing the morphological models is to create a new morphological class for any paradigm that exists in the language; with this, the number of classes is calculated up to 1500 for Czech [5] or 1000 for Russian [1]. These classes are artificial, created for the purposes of analysis.

The other possibility is to use the morphological models that already exist for generation, say, in case of Russian there are as few as about 40 morphological classes. These models are usually described in traditional grammars, because these grammars are oriented to generation. Besides, they correspond very well to the intuition of speakers. To be able to use these models, it is necessary to apply a method that allows for applying generation instead of direct analysis, because usually generation is much simpler than analysis. This method is known in artificial intelligence as "analysis through generation." In our case, it is applied as follows: first, the system generates all possible hypotheses based on the possible flexions, and then tries to generate the grammar forms according to each hypothesis using the corresponding stem and its morphological class taken from the dictionary. Note that the number of classes is small, while the peculiarities of words are described using morphological marks stored in the dictionary entries for specific words, for example, the presence of alternations, the absence of singular (*pluralia tantum*), etc. These marks are interpreted during the process of analysis/generation.

Obviously, it is much easier for development of a system to have a small number of morphological classes, which correspond very well to the intuition of speakers. Sometimes these classes already exist, but if not, it is easier to characterize the words in a given language applying the simple and intuitive classification.

We suggest to use during analysis the models created for generation. However, there is another possibility to apply the same models. Namely, it is possible to generate all possible wordforms beforehand and during the process of analysis just to search in the database that stores all these forms. This is another possibility to apply analysis through generation. Its advantage is the simplicity of the analysis algorithm:

it is just a lookup (note, however, that in any case an additional algorithm is to be developed for generation of all forms). Still, its disadvantage is the size of the dictionary that is much greater than that of the dictionary of stems. The exact number depends on the number of wordforms per lemma in a language, e.g., in Russian it is more than 30 times. Thus, the choice is: a large dictionary and a very simple algorithm versus small dictionary and more sophisticated algorithm. The latter can be viewed as compression of the dictionary (and a very good compression, indeed). There are other advantages of using of the algorithm of analysis over the database of wordforms: the algorithm possesses additional grammar knowledge. For example, processing of ungrammatical forms like *taked, the algorithm can understand what is meant and suggest the correct form *took*.

3   Approach

We suggest using static method of processing of stem allomorphs (all allomorphs are stored in the dictionary) and applying the natural morphological models created for generation based on "analysis through generation" procedure.

The first stage is data preparation. The words of a language should be characterized in terms of the morphological models used. Then, the stem dictionary is generated with all possible allomorphs of each stem. Note that the stem allomorphs should be marked according to the rule of their generation, for example, first, second, etc. stem. This information is necessary during wordform generation, namely, for choosing the correct stem allomorph.

The next stage is the development of the algorithm of morphological analysis. The following modules (parts of the algorithm) are necessary:

- Module of hypothesis generation (the correspondence between the flexions and the sets of possible values of grammar categories (flexion • values), e.g., in English, flexion –s can express plural for nouns or 3rd person singular for verbs, etc.).
- Module of choice of stem allomorphs (the correspondence between the sets of values of grammar categories of morphological classes and the number of the stem allomorph (values → stem allomorph number), e.g., in English, if we consider the verb stems *verify/verifi-* as allomorphs, then the first allomorph is used for the present tense (except for 3rd person, singular) and the second one for the past tense or present tense 3rd person singular, etc. This can be done using bit patterns, direct programming, etc. Note that we do not need the inverse correspondence because we apply this module only in generation.
- Module of choice of flexions: which flexion is used for a given set of grammar categories of a given class (values → flexion), e.g., in English, for plural the noun flexions –s or –es are used depending on the stem's final letters.
- Module of processing of irregular forms. All irregular grammar forms (irregular verbs, etc.) are stored in the dictionary with their lemma and the values of grammar categories (number, tense, etc.). Therefore, their analysis consists just in looking up in the dictionary (we should always check the hypothesis of the irregular form with zero flexion). Their generation is also consists in looking up in the dictionary—for the lemma and the corresponding values of grammar categories.

The generation procedure is very simple. Its input is a set of values of grammar categories and a string that identifies the word (stem allomorph or lemma). The procedure implies (1) obtaining the information from the dictionary (the morphological class, etc.), (2) choosing the correct stem allomorph, and (3) choosing the correct flexion (see the corresponding modules).

The analysis procedure also is not complicated. Its input is a character string. The procedure works as follows:

- Remove characters from the string one by one in order to find the possible flexion and the corresponding stem (zero flexion is always considered),
- Formulate the hypotheses for the flexion,
- Call the generation procedure for each hypothesis,
- Compare the result of generation with the input. If they coincide then the hypothesis is correct.

Note that it is important to apply generation because otherwise some incorrect forms would be accepted by the analyzer (overgeneration), for example: for *taked (instead of took), both the stem take- and the flexion -d (past tense) do exist, but they are incompatible, which is verified through generation (the correct form took for past tense will be generated and the forms do not coincide).

If there are several affixes in a word (for example, in Russian there are suffixes of participles), then this analysis procedure can be applied recursively. (This situation, however, is not typical for inflective languages.) In this case, the algorithm is to change the grammar information obtained from the dictionary to the grammar information that corresponds to these affixes (for example, those Russian participles have verbal stem but they have the same morphological class as adjectives).

4 Conclusions

We have presented the approach for developing systems of morphological analysis for inflective languages. It allows for spending less time and effort on this development. It is based on the static method of processing of stem allomorphs and the procedure of analysis known as "analysis through generation." These features allow using the morphological models that are oriented to generation. These models are much simpler and much more intuitive than those specially developed for analysis. Frequently these models can be taken from the traditional grammars.

We have applied this approach for the development of the systems of morphological analysis for Russian and Spanish with sufficiently large dictionaries (100,000 and 40,000 words, correspondingly). The development process was relatively simple and fast even for such morphologically rich language as Russian: it took about 6 months of development by one person for Russian (it would take less if we follow this approach from the very beginning) and about 2 months for Spanish of one master student. In both cases, the dictionaries oriented to generation were already available. Some part of the time was devoted to their preparation (transformation to database format and generation of the stem allomorphs). These systems are freely available for academic (see the author's contact address).

References

1. Gelbukh, A.F. Effective implementation of morphology model for an inflectional natural language. *J. Automatic Documentation and Mathematical Linguistics*, Allerton Press, vol. 26, N 1, 1992, pp. 22–31.
2. Hausser, Roland. *Foundations of Computational linguistics*. Springer, 1999, 534 p.
3. Koskenniemi, Kimmo. *Two-level Morphology: A General Computational Model for Word-Form Recognition and Production*. University of Helsinki Publications, N 11, 1983.
4. Malkovsky, M. G. *Dialogue with an artificial intelligence system* (in Russian). Moscow State University, Moscow, Russia, 1985, 213 pp.
5. Sedlacek R. and P. Smrz, A new Czech morphological analyzer AJKA. Proc. of *TSD-2001*. LNCS 2166, Springer, 2001, pp. 100–107.
6. Sidorov, G. O. Lemmatization in automatized system for compilation of personal style dictionaries of literature writers (in Russian). In: *Word by Dostoyevsky* (in Russian), Moscow, Russia, Russian Academy of Sciences, 1996, pp. 266–300.
7. Sproat, R. *Morphology and computation*. Cambridge, MA, MIT Press, 1992, 313 p.

Per-node Optimization of Finite-State Mechanisms for Natural Language Processing

Alexander Troussov[1], Brian O'Donovan[1], Seppo Koskenniemi[2], and
Nikolay Glushnev[1]

[1] IBM Dublin Software Lab, Airways Ind. Est., Cloghran, Dublin 17, Ireland.
`{atrousso, Brian_ODonovan, nglushnev}@ie.ibm.com`
[2] Oy IBM Ab. P.O.Box 265, 00101 Helsinki, Finland.
`Seppo.Koskenniemi@fi.ibm.com`

Abstract. Finite-state processing is typically based on structures that allow for efficient indexing and sequential search. However, this "rigid" framework has several disadvantages when used in natural language processing, especially for non-alphabetical languages. The solution is to systematically introduce polymorphic programming techniques that are adapted to particular cases. In this paper we describe the structure of a morphological dictionary implemented with finite-state automata using variable or polymorphic node formats. Each node is assigned a format from a predefined set reflecting its utility in corpora processing as measured by a number of graph theoretic metrics and statistics. Experimental results demonstrate that this approach permits a 52% increase in the performance of dictionary look-up.

1   Introduction

Natural language dictionaries can be compactly represented as Finite State Automata (FSAs) if word verification is seen as a process of moving from an input state to an acceptance state in a space of letter transitions. FSAs allow common elements of similar words to be factored out, which provides a more compact representation of dictionaries than hash-tables, and if the organization of nodes and transitions is optimized, traversal of an FSA need take no longer than hashing.

FSAs are most efficiently implemented with transition tables that enable rapid selection of links between states, where these links are stored in an array indexed by characters from the input language. However, this efficiency is purchased at the expense of considerable memory overheads. In [1] and [2] the problem was considered purely from the perspective of compression, whereas the primary goal of our research is directed at optimization for speed that balances the efficiency of node transition with the effect of a node's format on the size of the dictionary as a whole. The simplicity of finite-state processing means that efficiency hinges primarily on the speed of memory access. The classical memory organization of a computer is pyramidal, with small amounts of fast memory dedicated to registers and a cache, and greater amounts available to slower media such as disk. But traditional hardware and O/S approaches to optimal memory usage, such as pre-fetching, assume a regularity of access that is not valid for the highly transitional nature of finite-state processing.

A. Gelbukh (Ed.): CICLing 2003, LNCS 2588, pp. 221–224, 2003.

In this paper we suggest a systematic approach:

1. Ontologization of all useful node types in an FSA.
2. Classification of nodes according to their traffic-related role in an FSA.
3. A formal procedure for assigning a format to each node based on this role.

The finite state devices considered here are morphological dictionaries in which morphosyntactic information is attached to final end-states (though the approach generalizes to other FSA types). The optimization model is based both on an empirical analysis and on the following heuristic assumptions about the global structure of dictionaries:

1. The distribution of nodes ranked according to their out-degree is highly skewed. Empirical analysis reveals that nodes with high out-degree are associated with morpheme/grapheme bounds, while long filaments of nodes with only one in- and out-flowing link generally represent proper names, idioms and non-lexical entries.
2. The distribution of nodes ranked according to their frequency of usage is Zipf-like, with high-traffic nodes being less frequent than low-traffic nodes.
3. There is a positive correlation between a node's traffic and its out-degree.

2 Per-node Classification

Generally speaking, the classification of a node primarily reflects the traffic experienced by that node (especially if we assume the Markov property). Our classification is presented in the Table 1.

Each node in an FSA is assigned a format according to the classification provided in Table 1. "Heavy-traffic" nodes clearly require explicit lookup tables indexed by input characters, since their frequency of use mitigates the memory overheads of such tables. More problematic are the "Medium-traffic" nodes, which are those with many out-flowing links but which carry less traffic than "Heavy-traffic" nodes. Implementation of such nodes without the memory overhead of lookup tables is especially important for the efficient finite-state processing of ideographic languages. Goetz et. al. [2] has advocated that binary search be used for ideographic languages, while hash tables might also be useful if speed is the developer's primary concern.

For "Light-traffic" nodes with relatively few out-flowing links, a sequential list of transitions, ordered by an empirically-determined usage frequency, typically suffices. This ensures that the most useful transitions are accessed the quickest. Interestingly, the results of our experiments indicate that even global character frequency alone leads to efficient sorting of out-flowing links.

An empirical analysis reveals that a significant part of a dictionary is comprised of filament-like "letter chains", where the out-degree of several consecutive nodes is one. Recognition of letter chains provides scope for optimization by allowing an FSA to transit directly from the first node of a chain to the last. This method is known in the construction of word graphs as compaction, and the resulting directed acyclic graph (DAG) is called Compact DAG (see also path compression in [3]). In our approach, a dedicated node format is assigned to the head node of each letter chain, and it is the responsibility of this node/format to perform the necessary test to allow direct transition to the end of the chain.

Table 1. One-parametric classification of FSA dictionary nodes relative to both their out-degree and the frequency of their usage during corpora processing

One-Parametric Classification of FSA Dictionary Nodes

Classifi-cation of Nodes	"Start of a Chain": A chain is formed from nodes with only one out-flowing link (except the last node), which leads to another node in the chain. All nodes in the chain (except the first one) have exactly one in-flowing link.	"Light-Traffic": Typical nodes with more than one, but fewer than a dozen, out-flowing links.	"Medium-Traffic": Nodes with a dozen or more of out-flowing links. This format is used instead of the format of "Heavy nodes" when the memory is of concern.	"Heavy-Traffic": Frequently visited nodes, these typically also have a large number of out-flowing links.
Preferred format and technique for selection of apropos out-flowing links:	The information about intermediate nodes can be stored at the start of the chain to provide fast access from the first node in the chain to the last one.	Links are stored as a list of out-flowing links and they are sorted according to the frequency of their usage. Linear search.	Links are stored as an array of out-flowing transitions. Logarithmic search, hash tables.	Links are stored in an array with a size equal to the number of characters presented in the dictionary. Direct lookup.

3 Assignment of Polymorphic Formats to Nodes

A dictionary FSA for a given language/corpus is constructed as follows:

1. The input list of words (surface forms), is compiled into a letter tree, which is then minimized to reuse common prefixes and postfixes. Each word can be provided with additional information (its part-of-speech categories, etc.), which can be attached to the leaves (the terminals) of the letter tree; in this case two postfixes can be merged only if they lead to exactly the same information.
2. The unoptimized dictionary FSA is used to process a large corpus. For each node and each link in the FSA, its frequency of usage (traffic) is computed and stored.
3. The statistics collected in (2) is used to classify each node. First, chain detection is performed. Secondly, the top N most-visited nodes are classified as heavy-traffic nodes, where N is an empirical threshold. When dealing with alphabetical languages, all other nodes can be classified as light-traffic nodes, but for ideographic languages, a threshold on the number of out-flowing links is used to further discriminate between light- and medium-traffic nodes.

4. The optimized dictionary is compiled, with dedicated node formats assigned to each node to allow for optimal processing of the traffic through those nodes.

4 Experimental Results

Detailed experiments were done with an English dictionary. As a base case, an unoptimized dictionary is constructed, which simply uses sequential search to select transitions from each node (and where links are ordered according to the alphabetical order of input characters). This base-case processed an average of 9.130×2^{30} two-byte characters per hour (on an Intel Pentium III with 128MB of RAM running at 500MHz under Windows 2000). With an additional sorting of the out-flowing links in each node based on global character frequency, an 18% performance increase was obtained. However, the assignment of polymorphic node formats to each node based on traffic, as described in this paper, yielded a 52% performance increase over the base-case.

5 Conclusions and Future Work

The use of polymorphic node formats in FSA processing, as described in this paper, uniformly encompasses known FSA formats while supporting new formats not previously used in the FSA literature. We have yet to test our hypotheses about the global structural properties of dictionaries in a more general cross-linguistic manner; but our experimental results regarding the effects of optimization do suggest some empirical validity for these assumptions.

References

1. Kiraz, G.: Compressed storage of sparse finite-state transducers. In O. Boldt, H. Jurgensen, and L. Robbins, editors, Workshop on Implementing Automata WIA99 – Pre-Proceedings, Potsdam, July, 1999.
2. Goetz, T., Wunsch, H.: An Abstract Machine Approach to Finite State Transduction over Large Character Sets. Finite State Methods in Natural Language Processing 2001. ESSLLI Workshop, August 20–24, Helsinki.
3. Ciura, M. G., Deorowicz, S.: How to squeeze a lexicon. Software Practice and Experience, vol. 31, n. 11, pp. 1077–1090, 2001.

An Evaluation of a Lexicographer's Workbench Incorporating Word Sense Disambiguation

Adam Kilgarriff and Rob Koeling

Information Technology Research Institute (ITRI), Brighton, UK
Adam.Kilgarriff@itri.brighton.ac.uk, robk@cogs.susx.ac.uk

Abstract. NLP system developers and corpus lexicographers would both benefit from a tool for finding and organizing the distinctive patterns of use of words in texts. Such a tool would be an asset for both language research and lexicon development, particularly for lexicons for Machine Translation. We have developed the WASPBENCH, a tool that (1) presents a "word sketch", a summary of the corpus evidence for a word, to the lexicographer; (2) supports the lexicographer in analysing the word into its distinct meanings and (3) uses the lexicographer's analysis as the input to a state-of-the-art word sense disambiguation (WSD) algorithm, the output of which is a "word expert" for the word which can then disambiguate new instances of the word. In this paper we describe a set of evaluation experiments, designed to establish whether WASPBENCH can be used to save time and improve performance in the development of a lexicon for Machine Translation or other NLP application.

1 Motivations

On the one hand, Human Language Technologies (HLT) need dictionaries, to tell them what words mean and how they behave. On the other hand, the people making dictionaries (herafter, lexicographers) need HLT, to help them identify how words behave so they can make better dictionaries. This potential for synergy exists across the range of lexical data - in the construction of headword lists, for spelling correction, phonetics, morphology and syntax, but nowhere is it truer than for semantics, and in particular the vexed question of how a word's meaning should be analysed into distinct senses. HLT needs all the help it can get from dictionaries, because it is a very hard problem to identify which meaning of a word applies, and if the dictionary does not provide both a coherent and accurate analysis of what the meanings are, and a good set of clues as to where each meaning applies, then the enterprise is doomed. The MT version of the problem is to find the appropriate translation for a word in a given context, where the bilingual dictionary gives several possibilities, and this is just as hard. The lexicographer needs all the help they can get because the analysis of meaning is the second hardest part of their job [1], it occupies a large share of their working hours, and it is one where, currently, they have very little to go on beyond intuition. Synergy between HLT and lexicographer becomes a possibility with the advent of the corpus.

A. Gelbukh (Ed.): CICLing 2003, LNCS 2588, pp. 225–240, 2003.

Lexicographers have long been aware of their great need for evidence about how words behave, and, in the late 1970s and 1980s, English language dictionary publishers were rather quicker to pick up on the potential of large corpora than most parts of the HLT world. The pioneering project was COBUILD [2] and its first offering to the world, the Collins COBUILD English Dictionary came out in 1987.

The basic working methodology, in those early days, was the 'coloured pens' method. A lexicographer who was to write an entry for a word, say pike, was given the corpus evidence for pike in the form of a key-word-in-context printout, as in figure 1. They then read the corpus lines, identifying different meanings as they went along, assigning a colour to each meaning and marking each corpus line with the appropriate colour. Once they had marked all (or almost all - there are always anomalies) the corpus lines, they could then go back to write a definition for each sense, using, eg, the red corpus lines as the evidence for the first meaning, the green as the evidence for the second, the yellow as the evidence for the third, and so on.

In this scenario, note that a meaning, or word sense, corresponds to a cluster of corpus lines. This is a representation that HLT can work with. (It contrasts with a conception of word senses as mental objects, which is not useful to HLT.)

As corpus-based HLT took off, in the 1990s, researchers such as [4] explored corpus methods for word sense disambiguation (WSD). Here the correspondence between word senses and sets of corpus lines was taken at face value, with a set of corpus lines which were known (or believed) to belong to a particular sense being used as a training set. A machine-learning algorithm was then able to use the training set to induce a word expert which could decide which sense a new corpus instance belonged to.

1.1   The WASPBENCH System

Behind the current implementation of the English WASPBENCH lies a database of 70M instances of grammatical relations for English. These are 5-tuples:

$$< gramrel, word1, word2, particle, pointer >$$

gramrel can be any of a set of 27 core grammatical relations for English (including subject, subject-of, object, object-of, modifier, and/or, PP-comp), word1 and word2 are words of English (nouns, verbs or adjectives, lemmatized to give dictionary headword form; word2 may be null), particle is a particle or preposition, so that grammatical relations involving prepositions as well as two fully lexical arguments can be captured. For all relations except PP-comp it is null. Pointer points into the corpus, so we can identify where the instance occurs and retrieve its context if required. Examples of 5-tuples are

PP-comp,look,picture,at,1004683
object,   sip, beer,   -, 1005678

A65 1065	On Tuesday we opted for a more strenuous hike from Braithwaite village up the steep sloped of Grisedale pike .
A6R 13	Only when it was in the net did I realise what size it was and it weighed 26 ob 8 oz,'; added John who went on to bank five other pike , two of 8 lb 8 oz, and others of 10 lb, 11lb and 14 lb.
A6R 390	I hit the fish and stright away though it was a good one, but my son Tony has never caught a pike so I handed him the rod,'; said Lee.
A6R 825	Skimmers, roach and small perch from most Liverpool sections but pike active.
A6R 950	pike to 17 lb 2 oz showing.
A6R 1130	Roach at Bishop Monkton, pike around the canal mouth.
A7C 1528	Press forward every gallant man With hatchet, pike and gun!
AA0 92	Cardiff City: Wood; Rodgerson, Daniel, Barnard, Abraham, Gibbins, Morgan, Scott, pike , Kelly, Chandler.
ABL 650	I met him returning from one of the Penn ponds with the largest pike of the year swinging by his side and a look of sheer elation on his face.
AL3 19	The fishing habits of the angler banned from the British pike Championship for allegedly using photographs of the same fish to claim three separate and spectacular catches have landed him in trouble again.
ALU 269	Faulkner's local History mentions trout, pike , carp, roach, dace, perch, chub, barbel, smelt, flounder, shad, lamprey and eel all being caught in the river off Chelsea and also records nine salmon weighing 171 lbs.
ASN 2834	No Elsie they found nothing in Loch Craig but a huge pike .
ASW 863	Towards the close of the twelfth century the pike was used to counter cavalry charges, and remained in use in various forms until as late as the eighteenth century.

Fig. 1. BNC samples containing the noun *pike*

The database was prepared by parsing a lemmatised, part-of-speech-tagged version of the British National Corpus, a 100M word corpus of recent spoken and written British English.[1]

---

[1] http://info.ox.ac.uk/bnc

Using this database, WASPBENCH prepares a set of lists for each word1 in which, for each gramrel, the words which occur frequently and with high mutual information as word2 are identified and sorted according to their lexicographic salience. This set of lists is presented to the lexicographer for whom it is a useful summary of the word's behaviour. This is a word sketch [5].

The word sketch is a good starting point for the lexicographer to analyse the different meanings (step 1). They study it. All underlying corpus evidence is available at a mouseclick, in case they are unsure what contexts word1 occurs in gramrel with word2 in. They reach preliminary opinions about the different meanings the word has. They assign a short mnemonic label to each sense, and type the labels into a text-input box provided. They then hit the "set senses" button and the word sketch is updated, with each collocate now having a pull-down menu through which it can be assigned to one of the senses.

The lexicographer then spends some time –typically some thirty minutes for a moderately complicated word– assigning collocates to senses (step 2). The majority of high-salience $< collocate, gramrel >$ pairs relate to one sense of a word only (in accordance with Yarowsky's "one sense per collocation" dictum [6]), and it is usually immediately evident to the lexicographer which sense is salient, so the task is not unduly taxing. It is not necessary for the lexicographer to assign all, or any particular, collocate, and any collocate which is associated with more than one sense should be left unassigned.

When the lexicographer has assigned a good range of collocates, they press "submit". Then the WSD algorithm takes over, using the corpus instances where the collocates assigned by the lexicographer apply as the clusters of instances corresponding to a sense, and bootstrapping further evidence about how other corpus instances are assigned (step 3). The algorithm produces a word expert which can disambiguate new instances of the word.

1.2   WASPBENCH and Machine Translation (MT)

WASPBENCH is designed particularly with the needs of MT lexicography in mind. In that context, the components of the problem take on a slightly different form, sometimes with different names. A description of the same system in MT terms follows.

MT has long needed many rules of the form,

in context **C**, translate source language word **S** as target language word **T**

The problem has traditionally been that these rules are hard for humans to identify, and, as there is a large number of possible contexts for most words and a large number of ambiguous words, a very large number of rules is needed. In step (1), the word sketch, WASPBENCH identifies and displays to the user a good set of candidate rules but with the target word **T** unspecified. In step (2), it supports the assignment of target words, by the lexicographer, for a number of the rules. In step (3), it takes this small set of rules and uses a bootstrapping algorithm to automatically identify a very large set of rules, so the word can be appropriately translated wherever it occurs [7].

2   Evaluating WASPBENCH

Evaluating how successful we have been in developing the WASPBENCH presents a number of challenges.

- We straddle three communities - the (largely commercial) dictionary-making world, the (largely research) Human Language Technology (and specifically, WSD) world, and the (part commercial, part research) MT world. These three communities have very different ideas about what makes a technology useful.
- There are no precedents. WASPBENCH performs a function – corpus-based disambiguating-lexicon development with human input – which no other technology performs. We believe no other technology provides even a re-motely similar combination of inputs (corpus + human) and outputs (meaning analysis + word expert). This leaves us with no alternative products to compare it with.
- On the lexicography front: human analysis of meaning is decidedly 'craft' (or even 'art') rather than 'science'. WASPBENCH is, we hope, aiding the practitioners of this craft in doing their job better and faster. But, in the dictionary world, even qualitative analyses of the relative merits of one meaning analysis as against another are rare treats [8,9,10]. Quantitative evaluations are unheard of.
- A critical question for commercial MT would be "does it take less time to produce a word expert using WASPBENCH, than using traditional methods, for the same quality of output". We are constrained in pursuing this route because we do not have access to MT companies' lexicography budgets, and moreover consider it unlikely that MT companies would view the production of disambiguation rules as a distinct function in the way that we do. (Most existing MT systems take a highly domain-based view of word sense ambiguity. In this approach, once the domain is identified, it is assumed that ambiguity goes away, since words tend to only have one meaning and one translation within a given domain. The domain is usually fixed by the user selecting which lexicon they want to use. This strategy has taken MT a long way. It has effectively been the only option available for commercial MT for most words and language pairs, up until developments such as WASP-BENCH. It also serves as a useful corrective to the tendency in the WSD world to take the level of ambiguity displayed in paper dictionaries at face value, rather than taking a serious interest in the concept of domain. While clearly the solution for many ambiguity types, the domain-based view fails for many cases where words have multiple meanings/translations within a single domain, and is also hard to apply in situations where the user cannot realistically be asked to select the domain, such as web-page translation. For further discussion see [11,12,13,14])

In the light of these issues, we have adopted a 'divide and rule' strategy, setting up different evaluation themes for different perspectives. We have pursued five approaches:

- WASPBENCH as a WSD system, within the SENSEVAL evaluation exercise [15]
- the word sketches have been put to the test within a large scale commercial lexicography project; they were used as the main source of corpus evidence for a word's behaviour in the production of the Macmillan English Dictionary for Advanced Learners [16]; [17]
- three expert reports were commissioned from experienced lexicographers
- one set of experiments (with students at the Centre for Translation Studies, Leeds University[2]) explored the performance of WASPBENCH-based translations in comparison with translations produced by commercial MT systems
- a further set of experiments, with a larger group of subjects, explored the extent to which different individuals, working with the same data, produced consistent results.

It is the last evaluation strategy that we report on here. A report bringing together evidence from all evaluation approaches is in preparation.

The Setting

Following a March 2001 workshop designed to set the stage for India-UK collaboration in HLT [18] and interest generated there, the University of Brighton licenced WASPBENCH to Prof. Rajeev Sangal of the Indian Institute for Information Technology (IIIT) Hyderabad. This was the first time WASPBENCH had been used outside its development environment in Brighton, UK. WASPBENCH was installed and was then used in IIIT on a project which is developing an English-Hindi translation system. The goal was this: where an English word[3] had more than one possible Hindi translation, the WASPBENCH provides a computational environment and high-level HLT support for the lexicographer in "telling" the computer when it should be translated the one way, when the other.

In early 2002 we were seeking experimental subjects to evaluate WASPBENCH. We approached IIIT, who were glad to co-operate. We prepared datasets and experimental protocols and sent them to IIIT where the staff, who were already familiar with WASPBENCH, trained a group of students in its use and ran the experiments.

3   Experimental Setup

We asked the participants to work with the WASPBENCH to create word experts for the selected words. This task gave us information about how the users experienced using the workbench, either explicitly, by giving us feedback, or implicitly

---

[2] We would like to thank Prof. Tony Hartley for his help in setting this up.

[3] The word would have to be a noun, verb or adjective; WASPBENCH does not address grammatical words or, at the current time, adverbs.

by supplying us with data. This part of the experiment created the word experts. The other task was to evaluate the word experts. We applied them to a set of previously unseen test sentences and asked the participants to assess the results.

3.1   The Task

Creating the word experts. The main task for the participants was to use the WASPBENCH to create word experts for a list of selected ambiguous English words. The evaluation task focussed on translation. The user was asked to use the WASPBENCH in order to find out how the word was used in English (i.e. as represented by the BNC) and how the different uses of the word would be translated in a target language of the participant's choice. After the user has chosen the translations for the word and selected the clues giving evidence for when the word should receive a particular translation, the user submits the data and the WASPBENCH infers further rules to complete the word expert. The user is presented the rule set and can manually inspect it. If they are happy with the set, they can decide to submit the word expert and continue with the next word. If they are not happy with the rule set, they can return to the wordsketch definition form and add or amend the input. After submitting, the word expert is applied to a set of test sentences.

Assessing the results. Evaluating a word expert is like evaluating the work of a translator. The work of a translator can be judged by someone else, who can disagree on certain decisions made by the translator. The disagreement can be a matter of personal style. The assessment task here involves the same kind of problem. In this experimental paradigm we do not define beforehand what the desired translation is. Every subject may identify a different set of target translations for each word and even if they work with the same set, people might disagree on the preferred translation of a certain word in a particular context. There is just no gold standard and thus we cannot evaluate the decisions automatically. Therefore we asked the participants to assess the the word experts' judgements.[4]

The assessment task can best be introduced by looking at a screenshot. In figure 2 we present part of the evaluation screen with the results of applying the word expert made by participant 'one' for the noun bank to the set of 45 test sentences. The assesser is asked to enter their own number for identification purposes. The second column gives the test sentences with the word we are interested in (here bank) highlighted. The third column presents the word expert's translation. The assesser is asked to judge the correctness of the translation in this particular context in the fourth column. In case they disagree with the translation offered, they can pick their preferred translation from the pulldown menu in the fifth column (**Alternative**). This pulldown menu offers all the other suggested target translations for bank as defined by participant 'one'. In case the

---

[4] Similar difficulties were encountered in the Japanese SENSEVAL-2 machine translation task, and a similar strategy was adopted ([19]).

assesser thinks the proper target translation is not available, the choice 'other' is offered in the alternatives list and their choice can be entered in the last column (**Other**). After judging all 45 test sentences, the assesser is asked to submit the form by pressing the button in the right upper corner.

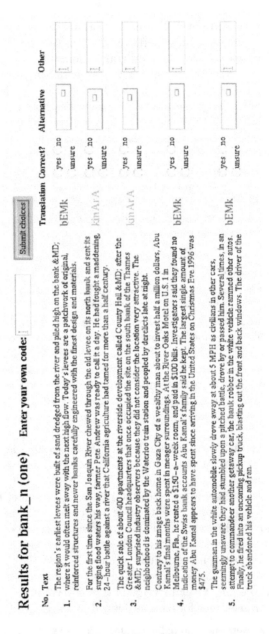

Fig. 2. Snapshot of the evaluation screen

3.2   Instruction and Available Time

Most participants had not worked with the WASPBENCH before. They were given a theoretical introduction and the opportunity afterwards to explore the user interface and its functionality by creating a word expert. The participants were allowed plenty of time to create the word expert and play with the WASPBENCH. They then applied the word expert to a set of test sentences and inspected the results, to conclude the introduction.

After the instruction session, approximately four days were allowed for working on the task: about two days for creating word experts and two for assessment. The participants were instructed to take their time to create the word experts, but to keep in mind that we did not expect perfection. In order to finish all 33 words in two working days, only approximately 30 minutes per word was available. Our first experiment taught us that that was not a reasonable thing to ask. Even though our first experiment showed that the speed at which the subjects created the word experts increased considerably as they became more familiar with the task and the workbench, more time was needed and we did not expect them to complete the full list. To ensure that every word on the list would be covered by equally many subjects, everyone was asked to start at a different position in the list.

3.3   Data

The Words. For the experiment we chose a set of words that are clearly ambiguous in English. We only selected words that were fairly, but not extremely, common (i.e. with 1,500 - 20,000 instances in the BNC). A total of 33 words were selected: 16 nouns, 10 verbs and 7 adjectives. Some of the words have just two clearly distinct meanings in English, others have more. There may of course also be further, more subtle meaning distinctions. All of the words were checked to confirm that the 'clearly distinct meanings' receive different translations in at least one of the languages at our disposal (Dutch, German and French). While we had identified a set of meanings for the words in the course of this process, this set was never shown to the participants. They were asked to create their own word expert with its own inventory of meanings/translations. This might result in different sets of target translation for different languages. In some languages two distinct different meanings might be translated with the same word, while subtle meaning differences might produce different translations in the target language. It is, of course, possible that, whenever more than participant was working on the same language, they disagreed on the one set of target translations.

The Test Data. In order to test the performance of the word experts, we selected for every word between 40 and 50 text fragments containing the target word. These fragments consisted of the complete sentence in which the word occurred plus one or two surrounding sentences. The test sentences were selected from the North American News Text Corpus.[5] Random samples were taken from

---

[5] Available from the Linguistic Data Consortium (www.ldc.upenn.edu).

the corpus and inspected for suitability. This was done to make sure that the samples were usable (some samples, like words from headlines, did not have much surrounding text) and to ensure that for every identified distinct meaning there were at least some test sentences available. If we had chosen a large set of test sentences from the corpus, we could have relied on pure random selection to take care of the proper meaning distribution, but a considerably larger sample than the 40 or 50 test sentences taken here would be necessary to rely on that.

The fact that we used an American news corpus for the test sentences and that the WASPBENCH currently uses the BNC for creating the word experts caused another problem: some words are used differently in British and American English, for example lot which has the 'parking space' meaning in American but not British English.

3.4   The Participants

A group of eighteen people were involved in the experiment. None of them had a specific lexicography or translation background, but all of them were post-graduates in linguistics or a closely related discipline (e.g. natural language processing). One of our goals for this experiment was to obtain data from several participants on the same words for the same target language. In the Leeds evaluation we worked with several people working on different languages. In order to minimize the effects of personal preferences we wanted to average the results from several (at least five) people working on the same word and target language. Most people worked with Hindi as target language (sixteen in total). Six of them were native speakers, the others were all fluent speakers of Hindi. Two subjects worked on other languages: Russian and Telugu. This was the mother tongue for both of them. All subjects had an excellent command of English, but were not necessarily fluent.

4   Evaluation of the Results

4.1   Summary of the Data

A total of 370 word experts were produced for the 33 words. This means that an average of 11.2 word experts per word are available. The minimum number of word experts per word was 9 and the maximum 13. As explained below, not all the results of applying the word experts to the test-data could be assessed. The results of a total number of 241 word experts was evaluated. This gives an average of 7.3 per word, with a minimum of 6 evaluated word experts for a word and a maximum of 10[6]. We are planning to evaluate the remaining 129 word experts at a later stage.

---

[6] For some of the words, one of the word experts was made for the target language Russian. This means that in a few cases we have a minimum of 5 different evaluated word experts that can be compared.

Total (241 word experts)

	Correct	Incorrect	Unsure	correct
All	6316	4011	485	58%
Nouns	3505	2014	236	61%
Verbs	1839	1238	101	58%
Adjectives	972	759	148	52%

Hindi (214 word experts)

	Correct	Incorrect	Unsure	correct
All	5712	3472	435	59%
Nouns	3179	1786	216	59%
Verbs	1683	1065	91	59%
Adjectives	850	621	128	53%

Hindi by native speakers (103 word experts)

	Correct	Incorrect	Unsure	correct
All	2721	1750	196	58%
Nouns	1608	928	94	61%
Verbs	762	571	56	55%
Adjectives	351	251	46	54%

Russian (22 word experts)

	Correct	Incorrect	Unsure	correct
All	523	430	33	53%
Nouns	326	228	20	57%
Verbs	98	109	2	47%
Adjectives	99	93	11	49%

Fig. 3. Summary of the India evaluation data

In figure 3 a summary of the results is presented. In 58% of the test sentences, the evaluator judged the word expert's prediction to be correct. In 33% the prediction was thought to be incorrect and in the remaining 5% they were not sure.

It is difficult to work out whether these results are good or bad. We would like to establish a "baseline" to compare WASPBENCH performance with.[7] With an average of 4.2 target translations per word (see figure 4) the WASPBENCH performs significantly better then the naive baseline that distributes the possible target translations evenly over the test sentences.A better baseline could arguably be set by assigning the most frequent occurring target translation to every sentence in the test set. However, this cannot be done once for all the participants, but needs to be done for every single word expert, due to the fact that different participants will often give different sense labels/translations for the same concept or take incompatible views of the words ambiguity. As mentioned above, test sentences were not a random sample of corpus instances containing the word, but were a subset of a random sample, chosen manually, to ensure that

---

[7] In our report on the results of the Leeds experiment we can compare with the machine translation results and we can conclude that the WASPBENCH outperforms those results.

a range of senses were covered. While this was necessary for experimental design, it complicates the issue of producing a baseline. A single random sample might well have produced 40 instances, all of the same meaning, implying a baseline of 100%, of little use for evaluating WASPBENCH. The opposite position of selecting test instances so that all senses were equally represented was considered, but rejected on the grounds that it was too far removed from the typically Zipfian facts of word frequency distribution. The approach adopted was a compromise.

4.2   Discussion

Considering the fact that the word experts were produced by inexperienced users in a relatively short amount of time (an average of 20.5 word experts in two days), we think that the overall results of the WASPBENCH are promising.

We expected a significantly better result for the nouns. It is often easier to determine the set of target translations for a noun than, for example, for a verb. Verbs often occur in constructions that are translated completely differently in the target language. This intuition is confirmed when compared to the results for the adjectives, but even though nouns do score overall better than verbs, the differences are small.

We did not find evidence for a difference in performance in the word experts between those that were produced by the native speakers of Hindi and by those that were non-native. Both the performance and the time needed for creating them were nearly identical.

Three of the participants volunteered to do the assessment task for their own word expert as well as for someone else's. The data from these three participants assessing their own word experts did not suggest any significant differences.

We expected decreasing success rates with increasing numbers of target translations. Although we do not have the space to give full results for every word, we have selected a few words in figure 5. The results for, for example, the nouns party and policy versus the noun line confirm this intuition. The verbs move versus pray and the adjectives flat versus funny are more evidence for this trend.

Some participants reported difficulties with loan words. Even though they experienced problems with particular sense of these words, the performance appeared to be better than average (see the figures for film and charge in figure 5). The other problematic cases reported were lexical gaps. The two words named explicitly proved to be very problematic. The results for the words float and moody were among the worst of the set.

One of our goals in this particular experiment was to find out how consistent the results are when several people work on the same data. We found that for most words the several word experts gave very similar results on the test data. The fluctuation in the results were strongly correlated with the number of target translations identified by the creator of the word sketch. Whenever the number of target translation identified by the participants was close to the average, the results for that word were close to the average.

Word	# Meanings	# Target translations	Word	# Meanings	# Target translations
bank	2	2.6	charge	3	4.7
chest	3	2.8	float	3	5.2
coat	3	2.6	move	3	6.3
film	3	2.7	observe	3	3.4
fit	3	4.9	offend	2	4.2
line	6	7.5	post	4	5.7
lot	4	3.6	pray	2	2.4
mass	3	6.4	ring	4	4.6
paper	3	4.3	toast	2	3
party	3	3.1	undermine	2	2.8
policy	3	2.2			
record	3	4.6	bright	4	4
seal	3	3.9	flat	4	7.4
step	2	4.4	free	5	3.8
term	3	5.4	funny	3	3.2
volume	3	4.9	hot	3	3.6
			moody	2	3.3
			strong	4	6.3

Fig. 4. Number of anticipated meanings and (average) number of target translations per word

Word	Correct	Incorrect	Unsure
film	74%	25%	1%
charge	65%	33%	2%
float	41%	48%	11%
moody	40%	52%	8%
party	72%	25%	3%
line	37%	54%	9%
policy	69%	29%	2%
move	29%	70%	1%
pray	86%	12%	2%
flat	43%	45%	12%
funny	66%	27%	7%

Fig. 5. The results for some individual words

5   User Experience with the Workbench

The evaluation task did not only provide data; it also gave us feedback on working with the workbench. Many comments were given on the presentation of the data, missing navigation abilities, buttons and correction facilities and other user-interface issues. We will not go into details here, but will incorporate suggestions into future releases of the workbench.

An important issue (also mentioned in the Leeds evaluation) is that people have difficulties with many of the grammatical relations, and instead, focus on example sentences. This is time consuming and it would be better if we could clarify the grammatical relations, either on the same screen, or on demand (for example by making help available).

A source of confusion and irritation is PoS tagger errors and errors made in predicting the grammatical relations. It makes clear that these components are critical for the usability of the workbench.

The participants also gave feedback on the evaluation task. Some of the issues raised had an impact on the number of word experts they could produce, others could influence the performance of their word experts. The most important remarks were about the assessment task. In the Leeds experiment, most of the subjects were native or near-native speakers of English. There was very little difference in time needed for creating the word experts between the Leeds group and the India group. However, most of the subjects in the Leeds group needed much less time for the assessment task than the India group. We underestimated the fact that for non-native speakers of English this task is much harder. For the native speakers it does not seem to be necessary to read the test sentences thoroughly. It is often enough just to look at the direct context of the ambiguous word to understand what the correct meaning of the word in this sentence is. It is much harder for the non-native speakers. They often want to understand the sentences properly before deciding on the correctness of the suggested translation. The lengthy test sentences (see the screenshot in figure 2) slowed down the progress of the assessment task considerably. As this had not been anticipated, not all the word experts could be evaluated.

As mentioned above, some participants reported that 'loan words' were problematic in cross evaluation cases. Although words like the noun film and the verb charge are used in the English form in Hindi for some of the senses, other senses are translated with a Hindi word. There are differences for several Indian languages with respect to which senses are translated. Some of the subjects experienced problems with assessing the results of a word expert made by someone whose mother tongue is different from the assesser.

6   Conclusions and Further Research

The evaluation experiment presented in this paper has given us a rich source of data. In this paper we have looked at this data from a few angles. The experiments taught us that the WASPBENCH is capable of organizing data in such a way that the users are able to create word experts in a consistent way.

Certain words are clearly causing problems. Identifying them beforehand, so special care can be taken for those, might improve the overall performance considerably. The case of lexical gaps, for example, needs extra attention. When words are significantly more ambiguous, it is probably worthwhile spending more time on creating the word expert. But it is probably not only the creator of the word expert who can improve on these words. It might be necessary to combine evidence from multiple sources, to decide which sense (or target translation) is the most suitable in a certain context. WASPBENCH currently uses a 'winner takes all' strategy for deciding which rule is applied for disambiguation; Sometimes an approach which accumulates evidence from different rules is better [20].

A nice aspect of the data we have gathered in this experiment is the reusability of the data. Modifications of the WSD engine in the WASPBENCH in the future can be evaluated by testing again with this data (although we are aware of the danger of overspecialising a system for a particular set of test data).

The feedback of the participants in both this experiment and in the Leeds experiment are very valuable for future developments of the WASPBENCH. Taking the workbench out of the laboratory and into the field is an important step in the development of a tool.

Acknowledgements. This work was supported by the UK EPSRC, under the WASPS project, grant GR/M54971. We would like to thank Amba Kulkarni and her colleagues at the IIIT for organising and supervising the experiments.

References

1. Kilgarriff, A.: The hard parts of lexicography. International Journal of Lexicography **11** (1998) 51–54
2. Sinclair, J.M., ed.: Looking Up: An Account of the COBUILD Project in Lexical Computing. Collins, London (1987)
3. COBUILD: The Collins COBUILD English Language Dictionary. *Edited by John McH. Sinclair* et al., London. (1987)
4. Gale, W., Church, K., Yarowsky, D.: A method for disambiguating word senses in a large corpus. Computers and the Humanities **26** (1993) 415–539
5. Kilgarriff, A., Tugwell, D.: Word sketch: Extraction and display of significant collocations for lexicography. In: Proc. Collocations workshop, ACL 2001, Toulouse, France (2001) 32–38
6. Yarowsky, D.: One sense per collocation. In: Proc. ARPA Human Language Technology Workshop, Princeton (1993)
7. Kilgarriff, A., Tugwell, D.: Wasp-bench: an MT lexicographer's workstation supporting state-of-the-art lexical disambiguation. In: Proc. MT Summit VIII, Santiago de Compostela, Spain (2001) 187–190
8. Fillmore, C.J.: Two dictionaries. International Journal of Lexicography **2** (1989) 57–83
9. Atkins, B.T.S., Levin, B.: Admitting impediments. In Zernik, U., ed.: Lexical Acquisition: Exploiting On-Line Resources to Build a Lexicon. Lawrence Erlbaum, Hillsdale, New Jersey (1991) 233–262

10. Atkins, B.T.S.: Then and now: Competence and performance in 35 years of lexicography. In: 10th EURALEX, Proceedings, Copenhagen (2002) 1–28
11. Edmonds, P., Kilgarriff, A.: Introduction to the special issue on evaluating word sense disambiguation systems. Natural Language Engineering (2002, forthcoming)
12. Magnini, B., Strapparava, C., Pezzulo, G., Gliozzo, A.: Using domain information for wsd. In: Proc. SENSEVAL-2: Second International Workshop on Evaluating WSD Systems, Toulouse, ACL (2001) 111–114
13. Vossen, P.: Extending, trimming and fusing wordnet for technical documents. In: Proceedings of the NAACL 2001 Workshop on WordNet and Other Lexical Resources, Pittsburgh (2001) http://www.seas.smu.edu/ rada/mwnw/papers/WNW-NAACL-105.pdf.
14. Buitelaar, P., Sacaleanu, B.: Ranking and selecting synsets by domain relevance. In: Proceedings of the NAACL 2001 Workshop on WordNet and Other Lexical Resources, Pittsburgh (2001)
15. Tugwell, D., Kilgarriff, A.: WASPBENCH: a lexicographic tool supporting wsd. In: Proc. SENSEVAL-2: Second International Workshop on Evaluating WSD Systems, Toulouse, ACL (2001) 151–154
16. Rundell, M., ed.: Macmillan English Dictionary for Advanced Learners. Macmillan, London (2002)
17. Kilgarriff, A., Rundell, M.: Lexical profiling software and its lexicographical applications – a case study. In: EURALEX 02, Copenhagen (2002)
18. McEnery, T., ed.: Language Engineering for South Asian Languages: workshop proceedings, University of Lancaster (2001) http://www.emille.lancs.ac.uk/lesal.htm.
19. Kurohashi, S.: Senseval-2 japanese translation task. In: Proceedings of Second International Workshop of Evaluating Word Sense Disambiguation Systems (SENSEVAL-2), Toulouse (2001) 37–40
20. Yarowsky, D., Florian, R.: Evaluating sense disambiguation performance across diverse parameter spaces. Journal of Natural Language Engineering (2002) In press Special Issue on Evaluating Word Sense Disambiguation Systems.

Using Measures of Semantic Relatedness for Word Sense Disambiguation

Siddharth Patwardhan[1], Satanjeev Banerjee[2], and Ted Pedersen[1]

[1] University of Minnesota, Duluth, MN 55812 USA
{patw0006,tpederse}@umn.edu, http://www.d.umn.edu/{~patw0006,~tpederse}
[2] Carnegie Mellon University, Pittsburgh, PA 15213 USA
banerjee+@cs.cmu.edu, http://www.cs.cmu.edu/~banerjee

Abstract. This paper generalizes the Adapted Lesk Algorithm of Banerjee and Pedersen (2002) to a method of word sense disambiguation based on semantic relatedness. This is possible since Lesk's original algorithm (1986) is based on gloss overlaps which can be viewed as a measure of semantic relatedness. We evaluate a variety of measures of semantic relatedness when applied to word sense disambiguation by carrying out experiments using the English lexical sample data of SENSEVAL-2. We find that the gloss overlaps of Adapted Lesk and the semantic distance measure of Jiang and Conrath (1997) result in the highest accuracy.

1 Introduction

Word sense disambiguation is the process of assigning a meaning to a word based on the context in which it occurs. The most appropriate meaning for a word is selected from a predefined set of possibilities, usually known as a sense inventory.

In this paper we present a class of dictionary–based methods that follow from the Adapted Lesk Algorithm of Banerjee and Pedersen [2]. The original Lesk algorithm [9] disambiguates a target word by selecting the sense whose gloss (or definition) has the largest number of words that overlap (or match) with the glosses of neighboring words. Banerjee and Pedersen extend the concept of a gloss overlap to include the glosses of words that are related to the target word and its neighbors according to the concept hierarchies provided in the lexical database WordNet [4]. This paper takes the view that gloss overlaps are just another measure of semantic relatedness, which is a point previously noted by Resnik [13]. In this paper we evaluate several additional measures of semantic relatedness when applied to word sense disambiguation using the general framework provided by the Adapted Lesk Algorithm.

Supervised learning algorithms also assign meanings to words from a sense inventory, but take a very different approach. A human manually annotates examples of a word with tags that indicates the intended sense in each context. These examples become training data for a learning algorithm that induces rules that are then used to assign meanings to other occurrences of the word. In supervised methods, the human uses the information in the dictionary to decide

A. Gelbukh (Ed.): CICLing 2003, LNCS 2588, pp. 241–257, 2003.
© Springer-Verlag Berlin Heidelberg 2003

which sense tag should be assigned to an example, and then a learning algorithm finds clues from the context of that word that allow it to generalize rules of disambiguation. Note that the learning algorithm simply views the sense inventory as a set of categories and that the human has absorbed the information from the dictionary and combined it with their own knowledge of words to manually sense–tag the training examples. The objective of a dictionary–based approach is to provide a disambiguation algorithm with the contents of a dictionary and attempt to make inferences about the meanings of words in context based on that information. Here we extract information about semantic relatedness from the lexical database WordNet (sometimes augmented by corpus statistics) in order to make such inferences.

This paper begins with an overview of the original Lesk algorithm and the adaptation of Banerjee and Pedersen. We review five other measures of semantic relatedness that are included in this study. These include measures by Resnik (1995), Jiang and Conrath (1997), Lin (1997), Leacock and Chodorow (1998), and Hirst and St. Onge (1998). We go on to describe our experimental methodology and results. We close with an analysis and discussion, as well as a brief review of related work.

2   The Lesk Algorithm

The original Lesk algorithm [9] disambiguates a target word by comparing its gloss with those of its surrounding words. The target word is assigned the sense whose gloss has the most overlapping or shared words with the glosses of its neighboring words.

There are two hypotheses that underly this approach. The first is that words that appear together in a sentence can be disambiguated by assigning to them the senses that are most closely related to their neighboring words. This follows from the intuition that words that appear together in a sentence must inevitably be related in some way, since they are normally working together to communicate some idea. The second hypothesis is that related senses can be identified by finding overlapping words in their definitions. The intuition here is equally reasonable, in that words that are related will often be defined using the same words, and in fact may refer to each other in their definitions.

For example, in The rate of interest at my bank is... a human reader knows that bank refers to a financial institution rather than a river shore, since each of these words has a financial sense. In WordNet the glosses of the financial senses of these three words overlap; the glosses of interest and bank share money and mortgage, and the glosses of interest and rate share charge.

The main limitation to this approach is that dictionary glosses are often quite brief, and may not include sufficient vocabulary to identify related senses. Banerjee and Pedersen suggest an adaptation based on the use of WordNet. Rather than simply considering the glosses of the surrounding words in the sentence, the concept hierarchy of WordNet is exploited to allow for glosses of word senses related to the words in the context to be compared as well. In effect, the glosses of surrounding words in the text are expanded to include glosses of those words to which they are related through relations in WordNet. Pedersen and Banerjee also suggest a variation to the scoring of overlaps such that a match of n consecutive words in two glosses is weighted more heavily than a set of n one word matches.

Suppose that bark is the target word and it is surrounded by dog and tail. The original Lesk algorithm checks for overlaps in the glosses of the senses of dog with the glosses of bark. Then it checks for overlaps in the glosses of bark and tail. The sense of bark with the maximum number of overlaps with dog and tail is selected. The adaptation of the Lesk algorithm considers these same overlaps and adds to them the overlaps of the glosses of the senses of concepts that are semantically or lexically related to dog, bark and tail according to WordNet.

3   WordNet

WordNet [4] is a freely–available electronic dictionary of nouns, verbs, adjectives and adverbs that has been developed at Princeton University. It organizes related concepts into synonym sets or synsets. For example: {car, auto, automobile, machine, motorcar} is a synset that represents the concept defined by the gloss, 4□wheeled motor vehicle; usually propelled by an internal combustion engine.

In addition to providing these groups of synonyms to represent a concept, WordNet connects concepts via a variety of relations. This creates a network where related concepts can be (to some extent) identified by their relative distance from each other. The relations provided include synonymy, antonymy, is□a, and part□of.

The concept hierarchies in WordNet generally do not cross part of speech boundaries, so semantic and lexical relations are confined to a particular part of speech. For nouns, an is□a relation exists between two concepts when one concept is□a□kind□of another concept. Such a concept is also known as a hypernym. For example, a car is a hypernym of motor vehicle. An is□a hierarchy also exists for verbs, although it represents is□way□of□doing, also known as troponomy. As an example, walking is a troponym of moving. Each of these hierarchies has a very general topmost node that is not related to a specific concept. As one traverses down from these topmost nodes the concepts become more specific or topical.

We use WordNet 1.7 which contains nine separate noun hierarchies containing 74,588 concepts joined by 76,226 is□a links. In order to allow for paths between all noun concepts in WordNet, we create a root node that subsumes the nine given hierarchies. Verb hierarchies provide less information about relatedness between separate concepts since there are 628 separate hierarchies for the 12,754 verb concepts. While these could all be joined by a root node, the result would be a tree structure that was very wide and would result in many different concepts being located at approximately the same path length from each other.

The measures of semantic relatedness considered in this paper focus on the noun is□a hierarchies in WordNet. These are the most developed relations in WordNet, comprising over 70% of the total relations for nouns. Each hierarchy can be visualized as a tree that has a very general concept associated with a root node and more specific concepts associated with leaves. For example, a root node might represent a concept like entity whereas leaf nodes are associated with carving fork and whisk broom.

Path lengths between concepts have been employed in other networks of concepts to represent semantic relatedness (e.g., [12]). However, this is only appropriate when the path lengths between concepts have a consistent interpretation. This is not the case with WordNet, since concepts higher in a hierarchy are more general than those lower in the hierarchy. Thus, a path of length one between two general concepts can suggest a large difference whereas one between two specific concepts may not. For example, in WordNet mouse and rodent are separated by a path of length one, which is the same distance that separates Ure iron and implement. The fact that path lengths can be interpreted differently depending on where they occur in WordNet has led to the development of a number of measures based on path lengths that incorporate a variety of correcting factors.

4   Measures of Semantic Relatedness

We make a distinction between relatedness and similarity, following Budanitsky and Hirst [3]. Semantic similarity is a kind of relatedness between two words that defines a resemblance. Semantic relatedness covers a broader range of relationships between concepts that includes similarity (or difference) as as well other relations such as isUaUkindUof, isUaUpartUof, isUaUspeciUcUexampleUof, isU theUoppositeUof to name but a few.

There are pairs of words that tend to occur together more often than we'd expect by chance. Sometimes this is indicative of a semantic relationship between the words. Even though these relations are quite diverse, humans can usually judge if a pair of words is more related than another. For example, a human would judge paper and pencil much more closely related than car and fork.

It would be useful to assign a value that characterizes the degree to which two words are related. The gloss overlaps discussed previously can be viewed as a very simple mechanism for assigning such values. For example, if two concepts share two words in their respective glosses, they might be considered to be more related than a pair of concepts whose glosses share one word.

What follows is a discussion of a number of measures that have been developed to assign values of semantic relatedness based on their relative position in a concept hierarchy, and possibly augmented by corpus–based information. All of these measures are based on the concept hierarchies as provided by Word-Net. Please note that in the rest of this paper concept and word sense are used somewhat interchangeably, since each concept in WordNet represents a distinct meaning that can be considered a word sense.

4.1   The Leacock–Chodorow Measure

The measure of Leacock and Chodorow [8] is based on the lengths of paths between noun concepts in an isUa hierarchy. The shortest path between two concepts is the one which includes the fewest number of intermediate concepts. This value is scaled by the depth of the hierarchy, where depth is defined as the length of the longest path from a leaf node to the root node of the hierarchy.

Thus, their measure of relatedness is defined as follows:

$$related_{lch}(c_1, c_2) = max[-log(ShortestLength(c_1, c_2)/(2 \cdot D))] \qquad (1)$$

$ShortestLength(c_1, c_2)$ is the shortest path length (having minimum number of nodes) between the two concepts and D is the maximum depth of the taxonomy (distance of the farthest node from the root node). Given our scheme of introducing a hypothetical root node that joins all the noun hierarchies, D becomes a constant of 16 for all nouns, meaning that the path length from this root node to the most distant leaf node is 16 in WordNet 1.7.

4.2   The Resnik Measure

Resnik [13] introduces a measure of relatedness based on his formulation of information content, which is a value that is assigned to each concept in a hierarchy based on evidence found in a corpus.

Before describing this measure of relatedness we first introduce the notion of information content, which is simply a measure of the specificity of a concept. A concept with a high information content is very specific to a particular topic, while concepts with lower information content are associated with more general, less specific concepts. Thus, carving fork has a high information content while entity has low information content.

Information content of a concept is estimated by counting the frequency of that concept in a large corpus and thereby determining its probability via a maximum likelihood estimate. According to Resnik, the negative log of this probability determines the information content of the concept:

$$IC(concept) = -log(P(concept)) \qquad (2)$$

If sense–tagged text is available, frequency counts of concepts can be attained directly, since each concept will be associated with a unique sense. If sense–tagged text is not available (which is the usual situation) it will be necessary to adopt an alternative counting scheme. Resnik [14] suggests counting the number of occurrences of a word type in a corpus, and then dividing that count by the number of different concepts/senses associated with that word. This value is then assigned to each concept. For example, suppose that the word type bank occurs 20 times in a corpus, and that there are two concepts associated with this type in the hierarchy, one for river bank and the other for financial bank. Each of these concepts would receive a count of 10. If the occurrences of bank were sense tagged then the relevant counts could simply be assigned to the appropriate concept.

In our experiments we choose to assign the total count to all the concepts and not divide by the number of possible concepts. Thus we would assign 20 to river bank and financial bank in the example above. This decision was based on the observation that by distributing the frequency count over all the concepts associated with a word type we effectively assign a higher relative frequency to those words having fewer senses. This would lead us to estimate a higher probability and therefore assign a lower value of information content to such concepts.

For example, suppose again that bank occurs 20 times and that there are two possible underlying concepts. Further suppose that carving fork also occurs 20 times but that it only has one associated concept. In the counting scheme of Resnik the two concepts associated with bank would have a higher information content than the single concept associated with carving fork. However, the term carving fork is certainly referring to just one concept, while occurrences of bank could be referring to either of the two possible concepts. As such it seems that the information content of carving fork should be at least as high as bank in this case.

Regardless of how they are counted, the frequency of a concept includes the frequency of all its subordinate concepts since the count we add to a concept is added to its subsuming concept as well. Note that the counts of more specific concepts are added to the more general concepts, but not from the more general to specific. Thus, counts of more specific concepts percolate up to the top of the hierarchy, incrementing the counts of the more general concepts as they proceed upward. As a result, concepts that are higher up in the hierarchy will have higher counts than those at lower more specific levels and have higher probabilities associated with them. Such high probability concepts will have low values of information content since they are associated with more general concepts.

The Resnik measure of semantic similarity [13] uses the information content of concepts along with their positions in the noun is‐a hierarchies of WordNet to compute a value for the semantic relatedness of the concepts. The principle idea behind his measure of semantic relatedness is that two concepts are semantically related proportional to the amount of information they share in common. The quantity of information common to two concepts is determined by the information content of the lowest concept in the hierarchy that subsumes both the given concepts. This concept is known as the lowest common subsumer of the two concepts. Thus, the Resnik measure of similarity is defined as follows:

$$sim_{res}(c_1, c_2) = IC(lcs(c_1, c_2)) \tag{3}$$

We note that this measure does not consider the information content of the concepts themselves, nor does it directly consider the path length. The potential limitation of this approach is that quite a few concepts might have the same least common subsumer, and would have identical values of similarity assigned to them. For example, in WordNet the concept of vehicle is the least common subsumer of jumbo jet, tank, house trailer, and ballistic missile. Therefore any pair of these concepts would receive the same similarity score.

4.3   The Jiang–Conrath Measure

Jiang and Conrath [7] use information content as defined by Resnik and augment it with a notion of path length between concepts. This results in a hybrid approach to computing semantic relatedness of pairs of concepts. This approach includes the information content of the concepts themselves along with the information content of their lowest common subsumer. The measure is determined by the formula:

$$dist_{jcn}(c_1, c_2) = IC(c_1) + IC(c_2) - 2 \times IC(lcs(c_1, c_2)) \tag{4}$$

This formula, however, results in a distance (or measure of unrelatedness) between the two concepts. Concepts that are more related have a lower score than the less related ones. In order to maintain consistency among the measures, we convert this measure of semantic distance into a measure of semantic relatedness via the following:

$$related_{jcn}(c_1, c_2) = \frac{1}{dist_{jcn}(c_1, c_2)} \tag{5}$$

4.4   The Lin Measure

The Lin measure [10] of semantic relatedness of concepts is based on his Similarity Theorem. It states that the similarity of two concepts is measured by the ratio of the amount of information needed to state the commonality of the two concepts to the amount of information needed to describe them.

The commonality of two concepts is captured by the information content of their lowest common subsumer and the information content of the two concepts themselves. This measure turns out to be a close cousin of the Jiang–Conrath measure, although they were developed independently:

$$related_{lin}(c_1, c_2) = \frac{2 \times IC(lcs(c_1, c_2))}{IC(c_1) + IC(c_2)} \tag{6}$$

This can be viewed as taking the information content of the intersection of the two concepts (multiplied by 2) and dividing it by their sum, which is analogous to the well-known Dice Coefficient.

4.5   The Hirst–St. Onge Measure

All of the above measures of semantic relatedness consider only the is‑a relations for nouns in WordNet. Hirst and St. Onge [6] introduce a measure of relatedness that considers many other relations in WordNet and is not restricted to nouns. The measure was originally intended to identify lexical chains, which are a series of words that are related and maintain coherence in a text.

As a result the Hirst–St. Onge measure assigns a relatedness score for word types rather than concepts. In order to make this measure suitable for our purposes, we eliminated one relation (extra strong) from the original formulation that focuses on word types rather than concepts.

This measure classifies all WordNet relations as horizontal, upward, or downward. Upward relations connect more specific concepts to more general ones, while downward relations join more general concepts to more specific ones. For example, is‑a is an upward relation while contains is considered to be a downward relation. Horizontal relations maintain the same level of specificity, where antonyms are an example.

The Hirst–St. Onge measure has four levels of relatedness: extra strong, strong, medium strong, and weak. An extra strong relation is based on the surface form of the words and therefore does not apply in our case since we are measuring the relatedness of word senses.

Two words representing the same concept have a strong relation between them. Thus, there is a strong relation between two instances of the same concept. There are two additional scenarios by which a strong relations can exist: First, if the synsets representing the concepts are connected via a horizontal relation then this constitutes a strong relation. Second, if one of the concepts is represented by a compound word and the other concept is represented by a word which is a part of the compound, and if there is any kind of synset relation between the two concepts, then there exists a strong relation between the two concepts.

The medium–strong relation is determined by a set of allowable paths between concepts that are described by Hirst and St. Onge [6]. If such a path exists between two concepts, then we have a medium–strong relation between them. The score or weight for the relation in this case is given by a formula that considers the path length between the concepts and the number of changes in direction of the path:

$$path\_weight = C - path\_length - (k \times number\_of\_changes\_in\_direction) \quad (7)$$

Following Budanitsky and Hirst, we use $C = 8$ and $k = 1$. The value of strong relations is defined to be 2*C. Thus, two concepts that exhibit a strong relation will receive a score of 16, two concepts with a medium strong relation will be scored as in the formula above, and two concepts that have no relation will receive a score of zero.

5   Disambiguation Using Semantic Relatedness

What follows is a description of the Adapted Lesk Algorithm of Banerjee and Pedersen. It starts by selecting a window of context that consists of the target word and some number of content words to the left and right that are known to WordNet. For the experiments in this paper, we use a window of three words, meaning that the glosses of the target word are compared with the glosses of the content words immediately to its left and right. However, if the target word occurs at the beginning or end of the sentence we adjust the window so that the two content words are to the right or left of the target word.

The algorithm identifies candidate senses for each word in the window of context based on the sense inventory in WordNet. If a word in the window is used as part of a compound, then the senses associated with that compound are the candidates. Otherwise, the candidate senses include those associated with the surface form of the word in the window as well as those of the base form of the word, as determined by the WordNet stemmer.

Most of the measures of semantic relatedness that we employ are intended for use with nouns; the only exceptions are the measures of Hirst–St. Onge and the gloss overlaps of the Adapted Lesk Algorithm. As such we only consider the noun senses of words found in the window of context. We do not part of speech tag the words in the windows of context. Instead, we identify the first word to the left and right of the target word that has a noun form that appears in WordNet, regardless of whether that word is actually used as a noun in that particular context. Our conjecture is that an adjacent verb or adjective that has a noun form will be more related to the target word than will a potentially more distant word that is used as a noun. Thus the window is formed by surrounding words that have noun forms regardless of their actual usage in that context.

After the candidate senses are determined, we measure the relatedness of the candidate senses of the target word to those of the surrounding words in the window of context. From this a score is computed for each sense of the target word that specifies how related it is to the senses of the words in the window of context. While the general framework of Banerjee and Pedersen supports two strategies for computing these scores, we employ their local paradigm.

This scoring method is similar to that of the original Lesk algorithm. The semantic relatedness of each sense of the target word is measured relative to every noun sense of the words in the window of context. The scores associated with each combination of senses are summed and used to assign a value to each candidate sense for the target word. The sense with the highest score is then assigned to the target word.

Candidate senses are scored by the original Adapted Lesk Algorithm using gloss overlaps. However, any measure of semantic relatedness could be used since the gloss overlaps simply produce a numeric score that indicates how many overlaps there are between the glosses of the senses of the target word and the glosses of the senses of the words in the window of context. The larger these scores, the more related the words. In this paper we extend the Adapted Lesk framework such that we can plug other measures of relatedness into the algorithm in place of gloss overlaps. All of the code used to calculate these measures and perform word sense disambiguation is available from the author's web pages.

6   Experimental Data

We compare the different measures of relatedness by employing them in the Adapted Lesk framework in place of gloss overlaps. We carried out word sense disambiguation experiments using the noun data from the English lexical sample task of Senseval-2. In particular, this consisted of of 1,754 instances from the evaluation portion of this data, where each instance is made up of three to four sentences where a single word (the target word) has been manually assigned its most appropriate sense from WordNet.

This results in 29 nouns that serve as target words, each of which has between 1 and 14 possible WordNet senses. Table 1 lists the base form of the target words and the number of instances available for that word. It also specifies the number of WordNet senses for the base form of the target word in column WN and the the total number of candidate senses considered for each word in column cand. The number of candidate senses is greater than the number of possible senses of the base form because target words may appear in multiple forms over a set of instances.

These various forms consist of morphological variants and compounds. For example, while art is the base form of one of the target words, it also occurs as a target word in the data as arts and art gallery. WordNet has a separate sense inventory for each form, so we will consider additional or different sets of senses depending on the form of the target word. The number of candidate senses shown is the total number of candidate senses considered across all the instances and is not specific to any particular instance or form of the word.

7   Experiments and Results

Our empirical evaluation follows the model of Budanitsky and Hirst [3], who compare the five measures of relatedness previously described when applied to context sensitive spelling correction. We use those same measures in this study in addition to the gloss overlaps from the Adapted Lesk Algorithm.

We use the local approach from Adapted Lesk with a three word window of context. The framework of Adapted Lesk was generalized so that it could perform word sense disambiguation based on each of the semantic relatedness measures discussed above in addition to the original gloss overlap measure.

Results are reported as per word and overall accuracy, where the number of correct instances is divided by the total number of instances. Table 1 shows the disambiguation accuracy attained when using each of the different measures of semantic relatedness. The results for the Resnik, Jiang–Conrath, Lin, Leacock–Chodorow, Hirst–St.Onge, and gloss overlap measures are shown in columns Res, Jcn, Lin, Lch, Hso and Lesk, respectively. The highest accuracy achieved for each word is shown in bold face, while the least is italicized. The overall accuracy for each measure is shown at the bottom of the table.

The measures of Resnik, Jiang–Conrath and Lin depend upon the corpus used to estimate information content. We carried out experiments using five sources of information content: SemCor (with and without sense tags), the Brown Corpus [5], the Penn [11], and the British National Corpus.

The Brown Corpus is a 1,000,000 token corpus of balanced English. SemCor is a sense tagged subset of the Brown Corpus that consists of about 200,000 sense-tagged tokens, many of which are associated with concepts that only occur one time. The Penn Treebank is a 1,000,000 token corpus of English taken from the Wall Street Journal. The British National Corpus (BNC) is by far the largest of these corpora as it is a 100,000,000 token balanced sample of English.

Table 1. Experimental Results

Word	Instance count	Senses WN	Senses cand	Res	Jcn	Lin	Lch	Hso	Lesk
art	98	4	14	0.41	0.54	0.42	0.44	*0.40*	**0.61**
authority	92	7	9	*0.14*	0.16	0.17	0.19	0.20	**0.27**
bar	151	13	21	0.21	0.23	**0.25**	*0.18*	0.25	0.21
bum	44	4	4	0.20	**0.73**	0.41	0.59	0.31	*0.13*
chair	69	4	7	0.37	0.33	0.46	*0.21*	0.44	**0.84**
channel	73	7	13	0.15	0.15	0.16	**0.23**	0.20	*0.10*
child	63	4	5	0.27	0.43	0.38	*0.02*	0.16	**0.62**
church	64	3	9	*0.37*	0.41	*0.37*	0.41	**0.48**	0.38
circuit	85	6	15	0.43	0.51	0.48	*0.34*	0.41	**0.53**
day	134	10	18	*0.12*	**0.43**	0.32	0.28	0.19	0.15
detention	32	2	5	0.61	0.81	0.61	*0.52*	0.63	**0.88**
dyke	28	2	2	0.73	0.86	0.77	*0.46*	0.61	**0.89**
facility	58	5	7	0.24	**0.34**	0.29	*0.21*	0.23	0.29
fatigue	43	4	6	*0.16*	0.42	0.22	**0.77**	0.44	**0.77**
feeling	51	6	7	*0.22*	**0.55**	0.27	0.53	0.26	0.49
grip	42	7	8	**0.22**	0.19	0.19	0.17	0.18	*0.12*
hearth	32	3	3	0.43	0.72	0.59	*0.38*	0.42	**0.75**
holiday	31	2	3	**0.55**	*0.16*	0.32	**0.55**	**0.55**	*0.16*
lady	53	3	8	0.36	*0.17*	0.19	**0.42**	0.36	*0.17*
material	69	5	10	0.44	**0.55**	0.44	0.40	0.38	*0.29*
mouth	57	8	8	0.12	0.12	0.11	*0.05*	0.20	**0.46**
nation	37	4	6	*0.18*	0.35	0.26	0.22	0.26	**0.59**
nature	44	5	6	0.10	0.11	*0.05*	0.11	**0.18**	0.16
post	78	8	12	0.16	**0.35**	0.19	*0.09*	0.15	0.31
restraint	45	6	7	0.31	**0.40**	0.33	0.36	0.30	*0.16*
sense	50	5	11	0.49	*0.40*	0.51	*0.40*	0.43	**0.50**
spade	33	3	4	**0.70**	*0.15*	0.56	0.21	0.40	0.59
stress	39	5	5	0.32	0.38	0.33	**0.44**	0.39	*0.31*
yew	28	2	3	0.66	0.79	0.73	*0.57*	0.70	**0.86**
Total	1723			*0.295*	0.380	0.331	0.305	0.316	**0.391**

We report the best results for each of these three measures in Table 1. The results for Jiang–Conrath and Lin are based on estimates of information content from the British National Corpus, while those of Resnik are based on the sense tagged version of SemCor. In addition, we provide the overall accuracies attained by each of these measures when their information content is determined from each of the indicated corpora in Table 2. Leacock–Chodorow, Hirst–St. Onge, and Adapted Lesk are not included here since they do not employ corpus information but instead only depend on information found in WordNet.

Table 2. Overall Accuracy Using Different Sources of Information Content

Corpus	Measure of Relatedness		
	Res	Jcn	Lin
SemCor	**0.295**	0.330	0.328
SemCor (untagged)	**0.295**	0.330	0.320
Brown Corpus	0.290	0.363	**0.331**
Penn Treebank	0.292	**0.380**	0.329
BNC	0.290	**0.380**	**0.331**

8   Analysis and Discussion

The gloss overlaps of Adapted Lesk and the Jiang–Conrath measure result in disambiguation that was significantly more accurate than the rest of the measures. The gloss overlaps of Adapted Lesk result in the highest overall accuracy (.391). In addition, it is the most accurate method for 13 of the 29 words. The next most accurate method overall was that of Jiang–Conrath when information content was estimated from the Penn Treebank or BNC (.380). This proved to be the most accurate method for 7 individual words.

Of the three measures based on information content, Jiang–Conrath was the only one that showed significant variations based on the corpora from which information content was estimated. It was most accurate with the British National Corpus and the Penn Treebank, and least accurate with SemCor (tagged and untagged).

Despite the very close similarity between the formulation of Jiang–Conrath and the Lin measure, there was a significant difference between them in accuracy for all corpora except SemCor (tagged and untagged). The accuracy of the Lin measure did not vary much with information content estimated from different corpora. The highest accuracy it attained was .331 and the lowest was .320. It was the least extreme of all the measures in that it was most accurate for one word and was the least accurate method for only two words. The Hirst–St. Onge measure (.316) was similarly conservative in that it was most accurate for four words and least accurate for just one.

The Leacock–Chodorow measure (.305) was most accurate for five words but least accurate for twelve words. Its overall accuracy was slightly higher than that of Resnik (.295), which was most accurate for three words and least accurate for six. Like the Lin measure, the accuracy associated with the Resnik measure did not vary a great deal with different sources of estimates for information content. The highest level was .295 and the lowest was .290.

These measures use a variety of different sources of information to determine the semantic relatedness of words. Leacock–Chodorow and Hirst–St. Onge rely on the structure of concept hierarchies; Resnik, Jiang–Conrath, and Lin augment this concept hierarchy with information content values estimated from corpora; and the Adapted Lesk Algorithm relies on gloss overlaps from WordNet.

The results attained by Leacock–Chodorow and Resnik suggest that simply relying on the concept hierarchy structure or information content values is not sufficient. The Jiang–Conrath measure combines the structure of WordNet with information content values taken from corpora and does extremely well and outperforms all other measures except the gloss overlaps of Adapted Lesk. This is an interesting result since the gloss overlaps are a completely different source of information.

8.1   Information Content Variations

We estimated information content from a number of corpora in order to study the effect of different amounts and types of data on disambiguation accuracy. Resnik's original experiments were with the Brown Corpus, while Lin and Jiang–Conrath used the sense–tagged version of SemCor.

We wanted to determine the effect of sense–tagged text on information content based measures. We expected sense–tagged text to be the best source of information content values, since each sense–tag represents a single concept and estimates derived from such data should be very reliable. We carried out disambiguation experiments using information content derived from the sense–tagged version of SemCor and then we repeated the experiment after removing the sense–tags.

Curiously enough, none of the three information content based measures performed significantly differently with the tagged and untagged versions of SemCor. We believe this is because many of the sense–tags in SemCor occur only once, thus creating a fairly sparse source of data. As a result the information content of the sense–tagged corpora is not significantly different than that of the untagged version.

We also wanted to assess the impact of increasing the size of the corpus from which information content values are estimated. Our initial experiments were done with SemCor, which has about 200,000 tokens. When carrying out the same experiments using the 1,000,000 token Brown Corpus and Penn Treebank, we observed that only Jiang–Conrath showed an increase in accuracy. Curiously enough, it performed considerably better with the Penn Treebank (.380) than it did with the more balanced Brown Corpus (.363). We say this is curious since the SENSEVAL-2 data does not seem terribly similar to typical Penn Treebank text.

Both Resnik and Lin performed at nearly the same level of accuracy regardless of the corpora from which the information content values were estimated. The Resnik measure was most accurate (.295) with SemCor whether it was sense–tagged or not, and least accurate with the Brown Corpus and BNC (.290). The Lin Measure was least accurate with the untagged version of SemCor (.320) and most accurate with the Brown Corpus and BNC (.331).

Our final experiment was with the British National Corpus (BNC), which is a 100,000,000 token sample of English. Despite the huge increase in size, Jiang–Conrath performed at the same level of accuracy as achieved with the Penn Treebank, and Resnik and Lin attained accuracy equal to (or less than) that of

SemCor. Thus, the very large increase in size of the corpus did not yield any benefit for word sense disambiguation. We are unclear as to why this would be the case, and consider this an important issue for future work.

8.2   Window Size Variations

The results reported earlier were based on window sizes of three, which include the target word and one content word to the right and left. We conducted several experiments with a window size of five, which includes the target word and two words to the right and left.

The most significant change in results when increasing the window size was with the Jiang–Conrath measure. For SemCor the accuracy rose to .341 with a window size of five (from .330) and for the BNC it attained .386 (from .380). As a result Jiang–Conrath achieves a level of accuracy that is essentially equal to that of the gloss overlaps of Adapted Lesk. The change of window size from three to five did not change the accuracy of Adapted Lesk.

The Lin measure with information content estimated from the Brown Corpus improved, rising from .331 to .341. The Resnik measure improved with respect to the Penn Treebank, which achieved .302 with a window size of five versus .292 with a window of three. In addition, the accuracy of the Hirst–St. Onge improved to .333 when the window size is five.

Thus, it appears that among the information content measures of Resnik, Lin, and Jiang–Conrath, the latter is the most able to take advantage of increased amounts of information. It is most accurate with a window size of five where its information content is estimated from the British National Corpus (.386). Given this same combination of window size and corpus, Lin achieves accuracy of .334 and Resnik reaches .298.

9   Related Work

A number of other methods to measure semantic relatedness of words have been proposed and used for word sense disambiguation. Agirre and Rigau [1] do not exactly describe a measure of semantic relatedness. Rather they introduce a notion of conceptual density and use this in the process of word sense disambiguation. This notion of conceptual density is again based on the WordNet is-a hierarchy. The process of disambiguation of a target word starts by considering all the possible senses of the target word and the senses of the words in the window of context of the target word (window sizes of five to 30 words were considered in their experiments). Sub-hierarchies in the WordNet is-a taxonomy are then determined, such that each sub-hierarchy contains one of the senses of the target word along with senses of word in the context. The conceptual density for each of these sub-hierarchies is computed as the ratio of the average number of hypernyms per node for the senses of the context words to the average number of hypernyms per node for all nodes of the sub-hierarchy. This ratio gives us the distribution or density of these senses in the sub–hierarchy. The sense of the target word in the sub–hierarchy with the largest conceptual density is selected as the implied sense. Though this method does not specify an exact formula for semantic relatedness of words, it appears to be built upon node counting techniques for measuring semantic relatedness and gives us yet another way to use the WordNet is⊡a hierarchy for word sense disambiguation.

Leacock and Chodorow [8] have used their measure to augment a supervised approach to word sense disambiguation that relies on local context, which are features that occur in close proximity to the target word. They use their measure (as well as Resnik's) to determine the relatedness between a noun in each test instance with nouns in the training data. If there is a noun in a test instance that does not occur in the training data, then the most related noun found in the training data is substituted in order to allow for disambiguation to proceed.

Lin [10] also used his measure of semantic relatedness to perform the task of word sense disambiguation. However, unlike the procedure followed in this paper, he used his measure of semantic relatedness to generate a list of local contexts for each target word. This list of context would then restrict the possibility of what could appear in the context of a given word for a particular sense. This was used to disambiguate new instances of the word.

10   Future Work

The two most accurate methods in this study were quite dissimilar. Adapted Lesk gloss overlaps are based on the definitions found within WordNet, while the measure of Jiang–Conrath is based on the concept hierarchy of WordNet and corpus statistics. This suggests that some combination of gloss overlaps, information content, and path lengths might result in improved accuracy.

We are aware that our method of estimating information content employs a different counting scheme than described by Resnik. In short, we do not divide frequency counts of word types by the number of associated concepts while Resnik does. We will carry out these same experiments using Resnik's estimation scheme. Our expectation is that the results will not vary significantly, since in general we believe that the concept counts are fairly noisy regardless of how they are made.

One of the curious results of these experiments was how little disambiguation accuracy was affected by changing the corpora from which information content values are estimated. The Resnik and Lin measures were fairly static in their performance regardless of the source of these estimates. The Jiang–Conrath measure improved with increasing corpus size, except when increasing to the very large British National Corpus, where it resulted in the same disambiguation accuracy as information content arrived at from the 100 times smaller Penn Treebank. Our next step it to estimate information content from corpora that is more like the data we are disambiguating to see if this changes the results.

A related point concerns the relatively low impact achieved by increasing the window size. We are curious as to why such a large increase in the information available to the disambiguation process would result in such minimal improvements. One possibility is that the very immediate context provides overwhelming evidence that is difficult to improve upon. In order to evaluate this idea we will carry out experiments using a two word window, that is the target word and one content word that precedes it.

The difficulties of using WordNet as a source of path lengths and gloss overlaps are well known. We have recently acquired Longman's Dictionary of Contemporary English (LDOCE) and intend to use its more limited concept hierarchy but richer and more regular glosses to carry out experiments similar to these. While the results of measures based on path lengths may suffer (since the hierarchy represented by LDOCE subject codes is fairly small) we are optimistic that the richer gloss information might result in better performance for Lesk inspired approaches.

11   Conclusions

We have shown that the Adapted Lesk Algorithm of Banerjee and Pedersen generalizes to a method of disambiguation based on semantic relatedness. We showed that several different measures of semantic relatedness work reasonably well in this framework, and that the gloss overlaps of Adapted Lesk and the Jiang–Conrath measure prove to be the most accurate for word sense disambiguation.

Acknowledgments. Satanjeev Banerjee is currently supported by the National Science Foundation under Grant No. REC–9979894. Ted Pedersen is partially supported by a National Science Foundation Faculty Early CAREER Development award (#0092784).

Any opinions, findings, conclusions, or recommendations expressed in this publication are those of the authors and do not necessarily reflect the views of the National Science Foundation or the official policies, either expressed or implied, of the sponsors or of the United States Government.

References

1. E. Agirre and G. Rigau. Word sense disambiguation using conceptual density. In *Proceedings of the 16th International Conference on Computational Linguistics*, pages 16–22, Copenhagen, 1996.
2. S. Banerjee and T. Pedersen. An adapted Lesk algorithm for word sense disambiguation using WordNet. In *Proceedings of the Third International Conference on Intelligent Text Processing and Computational Linguistics*, Mexico City, February 2002.
3. A. Budanitsky and G. Hirst. Semantic distance in WordNet: An experimental, application-oriented evaluation of five measures. In *Workshop on WordNet and Other Lexical Resources, Second meeting of the North American Chapter of the Association for Computational Linguistics*, Pittsburgh, June 2001.
4. C. Fellbaum, editor. *WordNet: An electronic lexical database.* MIT Press, 1998.

5. W. Francis and H. Kucera. *Frequency Analysis of English Usage: Lexicon and Grammar.* Houghton Mifflin, 1982.

6. G. Hirst and D. St. Onge. Lexical chains as representations of context for the detection and correction of malapropisms. In C. Fellbaum, editor, *WordNet: An electronic lexical database,* pages 305–332. MIT Press, 1998.

7. J. Jiang and D. Conrath. Semantic similarity based on corpus statistics and lexical taxonomy. In *Proceedings on International Conference on Research in Computational Linguistics,* Taiwan, 1997.

8. C. Leacock and M. Chodorow. Combining local context and WordNet similarity for word sense identification. In C. Fellbaum, editor, *WordNet: An electronic lexical database,* pages 265–283. MIT Press, 1998.

9. M. Lesk. Automatic sense disambiguation using machine readable dictionaries: How to tell a pine cone from a ice cream cone. In *Proceedings of SIGDOC '86,* 1986.

10. D. Lin. Using syntactic dependency as a local context to resolve word sense ambiguity. In *Proceedings of the 35th Annual Meeting of the Association for Computational Linguistics,* pages 64–71, Madrid, July 1997.

11. M. Marcus, B. Santorini, and M. Marcinkiewicz. Building a large annotated corpus of English: The Penn Treebank. *Computational Linguistics,* 19(2):313–330, 1993.

12. R. Rada, H. Mili, E. Bicknell, and M. Blettner. Development and application of a metric on semantic nets. *IEEE Transactions on Systems, Man and Cybernetics,* 19(1):17–30, 1989.

13. P. Resnik. Using information content to evaluate semantic similarity in a taxonomy. In *Proceedings of the 14th International Joint Conference on Artificial Intelligence,* Montreal, August 1995.

14. P. Resnik. WordNet and class–based probabilities. In C. Fellbaum, editor, *WordNet: An electronic lexical database,* pages 239–263. MIT Press, 1998.

Automatic Sense Disambiguation of the Near-Synonyms in a Dictionary Entry

Diana Zaiu Inkpen and Graeme Hirst

Department of Computer Science, University of Toronto, Toronto, Ontario, Canada, M5S 3G4
{dianaz,gh}@cs.toronto.edu

Abstract. We present an automatic method to disambiguate the senses of the near-synonyms in the entries of a dictionary of synonyms. We combine different indicators that take advantage of the structure on the entries and of lexical knowledge in WordNet. We also present the results of human judges doing the disambiguation for 50 randomly selected entries. This small amount of annotated data is used to tune and evaluate our system.

1 Near-Synonyms

Near-synonyms are words with close senses. They are described in dictionaries such as *Webster's New Dictionary of Synonyms* (Gove 1984) and *Choose the Right Word* (Hayakawa 1994) (hereafter CTRW). An entry in these dictionaries presents a cluster of near-synonyms, explains the core meaning that they share, and makes explicit the differences between them. The differences include stylistic, attitudinal, and denotational nuances (see Edmonds 2000, Hirst 1995 for more details). An example of a fragment of an entry in CTRW[1] is presented in Figure 1. CTRW contains 914 such entries.

We want to disambiguate the senses of the near-synonyms in each entry, as part of a bigger project which aims to automatically acquire knowledge of near-synonym differences from CTRW and other sources. A lexical knowledge-base of near-synonym differences is useful in an MT system to preserve not only the meaning of the sentences but also the nuances of meaning that words may carry and to avoid expressing unwanted nuances. Similarly, the lexical choice process in an NLG system can greatly benefit such information (Edmonds 2002). The first stage of the lexical acquisition process is presented by Inkpen and Hirst (2001).

In this paper, we present an algorithm for automatic sense disambiguation that takes advantage of the fact that the near-synonyms can help disambiguate each other, and the text of the entry is a rich context for disambiguation. We also present the agreement among judges in the task of annotating a small amount of data, which we use to both tune and evaluate our system.

2 Sense Disambiguation

Sense disambiguation means to select one or more senses in which a word is being used in a particular context. The task of disambiguating the meaning of near-synonyms is

---

[1] We are grateful to HarperCollins Publishers, Inc. for permission to use CTRW in our project.

A. Gelbukh (Ed.): CICLing 2003, LNCS 2588, pp. 258–267, 2003.
© Springer-Verlag Berlin Heidelberg 2003

Cluster: **acumen, acuity, insight, perception**

These nouns all refer to a highly developed mental ability to see or understand what is not obvious. **Acumen** has to do with keenness of intellect and implies an uncommon quickness and discrimination of mind. It requires acumen to solve an intricate problem in human relationships, or to emerge unscathed from a venture into penny stocks. . . . .

Acuity means sharpness or keenness, and is applied exclusively to perception: visual acuity; The intelligence test was used as a basis for judging the applicant's mental acuity. *See* KEEN, SENSATION, VISION, WISDOM. *Antonyms*: bluntness, dullness, obtuseness, stupidity.

Fig. 1. Part of the text of an entry in *Choose the Right Word* by S.I. Hayakawa. Copyright ©1987. Reprinted by arrangement with HarperCollins Publishers, Inc.

easier than the general task of word sense disambiguation (WSD). But it is not a simple task. As we show in section 3, disambiguating the meaning of the near-synonyms is not easy even for humans.

For each sense we need to decide whether it is relevant for the entry or not. For example, in Figure 1, *acumen* has two WordNet senses: acumen#n#1 glossed as "a tapering point", and acumen#n#2 glossed as "shrewdness shown by keen insight". The decision we want to make is that the second one is relevant for the entry, and the first one is not. More then one sense of a near-synonym can be relevant for an entry, so we view the problem as one of binary decisions: for each sense, decide whether it is relevant for the context or not. To disambiguate each sense, we compute the indicators described below. Then we combine them to decide if the sense is relevant.

In our task, the context is richer than in the general case of word sense disambiguation. We can use the full text of each entry (including the cross-references). For each entry in CTRW, we consider all senses of each near-synonym. We chose to use the WordNet1.7 sense inventory in order to integrate our word sense disambiguation program with other components in our project that use WordNet. The average polysemy for CTRW is 3.18 (for 5,419 near-synonyms there are 17,267 WordNet senses).

2.1   Intersection of Text and Gloss

Our main indicator of sense relevance is the size of the intersection of the text of the entry with the WordNet gloss of the sense, both regarded as bags of words. This is a Lesk-style approach (Lesk 1986). When we intersect the text with the gloss we ignore stopwords and the word to be disambiguated. (We experimented with stemming the words, but it did not improve the results.) The other near-synonyms occur in the text of the entry; if they happen to occur in the gloss, this is a good indication that the sense is relevant.

Sometimes the intersection contains only very common words that do not reflect a real overlapping of meaning. In order to avoid such cases, we weight each word in the intersection by its *tf·idf* score. The weight for the word i in the entry j is $tf\text{·}idf_{i,j} = n_{i,j} \log \frac{n_i}{N}$, where $n_{i,j}$ is the number of occurrences of the the word i in the entry j, n_i is the number of entries that contain the word i, and N is the total number of entries. While we could have imposed a general threshold for the intersection (if the score is lower than the threshold, the sense is not relevant), we preferred to train a decision tree to choose a series of thresholds to better fit the data (see section 2.6).

We also intersected the text of the entry with the glosses of related words, such as hyponyms, hypernyms, meronyms, holonyms, pertainyms for adjectives, and cause and entailment for verbs. The hyponym/hypernym glosses can be expected to work well because some of the near-synonyms in CTRW are in a hypernymy/hyponymy relation with each other.

2.2   Other Words in Synsets Being Near-Synonyms

Our next indicator is the other words in each synset. They reliably indicate a sense being relevant for the entry because the near-synonyms in the entry help disambiguate each other. For example, if the cluster is: *afraid, aghast, alarmed, anxious, apprehensive, fearful, frightened, scared*, when examining the senses of *anxious*, the sense corresponding to the synset `anxious#a#1, apprehensive#a#2` is relevant because the other word in the synset is *apprehensive*, which is one of the near-synonyms.

We also used the words in the synsets of related words, where by related words we mean words connected by a direct WordNet relation. If any of the words in the synsets of the words related to the sense under consideration happens to be a near-synonym in the same cluster, the sense can be judged as relevant.

2.3   Antonyms

The set of antonyms in the entry (the words following the keyword *Antonyms* in the text of the entry) is intersected with the set of WordNet antonyms of the current near-synonym. Figure 1 shows an example of antonyms in a dictionary entry. If two words share an antonym, they are likely to be synonyms. By extension, if the sense we examine has antonyms that intersect the antonyms of the cluster of near-synonyms, then the sense is relevant for the cluster. For this reason we can compare our results with the ones from Senseval2.

2.4   Systematic Polysemy

A word is systematically polysemous if its senses can be connected by a relation which is also used to connect all the senses of other systematically polysemous words. For example *window* and *door* have both sense that denote a moving barrier that closes an opening, and senses that denote the space in the wall.

We tested the hypothesis that if a word is polysemous in a systematic way, all its senses are included in a dictionary entry (because these senses act more like facets of the same sense). We did this experiment for nouns only, using CoreLex (Buitelaar 1998), a database of systematic polysemous classes covering around 40,000 nouns from WordNet 1.5. The 126 semantic types are derived by a careful analysis of sense distributions. We experimented with both the original CoreLex, and with a new version of CoreLex we built for WordNet1.7 using the same set of semantic types. This indicator selects as relevant all the senses of a noun that is in CoreLex (and therefore is systematically polysemous).

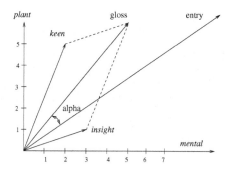

Fig. 2. Context vectors in a 2D space for the words *keen* and *insight*, for the WordNet gloss os the second sense of *accumen*,and for the CTRW entry from Figure 1.

2.5   Context Vectors

Sometimes, when the intersection of text and gloss is empty, it still could be the case that they are semantically close. For example, for the sense `reserved#a#2` with the WordNet gloss "marked by self-restraint and reticence", the intersection with the text of the CTRW entry *aloof, detached, reserved* is empty. The text of the entry happens to not use any of the words in the WordNet gloss, but the entry contains semantically close words such as *reluctant* and *distant*. By considering second-order co-occurrences (words that occur with the words of the text or of the gloss) the chance of detecting such similarity increases (Schütze 1998). One problem with this approach is that false positives can be also introduced.

We collected frequencies from the 100-million-word British National Corpus (BNC) (http://www.hcu.ox.ac.uk/BNC/). We chose the 2,000 most frequent words as dimensions, and the 20,000 most frequent words as features. By counting how many times each feature word co-occurs with a dimension word in BNC, we can represent them in the vector space of the dimensions. Then, the vectors of all feature words in an entry (except the near-synonym to be disambiguated) are summed to compute the context vector for the entry. The vectors of all words in a gloss are summed to get the context vector for the gloss. The cosine between the two vectors measures how close the two vectors are. The context vector for the entry will be the sum of many vectors, and it may be a longer vector than the context vector for the gloss, but this does not matter because we measure only the angle between the two vectors. Figure 2 presents a simplified example of context vectors for the second sense of *acumen*. For simplicity, only two dimensions are represented: *plant* and *mental*. Also, from the four content words in the gloss, three happen to be feature words, and only *keen* and *insight* are presented in the figure. The context vector of the gloss is sum of these two (or more) vectors. In a similar manner the context vector for the entry is obtained, and the cosine of the angle α between the two context vectors is used as an indicator for the relevance of the sense. Here, the cosine is 0.909, while the cosine between the context vector for the entry and the context vector for the first sense of *acumen* is only 0.839.

```
intersection_text_gloss > 4.41774 : Y (406.0/59.4)
intersection_text_gloss <= 4.41774 :
|   intersection_text_gloss_related_words > 23.7239 : Y (28.0/1.4)
|   intersection_text_gloss_related_words <= 23.7239 :
|   |   words_in_related_synsets = 0:
|   |   |   words_in_synset = 0:
|   |   |   |   intersection_text_gloss_related_words <= 4.61842 : N (367.0/62.5)
|   |   |   |   intersection_text_gloss_related_words > 4.61842 :
|   |   |   |   |   intersection_text_gloss_related_words <= 4.94367 : Y (4.0/1.2)
|   |   |   |   |   intersection_text_gloss_related_words > 4.94367 : N (42.0/14.6)
|   |   |   words_in_synset = 1:
|   |   |   |   intersection_text_gloss <= 1.19887 : N (16.0/8.9)
|   |   |   |   intersection_text_gloss > 1.19887 : Y (3.0/1.1)
|   |   words_in_related_synsets = 1:
|   |   |   intersection_text_gloss <= 0 : Y (24.0/4.9)
|   |   |   intersection_text_gloss > 0 :
|   |   |   |   corelex = 0:
|   |   |   |   |   cosine <= 0.856407 : Y (3.0/2.1)
|   |   |   |   |   cosine > 0.856407 : N (5.0/1.2)
|   |   |   |   corelex = 1:
|   |   |   |   |   intersection_text_gloss <= 3.44834 : Y (3.0/1.1)
|   |   |   |   |   intersection_text_gloss > 3.44834 : N (3.0/2.1)
```

Fig. 3. Simplified decision tree for the combination of indicators.

2.6   Using a Decision Tree to Combine Indicators

We use decision tree learning to determine the best combination of indicators. We use C4.5 (http://www.cse.unsw.edu.au/~quinlan/), a tree induction program, on our 904 data points. The attributes we employ for each data point are the values of the indicators: intersection text and gloss (numerical value), intersection of text and gloss of related words (numerical value), words in synset (0 or 1), words in synsets of related words (0 or 1), antonyms (0 or 1), membership in CoreLex (0 or 1), and the cosine between context vectors (numerical value). The classification is binary: Y/N, meaning relevant or not relevant for the entry. We obtain the class for each of our training examples from a standard solution we built (see section 3 for details about the standard solution). See Figure 3 for a simplified decision tree that combines indicators.

    We experimented with manual combinations, but we decided it is better to automatically derive a decision tree, because this learning mechanism has the ability to decide which indicators have more influence on the classification, and it can completely ignore indicators with low influence. We use the standard solution built in section 3 as training and test data in the decision-tree learning process. We could have split this data into a training set and a test set, but we chose to do 10-fold cross-validation, as a better method to estimate the error rate. Another advantage of using the decision tree is that it determines the thresholds for weighted intersection and for cosine.

3   Building a Standard Solution

The goal of using human judges in our work was twofold: to get a measure of how difficult the task is for humans, and to build a standard solution for use in evaluation. The standard solution also serves as training and test data for the decision tree used in section 2.6.

We had $k = 6$ judges (native or near-native speakers of English) doing the same job as the WSD program. We randomly selected 50 of the 914 clusters, containing 282 near-synonyms with 904 senses in total. The judges were presented with the text of the entry for each cluster, including antonyms and cross-references. For each near-synonym, all the WordNet senses (with their glosses and all the words in the synset) were listed, and the judges had to decide whether the sense is relevant for the cluster or not. The judges had no information about hypernyms, hyponyms, or antonyms.

There were 904 decisions the judges had to make. If we consider the decisions as votes, for 584 decisions, the judges voted 6–0 (or 0–6), for 156 decisions 5–1, and for 108 decisions 4–2. There were 56 ties (3–3).

The percent agreement among our judges was 85%. To get a more accurate measure the agreement among the k judges, we used the well-known kappa statistic (Siegel and Castellan 1988), (Carletta 1996), which factors in the agreement by chance. The chance agreement is 50.2% in our case. Therefore the kappa coefficient is $\kappa = 0.699$. The figures of agreement between pairs of two judges vary from 90% ($\kappa = 0.80$) to 78.8% ($\kappa = 0.57$). If we leave out one of the judges, who expressed a particular bias, we get a higher agreement of 86.8% ($\kappa = 0.73$).

We had the judges meet to discuss the ties. The discussion had a very small influence on the agreement figures (because the number of cases discussed was small), but it helped clarify the sources of disagreement. Senses which are "instances" or "proper names" (e.g. the sense "*the United States*" for the near-synonym *union*) were rejected by some judges as too specific, even if they were mentioned in the text of the entry. There was disagreement about intransitive senses of some transitive verbs (or the other way around). Another problem was posed by mentions of extended senses (literal or figurative senses) in the text. For example, the CTRW entry for *bombastic, orotund, purple, turgid* mentions that "these adjectives are used to describe styles of speaking or writing"; and later on: "turgid literally means swollen or distended". The question the judges had to ask themselves is whether this literal sense is included to the entry or not. In this particular case maybe the answer is negative. But it is not always clear whether the extended sense is mentioned by the lexicographer who designed the entry because the extended sense is very close and should be included in the meaning of the cluster, or whether it is mentioned so that the reader will be able to distinguish it. Some judges decided to include more often than exclude, while the other judges excluded the senses when they thought appropriate. If we omit one of the judges who expressed singular opinions during the discussion, we get a higher agreement of 86.8% ($\kappa = 0.73$).

In the standard solution, we decided to correct a few of the 56 cases of ties, to correct the apparent bias of some judges. We decided to include senses that are too specific or instances, but to exclude verbs with wrong transitivity. We produced two solutions: a more inclusive one (when a sense is mentioned in the entry, it was included) and a more exclusive solution (when a sense is mentioned, it was included only if the judges included it). The more inclusive solution was used in our experiments, but the results would change very little with the more exclusive one, because they differ only in 16 points out of 904.

Table 1. Accuracy for different combinations of indicators

Method	Accuracy
Baseline (select all senses)	53.5%
Antonyms	47.0%
Cosine (decision tree)	52.7%
CoreLex	54.2%
Words in synsets of hypernyms and hyponyms	56.4%
Intersection text & gloss of hypernyms and hyponyms (*tf·idf*)	61.0%
Words in synsets of related words	61.3%
Words in synset	67.1%
Intersection text & gloss of related words (*tf·idf*) (decision tree)	70.6%
Intersection text & gloss (no *tf·idf*)	76.8%
Intersection text & gloss (*tf·idf*) (decision tree)	77.6%
Best combination (no decision tree)	79.3%
Best combination (decision tree)	**82.5%**
Best combination (decision tree – Resnik's coefficient included)	**83.0%**

4   Results and Evaluation

Table 1 presents the results of using each indicator alone and in combinations with other indicators. We compare the results of our method with a standard solution (section 3 explains how the standard solution was produced). For the most of the indicators, we use the standard solution to quantify their potential. We define accuracy for our task as the number of senses correctly classified over the total number of senses.

For the indicators using *tf·idf* and for the cosine between context vectors we use a decision tree to avoid manually choosing a threshold; therefore the figures in the table are the results of the cross-validation. By manually combining indicators, the best accuracy we obtained was 79.3% for the attributes: intersection text and gloss (with a fixed threshold), words in synsets, and antonyms.

We found the best combination of indicators by training a decision tree as described in section 2.6. We achieve an accuracy of 83%, computed by 10-fold cross-validation. The indicators that contribute the most to improving the accuracy are the ones in the upper-part of the decision tree (Figure 3): the intersection of the text with the gloss, the intersection of the text with the glosses of the related words, the words in the synset, and the words in the synsets of the related words. The ones in the lower part (CoreLex and the cosine between context vectors) have less influence on the results. Their contribution is likely to be included in the contribution of the other indicators.

If the evaluation is done for each part-of-speech separately (see the first row in Table 2), it can be observed that the accuracy for nouns and verbs is higher than for adjectives. In our data set of 50 randomly selected near-synonym clusters, there are 276 noun senses, 310 verb senses, and 318 adjective senses. There were no adverbs in the test set, because there are only a few adverbs in CTRW.

Another indicator that we implemented after the previous experiments were done is Resnik's coefficient, which measures how strongly a word sense correlates with the

Table 2. Accuracy per part-of-speech.

Method	All	Nouns	Verbs	Adjectives
All indicators except Resnik's coefficient	82.6%	81.8%	83.2%	78.3%
All indicators including Resnik's coefficient	83.0%	84.9%	84.8%	78.3%
Only Resnik's coefficient	71.9%	84.0%	77.7%	–

words in the same grouping (in the case when we have groups of similar nouns). The algorithm was originally proposed by Resnik (1999) in a paper that presented a method for disambiguating noun groupings, using the intuition that when two polysemous words are similar, their most informative subsumer provides information about which sense of which word is the relevant one. The method exploits the WordNet noun hierarchy, and uses Resnik's similarity measure based on information content (Resnik 1999) (but see (Budanitsky 2001) for a critique of the similarity measure). We also implemented the same algorithm for verbs, using the WordNet verb hierarchy.

When we add Resnik's coefficient as a feature in the decision tree, the total accuracy (after cross-validation) increases slightly, to 83%. If Resnik's coefficient is included, the accuracy is improved for nouns and verbs (84.9% for nouns and 84.8% for verbs). The accuracy for adjectives is the same, because Resnik's coefficient is not defined for adjectives. If the only feature in the decision tree is Resnik's coefficient, the accuracy is high for nouns, as expected, and very low for verbs and for all parts of speech considered together.

In conclusion, the disambiguation method presented here does well for nouns and verbs, but it needs improvement for adjectives.

5   Comparison with Related Work

Senseval (http://www.itri.brighton.ac.uk/events/senseval/) had the goal of evaluating word sense disambiguation systems. We will refer here only to the experiments for the English language. Senseval2 used WordNet1.7 senses; therefore we can compare the Senseval2 results with my results, while bearing in mind that the words and texts are different (because of the nature of our task). Senseval2 had two tasks: all content words and selected words (the last one seems closer to our task). The precision and recall reported by the participating systems were all below 70%, and fancy supervised or unsupervised algorithms could beat a Lesk-baseline by only 2%. Our WSD program performs at least 13% better. We admit that our task is relatively easier than the general WSD task, because we have more context to help the disambiguation process. We report accuracy figures, but this is equivalent to reporting precision and recall, since we disambiguate all the near-synonyms (that is our algorithm handles all the instances). If we apply the method of computing precision and recall used Senseval2 to our case, we obtain the accuracy as we define it in section 4 (because in our task several senses of the same word can be considered correct, conjunctively). Our value for inter-annotator agreement (85%) is comparable to that of Senseval2 (85.5% for the English lexical sample task, according to the Senseval2 webpage).

Combining classifiers for WSD is not a new idea, but it is usually done manually, not on the basis of a small amount of annotated data. Stevenson and Wilks (2001), among others, combine classifiers (knowledge-sources) by using a weighted scheme.

An adapted Lesk-style algorithm for WSD that uses WordNet, but in a different manner, is presented by Pedersen and Banerjee (2002). They intersected glosses of all words in the context of a target word. The intersection is done pairwise, also considering intersections between glosses of a word and words related to the second word (by hypernymy, hyponymy, meronymy, etc.). They achieve an accuracy of 32%. Unlike Pedersen and Banerjee, we focus only on the target word (we do not use glosses of words in context), when we use the gloss of a near-synonym we include examples in the gloss, and we achieve high accuracy.

Schütze (1998) uses context vectors to cluster together all the contexts in which a word is used in the same sense. In this way it is possible to distinguish among word senses without using a sense inventory from a lexical resource. We use the context vectors as a measure of the semantic relatedness between the text of an entry and the gloss of a synset.

6   Conclusion and Future Directions

We have presented a method to disambiguate senses of the near-synonyms in dictionary entries. We also presented the inter-annotator agreement for the human task and analyzed the sources of disagreements. We built a standard solution and used it to tune and evaluate our automatic program.

We plan to reuse our WSD program in other components of our system. For example, nouns that describe situations have associated semantic roles; we can extract them by finding verb senses with the same meaning as the nouns. Moreover, we can use a similar WSD algorithm for disambiguating senses of peripheral concepts (nuances) expressed by near-synonyms.

Acknowledgments. We thank Eric Joanis, Jane Morris, Alex Budanitsky, and ZuZu Gadallah for participating in the judging task. Our work is financially supported by the Natural Sciences and Engineering Research Council of Canada and the University of Toronto.

References

Budanitsky, Alexander and Hirst, Graeme: Semantic distance in WordNet: An experimental, application-oriented evaluation of five measures. In *Proceedings of the Workshop on Word-Net and Other Lexical Resources, Second Meeting of the North American Chapter of the Association for Computational Linguistics (NAACL'2001)*, Pittsburgh (2001)

Buitelaar, Paul: An ontology of systematic polysemous classes. In *Proceedings of the International Conference on Formal Ontology in Information Systems (FOIS'98)*, Trento (1998)

Carletta, Jean: Assessing agreement on classification tasks: the kappa statistic. *Computational Linguistics*, 22(2) (1996) 249–254

Edmonds, Philip and Hirst, Graeme: Reconciling fine-grained lexical knowledge and coarse-grained ontologies in the representation of near-synonyms. In *Proceedings of the Workshop on Semantic Approximation, Granularity, and Vagueness*, Breckenridge, Colorado (2000)

Edmonds, Philip and Hirst, Graeme: Near-synonymy and lexical choice. *Computational Linguistics*, 28(2) (2002) 105–144

Gove, P.B. (ed.): *Webster's New Dictionary of Synonyms*. G.&C. Merriam Co. (1984)

Hayakawa, S.I.: *Choose the Right Word*. HarperCollins Publishers (1994)

Hirst, Graeme: Near-synonymy and the structure of lexical knowledge. In *Working notes, AAAI Symposium on Representation and Acquisition of Lexical Knowledge: Polysemy, Ambiguity, and Generativity*, Stanford University (1995) 51–56

Inkpen, Diana and Hirst, Graeme: Building a lexical knowledge-base of near-synonym differences. In *Proceedings of the Workshop on WordNet and Other Lexical Resources, Second meeting of the North American Chapter of the Association for Computational Linguistics*, Pittsburgh (2001)

Lesk, Michael: Automatic sense disambiguation using machine readable dictionaries: How to tell a pine cone from an ice cream cone. In *Proceedings of SIGDOC Conference*, Toronto (1986)

Pedersen, Ted and Banerjee, Satanjeev: An adapted Lesk algorithm for word sense disambiguation using WordNet. In *Proceedings of the 3rd International Conference on Intelligent Text Processing and Computational Linguistics (CICLing 2002)*, Mexico City, Mexico (2002)

Resnik, Philip: Semantic similarity in a taxonomy: an information-based measure and its application to problems of ambiguity in natural language. In *Journal of Artificial Intelligence Research*, 11:95–130, (1999)

Schütze, Hinrich: Automatic word sense discrimination. *Computational Linguistics*, 24(1) (1998) 97–123

Siegel, Sidney and Castellan, John N.: *Nonparametric Statistics for the Behavioral Sciences*. McGraw-Hill, Inc. (1988)

Stevenson, Mark and Wilks, Yorick: The interaction of knowledge sources in word sense disambiguation. *Computational Linguistics*, 27(3) (2001) 321–350

Word Sense Disambiguation for Untagged Corpus: Application to Romanian Language

Gabriela Şerban and Doina Tătar

Department of Computer Science, University "Babeş-Bolyai"
1, M. Kogalniceanu Street, Cluj-Napoca, Romania
{gabis, dtatar}@cs.ubbcluj.ro

Abstract. The task of disambiguation is to determine which of the senses of an ambiguous word is invoked in a particular use of the word [5,8]. It is known that the statistical methods produce high accuracy results for semantically tagged corpora [2]. Also, Word Net is a good source of information for WSD [3,4]. Since for Romanian language does not exist neither a corpus nor something similar with WordNet, we propose an algorithm for WSD which requires only information that can be extracted from untagged corpus. Our algorithm preserves the advantage of principles of Yarowsky [9,7,10] and adds the known high performance of a NBC algorithms. It learns to make predictions based on local context with only a few labeled contexts and many unlabeled ones.

Keywords: Word sense disambiguation, corpus.

1 Introduction

In [9], Yarowsky observed that there are constraints between different occurrences of contextual features that can be used for disambiguation. Two such constraints are *one sense per discourse* and *one sense per collocation*. These mean that the sense of a target word is highly consistent within a given discourse (document) and the contextual features (nearby words) provide strong clues to the sense of a target word.

Notational conventions used in the following are: w is the word to be disambigued (target word), $s_1, \cdots, s_K$ are possible senses for w, $c_1, \cdots, c_I$ are contexts of w in a corpus, $v_1, \cdots, v_J$ are words used as contextual features for disambiguation of w. The contextual features $v_1, \cdots, v_J$ occur in a fixed position near w, in a window of fixed length, centered or not on w ("unrestricted collocations" , in [6]).

A Naive Bayes Classifier (NBC) realizes the calculus of the sense s', which for the target word w and a given context c satisfies the relation [5]: $s' = argmax_{s_k} P(s_k \mid c) = argmax_{s_k} \frac{P(c \mid s_k)}{P(c)} P(s_k) = argmax_{s_k} P(c \mid s_k) P(s_k)$. The Naive Bayes assumption is that the contextual features are all conditional independent. This is not generally true, but there is a large number of cases in which the algorithm works well. Concerning the probabilities $P(v_j \mid s_k)$ and $P(s_k)$,

A. Gelbukh (Ed.): CICLing 2003, LNCS 2588, pp. 268–272, 2003.

these are calculated from a labeled (annotated) corpus. In our algorithm the probabilities $P(v_j \mid s_k)$ are re-estimated until all the contexts are solved.

2   A Bootstrapping Algorithm (BA) for WSD

The BA algorithm begins by identifying a small number of training contexts. This could be accomplished by hand tagging with senses the contexts of w for which the sense of w is clear because some seed collocations[9,10] occur in these contexts.

The notational conventions are as above: $C = \{c_1, c_2, \cdots c_I\}$ are contexts (windows) of w, as obtained with query w and with an on-line corpus tool (at us htdig and a Romanian corpus). Each c_i is of the form: $c_i = w_1, \ldots, w_t, w, w_{t+1}, \ldots, w_z$ where $w_1, w_2, \ldots, w_t, w_{t+1}, \ldots, w_z$ are words from the set $v_1, \ldots, v_J$ and t and z are selected by user.

Let us consider that the words $V = \{v^1, \cdots, v^l\} \subset \{v_1, \cdots, v_J\}$, where l is small (for example 2) are surely associated with the senses for w, such that the occurrence of v^i in the context of w determines the choice of a sense s^i for w (one sense per collocation). Here $\{s^1, \cdots, s^l\}$ is a subset of $\{s_1, \cdots, s_K\}$.

We mention that the set of words (V) used in the BA algorithm as contextual features for the disambiguation is very important; the disambiguation results are improved as the set V grows. This represents the first important characteristic of the BA algorithm.

These rules can be done generally as a decision list:

if $\mathbf{v^i}$ occurs in a context **c** of **w** **then** the sense of **c** is $\mathbf{s^i}$, $s^i \in S$ (1)

So, from the set of contexts obtained as query results, some contexts can be solved.

For our algorithm, we define a relation $\delta \subset W \times \mathcal{P}(W)$, where W is the set of all words and $\mathcal{P}(W)$ is the power set of W . If $w \in W$ is a word and $c \in \mathcal{P}(W)$ we say that $(w, c) \in \delta$ if $w \in c$ or, else, if exists a word $w1 \in c$ so that the words w and $w1$ have the same gramatical root (particularly c is a context).

So, a corresponding decision list has the following form:

if $(v, c) \in \delta$ and v has the sense $\mathbf{s_i}$ **then** the sense of the context **c** is $\mathbf{s_i}$

(2)

The decision list (2) improved with the relation δ represents the second important characteristic of the BA algorithm.

Algorithm

$C_{res} = \Phi$, determine the set $V = \{v^1, \cdots, v^l\}$
For each context c in C apply the rules:
   if $(v^i, c) \in \delta$ **then** the sense of c is s^i, $i = 1, \cdots, l$, $C_{res} = C_{res} \cup \{c\}$
$C_{rest} = C \backslash C_{res}$
While $C_{rest} \neq \Phi$ **do** :
   Determine a set V^* of words with a maximum frequency in C_{res}

$Define\ V = V \cup V^* = \bigcup_{j=1}^{K} V_{s_j},$
$where\ V_{s_j}\ is\ the\ set\ of\ words\ associated\ with\ the\ sense\ s_j\ (\ some\ V_{s_j}$
$can\ be\ \Phi)$
For $each\ c_i \in C_{rest}\ apply\ the\ BNC\ algorithm:$
$$s_i^* = argmax_s P(s \mid c_i) = argmax_s P(c_i \mid s) \times P(s)$$
$$C_{res} = C_{res} \cup \{c_i \mid P(s_i^* \mid c_i) > N,\ N\ fixed\ at\ 0.001\}$$
$$C_{rest} = C_{rest} \backslash C_{res}$$

In this algorithm: $P(c_i \mid s) = P(w_1 \mid s) \cdots P(w_t \mid s) P(w_{t+1} \mid s) \cdots P(w_z \mid s)$
and $P(w_i \mid s_j) = \begin{cases} 1 & if(w_i, V_{s_j}) \in \delta \\ \dfrac{nr.occ.w_i}{nr.\,total\,of\,words} & otherwise \end{cases}$

3 The Application for Words' Disambiguation

The application is written in JDK 1.4 and its goal is to find the correct sense for a given word (the target word) in some given contexts using the algorithm described in section 2.

3.1 Experiment

Our aim is to use the BA algorithm for the romanian language, to disambiguate the word poarta in some contexts obtained with an on-line corpus tool (at us htdig and a Romanian corpus).

We make the following specifications:

- the target word poarta has, in romanian language, four possible senses (two nouns and two verbs);
- we experiment our algorithm starting with 38 contexts for the target word;
- we start with four words as contextual features for the disambiguation (a single feature for each sense).

The accuracy of the BA algorithm in the proposed experiment is **60%**. We note that the accuracy of the disambiguation algorithm is calculated with the following formula

$$A = \frac{number\ of\ correctly\ solved\ contexts}{number\ of\ contexts} \tag{3}$$

The experiment at Hearst (1991) shows that to achieve a high precision in word sense tagging, the initial set must be large (20-30 occurrences for each sense).

We have to mention that, in our experiment, we associated a single occurrence for each sense (for an easier evaluation of the algorithm).

We make the following specifications:

- in the above experiment we grow the number of occurrences for each sense of the target word and we observe that: with two occurrences for each sense the algorithm's accuracy grows with **10%**, with three occurrences for each sense the accuracy grows with **15%**;

– we grow the number of input contexts (100) and we observe that the algorithm's accuracy grows with **15%**.

As a conclusion, if the number of words used as contextual features for the disambiguation and the number of contexts grow, the accuracy of the BA algorithm grows, too.

3.2   Experimental Comparison with the NBC Algorithm

In the case of the algorithm described in section 2 (BA - Bootstrapping Algorithm), the relation δ described in Equation 2 is very important. In order to illustrate the efficiency of the BA algorithm (with an without δ), we ran at the same time the NBC algorithm for the experiment proposed in subsection 3.1. We note that "BA without δ" is the BA algorithm (Section 2), in which a decision list has the form described in Equation 1.

The comparative experimental results obtained are shown in Figure 1. In Figure 1, we give, for each algorithm, a graphical representation of accuracy/context. More exactly, for a given algorithm, for the i-th context we represent the accuracy (see Equation 3) of the algorithm for the first i contexts. From Figure 1, it is obvious that the most efficient is the BA algorithm with the relation δ (at each step, the BA algorithm's accuracy is maximum).

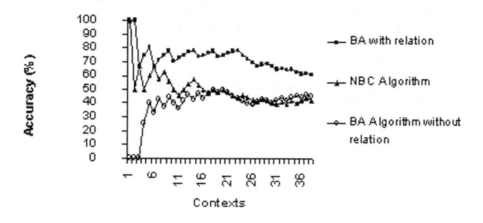

Fig. 1. The comparative experimental results

4   Further Work

Further work is planned to be done in the following directions: for assuring a better efficiency of the disambiguation, we plain to retain in a database the results of the learning process. We plain to study our approach in the context of combining labeled and unlabeled data with Co-Training as in [1]. Our own goal is to solve with our method the disambiguation for a query in a future QA-system in Romanian which is now in construction. We also planned to improve the application using a subroutine which determines all the synonyms for the initial features of the target word (a hierarchical clustering algorithm, which is already implemented).

References

1. A. Blum, T. Mitchell: Combining Labeled and Unlabeled Data with C-Training. Proceedings of the 11th Annual Conference on Computational Learning Theory (1998) 92–100
2. G. Escudero, L. Marquez, G. Rigau: Boosting applied to WSD. ACML,Barcelona, Spain (2000)
3. R. Mihalcea, D. Moldovan: An iterative Approach to WSD. Proceedings of FLAIRS (2000)
4. R. Mihalcea, D. Moldovan: A method for WSD of unrestricted text. Proceedings of the 37th Annual Meeting of the ACL, Maryland, NY (1999)
5. C. Manning, H. Schutze: Foundation of statistical natural language processing. MIT (1999)
6. T. Pedersen, R. Bruce: Knowledge Lean WSD. Proceedings of the Fifteenth National Conference on AI. Madison, WI (1998)
7. P. Resnik, D. Yarowsky : Distinguishing Systems and Distinguishing sense: new evaluation methods fot WSD. Natural Language Engineering, 1 (1998)
8. G. Serban, D. Tatar: A new algorithm for WSD. Studia Univ. Babes-Bolyai, Informatica. 2 (2001) 99–108
9. D. Yarowsky: Hierarchical Decision Lists for WSD. Kluwer Academic Publishers (1999)
10. David Yarowsky: Unsupervised Word Sense Disambiguation Rivaling Supervised Methods. Proceedings of ACL'95 189–196

Automatic Noun Sense Disambiguation*

Paolo Rosso[1], Francesco Masulli[2], Davide Buscaldi[3],
Ferran Pla[1], and Antonio Molina[1]

[1] Dpto. de Sist. Informáticos y Computación, U. Politécnica de Valencia, Spain
{prosso,fpla,amolina}@dsic.upv.es
[2] INFM-Genova and Dip. di Informatica, Università di Pisa, Italy
masulli@disi.unige.it
[3] Dip. di Informatica e Scienze dell'Informazione, Università di Genova, Italy
buscaldi@disi.unige.it

Abstract. This paper explores a fully automatic knowledge-based method which performs the noun sense disambiguation relying only on the WordNet ontology. The basis of the method is the idea of conceptual density, that is, the correlation between the sense of a given word and its context. A new formula for calculating the conceptual density was proposed and was evaluated on the SemCor corpus.

1 An Extension of the Conceptual Density

The task of Word Sense Disambiguation (WSD) consists of examining word tokens and specifying exactly which sense of each word is being used. The WordNet (WN) ontology, based on synsets (sets of synonyms), is the external lexical resource which is often used to perform the WSD task. In most of the WSD approaches, a word is disambiguated along with a portion of the text in which it is embedded, that is, its context. When the initial input source of information (i.e., the word and its context) is processed only together with the lexical knowledge source (e.g. WN), a fully automatic method which does not require any kind of training process is needed to perform WSD.

Conceptual Density (CD) is a measure of the correlation among the sense of a given word and its context. The foundation of this measure is the Conceptual Distance, defined as the length of the shortest path which connects two concepts in a hierarchical semantic net. The starting point for our work was the CD formula of Agirre and Rigau [1], which compares areas of subhierarchies:

$$\mathrm{CD}(c, m) = \frac{\sum_{i=0}^{m-1} \mathrm{nhyp}^i}{\sum_{i=0}^{h-1} \mathrm{nhyp}^i} \tag{1}$$

where c is the synset at the top of subhierarchy, m the number of word senses falling within a subhierarchy, h the height of the subhierarchy, and $nhyp$ the

---

* This work was supported by the Spanish Research Projects CICYT TIC2000-0664-C02 and TIC2000-1599-C01-01, and the VIDI of the Univ. Politécnica Valencia.

A. Gelbukh (Ed.): CICLing 2003, LNCS 2588, pp. 273–276, 2003.

averaged number of hyponyms for each node (synset) in the subhierarchy. The numerator expresses the expected area for a subhierarchy containing m marks (word senses), while the divisor is the actual area.

The synsets of the senses of the word to be disambiguated fall in different places in the hierarchy, and in most cases this means that the hierarchy can be partitioned into subhierarchies (we refer them as clusters), each containing exactly one sense of the word to be disambiguated (therefore, a word having six senses in WN should determine six partitions). When two or more senses of the word are one hyponym of each other the partition cannot be done. Therefore, in such conditions the word sense disambiguation cannot be carried out.

Formula 1 considers the averaged number of hyponyms of each node in the subhierarchy. Due to the fact that the averaged number of hyponyms for each node in WN1.6 is greater than in WN1.4 (the version which was used in the original work presented in [1]), we decided to consider only the relevant part of the subhierarchy determined by the synset paths (from c to an ending node) of the senses of both the word to be disambiguated and its context. The base formula is based on the M number of relevant synsets (corresponding to the marks m in Formula 1) divided by the total number nh of synsets of the subhierarchy.

$$baseCD(M, nh) = M/nh \qquad (2)$$

Formulas 1 and 2 do not take into account sense frecuency. It is possible that both formulas select subhierarchies with a low frecuency related sense. In some cases this would be a wrong election. This pushed us to modify the CD formula by including also the information about frequency that comes from WN:

$$CD(M, nh, f) = M^{\alpha}(baseCD)^{\log f} \qquad (3)$$

where M is the number of relevant synsets, α is a constant (the best results were obtained with α near to 0.10) , and f is an integer representing the frequency of the subhierarchy-related sense in WN (1 means the most frequent, 2 the second most frequent, etc.). This means that the first sense of the word (i.e., the most frequent) gets at least a density of 1 and one of the less frequent senses will be chosen only if it will exceed the density of the first sense. The M^{α} factor was introduced to give more weigth to the subhierarchies with a greater number of relevant synsets, when the same density is obtained among many subhierarchies.

We included some adjustment factors based on context hyponyms, in order to assign an higher conceptual density to the related cluster in which a context noun is an hyponym of a sense of the noun to be disambiguated (the hyponymy relation reflects a certain correlation between the two lexemes). We refer to this technique as to the Specific Context Correction (SCC). The idea is to select as the winning cluster the one where one or more senses of the context nouns fall beneath the synset of the noun to be disambiguated.

An idea connected to the previous one, was to give more weight to the clusters placed in deeper positions. We named this technique as Cluster Depth Correction (CDC). When a cluster is below a certain averaged depth (which was determined in an empirical way to be about 4) and, therefore, its sense of the noun to be disambiguated is more specific, the conceptual density of Formula 3 is augmented proportionally to the number of the contained relevant synsets:

$$CD * (depth(cl) - avgdepth + 1)^\beta \qquad (4)$$

where $depth(cl)$ returns the depth of the current cluster (cl) with respect to the top of the hierarchy; $avgdepth$ is the averaged depth of all clusters in the subhierarchies obtained from Semcor; its value was empirically determined to be equal to 4; and β is a constant (the best results were obtained with $\beta = 0.70$).

Finally, we investigated the possibility of expanding the context with the gloss of the noun to be disambiguated. This led to worse results, since the gloss was examined without considering the syntactic category of its words and a certain "noise" was introduced as consequence of considering all lexemes as possible nouns. A refinement was done by considering only monosemic words of the gloss but, in spite of that, the performance for the noun disambiguation task did not increase. In order to consider only nouns, we first Part-Of-Speech tagged the gloss. We used a POS tagger based on Lexicalized-HMM. This tagger was evaluated achieving a precision of 96.8% on the Wall Street Journal corpus [6].

2   Experimental Results and Conclusions

The first goal of our work was to determine an effective window context size. Like many other researchers have done [4], we have carried out WSD experiments using the Semcor corpus[1]. The best results in term of precision were obtained with a context window size of 2 nouns, confirming that closer nouns give a more precise definition of the context than farther ones. The drawback of this approach is the average recall (around 60%). This is mainly due to the fact that many nouns have senses that differ slightly one from each other. This can be viewed in a hierarchy as deep clusters with only one synset inside them (corresponding to the sense of the noun to be disambiguated). In most cases, there are no context nouns falling in these "singular" clusters, and the result is that sense disambiguation cannot be done.

We combined different correction models (SCC and CDC) over the whole SemCor corpus and for different window sizes (two, four and six). All these experiments outperformed the baseline precision (76.04%) and the baseline recall (23.21%)[2]. The best precision measure of 81.48% was obtained without any correction factor and with a very small window of size two (recall 60.17% and coverage 73.81%). Using the SCC technique, although precision was not affected significantly, we obtained only small improvements on recall and coverage measures. With regard to the CDC technique, the results did not differ significantly to those obtained with the previous correction factor. Improvements on recall

---

[1] The results were obtained over the 19 randomly selected SemCor files: br-a01,b13,c01,d02,e22,r05,g14,h21,j01,k01,k11,l09, m02,n05,p07,r04,r06,r08,r09.

[2] The baseline precision was calculated assigning the most frequent sense to every noun, whereas the baseline recall was calculated for monosemic nouns only.

(61.27%) and coverage (77.87%) measures were obtained increasing the size of the context window. Recall remained approximately around 60% and varied slightly even when considering many context nouns (e.g. six), whereas coverage improved even if at the price of obtaining a lower precision measure.

For each noun to be disambiguated, we investigated the possibility of expanding its context adding the gloss, excluding the example phrases. In order to reduce the "noise" introduced considering all the words of the gloss, only monosemic words were added to the context of the noun to be disambiguated. In a second approximation, we POS-tagged the words of the gloss and extracted only its monosemic nouns which were included in the context.

The tests with this "expanded context" were conducted over the first 10 files from Brown1 of SemCor, and the CDC factor was also employed. The results of averaged P(recision), R(ecall) and C(overage) are the following: CDC model and gloss P=78.42%, R=61.86% and C=78.80%; CDC model and POS-tagged gloss P=80.77%, R=62.42% and C=77.24%; CDC model and no gloss P=80.91%, R=62.19% and C=76.81%. In order to have a certain balance in terms of precision / recall, a window size of 4 (previous to its expansion with the monosemic nouns of the gloss) was used in the experiments. The size of the expanded context was 5.92 on average (i.e., it contained 6 nouns approximately).

Without POS-tagging the gloss, even considering only its monosemic words, the recall decreased slowly and the precision decreased by an average of more than 2% with respect to the precision obtained without the gloss. The POS-tagging preprocess of the gloss permitted to obtain improvements both on recall and coverage without practically losing in precision. These results are promising if we compare them to those obtained using the original CD formula [1] (precision 81.97% vs. 66.4% and recall 69.02% vs. 58.8% for the file br-a01 of SemCor) especially if we consider that the much more fine-grained 1.6 version of WN was used and only a very small context window size of two to four nouns was needed.

At the moment, we are applying the proposed WSD method to sense-tagged XML documents retrieval [3]. Further work needs to be done to perform the all-word disambiguation task, the evaluation of the method against the Senseval corpus and the comparison with other recent approaches [2,5].

References

1. E. Agirre, G. Rigau, A Proposal for Word Sense Disambiguation using Conceptual Distance. In Proceedings of RANLP, 1996.
2. D. Fernández-Amorós, J. Gonzalo and F. Verdejo. The role of conceptual relations in Word Sense Disambiguation. In Proceedings of NLDB-01, 2001.
3. M. Mesiti, P. Rosso, M. Merlo, A Bayesian Approach to WSD for the Retrieval of XML Documents. In Proceedings of JOTRI, Valencia, Spain, 2002, pp. 11–18.
4. R. Mihalecea, D. Moldovan, Semantic Indexing using WordNet Senses. In Proceedings of the Workshop on Recent Avances in NLP and IR, 2000.
5. A. Montoyo, Desambiguación léxica mediante Marcas de Especificidad. Ph.D. Thesis, Universidad de Alicante, 2002.
6. F. Pla, A. Molina, Part-of-Speech Tagging with Lexicalized HMM. In Proceedings of RANLP, Tzigov Chark, Bulgaria, 2001.

Tool for Computer-Aided Spanish Word Sense Disambiguation[*]

Yoel Ledo Mezquita[1, 2], Grigori Sidorov[1], and Alexander Gelbukh[1]

[1] Center for Computing Research (CIC),
National Polytechnic Institute (IPN),
Av. Juan de Dios Bátiz, esq. Miguel Othón de Mendizábal,
Mexico D. F., Zacatenco, CP 07738, Mexico
{ledo, sidorov, gelbukh}@cic.ipn.mx, www.gelbukh.com

[2] Telematics Department, CUJAE, Cuba
ledo@tesla.ispjae.edu.cu

Abstract. We present a system for for computer-aided WSD mark-up of texts in Spanish. The system is is based on Anaya dictionary, uses a Spanish morphological analyzer and a WSD method based on Lesk algorithm (along with the other standard strategies). This tool reduces time and effort for preparation WSD-marked corpora in Spanish. We also discuss the requirement for such type of systems, which our particular system satisfies only partially.

1 Introduction

Words in a typical explanatory dictionary have different senses; this is known as polysemy. However, in a text each word occurrence corresponds to only one of these dictionary senses. The problem of determining this word sense used in a given text is referred to as word sense disambiguation (WSD). There are different methods for WSD that can be classified into two main groups: statistical methods [1, 4, 6, 10] and methods based on knowledge sources [3, 7, 8, 5].

The methods of either type require preliminary data preparation both for automatic learning and for automatic verification of results that permits to evaluate the quality of the method. Hence the necessity for a tool that would allow for manual or computer-aided sense marking in texts. We do not call it "semi-automatic" since the important decisions are taken by the human and not by the computer; an automatic or semiautomatic tool of this kind is currently impossible since modern WSD methods still have low precision.

In the rest of the paper, we first discuss the requirements for an "ideal" tool of this kind, and then describe the system we developed for Spanish, which satisfies the most part of these requirements.

---

[*] Work done under partial support of Mexican Government (CONACyT, SNI), IPN, Mexico (CGEPI, COFAA, PIFI), and RITOS-2.

A. Gelbukh (Ed.): CICLing 2003, LNCS 2588, pp. 277–280, 2003.

2 Requirements for a WSD Markup Tool

It is desirable that a system for computer-aided WSD markup of texts in any language be able to:

- Pass automatically to the next word in the text that can have different senses and present to the user a list of possible senses of each word (the words having only one sense can be marked automatically),

    In particular, the program should skip auxiliary words because their senses normally are irrelevant for WSD. However, the user should be able to manually choose the words that the program normally skips.

- Give the user a possibility to choose one or several senses that the word has in the given context with the minimum number of actions (clicks and movements),

- Suggest automatically the most probable sense(s) and then wait for a user confirmation.

    If the task is that multiple senses are allowed, then the confirmation is just a click on the OK button. However, if exactly one sense is to be chosen, then the user is to choose one sense from this small list; the senses should be ordered according to their probabilities so that in the majority of the cases the user could click at the OK button, which is equivalent to select the first one.

The system that skips auxiliary words and calculates the probabilities of word senses should use various procedures of linguistic analysis, namely:

- Processing of the given language's morphology:

    - Automatic morphological analysis,
    - Generation of lemmas,
    - Resolution of parts of speech (POS) ambiguity and ordering of lemmas according to the probabilities of their parts of speech in the text. If syntactic analysis (full or partial) is used for these purposes, then lemmas should be ordered according to the results of syntactic analysis.

- Implementation of different WSD strategies or their combinations (the user should have the possibility to choose the desired combination of these methods):

    - Statistical and/or knowledge-based methods. In addition, the option should be included to order the lemmas according to the POS probability, according to the WSD strategy, or some combination,
    - "Always first sense" strategy: the sense that is listed first in the dictionary is taken; this is rather good strategy because lexicographers tend to order senses intuitively according to their "importance" which in many cases coincides with their frequency in texts, see some considerations in [7],
    - "One sense per document" strategy [10]: the system supposes that the sense once used in the document will be repeated in the same document. For the first occurrence of the word, the sense is to be chosen by user and; for this, other strategies should be applied for suggesting the most probable sense, but all other occurrences of this word in the document are supposed to have the same

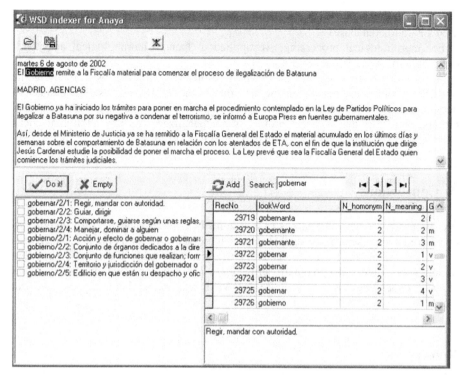

Fig. 1. Screenshot of the system.

sense. In addition, in this case the system should have an option of cleaning up all the data about the used word senses, in case if there are several documents in the file being processed.

We do not mention here some additional features: for example, what should be done in case that the dictionary is changed—say, some senses are merged or a new sense appears? The system should have a mode to reprocess the texts without unnecessary repetition of a manual work.

2   Tool We Developed

We developed such a tool for Spanish (Fig. 1). Of the requirements discussed above, the only one that our system does not implement is the resolution of POS ambiguity. Also, of the WSD strategies we have implemented only a version of the Lesk algorithm [7]; finally, we did not implement any graphical interface for combination of different WSD methods (this is changed directly in the program code if needed).

We used Anaya dictionary as the source for words and senses. This dictionary has more than 30,000 headwords. We preferred it over Spanish WordNet [9] because the latter has definitions in English while our WSD method needs definitions in Spanish.

It is possible to use any other explanatory dictionary in the corresponding format (we used a Paradox database).

For morphological processing, we applied a Spanish morphological analyzer / generator developed in our laboratory [1].

According to our experiments, the best results are achieved by combining the strategy of "one sense per document" and one of the WSD methods. The number of necessary clicks is more than 25% less in comparison with marking without system prompt. Note that the incorrect prompt is not penalized with any additional clicks because we use a mode in which only one sense is allowed.

3   Conclusions

We discussed the desired features of a system for computer-aided WSD marking of texts. We have presented a system for Spanish based on Anaya dictionary, which uses Spanish morphological analyzer and a WSD method based on the Lesk algorithm (along with some other standard strategies). The developed computer-aided tool allows for spending less time and effort for WSD text preparation in comparison with purely manual work.

References

1. Gelbukh, A. and G. Sidorov (2002). Morphological Analysis of Inflective Languages Through Generation. *J. Procesamiento de Lenguaje Natural*, No 29, September 2002, Spain. pp. 105–112.
2. Karov, Ya. and Edelman, Sh. (1998) Similarity-based word-sense disambiguation. *Computational linguistics*, Vol. 24, pp. 41–59.
3. Lesk, M. (1986) Automatic sense disambiguation using machine-readable dictionaries: how to tell a pine cone from an ice cream cone. *Proceedings of ACM SIGDOC Conference*. Toronto, Canada, pp. 24–26.
4. Manning, C. D. and Shutze, H. (1999) *Foundations of statistical natural language processing*. Cambridge, MA, The MIT press, 680 p.
5. McRoy, S. (1992) Using multiple knowledge sources for word sense disambiguation. *Computational Linguistics*, Vol. 18(1), pp. 1–30.
6. Pedersen, T. (2002) A baseline methodology for word sense disambiguation. In A. Gelbukh (ed.) *"Computational linguistics and intelligent text processing"*, LNCS 2276, Springer, 2002, pp 126–135.
7. Sidorov G. and A. Gelbukh (2001). Word sense disambiguation in a Spanish explanatory dictionary. Proc. of *TALN-2001* (*Tratamiento automático de lengauje natural*), Tours, France, July 2–5, 2001, pp 398–402.
8. Wilks, Y. and Stevenson, M. (1999) Combining weak knowledge sources for sense disambiguation. Proceedings of *IJCAI-99*, 884–889.
9. *WordNet: an electronic lexical database*. (1998), C. Fellbaum (ed.), MIT, 423 p.
10. Yarowksy, D. (1992) Word-sense disambiguation using statistical models of Roget's categories trained on large corpora. Proceeding of *Coling-92*, Nante, France, pp. 454–460.

Augmenting WordNet's Structure Using LDOCE

Vivi Nastase and Stan Szpakowicz

School of Information Technology and Engineering,
University of Ottawa,
Ottawa, Ontario, Canada
{vnastase, szpak}@site.uottawa.ca

Abstract. We propose an algorithm that will augment the structure of *WordNet* with links between the noun and verb hierarchies, by using word definitions extracted from *Longman's Dictionary of Contemporary English*. The results obtained show that a simple algorithm gives promising results, and additional resources could bring substantial improvement.

1 Introduction

WordNet covers nouns, verbs, adjectives and adverbs. The hierarchies of adjectives and adverbs are connected to the noun hierarchy through the pertainym links. The verb hierarchy is isolated from the other three components of WordNet . Linking all these structures would offer interesting resources for a variety of NLP tasks, such as language generation or semantic analysis. [Miller, 2001] has stated that future versions of WordNet will offer more links between the existing senses, notably noun-verb links. We use WordNet 1.6.

A manual analysis of glosses in WordNet has shown that it would be difficult to establish a connection between the nominal and verbal forms of a word using only this information. Glosses were not written in a controlled vocabulary, or with the intention of revealing relations between the gloss of a certain sense and the other closely connected senses.

For example, there is no overt, lexically expressed, connection between the words:

ship (noun) - a vessel that carries passengers or freight

ship (verb) - transport commercially

We have therefore decided to look elsewhere for help with finding connections between nouns and verbs. What we want is a phrase that shows a lexically explicit link between two words. Dictionary definitions contain relations of the following kind:

$DenominalVerb = Phrase(Noun)$

where $Phrase(Noun)$ includes $Noun$ – the noun that corresponds to the denominal verb. We expect the verb from $Phrase$ and its connection with $Noun$ to indicate the relation between $DenominalVerb$ and $Noun$. For example, if $Noun$ is the syntactic object of the main verb *be* in $Phrase$, then the relation between $DenominalVerb$ and $Noun$ is AGENT, as in the following example (from LDOCE):

A. Gelbukh (Ed.): CICLing 2003, LNCS 2588, pp. 281–294, 2003.
© Springer-Verlag Berlin Heidelberg 2003

host (verb) = to be the **host** on a radio or television programme

The availability of such definitions has convinced us to look into the usefulness of dictionaries for the task of finding relations between noun and verb senses in WordNet .

LDOCE is an attractive lexical resource for this problem because its definitions are written in a controlled vocabulary of 2000 words. Words that are not included in this set but appear in the dictionary can also be used in definitions, but they are treated as references. This is why definitions tend to look like patterns that are instantiated for each word. Also, if a noun and a verb are semantically related, the vocabulary constraints on the definitions make it quite likely that one will appear in the definition of the other. The pair **ship**(verb)/**ship**(noun) shows promising lexical commonality when looked up in LDOCE :

ship (verb) ▯ to send or carry something by **ship**

ship (noun) ▯ a large boat used for carrying people and goods across the sea

(Contrast this with the other sense of the noun **ship**: a large spacecraft or aircraft.)

Definitions that connect a noun and a verb not only help discover that there is a connection between those specific senses of the two words. We also want an indication of what the relation might be. The preposition *by* in the example above suggests an INSTRUMENT relation. Glosses in WordNet, even when they are good indicators that two words are related (they use similar words), are not always helpful in discovering the relation.

2   Related Work

Work on extending WordNet has focused on several aspects.

[Hearst, 1998] proposes an algorithm that discovers hyponym relations between entries in WordNet that are not already linked so. Given word/hyponym pairs, Hearst's system searches corpora for lexicosyntactic patterns indicative of the hyponym relation. It then uses these patterns to discover other connected concepts. If WordNet entries exist for those concepts, it proposes links between these entries. The identified patterns unambiguously signal hyponym relations. Other relations are not explored.

[Harabagiu, Miller, and Moldovan, 1999] present ideas for increasing the connectivity of WordNet by disambiguating the senses of the words in the glosses, and connecting, through topical relations, the defined sense with the senses that occur in the definition. As a first step the glosses are disambiguated, then transformed into first-order predicate logic based on the syntactic tree of the gloss. The next step transforms this logical form into a semantic form. A pair of senses is assigned either a semantic role (such as a-kind-of or a-part-of) or a thematic role (such as agent or experiencer) based on the syntactic roles and the semantic relations already in WordNet .

[Mihalcea and Moldovan, 2001a] present a progress report on this work. No results are reported yet on the assignment of any of the relations.

The use of WordNet in word-sense disambiguation has revealed the fact that the resource is too fine-grained for certain tasks, leading then to work on decreasing its granularity [Mihalcea and Moldovan, 2001b].

[Mendes and Chaves, 2001] include qualia information in synsets to enhance WordNet 's performance with respect to natural language automated reasoning. The use of qualia features would reduce redundancy in WordNet , by addressing the cases when new synsets have been put in WordNet because they did not quite fit closely related existing synsets.

[Montoyo, Palomar and Rigau, 2001] experiment with enriching WordNet with classification systems. Synsets in WordNet are tagged with categories extracted from a general domain classification system.

3   Finding the Connection between a Noun and a Verb

In order to connect the noun with its verbal counterpart, we perform the following steps (the selected elements are set in bold):

1. Establish a pair (noun, denominal verb), for example:
   (hammer, to hammer)
2. Pick the appropriate sense from LDOCE for the denominal verb:
   a) **to hit something with a <u>hammer</u> in order to force it into a particular position or shape**;
   b) to hit something many times, especially making a loud noise; ...
3. Connect the denominal verb definition with the appropriate definition of the corresponding noun:
   a) **a tool with a heavy metal part on a long handle, used for hitting nails into wood**;
   b) a tool like this with a wooden head used to make something flat, make a noise, etc;
   c) a wooden part of a piano that hits the strings inside to make a musical sound;
   ...
4. Connect the verb definition in LDOCE with the corresponding verb sense in WordNet :
   a) **beat with or as if with a hammer**;
   b) of metals;
5. Connect the noun definition in LDOCE with the corresponding noun sense in WordNet :
   a) the part of a gunlock that strikes the percussion cap when the trigger is pulled;
   b) **a hand tool with a heavy rigid head and a handle; used to deliver an impulsive force by striking**; ...
6. Connect the noun and the verb senses in WordNet , inserting a relation if possible:
   hammer (noun) → INSTRUMENT → **hammer** (verb)

4   Augmenting *WordNet* 's Structure

Our algorithm for finding links between nouns and verbs will proceed following the six steps described in **Section 3**.

4.1   Noun-Verb Pairs

We have started the experiment with the intention of looking at denominal verbs. Since the purpose of this experiment is only to see if the algorithm we propose gives promising results, we try to make the task as simple as possible. We avoid bringing in resources other than those required (WordNet and LDOCE), and we choose denominal verbs whose form is homonymous with the noun form, to avoid further processing. With the use of a lemmatizer, this constraint can be relaxed, and the algorithm applied to (noun,denominal verb) pairs which have similar, but not identical, forms.

Because of these working assumptions, we did not need to start with a list of pairs, but only with a list of verbs, from which we will choose the denominal ones, as it will be described in the next step.

4.2   Recognizing Denominal Verbs

As we said in the preceding subsection, we start with a list of verbs. In order to identify the denominal ones, we will use the definitions. We have automatically extracted a small sample of verb definitions from a Web version of LDOCE . In order to recognize the denominal verbs, we note that a noun will be used in the definition of the denominal sense of the homonymous verb. This is the criterion according to which we pick from the possible definitions the one (ones) for the denominal sense, if the verb has any such sense. This processing gives 342 definitions.

We have observed that LDOCE is organized in the following manner: for each word form that can belong to several syntactic classes, there will be numbered instances of this word to distinguish between the definitions for each such class. Example: iron1 will be used to access the definitions for the noun iron and iron2 for the verb to iron. We have also observed that in the case of denominal verbs, the noun is defined first (it will have the index 1).

We have incorporated these observations in the algorithm and extracted the definitions for the second form of every word in the list (that is, with index 2). The following phenomenon occurred: some of the verbs in the list were not denominal, but they were either deadjectival (e.g. to better, to clean), or they had deverbal noun counterparts (e.g. approach, associate). In the case of the deadjectival verbs the script extracted correctly the definitions for the deadjectival sense of the verb. In the case of proper verb with a deverbal noun pair, the script extracted the definition of the noun, since the verb was considered primary and had the index 1.

We have not eliminated these cases from the list, since the algorithm we propose is general enough to handle (noun, denominal verb), (adjective, deadjectival verb) and (verb, deverbal noun) pairs equally well.

For the present experiment we have used definitions of words alone, but no definitions of idioms or examples of usage.

In the more general case of nouns and verbs related by derivation, we can start either with the sense of the verb, or the sense of the noun, depending which definition explains the relation. For example, in the case of the noun traveller and the verb travel, we would pick the sense definition for one of these words that contains the other. In this case it is the definition of the noun that works best:

traveller (noun) - someone who is on a journey or someone who **travels** often

In this case a lemmatizer should help detect in the definitions variations of the word form under analysis.

At this point we have tested the use of LDOCE in the task of introducing links between (noun, denominal verb), (adjective, deadjectival verb) and (verb, deverbal noun) pairs, by comparing the number of definitions extracted with the number of definitions extracted from WordNet under the same assumptions. We pick definitions from WordNet that contain the same word as the one defined, for the same words (and with the same part of speech) we used to extract definitions from LDOCE . We have found 52 definitions in WordNet , as opposed to 342 in LDOCE .

4.3 Word-Sense Disambiguation in LDOCE

The controlled vocabulary restriction also helps in matching the correct (noun, denominal verb), (adjective, deadjectival verb) or (verb, deverbal noun) definitions, because they use similar concepts in their definition. Example:

iron (verb) - to make clothes smooth using an **iron**
iron (noun) - a thing that you use for making clothes smooth, which has
                  a heated flat metal base

For comparison here are the other definitions of the noun **iron**:

- a common hard metal that is used to make steel, is magnetic and is found in very small quantities in food and blood;
- a golf club made of metal rather than wood;
- a chain used to prevent a prisoner from moving.

To simplify the presentation, in what follows we will refer only to (noun, denominal verb) pairs, but the considerations are also valid for (adjective, deadjectival verb) and (verb, deverbal noun) pairs. Differences will be mentioned explicitly.

The algorithm that pairs definitions is very simple. It takes the definition of the denominal verb, and selects the definition of the corresponding noun that overlaps the most (simple word list intersection, no lemmatization). We filter some stop words from the intersection ({ a, an, the, this, that, on, for, to, of, and, etc, or, in, it, is}), and we filter out duplicates. For *iron*, for example, we would intersect the list of unique words corresponding to the verb definition, with the lists corresponding to the noun definitions:
{to,make,clothes,smooth,using,an,iron}

{ a, thing, that, you, use, for, making, clothes, smooth, → {clothes,
which, has, a, heated, flat, metal, base}   smooth}
{ a, common, hard, metal, that, is, used, to, make, steel, is, → { make }
magnetic, and, is, found, in, very, small, quantities, in, food,
and, blood}
{ a, golf, club, made, of, metal, rather, than, wood}   → {}
{ a, chain, used, to, prevent, a, prisoner, from, moving}   → {}

Some definitions cannot be paired automatically, because the definition of
the verb provides too little information:

drum (verb) - to play a **drum**

drum (noun) - a musical instrument made of skin stretched over a circular
    frame that you hit with your hand or a stick
    - something that looks like a drum, especially part of a ma-
    chine
    - a large round container for storing liquids such as oil, chem-
    icals, etc.

Without a connection between play and musical instrument we cannot establish a link between these two senses.

4.4 Word-Sense Disambiguation in WordNet

Mapping from WordNet to LDOCE was attempted before.

[Knight and Luk, 1994] perform semi-automatic mapping of nouns from
WordNet to LDOCE as part of their larger endeavour of building a large-scale
knowledge base. The mapping is performed in two steps. One is based on glosses
in WordNet and definitions in LDOCE , the other on the IS-A hierarchy in
WordNet and the semantic code and genus sense hierarchies in LDOCE . The
experiments were performed on a very early version of WordNet (1.4), where not
all words had a gloss attached.

[Kwong, 2001] uses LDOCE as an intermediary step in mapping between
WordNet and Roget□s Thesaurus WordNet and LDOCE senses of a word are
mapped onto each other according to the best overlap between an LDOCE definition and a synset, its gloss and its hypernym set in WordNet .

Our disambiguation process actually consists of two subtasks, one for each
member of the pair under analysis. For each verb, adjective and noun, we extract
from WordNet the synset and the gloss for each sense of the word. We gather all
these words on a list.

Example: **apprentice** (noun)

 Gloss - works for an expert to learn a trade

 Synset - apprentice, learner, prentice

 List - {apprentice, learner, prentice, works, for, an, expert, to, learn, a,
    trade}

We choose those word senses in WordNet whose lists overlap the most with
the definition of the word in LDOCE . We have tried several methods of computing the overlap: filter / do not filter the word defined; filter / do not filter

stop words; always choose a unique WordNet sense / choose a unique WordNet sense only if there is overlap between the definitions[1]

For reasons of space we will not present the results for all these experiments. In the **Section 5** we present agreement measures for the best of these generated files (exclude the word under analysis from the intersection, no filtering of stop words, pick the unique sense of the word in WordNet).

4.5   Linking the Noun with the Denominal Verb

On-line dictionaries, in particular LDOCE , are an attractive source of lexical knowledge. Initiatives to organize this information into a more NLP-friendly format include discovery of links between dictionary entries.

[Markowitz et al., 1986] used very simple patterns to discover a variety of relations (hypernym-hyponym, member-set, generic agent), differentiation indicators between action / stative verbs and adjectives, and collocational information (for example, noun definitions starting with: {any NP} indicate taxonomic relations).

[Jensen and Binot, 1987] link word senses in LDOCE to disambiguate prepositional attachment. Given a sentence with a prepositional attachment ambiguity, they use LDOCE definitions of the verb, complement noun and the noun in the prepositional phrase (PP) to decide where to attach the PP. For this purpose they apply certain heuristics based on the lexicosyntactic information from the definitions. A certainty factor is computed to help choose between ambiguous attachments. The heuristics characterize two semantic relations, instrument and part-of. A syntactic parser processes the sentences under analysis, and the dictionary definitions.

[Dolan et al., 1993] try to transform an on-line version of LDOCE into a graph-structured knowledge base. The vertices of the graph are the words in the dictionary, and the edges are lexical relations extracted from the definitions. Approximately 25 relation types for verbs and nouns are recognized (for example Location, Part-of, Purpose, Hypernym, Time). The algorithm employs lexical patterns and syntactic information in the definitions. It focuses on linking specific words in the definition based on these indicators. The shortcoming may be that the word defined is linked to other words in its definition, and not to corresponding word senses.

We are interested in using LDOCE definitions to discover the nature of links between specific pairs of words. At this point we have established the connection between words senses in WordNet through LDOCE . Now we must link word-sense pairs, and label the links to show how words themselves are related. WordNet already has some links between words in different parts of speech, but the link is generically called pertainym.

---

[1] The last choice refers to situations when a word has exactly one sense in *WordNet* , and the definition in *LDOCE* does not overlap with the list of words in the *WordNet* synset and gloss. It may be that there is no corresponding *WordNet* sense for the sense in *LDOCE* , or that the definitions use completely different words.

We have deliberately chosen LDOCE to get definitions from which we can extract the nature of the link between the two words in the pair. First we have to establish a set of possible labels, and then search the definitions for patterns indicative of these labels. We can use a machine learning system to extract patterns from the definitions of the words.

The starting point for the labelling task was a set of 50 relations which our research group has developed for the semantic analysis of texts [Nastase and Szpakowicz (2001)]. For this particular task, the judges have tagged the LDOCE definitions with semantic labels according to the following process:

> For every word whose definition we analyse, build a semantic net which describes its relations with possible arguments. One of these arguments must be the word's homonym that appears in the definition.

Example:
  anchor (verb) - to lower the **anchor** on a ship or boat to hold it in one place.

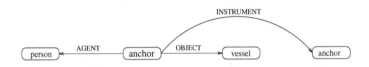

In this case the relation between **anchor**(verb) and **anchor**(noun) will be labelled INSTRUMENT.

After tagging, we have generated data for the machine learning process. Each of the definitions is a training example. The relation we assign will be the target attribute, and there are two more attributes - the part of speech of the word that is defined, and the definition itself which is represented as a bag of words.

We use C5.0 and RIPPER - machine learning systems that build rules based on the attributes that describe the data. We choose rule-based systems because we expect to see some of the indicators that the human judges have used in determining the label to be associated with a certain definition.

5   Results

Each of the steps of the algorithm presented in **Section 4** generates results whose accuracy we need to test.

The nature of the data and the tasks prevents us from computing precision measures because disambiguation and relation assignment tasks give ambiguous results even when performed by human judges. The best we can do in these circumstances is to compute agreement measures between the performance of the system and the performance of the two human judges we employ [Carletta, 1996], [Siegel and Castellan, 1988].

If the agreement of the system and each of the human judges is comparable to the agreement between the judges, we consider that the performance of the system is good (comparable to the performance of a human for the same task).

In order to show the agreement between a pair of judges we use the kappa statistic:

$$\kappa = \frac{Agreement_{observed} - Agreement_{chance}}{1 - Agreement_{chance}}$$

This statistic is used to compute the agreement measure for classification tasks. The kappa coeficient ranges from -1 to 1. A score of -1 shows complete disagreement between the judges, and a score of 1 shows perfect agreement. A score above 0.6 is considered to show good agreement.

The **observed agreement** is the percentage of instances on whose classification the judges agree.

The **chance agreement** is the probability that the two judges agree after randomly classifying instances.

The tasks we tackle are not classification, but word sense disambiguation and semantic relation assignment tasks. To make it even more complicated, in the WordNet disambiguation task the judges (but not the computer) are allowed to pick several possible senses, because the granularity of the resource usually precludes uniqueness. Similar problems may occur with LDOCE . Because of this, the cardinality of the sets selected by each judge may be different. The kappa statistic will be then adapted as follows:

- $Agreement_{observed}$ will be the percentage of the instances that both judges classify in the same way. It will be computed against the average number of definitions over the two sets that each judge creates.
- $Agreement_{chance}$ will be the probability that the two judges assign the same word sense to the words involved. For this we will find the average number of senses in each resource. The average number of senses for the words we use in WordNet is 3.56, and the average number of senses in LDOCE is 3.55^{2}. We denote by $P(Judge_X, Sense_N)$ the probability that $Judge_X$ picks $Sense_N$ for a certain word. The chance agreement will then be the probability that both judges in a pair will pick the same sense:

$$Agreement_{chance} = P(Judge_1, Sense_N) * P(Judge_2, Sense_N)$$

But

$$P(Judge_1, Sense_N) = P(Judge_2, Sense_N) = P(Sense_N) = (Average_{\#of\_senses})^{-1}$$

Then the chance agreement will be

$$Agreement_{chance} = 3.56^{-1} * 3.56^{-1} \approx 0.08 \quad \text{for } WordNet$$
$$Agreement_{chance} = 3.55^{-1} * 3.55^{-1} \approx 0.08 \quad \text{for } LDOCE$$

---

[2] We have eliminated from the definitions extracted from *LDOCE* the definitions of idioms and the examples of usage.

Table 1. Pairwise Agreement on Word-Sense Disambiguation

In *LDOCE*

Pair	Avg# of def	Agr_{obs}	Kappa
$(Syst, Jdg_1)$	305	0.62	0.59
$(Syst, Jdg_2)$	284	0.70	0.67
(Jdg_1, Jdg_2)	347	0.81	0.79

In *WordNet*

Pair	Avg# of def	Agr_{obs}	Kappa
$(Syst, Jdg_1)$	–	0.70	0.67
$(Syst, Jdg_2)$	–	0.62	0.59
(Jdg_1, Jdg_2)	722.5	0.73	0.71

5.1   Word-Sense Disambiguation in LDOCE

The system pairs nouns and verbs in LDOCE based solely on their definitions. In order to evaluate the performance of the system for this task, two human judges have manually picked definitions from LDOCE corresponding to the definitions of denominal verbs. There were 342 target definitions, for which pairs were required. Agreement was computed between the two judges, and between the system and each of the judges.

Out of the maximum 342 pairs, the system recognized only 245. In computing the agreement between the system and the human judges, we consider that for the 98 definitions for which the system could not find a pair, there was no agreement, in addition to the pair on which there is no agreement as shown by different choices.

Because each of the parties involved has picked a different number of definitions, in the percentages computed we will use the average of examples picked between the members of the pair.

The pairing would improve if we lemmatize the words in the definitions, as the following example shows:

package (verb) - to put something in a special package ready to be_sold
package (noun) - the box, bag, etc. that foods are put in for_selling

There is no link between the definitions because the system does not recognize the two different forms of the verb sell.

5.2   Word-Sense Disambiguation in WordNet

The system chooses a definition from WordNet for each member of the pair from LDOCE . Only definitions for the words in the pairs picked by the system in the LDOCE disambiguation step are chosen. The maximum number of definitions that could be selected from WordNet is 684 (342 pairs). The system selected 638 definitions.

The agreement between the human judges and the system was computed as before, using the probability that a pair of judges will pick the same sense for a word in WordNet as the chance agreement. The observed agreement is the percentage of instances on which the judges agree, computed against the average number of definitions picked by each of them.

The average number of senses in WordNet for the words under consideration is 3.56. The human judges were allowed to pick several senses from WordNet for one sense in LDOCE . The granularity of WordNet has proven to be too fine for certain word-sense disambiguation tasks, as shown by comparative results on coarse-grained and fine-grained WordNet in SENSEVAL competitions [Edmonds and Killgarriff, 2001]. The system, however, was restricted to pick at most one WordNet sense per LDOCE sense. $Judge_1$ has picked 762 definitions, $Judge_2$ 687 and the system 638 (a maximum of one per LDOCE sense). In analysing the performance of the system, we will use 684 as a base for computing the agreement percentages (the maximum number of definitions to be picked). A human judge can decide that several WordNet senses match a given LDOCE sense. If the system picks any of those, it is considered that it has disambiguated correctly. Therefore the average number of definitions is not relevant to the system's performance, and we will use it only when computing the agreement between the human judges.

The kappa statistic shows that there is good agreement between the system and the human judges, and between the human judges.

5.3   Labelling the Links with Semantic Relations

We have assigned semantic relations to the links established in LDOCE , based on a list of semantic relations developed by our research group. We have assigned the relations presented in Table 2

Both machine learning systems that we tried, C5.0 and RIPPER, perform better in a binary classification task as opposed to an n-classification task. We have therefore split our task of learning 20 relations into 20 binary learning problems. Out of these classification tasks, we have selected the ones where there are more than 10 examples for the positive class. We are left with the following relations: AGENT, CO-INSTRUMENT, INSTRUMENT, EFFECT, LOCATION AT, LOCATION TO, OBJECT, PRODUCT, PURPOSE.

For each of these relations we have run RIPPER and C5.0 to build rules. We expected to see in these rules what the system finds as indicators from the definitions. RIPPER generates rules of the following format:

$$Value_{TargetAttr} : -Attr_1 = Value_{Attr1}, ..., Attr_N = Value_{AttrN}(NC/NM)$$

where $Value_{AttrX}$ is one of the possible values of $Attr_X$, NC is the number of examples that the rule classifies correctly, NM is the number of examples that the rule misclassifies. As expected, the INSTRUMENT relation seems to be characterized mostly by the words using, with and by. RIPPER has generated the following rules for this relation:

inst :- using=t (38/1).

inst :- with=t, cover=f (30/6).

inst :- by=t, protect=f, surface=f (19/4).

Word = t means that $Word$ should be in the example (the definition under analysis), and Word = f means that the word should not be in the example, if we assign it to the particular class indicated by the rule.

For example, the interpretation of the rule inst :- using=t (38/1) is as follows:

Table 2. Semantic relations assigned

Relation	# ex	Sample Definition
agent	10	**host** - to be the **host** on a radio or television programme
co-agent	1	**crew** - to be part of the **crew** on a boat
co-instrument	46	**butter** - to spread **butter** on something
instrument	125	**anchor** - to lower the **anchor** on a ship or boat ...
cause	1	**sorrow** - to feel or express **sorrow**
direction	3	**target** - to aim something at a **target**
effect	53	**sound** - to make the **sound** of a letter in a word
exclusion	1	**dust** - to clean the **dust** from a surface ...
location at	14	**palm** - to hide something in the **palm** of your hand ...
location from	1	**shell** - to remove something such as beans or nuts from a **shell** or a pod
location through	3	**coast** - to sail along the **coast** while staying close to land
location to	14	**cache** - to put information in a **cache**
manner	4	**mushroom** - to spread up into the air in the shape of a **mushroom**
object	22	**apprentice** - to make someone an **apprentice**
product	21	**compost** - to make plants, leaves, etc., into **compost**
property	2	**associate** - someone who has an **associate** degree
purpose	12	**help** - to be very useful or give a lot of **help**
source	4	**smell** - to have a particular **smell**
time through	4	**holiday** - to spend your **holiday** in a place, vacation
type	1	**hurdle** - to run in **hurdle** races

If the definition of a denominal verb V contains the word *using*, the relation between V and the corresponding noun is INSTRUMENT. This rule works correctly in 38 cases, and introduces an error in one case.

In finding patterns for the AGENT label, both RIPPER and C5.0 focus on be as an indicator. Manual analysis suggests that with additional information about the syntactic roles of the verb's main arguments, the system could produce better rules.

Apart from the INSTRUMENT class, the others are very small compared to the size of the data set. EFFECT is 15% of the data set, and is the second largest class. Because of this, the systems get less than 15% error by classifying all examples as negative by default. With appropriate misclassification costs, the target class and the negative examples are discriminated, but the rules key in on specific words, and have no generalization power.

6   Conclusions

We have shown a very simple algorithm to link word senses in WordNet and LDOCE . Without any other resource than the dictionary itself, the algorithm performs very well, and shows good agreement with human judges on the same task. Its performance is comparable with that of the human judges in disambiguating word senses in LDOCE and in WordNet based on definitions in LDOCE.

The main purpose of the experiment is to label links between pairs of senses in WordNet , using definitions of the corresponding senses in LDOCE . We have used relations from a list developed by our research group. We have tried several machine learning methods to extract rules or patterns from the definition that indicate the presence of certain relation. For some of the relations we found the pattern, or rather one of the patterns.

Many improvements can be brought to this experiment. The use of a lemmatizer to reduce the words in definitions (both in LDOCE and in WordNet) to their lemmas would enhance the performance of the algorithm at several stages:

- matching the definitions – a word may occur with different derivations in the two definitions that we want to match, for example:
  package (verb) - to put something in a special package ready to be sold
  package (noun) - the box, bag, etc. that foods are put in for selling
- learning the patterns – the dimensionality of the vectors used for learning would decrease by using one lemma to cover all possible inflected forms. This could also affect the size of the decision tree or rules that are built, since at different points, different forms of the same word will be used.

There is another way of improving the matching between definitions. Some of them use generic words like something, someone as in the example:

ship (verb) ☐ to send or carry something by **ship**
ship (noun) ☐ a large boat used for carrying people and goods across the sea

Something in the verb definition is the syntactic object of the verb carry. It could be changed to a variable, which would match the syntactic object of the verb carry, in the noun's definition.

There are also methods of improving the process of finding patterns in definitions that indicate the presence of a certain relation. Our machine learning experiments were simplistic, and used only the words in the definition as bags of words. Order and syntactic information was discarded. This can be improved by adding information extracted from a syntactic tree for the definition, by using also part-of-speech characterization of the words and not only the words themselves.

We analyzed manually the placement of nouns homonymous with denominal verbs. It turns out that the AGENT relation is well predicated by the presence of the noun in the syntactic object position of the verb be.

Adding syntactic knowledge efficiently is a challenging item of future work.

Acknowledgements. Partial funding for this work comes from the Natural Sciences and Engineering Research Council of Canada.

References

[Carletta, 1996] Jean Carletta. 1996. *Assessing Agreement on Classification Tasks: The Kappa Statistic*, Computational Linguistics, 22(2), pg. 249–254.

[Dolan et al., 1993] William Dolan, Lucy Vanderwende and Stephen D. Richardson. 1993. *Automatically Deriving Structured Knowledge bases from On-line Dictionaries*, Proceedings of PACLING 93, Vancouver, BC, Canada.

[Edmonds and Killgarriff, 2001] Phil Edmonds and Adam Killgarriff, editors. 2001. Proceedings of the Second International Workshop on Evaluating Word Sense Disambiguation Systems, Toulouse, France.

[Harabagiu, Miller, and Moldovan, 1999] Sanda Harabagiu, George Miller and Dan Moldovan. 1999. *WordNet 2 – A Morphologically and Semantically Enhanced Resource*, Proceedings of SIGLEX-99, University of Maryland, MA, USA.

[Hearst, 1998] Marti A. Hearst. 1998. *Automated Discovery of WordNet Relations*, WordNet : An Electronic Lexical Database, ed. Christiane Fellbaum, MIT Press, USA.

[Jensen and Binot, 1987] Karen Jensen and Jean-Louis Binot. 1987. *Disambiguating Prepositional Phrase Attachments by Using On-line Dictionary Definitions*, Computational Linguistics 13, no.3-4, pg. 251–260.

[Knight and Luk, 1994] Kevin Knight and Steve Luk. 1994. *Building a Large-Scale Knowledge Base for Machine Translation*, Proceedings of AAAI-94, Seattle, WA, USA.

[Kwong, 2001] Oi Yee Kwong. 1998. Aligning WordNet with Additional Lexical Resources Proceedings of COLING/ACL Workshop on Usage of WordNet in NLP Systems, Montreal, Quebec, Canada.

[Markowitz et al., 1986] Judith Markowitz, Thomas Ahlswede and Martha Evans. 1986. *Semantically Significant Patterns in Dictionary Definitions*, Proceedings of ACL 1986, New York, NY, USA.

[Mendes and Chaves, 2001] Sara Mendes and Rui Pedro Chaves. 2001. *Enriching WordNet with Qualia Information*, Proceedings of NAACL 2001, Workshop on WordNet and Other Lexical Resources, Pittsburgh, PA, USA.

[Mihalcea and Moldovan, 2001a] Rada Mihalcea and Dan Moldovan. 2001. eXtended WordNet: Progress Report, Proceedings of NAACL 2001, Workshop on WordNet and Other Lexical Resources, Pittsburgh, PA, USA.

[Mihalcea and Moldovan, 2001b] Rada Mihalcea and Dan Moldovan. 2001. *Automatic Generation of a Coarse Grained WordNet*, Proceedings of NAACL 2001, Workshop on WordNet and Other Lexical Resources, Pittsburgh, PA, USA.

[Miller, 2001] George Miller. 2001. *Invited talk at the Workshop on WordNet and other lexical resources*, NAACL 2001, Pittsburgh, PA, USA.

[Montoyo, Palomar and Rigau, 2001] Andres Montoyo, Manuel Palomar and German Rigau. 2001. *WordNet Enrichment with Classification Systems*,Proceedings of NAACL 2001, Workshop on WordNet and Other Lexical Resources, Pittsburgh, PA, USA.

[Nastase and Szpakowicz, 2001] Vivi Nastase and Stan Szpakowicz, 2001. *Unifying Semantic Relations Across Syntactic Levels*, Proceedings of RANLP, Tzigov Chark, Bulgaria.

[Siegel and Castellan, 1988] Sidney Siegel and N.J. Castellan, Jr. 1988. *Nonparametric Statistics for the Behavioural Sciences*. McGraw-Hill, second edition.

Building Consistent Dictionary Definitions

Karel Pala and Eva Mráková

NLP Laboratory, Faculty of Informatics, Masaryk University
Botanická 68, CZ-602 00 Brno, Czech Republic
{pala,glum}@fi.muni.cz

Abstract. This paper is focused on the syntactic and semantic structures of dictionary definitions (in Czech). The former are explored by means of the partial syntactic parser DIS and their main types are presented together with their frequencies obtained from the sample of thousands dictionary definitions. It is shown that it is important to know valency frames for nouns that serve as genus proximum parts of the dictionary definitions. Then the distinguisher parts of the definitions are examined and the conclusion is made about their semantic structures. It is pointed out that a special semantic metalanguage will be necessary for the description of the semantic structures of the distinguishers. As a base for such language the formalism of transparent intensional logic (TIL) is suggested.

1 Introduction

In this paper we are going to explore both syntactic and semantic structures of the dictionary definitions as they can be found in standard printed or machine dictionaries (as e.g. SSJČ or NODE). Particularly, we would like to pay attention to the usual ways of building dictionary definitions, and to examine whether and to what extent they reliably and systematically follow the standard principles of the formal description of language data. The results following from the presented analysis should be applied to building dictionary definitions (glosses) for Czech WordNet (being further developed in the frame of Balkanet Project) and also the new Czech Lexical Database.

When working with various standard dictionaries (such as SSJČ for Czech, or NODE for English) one can see that the lexicographers follow several general but rather pragmatic principles in building the dictionary definitions. In other words, the techniques applied in building the dictionary definitions are based on the selected general principles but we can hardly say that they form a consistent and complete theory. In this respect, it can be observed that there are considerable differences between semantic theories (see e.g. Leech 1974, Lyons 1977, Cruse 2000) and the lexicographer's practice. However, the dictionaries are still almost the only resources of the lexical data for NLP, thus we have to pay attention to them at the first place. Though lexicographers follow the mentioned general principles and use well established techniques it is no secret that many objections can be raised with regard to the consistency of the dictionary definitions, both from the syntactic and semantic point of view. The considerable

A. Gelbukh (Ed.): CICLing 2003, LNCS 2588, pp. 295–303, 2003.
© Springer-Verlag Berlin Heidelberg 2003

number of dictionary definitions represent quite often just examples (though recently selected carefully from corpora, see for example Cobuild).

In building dictionary definitions the following techniques have been certainly regarded as the standard ones:

- definitions using genus proximum (GP) and the distinguishers (typical for nouns),
- definitions using semantic components or features (primitives) (with verbs: kill = cause to die),
- definitions based on the relation of troponymy (verbs: e.g. talk ▯ whisper),
- definitions using synonymical explanations or just one word synonyms (typical for adjectives, clever ▯ bright),
- definitions based on collocational determination of the sense of the entry (typical for adjectives: good student, good mile).
- definitions exploiting various kinds of ad hoc descriptions or explanations (any POS),
- definitions based on the descriptions of events or situations (see e.g. definition of table:2 if you ask for a **table** in a restaurant, you want to have a meal there (Cobuild95, p.1697).

It is correct to say that the mentioned lexicographic techniques are not strictly related to any of the standard semantic theories, such as presented by Leech (1974) or Lyons (1977) and recently also by others (Cruse, 2000). For example, the spontaneous lexicographer's use of semantic components can be certainly linked rather freely to the theory of the semantic features (primitives) as we can find it in Leech (1974, p.89-122) but no standard dictionary exploits them systematically. Similarly, the meaning relations like synonymy, antonymy, homonymy and hyponymy as they are introduced, say, in Lyons (270-301), are used in standard dictionaries but rather spontaneously and without the necessary consistency. The obvious exception is, however, WordNet 1.5., or thesauri like Roget (Roget) but they can hardly be labelled as a "standard" dictionaries; unfortunately in its "dictionary part" containing glosses Wordnet 1.5 suffers from many inconsistencies as any other "standard" dictionary (this is shown in Pala, Smrz, 2002).

Moreover, the lexicographer's above mentioned and widely used techniques based on GP and distinguishers do not represent, as far as we know, an integrated part of any well established semantic theory though they are used frequently in many dictionaries. The only lexical resource in which the reasonably well defined hypero/hyponymy (H/H) relations can be found and are systematically exploited seems to be WordNet and lexical databases of this sort (according to our knowledge). If we look for other theoretical works that could serve as the theoretical basis for building formally more consistent dictionaries perhaps The Generative Lexicon by Pustejovsky (1995) seems to offer a reasonably firm ground on which this could be attempted. Project named Corelex (Buitelaar, 1998) seems to point in this direction as well but it can be hardly considered a standard dictionary either.

It can be pointed out that the need for a reasonable "dictionary theory" is obvious and the progress in the area of the lexical resources strongly depends on building such theory that will allow us to prepare the consistent and formally well constructed lexical databases or machine dictionaries from which also the classical dictionaries suitable for human user can be later and reasonably derived.

2   The Correspondencies between Syntactic and Semantic Structures of Dictionary Definitions

Here we will try to explore the main types of correspondencies between syntactic and semantic structures of dictionary definitions with respect to nouns as they can be found in Czech dictionary SSJČ.

2.1   The Syntactic Structures of Dictionary Definitions (in Czech)

It is our strong belief that if we want to make the building of the (semantically) consistent dictionary definitions more formal we have to know more about their formal structure. In other words, we should examine their syntactic structures and see what types can be found in this respect and how they can be related to the semantic organization of dictionary definitions indicated above. For this purpose we have chosen the representative Dictionary of Written Czech (SSJČ, 1960) that now exists also in the machine readable form (Pala, Smrz, 2001, Slovko).

To examine larger data from SSJČ we need a tool that would enable us to analyse the syntactic structures of dictionary definitions from SSJČ. For this purpose we have chosen a partial parser for Czech (Žáčková, 2002) which after a modification of the used rules can be used to parse dictionary definitions for nouns (and for verbs, adjectives and adverbs as well but here we will deal only with nouns). For the present purpose we have prepared a sample containing 10 000 dictionary definitions (with the following distribution: 40 % nouns, 30 % verbs, 15 % adjectives, 15 % adverbs). The goal is to find the main types of syntactic patterns appearing in the noun dictionary definitions as they occur in SSJČ and to make the possible generalizations.

Preliminary examination shows that the dictionary definitions display some regular syntactic structures which quite systematically correspond to the semantic organization of the dictionary definitions and indicate their individual parts.

2.2   Noun Definions in SSJČ

We are interested here in the semantic organization of the noun definitions, or in other words, in their "deep structure" and how it is related to their "surface" syntactic structures. It can be seen that they mostly "behave" in a standard way, typically, these definitions follow the classical dictionary definition pattern, i.e. first part of the definition consists of the genus proximum (GP) and the second one represents the distinguishers $(d_1, d_2, \ldots, d_n)$.

We can observe here a good parallelism between GP and the first noun group in the dictionary definitions. What also can be done is to check semiautomatically the heads of these noun groups against the corresponding nouns in Czech WordNet and to see how regularly they contain the hyperonymical expressions (such as furniture in our example group of selected furniture nouns) – this can be done by comparing them with the corresponding H/H trees in WordNet (see below).

At the first glance we can see that the distinguishers are expressed in several ways: as noun groups, relative sentences, adjectival phrases with complements or as prepositional groups. The closer examination, however, shows that the picture is more complicated and the corresponding surface syntactic structures are much richer (see below). Thus the parsing of the dictionary definitions should discover the inventory of the syntactic structures that may correspond to the GP + d_1, d_2, . . . , d_n scheme. We give some typical examples from SSJČ together with their English equivalents from NODE. Angle brackets in Czech descriptions mark out the particular groups (and their cases in which they may occur).

stůl: $<$kus$>_{ng1}$ $<$nabytku$>_{ng2}$ $<$tvořený$>_{ap}$ $<$(vodorovnou) deskou$>_{ng7}$ $<$na nohach$>_{png6}$ $<$nebo$>_{conj}$ $<$na podstavci$>_{png6}$
table: a piece of furniture with a flat top and one or more legs, providing a level surface on which objects may be placed, and which can be used for such purpose as eating, writing, working or playing games

židle: $<$přenosný kus$>_{ng1}$ $<$nabytku$>_{ng2}$ $<$(s opěradlem)$>_{ng7}$ $<$k seze-ní$>_{png3}$ $<$pro jednu osobu$>_{png4}$
chair: a separate seat for one person, typically with a back and four legs

křeslo: $<$pohodlné sedadlo$>_{ng1}$ $<$s opěradly$>_{ng7}$
armchair: a large, comfortable chair with side supports for a person's arm

skříň: $<$vyšší kus$>_{ng1}$ $<$nabytku$>_{ng2}$ $<$na ukládaní různych předmětů$>_{png4}$ $<$nebo$>_{conj}$ $<$na věšení šatstva$>_{png4}$
cupboard: a piece of furniture with a door and usually shelves, used for storage, wardrobe

letadlo: $<$zařízení$>_{ng1}$ $<$schopné$>_{ap}$ $<$letaní$>_{ng2}$ $<$k dopravě$>_{png3}$ $<$vzduchem$>_{ng7}$
aeroplane: a powered flying vehicle with fixed wings and weight greater than that of the air it displaces

3   Parsing Syntactic Structures of Dictionary Definitions (in Czech – SSJČ)

The frequencies of the different definition types is shown in Table 1. Basic tables show the main types of the syntactic patterns found within the noun dictionary definitions in SSJČ. When we tried to extent the recall of the parser rules the time necessary for the analysis has increased enormously since the mechanism of the partial analysis is obviously not suitable for the exhaustive parsing. (Processing approx. 3700 entries took about 3 days.)

Table 1. Frequencies of the different deffinition types.

	1st file	2nd file	syntactic structure
# entries	3672	5935	
not processed (%)	21.0	20.3	
processed (%)	79.0	79.7	
from processed:			
def1 (%)	13.0	11.6	E = one-word-synonym
def2 (%)	62.7	63.2	E = (Ng | Pg)+
def3 (%)	18.0	18.5	E = (Ng | Pg)+ Ap (Ng | Pg)+
def4 (%)	2.3	2.0	E = Ng Sr
def5 (%)	0.1	0.1	E = (Ng | Pg)+ Ap (Ng | Pg)+ Sr
def6 (%)	3.4	4.2	E = [kdo|co|někdo|něco] .*
def7 (%)	0.4	0.4	E = [schopnost|neschopnost] .*

E in the examples of syntactic structures stands for the defined word (it is simple nominal group) in the definition. Ng can represent both simple nominal groups but also quite complicated recursive nominal groups (including the groups with coordination and genitive groups). Pg represents prepositional noun and pronoun groups (usually we use separate nonterminals Png and Ppg). Standard conventions of context-free syntax are used: (+ sign represents one or more repetition, * represents zero or more repetition, | stays for alternative etc.).

It can be observed that the type of definition labelled def5 is not very frequent, but the question is whether the definitions of this type can be classified under def4/def3, ev. to which category they belong. def6 a def7 represent very specific types of the definitions established only on the base of the specific key word like kdo (who) that do not belong into any of the previous category.

It can be said the definitions of the entries for whose no structure has been found usually can be intuitively classified as belonging to some of the groups 1-5. However, they display very complicated structures (e.g. very complicated attributive noun groups), that prevent the parser (the particular rules in it) from recognizing them. There are only few entries that do not belong into any of the introduced groups/categories, for example nazor, že... (the opinion that...).

The examples of the analyses of the individual definitions is given in Table 2. Angle brackets mark out the particular groups forming definition body. Labels

Table 2. Examples of the different definition types.

type	example (literal translation)
def1	**droždí** $= <kvasnice>_{ng1}$ ($<yeast>$)
def2	**afix** $= <společné\ označení>_{ng1} <pro\ předpony\ a\ přípony>_{png4}$ ($affix = <common\ label><for\ prefixes\ and\ suffixes>$)
def3	**balneografie** $= <obor>_{ng1} <lékařství>_{ng2} <zabývající\ se>_{ap}$ $<vědeckým\ popisem>_{ng3} <lázní>_{ng2} <a>_{conj} <léčivých\ vod>_{ng2}$ ($balneology = <field><of\ medicine><dealing\ with>$ $<scientific\ description><of\ spas><and><sanative\ waters>$)
def4	**akumulátor** $= <zásobník>_{ng1} <elektrické\ energie>_{ng2}$ $<,\ která\ v\ něm\ byla\ dříve\ nahromaděna\ chemicky>_{sr}$ ($accumulator = <store><of\ electric\ energy>$ $<that\ was\ accumulated\ into\ it\ previously\ by\ chemical\ processes>$)
def5	**konstantan** $= <slitina>_{ng1} <mědi>_{ng2} <a>_{conj} <niklu>_{ng2}$ $<vyznačující\ se>_{ap} <velikým\ elektrickým\ odporem>_{ng3}$ $<,\ který\ se\ málo\ mění\ teplotou>_{sr}$ ($constantan = <alloy><of\ copper><and><nickel>$ $<displaying><a\ strong\ electrical\ resistance>$) $<which\ causes\ only\ small\ changes\ in\ temperature>$)
def6	**falšovatel** $= <kdo>_{keyw}$ něco falšuje ($falsifier = <who>$ falsify something)
def7	**výrazovost** $= <schopnost>_{keyw}$ něco vyjádřit, vyjadřovat ($expressiveness = <ability>$ to express something)

used here are more specific then the ones used in the formal desriptions of the particular definitions (but it is easy to transform them to the respective general form).

If we examine the relations between syntactic and semantic structures of several selected definitions for the nouns like přístroj (apparatus), zařízení (device), stroj (machine) or nauka (doctrine) and obor (discipline) we can observe that the meaning of the nouns determines closely their valency frames which then decide about the syntactic structure of the definition. It can be also observed that the semantic nature of the headword also determines the meaning of genus proximum – e.g. in the case of ampermetr (ammeter) it has to be obviously apparatus which is further determined by the distinguishers describing the purpose of the apparatus – that it is designed for measuring, recording, determining, displaying etc. If our goal is to be able to process the dictionary definitions formally (algorithmically), then we have to deal with their valency frames as it can be demonstrated for the noun přístroj valency frames for přístroj contain the prepositions k (to) with dative, na (on) with accusative, pro (for) with accusative. Apart from this noun přístroj can co-occur with a relative sentence and with verbal adjectives like měřící (measuring), zapisující, zaznamenávající (recording), určující (determining) etc. Some examples of typical beginnings of definitions with the keyword přístroj (apparatus) and their formal structures follow.

přístroj k měření <čeho>	<png3><ng2>	(for measuring)
přístroj na měření <čeho>	<png4> <ng2>	(to measure)
přístroj pro studium	<png4>	(for studying)
přístroj, jímž, kterým, který	<srel>	(that, with what...)
přístroj zapisující změny	<adj><ng4>	(recording changes)
přístroj ukazující změny	<adj><ng4>	(displaying changes)
přístroj měřící kmitočet	<adj> <ng4>	(measuring frequency)
přístroj udávající rychlost	<adj><ng4>	(determining speed)
přístroj určující, kdy	<adj><srel>	(determining when...)

As to semantic structure of the dictionary definitions, if we take the parsed syntactic structures of the processed dictionary definitions and extract their head noun groups representing (according to the parser) the GP pattern we obtain a list of expressions that are hyperonyms of the headwords in the dictionary definitions. This result can be regarded as reliable enough, thus in this way confirming our starting assumption that GP patterns can be processed and obtained from the dictionary definitions rather automatically.

The next question is in what extent one can try to recognize the semantic structure of the distinguishers and if it can be done in a semi-automatic way. If we have a look at the distinguishers in our examples for apparatus (přístroj) we can see that typically they describe what the particular apparatus does, i.e. the activity of measuring, recording, determining, displaying... Thus we need to have a lexical (knowledge) database that knows everything about these devices and also formal means that would allow us to describe what the particular apparatus does, i.e. a set of predicates within an appropriate logical formalism, e.g. transparent intensional logic – TIL (Horák, 2002) that would allow us to describe the particular activities semantically.

In Table 3 we show the same data for the selected items which contains Table 1 for the complete test files of the definition samples. In addition to the percentual representation of the particular definition types are shown also actual numbers of the appropriate examples (first column for every selected word). The meanings of labels used in this table are the following: all – number of definitions with the selected keyword, nonproc – those definitions from the above mentioned which were not processed by the parser, proc – processed definitions (all – nonproc), def1-def4 – numbers (percentages) of the particular definition types.

It can be observed that apparatus, device and instrument display very similar distribution of the definition types (also stroj (machine) could be included into this group). This feature could be expected due to the similar meaning of all these words.

On the other hand, discipline and doctrine are semantically close as well but their distributions of definition types are quite different. The reason is that valency frames of these wors are different. Definitions with the keyword nauka (discipline) almost always starts with nauka o (def2, doctrine about), whereas obor (discipline) is very often obor zabývající se <čím> (def3, discipline dealing with). Definitition type distributions of nauka (discipline) and činnost (activity)

Table 3. Different deffinition types for the selected items.

	přístroj (apparatus)		zařízení (device)		nástroj (instrument)		obor (discipline)	
all	174		118		43		22	
nonproc	19	10.9%	19	16.1%	5	11.6%	3	13.6%
proc	155	89.1%	99	83.9%	38	88.4%	19	86.4%
def1	0	0.0%	0	0.0%	0	0.0%	1	5.2%
def2	140	90.3%	88	88.9%	32	84.2%	7	36.8%
def3	8	5.2%	3	3.0%	3	7.9%	11	50.0%
def4	7	4.5%	8	8.1%	3	7.9%	0	0.0%

	nauka (doctrine)		činnost (activity)		místnost (room)		stroj (machine)	
all	85		71		63		51	
nonproc	11	12.9%	1	1.4%	8	12.7%	3	5.9%
proc	74	87.1%	70	98.6%	55	87.3%	48	94.1%
def1	0	0.0%	0	0.0%	0	0.0%	1	2.1%
def2	72	97.3%	68	97.1%	48	87.3%	45	93.7%
def3	2	2.7%	2	2.9%	7	12.7%	1	2.1%
def4	0	0.0%	0	0.0%	0	0.0%	1	2.1%

are also similar. These are also semantically close words, but the distribution similarity here follows from the fact that most frequent definition structures of them – nauka o (doctrine about) and Činnost <kohoČČceho> (activity of st or sb) – belong to the same definition type (def2).

Definitions of the type def6 a def7 could not occur in our sample at all (because of the selected keywords); the occurence of def5 is not very likely here as well. There are not almost any definitions of type def1 which also follows from the selection of keywords.

4   Conclusions

We can conclude that this sort of analysis appears to be useful and helps in testing the noun dictionary definitions for their syntactic and semantic consistency. Its results can be, in our opinion, applied later to semi-automatic preparation of the dictionary definitions thus saving a considerable amount of manual work. Therefore the following steps will be taken in building dictionary definitions (glosses) for the developed Czech WordNet and prepared Czech Lexical Database as well:

- to use the different types of definitions for the different parts of speech in a systematic way, i.e. to use scheme GP + $d_1, d_2, \ldots, d_n$ mostly for nouns, the definitions based on semantic components and troponymy relations for verbs and synonymical explanations combined with collocational examples for adjectives and adverbs,
- to use the semantic classification of Czech verbs and integrate it appropriately into the dictionary definitions (glosses),

- to examine in a more detailed way the definitions with GP $+ d_1, d_2, \ldots,$ d_n pattern for nouns and to check whether the distinguishers can be inherited systematically between H/H trees, eventually to explore further how the properties represented by the distinguishers can be related and systematically organized,
- to examine whether the distinguishers can also capture the relation of meronymy or holonymy and in the positive case to find out how frequent it is,
- to explore more systematically the semantic structure the collocational examples using corpus data and integrate them systematically into the adjective dictionary definitions (glosses),
- the ultimate goal of the mentioned steps is to obtain the systematic, formal and consistent dictionary definitions (glosses) for the entries (possibly taking form of synsets) in the Lexical Database and Czech WordNet.

References

1. Balkanet Project, 2001.
2. Buitelaar, P.: Corelex. Systematic Polysemy and Underspecification. Ph.D. Thesis, Computer Science, Brandeis University, 1998.
3. Collins Cobuild English Dictionary, ed. by J. Sinclair. Cobuild. London, Harper Collins Publishers, 1995.
4. Horák, A.: The Normal Translation Algorithm in Transparent Intensional Logic (for Czech). Ph.D. Thesis, Faculty of Informatics, Brno, March, 2002.
5. Leech, G., N.: Semantics. Harmondsworth, Penguin, 1974.
6. Levin, B.: English Verb Classes and Alternations. The University of Chicago, Chicago Press, Chicago, 1993.
7. Lyons, J.: Semantics. Cambridge University Press, Cambridge, 1977.
8. New Oxford Dictionary of English. edited by P. Hanks. Oxford University Press, Oxford, 1998.
9. Pala, K. and Smrž, P.: Slovko, Bratislava, 2001.
10. Pala, K. and Smrž, P.: Glosses in WordNet 1.5 and their Standardization, accepted at LREC, 2002.
11. Pustejovsky, J.: The Generative Lexicon, A Bradford Book, MIT Press, Cambridge, 1995.
12. Havránek B. et al.: Slovník spisovného jazyka českého (SSJČ, Dictionary of Written Czech), Academia, Praha, 1960.
13. Vossen, P.: EuroWordNet 1, 2, Final Report, University of Amsterdam, CD ROM, 1999.
14. Žáčková, E.: Partial Parsing (of Czech), Ph.D. Thesis, Masaryk University, Brno, 2002.

Is Shallow Parsing Useful for Unsupervised Learning of Semantic Clusters?

Marie-Laure Reinberger and Walter Daelemans

CNTS – University of Antwerp – Belgium
{reinberg,daelem}@uia.ua.ac.be

Abstract. The context of this paper is the application of unsupervised Machine Learning techniques to building ontology extraction tools for Natural Language Processing. Our method relies on exploiting large amounts of linguistically annotated text, and on linguistic concepts such as selectional restrictions and co-composition.

We work with a corpus of medical texts in English. First we apply a shallow parser to the corpus to get subject-verb-object structures. We then extract verb-noun relations, and apply a clustering algorithm to them to build semantic classes of nouns. We have evaluated the adequacy of the clustering method when applied to a syntactically tagged corpus, and the relevance of the semantic content of the resulting clusters.

Keywords. Semantics, knowledge representation, machine learning, text mining, ontology, selectional restrictions, co-composition.

1   Introduction

Semantic representations are useful for many natural language processing tasks, including information retrieval, word sense disambiguation, and automatic translation. However, in order to deal adequately with problems such as polysemy, these representations should be sufficiently rich and fine-grained. Today, the use of powerful and robust language processing tools such as shallow parsers allows us to parse large text collections and thereby provide potentially relevant information for extracting semantic knowledge. In order to decide what information is relevant for modeling semantic representations, we need strong linguistic hypotheses to guide the automatic extraction process. In this paper, we present a first step in an attempt to build tools for ontology extraction from scratch, on the basis of specific domain texts. At the same time, we intend to process as much as possible using strictly unsupervised methods on linguistically annotated texts.

We will present here in a first section our linguistic assumptions, followed by a description of the syntactic analysis we perform, a description of the semantic information extraction process, and an evaluation of our results.

A. Gelbukh (Ed.): CICLing 2003, LNCS 2588, pp. 304–313, 2003.

2   Linguistic Assumptions

Due to the richness and the diversity of the information that a word may carry, efficient lexical semantic representations should contain a multitude of information of different kinds. In addition to the usual lexical information, these representations should include for example pragmatic information or knowledge of the world that might be useful to cope with problems such as ambiguity. In line with other data-oriented approaches to semantics, we start from the assumption that most of this information is present in plain texts in the way the words are organized and combined together to form complex expressions. The information that allows us to combine the right words together in order to produce meaningful expressions is assumed to be embedded in such texts, contained in the relations between the words of a complex expression. We take a broad perspective on these relations in that we do not restrict them to the hypernym/hyponym and meronymic relations, but that we also focus on information about the functionality of the concepts associated to a word (its uses, capacities etc.) that can be found in the way nouns and verbs, or nouns and adjectives are combined. The main problem lies then in finding a convenient way to get this information and retrieving it in an efficient way. We have chosen to begin this study by focusing on an unsupervised method, in order to gain insight in how far we could get (in terms of amount of and grain-size of the retrieved information) without human expertise.

An important assumption underlying our method is the hypothesis that syntax and semantics are not independent in natural language. They are closely related and interconnected, and we will refer here to this assumption as the principle of selectional restrictions: the syntactic structure of an expression provides relevant information about its semantic content.

The second hypothesis concerns the notion of co-composition [1]. Co-composition is an operation that occurs in the construction of meaning. If two elements compose an expression, each of them imposes semantic constraints on the other. In our studies, this is applied to the syntactic group noun-verb: the verb imposes restrictions on the noun, but the noun as well constrains the verb. In other words, each word in a noun-verb relation participates in building the meaning of the other word in this context ([2], [3]).

Related to these assumptions, we can then define two major tasks: (i) accessing the information, and (ii) organizing the information. Of course those tasks are related as the nature of the information retrieved will in some way influence its future organization. Our purpose is to build a repository of lexical semantic information, ensuring evolvability and adaptability. This repository can be considered as a complex semantic network. We could also label it an ontology, considering that an ontology is a collection of organized knowledge relative to a particular domain. An important point is that we assume that the method of extraction and the organization of this semantic information should depend not only on the available material, but also on the intended use of the knowledge structure. There are different ways of organizing it, depending on its future use and on the specificity of the domain. In this paper, we deal with such a specific domain, but one of our future objectives is to test our methods and tools on different domains. This brings us to the choice, composition, and annotation of our corpus.

3   Syntactic Analysis

We take a special interest in the compositional aspects of noun-verb relations. In order to provide information about these relations automatically in our corpus, we used the memory-based shallow parser which is being developed in Tilburg and Antwerp [4][1]. This shallow parser takes plain text as input, performs tokenization, POS tagging and phrase boundary detection, and finally finds grammatical relations such as subject-verb and object-verb relations, which are particularly useful for us. The software was developed to be efficient and robust enough to allow shallow parsing of large amounts of text from various domains.

In exploratory research, we used the Wall Street Journal corpus, but its vocabulary seemed not specific enough for our method, as we did not get enough occurrences for the different noun-verb pairs, at least for this first set of experiments on which we wanted to test the method. Consequently, we decided to test on texts representing more specific domains, and we used publicly available Medline abstracts, focusing on a particular medical subject. Our corpus is composed of the Medline abstracts retrieved by the Medline search engine under the queries "hepatitis A" and "hepatitis B". It contains about 4 million words. The shallow parser was used to provide a linguistic analysis of each sentence of this corpus, allowing us to retrieve semantic information of various kinds.

4   Semantic Information Extraction

Our method can be divided into two tasks. In a first step, we have used the syntactic information to perform a clustering of the nouns according to their relations with the verbs of the corpus. The second step will consist in building hierarchical relations between the clustered nouns, and between nouns and verb, making use of the results of the clustering.

4.1   Clustering

Method

As was mentioned earlier, the output of the shallow parser allows us to distinguish between noun-verb relations, where the noun appears as a subject in the expression, and noun-verb relations where it appears as an object. This lead us to focus particularly on the relation noun-verb and to use this information to operate a clustering on the nouns according to the verbs they combine with[2].

---

[1] See http://ilk.kub.nl for a demo version.

[2] With *noun*, we refer to the head of an NP having a subject or object relation with the verb.

Considering that most words have more than one meaning, we perform a soft clustering, in order to allow a word to belong to different clusters([5]) that represent different uses or meanings for this word.

The first step of the algorithm consists of processing the parsed text to retrieve the co-occurring noun-verb pairs, and remembering whether the noun appeared in a subject or in an object position. This step is performed with the use of a stoplist that skips all pairs implying the verbs to be or to have. We want to point out that we are not implying by doing so that those two verbs do not provide relevant information. They simply are too frequent and have such a broad meaning that we cannot, with this method and at this stage of the experiments, take them into account. We select then from the list we get the most frequent co-occurrences: the 100 most frequent noun-verb relations with the nouns appearing in the subject group, and the 100 most frequent relations where the noun is part of the object group. What we obtain is a list of verbs, each verb associated with a list of nouns that co-occur with it, either as subjects only or as objects only. Here is an extract of the list:

- acquiring_o: hepatitis infection virus disease
- associated_o: diseases cirrhosis DNA polymerase carcinoma HCC
- compensated_o: liver cirrhosis disease
- decompensated_o: liver cirrhosis disease
- decreased_s: rates prevalence serum incidence proportion number percentage
- estimated_s: prevalence rate virus incidence risk
- estimate_o: prevalence incidence risk number
- transmitted_o: hepatitis infection disease

The next step consists of clustering these classes of nouns according to their similarity. The similarity measure takes into account the number of common elements and the number of elements that differ between two classes of nouns. Each class is compared to all other classes of nouns. For each pair of classes C1-C2, the program counts the number of nouns common to both classes (sim), the number of nouns only present in C1 (dif1) and the number of nouns only present in C2 (dif2). If sim, dif1 and dif2 respect some predefined values the matching is considered to be possible. After the initial class has been compared to all other classes, all the possible matchings are compared and the one producing the largest new class is kept (in case of ties, the first one is kept). Each time a new cluster is created, the 2 classes involved are removed from the processed list. The whole process is iterated as long as at least one new matching occurs, resulting in the creation of a new cluster. We will describe the measures we used in the next section, along with the evaluation of the clustering.

Results

We display in Table 1 some examples of steady clusters that appear in the results for each experiment in a series of experiments. Intuitively, the examples reported here seem to make sense, given the verbs they are associated to. For example, the

Table 1. Examples of extracted clusters

complete(o) starting(o)	contain(o)	develop(o) induce(o)	analyse(s) identify(s)	decrease(s) estimate(o)
immunization	antigen	hepatitis	aim	incidence
vaccine	virus	infection	objective	risk
vaccination	hepatitis	disease	purpose	proportion
	protein	cirrhosis	study	rate
	serum	carcinoma		

nouns associated to the verbs *to decrease* and *to estimate* all name something that can be counted or represented by a number. The nouns associated to the verb *to complete* name something that can be fragmented or incomplete.

As we have used soft clustering, some words are associated to more than one cluster. This is the case for the word "hepatitis", e.g., which appears of course very often in this corpus. As shown in the table, "hepatitis" is associated with other diseases in the cluster of nouns representing nouns that can be combined with "to develop", and associated with other nouns representing things that can be considered as parts of a more important entity with the verb "to contain". But this anecdotal, intuitive approach does not tell us a lot about the general, objective, relevance of our clusters. Therefore, we need a method to measure this relevance, to ensure that the clusters indeed contain related words.

4.2   Evaluation of the Clusters

We evaluate our clustering method at two different levels. The first level concerns the relevance of the clusters: do they associate semantically related words? The second level concerns the method itself: is the syntactic tagging really useful, or could we perform interesting clusters from unparsed text as well?

Relevance Level

We evaluated the relevance of the clusters with the help of WordNet. Considering that we cannot automatically label the relations that unite the nouns of our clusters, we hoped that the variety of relations proposed by WordNet would fit the relations our clustering algorithm has built. The semantic information provided by WordNet is only used in the evaluation process. We do not intent to correct or enlarge the clusters with this information, as we wish to stay as much as possible within the paradigm of unsupervised learning.

We have extracted from WordNet all possible pairs consisting of two words present in the clusters, where the words of these pairs were linked in WordNet by a relation of synonymy, hypernymy, hyponymy or meronymy. The next step consisted of checking the presence of those pairs in the clusters. Of course, as the domain is very specific, not all the nouns present in the clusters are included

Table 2. Comparison of the percentage of words clustered and the average length of the clusters

	Number of clusters	Number of words	% of words clustered	Av. length of clusters
E1.1	120	153	94%	8.87
E1.2	28	105	64%	10.71
E2.1	155	148	91%	5.39
E2.2	32	108	66%	9.81

Table 3. Recall and negative recall values for the different clustering experiments

	Number of WordNet pairs	Recall on the pairs	Number of incorrect pairs	Negative recall
E1.1	108	75%	11628	32%
E1.2	75	57%	5460	21%
E2.1	77	74%	10878	19%
E2.2	77	65%	5778	21%

in WordNet. Here are some examples of word pairs that could be extracted from WordNet:

hepatitis – disease (hypernymic relation)
blood – cells (meronymic relation)
aim – purpose (synonym)

Due to the fact that we are aiming at elaborating tools, we concentrate on experimenting and testing. Therefore, our clustering is not yet supposed to classify as many nouns as possible. As we have reduced the input to the clustering method to the 100 most frequent relations noun(subject)-verb and the 100 most frequent relations noun(object)-verb, the set of nouns was limited to 163 (some nouns appearing in the two sets). In the first experiment (E1.1), our criteria were that two classes of nouns could be merged if they had more than 2 common elements (sim>2), and not more than 5 different elements (dif<6). Once the clustering process ended, we considered as clusters the sets that contained at least 3 nouns. From the initial set of 163 nouns, 153 were clustered, which represents 94% of them (see Table 2).

We then fed WordNet with those 153 words, and we retrieved 108 pairs of words. As 27 of those pairs failed to appear in the clusters, we got, according to the "WordNet sample" a recall of 75%. An evaluation of the precision score was difficult to settle as we do not have a gold standard of the "real" clusters. We therefore estimate a "negative recall", by generating incorrect pairs of words, and checking how many of them are present in the clusters. Those pairs are composed from non-related nouns, according to WordNet. We have generated about 11,000 pairs, of which about a third were present in the clusters, which in other words correponds to a negative recall of 32%. As the clustering is only a first step in an unsupervised ontology extraction process, it seemed sensible to focus on limiting the rate of errors and improve the results using other methods rather than investigating the mistakes. In order to improve the negative recall, we ran a new range of experiments (E2.1) where we allowed for more clusters to be formed (dif-sim<1). We kept the clusters containing two elements, but we eliminated the big clusters. A cluster was considered as too big when it contained more than 20 items, a number based on the biggest class associated to one verb. The same evaluation showed that about the same rate of words were clustered (91%). We obtained a good recall (74%), and a better negative recall (19%).

The elimination of the big clusters improves the precision score and is balanced by the creation of more small clusters, which improves recall. The weakness of both sets of results lies in the high number of clusters produced: 120 clusters for the first experiment, and 155 clusters for the second.

We tried to reduce the number of clusters by removing the smaller ones from both sets of previous results (experiments E1.2 and E2.2). We obtained for E1.2 a group of 28 clusters, which corresponds to 64% of the words, with a negative recall of 19%, but a recall of only 57%. The results for E2.2 were quite similar with a better recall of 65%. We conclude from this that relevant information can be found in the small-sized clusters, and that by removing the small clusters, we lose this information without improving the negative recall measure.

The experiment that rates the best score according to our objectives is experiment E2.1. It gives us the lowest negative recall, a good recall, and a high rate of the set of initial words are clustered. Its weak point is the numerous clusters generated. But this clustering is only the first result in an ontology extraction tools process, and the next steps will aim at improving the results of the clustering and making the clusters more precise.

A summary of the results discussed above appears in tables 2 and 3.

Efficiency Level

The second step of our evaluation consisted in comparing the results of the clustering algorithm on parsed text with the results we would get processing on plain text, in order to get a baseline. Our hypothesis is that the clustering performed on a syntactically analyzed text is more accurate than one performed on raw text. But we are also interested in the magnitude of the difference in performance between both methods: is it really worth the trouble to analyze the corpus syntactically, or can we get useful results already with raw text, results that we could then improve by retrieving more semantic information from more text?

We ran a set of experiments on plain text, using bi-grams as the equivalent for plain text of the noun-verb pairs in the annotated text. We have compared the two methods on the basis of the number of words clustered. The clustering on annotated text worked on 163 words corresponding to the 200 most frequent

Table 4. Percentage of words clustered using parsed text and using plain text

	Nb of clusters	Nb of words	Nb of words clustered	% of words clustered
E2.1	155	163	148	91%
4000 m.f.bg	38	1663	206	12%
5000 m.f.bg	52	1931	263	14%

Table 5. Recall and negative recall values for the clustering on parsed text and on plain text

	Nb of correct pairs	Recall	Nb of negative pairs	Negative recall
E2.1	77	74%	10878	19%
4000 m.f.bg	51	29%	21037	6%
5000 m.f.bg	75	27%	34641	5%

relations, of which 148 were clustered in experiment E2.1. In the bigram experiment, it appeared that considering the 4000 most frequent bigrams corresponded to 1663 words and that 206 of those words were clustered at the end of the process. We ran the clustering algorithm on different numbers of bigrams, and the results were quite similar. As shown in Table 4, and considering that the bigrams, even with the use of a stoplist, select all kinds of words, the percentage of words contained in the clusters was very low, which means that a lot of words have to be taken into account to cluster only a (comparatively) small number of nouns. As expected, the recall on the clusters using the WordNet pairs was low, and never reaching more than 30%. The best measure we obtained for all bigram sets was the negative recall, which never went over 6%. We give the results in Table 5 for the 4000 and the 5000 most frequent bigrams. We can see there that a difference of 1000 bigrams does not change significantly the recall values.

The results we get show that the use of annotated text improves the rate of words clustered and the recall. The difference of those two rates is important enough to balance the better negative recall, and to let us consider that performing a syntactic analysis prior to the clustering is useful.

5   Ongoing Work: Labeling and Building a Hierarchy

The next task in our project consists of labeling the relations between the nouns and building a hierarchy. To further pursue an unsupervised approach, the semantic labeling should be done automatically. We therefore do not intent to use WordNet and the different relations it proposes, but will try to get those semantic relations directly from the corpus.

The clustering we are performing does not provide any information concerning the kind of relations between the clusters, hence between the words. However, the different elements of a cluster have something in common that can be specified as a relation. We can focus on two types of information: the relations between words belonging to the same cluster, and the relations between the clusters of nouns and the verbs associated to them according to the relation verb-noun (subject or object). We are planning to perform this by using methods involving pattern matching or association rules ([6]), and automatic methods for constructing hierarchies ([7], [8]).

6   Conclusions and Perspectives

We have shown that unsupervised learning methods can be used to retrieve semantic information from text when a shallow syntactic analysis is available. This syntactic analysis proved to be useful as the clustering performed on the parsed text gave better results than the one performed on plain text. The next step of this research is to elaborate the conceptual knowledge sets for the clusters of nouns. Another interesting extension would consist in considering the groups of verbs associated to the clusters of nouns. That information could allow us to cluster the verbs and get selectional preferences associated with classes of verbs, but also to relate nouns to verbs, where these relations represent the semantic functions of the concept associated with the noun. Yet another issue is the retrieval of the prepositions that introduce a nominal complement and use this information to make the information associated with nouns more specific.

Acknowledgments. This research was carried out in the context of the Onto-Basis project, sponsored by IWT (Institute for the Promotion of Innovation by Science and Technology in Flanders).

References

1. Pustejovsky, J.: The Generative Lexicon. MIT Press (1995)
2. Gamallo, P., Agustini, A., Lopes, G.P.: Selection restrictions acquisition from corpora. In: Proceedings EPIA-01, Springer-Verlag (2001)
3. Gamallo, P., Agustini, A., Lopes, G.P.: Using co-composition for acquiring syntactic and semantic subcategorisation. In: Proceedings of the Workshop SIGLEX-02 (ACL-02). (2002)
4. Daelemans, W., Buchholz, S., Veenstra, J.: Memory-based shallow parsing. In: Proceedings of CoNLL-99. (1999)
5. Faure, D., Nédellec, C.: Knowledge acquisition of predicate argument structures from technical texts using machine learning: The system asium. In: Proceedings EKAW-99. (1999)
6. Maedche, A., Staab, S.: Semi-automatic engineering of ontologies from text. In: Proceedings of SEKE-00. (2000)
7. Caraballo, S.A.: Automatic construction of a hypernym-labeled noun hierarchy from text. In: Proceedings ACL-99. (1999)

8. Berland, M., Charniak, E.: Finfing parts in very large corpora. In: Proceedings ACL-99. (1999)
9. Agirre, E., Martinez, D.: Learning class-to-class selectional preferences. In: Proceedings CoNLL-01. (2001)
10. Caraballo, S.A., Charniak, E.: Determining the specificity of nouns from text. In: Proceedings SIGDAT-99. (1999)
11. Gamallo, P., Gasperin, C., Agustini, A., Lopes, G.P.: Syntactic-based methods for measuring word similarity. In: Proceedings TSD-01, Springer-Verlag (2001)
12. Maedche, A., Staab, S.: Ontology learning for the semantic web. IEEE Intelligent Systems **16** (2001)
13. McCarthy, D., Carroll, J., Preiss, J.: Disambiguating noun and verb senses using automatically acquired selectional preferences. SENSEVAL-2 (2001)
14. Wagner, A., Mastropietro, M.: Collecting and employing selectional restrictions. Technical report (1996)

Experiments on Extracting Semantic Relations from Syntactic Relations

Caroline Varaschin Gasperin and Vera Lúcia Strube de Lima

Faculdade de Informática
PPGCC, PUCRS
Av. Ipiranga, 6681
90619-900 Porto Alegre, RS, Brasil
{caroline,vera}@inf.pucrs.br

Abstract. This work presents the results of the application of a technique for automatic extraction of semantic relations among words from a corpus. The technique used is the one proposed by Grefenstette in [1]. We brought contributions to the syntactic context notion in [1], aiming to improve the identification of semantically related words. Then, we carried on three different experiments using a Portuguese language corpus: the first one compares the original Grefenstette's technique with the technique modified with our contributions, the second experiment investigates which syntactic relation is more relevant when identifying semantic relations, and the last experiment investigates the influence of the parser errors on the quality of the extracted semantic relations. Results and their analyses are detailed in this article.

1 Introduction

Identifying semantic relations among words in a corpus is an useful task mainly for automatic thesaurus/ontology building. A thesaurus can improve considerably the precision of systems for information retrieval, information extraction, document classification, machine translation, text summarization, and others.

This work presents an extension of Grefenstette's [1] strategy to obtain semantically similar words from corpora. This is a knowledge-poor syntax-based technique, like the ones in [2,3]. There are other kinds of techniques [4,5,6] that don't use syntactic information.

Grefenstette's technique includes basically three steps: extracting the syntactic contexts of each noun in the corpus, comparing each pair of nouns using their syntactic contexts through a similarity measure, and building lists of most similar nouns for each noun in the corpus.

The two main points that differentiate Grefenstette's technique from other syntax-based techniques to identify semantic relations between words are: the notion of syntactic context and the similarity measure.

According to Grefenstette, each word that is syntactically related to a noun is part of its syntactic context. This way, each adjective, noun or verb that share a syntactic relation with a noun is recorded as a syntactic context of the noun.

A. Gelbukh (Ed.): CICLing 2003, LNCS 2588, pp. 314–324, 2003.
© Springer-Verlag Berlin Heidelberg 2003

The similarity measure used by Grefenstette is a weighted version of Jaccard's measure, which assigns weights to each context extracted from the corpus, according to context frequencies in local (word) and global (corpus) scope.

Our extension to Grefenstette's technique is focused on the notion of syntactic context. We observed that some useful fine-grained syntactic information available in the corpus were not considered by Grefenstette when extracting the syntactic contexts. Our hypothesis is that this information could help considerably in identifying semantic relations between words. So, we decided to include the fine-grained information into the syntactic contexts.

We carried on experiments to validate Grefenstette's technique for Portuguese language, and also to validate the proposed extensions. The corpus used in the experiments consists of a 1,262,000-word subset of the FOLHANOT corpus, formed by news texts written in Brazilian Portuguese and syntactically analysed by the parser PALAVRAS [7].

We present a sample of the results, that is constituted by lists of words semantically related to some selected nouns. The analysis of such results is detailed, and a comparison between the lists generated through the original Grefenstette's technique and the lists generated through the extended technique proposed is shown.

We also carried on other two experiments: one to investigate which syntactic relation is more relevant when identifying semantic relations, and another to investigate the influence of the parser errors on the homogeneity of the generated lists of semantic related words.

In the next sections, we explain our contribution to Grefenstette's syntactic context notion. In section 3, we report our experiments to validate the proposed contributions. In section 4, we report our experiment to identify the most relevant syntactic relation. In section 5, we report our experiment to investigate the parser influence on the homogeneity of the word lists. In section 6, we present our concluding remarks. Finally, in section 7, we present the future phases of this work.

2   Syntax-Based Technique Adopted

Grefenstette's work [1] presents a syntax-based technique to automatically extract semantic relations between words. (This task is the opposite to the one considered in [8], where possible syntactic relationships are shown to be predictable basing on the semantic similarity between words.) The technique adopted consists on extracting syntactic contexts for each noun in a partially parsed corpus. Each syntactic relation between a noun and another word generates a syntactic context for this noun. The following nominal syntactic relations are considered: ADJ (an adjective modifies a noun), NN (a noun modifies another noun) and NNPREP (noun modifies another noun, using a preposition).

Verbal syntactic relations are also considered: SUBJ (a noun is the subject of a verb), DOBJ (a noun is the direct object of a verb) and IOBJ (a noun is the indirect object of a verb). Table 1 shows examples of some syntactic contexts.

To find the semantic similarity between the nouns, one compares them through their syntactic contexts, using as similarity measure a weighted version of the binary Jaccard measure [1]. The weighted Jaccard measure considers a global and a local weight for each context. The global weight takes into account the amount of different words associated

Table 1. Examples of binary syntactic dependencies

Sentence	Noun	Contexts
A cidade inicia a colheita da maior safre de sua história. (The city begins the crop of the largest production of its history.)	*cidade*	<SUBJ, *iniciar*>
	colheita	<DOBJ, *iniciar*> <*safra*>
	safra	<*grande*> <*história*>

with a given syntactic context in the corpus. The local weight is based on the frequency of occurrence of the context with a given word.

By computing the similarity measure of all word pairs in the corpus, it's possible to generate the list of the most similar words to each word in the corpus.

2.1 Adaptations to Portuguese

Grefenstette relates [1] the experiments to validate his technique on identifying semantically similar words using English language corpora. Nevertheless, we applied the Grefenstette's technique over a Portuguese corpus. We identified some points that had to be modified when using a Portuguese corpus:

- using a Portuguese language parser or a parsed Portuguese corpus;
- ignoring the syntactic relations NN, that do not occur in Portuguese: in general, the NN relations in English, are NNPREP in Portuguese. For example, the expression *planet area* (<NN, *area*, *planet*>) is written in Portuguese as *área do planeta* (<NNPREP, *área*, *planeta*>), using the preposition *de* ("of").

2.2 Extentions to the Notion of Syntactic Context

We observed that Grefenstette doesn't use all the information contained in the syntactic dependencies in the corpus.

Considering other similar techniques ([3], [2]) and the hypothesis of new sorts of contexts or information that could enrich the existing contexts, we could extend the notion of syntactic context adopted in [1].

We propose the following four extensions to the Grefenstette's notion of syntactic context.

Explicit syntactic relation in context. According to Grefenstette's notation, the contexts extracted from nominal relations (namely NN, ADJ, and NNPREP modifiers) do not keep the name of the particular syntactic relation. Grefenstette differentiates just the contexts derived from verbal syntactic relations (SUBJ, DOBJ e IOBJ). This way, words that function as adjectives and nouns generate identical contexts, even when they have different functions. For example, from the expressions *a obrigação do técnico* ("the obligation of the technician") and *o relatório técnico* ("the technical report") the same syntactic context *<técnico>* for the words *obrigação* and *relatório* would be extracted, which is not correct for Portuguese. On the other hand, if the syntactic relation was explicitly indicated in the context, the noun *obrigação* would receive the context *<NNPREP, técnico>* and the noun *relatório* would receive *<ADJ, técnico>*.

We believe the explicit indication of the syntactic relation in the context contributes to a better word discrimination.

Syntactic relation direction in context. In [2], when syntactic contexts are extracted, they are bidirectional. That is, it is recorded that word $p1$ is modified by word $p2$, and also that word $p2$ modifies $p1$. Consequently, the number of contexts extracted for each word increases. We believe that the higher is the number of syntactic contexts to describe word behaviour, the higher is the reliability of the results of the comparison with other words.

To represent the direction of the syntactic relation, a direction indicator is included in the context, which is determined on the point of view of the head of the syntactic relation. The nominal syntactic relations ADJ and NNPREP are recorded as $^\uparrow$ADJ and $^\uparrow$NNPREP in the contexts of the head noun of the relation, and as $^\downarrow$ADJ and $^\downarrow$NNPREP in the contexts of the modifier word (adjective or noun, respectively). The verbal syntactic relations SUBJ, DOBJ e IOBJ are recorded as $^\uparrow$SUBJ, $^\uparrow$DOBJ and $^\uparrow$IOBJ in the syntactic contexts of the head verb, and as $^\downarrow$SUBJ, $^\downarrow$DOBJ and $^\downarrow$IOBJ in the contexts of the noun.

Consequently, the fact of considering syntactic contexts for adjectives and verbs allows the generation of lists of semantically related adjectives and lists of semantically related verbs. Grefenstette, in [1], just related tests comparing nouns, since he just recorded the syntactic contexts of the nouns, not considering nouns as contexts of the adjectives and verbs that were syntactic related to them. In [9] we present successful experiments on generating lists of adjectives and verbs.

Syntactic relation SOBJ. We propose to consider a new sort of syntactic relation, which associates the subject and the object of a verb. This one is not a syntactic relation usually presented in grammars, but we believe this relation has relevant semantic information to discriminate nouns, because the verb imposes semantic restrictions to its subject and to its objects.

This new sort of syntactic relation is represented by SOBJ. For example, in the expression *a doença causou a morte* ("the disease caused the death"), it is extracted the context $<^\uparrow SOBJ, morte>$ to the word *doença*, and the context $<^\downarrow SOBJ, doença>$ to the word *morte*.

Prepositions in syntactic relations NNPREP and IOBJ in context. According to Grefenstette's technique, when binary dependencies within the syntactic relation NNPREP or IOBJ are extracted, the prepositions that are present in the original corpus expressions are ignored. Nevertheless, we believe that these prepositions have relevant semantic information to discriminate words.

For example, consider the following expressions: *marca da camisa* ("the brand of the shirt") and *marca na camisa* ("a mark in the shirt"). According to Grefenstette's syntactic context notion, the same context <*camisa*> is extracted for the noun *marca* in both expressions. Nevertheless, the preposition *de* ("of") brings a different syntactic dependency than the one for the preposition *em* ("in"). So, aiming to extracting semantic regularities, the prepositions should be considered as part of the syntactic contexts.

3   Experiment 1

The first experiment we did was to validate the Grefenstette's technique and the proposed extensions over a Portuguese corpus.

We established a five-step procedure for this first experiment:

1. extracting the syntactic contexts from the corpus;
2. creating different sets of syntactic contexts: we created two sets for noun contexts - one set according to Grefenstette's syntactic context notion and another according to the extended notion, to be compared;
3. calculating the word similarity (using the weighted Jaccard similarity measure);
4. building the lists of similar words: using each context set, we generated a list of similar words for each noun of the corpus.

To appreciate the results of the experiments, we randomly selected the lists of 10 nouns with different occurrence frequencies in the corpus.

The two lists for each selected noun (lists generated with contexts according to each syntactic context notion, Grefenstette's and extended ones) were compared to identify the contribution of the extension of the syntactic context notion considering improvement on the homogeneity of the lists of related nouns.

To analyse the word lists, we took a subjective measure, the homogeneity, that means: if a list contains several words that we consider semantically related to the given word, this list is homogeneous. We didn't find any systematic measure that could represent the lists homogeneity.

On Table 2, we present the lists of the nouns semantically related to this 10 nouns. The rows G of the table correspond to the lists generated from Grefenstette's technique, and the rows E correspond to the lists generated from the extended technique.

We can state that the lists contain several semantically related nouns. The E lists are noisier than the G lists; for the most part, more semantically related words are present in the second lists, and even words that appear in both lists are well positioned[1] in the G lists.

For instance, the list of the noun *mês* contains: co-hyponyms like *março, setembro, agosto*; holonyms like *ano, década*; meronyms like *dia, hora*. The list of the noun *mês* generated from the set of extended contexts is considered more homogeneous than the list generated from the set of Grefenstette's contexts, because:

– nouns that appear in both lists, like *agosto*, are well positioned in the second list. Its position in the list is improved due to new contexts shared by *agosto* and *mês*, like

---

[1] Ordering in the list of related words is related to the similarity value: the first word in the list is more closely related to the given word than the last word in the list.

Table 2. Lists of semantically related nouns

cultura/ culture	G	produção/production teatro/theatre população/population imprensa/press capital futebol/soccer jornal/newspaper filme/film cidade/city TV evento/event grupo/group música/music banda/band mercado/market
	E	teatro/thetre produção/production revista/magazine música/music cinema edição/edition banda/band experiência/experience população/population arte/art peça/play tradição/tradiction capital literatura/literature imprensa/press
feijão/ bean	G	sul-africanas/south-african preparado/prepared decepção/deception Casa/house grana/money exército/army minoria/minority molho/sauce Homem/man pastel/pastry Barão/baron grão/grain boné/cap fruto/fruit barro/clay
	E	soja/soy carne/meat trigo/wheat milho/corn leite/milk arroz/rice cesta/basket grão/grain massa/pasta frango/chicken sugestão/sugestion molho/sauce palestra/lecture fio/line exército/army
inflação/ inflation	G	custo/cost índice/index taxa/tax faturamento/invoice reajuste/ajust investimento/investiment juro/interest salário/salary média/average contrato/contract variação/variation expectativa/expectation moeda/currency velocidade/speed pista/track
	E	taxa/tax custo/cost salário/salary juro/interest média/average índice/index faturamento/invoice investimento/investiment nível/level variação/variation produtividade/productivity contrato/contract alíquota/aliquot preço/price velocidade/speed
mês/ month	G	dia/day semana/week ano/year edição/edition hora/hour final fase/phase eleição/election início/beginning vez/time domingo/Sunday década/decade volume US$ agosto/August
	E	semana/week dia/day agosto/August ano/year março/March edição/edition final setembro/September hora/hour década/decade outubro/October eleição/election janeiro/January dezembro/December junho/June
perda/ loss	G	aumento/rise redução/reduction ganho/profit variação/variation economia/saving crescimento/growth ausência/absense investimento/investment alta/increase média/average expansão/expansion reajuste/adjust faturamento/invoice queda/fall salário/salary
	E	reajuste/adjust aumento/rise crescimento/growth alta/increase economia/saving faturamento/invoice custo/cost prejuízo/injury valor/value redução/reduction salário/salary ausência/absense investimento/investment variação/variation diminuição/decrease
pesquisa/ research	G	estudo/study teste/test dado/datum resultado/result programa/program lançamento/publication projeto/project filme/film trabalho/work plano/plan negócio/business lista/list número/number reunião/meeting experiência/experience
	E	estudo/study teste/test trabalho/work dado/datum resultado/result programa/program plano/plan campanha/campaign empresa/company projeto/project artigo/article grupo/group lançamento/publication experiência/experience produção/production
proprietário/ proprietor	G	dono/owner morador/resident japonês/Japanese concessionária/concessionaire gerente/manager treinador/trainer editor Gol/gol seguradora/insurance_agency associado/associate habitante/inhabitant assistente/assistant emenda/emend produtor/producer bicheiro/illegal_banker
	E	dono/owner editor comerciante/seller gerente/manager trabalhador/worker menina/girl prefeito/mayor favorito/favorite morador/resident propriedade/property crédito/credit governador/governor japonês/Japanese dona/owner associado/associate
região/ region	G	rua/street cidade/city praia/beach hotel ilha/island bairro/district água/water parque/park pista/track centro/middle bar viagem/trip capital local/place escritório/office
	E	cidade/city ilha/islan bairro/district praia/beach rua/street banco/bank Banco/bank capital centro/middle interior população/population festa/party bar condomínio/condominium restaurante/restaurant

$<^\downarrow$NNPREP_de, *desempenho*$>$, $<^\downarrow$NNPREP_de, *edição*$>$, $<^\downarrow$NNPREP_de,*dia*$>$. Besides those contexts, other ones that were already shared had their global weights increased. This is the case of the context $<^\uparrow$NNPREP, *PROP*$>$, that is more common in the G set, and the context $<^\uparrow$NNPREP_de, *PROP*$>$, that takes part of the E set of contexts with lower frequency. This context is more rare than the first one (consequently, it has a higher weight), because in the second context set there are also the contexts $<^\uparrow$NNPREP_em, *PROP*$>$, $<^\uparrow$NNPREP_para, *PROP*$>$, $<^\uparrow$NNPREP_a, *PROP*$>$, which divided the occurrences of the context $<^\uparrow$NNPREP, *PROP*$>$ of the first context set.

– nouns as *março*, *setembro* and *outubro* appear just in the second list (E). In the case of *março*, contexts like $<^\downarrow$NNPREP_de, *dia*$>$, $<^\downarrow$NNPREP_de, *fim*$>$, $<^\downarrow$NNPREP_de, *inflação*$>$ increase its similarity with *mês*.

We believe the E lists are more homogeneous because the similarity computation is based on more contexts and some of this contexts are more precise than the ones used by Grefenstette. Lists of less frequent words tend to improve more than lists of frequent words, since the number of contexts shared between the less frequent words is low, and it allows that an increment in a context weight or the sharing of a new context produces a significative increase in the similarity value.

4   Experiment 2

Our second experiment is investigating which syntactic relation is more relevant when identifying semantic relations. We established the following four-step procedure for each syntactic relation considered (ADJ, NNPREP, SUBJ, DOBJ, IOBJ, SOBJ):

1. extracting the given sort of syntactic contexts from the corpus;
2. calculating the word similarity from that contexts (using the weighted Jaccard similarity measure);
3. building the lists of similar words.

The lists for each one of the 10 selected nouns were generated from 6 differents sets of contexts. Each list was compared with the list generated using all sorts of contexts together, according to the extended notion of contexts. These comparisions aim to estimate in what extent each syntactic relation contributes on identifying semantic relations among nouns. To do that, we:

1. observed the position (1 to 15) of each noun that was present in both lists;
2. assigned a weight corresponding to the position variation of each word in each list;
3. computed a similarity coeficient between the lists, considering the position variation of the nouns.

So, comparing the 6 lists of each one of the 10 selected nouns with the corresponding complete list, we conclude that the most relevant syntatic relation, the one that has more influence on the similarity computation, is the NNPREP. We believe it's because this syntactic relation is the one that generates the higher number of contexts. The less relevant syntactic relation showed to be the IOBJ, which has less influence on the similarity computation.

5   Experiment 3

The third experiment consists on investigating the influence of parser errors on the quality of the extracted semantic relations. To measure the correctness of the syntactic contexts extracted from the corpus, it was necessary to compare them manually with the original expressions in the corpus, looking for parsing problems. So, we adopted the following procedure:

1. selecting a portion of the FOLHANOT corpus to be manually analysed: this portion contains around 7,500 words, where around 2,000 are nouns;
2. extracting the syntactic contexts of all the words of this portion;
3. comparing manually the extracted contexts with the original expressions in the corpus, and then correcting the wrong ones and including the missing ones;
4. building the lists of similar words: using the set of uncorrected contexts, and another set with the corrected ones.

The process of correcting and classifying the corrected contexts showed us that: 86.23% of the contexts were correctly parsed, 8.66% were incorrectly parsed, and 4.98 weren't extracted due to a parsing error. The erroneuos contexts relate words that are not syntactically related, which leads us to estimate false semantic relations. The missing contexts could indicate or reinforce the syntactic relation between words.

Some pareser errors were more frequent than the others, so we distinguished them according to specific points. Table 3 shows the most frequent parsing problems that generated the erroneous and missing contexts, their percentage of occurrence and some examples.

It should be noted that, that some errors concern actual linguistic decisions made in the parsing process. For example, the PoS marking of past participles as verbs, not matter whether they are adjectively used or not.

After coorecting the syntactic contexts, we used them to extract the semantic relations among the nouns. Table 4 presents the lists of semantically related words to some nouns in the corpus. The rows U of the table show the lists generated from the uncorrected contexts of the selected portion of the corpus, and the rows C correspond to the lists generated from the corrected contexts.

To have a good homogeneity level, the used portion of the corpus should be larger. But in this experiment we focus on the differences between the lists. We can observe that the C lists are more homogeneous than the U lists. They are smaller and less noisy. For example, when considering the uncorrected contexts, the word *universidade* shared contexts with the words *época*, *ferrovia* and *produtor*, that do not seems to be semantically related to *universidade*. So, when correcting the contexts, the shared ones were eliminated and the words relation disappeared.

6   Concluding Remarks

Performing a global study of the experiment results, it is possible to point to the following remarks:

Table 3. Most frequent parsing errors

Errors	Occurrence	Examples
Prepositional phrase as adverbial phrase and vice-versa	22.87	*disputar o campeonato na Holanda* (dispute the championship on The Netherlands): *na Holanda* should be tagged as adverbial phrase
Proper nouns as common nouns	18.45	*Barreiras* (organization name) was treated as the common noun meaning barrier or barricade; *Folha* (newspaper name) was treated as the common noun meaning leaf
Incorrect subject, direct object or indirect object tags	17.71	*impediu o plantio de feijão* (prohibited the plantation of beans): *de feijão* should be a prepositional phrase instead of an indirect verb object
Prepositional attachment errors	11.07	*expansão de soja na fronteira* (soy expansion on the boundary): *fronteira* is attached to *soy* but should be attached to *expansão*
Adjective as verb	9.96	*ano passado* (last year): *passado* should be tagged as adjective instead of a verb form of to pass; *pesquisas confiáveis* (reliable research): *confiáveis* should be an adjective, not the verb *to rely on*
Adjective as noun and vice-versa	8.11	*quinta*: referring to *quinta-feira* (Thursday) instead of the ordinal number *quinto* (fifth); *alta de preço* (price increase): *alta* referring to *the increase* instead of the adjective *tall*
Verb as noun and vice-versa	5.90	*firma* (firm): tagged as the verb "to firm" instead of the noun "firm"
Preposition *a* as determiner and vice-versa	1.47	*se destina a implantação* (it is destinated to the implantation)

Table 4. Semantically related words

plantio/planting	U	cavalo/horse produtor/producer produção/production
	C	colheita/crop produção/production
cavalo/horse	U	condição/condition animal plantio/planting produtor/producer produção/production
	C	animal produção/production
ha/hectare	U	lavoura/crop quilo/kilo monocultura/single_culture milho/corn palanque/platform projeto/project início/beginning nelore gado/cattle cultura/culture milhão/million US$
	C	lavoura/crop monocultura/single_culture quilo/kilo início/beggining hectare projeto/project etapa/phase exposição/exposition milhão/million produção/production US$
maioria/most	U	receita/recipe vantagem/advantage cliente/customer bezerra/heifer alíquota/aliquot modelo/model gerente/manager variedade/variety técnico/technician programa/program irrigação/irrigation agricultor/farmer praga/plague processo/process produtor/producer
	C	vantagem/advantage receita/recipe
universidade/ university	U	época/epoch ferrovia/railroad produtor/producer
	C	

- different kinds of semantic relations could be identified between the given word and the words in the list;
- the extensions proposed to Grefenstette's syntactic context notion [1] allowed to increase the homogeneity of the noun lists.
- the NNPREP relation is the one that has more influence on computing the similarity, since it is the relation that generates more contexts;
- parsing errors in the corpus decrease the quality of the word lists.

To continue this work, we intend to cluster the lists of similar words to identify the different word meanings when treating polissemic ones. Another point is to look for more representative sets of syntactic contexts for each word in the corpus: because of the Zipf law, in traditional corpora most words of the language are not represented by the number of occurrences sufficient for reliable statistical decisions. One way to deal with this problem is the use of representative corpora collected from Internet [10]. Another possible approach is use existing dictionaries of collocations [11].

Overall, we belive the most important work to be done is to develop an evaluation procedure to measure the homogeneity of the word lists. We plan to implement systematic measures like the one presented in [12] as a pseudo-disambiguation task.

Besides that, a study should be done to observe if each syntactic relation implies on identifying an specific semantic relation. The classification of the semantic relations encountered could be different of more detailed than the usual linguistic classification as synonym, antonym, hyponum, meronym, etc.

Acknowledgements. We would like to thank NILC and AC/DC project for turning the corpus used in our experiments available, and CNPq/Brazil for the DTI grant to the first author (on COMMOn-REFs project) and for the Research Productivity grant to the second author.

References

1. Grefenstette, G.: Explorations in Automatic Thesaurus Discovery. Kluwer Academic Publishers, USA (1994)
2. Lin, D.: Automatic retrieval and clustering of similar words. In: Proceedings of the COLING-ACL'98, Montreal (1998)
3. Ruge, G.: Automatic detection of thesaurus relations for information retrieval. In: Foundations of Computer Science. Springer, Berlin (1997) 499–506
4. Park, Y.C., Han, Y.S., Choi, K.S.: Automatic thesaurus construction using bayesian networks. In: Proceedings of the 1995 International Conference on Information and Knowledge Management, Baltimore (1995) 212–217
5. Pacey, M.: The use of clustering techniques to reveal semantic relations between words. In Renouf, A., ed.: Explorations in Corpus Linguistics. Rodopi, Amsterdam (1998) 269–280
6. Thanopoulos, A., Fakotakis, N., Kokkinakis, G.: Automatic extraction of semantic relations from specialized corpora. In: Proceedings of COLING'2000, Saarbrücken (2000)
7. Bick, E.: The Parsing System Palavras: Automatic Grammatical Analysis of Portuguese in a Constraint Grammar Framework. PhD thesis, Århus University, Århus (2000)

8. Bolshakov, I., Gelbukh, A.: Heuristics-based replenishment of collocation databases. In Ranchhod, E., Mamede, N., eds.: Lecture Notes in Computer Science N 2389: Advances in Natural Language Processing. Springer-Verlag (2002)
9. Gasperin, C.V.: Extração automática de relações semânticas a partir de relações sintáticas. Master's thesis, PUCRS, Porto Alegre (2001)
10. A. Gelbukh, G. Sidorov, L.C.H.: Compilation of a spanish representative corpus. In: Lecture Notes in Computer Science N 2276: Computational Linguistics and Intelligent Text Processing. Springer-Verlag (2002) 285–288
11. Bolshakov, I., Gelbukh, A.: A very large database of collocations and semantic links. In et al., M.B., ed.: Lecture Notes in Computer Science N 1959: Natural Language Processing and Information Systems. Springer-Verlag (2001) 103–114
12. Lee, L.: Measures of distributional similarity. In: 37th Annual Meeting of the ACL. (1999) 25–32

A Method of Automatic Detection of Lexical Relationships Using a Raw Corpus

Héctor Jiménez-Salazar

Facultad de Ciencias de la Computación
B. Universidad Autónoma de Puebla
C.U. 72570, Puebla, México
hjimenez@fcfm.buap.mx

Abstract. This work presents some results on the application of a criterion used to compare the senses of a pair of words. A measure that involves the senses of words was used to reinforce hypothesis like hyponymy relationship between the words.

1 Introduction

Information Retrieval Systems (IRS) use lexical relationships (hyponymy, synonymy, holonymy, etc.) in order to improve its performance. In particular, query expansion techniques help to solve this task [4,2]. The problem is to construct these lexical resources for different domains. In [6], for two words x and y, the relation x hyperonym of y is obtained, through the subsumption notion: x subsumes y if $A_y \subset A_x$, where A_w denotes the set of contexts (documents, sentences, etc.) that contain the word w. For hyperonyms in general $A_y \subset A_x$ is not satisfied, but 80% of the members of A_y are in A_x.

We are interested in the exploration of several lexical relationships. In the present work the problem of comparing two sets is faced by computing how much a set is included in another; this is the base to define the quantity subsumption ratio. We specifically use the features of the contexts instead of the contexts. Features of a context follow the IRS idea of document representation by index terms. Now, the inclusion property of x subsumes y is expressed in the framework of formal concepts by duality: $B_x \subset B_y$, where B_w is the set of features that each member of A_w holds.

Thus, we will conceive the contexts that use a word w (a subset of A_w) with the same meaning as instances of a concept. In the formal concept theory [1] we can compare two concepts using its components, namely intent and extent. The extent is the set of objects which are instances of the concept, and the intent is the set of features that are satisfied by all the objects ascribed to the concept. In this approach, a concept is more general than another if the extent of the former contains the extent of the latter or, equivalently, if the intent of the former is contained in the intent of the latter. This supports the use of the intent to compare the sets of contexts.

A. Gelbukh (Ed.): CICLing 2003, LNCS 2588, pp. 325–328, 2003.
© Springer-Verlag Berlin Heidelberg 2003

The next section specifies the notion of subsumption ratio. Next the experiment carried out is described, and at the end the conclusions of this work are presented.

2   Subsumption Ratio

Let us consider a corpus T and the set of all sentences that use in T the word w, A_w, and let $A_w^i \in A_w$. We may represent A_w^i by its index terms or features, B_w^i, i.e. the most representative words of A_w^i with respect to A_w. To determine the representative terms, $v \in B_w^i$, the discrimination value model is used ([5] presents this model). Discrimination value model defines the document frequency of v, df_v, as the number of documents that contain the term v. Thus, for some i, $v \in B_w^i$ if $df_v \in [n_w/100, n_w/10]$, where $n_w = \#A_w$. Let us denote the k-th sense of the word w by w_k. w_k will be represented by some subset $A(w_k) \subset A_w$, where each context, member of $A(w_k)$, uses the same sense of w. A_w may be partitioned to group the most similar $A_w^i \in A_w$ that represent w_k. For this task we use B_w^i instead of A_w^i. Thus, we may represent the concept of the k-th sense of w with the extent $A(w_k)$ and the intent $B(w_k)$. The goal is to compare different meanings of two words, through its intents to conclude a semantic relationship between them. We define the subsumption ratio of x_i to y_j as:

$$\rho(x_i, y_j) = \frac{\#(B(x_i) \cap B(y_j))}{\#B(x_i)}$$

where $B(w_k)$ is the set of features of the k-th sense of the word w. Note that $B(x_i) \cap B(y_j)$ is the intent of a more general concept. Certainly if $B(x_i) \subset B(y_j)$ then $\rho(x_i, y_j) = 1$. Thus, we can use the ratio of features in $B(x_i)$ that are in $B(y_j)$ to indicate how much x_i subsumes y_j. If $\rho(x_i, y_j)$ is high then x_i will subsume y_j with degree $\rho(x_i, y_j)$. This point is directly related with the riches of the corpus.

Besides, we need to compute $\rho(y_j, x_i)$ which will complement the knowledge about x_i and y_j. For example, if both ratios have a high value we can strengthen the hypothesis of synonymy relationship between those word senses. From the previous remark it can be established the conditions to find some relationship between two word senses. Fixing the words x and y, and denoting $\rho(x_i, y_j)$ by ρ_{ij}, we propose the following rules:

y_j **synonym of** x_i: ρ_{ij} is high and ρ_{ji} is high
y_j **hyponym of** x_i: ρ_{ij} is high and ρ_{ji} is low
strongly related: ρ_{ij} is high and ρ_{ji} is medium
weakly related: ρ_{ij} is low and ρ_{ji} is medium
very low relation: ρ_{ij} is low and ρ_{ji} is low

This classification has implicit two thresholds μ_1, the maximum for low values of ρ_{ij} and μ_2, the maximum for medium values of ρ_{ij}.

3   Experiment

The corpus[1] (10Mb) is composed of 2057 articles, 61,216 sentences, a vocabulary of 136,988 signs (different words including punctuation, abbreviations and numbers) and 18,092 stems. The frequency of words was observed to choose those words that could provide sufficient contexts to the processing. Stop words were removed and the remaining words were stemmed. The test was performed on the words: triunfo 'triumph', victoria 'victory', militar 'military', coronel 'colonel', teniente 'lieutenant', avion 'plane', aeroplano 'airplane', aeropuerto 'airport', and hijo 'son' whose frequencies are 120, 140, 520, 251, 100, 590, 62, 166, 507, respectively. In the experiment were carried out the next steps:

1. Given a word w:
   a) To obtain A_w.
   b) To represent each member $A_w^k \in A_w$ by B_w^k, using the discriminator terms contained in A_w.
   c) To partition the collection A_w according to the most similar uses of w: $A(w_1), A(w_2), \ldots A(w_p)$, $(A_w = \cup_{q \le p} A(w_q))$. In this task Jaccard similarity measure is used. $A(w_k)$ has the corresponding $B(w_k)$; each pair $(A(w_k), B(w_k))$ represents a sense w_k.
2. Given two cluster collections corresponding to x and y, all pairs (taking only the largest groups) are produced, then $\rho(x_i, y_j)$ and $\rho(y_j, x_i)$ are applied, where i and j range from 1 to the number of elements in the cluster collection of x's and y's, respectively.
3. The highest values of $\rho(x_i, y_j)$ and $\rho(y_j, x_i)$ and its difference (Δ_{max}) are used to classify the dominant relationship between x and y.

Table 1. Classification with the subsumption ratio.

x-y	Δ_{max}	i,j	$\rho(x_i, y_j)$	$\rho(y_j, x_i)$	Class
triunfo-victoria	0.09	1,1	0.54	0.45	synonym
militar-teniente	0.40	2,2	0.50	0.08	hyponym
militar-coronel	0.48	3,2	0.66	0.18	hyponym
aeroplano-avión	0.63	2,1	0.02	0.66	hyponym
aeropuerto-avión	0.54	2,2	0.31	0.85	strongly related
aeropuerto-aeroplano	0.31	2,2	0.36	0.05	weakly related
hijo-aeropuerto	0.07	4,2	0.18	0.10	unrelated

In the table 1 we used the thresholds $\mu_1 = 0.2$ and $\mu_2 = 0.4$. For $x =$"militar" the number of largest clusters was six and for $y =$"teniente" was two, which gives 12 combinations. Both values $\rho(x_i, y_j)$ and $\rho(y_j, x_i)$ were calculated and plotted

---

[1] It is a collection of selected articles from the Mexican newspaper *El Universal*, titled *80 Años Informando (1916-1996)* '80 years of information'.

for each one of these combinations. The graph is shown at fig. 1-b. The first half of the graph corresponds to one sense of x varying all senses of y. The similarity matrix obtained in the clustering process was used to visualize the main senses of the word militar (see fig. 1-a), this is an iso-analogical representation of the word senses [3].

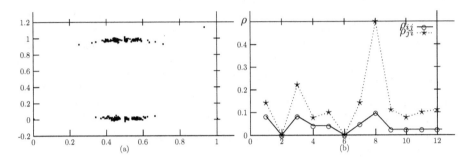

Fig. 1. (a) Clusters of contexts for *militar*. (b) Subsumption ratio for *teniente* and *militar*.

4   Conclusions

In this paper we have defined a measure based on the subsumption notion and formal concept theory in order to know the degree of relationship between two senses of words. This measure uses only a raw corpus and its advantage is that no domain knowledge is required. For this approach we have shown some examples but it is necessary an exhaustive test.

References

1. Davey, B. & Priestley, H.: *Introduction to lattices and order*, Cambridge Mathematical Textbooks, 1990.
2. Gelbukh, A.: Lazy query enrichment: a simple method of indexing large specialized document bases, *Proc.DEXA-2000 11th Int. Conf. and Workshop on Databases and Expert Systems Applications*, 2000.
3. Lavalle-Martínez, J.: *Representación isoanalógica de objetos n-dimensionales*, M.Sc. Thesis, CINVESTAV (México), 2000.
4. Mandala, R.; Tokunaga, T. & Tanaka, H.: Combining multiple evidence from different types of thesaurus, *Proc. 22nd International Conference ACM-SIGIR*, 191–197, 1999.
5. Salton, G.; Yang, C.S. & Yu, C.T.: A theory of term importance in automatic text analysis, *Journal of American Society for Information Science*, 26(1), 33–44, 1975.
6. Sanderson, M. & Croft, W.B.: Deriving concept hierarchies from text, *Proc. 22nd International Conference ACM-SIGIR*, 206–213, 1999.

Sentence Co-occurrences as Small-World Graphs: A Solution to Automatic Lexical Disambiguation

Stefan Bordag

Universität Leipzig, Institut für Informatik,
Augustusplatz 10-11, 04109 Leipzig
sbordag@informatik.uni-leipzig.de

Abstract. This paper presents a graph-theoretical approach to lexical disambiguation on word co-occurrences. Producing a dictionary similar to WordNet, this method is the counterpart to word sense disambiguation and thus makes one more step towards completely unsupervised natural language processing algorithms as well as generally better understanding of how to make computers meaningfully process natural language data.

1 Introduction

Automatic disambiguation of lexically ambiguous words is generally a two-tiered problem. First, a dictionary containing information necessary for the disambiguation is needed. In this dictionary all meanings for each word are listed. Second, this dictionary is used to determine which word sense is the appropriate one in a given piece of text. This last step has already been researched to a wide extend, see [C. D. Manning & H. Schütze 1999] for an overview. Recognition of the correct word meaning with the help of a manually created dictionary usually presents no serious problems anymore, given that the analysed text is long enough and, what is more important, that the word is actually in the dictionary. This last condition is also the most difficult one to fulfill, as creating a complete dictionary manually would be very time consuming to say the least. Therefore an algorithm which could produce at least a partially filled dictionary (in form similar to WordNet, see also [S. Banarjee, T. Pedersen 2002]) would certainly contribute to Information Retrieval systems as well as lead to a better understanding of statistical properties of natural language usage. As a side effect, the effectiveness of Information Retrieval systems could indeed be improved because for any desired semantical field, a dictionary could be created based on an appropriate corpus.

Using results of previous work of colleagues at the 'Deutscher Wortschatz Leipzig' corpus, who investigate the properties of co-occurrences of word forms in the German language for extraction of semantic information, see [F. Schmidt 1999], it was possible to develop such an algorithm. Based on purely statistical methods it distinguishes the most apparent contexts of a given word form. There are different kinds of co-occurrences of words in sentences such as left-neighbour (which words occur significantly often on the left side of the given word), right-neighbour (same on the right side) or whole sentence (which words occur significantly often together with a given word in a sentence – note that this is a symmetrical relationship). To solve the

A. Gelbukh (Ed.): CICLing 2003, LNCS 2588, pp. 329–332, 2003.
© Springer-Verlag Berlin Heidelberg 2003

problem of lexical disambiguation, the whole sentence co-occurrences were used but others might be useful as well, although the property of being symmetrical is important. A further important aspect of the Deutscher Wortschatz corpus is that it contains word forms along with frequency and all sentences as opposed to collecting only lemmas.

2   The Graph-Theoretic Approach

The algorithm is based on the mentioned co-occurrences of word forms as well as the recently discovered properties of so-called "small-world-graphs" (which are a special kind of a graph), see [D. J. Watts, S.H. Strogatz 1998] for the first paper on that topic and [R. Ferrero i Cancho, R. V. Solé 2001] for an application to language. A graph representing relationships between words in a language can be constructed by viewing the co-occurrences of two words as a relationship of two nodes which are connected, if these words are co-occurrences, and are not connected, if they are not co-occurrences. The resulting graph looks like a random graph, but it is not. Where a random graph has small average shortest paths from any point to any other, it also has only a small clusteredness (clusteredness is calculated by observing how often a node A is connected to another node C if A and B are connected and B and C as well). A graph of co-occurrences has instead a very high clusteredness while still having small shortest paths between any two of its points. This again is unlike the regular graph, which also has a high clusteredness, but extremely long shortest paths between two points of the graph.

The fact that small worlds thereby lie 'somewhere between' the regular graphs and the random graphs is due to a special kind of organization of the graph. First, there are so-called 'long-range nodes', which have connections to many clusters, thereby providing those clusters with a shortcut to many others without lowering the clusteredness coefficient, because there aren't many such long-range nodes in the graph compared to the overall number of nodes. Common verbs, articles and other function words are the representants of these long-range words. Second, the clusters by themselves are highly interwoven, so that it is often possible to traverse only a small number of clusters and reach any other, although this way the paths are longer then when taking shortcuts. These facts might become interesting for psycholinguistic research concerned with lexical access mechanisms.

Exploiting the fact that, though the words in the co-occurrence graph are arranged in clusters, these clusters are not maximal (i.e. not all nodes are connected with each other), the algorithm computes the nearest neighbours of a word, split into the different clusters. As the clusters are not maximal, performing the algorithm for each word of the same clusters usually results in slightly different word sets. The algorithm is further based on the assumption that three given words together almost never are ambiguous (an example is 'Gold Silber Kupfer' – 'gold silver copper', a counter example is 'Gold Silber Bronze' – 'gold silver bronze' as these still can mean either metals or Olympic games awards). Under this assumption it is enough to provide two more words in order to fully specify the required word sense in the given text.

The algorithm begins with creating triplets of words related to the input word. This is achieved by taking the direct neighbours of the input word, creating all possible pairs from them and then adding the input word to each pair. For each item in the resulting set of triplets, a set of words can be determined, which are connected to each member of the triplet, represented as a word vector over the corpus. It is clear that if the three words are from one cluster containing more then these three words, all or most of the other words from this cluster must be returned by this – otherwise nothing is returned[1]. A set of word triplets along with a word vector for each triplets is the result. The word vectors can then be clustered using a clustering algorithm, for example hierarchical agglomerative clustering (HAC), see [H. Läuter, R. Pincus 1989] for detailed mathematical discussion. After clustering, the sets of triplets are grouped together on the base of their word vectors. By merging the words from the word vectors for each group, groups of words occur, which correspond to the different clusters in the co-occurrence graph. Each of these clusters represent then one of the word's meanings or better: usage contexts.

3 Examples and Discussion of Results

As an example the German word 'Stich' was disambiguated, which has several completely different meanings: 1. a hole left after thrusting a knife into something (κ_3), 2. a certain move in the popular card game 'Skat' (κ_2), 3. 'Michael Stich', a famous tennis player (κ_1) and 4. an art product (usually on copper) made with the help of a special needle. The algorithm was able to find the first three (and most frequent) distinguishable word clusters and one group of words, B, which could not be clustered. Noteworthy is that apart from other items in this example, this set contains the linguistic collocation (idiomatic phrase) of 'letting someone down', in German 'jemanden im Stich lassen' or differently formulated, 'to feel let down' – 'sich im Stich gelassen zu fühlen'. If the word to be disambiguated is a part of an idiomatic expression, then the other constituents of this expression will usually be found in the set B, as such idiomatic expressions often let words occur statistically significant often together in a sentence without there being a semantically based correlation.

Stich

κ_1	ATP Achtelfinale Agassi Alleinspieler Andre Andrej Antwerpen As Asse Atout Aufschlag Australian Australier Ball Becker Beckers Bernd Biscayne Boris Break Breaks Brust Bälle Carl-Uwe Carlos Cedric Centre Chang Claus Coach Coeur [...]
κ_2	Alleinspieler As Bube Dame Fehler Gegenspieler Herz Herz- Herz-As Herz-Bube Herz-Buben Herz-Dame Herz-König Hinterhand K Karo Karo- Karo-As Karo-Bube Karo-Buben Karo-Dame Karo-Karten Karo-König Karte Kreuz- Kreuz-As [...]
κ_3	Bauch Brust Herz Messer Oberschenkel Schulter Stiche gestochen schlug stach verletzte versetzte zog
B	**gelassenen fühlte gelassene ließen** Groeneveld Herzgegend **lasse** Riglewski

---

[1] Except for the long-range nodes, which are connected to almost every word in the corpus. But these can be easily filtered out by word form frequency.

The success of the algorithm depends on the kind of corpus on which the algorithm is used. It is obvious that when using a certain corpus, the results can differ very much in comparison to application on another corpus. The 'Deutscher Wortschatz' corpus is mainly based upon printed media, which results in some topics being underrepresented while others are overrepresented. This can be seen in the given example: the group from 'Stich' as corresponding to 'Michael Stich' is by far larger than the group for the 'wound'. This illustrates that words concerning sports, politics or even medicine can be treated well, while words from other fields like literature, art and science that are not frequent in newspapers cannot be treated well. This can also be seen from the fact that there is not the slightest trace of the fourth meaning of 'Stich' in the data.

Further research will go in the direction of automatic categorization based upon the presented algorithm and some given precategorization of a small set of words. In Information Retrieval this categorization can be used for a dimensionality reduction, see [F. Sebastiani 2001] for an overview. It is still to be investigated how the unsymmetrical co-occurrence types mentioned above can contribute to the process and how the unbalance in the representation of certain topics can be neutralized.

References

1. S. Banarjee, T. Pedersen. An adapted Lesk Algorithm for Word Sense Disambiguation Using WordNet. In A. Gelbukh (Ed.), Computational Linguistics and Intelligent Text Processing, Lecture Notes in Computer Science N 2276, Springer-Verlag, 2002.
2. S. Bordag. Vererbungsalgorithmen von semantischen Eigenschaften auf Assoziationsgraphen und deren Nutzung zur Klassifikation von natürlichsprachlichen Daten, Diplomarbeit, Universität Leipzig, Institut für Mathematik und Informatik, 2002.
3. R. Ferrero i Cancho, R. V. Solé. The Small-World of Human Language. 2001. (http://www.santafe.edu/sfi/publications/)
4. H. Läuter, R. Pincus. Mathematisch-statistische Datenanalyse, Akademie-Verlag Berlin, 1989.
5. C. D. Manning & H. Schütze. Foundations of statistical natural language processing, 1999.
6. F. Sebastiani. Machine Learning in Automated Text Categorization, 2001.
7. F. Schmidt. Automatische Ermittlung semantischer Zusammenhänge lexikalischer Einheiten und deren graphische Darstellung, Diplomarbeit, Universität Leipzig, 1999.
8. D. J. Watts, S.H. Strogatz. Collective dynamics of 'small-world' networks, Nature 393:440–442, 1998.

Dimensional Analysis to Clarify Relations among the Top-Level Concepts of an Upper Ontology: *Process, Event, Substance, Object*

Patrick Cassidy

MICRA, Inc., Plainfield, NJ 07062
cassidy@micra.com

Abstract. To achieve a human level of understanding of natural language, cognitive systems need a representation of knowledge that can distinguish nuances of meaning as well as preserve intended ambiguity. Among the most important of the basic concepts in such a knowledge base are the representations for *events* and *processes*, and also for *objects* and *substances*. Although each concept in these related pairs of concepts appears distinct intuitively and linguistically, the distinction is sometimes lost when the concepts are formalized. In different ontologies one finds a variety of different representations for these four fundamental concepts. This paper presents a new representation which uses an extension of dimensional analysis to qualitative dimensions to provide distinct and logically well-defined yet intuitively acceptable definitions for these four fundamental concepts, and specifies how they relate to other fundamental concepts in an upper ontology. In this analysis, processes extended through time result in events, and substances extending through space constitute objects. These representations are expected to be better suited than alternatives for representing the nuances of meaning in linguistic utterances.

1 Introduction

The intuitive notion of an "event" is a concept which is fundamental to much of human reasoning, and a frequent topic of linguistic communication. An event is a series of changes in real-world objects occur which have a more or less well-defined beginning and end (e.g. *a movement, a decisive battle, the destruction of Gommorha, the 2000 Olympic Games*), and people can refer to such happenings as conceptual units which usually take the form of a noun, and can have properties which are expressed linguistically as adjectives. Events may recur, in the sense that similar occurrences that can be categorized as belonging to the same class can have multiple instances in our real world of experience. Thus we may attend many *beautiful weddings*, or view many *thrilling parades*, and it is reasonable to use the similarities between individual instances of such happenings to label them with a common name. In order to represent such happenings in a computer database, so as to allow a computer to reason about them as accurately as people do, we need to be concerned with: (1) what actually happens to the physical objects participating in an event, as can be determined by measurements on the objects; (2) how such happenings are

A. Gelbukh (Ed.): CICLing 2003, LNCS 2588, pp. 333–346, 2003.

viewed by humans; as evidenced by the terms and phrases people use to refer to such happenings, when they communicate with each other in natural language; and (3) how our logical representations can capture all of the *important* aspects of both the physical reality as well as the common perception of such events[1].

Closely related to *Event* is the notion of *Process*, which also encompasses changes in objects over time, but contains more of an intuition of something happening at some point of time, and does not by itself specify a starting or ending point. Thus the process *John running* may exist at any one of many points of time, in many different unrelated time intervals. If we discuss the process of *John running* during some specific time interval, however (e.g. a race), what happens in that interval may be viewed as a discrete event. According to this view, every process, extended over a particular time interval, gives rise to an event. Conversely, every event is the result of some process. Both of the notions of event and process are useful and frequently used, and give rise to alternate basic but distinct linguistic representations for something happening, respectively with or without being bound within some particular period of time. We here present a formalization of this relation between *Process* and *Event* which captures the linguistic intuition within a precise logical specification.

There have been different opinions about the fundamental nature and linguistic representation of events. A diverse selection of views regarding the linguistic labels for events, particularly with respect to the aspectual properties of event descriptions, has been presented in Higginbotham, Pianesi and Varzi [1]. Much of the analysis of *Event* and *Process* has been directed toward the identification of the participants in the events, motivated by the accessibility of the surface syntactical forms for such roles within linguistic utterances. In the present paper the focus is not on the participants in an event, nor on causal relations between events, agents, and the properties of objects, nor on the syntactic forms taken by the participants, nor on the different types into which events can be classified, but on the fundamental question of how to represent **what has changed** in the course of an *Event* or *Process*, and how these two concepts are related. This representation may be elaborated further to include such other aspects of events.

A *Process* is the formalization of the notion of something happening, without reference to a specific bounded time interval, (e.g. *John is running*). This notion may be nominalized, and will then often be expressed in English as a gerund in the *-ing* form, (e.g., *John's running,* the pleasures of *cooking*) without an article. Properties of processes may be expressed as adjectives (*strenuous running* can cause ...), or as adverbs (*running strenuously* can cause ...). By contrast, events do not take adverbial modifiers (e.g. *decisively winning* but not **a decisively win*). Linguistically and intuitively there appears to be a clear distinction between *Event* and *Process*, which should be reflected in our representations. However, linguistic phrases are sometimes ambiguous, and might refer to either an event or its associated process, introducing

---

[1] To emphasize the notion of the *important* (or *relevant*) aspects of reality and thought is essential. With a few exceptions, our representations of physical reality will be necessarily incomplete, and the aspects of reality that are abstracted out for our representation serve our practical purpose. Different representations (or theories or hypotheses) may be used to serve different purposes, but if these representations are intended to refer to the same consensus reality, each should be logically compatible with the others, i.e. should not lead to contradictory conclusions from the same data. Here we are concerned with finding a representation of the highest-level concepts on which has the widest range of applications.

some potential confusion. In addition, because every process gives rise to at least one and potentially many events, and conversely every non-atomic event is the result of some process proceeding over time, there is an intimate logical and causative connection between the two distinct concept types which has led in some cases to the creation of ontologies where the distinction is unclear or absent.

The relationship between *Event* and *Process* bears a certain analogy with the relationship between the concepts of *Substance* and *Object*. It has been noted that processes may be subdivided into temporal parts which still retain the same process identity, and quantities of a substance may be divided into spatial parts which still retain the same substance identity. In English, substances are referred to by mass nouns, and objects by count nouns. Thus the concept of a substance is qualitatively different from that of an object, and one may say that a certain object is **composed of** a particular substance (a *bar of gold*, or a *rod made of iron*). From the linguistic evidence, there appears to be clear cognitive distinctions between process and event on one hand, and also between substance and object on the other hand. But multiple objects and repeated processes make the distinction fuzzier. Jackendoff [2] has observed that ". . . plurals behave in many respects like mass nouns, and repeated events behave like processes". Others have noted some similarity between the intuitive and linguistic behavior of substances and processes. For example, in their discussion of the CYC Ontology, Lenat and Guha [3] also note the similarity between the homogeneous behavior of both substances and processes, leading them to refer to a substance as "physical stuff" and a process as "temporal stuff". As we shall discuss later, multiple objects and events can form **quasi- homogeneous** entities, provided that one can defocus one's attention from the individual entities and view the group at a level of **granularity** greater than the individual. We will see that it is the selection of a level of granularity that can determine whether the same extended entity is viewed as homogeneous "stuff" or a collection of discrete individuals.

The above distinctions, when formalized, are sometimes less than clear. The CYC Upper Ontology [4] released publicly shows no clear distinction in its hierarchy between substance and object. Specific substances are represented as some quantity of substance, (e .g. "plastic" is the collection of all instances of *a piece of plastic*). In CYC a process is represented as a subclass of event; e.g. a #$EnergyConversionProcess is a subclass of #$PhysicalEvent (though distinguished by also being an instance of #$TemporalStuffType). Thus the subclass relation between *Process* and *Event* confuses what should be a clear distinction. In contrast, John Sowa [5] has suggested that a continuous process can be represented as a differential function, which accurately reflects the common mathematical representation of processes in physics and chemistry. He then considers a discrete process as better represented as a series of events separated by states, and for computational convenience as a Petri Net. The representation of Processes in the Situation Calculus, Event Calculus, and within the Process Specification Language has focused on representations of intuitively discontinuous processes which can be decomposed into atomic units of *Event* (or *Action*) and *State* (or *Situation*). Sowa points out that such a discontinuous process can be represented as a **Discrete Process** and mapped into the representation of a continuous process, and this allows both views of *Process* to be represented within one consistent formalism. Nevertheless **Discrete Process** is viewed as a subclass of Process. We suggest here that such representations of discontinuous processes result from the unfortunate linguistic ambiguity of the word **Process**, which, in industrial settings is used as a synonym for **Procedure**, i.e. a specified series of **Events** which are designed to achieve some practical goal. Although it is possible to specify a type of discontinuous process which is a subtype of continuous process, an industrial "process" which consists of a series of discrete steps is more accurately a subtype of *Event*. The task of this paper is to provide a clear formalization of this alternative representation.

To formalize the above interpretations of *Process* and *Event*, we wish here to provide a small extension to Sowa's analysis to show that the intuitive distinctions between *Process* and *Event* can be represented so as to make the distinction clear and logically precise, yet accommodate both continuous and discrete process representations, while retaining the intuitive behavior expected from linguistic expressions and everyday experience. To provide additional motivation for the analysis presented here, we use an extension of the techniques of dimensional analysis as used in the physical sciences, extending it to qualitative dimensions that can help clarify the differences that need to be preserved and properly represented.

In order to properly define *Process* and *Event*, certain other fundamental building-block concepts are required. These are describe here briefly, and their preferred arrangement within a top-level ontology is suggested. We then discuss the analogous relation of *Substance* to *Object*. The atemporal objects defined in this way can also be related to the time-extended four-dimensional objects proposed by perdurantist philosophers as described by Loux [6]. However, discussing those relations would require considerably more space than is available here. Some additional related definitions are contained in a longer document available on the Internet[2], or directly from the author.

2   Representation Formalism

The definitions of the foundation concepts of *Set*, *Class*, *Relation*, and *Subclass* are those used in the Ontolingua [7] Frame-Ontology, and the details will not be repeated here, so as to focus on the aspects of representation that are most relevant to the distinctions we wish to make. The logical relations and predicates will be expressed in the KIF [8] notation, using some of the SKIF extensions proposed by Hayes and Menzel [9], such as row variables. The logical operators *and, or, not, equals, implies*, and the quantifiers, *forall* and *exists* are used as in KIF notation. Some of the definitions of classes in this analysis use quantification over relations, and thus go somewhat beyond the usual first-order uses of the KIF notation. These notations are not defined here.

In this discussion, the term "predicate" will be used to mean a logical sentence of the form (?R ?arg1 @arglist), where ?R is some defined *Relation* between entities in the ontology, ?arg1 is an argument which is an instance of an entity (corresponding to the *domain* of a binary relation), and @arglist is a row variable, being a list of other instances or classes of entities filling the other argument positions of the relation.

The hierarchy of the topmost classes of the ontology which are relevant to this discussion is presented in the longer paper as an indented list.

---

[2] Available at: http://www.micra.com/process/prcevent.doc

3 Dimensional Analysis

The procedure of *dimensional analysis* is familiar to students of the physical sciences performing calculations in which measures expressed in physical units of measurement are multiplied or divided. As one form of check on the correctness of the calculation, the dimensional units themselves are treated as algebraic symbols and are multiplied or divided for each corresponding manipulation of the numbers associated with the units of measure. The resulting derived unit of measure, which is commonly some product or ratio of the fundamental units, can be compared against the expected resulting unit, as a precaution against some inadvertent miscalculation. The Systeme Internationale recognizes seven fundamental physical units: kilo**gram**, **meter**, **second**, **mole**, candela, **ampere**, and **kelvin**. Other measures are either multiples of these fundamental units or composite measures derived by multiplication or division of the basic units. Physical measures are scalar, expressed as a real number followed by the unit of measure (e.g. 4.33 grams). The derived unit *density*, for example, would have the units of kilograms per cubic meter ($kg \bullet m^{-3}$). For our purpose in organizing the top level of an ontology we will use these basic units and also add the qualitative dimensions of *AttributeValue*, *SubstanceType*, and *Object* (which in some cases may be a composite dimensional unit). Manipulations of these qualitative dimensions in a manner analogous to those with scalar physical dimensions can assist in clarifying distinctions among some of the most general concepts of an upper ontology. *AttributeValue* is defined as the value of one the variable arguments of a predicate having some entity as its domain. Such *AttributeValues* may include quantifiable physical properties such as mass and velocity, or more intangible qualitative attributes such as monetary value, happiness, ownership, or existence. Each *SubstanceType* is specific to some distinct kind of definable substance, of which there may be many millions. Each *PureChemicalSubstance*, for example, has a defined atomic composition and molecular structure, but in the real world almost all substances encountered (e.g. tap water) are mixtures of *PureChemicalSubstance*, and each such mixture will count as a different *Substance* on the *SubstanceType* dimension. This is not a metric dimension, it is more appropriately considered as a composite dimension. For the purposes of this discussion, the component dimensions need not be specified, and *SubstanceType* can be taken as a primitive. The notions of *AttributeValue* and *SubstanceType* as dimensions are useful primarily for analyzing relations and specifying distinctions between higher-level concepts, and are not themselves logical components of the definitions, nor do they figure directly in reasoning about these higher-level concepts. The qualitative dimension of *PhysicalObject* will be shown to be composable from *PhysicalSubstance* and *Space*.

As an example of simple dimensional analysis in physics, we can consider the formula relating force to acceleration, $\mathbf{F=m \bullet a}$, where the symbol "$\bullet$" represents multiplication, the mass **m** is in kilograms, and the acceleration **a** is in meters per second per second ($meter \bullet second^{-2}$). Thus the force **F** has the dimension $kilogram \bullet meter \bullet second^{-2}$. If one wants to calculate the amount of work performed by exerting a force through some distance **d**, the calculation requires a simple multiplication of force and distance (assuming the simplest case of movement in the direction of the force): Work = $\mathbf{F \bullet d}$ = $\mathbf{m \bullet a \bullet d}$ and the resulting units are kilogram•meter^2•second^{-2}, which is correct as the dimensions for the unit of work (or energy), the Joule.

For the qualitative dimensions we will use in this analysis, a group of entities of the same type will have the same qualitative dimension as the component entities. Thus, a group of physical objects will have the qualitative dimension of a physical object. A group of events will have the same dimension as a single event. It is important not to use qualitative dimensions in this analysis literally as elements in mathematical calculations, as one can with the physical dimensions. The analogy lies rather with the ability to combine dimensions precisely though non-mathematically, so as to recognize what entities are dimensionally incompatible with others.

4 Basic Concepts

The basic concepts required to provide a rationale for the definitions of *Process* and *Event* can be only briefly described here. The basic concept classes required, in addition to the fundamental ones adopted from KIF, are: *Object*, *Attribute*, *Group*, *System*, *Time*, *Function*, *State*, *GrainSize*, *PhysicalSubstance*, and *Space* (for PhysicalObjects equivalent to *Volume*). From these the entities *Process* and *Event* can be derived. Other more abstract concepts may be used to define the basic concepts of concern here, but that analysis is not needed for the present discussion. The topmost concept class, of which all other concept classes are subclasses, is here labeled *Entity*.

4.1 Object

Object is a primitive notion in most ontologies, and is at the topmost level of the PUO ontology (*P*roposed *U*pper *O*ntology), which embodies the ontological principles discussed here. Nevertheless, in this analysis, the qualitative dimension of *Object* will be shown to be a composite dimension, with the more primitive dimensions of *SubstanceType* and space as components.

Every Object must have at least one attribute (which can be a location), and is disjoint from *Attribute*, *Predicate*, *Event*, *Process*, *State*, and *Space*. Attributes may modify Objects, Processes, Events, or other Attributes, but an *ObjectAttribute* (a type of *AttributeValue*) must modify some *Object*. Formally, the fact that *Object* is disjoint with *Attribute* can be represented by the predicate:

$$\textbf{(disjoint Object Attribute)} \qquad (1)$$

A *PhysicalObject* is an *Object* that has mass and exists in space-time.

4.2 Attribute

Each *Attribute* necessarily relates to some other Entity, and cannot exist independently. The values of *Attributes* which may change over time are sometimes called *fluents*, and the values of such attributes are the ones that are of interest in defining Processes and Events. The value of an Attribute, the *AttributeValue*, is one of the basic qualitative dimensions used in this analysis.

The most common relation in the PUO that relates objects to their attributes is the ternary relation *hasAttribute*, for which the arguments are an instance of *Entity*, a class of *Attributes*, and an *AttributeValue* which is an instance of that class of attributes. Generally, the hasAttribute relation as applied to Objects has the form:

(hasAttribute Object ObjectAttributeType ObjectAttribute)   (2)

The argument "ObjectAttributeType" specifies a class of attributes, and "ObjectAttribute" specifies an instance of an attribute. For example, to say that a car Car0123 has a color which is "InfernoRed", the predicate would state:

(hasAttribute Car0123 SurfaceColor InfernoRed)   (3)

where InfernoRed is an instance of SurfaceColor. Some attributes have quantitative AttributeValues which are composed of more than one component, such as measurements, which have a quantity plus a unit of measure. Such AttributeValues may be reified to fit in the above formalism. Alternatively, they can be represented as higher-arity relations, as below:

(hasAttribute Rocket0123 AltitudeAboveSeaLevel 35.7 Mile)   (4)

Predicates that relate to real-world situations (as contrasted with terminological definitions) will contain some reference to the time point or interval at which the assertion is true. They may be contained within a wrapper provided by a special type of predicate which is an *Assertion*, or alternatively *Time* may be a required element in the predicates on physical objects. In the latter case the predicate might take a form as below, with the time as the last argument:

(hasAttribute Rocket0123 AltitudeAboveSeaLevel 35.7   (5)
Mile GMT2002Jan06:10:54.345)

In either formalism, the set of AttributeValues (e .g 37.5 miles) of such predicates at different points in time may be represented as a function which specifies the value of the attribute at each point in time. A continuous process may be represented as such a function, as discussed by Sowa[5].

4.3 Group

A *Group* as defined here is an assemblage of one or more component entities, may be defined either extensionally or intensionally, but is not a type of mathematical set. The special functions that are used to represent physical processes are instances of *PhysicalGroup;* a subclass of *Group*. These functions are similar in some respects to the relations defined in set theory, but they are not mathematical objects and they have a location in space-time. Like the processes and events they represent, instances of such groups may be described by attributes appropriate to physical entities. One restriction on *Group* is that no *Group* can be a component entity of itself. Formally, *Process* and *Event* are subclasses of *PhysicalGroup*.

4.4 System

A System is a *Group* of *Object*s plus their *Attributes* and all relations between the component *Object*s, and the *Processes* involving those *Objects*. A *System* may have one or more than one *Object*. and the *Object*s may be composed of parts (which are not defined here).

The objects in a system may have predicates relating them to objects outside the system, and their relations to those objects may be significant in the analysis of processes. However, the properties of objects outside the system are not an element of the state of a system, and are not considered as directly affecting the processes within the system.

4.5 Time

Time is defined here as a physical metric dimension, isomorphic to the real line. Unlike the spatial dimensions, time is measured by a clock. Intervals of time may be open, closed, or open on one end, but in all cases the size of the time interval is determined by the difference in the values of the time points which define the two ends of the interval. Each *TimePoint* is contained within some *TimeInterval*. Other relations of time intervals are as described in the DAML-Time ontology [12].

4.6 Function

A *Function* is a *Relation* for which there is only one instance of the first argument for each instance of the set of remaining arguments. A *Relation* is defined similarly to relation in KIF, but is a subclass of *Group* (rather than MathematicalSet) and is not an abstract entity, but can have location in space and time.

4.7 State

A *State* of a *System* is the group of *AttributeValue*s for the attributes (e.g. temperature, location, rate) of the objects and processes in that *System*. This differs from the use of this term in PSL [10] and certain other ontologies. For a *PhysicalSystem*, the less ambiguous term would be *InstantaneousState* which is the set of values at one *TimePoint* for those *AttributeValue*s. *Time* is defined by a clock which may be outside the system. The most important predicates will in general be those assigning attributes (such as quantity, location, and physical properties) to the objects and specifying the relations of objects in the system to each other. This definition of *InstantaneousState* is similar to the notion of **Situation** in situation calculus, but differs in its precise relations to other entities. Two important subclasses of *InstantaneousState* are *BeginningState* and *EndingState*, being respectively the *InstantaneousState*s holding at the *TimePoint* which defines the *BeginingPoint* and the state at the *EndPoint* of an *Event*. At the user's discretion, only a subset of such predicate argument values may be used, namely those that are to be modeled in a cognitive system.

4.8 GrainSize

A *GrainSize* is either a unit of a metric space, or some number of entities, which sets a lower limit on the size of an entity in order for it to be considered homogeneous. The example in the next section shows how it is used with *PhysicalSubstance*.

4.9 PhysicalSubstance

A *PhysicalSubstance* is, unlike in CYC, not considered as a piece of some substance (e.c. gold), but something more abstract. *PhysicalSubstance* is one of the qualitative dimensions, which can be used as a primitive concept which is intimately connected to the concept of an *Object*. It is intended to be homogeneous, and is thus dependent on the notion of granularity – it has an associated grain size, and an object can be composed of a particular substance only if the object is several times the grain size of that substance. If a *PhysicalObject* does not extend at least four grains (of some *PhysicalSubstance*) in each spatial dimension, it must be considered as a collection of individual objects, and not composed of that *PhysicalSubstance*. Thus a *PhysicalSubstance* cannot in general be indefinitely divided and still remain the same substance. This concept of *Substance* is unrelated to the **Substance** of Aristotle, e.g. as described by Loux [6].

Where the ontologist wishes to represent a *Substance* as continuous (e.g. for simplified mathematical treatment), the grain size of that *Substance* for that object may be set to zero. This permits the use of functions which are densely continuous in the mathematical sense. In many situations, the calculations thus performed are accurate to within the limits of measurement and can be viewed as approximations to some (perhaps unknown) more accurate theory.

5   The Representation of Process and Event

With the above concepts, we can now define *Process* and *Event* in a way that clearly distinguishes between them while preserving the intuitions contained in several earlier representations.

Following Sowa [5] we will consider a *ContinuousPhysicalProcess* as being a *Group* of *Functions* describing the *InstantaneousState* of a system as a function of time, and whose granularity is zero for both *Time* and *AttributeValues*. The rate of change of the *AttributeValues* of a *System* would be the derivative of that function.. The present representation differs somewhat from Sowa's in the manner in which periods of stasis (time intervals with no change of attribute values) are represented. As specified in the definition above, the *InstantaneousState* of a system is the set of all those *AttributeValues* that the ontologist chooses to represent, at a particular *TimePoint*. Those *AttributeValues* will be the values of the arguments of certain predicates in which an object or process of the system is an instance of the predicate domain. Each distinguishable process (e.g. rusting) will have distinctive and characteristic changes in the values of specific arguments as a function of time. A *PrimitiveProcess* would be the function describing the changes with time for only one of the *AttributeValues* of that *System*. These values are what are called the "fluents" in some other representations, i.e. those attribute values which change over time as a process progresses. A *ComplexProcess* will be a *Group* of *Functions* representing changes with time of more than one *AttributeValue*.

As mentioned above, an event is intuitively understood as some change or changes occurring in a system within some bounded time interval. It follows that any two time points within the time course of a process can be used to identify the boundaries of a named *Event*. The event would consist of all the perceptible changes during that time interval. This definition can be used to represent a diverse array of events, and it is the definition of *PhysicalEvent* which will be used here. Sowa also notes that arbitrary time points may be marked in the representation of a continuous process, but he does not specifically identify the intervals between such points as defining individual events.

The suggestion that arbitrary Events may be defined as a result of a continuous Process at first may seem to violate the intuition that events should have reasonably well-defined starting and ending points, and for many events that intuition is true. It is natural that a naive person or an ontologist choosing to define a specific event will use beginning and ending time points that have some significance, usually periods of relative stasis for the variables of interest. But there is no compelling reason to create any restriction in this ontology against using arbitrary starting and ending time points for *Events*.

The relationship between a *Process* and an *Event* in this representation therefore may be expressed by saying that operation of a *Process* over some interval of time results in an *Event*: (**hasResult Process Event TimeInterval**). Conversely, every *Event* is the result of some corresponding *Process* operating over some interval of time.

The dimensional analysis of these definitions will help to make the difference between *PhysicalProcess* and *PhysicalEvent* more distinct. The distinctive character of a *PhysicalProcess* is the change of specific values of attributes over time. Its "dimension" would therefore most appropriately viewed as change of *AttributeValue* per *TimeInterval*. The resulting conceptual dimension is therefore **AttributeValue•TimeInterval**$^{-1}$. This conforms to the representation of Sowa [5], where differential equations are recognized as the appropriate mathematical specification for many continuous physical processes. A *PhysicalEvent*, however, is the totality of all changes that occur within a time interval, i.e. a *Group* of changes in *AttributeValues*. Changes in both attribute values and time intervals are involved. Representing an *Event* as a group of changes suggests the mathematical analogy of an integral function of the associated *Process*, which would give a dimension of **AttributeValue•TimeInterval.** This, however, would be misleading since it would suggest that a change of twice the magnitude in half the time of another change would be an equivalent event. The time dimension is important, not only in the magnitude of the interval, but also in its absolute location on the time line. A simple arithmetical summation of the two units involved is also precluded by the incommensurable units for attributes and time. The appropriate conceptual dimension for *PhysicalEvent*, then should be a complex concatenated dimension, specifically the pair (**AttributeValue, TimeInterval).** As emphasized in the introduction, these conceptual dimensions do not participate directly in any logical inferencing processes, and should not be viewed as providing information about the physical nature of the *Events* and *Processes* represented, but they can be useful to help tease apart the subtly interrelated conceptual elements contained within these fundamental concepts. The important point is that the conceptual dimensions of *Process* and *Event* are different, and **neither class can be a subclass of the other**.

The above analysis focused on continuous processes, where the *GrainSize* is zero for both *AttributeValue* and *TimeInterval*. For realistic physical processes, there is some minimum measurable difference in both attributes and in time. These minimum values serve in effect as the *GrainSize* for *PhysicalProcesses*. If the differences in all of the relevant attributes of a process are always measurable within the smallest represented time interval, the process will appear to be homogeneous, i..e. the process may be divided down to the grain size, and the nature of the process will appear to be similar within each division.. This is the sense in which processes appear to be divisible, like substances. It will be true only if the grain size is small enough so that each measurement shows some change in all the *AttributeValue*s whose changes define the *Process*. However, if all attributes remain constant for some measurable time interval, the *Process* may appear to be discontinuous, i.e. periods of change followed by periods of stasis. A *DiscontinuousProcess* includes periods of stasis (the *NullProcess*) and is not homogeneous.

It is necessary here to emphasize that these logical structures are only **representations** of reality chosen to serve a specific purpose. They are abstractions that leave out some details of reality. The ontologist is therefore free to choose the grain size that suits the purpose at hand, and where one ontologist may choose a grain size that makes a process effectively homogeneous, another may choose a larger grain size that makes the represented process discontinuous. The representations will be logically consistent, provided that the grain size is explicitly stipulated, as required for every *Process*.

5.1 Special Cases of Event

It is often not necessary for an ontologist to be concerned with the details of the process that produces a *PhysicalEvent*, but only with the difference in the *InstantaneousState*s at the beginning and ending *TimePoint*s of the *PhysicalEvent*. Such an Event may be treated as an *AtomicEvent*, i.e. one in which only the before-and-after states are represented explicitly. Where one application developer may be interested only in the results of an explosion, for example, an explosives expert may be concerned with the millisecond-by-millisecond progress of the detonation and the details of how its effects are generated.

A special and problematic case of *AtomicEvent* is the idealized and physically unrealistic but sometimes useful concept of an instantaneous *PhysicalEvent,* which might be viewed as the result of a *PhysicalProcess* that takes zero time. However, allowing such a *PhysicalEvent* could cause a logical contradiction, if a *PhysicalSystem* were allowed to have two different attribute values at the same time point. If an *InstantaneousEvent* is properly defined, such a contradiction can be avoided. But for conformance to physical reality, every *PhysicalEvent* should be represented as taking place over some non-zero interval of time, which can be smaller than the smallest measurable time interval, provided that the beginning and ending time points are never considered as identical. The *PhysicalProcess* that produces that *PhysicalEvent* must operate within that non-zero *TimeInterval*.

A special, limiting case of a continuous Process may be termed the *NullProcess*, i.e. a *PhysicalProcess* in which no *AttributeValue*s for the *System* change by more than the specified *GrainSize*, within some *TimeInterval*. A linguistic label might be "stasis" – nothing is happening. A *NullProcess* operating over some period of time will result in a special, limiting case of *Event*, the *NullEvent*, i.e. an *Event* during which no relevant *AttributeValue*s change. This *NullEvent* is identical to what has been called a **State** in certain process representations, such as PSL and in the Petri Nets described in Sowa [5]. Hobbs and Pustejovsky [11] also consider states and circumstances as a subtype of Event. For the sake of making the terminology of the PUO ontology closer to that of other treatments, the *NullEvent* could also be assigned a synonym, a "PersistentState", with no difference in meaning. Regardless of the terms used, the basic concept, that some attributes of objects may remain unchanged over time, is the same and can in all cases be represented as a *ContinuousProcess* with null changes. This concept will be useful in analysis of discontinuous processes.

6   Discontinuous Processes

To the extent currently measurable, at the fundamental physical level all physical processes are physically continuous in time, although when observing instruments have insufficient resolution, certain events may appear instantaneous. Nevertheless, many important processes and practical procedures seem to be naturally decomposable into discrete periods of time when something significant changes, followed by periods when no significant change occurs. Sowa [5] has provided a summary of the various ways that such decomposable processes ("**discrete processes**") may be represented, as alternating units of **Events** when some perceptible change occurs, and **States** when no significant change occurs. As mentioned above, the **States** (intervals of time when specific fluents are "constant") are logically indistinguishable from *NullEvents*. Thus a series of Events interspersed with *NullEvents* is, in the view of our proposed ontology, actually a *ComplexEvent*, and has the conceptual dimensions of *PhysicalEvent*. The "discrete process" represented by Sowa as Petri Nets would, in our view, be a subclass of *PhysicalEvent*, with the same conceptual dimension. The representation of discrete processes as Directed Acyclic Graphs is consistent with the above representation of all *PhysicalProcesse* as fundamentally continuous. Though the each **discrete process** would, in the current view, be a subtype of *PhysicalEvent* , it can be mapped to a continuous process by an **Embedding** as described by Sowa. The difference in terminology can be resolved by agreement on the use of appropriate synonyms for the same concepts.

7   Substance and Object

The familiar "substances" of everyday life, such as water, air, steel, milk, glass, or coffee, have been represented in different ways in different ontologies. Linguistically, they are treated as mass nouns rather than count nouns, and to reflect this distinction, an ontology should be able to discriminate substances from objects.

In CYC substances are represented as the collection of all objects consisting of that substance; e.g. for glass, the CYC documentation states: "Each element of #$Glass is a piece of glass; e.g., a wine bottle, a plate glass window, a microscope slide, a crystal water goblet, the mirrors of a reflecting telescope." Thus the class "#$Glass" in effect is a class of all pieces of glass; and this representation is similar in CYC for other substances. The distinction between objects and substances in CYC is not directly reflected in the hierarchy, but is achieved by assigning specific classes as instances of either #$ExistingStuffType or #$ExistingObjectType. We feel that such indirect assignment of important properties unnecessarily obscures their meaning, and for clarity believe that substances and objects should be differentiated within the class hierarchy. More seriously, the assignment of one entity as a subclass of another of different conceptual dimension risks creating a logical inconsistency.

To achieve the clear differentiation of *PhysicalSubstance* and *PhysicalObject* we consider a *PhysicalSubstance* to be an *Entity* which is one point in a qualitative dimension of *PhysicalSubstanceType*, and a quantitative dimension of *Density*. The conceptual units would therefore be **PhysicalSubstanceType•Mass•Volume^{-1}**. As a concept which has an associated property of homogeneity, each substance must be associated with a specific granularity. Therefore a *PhysicalObject* which is composed of some *PhysicalSubstance*, must have a size of at least four *GrainSizes* in each length dimension; otherwise it must be viewed as an aggregate of individual objects or parts.

For each case of a homogeneous *PhysicalSubstance* (e.g. water) there are two associated concepts, a *QuantityOfSubstance* and a *PhysicalObject*. A *QuantityOfSubstance* corresponds to some volume of space filled with that substance. For a *PhysicalSubstance*, i *QuantityOfSubstance* would have a mass which is the product of its density times the volume occupied by the *PhysicalSubstance*, (e.g. ten milliliters of water having a mass of ten grams). This concept, however, represents only a *generic* quantity of that substance, of which there may be may instances. A homogeneous *PhysicalObject* is formed by a *QuantityOfSubstance* which fills some *specific* region of space, e.g. the 200 ml of water sitting in a specific glass on my table, or the thirty ounces of wood in my baseball bat.. Both of these concepts have the same qualitative dimension:

$$(\textbf{SubstanceType•Mass•Volume}^{-1}) \bullet \textbf{Volume} = \textbf{SubstanceType•Mass} \qquad (6)$$

A homogeneous *PhysicalObject* can be divided, and the result would be two *PhysicalObject*s of the same composition, and if the object is large enough, two quantities of the same substance. But the division process may not go on indefinitely, and it will fail when it reaches the level of the grain size of the substance.

This representation of *PhysicalSubstance* provides a natural and precise way to represent mixtures of substances, whether macroscopically heterogeneous, such as cement, or microscopically homogeneous, such as aqueous solutions. The details are beyond the scope of this paper.

8 Conclusion

The use of conceptual dimensional analysis for *Event* and *Process* helps to clarify the distinction between Process and Event that is evident in linguistic utterances. The suggestions above for representation of the relation between Process and Event can form a firm logical basis for reasoning about what actually happens in all kinds of processes. A working demonstration of the use of this representation in a practical computational system, has not yet been attempted, however, and this fundamental ontology has as yet not been shown to be superior to others previously suggested.

References

1. James Higginbotham, Fabio Pianesi and Achille C. Varzi, *Speaking of Events* (New York, Oxford University Press, 2000).
2. Ray Jackendoff, *Semantic Structures* (Cambridge, Mass., MIT Press, 1990).
3. Lenat and Guha [1990] Douglas B. Lenat and R. V. Guha, *Building Large Knowledge-Based Systems: Representation and Inference in the CYC Project.* (Reading, Mass., Addison-Wesley)
4. CYC Upper Ontology. Available from Cycorp at http://www.cyc.com.
5. John F. Sowa, *Processes and Causality* [preprint, 2002]
   Available at: http://www.jfsowa.com/ontology/causal.htm.
6. Michael J. Loux, *Metaphysics* (New York, Routledge, 1998).
7. Ontolingua Theory Frame-Ontology. Available from:
   http://www.ksl.stanford.edu/htw/dme/thermal-kb-tour/frame-ontology.html
8. M. R. Genesereth and R. E. Fikes, *Knowledge Interchange Format, Version 3.0 Reference Manual*, Tech. Report KSL-92-86, Knowledge Systems Laboratory, June 1992.
9. Patrick Hayes and Christopher Menzel, A Semantics for the Knowledge Interchange Format. pp. 13–20 in the Proceedings of the Workshop on the IEEE Standard Upper Ontology, Aug. 6, 2001, Seattle Washington (in association with IJCAI-2001).
10. Process Specification Language. National Institutes of Standards and Technology, *The PSL Ontology*, available at http://www.mel.nist.gov/psl/psl-ontology/.
11. Jerry Hobbs and James Pustejovsky, *Annotating and Reasoning about Time and Events.* http://ww.cs.rochester.edu/~ferguson/daml/hobbs-pustejovsky.pdf (preprint, 2002).
12. Jerry R. Hobbs, A DAML Ontology of Time,
    http://www.cs.rochester.edu/~ferguson/daml/daml-time-20020830.txt

Classifying Functional Relations in Factotum via WordNet Hypernym Associations[*]

Tom O'Hara[1] and Janyce Wiebe[2]

[1] Department of Computer Science
New Mexico State University
Las Cruces, NM 88003
`tomohara@cs.nmsu.edu`
[2] Department of Computer Science
University of Pittsburgh
Pittsburgh, PA 15260
`wiebe@cs.pitt.edu`

Abstract. This paper describes how to automatically classify the functional relations from the FACTOTUM knowledge base via a statistical machine learning algorithm. This incorporates a method for inferring prepositional relation indicators from corpus data. It also uses lexical collocations (i.e., word associations) and class-based collocations based on the WordNet hypernym relations (i.e., *is-subset-of*). The result shows substantial improvement over a baseline approach.

1 Introduction

Applications using natural language processing often rely predominantly upon hierarchical semantic relations (e.g., is-a, is-subset-of, and is-part-of), along with synonymy and word associations. These are readily available in lexical resources such as Princeton's WordNet [1] or can be extracted directly from corpora [2]. Other types of relations are important, although more difficult to acquire. These correspond to dictionary differentia [3], that is, the distinguishing relations given in definitions. Differentia provide information such as attributes, typical functions, and typical purpose. This paper shows how to infer such relations from examples in a knowledge base (KB). For the purpose of this work, the term functional relations refers to these non-hierarchical relations, excluding attributes.

The FACTOTUM semantic network [4] developed by Micra, Inc. makes explicit many of the functional relations in Roget's Thesaurus.[1] Outside of proprietary resources such as Cyc [5], Factotum is the most comprehensive KB

---

[*] Patrick Cassidy of Micra, Inc. kindly made Factotum available and provided valuable input on the paper. Michael O'Hara helped much with the proofreading. The first author is supported by a generous GAANN fellowship from the Department of Education. Some of the work used computing resources at NMSU made possible through MII Grants EIA-9810732 and EIA-0220590.
[1] Factotum is based on the public domain version of Roget's Thesaurus. The latter is freely available via Project Gutenberg (http://promo.net/pg), thanks to Micra, Inc.

A. Gelbukh (Ed.): CICLing 2003, LNCS 2588, pp. 347–359, 2003.
© Springer-Verlag Berlin Heidelberg 2003

with respect to functional relations. OpenCyc[2] does include definitions of many non-hierarchical relations. However, there are not many instantiations (i.e., relationship assertions), because it concentrates on the higher level of the ontology.

This paper is organized as follows: Section 2 presents more background on the usefulness of differentiating relations, and discusses the main differentiating relations in Factotum. Section 3 shows how corpora can be used to infer clue words for these relations. Section 4 presents results from experiments on classifying the functional relations in Factotum. Section 5 discusses related work. The last section summaries the paper's contributions and mentions areas for future work.

2   Background

2.1   Importance of Non-hierarchical Semantic Relations

Distinguishing features play a prominent role in categorization. For instance, in Tversky's [6] influential contrast model, the similarity comparison incorporates factors specific to either term, as well as factors common to both, Tversky also conducted experiments [7] showing that, in certain cases, the distinctive features are given more weight than common ones. Similar results are reported by Medin et al. [8].

Conceptual knowledge for natural language processing is commonly organized into hierarchies called ontologies (e.g., the Mikrokosmos ontology for machine translation [9]). The concepts in these hierarchies are usually partially ordered via the instance and subset relations (i.e., is-a and is-subset-of). Each is a relation of dominance, which Cruse [10] considers as the defining aspect of hierarchies. He points out that an important part of hierarchies is the differentiation of siblings. This is the role of conceptual differentia , that is, the semantic relations that distinguish sibling concepts. Without these relations, the information in hierarchical lexicons would only indicate how the lexicalized concepts represented are ordered without indicating the differences among the concepts.

Manually-derived lexicons, such as the Mikrokosmos English lexicon [11], often contain differentia in the rich case-frame structures associated with the underlying concepts. This contrasts with semi-automatically derived lexicons such as WordNet [1], which emphasize the lexical hierarchy but not the underlying semantics. For instance, Mikrokosmos[3] averages about 2.4 properties per concept (including some inverse relations), whereas WordNet[4] only averages 1.3 (including inverses).[5] This suggests that the reason large-scale lexicons tend to incorporate less differentia is due more to the difficulty in acquiring the

---

[2] Version 0.7 of OpenCyc, a publicly available subset of Cyc (www.opencyc.org).

[3] 1998 version of Mikrokosmos (crl.nmsu.edu/Research/Projects/mikro/index.html).

[4] Version 1.7 of WordNet (www.cogsci.princeton.edu/~wn).

[5] *Properties* refers to functional relations, attributes and part-whole relations (e.g., *is-member-meronym-of*), excluding just the instance and subset relations. WordNet 1.6 only averages 0.64 properties, so version 1.7 represents a substantial improvement.

information than to the relative worth of the information. Factotum compares favorably in this respect, averaging 1.8 properties per concept. OpenCyc provides the highest average at 3.7 properties per concept (with an emphasis on argument constraints and other usage restrictions).[6]

Hirst [12] advocates adding case structures to standard dictionaries, in the same manner that learner's dictionaries indicate verbal subcategorization frames. This would provide a common resource for more-detailed language knowledge, useful for humans as well as for computerized processing.

Work in formal semantics tends not to cover functional relations much, although there are some notable exceptions. Pustejovsky's Generative Lexicon theory accounts for them in his qualia structure [13]. Mel'čuk's Meaning Text Theory [14] accounts for them via lexical functions in his Explanatory Combinatorial Dictionary. Both of these theories are quite influential, adding more support that functional relations are desirable although perhaps difficult to acquire. Heylen [15] discusses the connection between the two theories.

2.2   Factotum

The FACTOTUM semantic network [4] is a knowledge base derived initially from the 1911 version of Roget's Thesaurus. Part of purpose is to make explicit the relations that hold between the Roget categories and the words listed in each entry. It incorporates information from other resources as well, in particular the Unified Medical Language System (UMLS), which formed the basis for the initial set of semantic relations.

Figure 1 shows a sample from Factotum. This illustrates that the basic Roget organization is still used, although additional hierarchical levels have been added. The relations are contained within double braces (e.g., "{{has_subtype}}") and generally apply from the category to each word in the synonym list on the same line. Therefore, the line with "{{result_of}}" indicates that conversion is the result of transforming, as shown in the semantic relation listing that would be extracted.[7] There are over 400 relations instantiated in the semantic network. Some of these are quite specialized (e.g., has-brandname). In addition, there are quite a few inverse functions, since most of the relations are not symmetrical. Certain features of the semantic network representation are currently ignored during the relation extraction. For example, relation specifications can have qualifier prefixes, such as an ampersand to indicate that the relationship only sometimes holds.

Table 1 shows the most common relations in terms of usage in the semantic network, and includes others that are used in the experiments discussed later.[8]

---

[6] These figures are derived by counting the number of relations excluding the instance and subset ones. OpenCyc's comments and lexicalizations are also excluded (implicit in Factotum and WordNet). The count is then divided by the number of concepts.

[7] For clarity, some of the relations are renamed to make the directionality more explicit, following a suggestion for their interpretation in the Factotum documentation.

[8] The database files and documentation for the semantic network are available from Micra, Inc. via ftp://micra.com/factotum.

A6.1.4 CONVERSION (R144)

#144. Conversion.

N. {{has_subtype(change, R140)}} conversion, transformation.
{{has_case: @R7, initial state, final state}}.
{{has_patient: @R3a, object, entity}}.
{{result_of}} {{has_subtype(process, A7.7)}} converting, transforming.
{{has_subtype}} processing.
transition.

⇒

⟨change, *has-subtype*, conversion⟩   ⟨change, *has-subtype*, transformation⟩
⟨conversion, *has-case*, initial state⟩   ⟨conversion, *has-case*, final state⟩
⟨conversion, *has-patient*, object⟩   ⟨conversion, *has-patient*, entity⟩
⟨conversion, *is-result-of*, converting⟩   ⟨conversion, *is-result-of*, transforming⟩
⟨process, *has-subtype*, converting⟩   ⟨process, *has-subtype*, transforming⟩
⟨conversion, *has-subtype*, processing⟩

Fig. 1. Sample entry from Factotum with extracted relations

The functional relations are shown in boldface. The exclusion of the meronymic or part-whole relations (e.g., is-conceptual-part-of) accords with their classification by Cruse [10] as hierarchical relations. Note that the usage counts just reflect relationships[9] explicitly labeled in the KB data file. For instance, this does not account for implicit has-subtype relationships based on the hierarchical organization of the thesaural groups.

Table 2 shows the relation usage in WordNet version 1.7. This shows that the majority of the relations are hierarchical (is-similar-to can be considered as a hierarchical relation for adjectives). Therefore, the information in Factotum complements WordNet through the inclusion of more functional relations.

3   Inferring Relation Markers

Note that Factotum does not indicate the way the relationships are expressed in English. WordNet similarly does not indicate this, but does include definition glosses that can be used in some cases to infer the relation markers (i.e., generalized case markers). For example,

Factotum: ⟨drying, is-function-of, drier⟩

WordNet: {dry#1, dry_out#3} remove the moisture from and make dry
{dryer#1, drier#2} an appliance that removes moisture

Therefore, the Factotum relations cannot be used as is to provide training data for learning how the relations are expressed in English. This contrasts with corpus-based annotations, such as Treebank II [16] and FrameNet [17], where the relationships are marked in context.

---

[9] For clarity, *relationships* refers to relation instantiations, and *relations* to the types.

Table 1. Sample relations from Micra's FACTOTUM. Boldface relations are used in the experiments in Section 4.

Relation	Usage	Description
has-subtype	37355	inverse of *is-a* relation
is-property-of	7210	object with given salient character
is-caused-by	3203	indicates force that is the origin of something
has-property	2625	salient property of an object
has-part	2055	a part of a physical object
has-high-intensity	1671	intensifier for the property or characteristic
has-high-level	1564	implication for the activity (e.g., intelligence)
is-antonym-of	1525	generally used for lexical opposition
is-conceptual-part-of	1408	parts of other entities (in case relations)
has-metaphor	1313	non-literal reference to the word
causes$_{mental}$	1208	motivation (causation in the mental realm)
uses	1157	a tool needing active manipulation
is-performed-by	1081	human actor for the event
performs$_{human}$	987	human role in performing some activity
is-function-of	983	artifact that passively performs the function
has-result	977	more specific type of *causes*
has-conceptual-part	937	generalization of *has-part*
is-used-in	930	activity or some desired effect for the entity
is-part-of	898	distinguishes part from group membership
causes	866	inverse of *is-caused-by*
has-method	830	method used to achieve some goal
is-caused-by$_{mental}$	810	inverse of *causes$_{mental}$*
has-consequence	785	causation due to a natural association
has-commencement	663	state that commences with the action
is-location-of	655	absolute location of an object
requires	341	object or sub-action necessary for an action
is-studied-in	331	inquires into any field of study
is-topic-of	177	document or other communication for the subject
produces	166	what an action yields, secretes, generates, etc.
is-measured-by	158	instrument or method for measuring something
is-job-of	117	occupation title for a job function
is-patient-of	101	action that the object participates in
is-facilitated-by	98	object or sub-action aiding an action
is-biofunction-of	27	biological function of parts of living things
was-performed-by	22	*is-performed-by* occurring in the past
has-consequence$_{object}$	21	consequence for the patient of an action
is-facilitated-by$_{mental}$	9	trait that facilitates some human action

However, given the increased coverage of the web, the relation markers can be inferred. For example, each of the relationships can be used in proximity searches involving the source and target terms. For example, using AltaVista's Boolean search[10], this can be done via 'source NEAR target'. Unfortunately, this

---

[10] AltaVista's Boolean search is available at www.altavista.com/sites/search/adv.

Table 2. Relation usage in WordNet (version 1.7)

Relation	Usage	Description
has-hypernym	88381	superset relation
is-similar-to	22492	similar adjective synset
is-member-meronym-of	12043	constituent member
is-part-meronym-of	8026	constituent part
is-antonym-of	7873	opposing concept
is-pertainym-of	4433	noun that adjective pertains to
also-see	3325	related entry (for adjectives and verbs)
is-derived-from	3174	adjective that adverb is derived from
has-verb-group	1400	verb senses grouped by similarity
has-attribute	1300	related attribute category or value
is-substance-meronym-of	768	constituent substance
entails	426	action entailed by the verb
causes	216	action caused by the verb
has-participle	120	verb participle

technique would require detailed post-processing of the web search results, possibly including parsing in order to extract the patterns. As an expedient, common prepositions[11] are included in a series of proximity searches to find the preposition occurring the most with the terms. For instance, given the relationship ⟨drying, is-function-of, drier⟩, the following searches would be performed.

drying NEAR tendril NEAR of
drying NEAR tendril NEAR to
...
drying NEAR tendril NEAR "because of"

To account for prepositions that occur frequently (e.g., 'of'), mutual information (MI) statistics [2] are used in place of the raw frequency when rating the potential markers. These are calculated as follows:

$$MI_{prep} = log_2 \frac{P(X,Y)}{P(X) \times P(Y)} \approx log_2 \frac{f(\text{source NEAR target NEAR prep})}{f(\text{source NEAR target}) \times f(\text{prep})}$$

Such checks are done for the 25 most common prepositions to find the preposition yielding the highest mutual information score. Using this metric, the top three markers for the ⟨drying, is-function-of, drier⟩ relationship are 'during', 'after', and 'with'.

This technique can readily be extended to finding relation markers in foreign languages, such as Spanish, given a bilingual dictionary. Ambiguous translations pose a complication, but in most of these cases, similar relation markers

---

[11] The common prepositions are determined from the prepositional phrases assigned functional annotations in Penn Treebank II [16].

should be likely unless the relations between the alternative meaning pairs diverge significantly.[12] For example, when the process is applied to the translated relationship for the example, namely ⟨secar, is-function-of, secarador⟩, the top three markers are 'con', 'de', and 'para'.

4 Classifying the Functional Relations

4.1 Methodology

Given the functional relationships in Factotum along with the inferred relation markers, machine learning algorithms can be used to infer what relation most likely applies to terms occurring together with a particular marker. Note that the main purpose of including the relation markers is to provide clues for the particular type of relation. Because the source term and target terms might occur in other relationships, associations based on them alone might not be as accurate. In addition, the inclusion of these clue words (e.g., the prepositions) makes the task closer to what would be done in inferring the relations from free text. In effect, this task is preposition disambiguation, using the Factotum relations as senses.

A straightforward approach for preposition disambiguation would use standard feature sets for word-sense disambiguation (WSD), such as those used in the SENSEVAL competitions [19,20]. These include syntactic features for the immediate context (e.g., the parts-of-speech of surrounding words). More importantly, WSD feature sets include semantic features based on collocations (e.g., word associations). The latter can be highly accurate, but might over-fit the data and generalize poorly. To overcome these problems, class-based collocations are also incorporated, using WordNet hypernym synsets.

Figure 2 gives the feature settings used in the experiments. These are similar to the settings used by the GRLING-SDM system in the first SENSEVAL competition [21], except for the inclusion of the hypernym-based collocations.

Word collocation features are derived by making two passes over the training data. The first pass tabulates the co-occurrence counts for the words in a window around the target word and each of the classification values or categories (e.g., the preposition senses). These counts are used to derive a conditional probability estimate of each class value given the various potential collocates. Those exceeding a certain threshold are collected into a list associated with the class value, making this a "bag of words" approach. As shown in Figure 2, a potential collocate is selected whenever its co-occurrence with the class category increases the probability for the latter by 20%. The second pass determines the value for the collocational feature of each classification category by checking whether the current context has any of the associated collocation words. For the test data, only the second pass is made, using the collocation lists derived from the training data.

---

[12] Sidorov et al. [18] illustrate the differences that might arise for terms referring to non-adults in English, Spanish, and Russian.

Features:

POS_{source}:	part-of-speech of the source term
POS_{target}:	part-of-speech of the target term
Prep:	preposition serving as relation marker (or 'n/a' if not inferable)
WordColl$_i$:	true if context contains any word collocation for relation i
HypernymColl$_i$:	true if context contains any hypernym collocation for relation i

Collocation selection:

Frequency constraint:	$f(word) > 1$
Conditional independence threshold:	$\frac{p(c|coll)-p(c)}{p(c)} >= 0.2$
Organization:	per-class-binary grouping [22]

Model selection:
Decision tree (via Weka's J48 classifier [23])
10-fold cross-validation

Fig. 2. Features used in semantic role classification experiments

In generalizing this to a class-based approach, the potential collocational words are replaced with each of their hypernym ancestors from WordNet. Since the co-occurring words are not sense-tagged, this is done for each synset serving as a different sense of the word. (Likewise, in the case of multiple inheritance, each parent synset is used.) For example, given the co-occurring word "money", the counts would be updated as if each of the following tokens were seen, shown grouped by sense.

1. {medium_of_exchange#1, monetary_system#1, standard#1, criterion#1, measure#2, touchstone#1, reference_point#1, point_of_reference#1, reference#3, indicator#2, signal#1, signaling#1, sign#3, communication#2, social_relation#1, relation#1, abstraction#6}
2. {wealth#4, property#2, belongings#1, holding#2, material_possession#1, possession#2}
3. {currency#1, medium_of_exchange#1, monetary_system#1, standard#1, criterion#1, measure#2, touchstone#1, reference_point#1, point_of_reference#1, reference#3, indicator#2, signal#1, signaling#1, sign#3, communication#2, social_relation#1, relation#1, abstraction#6}

Thus, the word token 'money' is replaced by 41 synset tokens. Then, the same two-pass process described above is performed over the replacement tokens. Although this introduces noise due to ambiguity, the conditional-independence selection scheme [22] compensates somewhat (e.g., by selecting hypernym synsets that only occur with specific categories).

Figure 3 contains sample feature specifications from the experiments discussed in the next section. This shows that 'n/a' is used whenever a preposition marker for a particular relationship cannot be inferred. For brevity, the feature specification only includes collocation features for the most frequent relations. Sample collocations are also shown for the relations. In the word collocation case, the occurrence of 'similarity' is used to determine that the is-caused-by feature (HC_1) should be set on for the first two instances; however, there is no corresponding hypernym collocation due to conditional-independence filtering. Although 'new' is not included as a word collocation, one of its hypernyms, namely 'Adj:early#2', is used to determine that the has-consequence feature (HC_3) should be on in the last instance.

Relationships from Factotum with inferred markers:
⟨similarity, *is-caused-by*, connaturalize⟩   n/a
⟨similarity, *is-caused-by*, rhyme⟩   by
⟨approximate, *has-consequence*, imprecise⟩ because
⟨new, *has-consequence*, patented⟩   with

Word collocations only:

Relation	POS_s	POS_t	Prep	WC_1	WC_2	WC_3	WC_4	WC_5	WC_6	WC_7
is-caused-by	NN	VB	n/a	1	0	0	0	0	0	0
is-caused-by	NN	NN	by	1	0	0	0	0	0	0
has-consequence	NN	JJ	because	0	0	0	0	0	0	0
has-consequence	JJ	VBN	with	0	0	0	0	0	0	0

Sample collocations:
is-caused-by   {bitterness, evildoing, monochrome, *similarity*, vulgarity, wit}
has-consequence   {abrogate, frequently, insufficiency, nonplus, ornament, useless}

Hypernym collocations only:

Relation	POS_s	POS_t	Prep	HC_1	HC_2	HC_3	HC_4	HC_5	HC_6	HC_7
is-caused-by	NN	VB	n/a	0	0	0	0	0	0	0
is-caused-by	NN	NN	by	0	0	0	0	0	0	0
has-consequence	NN	JJ	because	0	0	0	0	0	0	0
has-consequence	JJ	VBN	with	0	0	1	0	0	0	0

Sample collocations:
is-caused-by   {N:hostility#3, N:inelegance#1, N:humorist#1, V:stimulate#4}
has-consequence   {V:abolish#1, *Adj:early#2*, N:inability#1, V:write#2, V:write#7}

Combined collocations:
The combination of the above specifications:
that is, ⟨Relation, POS_s, POS_t, Prep, WC_1, ... WC_7, HC_1, ... HC_7⟩.

where POS_s and POS_t are the parts of speech for the source and target terms, and the relations for the word and hypernym collocations (WC_i and HC_i) follow:
    1. *is-caused-by*   2. *is-function-of* 3. *has-consequence* 4. *has-result*
    5. *is-caused-by$_{mental}$* 6. *is-performed-by* 7. *uses*

Fig. 3. Sample feature specifications for the different experiment configurations. The collocation features are not shown for the low frequency relations.

4.2   Results

For this task, the set of functional relations in Factotum are determined by removing the hierarchical relations (e.g., has-subtype and has-part) along with the attribute relations (e.g., is-property-of). In addition, in cases where there are inverse functions (e.g., causes and is-caused-by), the most frequently occurring relation of each inverse pair is used. This is done because the approach currently does not account for argument order. The boldface relations in the listing shown earlier in Table 1 are those used in the experiment. Only single-word source and target terms are considered to simplify the WordNet hypernym lookup. The resulting dataset has 5959 training instances. The dataset also includes the inferred relation markers, thus introducing some noise.

Table 3 shows the results of the classification. The combined use of both collocation types achieves the best overall accuracy at 71.2%, which is good considering that the baseline of always choosing the most common relation (is-caused-by) is 24.2%. This combination generalizes well by using hypernym collocations, while retaining specificity via word collocations. Note that the classification task is quite challenging, given the large number of choices and high entropy [24].

Table 3. Functional relation classification, using inferred prepositions along with source and target. The accuracy figures are averages based on 10-fold cross validation. The gain in accuracy for the combined experiment versus the word experiment is statistically significant at $p < 0.01$ (via a paired t-test).

Experiment	Accuracy	Stdev
Word	68.4	1.28
Hypernym	53.9	1.66
Combined	71.2	1.78

# Instances:	5959
# Classes:	21
Entropy:	3.504
Baseline:	24.2

5   Related Work

Recently there has a bit of work related to preposition disambiguation and semantic role classification. Litkowski [25] presents manually-derived rules for disambiguating 'of'; Srihari et al. [26] present manually-derived rules for disambiguating prepositions used in named entities. Gildea and Jurafsky [27], as well as Blaheta and Charniak [28], address the more general problem of assigning semantic roles to arbitrary constituents of a sentence. We provide a detailed comparison elsewhere [29], including other work in preposition disambiguation. Syntactic functional relations are important as well. Dini et al. [30] show how relations extracted from parse annotations facilitate word sense disambiguation.

Scott and Matwin [31] also use WordNet hypernyms for classification, in particular topic detection. Their approach is different in that they include a numeric density feature for each synset that subsumes words appearing in the document, potentially yielding hundreds of features. We just have a binary feature for each of the relations being classified. They only consider nouns and verbs, whereas we also include adjectives.[13] As with our approach, they consider all senses of a word, distributing the alternative readings throughout the set of features. Gildea and Jurafsky [32] instead just select the first sense for their hypernym features.

Factotum has been used in other language processing research. Cassidy [4] shows how control of inference might be done for Factotum and discusses its use in word sense disambiguation. Bolshakov et al. [33] discuss the translation of Factotum into Russian and the complications due to the mismatch in the lexicalization of various concepts. Gelbukh [34] shows how Factotum can be useful for word-sense disambiguation and related tasks (e.g., machine translation) via path-based distance measures derived from the network. Follow-up work [35] discusses additional tasks that can be solved via the path minimization approach, such as resolving prepositional phrase attachment. This also describes more customizations to the standard shortest-paths algorithms for use in language processing applications (e.g., dealing with the different types of links in the semantic network).

6   Conclusion

Factotum provides complementary information to that contained in WordNet and other lexical resources. This paper shows how automatic classification of the functional relations from this data can be done, using a combination of word and hypernym collocations. The approach achieves good accuracy (71.2%), which is nearly three times the baseline. We also illustrate how relation markers can be inferred using corpus-based techniques (via AltaVista's proximity search).

Recent work by Gildea and Jurafsky [32] illustrates the use of mappings from FrameNet's fine-grained relations to coarse-grained ones more commonly used in computational linguistics. This suggests a method for converting annotations from one lexical resource to another. Future work will pursue this with Factotum and other knowledge bases such as OpenCyc. We will also investigate more fully the inference of relation markers for foreign languages (e.g., via proximity searches of the source and target terms from the translated semantic network produced by Gelbukh's technique [35]).

References

1. Miller, G.: Special issue on WordNet. International Journal of Lexicography **3(4)** (1990)
2. Manning, C.D., Schütze, H.: Foundations of Statistical Natural Language Processing. MIT Press, Cambridge, Massachusetts (1999)

---

[13] The adjective hierarchy is augmented by treating *is-similar-to* as *has-hypernym*. Adverbs would be included, but there is no hierarchy for them. Adverbs are related to adjectives via *is-derived-from*, so future work might treat these as *has-hypernym*.

3. Landau, S.: Dictionaries: The Art and Craft of Lexicography. Second edn. Cambridge University Press, Cambridge (2001)
4. Cassidy, P.J.: An investigation of the semantic relations in the Roget's Thesaurus: Preliminary results. In: Proc. CICLing '00. (2000)
5. Lenat, D.B.: Cyc: A large-scale investment in knowledge infrastructure. Communications of the ACM **38(11)** (1995)
6. Tversky, A.: Features of similarity. Psychological Review **84(4)** (1977) 327–352
7. Gati, I., Tversky, A.: Weighting common and distinctive features in perceptual and conceptual judgements. Cognitive Psychology **16** (1984) 341–370
8. Medin, D.L., Goldstone, R.L., Gentner, D.: Respects for similarity. Psychological Review **100** (1993) 252–278
9. Mahesh, K., Nirenburg, S.: A situated ontology for practical NLP. In: Proc. Workshop on Basic Ontological Issues in Knowledge Sharing. (1995) International Joint Conference on Artificial Intelligence (IJCAI-95), Aug. 19-20, 1995. Montreal, Canada.
10. Cruse, D.A.: Lexical Semantics. Cambridge University Press, Cambridge (1986)
11. Onyshkevych, B., Nirenburg, S.: A lexicon for knowledge-based MT. Machine Translation **10(2)** (1995) 5–57 Special Issue on Building Lexicons for MT.
12. Hirst, G.: Why dictionaries should list case structures. In: Proc. Conference on Advances in Lexicography. (1986) University of Waterloo, November.
13. Pustejovsky, J.: The Generative Lexicon. MIT Press, Cambridge, MA (1995)
14. Mel'čuk, I.A., Polguere, A.: A formal lexicon in the meaning-text theory (or how to do lexica with words). Computational Linguistics **13 (3-4)** (1987) 261–275
15. Heylen, D.: Lexical functions, generative lexicons and the world. In Saint-Dizier, P., Viegas, E., eds.: Computational Lexical Semantics. Cambridge University Press, Cambridge (1995) 125–140
16. Marcus, M., Kim, G., Marcinkiewicz, M.A., MacIntyre, R., Bies, A., Ferguson, M., Katz, K., Schasberger, B.: The Penn Treebank: Annotating predicate argument structure. In: ARPA Human Language Technology Workshop. (1994)
17. Fillmore, C.J., Wooters, C., Baker, C.F.: Building a large lexical databank which provides deep semantics. In: Proceedings of the Pacific Asian Conference on Language, Information and Computation. (2001) Hong Kong.
18. Sidorov, G., Bolshakov, I., Cassidy, P., Galicia-Haro, S., Gelbukh, A.: 'Non-adult' semantic field: comparative analysis for English, Spanish, and Russian. In: Proc. 3rd Tbilisi Symposium on Language, Logic, and Computation. (1999)
19. Kilgarriff, A., Palmer, M.: Introduction to the special issue on SENSEVAL. In *Computers and the Humanities* [36] 15–48
20. Edmonds, P., Cotton, S., eds.: Proceedings of the SENSEVAL 2 Workshop. Association for Computational Linguistics (2001)
21. O'Hara, T., Wiebe, J., Bruce, R.F.: Selecting decomposable models for word-sense disambiguation: The grling-sdm system. In *Computers and the Humanities* [36] 159–164
22. Wiebe, J., McKeever, K., Bruce, R.: Mapping collocational properties into machine learning features. In: Proc. 6th Workshop on Very Large Corpora (WVLC-98), Montreal, Quebec, Canada, Association for Computational Linguistics SIGDAT (August 1998) 225–233
23. Witten, I.H., Frank, E.: Data Mining: Practical Machine Learning Tools and Techniques with Java Implementations. Morgan Kaufmann (1999)
24. Kilgarriff, A., Rosenzweig, J.: Framework and results for English SENSEVAL. In *Computers and the Humanities* [36] 15–48

25. Litkowski, K.C.: Digraph analysis of dictionary preposition definitions. In: Proceedings of the Association for Computational Linguistics Special Interest Group on the Lexicon. (2002) July 11, Philadelphia, PA.
26. Srihari, R., Niu, C., Li, W.: A hybrid approach for named entity and sub-type tagging. In: Proc. 6th Applied Natural Language Processing Conference. (2001)
27. Gildea, D., Jurafsky, D.: Automatic labeling of semantic roles. In: Proc. ACL-00. (2000)
28. Blaheta, D., Charniak, E.: Assigning function tags to parsed text. In: Proc. NAACL-00. (2000)
29. O'Hara, T., Wiebe, J.: Classifying preposition semantic roles using class-based lexical associations. Technical Report NMSU-CS-2002-013, Computer Science Department, New Mexico State University (2002)
30. Dini, L., Tomaso, V.D., Segond, F.: Word sense disambiguation with functional relations. In: Proc. First International Conference on Language Resources and Evaluation (LREC). (1998) 28–30 May 1998, Granada, Spain.
31. Scott, S., Matwin, S.: Text classification using WordNet hypernyms. In Harabagiu, S., ed.: Use of WordNet in Natural Language Processing Systems: Proceedings of the Conference, Somerset, New Jersey, Association for Computational Linguistics (1998) 38–44
32. Gildea, D., Jurafsky, D.: Automatic labeling of semantic roles. Computational Linguistics **28(3)** (2002) 245–288
33. Bolshakov, I., Cassidy, P., Gelbukh, A.: Russian Roget: Parallel Russian and English hierarchical thesauri with semantic links, based on an enriched Roget's Thesaurus. In: Proc. Annual International Conf. on Applied Linguistics Dialogue-95, Moscow, Russia (1995) 57–60
34. Gelbukh, A.F.: Using a semantic network for lexical and syntactical disambiguation. In: Proc. CIC-97, Nuevas Aplicaciones e Innovaciones Tecnológicas en Computación. (1997) 352–366 Simposium Internacional de Computación, CIC, IPN, Mexico City, Mexico.
35. Gelbukh, A.F.: Using a semantic network dictionary in some tasks of disambiguation and translation. Technical report, CIC, IPN, Mexico (1998) Serie Roja, N 36.
36. Kilgarriff, A., Palmer, M., eds.: Computers and the Humanities: Special Issue on SENSEVAL. Volume 34 (1–2). Kluwer Academic Publishers, Dordrecht, The Netherlands (2000)

Processing Natural Language without Natural Language Processing

Eric Brill

Microsoft Research
One Microsoft Way
Redmond, Wa. 98052
brill@microsoft.com

Abstract. We can still create computer programs displaying only the most rudimentary natural language processing capabilities. One of the greatest barriers to advanced natural language processing is our inability to overcome the linguistic knowledge acquisition bottleneck. In this paper, we describe recent work in a number of areas, including grammar checker development, automatic question answering, and language modeling, where state of the art accuracy is achieved using very simple methods whose power comes entirely from the plethora of text currently available to these systems, as opposed to deep linguistic analysis or the application of state of the art machine learning techniques. This suggests that the field of NLP might benefit by concentrating less on technology development and more on data acquisition.

1 Introduction

Despite decades of research and development, we can still only create machines with the most rudimentary natural language processing capabilities. One of the greatest barriers to advanced natural language processing is our inability to overcome the linguistic knowledge acquisition bottleneck. It turns out that building a robust, scalable NLP system is vastly more difficult than would appear at first blush. Language is complex and highly idiosyncratic, or, in the words of Edward Sapir: "Unfortunately, or luckily, no language is tyrannically consistent. All grammars leak." [11] Over the years, there has been an ongoing debate as to how best to improve NLP systems: via better linguistics or more powerful machine learning, or perhaps some hybrid of the two. During this time, the amount of on-line text has ballooned from the ubiquitous million-word Brown corpus and few million-word Penn Treebank to close to a trillion words currently accessible on the Web. We believe this huge increase in available text has huge implications for the debate on how best to proceed toward our goal of building machines with sophisticated language processing abilities.

Much of the challenge NLP is faced with involves generalizing from the finite to the infinite. Given a finite set of training instances for a learning algorithm or a set of development instances for creating a hand-crafted system, we attempt to generalize to cover the infinite set of instances the system could potentially encounter. From an engineering perspective, the importance of generalization is proportional to the

A. Gelbukh (Ed.): CICLing 2003, LNCS 2588, pp. 360–369, 2003.
© Springer-Verlag Berlin Heidelberg 2003

percentage of strings the system will encounter that did not appear in the original training set. At one extreme, if the training set is complete, i.e. it contains all strings the system will encounter, then there is no need for generalization; we can simply hard code the behavior for each such string. However, if our training set only covers a small percentage of future instances then performance will be abysmal without proper string generalization.

It has long been a tenet of natural language processing that the first step in any NLP pipeline is for the system to first syntactically annotate a string (e.g. with morphological analysis, parts of speech, named entity labels, syntactic structure) and then possibly also semantically label the string (e.g. with lexical meaning, logical form). This, in part, serves the purpose of string generalization. A system can operate on the generalized annotated string, thereby attaining better coverage than would be possible without these linguistic preprocessing steps. Although many linguistic generalization components have been developed, they still have not brought with them the level of generalization necessary for a computer to perform advanced natural language processing.

In this paper, we suggest that in the end, true progress might very well come not from the traditional areas investigated by our field, but rather simply by employing simple techniques over the vast text collections now readily available (and preparing relevant text collections where none currently exist). We discuss some recent work that suggests that concentrating our efforts on data acquisition rather than linguistic technology advancement might be the most fruitful path to follow.

2   Confusion Set Disambiguation[1]

The amount of readily available on-line text has reached hundreds of billions of words and continues to grow. Yet for most core natural language tasks, algorithms continue to be optimized, tested and compared after training on corpora consisting of only one million words or less. We evaluated the performance of different learning methods on a prototypical natural language disambiguation task, confusion set disambiguation, when trained on orders of magnitude more labeled data than has previously been used.

Confusion set disambiguation is the problem of choosing the correct use of a word, given a set of words with which it is commonly confused. Example confusion sets include: {principle, principal}, {then, than}, {to, two, too}, and {weather, whether}. Numerous methods have been presented for confusion set disambiguation. The more recent set of techniques includes multiplicative weight-update algorithms [5], latent semantic analysis [7], transformation-based learning [10], decision lists [12], and a variety of Bayesian classifiers (e.g. [6]). In all of these approaches, the problem is formulated as follows: Given a specific confusion set (e.g. {to, two, too}), all occurrences of confusion set members in the test set are replaced by a marker; everywhere the system sees this marker, it must decide which member of the confusion set to choose.

Confusion set disambiguation is one of a large class of much studied natural language problems involving disambiguation from a relatively small set of

---

[1] The work described here originally appeared in [1].

alternatives based upon the string context in which the ambiguity site appears. Other such problems include word sense disambiguation, part of speech tagging and some formulations of phrasal chunking. One advantageous aspect of confusion set disambiguation, which allows us to study the effects of large data sets on performance, is that labeled training data is essentially free, since the correct answer is surface apparent in any collection of reasonably well-edited text.

2.1   Learning Curve Experiments for Confusion Set Disambiguation

This work was partially motivated by the desire to develop an improved grammar checker. Given a fixed amount of time, we considered what would be the most effective way to focus our efforts in order to attain the greatest performance improvement. Some possibilities included modifying standard learning algorithms, exploring new learning techniques, and using more sophisticated features. Before exploring these somewhat expensive paths, we decided to first see what happened if we simply trained an existing method with much more data. We generated learning curves for various machine learning algorithms: winnow, perceptron, naïve Bayes, and a very simple memory-based learner. For the first three learners, we used the standard collection of features employed for this problem: the set of words within a window of the target word, and collocations containing words and/or parts of speech. The memory-based learner used only the word before and word after as features.

We collected a 1-billion-word training corpus from a variety of English texts, including news articles, scientific abstracts, government transcripts, literature and other varied forms of prose. This training corpus is three orders of magnitude greater than the largest training corpus previously used for this problem. We used 1 million words of Wall Street Journal text as our test set, and no data from the Wall Street Journal was used when constructing the training corpus. Each learner was trained at several cutoff points in the training corpus, i.e. the first one million words, the first five million words, and so on, until all one billion words were used for training. In order to avoid training biases that may result from merely concatenating the different data sources to form a larger training corpus, we constructed each consecutive training corpus by probabilistically sampling sentences from the different sources weighted by the size of each source.

In Figure 1, we show learning curves for each learner, up to one billion words of training data. Each point in the graph is the average performance over ten confusion sets for that size training corpus. Note that the curves appear to be log-linear even out to one billion words. These results suggest that natural language technologists may want to carefully consider the trade-off between spending time and money on algorithm development versus spending it on corpus development. At least for the problem of confusion set disambiguation, none of the learners tested is close to asymptoting in performance at the one million word training corpus size commonly employed by the field. Note also that the relative differences in performance between learning algorithms trained on a million words is dwarfed by the improvement to all systems when trained on orders of magnitude additional data. This draws to question the utility of the sort of incremental improvements in accuracy on a fixed (typically very small) training corpus that currently account for a large percentage of NLP research.

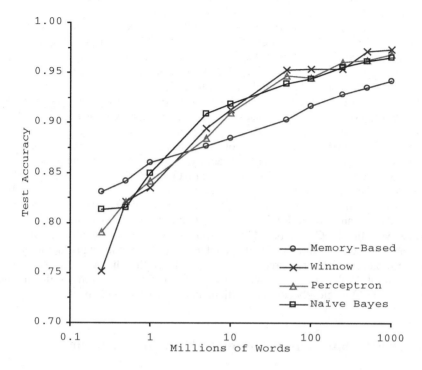

Fig. 1. Learning Curves for Confusion Set Disambiguation

3 Lexical Probabilities and Language Modeling

Another core natural language task is the problem of language modeling – predicting the next word given the history of previous words. An ngram model estimates the probability of a word wi given the history as $P(w_i \mid w_{i-1} .. w_{i-n-1})$. On the surface, this seems like a terribly inadequate model, and one would assume that success at this task would require deep linguistic analysis. Despite the obvious weaknesses, the ngram language model has proven to be extremely effective for speech recognition. There are two major problems with these models: (1) representational inadequacies and (2) insufficient training data for probability estimates. The first problem cannot readily be solved. For the second, again a problem of string generalization, could big gains come again simply by throwing more data at the problem, or is this a case where true linguistic generalization is necessary? Two recent papers address this issue.

In [13], Zhu and Rosenfeld use the World Wide Web as a large corpus from which they can extract trigram probabilities to augment a domain-specific language model trained on a much smaller corpus. Using a search engine that returns frequency counts for a query, one can estimate $P_{web}(w_3 \mid w_1, w_2)$ (the probability of w_3 following

w_1, w_2 in text on the Web) by querying the search engine with the two queries "w_1 w_2 w_3" and "w_1 w_2" and computing $P_{web}(w_3 \mid w_1, w_2) = count(w_1 w_2 w_3)/count(w_1 w_2)$.

Zhu and Rosenfeld used the 103 million word Broadcast News corpus to build their original language model. They found that about 40% of the trigrams that appeared in their test set were not present in their training corpus, whereas only 10% of the trigrams were not present on the searchable Web (which they estimate at the time of their experiments to be approximately 100 billion words). They were able to obtain a significant decrease in speech recognition word error rate using a language model created by interpolating the Broadcast News language model with that from the Web, compared to using the Broadcast News language model alone.

Keller et al. [8] looked at a similar problem. They studied to what extent the Web could be used to get reliable bigram probability estimates for noun-noun, adjective-noun and verb-object bigrams. They observed that their Web-obtained bigram counts were on the order of 759 to 977 times greater than those obtained using the 100 million word British National Corpus (BNC). Since Web data is very noisy and unbalanced compared to the BNC, they next studied to what extent the Web counts correlate with the BNC counts. They found a very high correlation coefficient, indicating that the vast amount of text available on the Web outweighs the noisy and unbalanced nature of this resource. As further evidence that the Web-derived counts are meaningful, Keller et al. demonstrate that, for adjective-noun bigrams, the bigram counts from the Web closely correlate with human plausibility judgments.

4   AskMSR: Data-Driven Automatic Question Answering[2]

The goal of a question answering system is to retrieve 'answers' to questions rather than full documents or even best-matching passages as most information retrieval systems currently do. The TREC Question Answering Track which has motivated much of the recent work in the field focuses on fact-based, short-answer questions such as *"Who killed Abraham Lincoln?"* or *"How tall is Mount Everest?"*

We have developed a question answering system, AskMSR. The design of our question answering system is again motivated by the idea that significant improvements in accuracy can be attained simply by increasing the amount of data used for learning. Following the same guiding principle we take advantage of the tremendous data resource that the Web provides as the backbone of our question answering system. Many groups working on question answering have used a variety of linguistic resources – part-of-speech tagging, parsing, named entity extraction, semantic relations, dictionaries, WordNet, etc. We chose instead to focus on the Web as gigantic data repository with tremendous redundancy that can be exploited for question answering. The Web, which is home to billions of pages of electronic text, is orders of magnitude larger than the TREC QA document collection, which consists of fewer than 1 million documents. This is a resource that can be usefully exploited for question answering. We view our approach as complimentary to more linguistic approaches, but have chosen to see how far we can get initially by focusing on data per se as a key resource available to drive our system design.

---

[2] The work described here originally appeared in [4].

Automatic QA from a single, small information source is extremely challenging, again because of the difficulty of accurate string generalization. Since there is likely to be only one answer in the source to any user's question, a system has to adequately generalize across a large number of potential answer surface realizations in order to effectively identify the answer to a question. Given a source, such as the TREC corpus, that contains only a relatively small number of formulations of answers to a query, we may be faced with the difficult task of mapping questions to answers by way of uncovering complex lexical, syntactic, or semantic relationships between question string and answer string. The need for anaphor resolution and synonymy, the presence of alternate syntactic formulations and indirect answers all make answer finding a potentially challenging task. However, the greater the answer redundancy in the source data collection, the more likely it is that we can find an answer that occurs in a simple relation to the question. Therefore, the less likely it is that we will need to resort to solving the aforementioned difficulties facing natural language processing systems.[3]

4.1 Utilizing Data Redundancy in Automatic Question Answering

We take advantage of the redundancy (multiple, differently phrased, answer occurrences) available when considering massive amounts of data in two key ways in our system.

Enables Simple Query Rewrites. The greater the number of information sources we can draw from, the easier the task of rewriting the question becomes, since the answer is more likely to be expressed in different manners. For example, consider the difficulty of gleaning an answer to the question *"Who killed Abraham Lincoln?"* from a source which contains only the text *"John Wilkes Booth altered history with a bullet. He will forever be known as the man who ended Abraham Lincoln's life,"* versus a source that also contains the transparent answer string, *"John Wilkes Booth killed Abraham Lincoln."*

Facilitates Answer Mining. Even when no obvious answer strings can be found in the text, redundancy can improve the efficacy of question answering. For instance, consider the question: *"How many times did Bjorn Borg win Wimbledon?"* Assume the system is unable to find any obvious answer strings, but does find the following sentences containing "Bjorn Borg" and "Wimbledon", as well as a number:

(1) ***Bjorn Borg*** *blah blah* ***Wimbledon*** *blah blah* **5** *blah*
(2) ***Wimbledon*** *blah blah blah* ***Bjorn Borg*** *blah* **37** *blah.*
(3) *blah* ***Bjorn Borg*** *blah blah* **5** *blah blah* ***Wimbledon***
(4) **5** *blah blah* ***Wimbledon*** *blah blah* ***Bjorn Borg***.

By virtue of the fact that the most frequent number in these sentences is 5, we can posit that as the most likely answer.

---

[3] For other examples of systems that capitalize on answer redundancy to improve performance, see [3, 9].

4.2 AskMSR System Architecture

The architecture of our system can be described by four main steps: query-reformulation, n-gram mining, filtering, and n-gram tiling. In the remainder of this section, we will briefly describe these components (see Figure 2).

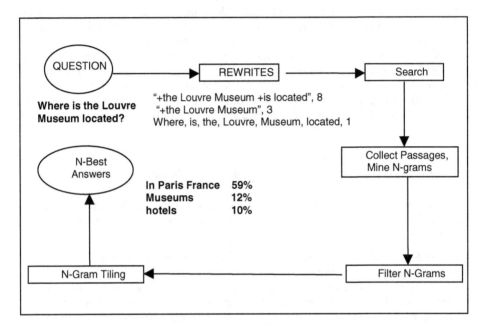

Fig. 2. Overview of the AskMSR Question-Answering System

4.2.1 Query Reformulation

Given a question, the system generates a number of weighted rewrite strings which are likely substrings of declarative answers to the question. For example, *"When was the paper clip invented?"* is rewritten as *"The paper clip was invented"*. We then look through the collection of documents in search of such patterns. Since many of these string rewrites will result in no matching documents, we also produce less precise rewrites that have a much greater chance of finding matches. For each query, we generate a rewrite which is a backoff to a simple ANDing of all of the non-stop words in the query.

The rewrites generated by our system are simple string-based manipulations. We do not use a parser or part-of-speech tagger for query reformulation, but do use a lexicon for a small percentage of rewrites, in order to determine the possible parts-of-speech of a word as well as its morphological variants. Although we created the rewrite rules and associated weights manually for the current system, it may be possible to learn query-to-answer reformulations and their weights.

4.2.2 N-Gram Mining

Once the set of query reformulations has been generated, each rewrite is formulated as a search engine query and sent to a search engine from which page summaries are collected and analyzed. From the page summaries returned by the search engine, n-grams are collected as possible answers to the question. For reasons of efficiency, we use only the page summaries returned by the engine and not the full-text of the corresponding web page.

The returned summaries contain the query terms, usually with a few words of surrounding context. The summary text is processed in accordance with the patterns specified by the rewrites. Unigrams, bigrams and trigrams are extracted and subsequently scored according to the weight of the query rewrite that retrieved it. These scores are summed across all summaries containing the n-gram (which is the opposite of the usual inverse document frequency component of document/passage ranking schemes). We do not count frequency of occurrence within a summary (the usual tf component in ranking schemes). Thus, the final score for an n-gram is based on the weights associated with the rewrite rules that generated it and the number of unique summaries in which it occurred.

4.2.3 N-Gram Filtering

Next, the n-grams are filtered and reweighted according to how well each candidate matches the expected answer-type, as specified by a handful of handwritten filters. The system uses filtering in the following manner. First, the query is analyzed and assigned one of seven question types, such as *who-question, what-question,* or *how-many-question*. Based on the query type that has been assigned, the system determines what collection of filters to apply to the set of potential answers found during the collection of n-grams. The candidate n-grams are analyzed for features relevant to the filters, and then rescored according to the presence of such information.

A collection of 15 simple filters were developed based on human knowledge about question types and the domain from which their answers can be drawn. These filters used surface string features, such as capitalization or the presence of digits, and consisted of handcrafted regular expression patterns.

4.2.4 N-Gram Tiling

Finally, we applied an answer tiling algorithm, which both merges similar answers and assembles longer answers from overlapping smaller answer fragments. For example, "A B C" and "B C D" is tiled into "A B C D." The algorithm proceeds greedily from the top-scoring candidate – all subsequent candidates (up to a certain cutoff) are checked to see if they can be tiled with the current candidate answer. If so, the higher scoring candidate is replaced with the longer tiled n-gram, and the lower scoring candidate is removed. The algorithm stops only when no n-grams can be further tiled.

In our experiments with AskMSR, we found that when AskMSR used only the TREC corpus the results were about half as good as those obtained using the entire Web, another example of a huge performance gain coming solely by using orders of magnitude additional data.

5 What If an Annotated Corpus Is Needed?[4]

In the examples presented above, we have demonstrated that big gains are possible on a number of different tasks solely by vastly increasing the size of the training corpus. However, all of these tasks had the property that they could benefit from *unannotated* data. There are many tasks for which annotated data is necessary. Is it feasible to think of, for instance, ever having a billion-word Treebank to use as training material for tagging, parsing, named entity recognition, and other applications? Perhaps not, but let us run through some numbers.

To be concrete, assume we want a billion words annotated with part of speech tags at the same level of accuracy as the original million word corpus.[5] If we train a tagger on the existing corpus, the naïve approach would be to have a person look at every single tag in the corpus, decide whether it is correct, and make a change if it is not. In the extreme, this means somebody has to look at one billion tags. Assume our automatic tagger has an accuracy of 95% and that with reasonable tools, a person can verify at the rate of 5 seconds per tag and correct at the rate of 15 seconds per tag. This works out to an average of $5*.95 + 15*.05 = 5.5$ seconds spent per tag, for a total of 1.5 million hours to tag a billion words. Assuming the human tagger incurs a cost of \$10/hour, and assuming the annotation takes place after startup costs due to development of an annotation system have been accounted for, we are faced with \$15 million in labor costs. Given the cost and labor requirements, this clearly is not feasible. But now assume that we could do perfect error identification, using sample selection techniques. In other words, we could first run a tagger over the billion-word corpus and using sample selection, identify all and only the errors made by the tagger. If the tagger is 95% accurate, we now only have to examine 5% of the corpus, at a correction cost of 15 seconds per tag. This would reduce the labor cost to \$2 million for tagging a billion words. Next, assume we had a way of clustering errors such that correcting one tag on average had the effect of correcting 10. This reduces the total labor cost to \$200k to annotate a billion words, or \$20k to annotate 100 million. Suppose we are off by an order of magnitude; then with the proper technology in place it might cost \$200k in labor to annotate 100 million additional words.

As a result of the hypothetical analysis above, it is not absolutely infeasible to think about manually annotating significantly larger corpora. Given the clear benefit of additional annotated data, we should think seriously about developing tools and algorithms that would allow us to efficiently annotate orders of magnitude more data than what is currently available.

6 Conclusions

In this paper, we have shown that great improvements in accuracy can be attained at a number of natural language tasks solely by increasing the amount of training data used. Most NLP systems are currently derived from relatively small training corpora.

---

[4] This discussion is taken from [2].

[5] We assume an annotated corpus such as the Penn Treebank already exists, and our task is to significantly grow it. Therefore, we are only taking into account the marginal cost of additional annotated data, not start-up costs such as style manual design.

The fact that huge gains are possible from large increases in training data size, and that we now have access to vast amounts of on-line text, suggests that it might make sense for the community to put a much greater emphasis on obtaining significantly larger training corpora, and developing the tools that will allow us to effectively access, annotate and make optimal use of such a resource.

References

1. Banko, M. and Brill, E. Scaling to Very Very Large Corpora for Natural Language Disambiguation. Proceedings of the Association for Computational Linguistics, 2001.
2. Banko, M. and Brill, E. Mitigating the Paucity-of-Data Problem: Exploring the Effect of Training Corpus Size on Classifier Performance for Natural Language Processing. Human Language Technologies Conference, 2001.
3. C. Clarke, G. Cormack and T. Lyman. Exploiting redundancy in question answering. In *Proceedings of SIGIR'2001*.
4. Dumais, S., Banko, M., Brill, E., Lin, J. and Ng, A. Web question answering: is more always better? In *Proceedings of SIGIR 2002*.
5. Golding, A.R. and Roth, D. A Winnow-Based Approach to Context-Sensitive Spelling Correction. Machine Learning, 34:107–130.
6. Golding, A.R. and Schabes, Y. Combining trigram-based and feature-based methods for context-sensitive spelling correction. In Proc. 34th Annual Meeting of the Association for Computatoin Lingusitcs. Santa,Cruz, Ca.
7. Jones, M. P. and Martin, J. H. Contextual spelling correction using latent semantic analysis.
8. Keller, F., Lapata, M. Ourioupina, O. Using the Web to Overcome Data Sparseness. In Proceedings of the Conference on Empirical Methods in Natural Langauge Processing.
9. Kwok, C., Etzioni, O. and Weld, D. (2001). Scaling question answering to the Web. In *Proceedings of WWW'10*.
10. Mangu, L and Brill, E. Automatic rule acquisition for spelling correction. In Proc. 14th International Conference on Machine Learing. Morgan Kaufmann.
11. Sapir, E. Language: An Introduction to the Study of Speech. 1921.
12. Yarowsky, D. Decision lists for lexical ambiguity resolution: Application to accent restoration in Spanish and French. In Proc. 32nd Annual Meeting of the Association for Computational Linguistics, Las Cruces, NM.
13. Zhu, X. and Rosenfeld, R.. *Improving Trigram Language Modeling with the World Wide Web*. In proceedings of International Conference on Acoustics, Speech, and Signal Processing, 2001.

The Design, Implementation, and Use of the Ngram Statistics Package

Satanjeev Banerjee[1] and Ted Pedersen[2]

[1] Carnegie Mellon University, Pittsburgh, PA 15213 USA
[2] University of Minnesota, Duluth, MN 55812 USA
`http://www.d.umn.edu/~tpederse/nsp.html`

Abstract. The Ngram Statistics Package (NSP) is a flexible and easy–to–use software tool that supports the identification and analysis of Ngrams, sequences of N tokens in online text. We have designed and implemented NSP to be easy to customize to particular problems and yet remain general enough to serve a broad range of needs. This paper provides an introduction to NSP while raising some general issues in Ngram analysis, and summarizes several applications where NSP has been successfully employed. NSP is written in Perl and is freely available under the GNU Public License.

1 Introduction

A simple model of written text is as a series of symbols that carry some meaning when considered as a whole. We may wish to treat those symbols as phrases, words, or characters depending on our motivations. Ngrams are a simple representation that suits this view of written language. An Ngram is a sequence of N units, or tokens, of text, where those units are typically single characters or strings that are delimited by spaces. However, a token could also be a fixed length character sequence, strings with embedded spaces, etc. depending on the intended application.

The identification of Ngrams that are interesting in some way is a fundamental task in natural language processing. An Ngram might be considered interesting if it occurs more often than would be expected by chance, or has some tendency to predict the occurrence of other phenomena in text. There is a long history of research in this area. Character Ngrams were used by Shannon [10] to estimate the per–letter entropy of the English language. In the last decade there has been a large amount of work in developing corpus–based techniques to identify collocations in text (e.g., [2], [3], [6], [9]).

This paper describes the Ngram Statistics Package (NSP), a general purpose software tool that allows users to define Ngrams as they wish and then utilize standard methods from statistics and information theory to identify interesting or significant instances of Ngrams in large corpora of text.

Earlier versions of this package were known as the Bigram Statistics Package (BSP). This was first released in November 2000 (v0.1) and was limited to dealing

A. Gelbukh (Ed.): CICLing 2003, LNCS 2588, pp. 370–381, 2003.
© Springer-Verlag Berlin Heidelberg 2003

with two word sequences (bigrams). In June 2001 BSP became NSP (v0.5) and was extended to handle Ngrams. As of this writing NSP is at v0.51 and remains an active project, with future releases planned.

What follows is a summary of NSP designed to acquaint a potential user with a few of the many features of the package. We also review general issues of Ngram processing, and briefly discuss research that has incorporated NSP.

2   Tokenization of Text

The typical first step of any natural language processing application is tokenization. The symbols that make up a text file are divided into tokens which represent the smallest indivisible units in that text. Tokens are often defined to be space delimited alphanumeric strings or individual ASCII characters, but could take many other forms depending on the application.

NSP is designed to allow the user to define tokens through the use of Perl regular expressions. In particular we define a token as a contiguous sequence of characters that match one of a set of regular expressions. These may be user-provided (via the --token option) and must be Perl regular expressions. If the user does not provide a token definition, the following two regular expressions provide a default, where the backslashes delimit a Perl regular expression:

/\w+/ → a contiguous sequence of alpha–numeric characters
/[\.,;:\?!]/ → a single punctuation mark

This default says that a token is either an alpha–numeric character string or an individual punctuation mark. Thus in President George W. Bush visits with guests the tokens are: President<>, George<>, W<>, .<>, Bush<>, visits<>, with<>, and guests<>.

In our notation tokens are terminated by the meta–character <>, and Ngrams composed of N tokens are represented by concatenating the <> terminated tokens one after another. Such a representation is required since tokens may include embedded spaces and using white space as a delimiter isn't possible. For example, George W. Bush<> represents a single token that starts with G, ends with h and includes two embedded spaces. This token could then be paired with another to create a bigram, as in President<>George W. Bush<>.

The NSP default definition of a token as a string of alphanumerics or a single punctuation mark may not be suitable in all cases. For example, we may not want to treat George<>, W.<>, and Bush<> as three separate tokens but as one, since they represent a single entity known as George W. Bush<>. On the other hand, in Welcome ⬚rst⬚time home buyers! should the string ⬚rst⬚ time be two tokens or one? Further, do we wish to distinguish between ⬚rst⬚ time and ⬚rst time? What about punctuation marks; should they be a part of the previous word, a token by themselves or should they be ignored? Similarly, there are various choices to be made in dealing with numbers, symbols, dates, abbreviations, etc. The lack of a universally appropriate definition for tokens motivates our desire to support a very flexible notion of tokenization in NSP.

Tokenization in NSP is done via the program `count.pl`. It converts the input file into one long string by replacing new–line characters with spaces. This string is then matched against the user–provided regular expressions (or the system defaults). Every regular expression specified is checked (in order) to see if any of them match the string starting with the first character of the input string. If none match, then the first character of the input string is considered a non token and is removed and henceforth ignored. Otherwise the matching process stops at the first regular expression that yields a match. The longest sequence of characters (starting with the first character of the input string) that matches this regular expression is then identified as the next token and removed from the string. This process continues until the entire string has been matched and all the text identified as either tokens or not.

For example, assume that the following two regular expressions are being used to define tokens: /George W. Bush/, /\w+/. That is, the string George W. Bush<> will be considered a token, and so will every other unbroken sequence of alpha numeric characters. Thus, given the sentence President George W. Bush visits with guests the output tokens are President<>, George W. Bush<>, visits<>, with<> and guests<>. Note that after President<> has been recognized as a token and removed, the resulting string George W. Bush visits with guests is matched by both regular expressions. However since regular expression are checked in the order in which they are provided, and the matching process stops at the first successful match, the resulting token is George W. Bush<> instead of just George<>. Thus the ordering of regular expressions in the token definition imposes a sort of priority, and it should be clear to a user that different orderings of a set of regular expressions can result in different tokenizations.

3   From Tokens to Ngrams

Once tokens are identified, `count.pl` assembles sequences of N tokens into Ngrams. Typically Ngrams are formed of contiguous tokens, that is tokens that occur one after another in the input corpus. Given President George W. Bush visits with guests and the token definition regular expression /\w+/, the possible bigrams (Ngrams with N = 2) are: President<>George<>, George<>W<>, W<>Bush<>, Bush<> visits<>, visits<>with<>, and with<>guests<>. Similarly, the possible trigrams (Ngrams with N =3) are: President<>George <>W<>, George<>W<>Bush<>, W<>Bush<>visits<>, Bush<>visits <>with<>, and visits<>with<>guests<>.

It may also be necessary to identify Ngrams from non contiguous tokens, that is tokens separated by some number of intermediate tokens. For example, given the text President George W. Bush, it may be advantageous to identify the bigrams President<>Bush<> and George<>Bush<> and the trigram President<>George<>Bush<> in addition to the sequential bigrams described above. This is useful when one wants to report having observed the bigram

George<>Bush<> even when those two tokens are separated by the intervening token W<>.

To allow Ngrams to be formed from non–contiguous tokens, count.pl provides a --window option. This defines a window of k contiguous tokens, where the value of k is greater than or equal to the value of N. An Ngram can be formed from any N tokens as long as all the tokens belong to a single window of size k. Further the N tokens in the Ngram must occur in exactly the same order as they do in the original window of text.

Thus given a window size of k and an Ngram size of N, we have ^kC_N (k choose N) Ngrams per window. For example, consider again the text President George W. Bush visits with guests The following are all the possible bigrams for a window size of 3: President<>George<>, President<>W<>, George<>W<>, George<>Bush<>, W<>Bush<>, W<>visits<>, Bush<> visits<>, Bush<>with<>, visits<>with<>, visits<>guests<>, and with <>guests<>.

4   Counting Ngram Frequencies

Having tokenized a given corpus of text and from that constructed Ngrams, the program count.pl counts the number of times each Ngram occurs in the corpus. It outputs the frequency of each unique Ngram, as well as the frequencies of the various combinations of tokens that make up the Ngram.

4.1   Counting Bigrams

Suppose NSP is counting two token sequences of alphanumeric strings. The output of count.pl consists of a count of the total number of bigrams in the corpus, followed by a list of all the unique bigrams and their associated frequency counts. Here we show a small example, which just shows a single bigram and its counts:

1,319,237
George<>Bush<>27 134 463

The value 1,319,237 is the number of bigrams found in the corpus, and can be thought of as the sample size. Note that this is not a count of the unique bigrams but rather the total number of bigrams without regard to repetition. The next line represents the bigram George<>Bush<> and shows that the bigram itself has occurred 27 times in the corpus. Further, the token George<> has occurred as the "left hand" token in 134 bigrams in the corpus, which includes the 27 instances of the bigram George<>Bush<> itself. Similarly the token Bush<> has occurred as the "right hand" token in 463 bigrams, 27 of which are George<>Bush<>.

The format of the count.pl output is a compact representation of a typical two–by–two contingency table. For example in Table 1, the four internal cells

Table 1. Contingency table for *George<>Bush<>*

	Bush	!Bush	
George	27	107	134
!George	436	1,318,667	1,319,103
	463	1,318,774	1,319,237

categorize the 1,319,237 bigrams in the corpus into four disjoint sets: 27 instances
of the bigram George<>Bush<>, 436 bigrams that have Bush<> as the second
token and do not have George<> as the first token, 107 bigrams that have
George<> as the first token and do not have Bush<> as the second token, and
the remaining 1,318,667 bigrams that have neither George<> as the first token
nor Bush<> as the second token.

Observe that the rest of the contingency table can be reconstructed from
the internal cell count 27, the marginal frequencies 134 and 463, and the sample
size of 1,319,237. Note that the sample size will be the same regardless of which
Ngram from the corpus is under consideration. Thus, this value need only be
represented once in the count.pl output.

4.2   Counting Ngrams

Although counting bigrams is the default behavior of program count.pl, the
user can set the value of N through the option --ngram. For trigrams and longer
Ngrams, frequency values of various combinations of tokens are also computed.
For example consider the following output after creating and counting trigrams:

1,316,737
President<>George<>Bush<>2 338 134 463 3 2 27

The sample size is 1,316,737 and indicates the total number of trigrams in the corpus. The next line gives counts for the trigram President<>George<>Bush<>,
which occurs in the corpus exactly twice. Further, the token President<>
occurs as the first token in 338 trigrams, the token George<> occurs as the
second token in 134 trigrams and the token Bush<> occurs as the third token
in 463 trigrams in the corpus. Finally the tokens President<> and George<>
occur simultaneously as the first and second tokens in 3 trigrams, the tokens
President<> and Bush<> occur as the first and third tokens in 2 trigrams and
the tokens George<> and Bush<> occur as the second and third tokens in 27
trigrams.

This data is represented in Table 2. Here, the 1,316,737 trigrams are broken
up into eight categories depending upon whether they contain or do not contain
the three particular tokens in the three specific positions. Observe that count.pl
only produces the minimum number of frequencies required to reconstruct the
table. This is particularly important as the value of N grows larger.

Table 2. Contingency tables for *President<>George<>Bush<>*

		Bush	!Bush	
President	George	2	1	3
President	!George	0	335	335
!President	George	25	106	131
!President	!George	436	1,315,832	1,316,268
		463	1,316,274	1,316,737

When given an Ngram, count.pl represents its leftmost token as w_0, the next token as w_1, and so on until w_{n-1}. Further let $f(a, b, ..., c)$ be the number of Ngrams that have token w_a in position a, token w_b in position b, ... and token w_c in position c, where $0 <= a < b < ... < c < n$. Then, given an Ngram, the first frequency value reported is $f(0, 1, ..., n - 1)$; this is the frequency of the Ngram itself. This is followed by n frequency values, $f(0)$, $f(1)$, ..., $f(n - 1)$; these are the frequencies of the individual tokens in their specific positions in the given Ngram. This is followed by (n choose 2) values, $f(0, 1)$, $f(0, 2)$, ..., $f(0, n - 1)$, $f(1, 2)$, ..., $f(1, n - 1)$, ... $f(n - 2, n - 1)$. This is followed by (n choose 3) values, $f(0, 1, 2)$, $f(0, 1, 3)$, ..., $f(0, 1, n-1)$, $f(0, 2, 3)$, ..., $f(0, 2, n-1)$, ..., $f(0, n - 2, n - 1)$, $f(1, 2, 3)$, ..., $f(n - 3, n - 2, n - 1)$. And so on, until (n choose n-1), that is n, frequency values $f(0, 1, ..., n - 2)$, $f(0, 1, ..., n - 3, n - 1)$, $f(0, 1, ..., n - 4, n - 2, n - 1)$, ..., $f(1, 2, ..., n - 1)$.

This gives us a total of 2^{n-1} possible frequency values for Ngrams of size n. We call each such frequency value a frequency combination, since it expresses the number of Ngrams that have a given combination of one or more tokens in one or more specific positions. By default all such combinations are output, exactly in the order shown above. However the total number of frequency values grows exponentially with the value of n, that is the Ngram size under consideration. Since computing, storing and later displaying such a large number of frequency values can be both very resource intensive as well as unnecessary, the package gives the user the capability to specify which frequency combinations he wishes to have computed and displayed. Specifically the user can use the option --set_freq_combo to provide program count.pl with a file containing the inputs to the hypothetical $f()$ function above to specify which frequency combinations she desires to have counted. For example, to compute only the frequencies of the trigrams and those of the three individual tokens in the trigrams (and not of the pairs of tokens), the user can tell the package just to count the following $f()$ functions: $f(0, 1, 2)$, $f(0)$, $f(1)$, and $f(2)$. This will result in the following counts:

President<>George<>Bush<>2 338 134 463

The only difference from the previous example is the fact that the frequency values $f(0, 1)$, $f(0, 2)$ and $f(1, 2)$ are not output. However, there are considerable internal differences as any frequency combinations that are not requested are not counted, thus realizing a considerable savings in computation time and memory utilization for large corpora and larger values of N.

4.3   Ngram Filters

Often it is necessary to filter the entire set of Ngrams and observe only a small subset of all the possible Ngrams in a given input text. For example sometimes Ngrams made up entirely of function words are not interesting and one may wish to stop or ignore them. This package provides two different mechanisms through which to create smaller subsets of Ngrams.

In the first mechanism, the user may use the option `--stop` to pass to program `count.pl` a file containing a list of stop words, and Ngrams that are made up entirely of these words will not be created. For example if the user provides the words the and of as stop words, then given the sentence He is one of the worst kinds, the bigram of<>the<> will not be created. However bigrams one<>of<> and the<>worst<> will continue to be created since they are not made up entirely of stop–words and have at least one word not in the stop list. This stopping technique is particularly useful during the creation of non–contiguous Ngrams when Ngrams composed entirely of function words become more likely.

In the second mechanism, the user may specify a frequency cutoff . Every Ngram that occurs less than some specified number of times can be ignored (option `--remove`), in which case they are excluded from the sample size and do not affect any frequency counts, or they can be counted but simply not displayed (option `--frequency`), in which case they are included in the sample size and affect the various frequencies. The first case assumes that Ngrams that occur less than the cut–off number of times are not significant enough to include in overall counts, while in the second case these low frequency Ngrams affect the overall counts but are not displayed in the `count.pl` output. These are radically different approaches to counting, and both are appropriate under certain circumstances. The user must choose between these cut–off mechanisms with some care so as to avoid unexpected results.

5   Measures of Association for Ngrams

Once a user has identified and counted Ngrams and their components via the `count.pl` program, NSP allows a user to go on and apply various measures of association to that data with the program `statistic.pl`. Such measures judge whether the tokens that make up the Ngram occur together more often than would be expected by chance. If so, then the Ngram may represent a collocation or some other interesting phenomena.

A measure that returns a score that can be assigned statistical significance is referred to more precisely as a test of association. Examples supported in NSP include the log–likelihood ratio, Fisher's exact test, and Pearson's chi–squared test. Measures that do not allow for significance to be assigned to their value include the Dice Coefficient and pointwise Mutual Information. When discussing both kinds of techniques we refer to them generically as measures of association and use the more specific term test of association when appropriate.

5.1 Background

To support measures of association on Ngrams, NSP implicitly defines N random binary variables $W_i, 0 \leq i < N$, where W_i represents the ith token in the Ngram. Each of these variables indicate whether or not a particular token occurs at the given position. For example, the variable W_0 could represent whether or not George<> occurs in the first position of the Ngram.

In Table 1 the first row of the contingency table represents all Ngrams such that $W_0 = $ George<> (it occurs), while the second row represents all Ngrams such that $W_0 \neq$ George<> (it does not occur). Similarly, the first column represents all Ngrams such that $W_1 = $ Bush<> while the second column represents all Ngrams such that $W_1 \neq$ Bush<>.

Tests of association between two random variables typically set up a null hypothesis that holds if the two random variables are independent of each other. A pair of words that fail this test might then be considered to be related or dependent in some way, since they have failed to exhibit statistical independence. Formally speaking, for two words that make up a bigram to be considered independent, we would expect the probability of the two words occurring together to be equal to the product of the probabilities of the two words occurring separately.

For example, if the bigram under consideration is George<>Bush<>, the probability of its occurrence could be represented by $P(W_0, W_1)$. For these two words to be considered independent this joint probability would have to be equal (or nearly so) to the product of the probabilities of the individual words George<> and Bush<>, represented by $P(W_0)$ and $P(W_1)$. Thus, these tests of association are based on the formal definition of statistical independence, i.e., $P(W_0, W_1) = P(W_0)P(W_1)$. To reject the hypothesis of independence, one must find that the value of $P(W_0, W_1)$ that is based on observed frequency counts diverges from the expected values that are based on the hypothesis of independence.

For Ngrams where $N \geq 3$, there are numerous ways to formulate a null hypothesis. With more than 2 random variables, the null hypothesis can capture a wider range of possible models than simple independence. Here we are moving from tests of association into the more general realm of statistical model evaluation. For example, when $N = 3$, one can formulate the null hypothesis that the observed probability of a trigram reflects that the three words are completely independent of one another, or that two of the words are dependent on each other but independent of the third. In these cases the null hypotheses could be formulated as: $P(W_0)P(W_1)P(W_2)$ or $P(W_0, W_1)P(W_2)$ or $P(W_0)P(W_1, W_2)$ or $P(W_1)P(W_0, W_2)$.

Each of these null hypotheses represents a different hypotheses, and the expected values for each could be compared to the observed value of $P(W_0, W_1, W_2)$

to determine how closely the observed values correspond with the expected values. Recall from the previous section that program `count.pl` allows the user to compute all such frequencies through the option `--set_freq_combo`. Thus the package allows the user to create a wide range of null hypotheses particularly as N grows larger.

5.2   Implementation

Given the observed frequencies from `count.pl`, a user can apply a measure of association to determine if the words in an Ngram are somehow related. Although this package implements several measures of association, the primary design goal was to facilitate the quick and easy implementation by the user of their own favorite measures. This is achieved via the program `statistic.pl`, which is the tool designed to process the list of Ngram counts produced by `count.pl` and apply measures of association to that data.

The program `statistic.pl` remains unchanged regardless of the measure of association it is performing. This is achieved by requiring that a measure be implemented as a Perl module that exists as a file separate from the rest of the program and is plugged into `statistic.pl` at run–time. Such a module must follow a set of rules that specify the interface between it and `statistic.pl`. For each Ngram in the corpus, `statistic.pl` passes to the module the size of the corpus and the various frequency values associated with the Ngram. The module is then expected to return a floating point number that expresses the degree to which the tokens that make up the given Ngram are associated with each other. Mechanisms exist for the module to throw exceptions so that `statistic.pl` can exit gracefully.

A module that implements a measure of association must export two functions to `statistic.pl`: `initializeStatistic()` and `calculateStatistic()`. The former is the first function called by `statistic.pl` and is used to pass to the module such information as the Ngram size, the total number of Ngrams in the corpus and a data structure containing the list of frequency combinations associated with each Ngram in this dataset. For every Ngram, `statistic.pl` calls function `calculateStatistic()` and passes to it all the frequency values associated with that Ngram. This function is expected to return a floating point value proportional to the degree of association for the Ngram in question.

Besides these two functions, the user may also implement and export three more functions: `errorCode()`, `errorString()` and `getStatisticName()`. The first two can be used to throw exceptions while the last can be used to return a string containing the name of the measure; if returned, this string is used in the formatted output of the program.

The advantage of this design is that it allows the user to concentrate entirely on the mechanism of the statistical measure without concern to the rest of the infrastructure. For example the processing of the list of Ngrams in the corpus of text, the counting and storage of their frequency values, etc is already taken care of. The author of a new measure need only focus on the measure's inputs, outputs and internal computation.

6   Comparing Ranked Lists of Ngrams

NSP is designed not only to create and analyze Ngrams in a corpus of text, but also to allow the user to study the effect of new measures of association. Section 5 describes how the user can implement a new measure and integrate it into the package. NSP also provides a program `rank.pl` that allows a user to compare two ranked lists of Ngrams and determine how much they differ with respect to each other. Thus if a user introduces a new measure it is possible to determine how much it resembles or differs from some existing ones.

`rank.pl` implements the Spearman's Rank Correlation Coefficient to compare two measures of association. This coefficient measures the correlation between two different rankings of a list of items. Specifically, given a set of Ngrams and their frequencies as observed in a corpus of text, we rank them according to each of the two measures of association, and then compute the correlation between these two different rankings using equation 1.

$$r = 1 - \frac{6 \sum_{i=1}^{i=n} D_i^2}{n(n^2 - 1)} \tag{1}$$

In this equation, n is the total number of unique Ngrams in the corpus, D_i is the difference between the rankings of Ngram i in the two lists and r is the value of the correlation. The value of r ranges from -1 to +1. A value of 0 implies no correlation between the two lists, while values that are further away from 0 imply greater correlation where the sign of the value indicates positive or negative correlation.

7   Applications of the Ngram Statistics Package

The range of applications in which NSP has been utilized reflects the generality with which Ngrams can be employed.

An original motivation for developing NSP was to support the second author's work in word sense disambiguation. He has developed a supervised approach to word sense disambiguation that learns decision trees of bigrams from sense–tagged corpora (e.g., [7], [8]). In this approach a word is disambiguated based on the word bigrams that occur nearby. This approach has proven to be relatively successful and is quite easy to implement, at least in part due to NSP.

The language independence of Ngrams and NSP is demonstrated by several applications with Dutch that identify collocations that involve non–content words. Bouman and Villada [1] use NSP to identify collocational prepositional phrases, while van der Wouden [11] uses it to determine a variety of non–content collocations in Dutch text.

The range of possible applications for Ngrams and NSP is illustrated by the following projects. Zaiu-Inkpen and Hirst [13] extend a database of near–synonyms with information about their collocational behavior. Lopez et. al. [5] use information about word bigrams to take the place of parses when no parse was available in performing word alignment of parallel text. Gill and Oberlander

[4] compare the writing styles of introverts and extroverts by identifying word bigrams used by one group but not the other in written text.

8   Future Work

There are a number of possible enhancements to NSP that will be carried out in the next few years.

Ngrams are counted by storing them in a hash table. This poses no problems for relatively large corpora of a few million tokens, but to process 100 million token corpora a more efficient mechanism must be developed. One possibility would be the use of suffix trees as described by Yanamoto and Church [12].

NSP version 0.51 provides a small number of measures of association that are only implemented for bigrams. We are beginning to implement measures for trigrams and will include those in future releases. In addition, NSP is now geared towards ASCII text. We attempted to incorporate Unicode support as provided in Perl 5.6 but found that it was not yet stable. We are hopeful that this situation will improve with Perl 5.8 and allow NSP to support Unicode.

At present NSP is a stand–alone package that runs from the command line. We plan to implement it as a set of library modules that will allow it to be included in programs and also to take advantage of some of the object oriented features that Perl supports. We also plan to provide a graphical interface with Perl/Tk in addition to the command line support. In conjunction with this we would increase the graphs and charts available to the user for exploring their data.

Acknowledgments. The Ngram Statistics Package was implemented by the first author while he was at the University of Minnesota, Duluth. During 2000-2001 he was supported by a Grant-in-Aid of Research, Artistry and Scholarship from the Office of the Vice President for Research and the Dean of the Graduate school of the University of Minnesota. In 2001-2002 both authors were supported by a National Science Foundation Faculty Early CAREER Development award (#0092784). The first author is currently supported by the National Science Foundation under Grant No. REC–9979894.

Any opinions, findings, conclusions, or recommendations expressed in this publication are those of the authors and do not necessarily reflect the views of the National Science Foundation or the official policies, either expressed or implied, of the sponsors or of the United States Government.

References

1. G. Bouman and B. Villada. Corpus–based acquisition of collocational prepositional phrases. *Computational Linguistics in the Netherlands (CLIN)*, 2002.
2. K. Church and P. Hanks. Word association norms, mutual information and lexicography. In *Proceedings of the 28th Annual Meeting of the Association for Computational Linguistics*, pages 76–83, 1990.

3. T. Dunning. Accurate methods for the statistics of surprise and coincidence. *Computational Linguistics*, 19(1):61–74, 1993.
4. A. Gill and J. Oberlander. Taking care of the linguistic features of extraversion. In *Proceedings of the 24th Annual Conference of the Cognitive Science Society*, pages 363–368, Washington, D.C., 2002.
5. A. Lopez, M. Nossal, R. Hwa, and P. Resnik. Word–level alignment for multilingual resource acquisition. In *Proceedings of the 2002 LREC Workshop on Linguistic Knowledge Acquisition and Representation: Bootstrapping Annotated Language Data*, 2002.
6. T. Pedersen. Fishing for exactness. In *Proceedings of the South Central SAS User's Group (SCSUG-96) Conference*, pages 188–200, Austin, TX, October 1996.
7. T. Pedersen. A decision tree of bigrams is an accurate predictor of word sense. In *Proceedings of the Second Annual Meeting of the North American Chapter of the Association for Computational Linguistics*, pages 79–86, Pittsburgh, July 2001.
8. T. Pedersen. Machine learning with lexical features: The Duluth approach to Senseval-2. In *Proceedings of the Senseval-2 Workshop*, pages 139–142, Toulouse, July 2001.
9. T. Pedersen, M. Kayaalp, and R. Bruce. Significant lexical relationships. In *Proceedings of the Thirteenth National Conference on Artificial Intelligence*, pages 455–460, Portland, OR, August 1996.
10. C. Shannon. Prediction and entropy of printed English. *The Bell System Technical Journal*, 30(50–64), 1951.
11. T. van der Wouden. Collocational behavior in non content words. In *ACL/EACL Workshop on Collocations*, Toulouse, France, 2001.
12. M. Yanamoto and K. Church. Using suffix arrays to compute term frequency and document frequency for all substrings in a corpus. *Computational Linguistics*, 27(1):1–30, 2001.
13. D. Zaiu Inkpen and G. Hirst. Acquiring collocations for lexical choice between near synonyms. In *SIGLEX Workshop on Unsupervised Lexical Acquisition, 40th meeting of the Association for Computational Linguistics*, Philadelphia, 2002.

An Estimate Method of the Minimum Entropy of Natural Languages

Fuji Ren[1], Shunji Mitsuyoshi[2], Kang Yen[3], Chengqing Zong[4], and
Hongbing Zhu[5]

[1] Faculty of Engineering, The University of Tokushima
Tokushima, 770-8506 Japan
ren@is.tokushima-u.ac.jp
[2] Department of Research, A.G.I. Inc.
Tokyo, 106-0043 Japan
syunji@agi-web.co.jp
[3] Dept. of Electrical and Computer Eng., Florida Int'l University
Miami Florida 33174
yenk@fiu.edu
[4] Institute of Automation, Chinese Academy of Science
Beijing, 100080 China
cqzong@sycamore.ia.ac.cn
[5] Faculty of Engineering, Hiroshima Kokusai Gakuin University
Hiroshima, 739-0321 Japan
kohe@wuchang.cs.hkg.ac.jp

Abstract. The study of minimum entropy of English has a long history and has made a great progress, but only a few studies on other languages have been reported in literature so far. In this paper, we present a new method to estimate the minimum entropy of character in natural languages, based on two hypotheses of conservation of information quantity. We also verified the hypotheses empirically through experiments with two natural languages, Japanese and Chinese.

1 Introduction

Entropy, introduced by Shannon in 1948, is a standard measure for the quantity and uncertainty of information. In the early time of the development of information theory, the study of the entropy of natural languages was hindered by the availability of large enough databases and capable machines. Then the dramatic improvement in computer capability and the increase of corpus have accelerated this study.

Shannon has estimated the entropy of a character in English by using the appearance frequency of character groups[4]. With the assumption that each character occurs with the same probability, entropy F_0 is computed. Entropy F_1 is sought with the appearance probability of each character, then entropy F_2 is calculated by means of character pairs. He thought that he could have got entropy H as a limiting value of F_n if he had expanded the range of a character

A. Gelbukh (Ed.): CICLing 2003, LNCS 2588, pp. 382–392, 2003.

group. Here F_n is called entropy of n-gram. If n is small enough, F_n can be computed through the appearance frequency of character group from a corpus.

Brown et al at IBM,[5,6] using a model based on tri-gram of character, computed the entropy for all printable ASCII characters. They conducted an experiment by using a corpus of about 600 million characters to develop a language model of token unit. Then they applied this model to about 6 million characters to calculate the minimum entropy. It has been reported that the minimum entropy of a character is 1.75 bits.

Asai estimated entropy of Japanese by statistically processing the results of human estimation[3]. He randomly extracted sentences of 5, 8, 10, 15, 20 and 50 characters from newspapers. Then, making out questionnaires by deleting the 5th, 8th, ..., 50th character respectively, he asked testees to guess the deleted character. The process was repeated if the testees guessed wrong answers. After substituting of P_i, the probability of guessing correctly in the ith trial, into Shannon's entropy formula, he obtained the value of entropy. The character total used in his experiment was only 1,500. It was pointed out that this estimation method using the results of human estimation was insufficient in many respects[2].

In recent years, researchers have estimated entropy of Japanese by means of n-gram model of a morpheme unit[2]. This method is based on the following fact: when a model is made to estimate the output for a given information source, its cross-entropy defines the upper limit of its information quantity. So far, in many studies a tri-gram model has been chosen, which is empirically effective, but it has a drawback that the changes of entropy in a longer preceding context are not clear. Thus, n-gram model of a morpheme unit has been utilized to compute information quantity per character in Japanese. The experiment on EDR corpus has shown that information quantity per character is 4.30 bits when $n = 16$. In addition, their studies have indicated that raising the degree of the model decreases information quantity only a little, but enlarging the corpus decreases it quite a lot.

In this paper, we propose a new method for the estimation of minimum entropy of character in languages with many characters, such as Japanese and Chinese. This method is based on the hypotheses of conservation of information quantity. The main features of this method are: (1) with a large quantity of translation corpus, this method enables us to estimate the minimum entropy without calculating the probability, (2) the fluctuation of the ratio between character quantities in two languages becomes negligible when the scale of translation corpus increases, and (3) requirements on computer capacity and speed are not critical.

In the following, Section 2 introduces the concept of minimum entropy in natural languages. Section 3 describes a new estimating method of minimum entropy of character in natural languages, based on two hypotheses of conservation of information quantity. Section 4 discusses the collection of translation corpus between Japanese and English and the experiment of estimating the minimum entropy of Japanese. The results of the similar analysis on Chinese are presented in Section 5. Section 6 provides an empirical proof of conservation of information quantity. Section 7 draws the conclusion.

2   Minimum Entropy of Natural Languages

The character rows of a natural language have habits, which can be measured to some extents[1,7]. For example, if you see "q" in a head of a character row in English, you can immediately say that the next character is "u". Since the relation is fixed, no extra information is gained. Shannon proposed a standard called "information quantity" to measure this kind of redundancy. Suppose a phenomenon has a probability of P, then its information quantity I is defined by

$$I(P) = log_2 \frac{1}{P} = -log_2 P \qquad (1)$$

Since "u" comes after "q" in character rows all the time, the information quantity of "u" after "q" is $I(P) = 0$ because $P(u \mid q) = 1$.

Assume that the probabilities of each character in a character row consisting of n characters are $P_1, P_2, ..., P_n$. The entropy per character, H, is defined by

$$H = -\sum_{i=1}^{n} P_i log_2 P_i \qquad (2)$$

For example, suppose that the character total of Chinese is 12,370 and every character occurs with the same probability, we can say the entropy of a Chinese character is 9.65 bits.

$$-\sum_{i=1}^{12370} \frac{1}{12370} log_2 \frac{1}{12370} = 9.65 \qquad (3)$$

The entropy per character for each of 75 Japanese Hirakana characters with the same probability of occurrence only has a value of 6.23 bits.

3   Estimation of Minimum Entropy Based on a Hypothesis of Conservation of Information Quantity

Although the study on entropy of character in English has an advantage due to its small character total, it is still a difficult task in general. The task becomes worse for languages with large character total, such as Japanese and Chinese. Therefore, it is believed that a more accurate value for the minimum entropy in character can be achieved as the processing capacity of a computer improves and a large scale of machine-readable corpus is available. We have studied a new method to estimate the minimum entropy of character in languages with large character total. In this paper, we propose this estimating method of minimum entropy of character in natural languages, based on two hypotheses of conservation of information quantity.

Hypothesis 1 The information quantity Q in a writing is the product of its character total M and its minimum entropy per character H.

$$Q = H \times M \tag{4}$$

Hypothesis 2 If each writing in diffrent languages has the same content, the information quantities of each writing are approximately equal to one another.

According to Hypothesis 2, the relationship between the minimum entropy and the character total in multiple languages is described by

$$M_i \times H_i = M_k \times H_k + \alpha \tag{5}$$

Here α is the fluctuation coefficient. As M_i and M_k approach infinite, the fluctuation coefficient comes to zero, and the above formula reduces to

$$M_i \times H_i = M_k \times H_k \tag{6}$$

We call this as the estimation formula of minimum entropy based on conservation of information quantity. With respect to three languages of Japanese, Chinese and English, the following formula has been established.

$$M_e \times H_e = M_j \times H_j = M_c \times H_c \tag{7}$$

Here, M_e, M_j, and M_c and H_e, H_j, and H_c are the character total of a writing and the minimum entropy of a character in English, Japanese, and Chinese, respectively.

To reach the minimum entropy of character in English, Shannon used Jip's Law. First, he got the entropy of a word, and then converted it into the entropy of a character, which gave a value of 2.62 bits. Moreover, taking the space between words into consideration, this value becomes 2.14 bits. Through the experiment of testees' forecasting alphabet, Shannon showed the minimum entropy of a character in English is in the range between 0.6 to 1.3 bits, using 100 characters immediately before the character to be estimated. On the other hand, Brown et al, using a language model based on tri-gram of characters, computed the minimum entropy of character and found its value was 1.75 bits. Since Shannon's estimation has been criticized in many respects, in the following discussion we take 1.75 bits as the minimum entropy of character in English.

Using the character total relations between English and Japanese as well as between Japanese and Chinese, we can calculate minimum entropy of character in Japanese and Chinese as follows.

$$H_j = \frac{M_e}{M_j} \times H_e = R_{ej} \times H_e \tag{8}$$

$$H_c = \frac{M_j}{M_c} \times H_j = R_{jc} \times H_j \tag{9}$$

Here R_{mn} is the ratio of characters between languages m and n.

4   Estimation of Minimum Entropy of Character in Japanese

The formulae (8) and (9) indicate that the character total ratio in writings in English and Japanese enables us to estimate the minimum entropy of Japanese from that of English. Here the problem to be solved is how to precisely compute the character total ratio between English and Japanese. In general, R_{ej} varies, depending on the types of writings and whether the corpus is an original or a translation version. For the former, once the scale of translation corpus surpasses a level, the scattering of R_{ej}, due to the types of writings and translators, seems to be absorbed. For the latter, after collecting both the corpus of Japanese original and English translation and that of English original and Japanese translation, the relation of R_{ej} can be studied.

Table 1. Information of Japanese-English Translation Corpus

No	E_n (TE_n)	J_n (TJ_n)	nR_{ej}	jR_{ej}
1	7661 (7661)	2681 (2681)	2.858	2.858
2	12614 (20275)	4966 (7647)	2.540	2.651
3	5597 (25872)	2259 (9906)	2.478	2.612
4	11298 (37170)	5250 (15156)	2.152	2.452
5	20648 (57818)	7509 (22665)	2.750	2.551
6	24913 (82731)	8892 (31557)	2.802	2.622
7	14450 (97181)	5041 (36598)	2.866	2.655
8	12989 (110170)	4506 (41104)	2.883	2.680
9	23673 (133843)	8821 (49925)	2.684	2.681
10	23403 (157246)	8842 (58267)	2.805	2.699
11	256330 (413576)	113968 (172235)	2.249	2.401
12	15579 (429173)	6648 (178883)	2.346	2.399
13	118192 (547365)	44412 (223295)	2.661	2.451
14	473921 (1021286)	186702 (409997)	2.538	2.491
15	29854 (1051140)	9939 (419936)	3.004	2.503
16	636719 (1687859)	240618 (660554)	2.646	2.555
17	27342 (1715201)	12886 (673440)	2.122	2.547
18	434183 (2149384)	164170 (837610)	2.645	2.566
19	27717 (2177101)	9538 (847148)	2.906	2.570
20	652372 (2829473)	242380 (1089528)	2.692	2.597
21	224366 (3053839)	99938 (1189466)	2.245	2.567
22	76466 (3130305)	25733 (1215199)	2.972	2.576
23	94897 (3225202)	34753 (1249952)	2.731	2.580
24	872727 (4097929)	342893 (1592845)	2.545	2.573
25	606056 (4703985)	230094 (1822939)	2.634	2.580
26	600502 (5304487)	236404 (2059343)	2.540	2.576
27	338184 (5642671)	142550 (2201893)	2.372	2.563
28	30475 (5673146)	10514 (2212407)	2.899	2.564

For each data set, Japanese character total, English character total, cumulative total, and nR_{ej} are shown in Table 1 and the meaning of their abbreviations is given below.

$E_n(TE_n)$: English character total (Cumulative English character total)
$J_n(TJ_n)$: Japanese character total (Cumulative Japanese character total)
nR_{ej}: Ratio of English and Japanese character totals in the nth Japanese-English corpus
jR_{ej}: Ratio of cumulative English and Japanese character totals in the Japanese-English corpus

Although the value of the ratio of English-Japanese character total to that of cumulative English-Japanese character total fluctuates row by row in Table 1, the accumulated value jR_{ej} approaches to its equilibrant value 2.56.

According to formula (8), the minimum entropy per character in Japanese is computed from the formula below with value of 4.48 bits.

$$H_{j1} = jR_{ej} \times H_e = 2.56 \times 1.75 = 4.48 \tag{10}$$

Following the same process for Japanese-English translation corpus in the previous section, English-Japanese translation corpus has been gathered and analyzed. For each data set, Japanese character total, English character total, cumulative total and eR_{ej} are shown in Table 2. Based on this table, the minimum entropy of one character in Japanese is estimated as 2.85 bits.

$$H_{j2} = eR_{ej} \times H_e = 1.63 \times 1.75 = 2.85 \tag{11}$$

As mentioned above, we estimated two minimum entropies of character in Japanese, using Japanese-English and English-Japanese translation corpora collected. For the appropriate value of minimum entropy of character in Japanese, we consider the following argument. While H_{j1} is a result of estimation from the corpus of Japanese original and English translation and H_{j2} is the one from the corpus of English original and Japanese translation, two values are different. The reason of the difference depends on whether the original language is Japanese or English. Regardless of Japanese and English, every language pair has the tendency that the translation has larger character total than the original. In general the following formulae are formed.

$$jR_{ej} = R_{ej} + \beta 1 \tag{12}$$

$$eR_{ej} = R_{ej} - \beta 2 \tag{13}$$

In these formulas, jR_{ej} is the ratio of cumulative character totals in Japanese and English for the corpus with Japanese original and English translation while eR_{ej} is the ratio of cumulative character totals in English and Japanese for the corpus with English original and Japanese translation. In addition, $\beta 1$ and $\beta 2$ are positive fixed numbers and are called fluctuation factors of character total ratios occurred in translation. $\beta 1$ and $\beta 2$ are generally in terms of statistics

Table 2. Information of English-Japanese Translation Corpus

No	E_n (TE$_n$)	J_n (TJ$_n$)	nR$_{ej}$	eR$_{ej}$
1	37598 (37598)	21747 (21747)	1.729	1.729
2	33870 (71468)	18465 (40212)	1.834	1.777
3	44929 (116397)	24497 (64709)	1.834	1.799
4	39937 (156334)	22567 (87276)	1.770	1.791
5	42904 (199238)	21456 (108732)	2.000	1.832
6	153941 (353179)	77644 (186376)	1.983	1.895
7	204919 (558098)	140788 (327164)	1.456	1.706
8	716347 (1274445)	516394 (843558)	1.387	1.511
9	117386 (1391831)	79813 (923371)	1.471	1.507
10	343030 (1734861)	225047 (1148418)	1.524	1.511
11	636719 (2371580)	240618 (1389036)	2.646	1.707
12	562091 (2933671)	385070 (1774106)	1.460	1.654
13	61140 (2994811)	37883 (1811989)	1.614	1.653
14	368538 (3363349)	198209 (2010198)	1.859	1.673
15	792420 (4155769)	481893 (2492091)	1.644	1.668
16	567153 (4722922)	388597 (2880688)	1.459	1.640
17	471576 (5194498)	297656 (3178344)	1.584	1.634
18	142298 (5336796)	93219 (3271563)	1.526	1.631

with enough data quantity and are almost the same. Based on the premise, the following formula is formed.

$$R_{ej} = \frac{jR_{ej} + eR_{ej} + (\beta 2 - \beta 1)}{2} = \frac{jR_{ej} + eR_{ej}}{2} \tag{14}$$

According to the analysis above, R_{ej} has value 2.09 as indicated below.

$$R_{ej} = \frac{jR_{ej} + eR_{ej}}{2} = \frac{2.56 + 1.63}{2} = 2.09 \tag{15}$$

Thus the estimation formula of minimum entropy indicates that the value of H_j can be calculated from

$$H_j = R_{ej} \times H_e = 2.09 \times 1.75 = 3.65 \tag{16}$$

5   Estimation of Minimum Entropy of Character in Chinese

Following the same procedure in the previous experiment of estimating the minimum entropy of character in Japanese, we can seek the minimum entropy of character in Chinese by using the character total ratio of Japanese and Chinese writings. Using Chinese novels and their Japanese translations as source data, CJ-Corpus is created[9,10]. Analyzing data with the same method in the previous section, when an original is in Japanese and a translation is in Chinese,

jR_{jc} is 1.44; and cR_{jc} is 1.66 when an original is in Chinese and a translation is in Japanese. Therefore, R_{jc} is 1.55. Following the same analysis in the previous section, based on the estimation formula of minimum entropy, H_c is 5.66 bits.

6 Empirical Proof of "Conservation of Information Quantity"

In this section we will use an empirical method to verify the validity of the hypotheses of "conservation of information quantity." In section 4, the character-total ratios in Japanese and English computed from JE-Corpus and EJ-Corpus have different values, 2.56 and 1.63, respectively. Consider that the minimum entropy of character in English or Japanese is fixed. This statement seems to contradict our hypothesis 2 that the product of the minimum entropy of character and the character total of any document is fixed regardless of languages. But, in general a translation version of a document will have a larger value in character total. This problem can be handled by introducing "fluctuation factors," $\beta 1$ and $\beta 2$, to the character total ratios as indicated in formulae (12) and (13).

Based on a large quantity of data, we consider that in terms of statistics $\beta 1$ and $\beta 2$ are almost the same. Thus the formulae (12) and (13) are valid. In addition, to verify the validity of our hypotheses, we will conduct an empirical proof in the following.

To verify those two hypotheses of "conservation of information quantity," we adopt the following argument.

Assuming that the hypotheses of conservation of information quantity are correct, for example, the entropy of character in Chinese estimated in the order of "English → Japanese → Chinese" should generally agree to the one estimated in the order of "Japanese → English → Chinese."

Accepting the above argument, we have carried out the following experiment. Since we do not have Chinese-English (or English-Chinese) translation corpus, to create these collections is the first step. We have searched Web-sites, created both in Chinese and English, in China, United States, Hong Kong, Singapore etc., for experimental materials. With the consideration of quality and quantity of translations, we have chosen the writing of "SELECTED ESSAYS" in both Chinese and English, from the web sites of "Early News" as the corpus[8]. Table 3 shows the data of CE-Corpus and Table 4 the data of EC-Corpus. The meaning of the abbreviations used in the tables is given below.

$E_n(TE_n)$: English character total (Cumulative English character total)
$C_n(TC_n)$: Chinese character total (Cumulative Chinese character total)
nR_{ec}: Ratio of English and Chinese character totals in the nth English-Chinese (or Chinese-English)corpus
cR_{ec}: Ratio of cumulative Chinese and English character totals in the Chinese-English corpus

Table 3. Information of Chinese-English Translation Corpus

No	E_n (TE$_n$)	C_n (TC$_n$)	nR$_{ec}$	cR$_{ec}$
1	4246(4246)	1152(1152)	3.685	3.685
2	3958(8204)	1093(2245)	3.291	3.654
3	5075(13279)	1398(3643)	3.630	3.645
4	4955(18234)	1226(4869)	4.041	3.744
5	4690(22924)	1233(6102)	3.803	3.756
6	4473(27397)	1273(7375)	3.513	3.714
7	3667(31064)	946(8321)	3.876	3.733
8	4222(35286)	1237(9558)	3.413	3.691
9	2912(38198)	968(10526)	3.008	3.628
10	3421(41619)	970(11496)	3.526	3.620
11	3926(45545)	1108(12604)	3.543	3.613
12	4892(50437)	1242(13846)	3.938	3.642
13	4054(54491)	1101(14947)	3.682	3.645
14	4960(59451)	1194(16141)	4.154	3.683
15	4450(63901)	1225(17366)	3.632	3.679
16	5226(69127)	1262(18628)	4.141	3.710
17	3188(72315)	1027(19655)	3.104	3.679
18	5445(77760)	1833(21488)	2.970	3.618
19	5079(82839)	1246(22734)	4.076	3.643
20	4506(87345)	1213(23947)	3.714	3.647
21	3190(90535)	824(24771)	3.871	3.654
22	4774(95309)	1389(26160)	3.437	3.643
23	3292(98601)	1134(27294)	2.902	3.612
24	3962(102563)	1047(28341)	3.784	3.618
25	3450(106013)	922(29263)	3.741	3.622
26	4068(110081)	1266(30529)	3.213	3.605

eR_{ec}: Ratio of cumulative English and Chinese character totals in the English-Chinese corpus

Table 3 indicates that cR_{ec} has value of 3.61, and Table 4 shows 2.75. Therefore, R_{ec} has the value of 3.18.

$$R_{ec} = \frac{cR_{ec} + eR_{ec}}{2} = \frac{3.61 + 2.75}{2} = 3.18 \tag{17}$$

If the assumed hypotheses of "conservation of information quantity" are true, the entropy of character in Chinese estimated in the order of "English → Japanese → Chinese" should generally agree to the one estimated in the order of "Japanese → English → Chinese."

The entropy of character in Chinese was estimated in the order of "English → Japanese → Chinese," resulting in a value of 5.66 bits. To the contrary, based on the fact that H_j is 2.94 and H_e is 1.75, the estimated value of H_c in the order of "Japanese → English → Chinese" is 5.57 bits.

$$H_c = R_{ec} \times H_e = 3.18 \times 1.75 = 5.57 \tag{18}$$

Table 4. Information of English-Chinese Translation Corpus

No	E_n (TE$_n$)	C_n (TC$_n$)	nR$_{ec}$	eR$_{ec}$
1	5165(5165)	1869(1869)	2.763	2.763
2	3348(8513)	1183(3052)	2.830	2.789
3	2631(11144)	980(4032)	2.684	2.763
4	3598(14742)	1211(5243)	2.971	2.811
5	3406(18148)	1074(6317)	3.171	2.872
6	4229(22377)	1531(7848)	2.762	2.851
7	2968(24345)	1141(8989)	2.601	2.708
8	3689(28034)	1120(10109)	3.293	2.773
9	2414(30448)	1008(11117)	2.394	2.738
10	3002(33450)	1167(12284)	2.572	2.723
11	4077(37527)	1455(13739)	2.802	2.731
12	3781(41308)	1355(15094)	2.790	2.736
13	2953(44261)	1210(16304)	2.440	2.714
14	2862(47123)	877(17181)	3.263	2.742
15	1701(48824)	690(17871)	2.465	2.732
16	3496(52320)	1212(19083)	2.884	2.741
17	8162(60482)	2938(22021)	2.778	2.746

Estimating from both routes, the absolute error in entropies of character in Chinese is 0.9 bits and the relative error is approximately 1.6%. From the above result, we can draw the following conclusions.

- The quantity of translation corpus we collected is insufficient.
- The quality of translation corpus is inappropriate. For example, regarding Japanese-English translation corpus we collected, approximately 18% of English characters remain in Japanese translation.
- The area of translation corpus is partial. For instance, Chinese-English translation corpus consists of only the one in Singapore.

Nonetheless from the view point of statistics, an error of 1.6% indicates that the hypothesis proposed is experimentally acceptable.

7   Conclusion

In this paper, we present a new estimating method of minimum entropy of character in natural languages, based on a hypothesis of conservation of information quantity. The validity of this hypothesis has been verified by means of an empirical proof. The results of this study show that an estimate of minimum entropy of 3.65 bits for Japanese character by using 11 million character of Japanese-English parallel corpus and 5.66 bits for Chinese character with 14 hundred thousand character Japanese-Chinese parallel corpus.

Acknowledgments. We would like to thank all our colleagues participating in this project. This work has been partly supported by the Education Ministry of Japan under Grant-in-Aid for Scientific Research (14380166, 14022237).

References

1. K. Kita, T. Nakamura, M. Nagata, "Voice Language Processing," Morikita Publishing, Inc., 1996
2. N. Mori, O. Yamaji, "Estimating the Upper Limit of Information Quantity in Japanese Language," Information Processing Society Journal, Vol. 38, No. 11, pp. 2192–2199, 1997
3. K. Asai, "About Entropy in Japanese," Measuring Japanese Language, pp. 4–7, 1965
4. C.E. Shannon, "Prediction and Entropy of Printed English," Bell System Technical Journal, Vol. 30, pp. 50–64, 1951.
5. P.F. Brown, S.A.D. Pietra, R.L. Mercer, "An Estimate of an Upper Bound for the Entropy of English," Computational Linguistics, Vol.18, No. 1, pp. 31–20, 1992.
6. P.F. Brown, V.J.D. Pietra, P.V. deSouza, J.C. Lai, R.L. Mercer, "Class-Based n-gram Models of Natural Language," Computational Linguistics, Vol. 18, No. 4, pp. 467–479, 1992.
7. T.M. Cover, R.C. King, "A Convergent Gambling Estimate of the Entropy of English," IEEE Trans. on Information Theory, Vol.-IT-24, No.-4, pp. 413–421, 1978.
8. http://www.zaobao.com/bilingual/bilingual.html.
9. F. Ren, J. Nie, "The Concept of Sensitive Word in Chinese - Survey in a Machine-Readable Dictionary," Journal of Natural Language Processing, Vol. 6, No. 1, pp. 59–78, 1999.
10. L. Fan, F. Ren, Y. Miyanaga, K. Tochinai, "Automatic Composition of Chinese Compound Words for Chinese-Japanese Machine Translation," Transactions of Information Processing Society of Japan, Vol. 33, No. 9, pp. 1103–1113, 1992.

A Corpus Balancing Method for Language Model Construction

Luis Villaseñor-Pineda[1], Manuel Montes-y-Gómez [1], Manuel Alberto Pérez-Coutiño[1], and Dominique Vaufreydaz [2]

[1] Instituto Nacional de Astrofísica, Óptica y Electrónica (INAOE), Mexico
{villasen,mmontesg,mapco}@inaoep.mx
[2] Laboratoire CLIPS-IMAG, Université Joseph Fourier, France
Dominique.Vaufreydaz@imag.fr

Abstract. The language model is an important component of any speech recognition system. In this paper, we present a lexical enrichment methodology of corpora focused on the construction of statistical language models. This methodology considers, on one hand, the identification of the set of poor represented words of a given training corpus, and on the other hand, the enrichment of the given corpus by the repetitive inclusion of selected text fragments containing these words. The first part of the paper describes the formal details about this methodology; the second part presents some experiments and results that validate our method.

1 Introduction

The language model (LM) is an important component of any automatic speech recognition system. Its purpose is to reduce the search space in order to accelerate the recognition process. There are two kinds of language models: grammar based and statistical. The statistical LMs have the capability to use the statistical properties of language in context of two or more words. Because of this, statistical LMs are more flexible than the grammar based ones, and allow capturing situations closer to spoken language (where rules for written language are not always respected).

Statistical LMs are calculated from training corpora delimited by their vocabulary size, the treatment of unknown words, and others [3]. The size of the training corpus is an essential factor of a LM. Generally, a large corpus tends to have more contexts for each word, and thus tends to produce more accurate and robust LMs.

The construction of a corpus is not an easy task mainly because the written texts do not represent adequately many phenomenon of spontaneous speech. One way to diminish this problem is using web documents as data sources. Because many people around the world contribute to create the web documents, most of them has informal contents, and include many everyday as well as non-grammatical expressions used in spoken language. This situation allows not only the construction of very large corpora but also the creation of corpora combining good written grammatical text and free text closer to the spoken language [2, 7].

A. Gelbukh (Ed.): CICLing 2003, LNCS 2588, pp. 393–401, 2003.

Once a training corpus is constructed from the web several questions emerge. For instance, is the obtained corpus rich enough for the specified task? are the domain words well represented? can the corpus be enriched? In this paper, we present a methodology to respond to these questions. Basically, this methodology consists of two steps: i) a lexical analysis of the training corpus in order to identify its weaknesses relating to a given reference corpus[1], and ii) a lexical enrichment process of the training corpus focused on reducing the identified weaknesses, and obtaining a better LM.

The rest of the paper is organized as follows. Section 2 introduces formal concepts of the lexical analysis of a training corpus, and explains the identification of its bad represented words. Section 3 describes its enrichment process. Section 4 shows some experiment results that illustrate and validate our method. Finally, section 5 presents our conclusions and discusses future work.

2   Lexical Analysis of the Training Corpus

It is clear that the terms and expressions used in real dialogs considerably differ from those occurring in texts. For instance, we can expect that the frequency of occurrence of pronouns and verbs in the first and second person is not similar between a dialog among people and a written text. Therefore the aim of this analysis is to find those words having very different frequencies in two corpora (i.e. between a training corpus and a reference corpus). The identified words can be over or sub represented in the training corpus related to the reference one.

The method of lexical analysis of two corpora consists of two major stages:

1. Constructing the word probability distribution for each corpus (preprocessing stage).
2. Measuring the difference between the probability distributions of the corpora, and identifying the critical words (comparison stage)

These processes are described in the next two subsections.

2.1   Preprocessing Stage

This stage considers the creation of an index of the corpora. This index indicates the words used in the corpora, and their corresponding frequencies of occurrence in each corpus. We represent this index by an inverted file, and instrument it by a set of hash tables [4].

Once the index is built, a frequency $f_t^{C_i}$ is assigned to each word t. This frequency indicates the number of occurrences of the word t in the corpus C_i. Then, using these frequencies of the words, a probability distribution $D_i = \left\{ p_t^{C_i} \right\}$ of the

---

[1] A *reference corpus* is a set of samples for a given interaction including the linguistics phenomenon of the domain. These corpora are obtained from real (or almost real) conditions. In our case, we built the reference corpus using the technique of the Wizard of Oz (see section 4.1).

words in the corpus C_i is constructed, where $p_t^{C_i} = f_t^{C_i} \Big/ \sum_{j=1}^{n} f_j^{C_i}$ expresses the probability of occurrence of the word t in the corpus C_i. Here, n is the number of words considered by the index.

2.2 Comparison Stage

This stage aims, at a first step, determining the general difference between the corpora. Then based on this information, identifying the specific words mainly causing this difference (i.e. the set of disparate words of the training corpus).

2.2.1 Comparison of the Probability Distributions

In order to measure the lexical difference between the corpora, we compare their word probability distributions $D_i = \{ p_t^{C_i} \}$. Because we are interested in the general difference regardless of the direction, we propose a comparison measure *Diff* for two distributions: the quotient of the difference area and the maximal area. This measure reflects an overall difference of the corpora and does not measures individual proportions of difference of each individual word. More detail on this measure can be found in [5].

$$Diff = \frac{A_d}{A_m} \qquad \text{difference coefficient:}$$

$$A_d = \sum_{t=1}^{n} d_t \qquad \text{difference area}$$

$$A_m = \sum_{t=1}^{n} max\left(p_t^{C_e}, p_t^{C_r} \right) \qquad \text{maximal area}$$

$$d_t = \left| p_t^{C_e} - p_t^{C_r} \right| \qquad \text{word difference}$$

If the difference coefficient between the two probability distributions tends to 1, then there exists a considerable lexical difference between the corpora. On the contrary, if the difference coefficient tends to 0, then we can conclude that the corpora are lexically similar.

2.2.2 Identification of the Disparate Words

A global difference between the corpora is caused essentially by the abrupt differences d_t of some individual words. We call these words *disparate*, and defined them as those with a difference noticeably greater than the typical difference. Let d_μ be a "typical" value of d_t and d_σ be a measure of the "width" of the distribution (see below). Then a word t for which $d_t > d_\mu + (\alpha \times d_\sigma)$ is identified as a disparate word.

The tuning constant α determines the criterion used to identify an individual difference as noticeable.

$$d_\mu = \frac{1}{n}\sum_{t=1}^{n} d_t \qquad\qquad \text{average difference}$$

$$d_\sigma = \sqrt{\frac{1}{n}\sum_{t=1}^{n}(d_t - d_\mu)^2} \qquad \text{standar deviation of difference}$$

3   Lexical Enrichment of the Training Corpus

On the basis of the lexical analysis of the corpora (i.e. the comparison of the training and reference corpora), it is possible to determine, first, the appropriateness of the training corpus related to the reference one, and then, the set of poor represent words requiring to be enriched.

The appropriateness of the training corpus is determined by the difference coefficient. If this coefficient is closer to 0, then the word distributions of both corpora are similar, and thus the training corpus is adequate for the task at hand in accordance with the reference corpus. On the contrary, if the difference coefficient is closer to 1, then the word distributions of the corpora are very different, and there are not sufficient elements to generate a satisfactory LM.

For the situation where the difference coefficient is closer to 0, it is necessary to enrich the training corpus. The lexical analysis allows determining the set of bad-represented words (i.e. the set of disparate words). From them, the subset of sub-represented words is of particular interest to be enriched. We call them *critical words*.

Two different data sources can be used to obtain samples of the critical words, and thus enriching the training corpus. On one hand is a new group of documents obtained from the web; on the other hand is the reference corpus. Since we are interested in the creation of LMs for spoken language, and the spoken phenomenons are poorly represented in the web documents (for instance deictic and courtesy expressions; see section 4.2), we decided to use the reference corpus as data source.

Basically, our method proposes to enlarge the training corpus aggregating to it several times a set of selected phrases from the reference corpus. The following section describes the selection of these phrases and their incorporation to the training corpus.

3.1   The Process of Enrichment

Given the set of critical words W_c (i.e. the set of sub-represented words in the training corpus) the process of lexical enrichment of the training corpus consists of the following steps:

1. Construct the selected corpus C_s from the reference corpus C_r. This new corpus contains only those phrases from the reference corpus having one or more critical words (i.e. $C_s \subseteq C_r$ and $|C_s| \leq |C_r|$).[2] Some properties about the frequency of occurrence of its words are:

---

[2] The notation $|C_i|$ stands for the number of phrases in the corpus C_i.

$$\forall t \in W_c : f_t^{C_s} = f_t^{C_r}$$
$$\forall t \notin W_c : f_t^{C_s} \leq f_t^{C_r}$$

2. Calculate the deficit of occurrence of each single critical word. This deficit indicates the number of times the word $t \in W_c$ must be incorporated to the training corpus C_e in order to reach its probability of occurrence in the reference corpus.

$$deficit_t = (P_t^{C_r} - P_t^{C_e}) \times |C_e|$$

3. Determine the number of times (repetitions) the selected corpus must be aggregated to the training corpus. This number of repetitions $\hat{r}$ is calculated in order to fulfill the occurrence deficit of all critical words.

$$\hat{r} = max(R), \text{ where :}$$
$$R = \{r_t | t \in W_c\}$$
$$r_t = \frac{deficit_t}{f_t^{C_s}}$$

4. Construct the enriched training corpus C_{e+}. This step consists on aggregating $\hat{r}$ times the selected corpus to the training one. The resulting enriched training corpus satisfied the following condition: $|C_{e+}| = |C_e| + (\hat{r} \times |C_s|)$.

4 Experimental Results

This section shows some experiments that validate our method. This experiments use the corpus DIME as reference corpus, and the corpus WebDIME as training corpus. The following subsections describe both corpora, and presents the results for their lexical comparison, and for the lexical enrichment of the WebDIME corpus.

4.1 Description of the Corpora

4.1.1 The DIME Corpus

The DIME corpus is a multimodal corpus that provides empiric information for studying the use and interaction between spoken language, deictic gestures and the graphical context during human-computer interaction [8]. This corpus consists of a set of dialogs corresponding to the domain of kitchen design. This domain was selected because it is simple (most people can undertake it without previous experience), has a constrained language, and allows the use of deictic gestures.

For the construction of the DIME corpus, we used a so-called *Wizard of Oz* experiment. This experiment consists of a person (the wizard) playing the role of the system, and other person (the subject) solving tasks in the domain of interest with the help of the wizard [1].

Table 1. Main data of the DIME and WebDIME corpora

	DIME corpus	WebDIME corpus
Instances of lexical forms	27459	27,224,579
Lexical forms	1110	1110
Lines	5779	4,520,513

The construction, and the corresponding transcription, of the DIME corpus was performed within the context of the DIME project "Intelligent Multimodal Dialogs in Spanish" [6]. Table 1 resumes the main characteristics of this corpus.

4.1.2 The WebDIME Corpus

The creation of the DIME corpus was motivated by two different purposes: on one hand, the study of multimodal human-computer interactions, on the other hand, the construction of an automatic speech recognition system. Despite their richness for the first purpose, the DIME corpus is very small to be used for obtaining a statistical LM (i.e. to be used as training corpus). This situation motives us to collect a larger corpus from the web: the WebDIME corpus.

The WEbDIME corpus is a large set of phrases containing just the vocabulary for the domain of kitchen design (i.e. the same vocabulary of the DIME corpus). It was constructed from almost 30 gigabytes of Spanish web documents gathered by the CLIPS-Index web robot [7]. Basically, it consists of all the minimal blocks containing the words of the domain vocabulary found in the collected documents. The table 1 resumes the main characteristics of this corpus.

4.2 Results of Lexical Comparison between DIME and WebDIME

The following bullets resume the results from the comparison of the corpora:

- The difference coefficient is equal to 0.71. It indicates an important disparity among the proportions of occurrence of the vocabulary words in both corpora. This situation predicts the construction of an inadequate LM from the WebDIME corpus for the tasks of kitchen design.
- The set of critical words represents the 2.6% of the application vocabulary (see the table 2). This words are of three main kinds:
  - *Domain words* such as "refrigerator", "cupboard" and "stove". This is a serious problem since these words are very common in our application.
  - *Deictic words*, for instance, "there" and "here". This omission occurs because these words are common in a multimodal interaction but not in written texts.
  - *Courtesy expressions* including auxiliary verbs such as "can" and "would". These expressions are regular in Spanish spoken language but are almost null in written texts.

It is important to point out that in spite of the small number of critical words (just 29 words from a vocabulary of 1110), the damage caused to the LM may be substantial because it considers all usage contexts of these words. This supposition was confirmed by the experiments (see the section 4.3).

Table 2. The set of critical words of the WebDIME corpus

ahí (*there*)	esta (*this, this one*)	ponga (*put*)
ahora (*now*)	está (*is*)	puedes (*can*)
Alacena (*cupboard*)	éste (*this one*)	quieres (*would*)
alacenas (*cupboards*)	estufa (*stove*)	quiero (*would*)
aquí (*here*)	fregadero (*kitchen sink*)	refrigerador (*refrigerator*)
así (*so*)	hacia (*for*)	sí (*yes*)
bien (*well*)	mueble (*stuff*)	tenemos (*have*)
bueno (*good*)	okey (*okay*)	vamos (*lets go*)
dónde (*where?*)	pared (*wall*)	ver (*to see*)
esquina (*corner*)	poner (*to put*)	

4.3   Results of Lexical Enrichment of WebDIME Corpus[3]

The enrichment of the corpus WebDIME was done in two steps (see the section 3.1). First, we obtained a selected corpus C_s of 3278 phrases from the DIME corpus (C_r). Then, we aggregate 402 times these phrases to WebDIME (C_e) in order to build the WebDIME+ corpus (C_{e+}).

In order to estimate the adequacy of the enriched corpus, we evaluated the coverage of the resultant LM for the given task. Basically, we consider the following well-known measures: the perplexity, the n-gram hit factor, and the number of learned bigrams [3]. The table 3 compares the LMs constructed from the WebDIME and WebDIME+ corpora. These results demonstrate that the LM obtained from the new enriched corpus is better: the perplexity decreased, and the 2-gram hit factor and the number of learned bigrams increased.

Additionally, we performed another two experiments for validating our methodology. These experiments considered different ways of enriching the training corpus.

The first experiment consisted on varying the number of repetitions the selected corpus was aggregated to the WebDIME corpus. Table 4 shows the results of this experiment. In this table, WebDIME1 is a corpus conformed by WebDIME and only one repetition of the selected phrases; WebDIME262 contains 262 repetitions of the

Table 3. Evaluation of the obtained LMs

Training corpus	Perplexity	Bigram hit factor	Learned bigram
WebDIME	203.02	2797	163624
WebDIME+	16.42	3068	164462

selected corpus[4], and WebDIME800 contains 800 repetitions.

The results show that perplexity decreased considerably between WebDIME1 and the WebDIME+, and just a few between WebDIME+ and WebDIME800. Therefore, from table 4 it is clear that the WebDIME+ corpus maintains the best relation between

---

[3] All LMs used in the experiments were constructed by the same technique. Also, we reserved a subset of the DIME corpus for evaluation purposes. This subset was excluded for the construction of the selected corpus.

[4] 262 is the average of the repetitions of all critical words. The proposed calculus considers the maximum instead of the average (see section 3.1).

Table 4. Experiments aggregating different times the selected corpus

Training corpus	Perplexity	Bigram hit factor	Learned bigram	Diff
WebDIME1	60.21	3068	164462	0.72
WebDIME262	17.59	3068	164462	0.66
WebDIME+	16.42	3068	164462	0.64
WebDIME800	15.04	3068	164462	0.59

cost and benefit. Additionally, the table 4 shows a strong correlation between the perplexity and the difference coefficient.

In the second experiment the selected corpus was substituted by the complete DIME corpus (i.e. the construction of the selected corpus was eliminated from the procedure of section 3.1). Table 5 shows the results of this experiment. In this table, WebDIMED1 is the corpus conformed by WebDIME and one repetition of the reference corpus; and WebDIMED402 consist of WebDIME and 402 repetitions of the corpus DIME (i.e. the reference corpus).

Table 5. Experiments aggregating the reference corpus

Training corpus	Perplexity	Bigram hit factor	Learned bigram
WebDIMED1	121.76	2947	165124
WebDIMED402	17.59	2947	165124

The comparison of the results of tables 4 and 5 allows concluding that using a selected corpus is an advantageous strategy for compensating the deficit of the critical words (at least a better strategy than just aggregating the reference corpus). For instance, the results show that perplexity was less and 2-gram hit factor was greater when using the selected corpus.

5   Conclusions and Future Work

In this paper we presented a methodology for lexical corpora enrichment focused on the creation of statistical language models. This methodology consists of two major steps: first, a lexical comparison between the training and reference corpora that allows identifying the set of critical words (sub represented words) of the training corpus; second, the lexical enrichment of the training corpus.

The proposed methodology was experimented with the DIME and WebDIME corpora. The result of this experiment was the enriched corpus WebDIME+. We demonstrated that the adequacy of this new corpus for the task at hand was better than that for the original training corpus.

Additionally, we propose a new measure, the difference coefficient, to quantify the difference between two corpora. Our experiments demonstrate that, similar to traditional measures such as perplexity, this coefficient may be used to evaluate the adequacy of a corpus to a given domain.

As future work we plan to: 1) continue the evaluation of the obtained LMs over a speech recognition system, 2) propose a iterative method for corpora enrichment based on the dynamic calculus of the critical words and pertinent stop conditions, 3) extend the corpora comparison in order to consider syntactic information (such as part of speech tags).

Acknowledgements. This work was done under the partial support of CONACYT (project 31128-A), the "Laboratorio Franco-Mexicano de Informática (LAFMI)", and the Human Language Technologies Laboratory of INAOE.

References

1. Bernsen, N., H. Dybkjaer and L. Dybkjaer. Designing Interactive Speech Systems. From First Ideas to User Testing. Springer-Verlag. 1998.
2. Gelbukh, A., G. Sidorov and L. Chanona. Compilation of a Spanish Representative Corpus. In A. Gelbukh (Ed.) Computational Linguistics and Intelligent Text Processing, Lecture Notes in Computer Science N 2276, Springer-Verlag, 2002.
3. Jurafsky, D. and J. Martin. Speech and Language Processing. Prentice Hall. 2000.
4. Kowalski, G. Information Retrieval Systems: Theory and implementation. Kluwer Academic Publishers, 1997.
5. Montes y Góméz, M., A. Gelbukh and A. López-López. Mining the News: Trends, Associations and Deviations. Computación y Sistemas, Vol. 5, No. 1, IPN 2001.
6. Pineda, L. A., A. Massé, I. Meza, M. Salas, E. Schwarz, E. Uraga and L. Villaseñor. The DIME Project. Mexican International Conference on Artificial Intelligence MICAI-2002, Lecture Notes in Artificial Intelligence 2313, Springer-Verlag, 2002.
7. Vaufreydaz, D., M. Akbar and J. Rouillard. Internet Documents : A Rich Source for Spoken Language Modeling. Automatic Speech Recognition and Understanding (ASRU'99), Keystone, Colorado, USA, 1999.
8. Villaseñor, L., A. Massé and L.A. Pineda. The DIME corpus. 3er Encuentro Internacional de Ciencias de la Computación ENC-01, Aguascalientes, México, 2001.

Building a Chinese Shallow Parsed TreeBank for Collocation Extraction

Li Baoli[1], Lu Qin[2], and Li Yin[2]

[1] Department of Computer Science and Technology,
Peking University, Beijing, P.R. China, 100871
libl@pku.edu.cn
[2] Department of Computing, The Hong Kong Polytechnic University,
Hung Hom, Kowloon, Hong Kong
{csluqin, csyinli}@comp.polyu.edu.hk

Abstract. To automatically extract Chinese collocations and build a large-scale collocation bank, we are developing a one-million-word Chinese shallow parsed treebank. The treebank can be used not only as a training set for our shallow parser, but also as processed data from which collocations are extracted. This paper presents several issues related to this on-going project, such as our definition of shallow parsing used in Chinese collocation extraction, guideline preparation, and quality control.

1 Introduction

A collocation is a fixed usage of two or more words, occurring adjacently or separated by other words. The exact meaning of a collocation usually cannot be derived directly from the meaning of its components. Collocations are important for a number of applications, such as machine translation, computational lexicography, and so forth. Many studies on automatic collocation extraction have been conducted in the past decades [1, 2]. The techniques in these studies are mainly based on lexical statistics, including frequency, mean and variance, hypothesis testing, and mutual information.

We consider that collocations should be restricted within grammatically bound elements that occur in a particular order. Co-occurred words like *doctor – nurse* or *plane – airport* are not regarded as collocations. To determine whether two or more words form a collocation, syntactic information must be introduced. Shallow parsing can be used effectively to identify local structure of a sentence without the need for full parsing, thus it becomes a natural choice for collocation extraction.

In order to extract Chinese collocations automatically and build a large-scale collocation bank, we are developing a Chinese shallow parsed treebank. The treebank can be used not only as a training set for the shallow parser, but also as processed data from which collocations are extracted. Several efforts were made on building large scale Chinese full parsed treebanks for general purpose [3, 4], but little has been done to construct a shallow parsed treebank, especially for the purpose of collocation extraction. This motivated us to build a one-million-word shallow treebank.

A. Gelbukh (Ed.): CICLing 2003, LNCS 2588, pp. 402–405, 2003.

In this paper, we present several issues about how to build a Chinese shallow parsed treebank for collocation extraction. Section 2 gives our definition of shallow parsing used in collocation extraction. Section 3 discusses how to build such a shallow parsed treebank. Conclusion and future plans are given in Section 4.

2 Shallow Parsing for Collocation Extraction

Shallow or partial parsing is usually defined as the task of obtaining only a limited amount of syntactic information from running text. But this definition is equivocal, especially when used for an engineering project. Under the context of our project, shallow parsing for collocation extraction should be able to recognize basic blocks of a sentence where the boundary of syntactic chunks can be identified. The marking of the chunks can limit the identification of collocation either within a chunk or between chunks depending on the types of collocation we are looking for. As nested chunking sometimes can make training more difficult, we limit the nesting of chunks to only 2 levels at most. Any deeper syntactic structures are ignored. Consequently, our shallow parsed tree will be a tree of no more than 2 in height. For example, a sentence (a) in Figure 1 (on next page) is fully parsed as (b) in the LDC Chinese Treebank [3], whereas it is bracketed as (c) in our corpus. The sub-structures in the phrase "具体措施和政策要点 (concrete measures and essentials on policy)" are not annotated.

3 Some Issues in Treebank Annotation

3.1 Guideline Preparation

One important consideration in the preparation of the annotation guideline was to make it applicable to Chinese collocation extraction. The workload of the annotation must also be manageable. Consequently, the guideline must be simple and easy to follow and the result can be of reasonable quality within a specified time frame.

3.2 Word Segmentation and Part of Speech Tagging

Unlike English, there is no space between Chinese words. Thus word segmentation must be done as a necessary preprocessing step. To avoid the difficulties in defining the notion of words, we simply derived the wordlist used in our annotation from a widely used Chinese syntactical lexicon [5]. Moreover, to comply with the principles adopted in contemporary linguistic theories, we defined POS tags based on syntactic distribution rather than meaning and we have about 88 different POS tags.

One difference between our guideline and those of others is in the processing of repetitive structures, such as AA (e.g., 看看/see), ABAB (e.g., 研究研究/research), and A-一-A (e.g., 想一想/think). We regard such a repetitive structure as a single segmentation unit. In addition to POS tag, we further annotate its internal structure (e.g.

看看/v-AA). From this detailed information, we can easily obtain its stem, which will be helpful to identify collocations even in a small corpus.

```
(a) Raw data:

他/he 还/also 提出/propose 一/one 系列/series 具体/concrete 措施/measure 和
/and 政策/policy 要点/essential 。
(He also proposed a series of concrete measures and essentials on policy.)

(b) Parsed result in LDC-CTB:

(IP (NP-SBJ (PN 他))
   (VP (ADVP (AD 还))
      (VP (VV 提出)
         (NP-OBJ (QP (CD 一)
                     (CLP (M 系列)))
                 (NP (NP (ADJP (JJ 具体))
                         (NP (NN 措施)))
                     (CC 和)
                     (NP (NN 政策)
                         (NN 要点))))))
   (PU 。))

(c) Bracketed result in our treebank:

他/r [还/d 提出/v]V [[一/m 系列/n]QP [具体/a 措施/n 和/c 政策/n 要点
/n]NP-BL]/NP 。/w
```

Fig. 1. A sample sentence and its parsed result

3.3 Syntactic Bracketing

In our annotation, each clause ended with punctuations such as period (。), comma (，), semicolon (；), exclamation point (！), colon (：), and interrogation mark (？), is taken as a processing unit. The annotation is conducted in a Top-Down manner. When we process a clause, the main predicate is first recognized. Then each phrase with maximum length, which plays a distinct semantic role of the predicate, is bracketed. The concept of "phrase with maximum length" depends on contexts[1]. After recognizing the first level chunks, we further parse the chunks with nested structures. When extracting candidate collocations, we first consider the headwords of the first level chunks, and then the words within a chunk. We believe that when a chunk or a clause is too short, further annotation may not bring more benefits. In fact, simple statistical methods can filter false collocations derived from such chunks and small chunks can be easily parsed.

In our annotation, each bracket has zero or more structural or functional tags as well as a syntactic label (like [3]). For example, a noun phrase should be further annotated with its internal structure. If the internal structure is modifier-modified (e.g.,

---

[1] For example, "香港理工大学计算机系的学生" is a noun phrase with maximum length in the sentence "香港理工大学计算机系的学生很受欢迎", whereas "计算机系的学生" is such a maximum phrase in the sentence "计算机系的学生表演了精彩的节日".

漂亮的姑娘/beautiful girl), we only care about the headword when extracting collocations between different chunks. If the internal structure is parallel (e.g., 桌子椅子/tables and chairs), each component in the chunk will be considered.

3.4 Annotation Process and Quality Control

Our annotation is conducted in two phases: first, word segmentation and POS tagging, and second, syntactic bracketing. The treebank annotation is an iterative process, in which incremental refinement of guidelines, corpus, and tools, is done step by step. One supervisor and two annotators with linguistic background are involved in our project. The one-million-word original text corpus was selected from news reports, and mainly contains articles about economic development.

We take some measures to maintain the quality, i.e. annotation accuracy and inter-annotator consistency. Every annotator is assigned about 60% of the entire data to process. Thus about 20% of the data is randomly selected for double annotation. These cross-annotated texts could be used to measure the inter-annotator consistency. Moreover, the supervisor must check and re-annotate the same part based on the two annotators' work. The final result is used as gold standard to evaluate the annotation accuracy of each annotator.

4   Conclusion and Future Plans

We have discussed some issues in building a Chinese shallow parsed treebank, which include our definition of partial parsing used in collocation extraction, guideline preparation, and quality control. Till now, we have finished the first annotation phase, i.e. word segmentation and POS tagging, and a small part of texts have been syntactically bracketed. The final treebank is expected to be completed in June 2003.

As indicated above, our shallow parsed treebank contains very limited syntactic and semantic information. We plan to annotate the syntactic function of each chunk and the relationship between predicate chunk and other chunks in the future.

References

1. Christopher D. Manning, Hinrich Schutze: Foundations of Statistical Natural Language Processing. MIT Press (1999)
2. Smadja F.: Retrieving Collocations from text: Xtract, Computational Linguistics. 19:1(1994) 143–177
3. Fei Xia, et al.: Developing Guidelines and Ensuring Consistency for Chinese Text Annotation. In the Proceedings of the second International Conference on Language Resources and Evaluation (LREC-2000), Athens, Greece (2000)
4. Keh-Jiann Chen, et al.: the CKIP Chinese Treebank: Guidelines for Annotation. In: Building and Using Syntactically Annoted Corpora, Dordrecht: Kluwer (2000)
5. Yu Shiwen, et al.: the Grammatical Knowledge-base of Contemporary Chinese: a Complete Specification. Beijing: Tsinghua University Press (1998)

Corpus Construction within Linguistic Module of City Information Dialogue System

Roman Mouček and Kamil Ekštein

Department of Computer Science and Engineering,
University of West Bohemia, Plzeň, Czech Republic
{moucek,kekstein}@kiv.zcu.cz

Abstract. This paper deals with the methods of corpus constructions for computerized dialogue system used in city information center. The corpus of recorded, generated and simulated sentences is introduced. The usage of corpus and the corresponding results are presented.

1 Introduction

A very important application in the human-machine interaction area is the domain of computerized dialogue systems. The new computerized dialogue system developed at the University of West Bohemia, Czech Republic, in co–operation with Technical University in Dresden, Germany, and Pilsen City Council, is intended for Pilsen city information center. The aim of this dialogue system is to introduce a more natural dialogue between a user and computer. Many results are not used only for the developed dialogue system itself but they are intended for other research activities in our laboratories.

The dialogue system architecture is modular and it follows the architecture used in SUNDIAL project (described in [1]). It consists of word recognizer, module of linguistic analysis, dialogue manager, application database and speech synthesizer. This paper deals with one of the initial problems – corpus construction.

2 Corpus Construction

We used several methods during the corpus construction:

- dialogue recording,
- sentence generation,
- dialogue simulation.

The results of these methods are presented in the following sections. On the base of these results we decided there was no need to use another special methodology for corpus construction. Even so, we are able to cover more problems which are connected with the other parts of the dialogue system (analysis of user requirements, determination of system boundaries, domain selection, dialogue modelling and speech recognition).

A. Gelbukh (Ed.): CICLing 2003, LNCS 2588, pp. 406–409, 2003.

2.1   Corpus of Recorded Sentences

The first detailed analysis of the problem area had been carried out by Jana Schwarz, Institute of Slavistics, TU Dresden, Germany. She visited 12 information centers in different regions of the Czech Republic to cover differences in spoken language. About 500 dialogues were recorded with an overall length of more than 13 hours. These dialogues were transcribed and widely analyzed [4].

These real dialogues are nowadays used in the process of dialogue modelling. Another research group uses up these dialogues as a basis in their research of Czech spoken language and in the research of differences between spoken and written Czech.

The corpus of real dialogues is used within our dialogue system as:

- the source for analysis of user requirements,
- the source for determination of dialogue system boundaries,
- the first source for elaboration of syntactic construction used in spoken language,
- the typical word collocations and phrases used in tourist information centers,
- the first source for dialogue modelling.

For our purposes we eliminated all the sentences connected e.g. with the purchase and all the sentences that can be used only in human-human interaction. We obtained following results:

- we are not able to cover all the questions asked in tourists information centers by robust computerized dialogue system,
- we have to select only a subdomain of the problem area (two subdomains were selected – public transport and institution – with respect to the frequency of user questions, our experience and needs of Pilsen City Council.

2.2   Corpus of Generated Sentences

The corpus of recorded sentences was further analyzed to automatically create the sentence templates. There was developed a special program package using the method of a quantitative linguistic analysis working in two modes (generation of a set of templates describing the syntactic structure of real sentence and generation of a large corpus of unique training sentences on the basis of sentence templates and stochastic complex-free grammar, described in detail in [4]. The grammar rules had been several times reworked and experimentally completed by terminal symbols (possible words and word collocations which had not appeared in the real sentences before). Each nonterminal symbol (the basic element of the sentence template) is marked by its probability of occurrence. Then the whole corpus consists of more than 40.000 sentences.

The modified corpus of generated sentences (see Section 2.3) is used in our dialogue system as:

- the source for the training of speech recognizer [2],
- the source for the verification of sentence templates.

We obtained following results:

- the program package for sentence generation is very useful in the phase of speech recognition (the generation of sentences adds no information to the corpus but the corpus covers word collocations in the problem area as much as possible, and the corpus used as a language model respects the probability of occurrence of words and word collocations in the spoken language),
- it is sometimes very hard to decide which sentence is wrong because many syntactically wrong sentences can appear in spoken language,
- the number of wrong sentences in the corpus of generated sentences is 7.8%,
- thus the corpus of generated sentences can be used for training of a module of linguistic analysis.

2.3   Corpus of Simulated Sentences

The whole corpus of recorded dialogues (it means also corpus of generated sentences) covers too wide area to be elaborated in the module of linguistic analysis (see Section 2.1). Thus the corpus of real and generated sentences was divided by another program tool into several domains. The principles of domain analysis are described e.g. in [3]. Then the corpus for transport domain contains approximately 4.000 sentences and the corpus for institution domain about 5.000 sentences.

On the other side, the analysis of corpus of generated sentences for transport domain showed that this corpus still did not cover all common situations in spoken language in this domain. We also needed to simulate the change in the dialogue strategy if people speak to computer instead of human being. 15 university students and 50 people of different education and different social status were asked to simulate dialogues with computer in the domain of transport (especially local transport in Pilsen area). The process of the dialogue simulation was controlled by people experienced in human-computer interaction. The method "Wizard of Oz" was partly used.

The corpus of simulated sentences is used in our dialogue system as:

- the source completing the set of typical dialogues in selected domains,
- the second source for the program package generating sentence templates,
- the source for the comparison of sentence templates obtained from the recorded dialogues,
- the source for analysis of dialogue strategies in the case of human-computer interaction.

We obtained following results:

- the final corpus contains more then 8.000 sentences for transport domain,

– the final set of grammar rules contains 58% of grammar rules obtained by analysis of simulated sentences, it means that we were not able to complete most of the possible syntactic structures of spoken language in this specific area without additional dialogue simulation,

– the final number of terminal symbols (words and word collocations) contains only 14% of new items, it means that we were able to cover most of the vocabulary in the first step of sentence generation by experimental completion of grammar rules with terminal symbols in the transport domain,

– the proper and successful use of the method "Wizard of Oz" is very difficult and time-consuming.

3   Conclusion and Future Work

This paper describes the basic approaches to the corpus construction within computerized dialogue system intended for city information center. The corpora of recorded and simulated sentences serve as a base for generation of sentence templates. Then the corpus of generated sentences is created. This final corpus of generated sentences is used in the speech recognition module and in the linguistic module. The very preliminary results (the speech recognition module is still under construction) of the recognition accuracy rates show that the word recognition accuracy reaches 91.7% and the sentence recognition accuracy 69.1% (20 speakers and microphone quality). This paper shows the importance of the corpus of real sentences (e.g. the analysis of user requirements), the corpus of simulated sentences (e.g. the completion of possible syntactic structures) and the corpus of generated sentences (usage within speech recognition module and linguistic module). The usage of all methods described above enabled our team to solve many other problems during dialogue system construction.

Acknowledgement. This research is supported partly by the Grant of Czech Republic Ministry of Education, MSM 235200005 Information Systems and Technologies and partly by the Grant Agency of the Czech Republic under the grant GA 201/02/1553.

References

1. Eckert W.: Gesprochener Mensch–Maschine–Dialogue, PhD Thesis, Universität Erlangen–Nürnberg, Germany, 1995.
2. Ekštein K.: SpART I – An Experimental Automatic Speech Recognizer, In *Proceedings of SPECOM 2001*, Moscow, Russia, Oct 2001.
3. Mouček R., Taušer K.: Dialogue System for City Information Center, *Proceedings of the 6th World MultiConference on Systemics, Cybernetics and Informatics SCI 2002*, Orlando, USA, 2002, volume XII, pp. 563–567.
4. Schwarz J., Matoušek V.: Creation of a Corpus of Training Sentences Based on Automated Dialogue Analysis, *Proceedings of the 4th International Conference TSD 2001*, Železná Ruda, Czech Republic, Sep 2001.

Diachronic Stemmed Corpus and Dictionary of Galician Language*

Nieves R. Brisaboa, Juan-Ramón López, Miguel R. Penabad, and Ángeles S. Places

Dep. de Computación, Universidade da Coruña
{brisaboa, penabad}@udc.es, mon@dc.fi.udc.es,
asplaces@mail2.udc.es

Abstract. In this work we present a manually marked up corpus of Old Galician language (460 documents, 5,601,290 running words) and a diachronic dictionary extracted from it, as well as its potential applications, whose implementation is a topic of future work.

1 Introduction

In [7] we have described a tool for computer-aided stemming of documents written in languages with no orthographic regulation. Basically, the tool works as follows.

It is based on an approach that we call the *exhaustive approach*. The exhaustive approach consists in the definition of a collection of *lexemes* by means of exhaustive enumeration. A lexeme is the set of all different orthographic forms for a particular word and all its morphological forms. It is referred to by the lemma (dictionary form of the word—infinitive for verbs, singular for nouns, etc.) in its modern grammatical version. For example, English words *love*, *loving* and *luv* belong to the lexeme having LOVE—the well-written infinitive form—as its lemma.

Working with our system involves two phases: First, the documents must be analysed using the Document Analysis Module and included in the database. Then, users can perform different types of queries using the Database Querying Module. These two phases and their corresponding system modules shown in Fig. 1 are described below.

The Document Analysis phase is carried out by the Document Analysis Module of the system. The process of stemming each running word (wordform) of an input document is reduced to the comparison of the wordform with the content of each lexeme present in the database, determining its correct classification and thus its corresponding lemma.

For this process, the system is capable of working in two modes: Supervised mode and Non-Supervised mode. Supervised mode implies that the system *always* asks the user the lexeme to which the wordform must be assigned, maybe making a suggestion for a possible lexeme. Non-Supervised mode means that if the system can unambiguously assign the wordform to a lexeme then it will do it, and only in case of ambiguity it will ask the user.

* This work was partially funded by CICYT (TEL99-0335-C04-02)

A. Gelbukh (Ed.): CICLing 2003, LNCS 2588, pp. 410–414, 2003.

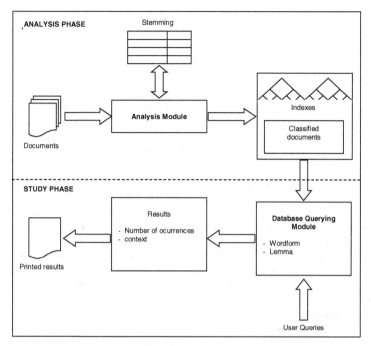

Fig. 1. How the mark-up tool works

The Database Querying Module is used to extract information from the analysed documents. It accesses all the documents in a corpus and, using the indexes created by the Analysis Module, allows for a number of basic kinds of searches: (1) *Wordform search:* to look for occurrences of a given spelling of a wordform; (2) *Lemma search:* to look for occurrences of all wordforms of a given lexeme.

Since the system presents some information about the document, such as its origin and date, it is a valuable tool for linguists studying the evolution of a language. For example, given a lemma, all the documents that contain it can be obtained. An exploration that considers the dates and places of writing of these documents gives a straightforward indication of the evolution of the word. On the other hand, the tool can also be used by other types of researchers, mainly from Humanities, to obtain information about the society of the time when the documents were written.

The rest of the paper is organized as follows. Section 2 describes the problems of stemming non-normative texts. Section 3 summarizes the corpus obtained as a result of application of the tool. Section 4 describes the possible applications of these results. Section 5 offers some conclusions and directions for future work.

2 Stemming Non-normative Texts

Every language has had a period where there were no strict orthographical, grammatical, or syntactical regulations to write in this language. Writers using a language in such period were not constrained by any kind of normative, so their writings reflect different variations of the language. There are, for example, Spanish texts from the

Mexican altiplano from the Colonial Period where 16 forms of the word "Iglesia" (church) can be found.[1] These variations make these documents of significant interest for linguistic researchers, as they reflect the real evolution of the language through time. Furthermore, there is also a community of researchers that is interested in studying the culture that is reflected in these texts.

However, this linguistic richness and these different variations make it impossible—or at least impractical—the use of conventional Natural Language Processing techniques (such as stemming) for supporting text retrieval. Such approaches based on the definition of a stemming algorithm that relies on the well-defined and well-known rules of the given language [3, 4], allow for the automatic and almost autonomous processing of documents (see, e.g., [1,5,6,8,9,10]). However, these stemming techniques (i.e. rules) are not appropriate for the documents written in a non-normalized language, because they assume that the texts are correctly written.

Without the possibility of stemming these texts, the automatic processing of the cultural heritage that they represent is not possible. This is true for texts in any language written before it became normative with strict orthographic and grammatical rules, but it is especially important for the study of non-literary works or writings by poorly educated people, because this really shows the evolution of a language.

Thus, for documents written without a clear and stable regulation, a different approach is needed. In this work we have applied a tool that follows the *exhaustive approach* by defining a wide and complete collection of *lexemes* that allow for systematic word comparisons.

3 Corpus Obtained

We have applied our tool to 460 documents (5,601,290 running words) in Old Galician language, from Middle Age to the present time.

Galician is the language spoken in Galicia, a region in the northwest of Spain. It is very close to Portuguese, having the same syntactic, morphological, and lexical base. After Spain and Portugal became different states, Galician entered a decline period suffering a sharp demotion for three centuries (16th to 18th). It continued being used but its exclusively oral use caused a strong dialectalization. During the 19th century, the literary, cultural, political, and historical recovery of Galician took place. Writers of this age had to "invent" their own orthographic regulations, all of them strongly influenced by the Spanish ones. Finally, since 1977, an official orthographic regulation exists but since it has many political implications, it has not been accepted by many Galician writers and philologists, who have proposed and support different alternative regulations. Four orthographic regulations exist nowadays. Thus, Galician texts are perfect examples of documents written in a non-normative language.

Using our tool with the mentioned documents we have obtained a diachronic stemmed corpus of Galician language. From this corpus, a dictionary can be extracted with the following structure:

```
wordform lemma time
```

where time is a list of the centuries, with frequencies, when the form was used, e.g:

```
yglezya iglesia {16:321,17:45,18:2}
```

---

[1] In Spanish, this word has only two forms: singular (*iglesia*) and plural (*iglesias*).

where 16 stands for years 1600s and 321 the number of occurrences found in the corpus. The dictionary contains 80,649 lexemes, and 196,678 wordforms.

In our experiments, we use a corpus of Galician language built by ourselves from many different sources, including Web documents, e-books, documents from digital libraries and parts of other corpora, most of them available in Internet. Most of the texts were collected from the Galician Virtual Library [414], the CORGA corpus, Galician Wordtheque and technical documents from different people. Texts were classified in categories: ECO (economy and society texts), JUS (legal texts), LIT (literature), NEW (newspapers), and TEC (science and technology). Table 1 shows a brief description of the sources:

Table 1. Corpus obtained

	# Documents	Size (MB)	# Words	# Wordforms	# Lexemes
ECO	129	4.0	544,075	42,839	18,489
JUS	157	3.3	508,539	32,822	15,319
LIT	99	13	2,260,291	110,722	42,862
NEW	65	10	1,733,210	88,029	38,901
TEC	10	3.6	555,175	45,340	20,438
Total:	460	34	5,601,290	196,678	80,649

4 Possible Applications

Most existing corpora, e.g., those collected from Internet [11], reflect only the contemporary state of the language. Unlike them, our manually stemmed corpus is diachronic since it contains documents from different epochs. We consider such a corpus (and the corresponding dictionary of lexemes as sets of wordforms) a valuable linguistic resource, which has the following potential applications both in automatic processing of non-normative texts and in the Humanities:

1. Data mining techniques can be applied to this dictionary to induce the forms absent from it. For example, if we know the variants *yglezya – iglesia, idiosincrazya – idiosincrasia*, etc., then we can automatically induce the correspondence *gimnázya – gimnasia* absent from the initial dictionary. This is useful for automatic or semiautomatic stemming of new documents.
2. One can suppose that stemming non-normative texts can be done on phonetic base: both the words from the corpus and the words from a contemporary (normative) dictionary are transcribed to the phonetic form and are compared in this form: *yglezya* -> [IGLESYA], *iglesia* -> [IGLESYA]. Though we did not implement such an algorithm, our dictionary can be used to estimate its accuracy.
3. Data mining techniques can be applied to this dictionary to discover the regularities in diachronic changes of the language. This is useful for linguistic study of the language as well as for the application discussed in the next item.
4. Automatic prediction of the changes of a specific word in a specific century can improve the accuracy of the automatic stemming describe in the item 1 above. Specifically, only the wordforms predicted for the given century should be taken into account in automatic stemming when processing documents with a known date.

5. Our dictionary, or its improved variant described in the item 4, can be used for automatic determination of the date of the document.

5   Conclusions

We have presented a manually marked up corpus of Old Galician language (460 documents, 5,601,290 running words) and a diachronic dictionary extracted from it, as well as its potential applications. Their implementation is a topic of future work.

References

1. Brisaboa, N. R., Callón, C., López, Juan-Ramón, Places, A. S., Sanmartín, G. Stemming Galician Texts. Lecture Notes in Computer Science (LNCS 2476),. Springer-Verlag (SPIRE'2002), pp. 91-97. Lisboa, Portugal, 2002.
2. Galician Virtual Library. http://bvg.udc.es
3. Gelbukh, A., Sidorov, G. Morphological Analysis of Inflective Languages Through Generation. J. *Procesamiento de Lenguaje Natural*, No 29, 2002.
4. Gelbukh, A., Sidorov, G. Approach to Construction of Automatic Morphological Analysis Systems for Inflective Languages with Little Effort. *Computational Liguistics and Intelligent Text Processing*. Lecture Notes in Computer Science N 2588, Springer-Verlag, 2003.
5. Honrado, A., Leon, R., O'Donnell, R. and Sinclair, D. A Word Stemming Algorithm for the Spanish Language. In *Proceedings of the 7th International Symposium on String Processing and Information Retrieval (SPIRE'2000) – IEEE Comp. Society.*, pp.139–145, España, 2000.
6. Kraaij, W., Pohlmann, R. Porter's stemming algorithm for Dutch. In L.G.M. Noordman and W.A.M. de Vroomen, editors, *Informatiewetenschap 1994: Wetenschappelijke bijdragen aan de derde STINFON Conferentie*, pp. 167–180, Tilburg, 1994.
7. López, J.R., Iglesias, E.L., Brisaboa, N.R., Paramá, J.R., Penabad, M.R. Base de datos documental para el estudio del español antiguo. In Proceedings of the *X Simposio Internacional en Aplicaciones de Informática (INFONOR'97)*, pp. 2–8.Chile, 1997.
8. Moreira, V., Huyck, C. A Stemming Algorithm for the Portuguese Language. In *Proceedings of the 8th International Symposium on String Processing and Information Retrieval (SPIRE'2001) – IEEE Computer Society*, pp.186-193, Chile, 2001.
9. Snowball Project. http://snowball.sourceforge.net.
10. Wechsler, M., Sheridan, P., Schäuble, P. Multi-Language Text Indexing for Internet Retrieval. In the *Proceedings of the 5th RIAO Conference Computer Assisted Information Searching on the Internet*. Montreal, Canada, 1997.
11. A. Gelbukh, G. Sidorov, L. Chanona-Hernández. *Compilation of a Spanish representative corpus. Computational Linguistics and Intelligent Text Processing*, Lecture Notes in Computer Science, N 2276, Springer-Verlag, 2002, pp. 285–288.

Can We Correctly Estimate the Total Number of Pages in Google for a Specific Language?[*]

Igor A. Bolshakov and Sofia N. Galicia-Haro

Center for Computing Research (CIC)
National Polytechnic Institute (IPN)
Mexico City, Mexico
{igor,sofia}@cic.ipn.mx

Abstract. It is argued that for some applications the total amount of web-pages actually stored in an Internet search engine for a specific language is relevant. It is shown that some elementary steps in getting statistics characterizing Google engine's database are bewildering: simple set theory operations gives evidently inconsistent results. Without claiming an ultimate precision, we propose a method of estimation of the total page amount for a given language in a given moment. It takes amounts of Google pages for the words most frequent in a representative text corpus, reorders these words, and gives maximum likelihood estimates for their contributions. The method is applied to Spanish and gives the results with theoretically calculated precision much higher than really needed while resting on such an error-prone mechanism outputting raw statistical data.

1   Google Is Extremely Unreliable in All Its Statistics

The most important modern application of Internet search engines like Google is the retrieval of information on commerce, politics, science, technologies, etc. The applications of Internet searches directly to the needs of computational linguistics are scarce [1, 2, 5]. However, such applications are reasonable and even topical. For example, we can imagine a text editing system accessing Goggle to clear up the prevailing orthography of a new term, to disambiguate the sense of a given word [1] or test availability of a given collocation in the language [3].

For computational linguistic purposes, we sometimes need to statistically measure amounts of web-pages containing specific words and collocations. These data should be weighted, i.e. divided by the total amount of web-pages, given a search engine, a specific language and a moment of time. For example, the criterion of that combination of words V and W is statistically stable enough to be considered collocation has the shape of the so-called mutual information inequality [7]:

---

[*] Work done under partial support of CONACyT, CGEPI-IPN, and SNI, Mexico. We are grateful to Prof. A. Gelbukh for his valuable advices and to D. Filatov for his help in calculations.

A. Gelbukh (Ed.): CICLing 2003, LNCS 2588, pp. 415–419, 2003.

$$\ln \frac{N(V,W)}{N_{\max}} > \ln \frac{N(V)}{N_{\max}} + \ln \frac{N(W)}{N_{\max}},$$

where $N(V,W)$ is the amount of web-pages where V and W co-occurred, $N(V)$ and $N(W)$ are amounts of their web-pages evaluated independently, $N_{\max}$ is the total web-page amount managed by Google for the given language.

We need accurate and actual data, since all statistics in large search engines are subject to variations from day to day and even during a day. Some general statistics about Google are published in its principal pages, but without their distribution between specific languages.

Seeking for a computational method resting on raw statistical data delivered by Google, we encounter some bewildering results from the very beginning.

Let us take two Spanish word of high statistical ranks (e.g., *que* and *de*) and pass them into Google. Then it may be seen that

$N(que) = 7,350,000;\ N(de\ \neg que) = 2,980,000;\ N(que) + N(de\ \neg que) = 10,330,000;$
$N(de) = 6,740,000;\ N(que\ \neg de) = 1,220,000;\ N(de) + N(que\ \neg de) = 8,960,000;$
$N(que\ \text{OR}\ de) = 7,440,000;\ N(de\ \text{OR}\ que) = 7,340,000.$

This implies that

- The operation OR, within the precision of ±0.7% of the mean value, does not depend on the order of the operands. This is OK.
- However, the three different ways of calculating the amount of pages where at least one word of the two is available give drastically differing results. Indeed, the summations without OR gives results differing in ±17.3% of their mean value, whereas the result of the OR operation differs from the mean value of the two in −23.6% .

From this we can infer that the OR operation should not be used at all, and any results without OR are also rather doubtful.

The other deficiency of Google is poor attribution of languages. We mean not only pages in one language attributed to other language (e.g., some pages in Portuguese are recognized as Spanish ones, and some pages in Ukrainian and Bulgarian recognized as Russian). Very confusing influence on statistics is exerted by the pages that are in essence text-deprived (ads, banners, etc. with short texts within a picture or alike), with some pseudo-texts in the pages' descriptions given in a formal language. We cannot guess what algorithm can assign such pages to a specific language. Numerous repetitions among web-pages also can be seen.

However, for our purposes, we hazard to propose below a method of calculating the full amount of pages in a specific language accessible in a given search engine at the current moment, neglecting all Google errors mentioned above. Our task is to determine the whole bulk in supposition that the Google-delivered data are reliable.

2   Method of Estimation

Our method can be formulated as follows.

1. A few tens of words (functional word forms, to put it more exactly) of a given language are taken, which are the most frequent in a text corpus of a rather high length. For our purposes, as few as $K_{max} = 24$ highest ranked forms proved to be sufficient.
2. The forms taken are ordered once more according to the amounts of web-pages where they occurred.
3. The number of pages $N_1 = N(W(1))$ for the first-rank form $W(1)$ is taken as the initial approximation to the N_{total} to be computed.
4. The cycle is started:

- The word $W(k_2)$ is searched ($k_2 = 2, 3, ..., K_{max}$), for which $N_2 = \max\{N(W(k_2)\neg W(1))\}$ is reached, where the pages without $W(1)$ are only taken into account. The N_2 is added to N_{total}.
- The word $W(k_3)$ is searched ($k_3 = 2, 3, ..., K_{max}, k_3 \neq k_2$), for which $N_3 = \max\{N(W(k_3)\neg W(1)\neg W(k_2))\}$ is reached, where the pages without $W(1)$ and $W(k_2)$ are taken into account. The N_2 is added to N_{total}, etc.

Such contributions of words without all previous ones could be taken up to $W(K_{max})$ or even further, but Google does not permits to use more that $K = 10$ elements in the search formula. So we are forced to stop calculation of N_{total} with the last increment $\max\{N(W(k_{10})\neg W(1)\neg W(k_2)\neg W(k_3) ...\neg W(k_9))\}$, i.e. with the 10th word among the K_{max} indicated above that gives the maximal contribution of pages not yet taken into account.

The rest words can be taken into further consideration in the supposition that no more than nine most influent words are cast away for each of them. This would evidently gives an oversized result.

To get a more realistic estimate and at the same time to evaluate the standard deviation of this estimate, let us approximate the random values $N_1, N_2 ..., N_{10}$ by the infinite exponential series

$$\tilde{N}_{total} \approx e^a (1 + e^{-u} + e^{-2u} + ...) = e^a / (1 - e^{-u}),$$

where $a \gg 1$ and $u > 0$ are determined through $N_1, N_2, ..., N_{10}$ by the maximum likelihood method [4]. This gives the following estimates for a and u:

$$\tilde{a} = \frac{2M_0(2K+1)}{K(K-1)} - \frac{6M_1}{K(K-1)}, \qquad \tilde{u} = \frac{6M_0}{K(K-1)} - \frac{12M_1}{K(K^2-1)},$$

where $M_0 = \Sigma_{i=1...K} \ln(N_i)$, and $M_1 = \Sigma_{i=1...K} \ln(N_i) i$. To estimate the dispersion σ^2 of the random values $\ln(N_i)$, the following formula is valid

$$\sigma^2 = \frac{1}{K} \sum_{i=1....K} (\ln(N_i) - \tilde{a} - \tilde{u} i)^2$$

In order to determine the dispersion $D(\tilde{N}_{total})$, we deliberately ignore the random nature of σ^2 and calculate the minimal covariation matrix of the random pair $\{a = \tilde{a}, u = \tilde{u}\}$, as if only these two are to be estimated. Indeed, the influence of σ^2 is measured by higher powers of its mean value, already rather small. In such a supposition, we construct a linear combination of the covariation matrix entries and the second partial derivatives of $\tilde{N}_{total}$ by a and u:

$$\mathbf{D}(\tilde{a}) = \frac{\partial^2 \tilde{N}_{\text{total}}}{\partial a^2}\, \mathbf{D}(\tilde{a}) + 2\frac{\partial^2 \tilde{N}_{\text{total}}}{\partial a\,\partial u}\, \mathbf{R}(\tilde{a},\ \tilde{u}) + \frac{\partial^2 \tilde{N}_{\text{total}}}{\partial u^2}\, \mathbf{D}(\tilde{u})$$

where the derivatives are taken in the point $\{a = \tilde{a},\ u = \tilde{u}\}$, and

$$\mathbf{D}(\tilde{a}) = \frac{2\sigma^2(2K+1)}{K(K-1)}\ ;\ \ \mathbf{R}(\tilde{a},\ \tilde{u}) = -\frac{6\sigma^2}{K(K-1)}\ ;\ \ \mathbf{D}(\tilde{u}) = \frac{12\sigma^2}{K(K^2-1)}\ .$$

Finally, this gives

$$\mathbf{D}(\tilde{N}_{\text{total}}) = \frac{2\sigma^2 e^a}{K(K-1)(1-e^{-u})}\left[(2K+1)+\frac{3e^{-u}}{(1-e^{-u})}+\frac{6e^{-u}(1+e^{-u})}{(K+1)(1-e^{-u})^2}\right],$$

where all values are taken in the estimate point $\{\ \tilde{a},\ \tilde{u}\ \sigma^2\}$.

After such calculations, the standard deviation $\sqrt{\mathbf{D}(\tilde{N}_{\text{total}})}$ should be compared with the value of $\tilde{N}_{\text{total}}$.

3   An Example: Spanish

To realize the proposed method, a PERL program was developed for accessing Google. The most frequent word forms were taken from LEXESP corpus of Spanish [6]. The form *es* is among them, but we have noticed that in too many cases it corresponds to the suffix *.es* in the e-mail addresses, so we ignore it in our calculations. The statistics and the results of the two sequential reordering of words are presented in the table, where the column 1 gives the most common forms ordered by their web-page amounts, the column 2 gives their specific page amounts in Google, column 3 gives the rank numbers of these forms in the corpus, and the column 4 gives the ranks assigned to the forms while moving on by our algorithm.

Form	Page amount, in 10^6	Rank in corpus	Rank while calculating	Form	Page amount, in 10^6	Rank in corpus	Rank while calculating
que	7.01	3	1	las	5.64	11	–
y	6.68	4	5	un	5.55	10	–
por	6.63	16	–	los	5.54	8	–
una	6.30	14	–	para	5.52	20	10
es	6.10	18	N/A	como	5.46	22	–
el	6.08	5	9	su	5.35	17	–
en	6.08	6	6	o	5.10	23	–
con	6.08	15	–	lo	5.06	19	–
la	6.07	2	8	al	4.85	21	–
de	6.00	1	2	a	4.81	7	3
del	5.99	12	7	sus	4.41	24	–
se	5.65	9	–	no	4.31	13	4

The cycle for the ten most influent words (without *es*) is given in other table and repeated in the figure, where the points representing N_i are given in logarithmic scale, while the straight line is the linear maximum likelihood approximation $\ln(N_i) \approx 15.43 - 0.52\,i$ with $\tilde{a} = 15.43$ and $\tilde{u} = 0.52$. Hence, $\tilde{N}_{total} = 12{,}431{,}000$ with the standard deviation $\sqrt{D(\tilde{N}_{total})} = 26{,}550$, that is only 0.2% of the measured value.

Page amount	Combination of words tested
7010000	que
4610000	de ¬que
362000	a ¬que ¬de
302000	no ¬que ¬de ¬a
225000	y ¬que ¬de ¬a ¬no
169000	en ¬que ¬de ¬a ¬no ¬y
126000	del ¬que ¬de ¬a ¬no ¬y ¬en
79300	la ¬que ¬de ¬a ¬no ¬y ¬en ¬del
63900	el ¬que ¬de ¬a ¬no ¬y ¬en ¬del ¬la
44300	para ¬que ¬de ¬a ¬no ¬y ¬en ¬del ¬la ¬el
12991500	**total**

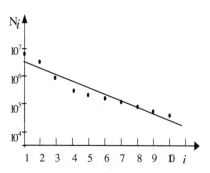

Such a deviation is totally negligible as compared to the suspected imprecision of the raw data, not mentioning their systematic changes in time. Our instrument evidently does not correspond to the job. We can only wait till Google's managers will make the raw statistics and set operations more reliable, to apply our algorithm. Till then our negative knowledge stays valid, and we can answer "no" to the question at the title.

However, we do have a tentative estimate just now: as Google testifies, at the moment of the measurements Spanish was represented in it by $\tilde{N}_{total} \approx 12{,}400{,}000$ pages.

References

1. Agirre, E., D. Martinez. *Exploring automatic word sense disambiguation with decision lists and the Web*. Proceedings of Semantic Annotation and Intelligent Annotation Workshop. Organized by COLING, Luxemburg, 2000.
2. Agirre E., D. Martinez. *Integrating selectional preferences in WordNet*. Proceedings of the First International WordNet Conference in Mysore, India, 21–25 January, 2002.
3. Bolshakov, I. A. *Detección y corrección de malapropismos en español mediante un sistema bi-etapa para comprobar colocaciones*. Memoria del Congreso Internacional de Computación CIC'2002. CIC-IPN, Mexico, noviembre, 2002.
4. Cramer, H. *Mathematical Methods of Statistics*. Princeton University Press. 1999.
5. Keller, F., M. Lapata, and O. Ourioupina. *Using the Web to Overcome Data Sparseness*. Proceedings of the Conference on Empirical Methods in Natural Language Processing. Philadelphia, Pennsylvania, USA. 2002.
6. LEXESP corpus. http://www.ub.es/edicions/libros/v14.htm, http://clic.fil.ub.es/ recursos/corpus.shtml.
7. Manning, Ch. D., H. Schütze. *Foundations of Statistical Natural Language Processing*. The MIT Press, 1999.

The Word Is Mightier than the Count: Accumulating Translation Resources from Parsed Parallel Corpora

Stephen Nightingale and Hideki Tanaka

ATR, Spoken Language Translation Research Laboratory
Keihanna, Kyoto, Japan
{night, tanakah}@slt.atr.co.jp

Abstract. Large, high-quality, sentence aligned parallel corpora are hard to come by, and this makes the Statistical Machine Translation enterprise more difficult. Even noisy corpora can provide useful translation resources not otherwise available though. Many investigations have used statistical methods to find word correspondences. Often such methods suffer from overgeneration, so to correct this we filter relevant translation candidates using a lexical post-process. This dictionary lookup is so effective in fact that it brings into question the value of the statistical methods. Using a dictionary lookup against all combinations of phrase pairs as a baseline, we compare three statistical methods and report the results. The three methods are (1) Mutual Information; (2) Expectation Maximization over word co-occurrence frequencies; and (3) EM over word alignments in every sentence. We also apply the dictionary lookup as a postprocess, to tackle overgeneration.

1   Introduction

Large, high-quality, sentence aligned parallel corpora are hard to come by, and this makes the Statistical Machine Translation enterprise more difficult. Even noisy corpora can provide useful translation resources not otherwise available though, particularly when compounds derived from parsed corpora are extracted and selectively filtered.

We can then use word-by-word dictionary lookups to select the maximal set of compositional and partially compositional compounds, to use as a baseline for assessing the statistical methods. The three statistical methods evaluated in this experiment are: (1) a Mutual Information calculation is used to correlate terms in parallel pieces of text; (2) the Expectation Maximization algorithm is used over frequencies of word occurrences, to yield a probabilistic dictionary; and (3) using the probabilistic dictionary derived from EM(1) as a starting point, we compute word alignments over each sentence in the corpus to produce a better probabilistic dictionary.

The first method, used by Fung and Church [5], treats each sentence as a bag of words in which only word frequency information is significant, the

A. Gelbukh (Ed.): CICLing 2003, LNCS 2588, pp. 420-431, 2003.

second method computes frequency information over all alignments, and the third treats each sentence as an ordered sequence of words: word frequency information is significant over the whole corpus, and word order is significant within each sentence. The latter two methods are essentially IBM Models 1 and 2 respectively, from the Candide framework [3].

Our results show that the exhaustive generation and dictionary lookup method perform best, but of the statistical methods, EM over word frequencies gives the better results. One issue is, therefore, why does the EM method outperform MI? The larger purpose of the work is to accumulate resources from bilingual corpora which cannot be directly used for Statistical Machine Translation, but may be useful for other corpus based MT work.

A standard reference for exploiting parallel texts is Melamed [7], and as part of a wide ranging investigation into translational equivalence he reviews all of the statistical methods discussed in this paper, though not in direct comparison against a single corpus. Still, several things have moved on since Melamed's investigation: in the first place, the availability of very substantial bilingual dictionaries such as Edict [2] allow a high degree of corroboration of statistically extracted word translations, including, significantly, personal and organization names. In the second place it is now possible to parse large corpora with adequate accuracy [4, 6], allowing a more systematic combination of the words which form compounds. Third, the availability for research purposes of an efficient implementation of the Expectation Maximization methods [1] allows experimentation against large corpora to proceed with some felicity. Thus, this paper is offered as a useful contribution to the field of automatic vocabulary extraction.

The investigation is structured as follows: In Section 2 the corpus and its preparation are described. The dictionary lookup method and the three term translation extraction methods are described in Section 3 together with the results from processing the NHK News corpus. In Section 4 the results are discussed and compared. Section 5 concludes.

2   The Corpus

The NHK News Corpus [8] includes 41.1K content-aligned news articles of Japanese an their free English translations. Each article has typically 4 - 10 sentences, and while the average length of a Japanese sentence is about 40 words, the English sentences average about 21 words in length. A typical example article pair concerns the debate in Japanese about the introduction of Daylight Savings Time. The first sentence of each article is given below, in which the English has 19 words and the Japanese about 36. Both sentences concern a meeting in Tokyo to discuss the introduction of daylight savings time to Japan, but the Japanese 有識者 (yuu shiki sya = "experts") expands to "representatives of labor business and consumer groups". Moreover the Japanese sentence contains an extra clause concerning the possible introduction of legislation, which accounts for part of the additional length. The notion of Daylight Savings Time is not well known in Japan, but widely used elsewhere, so the Japanese explanation of what it is, is

Table 1. Multiword Compounds

English Compound	Frequency	Japanese Compound	Frequency
joint news conference	110	調べ	205
civilians	110	合意 文書	205
chemical weapons	110	ポル・ポト 派	204
foreign ministry spokesman	109	青木 官房 長官	204
japanese banks	109	重点	204

omitted from the English. In the translation of this sentence then, there are some corresponding terms and some redundant elements. To a greater or lesser extent, the same situation holds true throughout the corpus, so reducing its utility for high quality statistical machine translation.

1(a) Representatives of labor business and consumer groups have met in tokyo to discuss introducing daylight saving time to japan

1(b) 夏の間　　　だけ 時計の針 を　　一時間　　進める　サマータイム 制度　　を
summertime only clock   OBJ one hour advance summertime system OBJ
日本　でも　導入する　よう 求める 有識者らの 会合　　が
Japan to also introduce like ask for experts   meeting NOM
きょう 東京　で 開かれており 国会 が　　立法化　　に　　向けて
today Tokyo in was opened Diet NOM legislation DAT facing
審議　　　に　入る　よう 訴える アピール など を　　採択します
discussion DAT enter like appeal appeal   other OBJ adopt

We separate the corpus into the coherent genre of Economy, Politics and International (labelled "EIP") articles, and Capital and Regional news (labelled "Capital"). The corpora have been prepared by parsing all sentences and article identifiers: the English using Charniak's parser [4], and the Japanese using Cabocha, a dependency parser [6]. For this experiment, only the content words in Noun Phrases are considered, and all other structures are filtered out. NP structures are analysed for Multiword Compounds (Terms) and these are treated as lexical units for statistical processing.

Some sample English and Japanese compounds are given in Table 1, with their frequencies. For example the term 'chemical weapons' occurs in the English corpus 110 times, while 青木官房長官 (aoki kanbou chyoukan) occurs 204 times in the Japanese corpus. The table is an extract from the complete NP set, so it includes both single and multiword compounds. For the purposes of this experiment only multiword compounds of frequency greater than 2 are used in the final, prepared corpus. The total EIP corpus contains about 4.7 million English words and 7.85 million Japanese words. After filtering for Noun Phrase compounds, the English retains about 1.25 million words in 528K terms, and the Japanese retains about 2 million words in 826K terms. Thus by selective filtration of multiword noun compounds, we are processing about 1/4 of the overall corpus. Both the EIP corpus and the Capital Corpus are summarized in Table 2. The Raw EIP corpus contains 29.6K article pairs, with 218K English sentences

Table 2. Corpus Statistics

ID	Partition	English	Japanese	Partition	English	Japanese
Articles		29.6K	29.6K		11.5K	11.5K
Sentences		218K	179.7K		86.2K	81.2K
All NPs	EIP	1.2M	2.98M	Capital	467.2K	1.35M
Unique NPs		57.2K	32.4K		37.1K	28.6K
Bags of NPs		29.6K	29.6K		11.5K	11.5K
Avg Bag Size		17.8	27.9		13.4	29.6

and 179.6K Japanese sentences. After parsing and filtering the English has 1.2M NPs, with 57.2K unique, and the Japanese has 2.98M NPs, with 32.4K unique. Each article is treated as a bag of NPs, retained in their original sequence, as the alignment is important to one of the term extraction methods described below. Thus the average English article has 17.8 multiword compounds and the average Japanese article has 27.9 multiword compounds. For the purposes of statistical processing these bags of NPs are tokenized, for computational efficiency, and treated as "sentences". The three statistical methods and the exhaustive generation are separately run over each of the EIP and Capital partitions.

3   Methods and Results

The overall experiment is concerned with the extraction of multiword noun compound translations. For each sentence pair there is a potential for any word in the English to be a translation of any word in Japanese, so in the average sentence pair there are 17.8 * 27.9 = 496 such pairs. If all the words were unique, summing over the whole corpus of 29.6K sentence pairs would give a total of 14.7 million word pairs, but there are many duplicates so the actual number is just over 6.4 million word pairs. Clearly not all of these pairs are translations, but we can use the distribution of co-occurrence information over the corpus to estimate the translations - indeed, this is the principle behind all the methods investigated in Melamed [7]. For example if the word 'Japan' occurs 3000 times among the English sentences, the word 日本 (Nihon) occurs 3000 times among the Japanese, and all these occurrences are in matched pairs, then we can with confidence say that 'Japan' is a translation of 日本. Conversely if the term 'lemon fizz' occurs 12 times and 総理大臣 (souri daijin = "prime minister") occurs 1500 times, and the number of co-occurrences is 4, we can infer that these are unlikely to be translations. We would like to find a method which searches the 6.4 million word pair space to find the pairs which are more likely to be translations, and eliminate the pairs which are less likely to be translations.

As a baseline we can exhaustively compute all 6.4 million word correspondences and use dictionary lookup of the component words. Since this includes terms which occur just two times, there is a small possibility that some pairs are chance co-occurrences, rather than translations of the corpus. The statistical methods described below might possibly give higher confidence of translation probability. Of the statistical methods, in the first case we computed the Mutual Information of potential noun compound translations, in the second we computed the probability of translation based on word frequencies using the EM algorithm, and in the third, we computed translation probabilities based on word frequency and word alignment, also using the EM algorithm. These methods are called MI, EM(1) and EM(2). The implementation is a modification of the EGYPT tools for Statistical Machine Translation [1], in particular 'Giza' was modified to compute the Mutual Information, and 'Whittle' was replaced by a tokenizer which identifies and tokenizes multiword compounds. The EM(1) and EM(2) methods involve running Models 1 and 2 of Giza, and postprocessing the probabilistic translations file.

All three of the statistical methods overgenerate, producing multiple possible translations for each term. Postprocessing of the results involves applying the same dictionary lookup as is described in the baseline method, and elimination of those compounds for which there is no common word.

Table 3. Digital Satellite Broadcasting(1)

Japanese	English
デジタル衛星放送	digital satellite broadcasting
デジタル衛星放送	digital broadcasting
デジタル衛星放送	broadcasting business
デジタル衛星放送	ten million
デジタル衛星放送	british newspaper
デジタル衛星放送	last summer

3.1   Exhaustive Generation and Dictionary Lookup

When we take the cross-product of all co-occurring pairs of compounds, there are 6.4 million pairs in the EIP corpus, and 2.06 million pairs in the Capital corpus. These constitute the entire sets of word pairs which can appear in the corpus, and the translation candidate sets yielded by the Mutual Information, and Expectation Maximization methods are subsets of this total. Since the unique vocabularies are 57.2K English and 32.4K Japanese terms, we would hope to find a set of co-occurrences somewhere close to these figures. In the total output files, there are pairs of compounds having no actual relation to each other, and the irrelevant correspondences are filtered out after comparing the component words of each term against a dictionary and finding the degree of overlap. To take as an example デジタル衛星放送 (dijitaru eisei housou) from the EIP corpus, for which a correct word for word translation is "digital satellite broadcasting", and a sample incorrect translation is "british newspaper". The output file gives 81 translation candidates for this term. Using EDICT, a freely available (for research purposes) on-line dictionary [2], we check every word pair in each term

Table 4. All Filters for 'Exhaustive Generation'

Corpus	Raw	Relevant	Unique	Absolute
EIP	6419882	243275	18546	3252
Capital	2068753	65284	7533	1037

translation pair, and eliminate all pairs for which there is no single word translation. The dictionary shows translations for デジタル =digital 衛星 =satellite 放送 =broadcasting, so "digital satellite broadcasting" with 3 dictionary lookups is acceptable as a translation and "british newspaper" with no dictionary lookups is discarded.

Table 3 gives a sample of the candidates for this term, 3 relevant and 3 not. Using a one word pair match in the dictionary as a criterion of relevance gives 26 Relevant entries for デジタル衛星放送 (dijitaru eisei housou). By processing all entries in the raw output files against the dictionary lookup the total candidate set is reduced from 6.4 million to 243275, though many of the entries in this refined dictionary are multiple translations of the same term.

As the "Relevant" measure only requires a single word overlap, it is possible that the complete translation of a multiword term is actually incorrect. An example from the output file confirms this. The English term "anti government guerrillas" has a correct translation of 反政府ゲリラ (han seifu gerira). This term also corresponds with 政府側 (seifu gawa, literally "the government side"), and also with ペルー政府 (peru seifu, literally "the Peruvian government"). These are both opposite in meaning to the English term. We might consequently like to find the best translation for each term and ignore misses. This set of unique candidates is achieved by picking the best score for each translation set, so in this example, "anti government guerillas" = 反政府ゲリラ has three matching lookups and is selected as the unique translation, while the other two alternatives match only one word and are discarded. This level of filtering reduces the entire translation set to 18546 Unique terms. It is these Unique translations which are the most useful contribution to the bilingual dictionary in a Machine Translation system. Still, this measure includes many pairs which are not precisely overlapping word-for-word, so we would really like to find an absolute baseline to measure the effectiveness of the three statistical term extraction methods. Now, there is a unique number of candidates for which there is an exact dictionary match: 2 correct lookups for a 2 word term, 3 correct lookups for a 3 word term and so on. The exhaustive generation method should extract all of these, and we can infer that whichever of the statistical extraction methods extracts the greatest number of these absolutely unique term translations is the best. Table 4 shows, in the "Absolute" column, that exhaustive generation extracts 3252 of these terms from the EIP corpus, and 1037 from the Capital corpus. With this information filtered from the exhaustively generated translation candidate set, we proceed to describe the statistical filtering methods, and their results.

3.2   Mutual Information

For each sentence pair, every co-occurrence of an English-Japanese term pair is counted. Using these co-occurrences and the corpus specific term frequencies the Mutual Information is calculated as:

$$MI = log\frac{ejcooccurrence * sentences}{efreq * jfreq} \tag{1}$$

For example the English term 'international currency system' occurs 9 times in the corpus, and the Japanese 国際通貨制度 (kokusai tsuuka seido) occurs 6 times, however they co-occur 6 times in parallel pieces. Their mutual information is calculated as:

$$MI = log\frac{(6 * 29620)}{(6 * 9)} = 8.09 \tag{2}$$

When the frequency of a pair of words is very low, the chance of a false positive is increased, as pointed out by Fung and Church [5], so word pairs with frequency 3 or less are not computed. Mutual Information values are calculated for the 6.4 million word pairs of the EIP corpus and of these, 681K entries have a non-zero value. As an example the term リ ツ ィ ン 大統領 (eritsin daitouryou) meaning 'President Yeltsin', occurs 1488 times with a non-zero MI value, and the correct translation has the highest Mutual Information value of 2.517. The Mutual Information result is calculated once only for each pair. In contrast, the following two methods involve the iterative estimation of parameters, and so must be calculated multiple times.

3.3   Expectation Maximization(1)

EM is a generate and test style, iterative algorithm for converging on good estimates of hidden parameters in a model. In this case the value we want to estimate is the probability of a Japanese word given an English word, or P(f|e). This is accomplished by Brown et al [3] in two complementary steps of accumulating counts of the connections between word f in F and word e in E, for all (e,f), and using these counts to estimate the translation probability, t(f|e) for all pairs (e,f) which reach a given cutoff; then using the updated translations to refine the count accumulation. In each iteration, the probabilities of more plausible candidates are promoted, and lower ranking candidates are eliminated. The probable translations approach a maximum value after some number of iterations; we use 15, as marginal improvements beyond this are tiny. The equation, which sums over the counts, is given in (3).

$$t(f|e) = \sum_{i=0}^{l} c(f_j|e_i) \tag{3}$$

The first iteration is the initialization step, yielding equal probabilities for all word pairs. The second iteration accumulates counts over all alignments and generates 6.26 million word correspondences. An alignment is defined by the correspondence between a position i in the English sentence and a position j in the Japanese sentence. The counts are summed over all alignments, so for all positions 0 to length l in the English, and 1 to length m in the Japanese, the counts are accumulated. Of these, the sum over all correspondences for each Japanese term is a probability of 1. Successive iterations winnow the total number of correspondences by eliminating lower ranking candidates and adjusting the probabilities, so 5.9 million remain after 3 iterations, 5.4 million after 4 iterations, until the 15th iteration when 1.43 million word correspondences remain. The probabilities of plausible translations are promoted at each iteration, so for エリツィン大統領 (eritsin daitouryou = President Yeltsin) after 2 iterations there are 3993 candidates and the most plausible "president yeltsin" has a probability of 0.192, after 3 iterations this candidate has a probability of 0.221 and there are still 3623 candidates, after 4 iterations there are 2840 candidates and "President Yeltsin" has probability 0.234, until finally after 15 iterations there are 504 remaining candidates and "エリツィン大統領 = President Yeltsin" has probability 0.231 (so the probability can sometimes reduce between iterations). With this number of candidates, there are many whose probability is very small due to infrequent co-occurrence. This set still includes many implausible translations, so in the next variant we take account of word alignments over the corpus, to promote the stronger candidate pairs and at the same time further reduce the total candidate set.

3.4   Expectation Maximization(2)

The model 1 algorithm given above computes word translation probabilities by summing over all alignments in a corpus, but without taking account of the actual word positions of the corresponding word pairs in each sentence pair. The second EM step computes the probability of a translation depending on the alignment, so depending on the position of the English word in its sentence, the position of the Japanese word in its sentence, and the lengths l and m respectively of the English and Japanese sentences. The starting position for EM(2) is the set of translation probabilities generated by EM(1). The translations in this table are refined by taking account of the relative co-occurrence positions in a sentence of each word pair. For this purpose EM(2) also generates a table of alignments, whose summation a(i|j,l,m) constitutes a set of distributions: for every pair of lengths (l,m) the probability that any word in position i is a translation of a word in position j, sums to 1. Equation (4) governs this EM algorithm.

$$Pr(f|e) = \prod_{j=1}^{m} \sum_{i=0}^{l} t(f_j|e_i) * a(i|j,m,l) \tag{4}$$

From the EM(1) translation table, an initial set of alignments is estimated in which the translation probability for any E-J word pair in any set of positions i in l and j in m is set to a uniform value. In each subsequent iteration, the counts of any word translation in position i with respect to position j are computed, and the translation of f_j with respect to e, summed over all alignments, is calculated. The final translation table cannot therefore be interpreted independently of the alignment table.

Using the 1.43 million probable translations for the EIP corpus generated by EM(1), we perform 15 iterations of EM(2) to generate a probable translations table with 1.15 million entries. Continuing with the President Yeltsin example, after 15 iterations there are 359 remaining candidates, and "エリツィン大統領 = President Yeltsin" has probability 0.24. This shows some improvement over EM(1) but still the candidate set includes many lexically unrelated pairs.

3.5   Postprocessing

The three methods described above extract different translation candidate sets, 681K for MI,, 1.43 million for EM(1) and 1.15 million for EM(2), but there is still a great deal of overgeneration in all of these cases. clearly many word pairs having no actual relation to each other, and in many cases the best candidate is not the one with the highest MI or probability score. We can however use the dictionary lookup method to refine the results. To take the previous example デジタル衛星放送 (dijitaru eisei housou) = "digital satellite broadcasting". The output files for MI, EM(1) and EM(2) give 21, 12 and 13 translation possibilities respectively for this term.

Table 5. Digital Satellite Broadcasting (2)

Method	Japanese	English	Comparator
EM(1)	デジタル衛星放送	digital satellite broadcasting	0.731011
	デジタル衛星放送	digital broadcasting	0.000579113
	デジタル衛星放送	broadcasting business	1.41765e-05
EM(2)	デジタル衛星放送	digital satellite broadcasting	0.785034
	デジタル衛星放送	digital broadcasting	0.00147203
	デジタル衛星放送	broadcasting business	4.03693e-05
MI	デジタル衛星放送	digital satellite broadcasting	7.26884

Using a minimum one word match as a criterion of relevance, Table 5 gives the list of Relevant entries for デジタル衛星放送 (dijitaru eisei housou) for each term extraction method. The EM(1) file reduces from 12 candidates to 3, including the correct "digital satellite broadcasting" with 3 dictionary overlaps, "digital broadcasting" with 2 overlaps, and "broadcasting business" with 1; similarly the EM(2) file reduces from 13 to the same 3 entries. The MI translation candidate output file is reduced from 21 to 1 entry, which is "digital satellite broadcasting".

By processing all entries in the raw output files against the dictionary lookup the MI candidate set is reduced from 681K to 46298, the EM(1) set goes from 1.43 million to 76996 and the EM(2) set reduces from 1.15 million to 65304.

Table 6. All Results

Corpus	Method	Raw	Relevant	Unique	Absolute
EIP	EM(1)	1431849	76996	17007	1193
	EM(2)	1155149	65304	16557	1161
	MI	681084	46298	11053	937
Capital	EM(1)	542789	24174	6787	773
	EM(2)	461101	21324	6604	726
	MI	260038	14455	4631	642

However there are still many entries in the refined dictionary with more than one translation for the same term.

Using the criterion of uniqueness developed in Section 3.1 reduces the EM(1) translation set to 17007, the EM(2) set to 16557 and the MI set to 11053, so the EM methods seem to perform significantly better than Mutual Information, by extracting more Relevant and more Unique translations. We saw from the exhaustively generated set some 3252 Absolute translations in the EIP corpus and 1037 in the Capital corpus, so these are the baselines against which to measure the effectiveness of the statistical methods. For EIP, Table 6 shows, in the "Absolute" column, that the EM(1) method extracts 1193 absolute translations for a recall of 36.7% (1193 *100 / 3252), EM(2) extracts 1161, for 35.7% recall, and MI extracts 937 absolute translations giving just 28.8% recall of the absolute translations. Similarly for Capital, EM(1) extracts 773 word-for-word translations (74.5% recall), EM(2) extracts 726 (70% recall) and MI extracts 642 exact translations (61.9% recall). On this measure then, EM(1) is just ahead of EM(2), and both EM methods are superior to Mutual Information. But still, all of the statistical methods fall well short of the figures yielded by exhaustive generation.

4   The Discussion

The effectiveness of the dictionary based post-process in finding Relevant and Unique candidate translations suggests that a maximal set can be extracted by putting no limits on word frequency, or overlap frequency, but by computing all co-occurring word pairs, and applying the post-process. When this is done the 6.4 million candidates in the EIP corpus generate 243K Relevant, 18.5K Unique and 3253 Absolute translations. The 2.06 million candidates in the "Capital" corpus generate 65.2K Relevant, 7.5K Unique and 1037 Absolute translations. There is however no way to rank alternate translations of the same term, so the Unique translations are a more effective measure than the Relevant, and since there are 18.5K unique translations out of a possible 32.4K Japanese vocabulary items, this gives a respectable coverage of 57% (and a slightly less respectable 33% coverage of the English vocabulary). The shortfall can be attributed to some combination of, (1) the dictionary fails to include relevant word-for-word translations, so falsely lowering the lookup count, (2) the fact that some correct translations may be wholly non-compositional, so a dictionary is ineffective, and (3) this content-aligned corpus includes some unknown number of terms in each population which are not translations in the corresponding article.

While these are better figures than any of the statistically extracted methods, there may be times when it is not possible to generate all possible candidate pairs. Or, more likely, there may be times when a dictionary lookup is impractical or less effective. For such times we would like to know which statistical method we can rely on to give us better quality results. We therefore compare the statistical methods against each other and against the exhaustive baseline.

The results given in Table 6 indicate that both EM variants perform better, since they extract more Relevant, Unique and Absolute translations across the board than MI. But on the face of it there is no particular reason why EM(1), which computes word pair correspondences over all alignments, should perform better than MI, which treats each sentence as a bag of words, and therefore ignores intra-sentential alignments. Some clue as to the differences can however be gained from examining the initial conditions. In their text alignment experiments, Fung and Church [5] used Mutual Information to extract word pair translations from a French-English corpus. They show in their work that mutual information results can be unreliable when the counts are small, and therefore they use T-scores to filter out insignificant mutual information values. They conclude that they need to see two words in at least 3 different sentence pairs to consider the results significant (with a 95% confidence level). They also suggest that higher frequency occurrences are unreliable and apply an upper limit of 20 instances. Our calculations above are computed with their limits in mind.

As a contrast, Brown et al [3] suggests only that frequency 1 words should be eliminated from the calculation. On this evidence, Brown et al were more confident of extracting good results using EM, from a wider spread of vocabulary frequencies: 2 to max, as opposed to 3 to 20. Our own work reported here takes account of these two differing sets of starting conditions. If we relax the starting conditions for MI to match the same frequency limits, there are 2.35 million non-zero MI values before filtering, and 118924 Relevant, 16339 Unique and 2137 Absolute values extracted. These figures (particularly the Unique ones) are more comparable with the Expectation Maximization results, though now the MI value is not being used as a discriminant.

Turning to a comparison between the Model 1 EM results and Model 2: if we are using the method to extract possible translations in a translation system with an absolute dictionary, then EM(1) extracts more plausibly Unique translations than EM(2), and the extra alignment training is not necessary. However the generation of multiple alternatives for any term or word is more of a virtue in a Statistical MT system, because in the higher models, the set of possible translations assembled by the Decoder is formed from both the Translation table, with its probabilities of translation, and the alignment table, with its probabilities that a certain word in position j of the Target sentence is a translation of a word in position i of the Source. So a lower probability alternative translation can win out, if its alignment probability is higher. In this case the set of translations generated by EM(1) is a starting condition for the training of the higher level model, which is trained with respect to these alignments and cannot be interpreted separately from them.

5   Conclusions

The advantage of parsing a corpus before translation training is that frequently co-occurring words can be grouped together and treated as unit terms. After tokenizing the terms, the compacted corpus can be processed more quickly. After generating the set of translation candidates, the use of a dictionary lookup to filter plausible candidates is the more powerful, because of the increased potential for matching one or more words in a candidate pair of multi-word terms. This gives us a way of corroborating the effectiveness of purely statistical methods of vocabulary extraction. The results of comparing Mutual Information and Expectation Maximization methods, when compared against the benchmark, show that good translation candidates can be extracted with greater confidence using EM than MI.

However, the results also show that wherever it is feasible to exhaustively compute the possible candidate set, and filter for good translations using a high-quality dictionary, this is the method we should prefer.

References

1. Al Onaizan et al: Statistical Machine Translation, Final Report Johns Hopkins University, Workshop 1999
2. Breen, J.W.: Building an Electronic Japanese-English Dictionary Presented at the Japanese Studies Association of Australia Conference, Brisbane, Queensland, Australia, July 1995
3. Brown et al: The Mathematics of Machine Translation: Parameter Estimation Computational Linguistics, vol 19, number 2, pp 263-311, 1993
4. Charniak, E.: Immediate Head Parsing for Language Models In Proceedings of the 39th Annual Meeting of the Association for Computational Linguistics, 2001
5. Fung, P. and Church, K.W.: K-Vec: A New Approach for Aligning Parallel Texts In Proceedings 15th COLING pp 1096-1102 (1994)
6. Kudoh, T. and Matsumoto, Y.: Japanese Dependency Structure Analysis Based on Support Vector Machines In Empirical Methods in Natural Language processing and Very Large Corpora, Pages 18–25, 2000
7. Melamed, I.D.: Empirical Methods for Exploiting Parallel Texts The MIT Press, Cambridge Massachussetts, 1998
8. Tanaka et al: Speech to Speech Translation System for Monologues – Data Driven Approach ICSLP, Denver Colorado, 2002

Identifying Complex Sound Correspondences in Bilingual Wordlists

Grzegorz Kondrak

Department of Computing Science,
University of Alberta,
Edmonton, AB, T6G 2E8, Canada
kondrak@cs.ualberta.ca
http://www.cs.ualberta.ca/~kondrak

Abstract. The determination of recurrent sound correspondences between languages is crucial for the identification of cognates, which are often employed in statistical machine translation for sentence and word alignment. In this paper, an algorithm designed for extracting non-compositional compounds from bitexts is shown to be capable of determining complex sound correspondences in bilingual wordlists. In experimental evaluation, a C++ implementation of the algorithm achieves approximately 90% recall *and* precision on authentic language data.

1 Introduction

All languages change through time. Table 1 gives an example of how much English has evolved within the last fourteen hundred years. Words that make up languages undergo sound changes (nfi → now) as well as semantic shifts ('guardian' → 'ward'). Lexical replacement is a process in which lexemes drop out of usage altogether, and are substituted by other, unrelated words (herigean → praise). Morphological endings change and disappear as well (-on in sculon).

Table 1. The first verse of Caedmon's *Hymn* and its modern English translation.

Old English:	Nū	sculon	herigean heofonrīces	weard
Modern English:	Now	we should	praise	heaven-kingdom's guardian

When two groups of people that speak a common language lose contact with each other, their respective languages begin to diverge, and eventually become mutually unintelligible. In such cases, we may still be able to determine that the languages are genetically related by examining cognates, that is words that have developed from the same proto-form. For example, French lait, Spanish leche, and Italian latte constitute a cognate set, as they are all descendants, or reflexes, of Latin lacte. In general, the longer the time that has passed since the linguistic split, the smaller the number of cognates that remain as a proof of a genetic relationship.

A. Gelbukh (Ed.): CICLing 2003, LNCS 2588, pp. 432–443, 2003.

Because of gradual changes over long periods of time, cognates often acquire very different phonetic shapes. For example, English hundred, French cent, and Polish sto are all descendants of Proto-Indo-European *kmtom (an asterisk denotes a reconstructed form). The semantic change can be no less dramatic; for example, English guest and Latin hostis 'enemy' are cognates even though their meanings are diametrically different. On the other hand, not all similar sounding words that have the same meaning are cognates. It can be a matter of chance resemblance, as in English day and Latin die 'day', or an instance of a borrowing, as in English sprint and Japanese supurinto. Borrowings are lexical items that have been incorporated (possibly in modified form) into one language from another.

An important phenomenon that allows us to distinguish between cognates and borrowings is the regularity of sound change. The regularity principle states that a change in pronunciation applies to sounds in a given phonological context across all words in the language. Regular sound changes tend to produce regular correspondences of phonemes in corresponding cognates. /d/:/t/ is a regular correspondence between English and German, as evidenced by cognate pairs such as day ⫽ tag, dry ⫽ trocken, and drink ⫽ trinken. Table 2 shows contains examples of a regular sound correspondence between four Romance languages. I prefer to use the term recurrent sound correspondences because in practice the matchings of phonemes in cognate pairs are more tendencies than hard-and-fast rules.

Table 2. An example of a recurrent sound correspondence in related languages.

Latin	Italian	Spanish	French	
nocte	notte	noche	nuit	'night'
octo	otto	ocho	huit	'eight'
lacte	latte	leche	lait	'milk'
factu	fatto	hecho	fait	'done'
tectu	tetto	techo	toit	'roof'

The determination of recurrent sound correspondences is the principal step of the comparative method of language reconstruction. Not only does it provide evidence for the relatedness of languages, but it also makes it possible to distinguish cognates from borrowings and chance resemblances. However, because manual determination of recurrent sound correspondences is an extremely time-consuming process, it has yet to be accomplished for many proposed language families. A system able to perform this task automatically from unprocessed bilingual wordlists could be of great assistance to historical linguists. The Reconstruction Engine [14], a set of programs designed to be an aid in language reconstruction, requires a set of recurrent sound correspondences to be provided beforehand.

The determination of recurrent sound correspondences is closely related to another task that has been much studied in computational linguistics, the identification of cognates. Cognates have been employed for sentence and word alignment in bitexts [16], improving statistical machine translation models [1], and inducing translation lexicons [10]. Some of the proposed cognate identification algorithms implicitly determine and employ recurrent sound correspondences [18, 15].

Although it may not be immediately apparent, there is a strong similarity between the task of matching phonetic segments in a pair of cognate words, and the task of matching words in two sentences that are mutual translations. The consistency with which a word in one language is translated into a word in another language is mirrored by the consistency of sound correspondences. The former is due to the semantic relation of synonymy, while the latter follows from the principle of the regularity of sound change. Thus, as already asserted by Guy [5], it should be possible to use similar techniques for both tasks.

The method of determining complex recurrent sound correspondences that I present here adopts the approach proposed in [13]. The idea is to relate correspondences between sounds in wordlists to translational equivalences between words in bitexts (bilingual corpora). The method induces models of sound correspondence that are similar to models developed for statistical machine translation. It has been shown [13] that the method is able to determine recurrent sound correspondences with high accuracy in bilingual wordlists in which less than 30% of the pairs are cognates. However, in the one-to-one model employed by the method, links are induced only between individual phonemes. This is a serious limitation because recurrent sound correspondences often involve clusters of phonemes. Many-to-many correspondences, such as the ones shown in Table 2, may either be only partially recovered or even completely missed by the algorithm.

This paper presents an extension of the approach described in [13], which overcomes its main limitation by adapting the algorithm for discovering noncompositional compounds (NCCs) in bitexts proposed by Melamed [16]. In Section 2, I review previous work on determination of recurrent sound correspondences. Melamed's approach to inducing models of translational equivalence is discussed in Section 3. Section 4 describes the algorithm for discovering noncompositional compounds. Section 5 contains some implementation details. Section 6 describes the data used for the experimental evaluation, and Section 7 is devoted to the evaluation itself.

2   Related Work

In a schematic description of the comparative method, the two steps that precede the determination of recurrent sound correspondences are the identification of cognate pairs [12], and their phonetic alignment [11]. Indeed, if a comprehensive set of correctly aligned cognate pairs is available, the recurrent sound correspondences could be extracted by simply following the alignment links. Unfortunately, in order to make reliable judgments of cognation, it is necessary to know in advance what the recurrent sound correspondences are. Historical linguists solve this apparent circularity by guessing a small number of likely cognates and refining the set of correspondences and cognates in an iterative fashion.

Guy [5] outlines an algorithm for identifying cognates in bilingual wordlists which is based on recurrent sound correspondences. The algorithm estimates the probability of phoneme correspondences by employing a variant of the χ^2 statistic on a contingency table, which indicates how often two phonemes co-occur in words of the same meaning. The probabilities are then converted into the estimates of cognation by means of some experimentation-based heuristics. Only simple, one-to-one phoneme correspondences are considered. The paper does not contain any evaluation on authentic language data, but Guy's program COGNATE, which implements the algorithm, is publicly available. The program does not output an explicit list of recurrent sound correspondences, which makes direct comparison with my method difficult.

Oakes [17] describes a set of programs that together perform several steps of the comparative method, from the determination of recurrent sound correspondences in wordlists to the actual reconstruction of the proto-forms. Word pairs are considered cognate if their edit distance is below a certain threshold. The edit operations cover a number of sound-change categories. Sound correspondences are deemed to be regular if they are found to occur more than once in the data. The paper describes experimental results of running the programs on a set of wordlists representing four Indonesian languages, and compares those to the reconstructions found in the linguistic literature. Section 7 contains a comparison of the recurrent sound correspondences identified by JAKARTA and the ones discovered by my method.

Because the tasks of determination of recurrent sound correspondence and the identification of cognates are intertwined, some of the bitext-related algorithms implicitly determine and employ recurrent sound correspondences. Tiedemann [18] considers automatic construction of weighted string similarity measures from bitexts. He includes three lists of the most frequent character "mappings" between Swedish and English, which correspond to his three mapping approaches (single characters, vowel and consonant sequences, and non-matching parts of two strings). However, because genetic cognates in the data seem to be outnumbered by borrowings, the lists contain few genuine correspondences. Mann and Yarowsky [15] take advantage of language relatedness in order to automatically induce translation lexicons. In their search for cognates, they discover most probable character "substitutions" across languages. In the provided French–Portuguese examples, phonologically plausible correspondences b:v, t:d mix with mere orthographic regularities c:q, x:s.

Knight and Graehl [9] in their paper on back-transliteration from the Japanese syllabic script katakana to the English orthography consider the sub-task of aligning the English and Japanese phonetic strings. They apply the estimation-maximization (EM) algorithm to generate symbol-mapping probabilities from 8,000 pairs of unaligned English–Japanese sound sequences. It is possible to view the sound pairs with the highest probabilities as the strongest recurrent correspondences between the two languages. Naturally, the existence of those correspondences is an artifact of the transliteration process, rather than a consequence of a genetic language relationship. Nevertheless, it may be possible to employ a similar approach to discover recurrent sound correspondences in genuine cognates. A drawback of the alignment model presented in the paper is an asymmetric, one-to-many mapping between the English and Japanese sounds, and a restricted set of edit operations that excludes both insertions and deletions. These restrictions are designed to make the models less expensive to compute.

3   The Word-to-Word Model of Translational Equivalence

In statistical machine translation, a translation model approximates the probability that two sentences are mutual translations by computing the product of the probabilities that each word in the target sentence is a translation of some source language word. A model of translation equivalence that determines the word translation probabilities can be induced from bitexts. The difficulty lies in the fact that the mapping, or alignment, of words between two parts of a bitext is not known in advance.

Algorithms for word alignment in bitexts aim at discovering word pairs that are mutual translations. A straightforward approach is to estimate the likelihood that words are mutual translations by computing a similarity function based on a co-occurrence statistic, such as mutual information, Dice coefficient, or the χ^2 test. The underlying assumption is that the association scores for different word pairs are independent of each other.

Melamed [16] shows that the assumption of independence leads to invalid word associations, and proposes an algorithm for inducing models of translational equivalence that outperform the models that are based solely on co-occurrence counts. His models employ the one-to-one assumption, which formalizes the observation that most words in bitexts are translated to a single word in the corresponding sentence. The algorithm, which is related to the expectation-maximization (EM) algorithm, iteratively re-estimates the likelihood scores which represent the probability that two word types are mutual translations. In the first step, the scores are initialized according to the G^2 statistic [4]. Next, the likelihood scores are used to induce a set of one-to-one links between word tokens in the bitext. The links are determined by a greedy competitive linking algorithm, which proceeds to link pairs that have the highest likelihood scores. After the linking is completed, the link counts are used to re-estimate the likelihood scores. Three translation-model re-estimation methods are possible: Method A calculates the likelihood scores as the logarithm of the probability of jointly generating the pair of words, Method B uses auxiliary parameters to represent an explicit noise model, and Method C conditions the auxiliary parameters on various word classes. The re-estimated likelihood scores are then applied to find a new set of links. The process is repeated until the translation model converges to the desired degree.

As demonstrated in [13], it is possible to adapt Melamed's algorithm to the problem of determining recurrent sound correspondences. The main idea is to induce a model of sound correspondence in a bilingual wordlist, in the same way as one induces a model of translational equivalence among words in a parallel corpus. After the model has converged, phoneme pairs with the highest likelihood scores represent the most likely recurrent sound correspondences.

The most important modification to the original algorithm is the substitution of the approximate competitive-linking algorithm of Melamed with a variant of the well-known dynamic programming algorithm [11], which computes the optimal alignment between two strings in polynomial time. Insertion and deletion of segments is modeled by employing an indel penalty for unlinked segments, rather than by null links used by Melamed. The alignment score between two words is computed by summing the number of induced links, and applying an indel penalty for each unlinked segment, with the exception of the segments beyond the rightmost link. In order to avoid inducing links that are unlikely to represent recurrent sound correspondences, only pairs whose likelihood scores exceed a set threshold are linked.

The algorithm for the determination of recurrent sound correspondences was evaluated on 200-word lists of basic meanings representing several Indo-European languages. The results show that the method is capable of determining recurrent sound correspondences in bilingual wordlists in which less than 30% of pairs are cognates, and that it outperforms comparable algorithms on the related task of the identification of cognates.

4 Discovering Non-compositional Compounds in Bitexts

The algorithm proposed in [13] can only discover recurrent sound correspondences between single phonemes. This limitation, which is directly inherited from Melamed's original algorithm, may prevent the algorithm from detecting many more complex correspondences, such as the ones in Table 2. A quite similar problem exists also in the statistical machine translation. Non-compositional compounds (NCCs) are word sequences, such as "high school", whose meaning cannot be synthesized from the meaning of its components. Since many NCCs are not translated word-for-word, their detection is essential in most NLP applications.

As a way of relaxing the one-to-one restriction, Melamed [16] proposes an elegant algorithm for discovering NCCs in bitexts. His information-theoretic approach is based on the observation that treating NCCs as a single unit rather than as a sequence of independent words increases the predictive power of statistical translation models. Therefore, it is possible to establish whether a particular word sequence should be considered a NCC by comparing two translation models that differ only in their treatment of that word sequence. For the objective function that measures the predictive power of a translation model $Pr(s,t)$, Melamed selects mutual information:

$$I(S;T) = \sum_{s \in S} \sum_{t \in T} Pr(s,t) \log \frac{Pr(s,t)}{Pr(s)Pr(t)},$$

where S and T represent the distributions of linked words in the source and target texts, and s and t are word tokens.

Melamed's approach to the identification of NCCs is to induce a trial translation model that involves a candidate NCC and compare the model's total mutual information with that of a base translation model. The NCC is considered valid only if there is an increase of the mutual information in the trial model. The contribution of s to $I(S;T)$ is given as:

$$i(s) = \sum_{t \in T} Pr(s,t) \log \frac{Pr(s,t)}{Pr(s)Pr(t)}.$$

In order to make this procedure more efficient, Melamed proposes inducing the translation model for many candidate NCCs at the same time.

A complex gain-estimation method is used to guess whether a candidate NCC is useful before inducing a translation model that involves this NCC. Each candidate NCC xy causes the net change Δ_{xy} in the objective function, which can be expressed as:

$$\Delta_{xy} = i'(x) + i'(y) + i'(xy) - i(x) - i(y),$$

where i and i' are predictive value functions for source words in the base translation model and in the trial translation model, respectively. $i'(x)$ is estimated on the assumption that the links involving x will not change in the trial translation model unless y occurs to the right of x:

$$i'(x) = i(x : RC \neq y),$$

where $(x : RC \neq y)$ denotes the set of tokens of x whose right context is y. Similarly,

$$i'(y) = i(y : LC \neq x),$$

where LC denotes word context to the left. Finally, $i'(xy)$ is estimated as follows:

$$i'(xy) = i(x : RC = y) + i(y : LC = x).$$

Given parallel texts E and F, the algorithm iteratively augments the list of NCCs. The iteration starts by inducing a base translation model between E and F. All continuous bigrams which are estimated to increase mutual information of the translation model are placed on a sorted list of candidate NCCs, but for each word token, only the most promising NCC that contains it is allowed to remain on the list. Next, a trial translation model is induced between E' and F, where E' is obtained from E by fusing each candidate NCC into a single token. If the net change in mutual information gain contributed by a candidate NCC is greater than zero, all occurrences of that NCC in E are permanently fused; otherwise the candidate NCC is placed on a stop-list. The entire iteration is repeated until reaching an application-dependent stopping condition.

The method was evaluated on a large English–French bitext containing transcripts of Canadian parliamentary debates (Hansards). In one experiment, after six iterations the algorithm identified on both sides of the bitext about four hundred NCCs that increased the mutual information of the model. Another experiment, which is particularly relevant for the application discussed in this chapter, showed that the method was capable of discovering meaningful NCCs in a data set consisting of spellings and pronunciations of English words (for example, ph was determined to be a NCC of English spelling because it consistently "translates" into the sound /f/). However, the full NCC recognition algorithm was not tested in any real application.

5   Implementation of the Algorithm

The NCC algorithm of Melamed has been adapted to the problem of determining complex sound correspondences and implemented as a C++ program named CORDI. The program takes as input a bilingual wordlist and produces an ordered list of recurrent sound correspondences. Method C discussed in Section 3 is used for the inducing of translation models, In Method C, phonemes are divided into two classes: non-syllabic (consonants and glides), and syllabic (vowels); links between phonemes belonging to different classes not induced.

Adjustable parameters include the indel penalty ratio d and the minimum-strength correspondence threshold t. The parameter d controls the behaviour of the alignment algorithm by fixing the ratio between the negative indel weight and the positive weight assigned to every induced link. A lower ratio causes the program to be more adventurous in positing sparse links. The parameter t controls the tradeoff between reliability and the number of links. The value of t implies a score threshold of $t \cdot \log \frac{\lambda^+}{\lambda^-}$, which is a score achieved by a pair of phonemes that have t links out of t co-occurrences. In all experiments described below, d was set to 0.15, and t was set to 1 (sufficient to reject all non-recurring correspondences). The maximum number of iterations of the NCC algorithm should also be specified by the user, but the algorithm may terminate sooner if two subsequent iterations fail to produce any candidate NCCs.

The NCC algorithm is adapted with one major change. After inducing a trial translation model between E' and F, the original algorithm accepts all candidate NCCs that contribute a positive net change in mutual information gain. For the detection of phoneme NCCs, I decided to accept all candidate NCCs that result in a recurrent sound correspondence that has a likelihood score above the minimum-strength threshold t described above. I found that the strength of an induced correspondence better reflects the importance of a phoneme cluster than the mutual information gain criterion.

6   The Algonquian Data

The test data suitable for the evaluation of the approach outlined above has to fulfill several requirements: it should be sufficiently large to contain many surviving cognates, the lexemes should be given in a consistent notation that allows for an automatic transcription into phonetic form, and, finally, the cognation information has to be provided in the electronic form as well, so that the performance of the program can be measured objectively. The last condition is perhaps the most difficult to satisfy. Even in the rare cases when machine-readable bilingual lexicons can be acquired, the cognation judgments would have to be laboriously extracted from etymological dictionaries. Note that optical scanning of phonetic symbols or unusual diacritics is is not feasible with the current state of technology.

Fortunately, the machine-readable Algonquian data [8] satisfy the above requirements. It consists of two parts that complement each other: the etymological dictionary, and the vocabulary lists from which the dictionary was produced.

The dictionary, which is also available in book form [7], contains 4,068 cognate sets, including 853 marked as nouns. Each cognate set is composed of a reconstructed proto-form and the corresponding cognates accompanied by short glosses in English. Nearly all cognates belong to one of the four principal Algonquian languages (Fox, Menomini, Cree, Ojibwa). The dictionary file is almost identical with the book version, and required only minimal clean-up. The lexemes are already in a phonemic transcription, so no sophisticated grapheme-to-phoneme conversion was necessary. A simple coding is used to express phonemes that lack ASCII equivalents: c for /š/, q for the glottal stop, etc. In the experiments described in this section, the dictionary file served as a source of the cognation information.

Table 3. The size of the Algonquian vocabulary lists.

Language	Dictionary only		Dictionary and lists	
	All words	Nouns	All words	Nouns
Fox	1252	193	4759	575
Menomini	2231	361	8550	1540
Cree	2541	512	7507	1628
Ojibwa	2758	535	6334	1023
Total	**8782**	**1601**	**27150**	**4766**

In contrast with the dictionary, the vocabulary lists can be characterized as noisy data. They contain many errors, inconsistencies, duplicates, and lacunae. The Fox file is incomplete. In the Menomini file, three different phonemes (/č/, /æ/, and the glottal stop) had been merged into one, and had to be painstakingly reconstructed on the basis of phonotactic constraints. As much as possible, the entries were cross-checked with the dictionary itself, which is much more consistent. Table 3 specifies the number of unique lexemes available for each language. It appears that only about a third of the nouns present in the vocabulary lists had made it into the dictionary.

7   Experimental Evaluation

In order to test the suitability of the NCC approach, an experiment was performed on a subset of the Algonquian data. The goal was to determine recurrent sound correspondences from noisy wordlists and evaluate them against the set of correspondences determined by Bloomfield [2,3]. Because of the large number of complex 1:2 and 2:2 recurrent sound correspondences, the Algonquian languages are ideal for testing the NCC approach.

The input data was automatically extracted from the raw vocabulary lists by selecting all pairs of noun lexemes that had at least one gloss in common. The end result of such an operation is bilingual wordlists containing both cognate and non-cognate pairs. The Cree–Ojibwa list served as the development set, and the Fox–Menomini list as the test set. The Cree–Ojibwa contained 732 pairs, including 242 (33.1%) cognate pairs. The Fox–Menomini list turned out to be even more challenging: it contained 397 word pairs, including only 79 (19.9%) cognate pairs.

Since the vowel correspondences in Algonquian are rather inconsistent, following Hewson [6], I decided to concentrate on consonants and consonant clusters. On the Fox–Menomini data, the algorithm terminated after 12 iterations, which took several minutes on a Sparc workstation. (Each iteration involves inducing anew both the base and the trial translation models.)

Table 4 compares the set of 31 correspondences enumerated by Bloomfield, which is adopted as the gold standard, with the set of 23 correspondences determined by CORDI, and eight correspondences identified by JAKARTA [17]. 20 recurrent sound correspondences identified by CORDI are correct, while the remaining three are wrong and can be traced to alignments of unrelated words. The resulting precision was therefore 87%.

Table 4. The Fox–Menomini consonantal correspondences determined by a linguist and by two computer programs. The correspondences shown in boldface are valid correspondences that were present in the input set of word pairs.

Bloomfield:	p:p t:t k:k s:s h:h h:q č:č š:s n:n m:m t:ht
	hp:hp hk:hk ht:qt hk:hk šk:sk č:hč **s:hs s:qs**
	š:qs s:hn s:qn **šk:hk p:hp** hč:qč k:hk hk:čk
	hp:sp hč:hč ht:ht š:hs n:hn
CORDI:	**p:p t:t k:k s:s h:h** č:č **š:s** p:č **n:n m:m t:ht**
	hp:hp hk:hk ht:qt hk:hk šk:sk č:hč **s:hs s:qs**
	š:qs s:hn s:qn hk:t t:sk
JAKARTA:	**p:p t:t k:k s:s h:h n:n m:m** h:hs

In order to determine why the number of recurrent sound correspondences established by Bloomfield was much greater than the number of recurrent sound correspondences produced by the program, I manually analyzed the 79 cognate pairs included in the input wordlist. I found that ʔ:hk and p:hp occur twice in the input, hɛ:qɛ occurs once, and the remaining seven complex correspondences do not occur at all. The h:q correspondence is dubious because it only occurs within clusters. Since, by definition, recurrent correspondences are those that occur at least twice, the recall on the test set was in fact $21/23 = 91\%$.

For comparison, on the same Fox–Menomini list, JAKARTA identifies only eight consonantal correspondences of which the single complex correspondence is not in Bloomfield's set. The resulting precision is comparable at 88%, but the recall is only 32%.

The results of the experiment are extremely encouraging. The accomplishment of a very high precision and recall on a test set composed of 80% noise confirms that the iterative statistical approach advocated here is highly robust. The impressive outcome should, however, be interpreted with caution. Because of the (unavoidably) small number of target correspondences, the change of a single classification makes a difference of about 5% in the resulting precision/recall figures. Moreover, the decision to ignore vowels and glides helped the program to focus on the right type of correspondences. Finally, the Algonquian consonantal correspondences are almost context-free, which nicely suits the program's principles.

8   Conclusion

I have proposed an original approach to the determination of complex sound correspondences in bilingual wordlists based on the idea of relating recurrent correspondences between sounds to translational equivalences between words. Through induction of statistical models that are similar to those developed for statistical machine translation, the method is able to recover recurrent sound correspondences from bilingual wordlists that consist mostly of unrelated pairs. The results presented here prove that the techniques developed in the context of statistical machine translation can be successfully applied to a problem in diachronic phonology. I am convinced that the transfer of methods and insights is also possible in the other direction.

Acknowledgments. I would like to thank Graeme Hirst, Radford Neal, and Suzanne Stevenson for helpful comments, to John Hewson for the Algonquian data, to Michael Oakes for assistance with JAKARTA, This research was supported by the Natural Sciences and Engineering Research Council of Canada.

References

1. Y. Al-Onaizan, J. Curin, M. Jahr, K. Knight, J. Lafferty, D. Melamed, F. Och, D. Purdy, N. Smith, and D. Yarowsky. Statistical machine translation. Technical report, Johns Hopkins University, 1999.
2. Leonard Bloomfield. On the sound-system of central Algonquian. *Language*, 1:130–156, 1925.

3. Leonard Bloomfield. Algonquian. In Harry Hoijer et al., editor, *Linguistic Structures of Native America*, volume 6 of *Viking Fund Publications in Anthropology*, pages 85–129. New York: Viking, 1946.
4. Ted Dunning. Accurate methods for the statistics of surprise and coincidence. *Computational Linguistics*, 19(1):61–74, 1993.
5. Jacques B. M. Guy. An algorithm for identifying cognates in bilingual wordlists and its applicability to machine translation. *Journal of Quantitative Linguistics*, 1(1):35–42, 1994. MS-DOS executable available at http://garbo.uwasa.fi.
6. John Hewson. Comparative reconstruction on the computer. In *Proceedings of the 1st International Conference on Historical Linguistics*, pages 191–197, 1974.
7. John Hewson. *A computer-generated dictionary of proto-Algonquian*. Hull, Quebec: Canadian Museum of Civilization, 1993.
8. John Hewson. Vocabularies of Fox, Cree, Menomini, and Ojibwa, 1999. Computer file.
9. Kevin Knight and Jonathan Graehl. Machine transliteration. *Computational Linguistics*, 24(4):599–612, 1998.
10. Philipp Koehn and Kevin Knight. Knowledge sources for word-level translation models. In *Proceedings of the 2001 Conference on Empirical Methods in Natural Language Processing*, pages 27–35, 2001.
11. Grzegorz Kondrak. A new algorithm for the alignment of phonetic sequences. In *Proceedings of NAACL 2000: 1st Meeting of the North American Chapter of the Association for Computational Linguistics*, pages 288–295, 2000.
12. Grzegorz Kondrak. Identifying cognates by phonetic and semantic similarity. In *Proceedings of NAACL 2001: 2nd Meeting of the North American Chapter of the Association for Computational Linguistics*, pages 103–110, 2001.
13. Grzegorz Kondrak. Determining recurrent sound correspondences by inducing translation models. In *Proceedings of COLING 2002: 19th International Conference on Computational Linguistics*, pages 488–494, 2002.
14. John B. Lowe and Martine Mazaudon. The reconstruction engine: a computer implementation of the comparative method. *Computational Linguistics*, 20:381–417, 1994.
15. Gideon S. Mann and David Yarowsky. Multipath translation lexicon induction via bridge languages. In *Proceedings of NAACL 2001: 2nd Meeting of the North American Chapter of the Association for Computational Linguistics*, pages 151–158, 2001.
16. I. Dan Melamed. *Empirical Methods for Exploiting Parallel Texts*. The MIT Press, Cambridge, MA, 2001.
17. Michael P. Oakes. Computer estimation of vocabulary in protolanguage from word lists in four daughter languages. *Journal of Quantitative Linguistics*, 7(3):233–243, 2000.
18. Jörg Tiedemann. Automatic construction of weighted string similarity measures. In *Proceedings of the Joint SIGDAT Conference on Empirical Methods in Natural Language Processing and Very Large Corpora*, College Park, Maryland, 1999.

Generating Texts with Style

Richard Power[1], Donia Scott[1], and Nadjet Bouayad-Agha[2]

[1] Information Technology Research Institute, University of Brighton
Lewes Road, Brighton BN2 4AT, UK
{richard.power,donia.scott}@itri.bton.ac.uk
[2] Departament de Tecnologia, University Pompeu Fabra
Passeig de Circumval-lació 8, Barcelona, Spain
Nadjet.Bouayad@tecm.upf.es

Abstract. We describe an approach for generating a wide variety of texts expressing the same content. By treating stylistic features as constraints on the output of a text planner, we explore the interaction between various stylistic features (from punctuation and layout to pronominal reference and discourse structure) and their impact on the form of the resulting text.

1 Introduction

Any reasonably complex message, comprising perhaps ten propositions, can be expressed in billions of ways in English or any other natural language. An important challenge for computational linguists is to understand the contextual and stylistic factors that make one version preferable to another. In the final chapter of 'Elements of Style' [1], E.B. White posed this problem by contrasting a memorable quotation from Thomas Paine:

These are the times that try men's souls.

with several alternative formulations of the same literal content, including:

Soulwise, these are trying times.

As White points out, recognising the absurdity of the second formulation is easy; explaining exactly why it is absurd is altogether harder. We describe in this paper an approach that addresses some aspects of stylistic variation, particularly those that apply at the structural level. This work is carried out within the context of natural language generation (NLG).

Most NLG systems are restricted to one style of text. Moreover, with the notable exception of Hovy's PAULINE, existing NLG systems cannot reason about the style(s) they produce; such decisions are hard-wired within the system [2]. Since style impacts on all aspects of text — from syntax and lexical choice through to discourse structure and layout — changing the style of the output texts of such systems can have far reaching implementational consequences. The approach we describe here achieves a wide variety of styles in a flexible and

A. Gelbukh (Ed.): CICLing 2003, LNCS 2588, pp. 444–452, 2003.

efficient manner, at least at the level of text planning. Where appropriate, it also gives control over stylistic choices to the user.

In describing a text as being 'good', one is really addressing two distinct classes of criteria. The first concerns correctness: does the text conform to the rules of the language? In other words, is it grammatical, is the punctuation correct, are the correct words chosen, and so forth. Clearly, one would rule out any text which does not satisfy such criteria. However, for a given content there will be a wide variety of correct texts, their number increasing exponentially with the size of the content (i.e., number of propositions). The second class of criteria relates to the suitability of the selected text compared with alternative 'correct' solutions.

The first criterion accounts for 'stylistic' rules that are applied to any situation of communication and whose violation hinders seriously the quality of the text. The second criterion brings us back to E.B. White's point: to what extent is a particular version of a text appropriate to the given situation of communication — e.g., the genre, the register, the idiosyncratic style of the author or the house style of the publisher?

In what follows, we provide a general description of our approach to the implementation of style at the level of text planning, taking into account the different types of stylistic rules. We exemplify our approach through a working example showing the operation of stylistic settings on the production of a text.

2   Hard and Soft Constraints

We treat stylistic rules as constraints and distinguish between the two classes of stylistic criteria through their classification as hard or soft constraints.

A hard constraint is a fatal defect; texts violating hard constraints should never be generated, regardless of their other merits. Among hard constraints we include correct structure, both as regards syntax and higher textual levels, and correct realization of rhetorical relationships. The system currently imposes about 20 such constraints during text planning, including the following:

- Spans linked by a subordinating conjunction (e.g., since) must occur within the same text-clause.
- The text-category hierarchy [3] must be respected: for instance, a text-sentence cannot contain a paragraph (unless the paragraph is indented).
- Vertical lists cannot be used for the arguments of a nucleus-satellite relation; the relation must be multinuclear.

Since soft constraints are non-fatal defects, there may be circumstances in which violations are accepted as a necessary evil. Many stylistic dilemmas arise because one soft constraint conflicts with another. For example, we may prefer to avoid the passive voice, but we also prefer to place the current discourse topic in subject position. How can such a conflict be resolved? Following Optimality Theory [4], the constraints could be arranged in an order of priority, but this leads to absurd anomalies: a single violation of one constraint might outweigh a hundred violations of constraints with lower rank. The alternative, which we adopt, is to compute for each solution a cost, weighting violations according to their relative importance. Style preferences defined by the user make their presence felt by modifying some of these weights.

For efficiency, it is obviously desirable that solutions violating hard constraints are eliminated before any candidates are generated. We have shown elsewhere [5] that this can be done by formulating text planning as a Constraint Satisfaction Problem, which can be solved by Constraint Logic Programming [6]. Briefly, the idea is that the features over which hard constraints are defined are represented by finite-domain variables, and that unacceptable combinations of values are ruled out before any specific solutions are generated.

To evaluate violations of soft constraints, we can find no sufficiently flexible alternative to a generate-and-test method. Several hundred candidate text plans are generated; each is assigned a cost by summing weighted scores for each violation; the solution with lowest cost is selected, and passed forward for tactical generation and formatting.

The obvious drawback to generate-and-test is that the number of candidates increases exponentially with complexity (roughly, with the number of elementary propositions in the semantic input). From informal experiments, we find that the number of candidate solutions is around 5^{N-1} for N elementary propositions, which means that even for a short passage containing a dozen propositions the text planner would find about 50 million solutions satisfying the hard constraints. One might try to address this problem by a statistical optimization method such as a genetic algorithm [7], but we think a more natural and informative method is to break up the problem into parts, so that at each stage only a manageable part of the total solution is constructed. For instance, when planning a text, the semantic material could first be distributed among sections, then perhaps among paragraphs, thus spawning many small-scale text-planning problems for which the search spaces would be measured in hundreds rather than billions.

We have followed this approach also in combining text planning with tactical generation. Once the best text plan has been selected, it remains fixed, no matter what further costs accrue during syntactic realization. Moreover, the realization of each proposition in the linear sequence is fixed before passing to the next proposition. The tactical generator thus explores various ways of realizing the first proposition, evelutes them according to soft constraint violations, and chooses the best; the resulting linguistic context is then taken into account when searching for the best realization of the second proposition.

3   A Working Example

3.1   The ICONOCLAST System

We have developed a system, ICONOCLAST, which generates texts for the domain of Patient Information Leaflets (PILs) — the package inserts which explain ingredients, side-effects, instructions for using the medicine, and so forth.

The user of the system can define the content of a leaflet by using the WYSI-WYM method [8], and can also vary the style of the generated text by sliding pointers along nine scales representing the following parameters:

Paragraph Length
Sentence Length
Frequency of Connectives
Frequency of Passive Voice
Frequency of Pronouns
Frequency of Semicolons
Frequency of Commas
Technical Level (use of technical terms)
Graphical Impact (use of vertical lists)

As examples of style profiles we have saved two configurations named 'Broadsheet' and 'Tabloid'[1]. The broadsheet style has long paragraphs and sentences, frequent use of passives, semicolons, and commas, relatively few pronouns, high technical level, and low graphical impact; the tabloid style is the reverse. With the broadsheet profile loaded, the output text for a short section of a PIL on 'Taking your medicine' might read as follows:

To take a tablet, remove the tablet from the foil, and swallow it with water.
If you take an overdose, tell your doctor immediately, or go to your hospital's Casualty Department.

The user might induce small changes in this text by using the sliders, for example by reducing the comma frequency or raising the pronoun frequency. Every time this is done, the system generates a new text from the current model and current style profile. Alternatively, the user might decide to change the style completely by loading the tabloid profile, with perhaps the following result:

To take a tablet:
　1 Remove it from the foil
　2 Swallow it with water
If you take an overdose
　• tell your doctor immediately, or
　• go to your hospital's Casualty Department.

3.2　Satisfying Hard Constraints

Figure 1 shows a simple model comprising two propositions linked by a 'cause' relation[2]. With standard settings for hard constraints, and two potential discourse connectives (since, consequently), our text planner generates eight candidate solutions for this input, including plans A and B in figure 2. After syntactic realization, the texts resulting from these plans were as follows:

---

[1] These labels should not be taken too seriously.
[2] Details of the semantic representation are presented in [9].

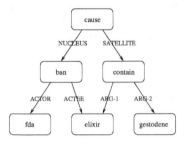

Fig. 1. Semantic Input

(A) Since Elixir contains gestodene, it is banned by the FDA.
(B) The FDA bans Elixir. It contains gestodene.

We will show later that under most settings of the style parameters, A is preferred to B; first, however, we say a little more about how these candidate solutions are obtained.

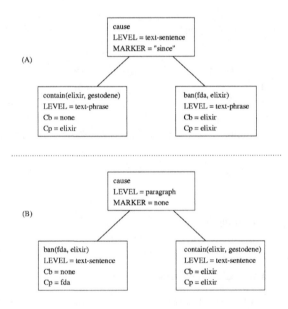

Fig. 2. Text Plans

The algorithm for producing plans like A and B, implemented in the Constraint Logic Programming language Eclipse [10], can be summarized as follows[3]:

---

[3] Details are available in [5].

1. A schematic plan is constructed by assigning one node to each rhetorical relation and to each elementary proposition. Since the semantic input in figure 1 has one rhetorical relation linking two propositions, we obtain a schematic plan with three nodes (figure 2).
2. Each node is assigned text-category variables [3]. A text-category comprises a LEVEL (e.g., section, paragraph, text-sentence) and an INDENTATION (relevant for texts with vertical lists). To simplify, we assume here that there are no indented constituents.
3. Each node (except the root) is assigned a POSITION variable representing its order in relation to its sisters. This variable is omitted from figure 2, where position is shown instead by left-to-right order on the page.
4. Nodes representing relations are assigned a MARKER variable whose value ranges over the relevant discourse markers (e.g., since and consequently for 'cause'), including an empty value (none) if the relation can be left implicit.
5. Nodes representing propositions are assigned Cb and Cp variables ranging over the potential backward and forward centers [11].
6. Constraints are defined over the solution variables so that ill-formed text plans cannot be generated.
7. All combinations of variables satisfying the hard constraints are enumerated; every such combination defines a candidate text plan to be submitted to further evaluation using soft constraints.

Note, incidentally, that the plans in figure 2 are still schematic: for instance, plan A needs to be elaborated so that the discourse connective since is coordinated with the first proposition.

3.3 Satisfying Soft Constraints

Having generated a set of candidate plans, including A and B, the program applies soft constraints in order to assign a cost to each plan. The cost is computed by checking for a series of violations at each node, penalizing each violation by a score that might depend on the current settings of the style parameters, and then summing over the whole plan. We list below some soft constraints that are currently implemented; note, however, that these constraints are provisional, and that so far we have no empirical basis either for choosing these particular constraints or for fixing their relative weights. The purpose of the list is to indicate some plausible stylistic constraints, and to show how they can be applied at the text-planning stage.

The first five constraints represent general principles of good style, unrelated to the style parameters controlled by the user.

Nucleus-Satellite Order
In most cases (including 'cause') the nucleus can be best emphasized by placing it in final position. A penalty is therefore imposed when the nucleus is placed first. Plan B violates this constraint.

Structure Branching
Right-branching structures are preferred to left-branching ones.

Rhetorical Grouping

Text plans that express rhetorical groupings explicitly are preferred to ones that leave them implicit. For instance, a plan which expressed three propositions by a paragraph of three sentences would be penalized if two of these propositions were grouped together in rhetorical structure.

Marker Repetition

If two rhetorical relations that are neighbours in the semantic input are expressed by the same discourse connective, a penalty is applied. This constraint would for example penalize a sentence in which since occurred twice.

Continuity of Reference

Three soft constraints based on centering theory are employed to score continuity of reference: they are salience ($Cp_N = Cb_N$), coherence ($Cb_N = Cb_{N+1}$) and cheapness ($Cp_N = Cb_{N+1}$) [12,13]. Plan B violates this constraint, since the Cp of the first proposition fails to predict the Cb of the second.

On the basis of these five constraints, plan A (no violations) will be preferred to plan B (two violations). However, this difference in favour of plan A might be over-ridden by costs resulting from the remaining constraints, which depend upon the style parameters controlled by the user.

Paragraph Length

Although no words have been generated yet, paragraph length can be measured from the number of propositions expressed in each paragraph. The cost is calculated as a deviation from an ideal length determined by the user.

Sentence Length

The length of each text-sentence is also measured by the number of propositions it contains, and scored by deviation from the user-controlled ideal length.

Connective Frequency

If the user requests frequent connectives, failure to use a discourse marker is penalized; conversely, if the user requests few connectives, the presence of a marker is penalized.

Passive Voice

Inclusions of passives in the output text are penalised if the user requests a low frequency of occurence, and vice versa for actives when a high frequency of passives are requested.

Semicolon Frequency

Following Nunberg's punctuation rules [3], every text-clause will end in a semicolon unless it is the final constituent of a text-sentence. If the user requests frequent semicolons, text-sentences with only one text-clause are penalized; if the user requests infrequent semicolons, text-sentences with more than one text-clause are penalized.

Graphical Impact

Under standard settings, the hard constraints allow vertical lists only for multinuclear relations (e.g. alternative, sequence). Failure to use an indented structure in such cases is penalized if the user has requested high graphical impact; the presence of an indented structure is penalized if the user has requested low graphical impact.

4   Conclusions

Although we have concentrated here on stylistic constraints at the level of text planning, the approach we take to optimization means that possibilities at other levels are also considered at no extra cost. For example, text planning constraints on the setting for the preferred center (i.e., Cp, the most salient referent) will rule out certain syntactic choices since even at the text-planning stage, the eventual use of the passive can be foreseen if the ACTEE of an action is the Cp. Similarly, constraints on text category will have a direct bearing on the appearance of semicolons.

The system we have developed has proved a useful research tool for investigating the interaction between stylistic goals. Through the generate-and-test method, one can quickly evaluate the consequences of a given stylistic choice and discover new constraints that should be added.

The system can also be viewed as an authoring tool that allows users to specify not only the content of a document to be generated — as in other systems, e.g., [14,15,16,17,8] — but also fairly fine-grained decisions over the style of the output text.

Finally, the system has the added capability of being self-critiquing: the user can, if he or she wishes, see the extent to which any or all of the generated versions deviates from what would in theory be ideal. This too is achieved at no extra cost.

References

1. Strunk, W., White, E.: The elements of style. MacMillan (1979)
2. Hovy, E.: Generating Natural Language under Pragmatic Constraints. Lawrence Erlbaum Associates, Hillsdale, NJ (1988)
3. Nunberg, G.: The Linguistics of Punctuation. CSLI, Stanford, USA (1990)
4. Kager, R.: Optimality Theory. Cambridge Textbooks in Linguistics. Cambridge University Press (1999)
5. Power, R.: Planning texts by constraint satisfaction. In: Proceedings of COLING-2000. (2000)
6. Hentenryck, P.V.: Constraint Satisfaction in Logic Programming. MIT Press, Cambridge, Mass. (1989)
7. Mellish, C., Knott, A., Oberlander, J., O'Donnell, M.: Experiments using stochastic search for text planning. In: Proceedings of the Ninth International Workshop on Natural Language Generation, Niagara-On-the-Lake, Ontario, Canada (1998) 98–107
8. Power, R., Scott, D.: Multilingual authoring using feedback texts. In: Proceedings of the 17th International Conference on Computational Linguistics and 36th Annual Meeting of the Association for Computational Linguistics, Montreal, Canada

9. Power, R.: Controlling logical scope in text generation. In: Proceedings of the European Workshop on Natural Language Generation, Toulouse, France (1999) 1–9

10. ECRC: Eclipse User manual. Technical report, European Computer Research Centre, Munich, Germany (1992)

11. Grosz, B., Joshi, A., Weinstein, S.: Centering: a framework for modelling the local coherence of discourse. Computational Linguistics 21 (1995) 203–225

12. Kibble, R., Power, R.: Using centering theory to plan coherent texts. In: Proceedings of the 12th Amsterdam Colloquium, Institute for Logic, Language and Computation, University of Amsterdam (1999)

13. Strube, M., Hahn, U.: Functional centering: Grounding referential coherence in information structure. Computational Linguistics (1999)

14. Caldwell, D., Korelsky, T.: Bilingual generation of job descriptions from quasi-conceptual forms. In: Proceedings of the Fourth Conference on Applied Natural Language Generation. (1994)

15. Paris, C., Vander Linden, K., Fischer, M., Hartley, A., Pemberton, L., Power, R., Scott, D.: A Support tool for writing multilingual instructions. In: Proceedings of the 14th International Joint Conference on Artificial Intelligence, Montreal, Canada (1995) 1398–1404

16. Power, R., Cavallotto, N.: Multilingual generation of administrative forms. In: Proceedings of the 8th International Workshop on Natural Language Generation, Herstmonceux Castle, UK (1996) 17–19

17. Sheremetyeva, S., Nirenburg, S., Nirenburg, I.: Generating patent Claims from interactive input. In: Proceedings of the 8th International Workshop on Natural Language Generation, Herstmonceux Castle, UK (1996) (1998) 1053–1059

Multilingual Syntax Editing in GF

Janna Khegai, Bengt Nordström, and Aarne Ranta

Department of Computing Science
Chalmers University of Technology and Gothenburg University
SE-41296, Gothenburg, Sweden
{janna, bengt, aarne}@cs.chalmers.se

Abstract. GF (Grammatical Framework) makes it possible to perform multilingual authoring of documents in restricted languages. The idea is to use an object in type theory to describe the common abstract syntax of a document and then map this object to a concrete syntax in the different languages using linearization functions, one for each language. Incomplete documents are represented using metavariables in type theory. The system belongs to the tradition of logical frameworks in computer science. The paper gives a description of how a user can use the editor to build a document in several languages and also shows some examples how ambiguity is resolved using type checking. There is a brief description of how GF grammars are written for new domains and how linearization functions are defined.

1 Introduction

1.1 Multilingual Authoring

We are interested in the problem of editing a document in several languages simultaneously. In order for the problem to be feasible, we use a restricted language. The idea is to use a mathematical structure (an object in type theory) as the basic representation of the document being edited. This structure describes the abstract syntax of the document. Concrete representations of the document in the various languages are expressed using linearization functions, one function for each language. The process of producing a concrete representation from the abstract object is thus deterministic, each abstract object has only one concrete representation in each language. The reverse problem (parsing) is not deterministic, a given concrete representation may correspond to many abstract objects (ambiguity). The way we resolve ambiguity is by having an interactive system, an ambiguity results in an incomplete abstract object which has to be completed by the user. For instance, in the phrase Dear friend it is not clear whether the friend is male of female, thus making a translation into Swedish impossible. In the corresponding abstract object there is a field for gender which has to be filled in by the user before the editing is complete.

Type theory is a completely formal language for mathematics developed by Martin-Löf in the 70's [9]. Versions of it are extensively used under the title of Logical Frameworks in various implementations of proof editors like Coq [19],

A. Gelbukh (Ed.): CICLing 2003, LNCS 2588, pp. 453–464, 2003.

Alf [8], and Lego [7]. The type system of type theory is not only used to express syntactic well-formedness, but also semantic well-formedness. This means that a syntactically well-formed term also has a meaning. Moreover, it is often possible to use type checking to resolve ambiguities that a weaker grammatical description cannot resolve.

1.2   The GF Niche – Meaning-Based Technique

Grammatical Framework (GF) is a grammar formalism built upon a Logical Framework (LF). What GF adds to LF is a possibility to define concrete syntax, that is, notations expressing formal concepts in user-readable ways. The concrete syntax mechanism of GF is powerful enough to describe natural languages: like PATR [18] and HPSG [13], GF uses features and records to express complex linguistic objects. Although GF grammars are bidirectional like PATR and HPSG, the perspective of GF is on generation rather than parsing. This implies that grammars are built in a slightly different way, and also that generation is efficient enough to be performed in real time in interactive systems. Another difference from usual grammar formalisms is the support for multilinguality: it is possible to define several concrete syntaxes upon one abstract syntax. The abstract syntax then works as an interlingua between the concrete syntaxes. The development of GF as an authoring system started as a plug-in to the proof editor ALF, to permit natural-language rendering of formal proofs [5]. The extension of the scope outside mathematics was made in the Multilingual Document Authoring project at Xerox [3]. In continued work, GF has been used in areas like software specifications [4], instruction texts [6], and dialogue systems [17]. In general, GF works for any domain of language that permits a formal grammar. Since LF is more general than specific logical calculi, it is more flexible to use on different domains than, for instance, predicate calculus.

1.3   The Scope of the Paper

The GF program implementing the GF grammar formalism is a complex system able to perform many NLP tasks. For example, it can do the morphological analysis of French verbs, construct a letter in several languages, and even greet you in the morning using a speech synthesizer. In this paper, however, we choose to restrict the topic and only look at GF as a multilingual authoring tool. For a more elaborated description of the system, we refer to [16,15].

The GF users can be divided into three competence levels:

– Author level
– Grammarian level
– Implementor level

On the author level all we can do is to work with pre-existing grammars. This level is described in Section 2. On the grammarian level we write grammars describing new language fragments. This, of course, requires acquaintance with the GF formalism. Examples of work on this level are given in Section 3. On both of these levels, we have some control, for example, over parsing algorithms to be used. However, the full control of parsing, linearization, graphics and other algorithms, is only accessible on the implementor level. Since GF is open source software, any user who wants can also become an implementor; but describing the implementor level is outside the scope of this paper.

2 The GF Syntax Editor

The graphical user interface implemented in the GF Syntax Editor hides the complexity of the system from the naive user. It provides access to the system functionality without requiring knowledge of the GF formalism. In this section we will show a simple example of GF syntax editing procedure.

When you start the GF editor you choose the topic and the languages you want to work with. For instance, we decide to work within the LETTER topic and want to have translations in four languages: English, Swedish, French and Finnish. You can create a new editing object by choosing a category from the New list. For example, to construct a letter, choose the Letter category (Fig. 1). In Fig. 2 you can see the created object in the tree form in the left upper part as well as linearizations in the right upper part. The tree representation corresponds to the GF language-independent semantic representation, the GF abstract syntax or interlingua. The linearizations area displays the result of translation of abstract syntax representation into the corresponding language using the GF concrete syntax.

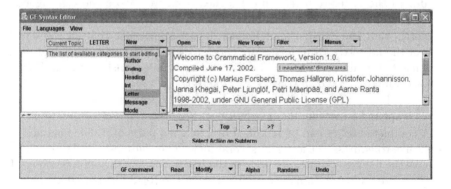

Fig. 1. The New menu shows the list of available categories within the current topic LETTER. Choosing the category Letter in the list will create an object of the corresponding type. The linearizations area contains a welcome message when the GF Editor has just been started.

According to the LETTER grammar a letter consists of a Heading, a Message and an Ending, which is reflected in the tree and linearizations structures.

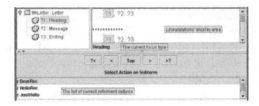

Fig. 2. The Abstract Syntax tree represents the letter structure. The current editing focus, the metavariable ?1 is highlighted. The type of the current focus is shown below the linearizations area. The context-dependent refinement option list is shown in the bottom part.

However, the exact contents of each of these parts are not yet known. Thus, we can only see question marks, representing metavariables, instead of language phrases in the linearizations.

Editing is a process of step-wise refinement, i.e. replacement of metavariables with language constructions. In order to proceed you can choose among the options shown in the refinement list. The refinement list is context-dependent, i.e. it refers to the currently selected focus. For example, if the focus is Heading, then we can choose among four options. Let us start our letter with the DearRec structure (Fig. 3(a)).

Now we have a new focus - metavariable ?4 of the type Recipient and a new set of refinement options. We have to decide what kind of recipient the letter has. Notice that the word Dear in Swedish and French versions is by default in male gender and, therefore, uses the corresponding adjective form. Suppose we want to address the letter to a female colleague. Then we choose the ColleagueShe option (Fig. 3(b)).

Notice that the Swedish and French linearizations now contain the female form of the adjective Dear , since we chose to write to a female recipient. This refinement step allows us to avoid the ambiguity while translating from English to, for example, a Swedish version of the letter.

Proceeding in the same fashion we eventually fill all the metavariables and get a completed letter like the one shown in Fig. 4(a).

A completed letter can be modified by replacing parts of it. For instance, we would like to address our letter to several male colleagues instead. We need first to move the focus to the Header node in the tree and delete the old refinement. In Fig. 5(a), we continue from this point by using the Read button, which invokes an input dialog, and expects a string to parse. Let us type colleagues.

The parsed string was ambiguous, therefore, as shown in Fig. 5(b), GF asks further questions. Notice that after choosing the ColleaguesHe option, not only the word colleague , but the whole letter switches to the plural, male form, see Fig. 4(b). In the English version only the noun fellow turns into plural, while in the other languages the transformations are more dramatic. The pronoun you turns into plural number. The participle promoted changes the number in the Swedish and French versions. The latter also changes the form of the verb have.

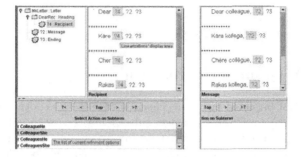

Fig. 3. (a) The linearizations are now filled with the first word that corresponds to *Dear* expression in English, Swedish, French and Finnish. The refinement focus is moved to the Recipient metavariable. (b) The Heading part is now complete. The adjective form changes to the corresponding gender after choosing the recipient.

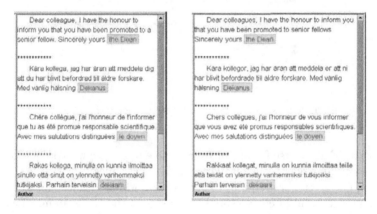

Fig. 4. (a) The complete letter in four languages. (b) Choosing the plural male form of the Recipient causes various linguistic changes in the letter as compared to (a).

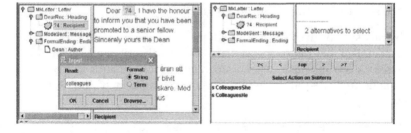

Fig. 5. (a) A refinement step can be done by using the Read button, which asks the user for a string to parse. (b) When the parsed string in (a) is ambiguous GF presents two alternative ways to resolve the ambiguity.

Both the gender and the number affect the adjective dear in French, but only the number changes in the corresponding Finnish adjective. Thus, the refinement step has led to substantial linguistic changes.

3   The GF Grammar Formalism

The syntax editor provided by GF is generic with respect to both subject matters and target languages. To create a new subject matter (or modify an old one), one has to create (or edit) an abstract syntax To create a new target language, one has to work on a concrete syntax. Target languages can be added on the fly: if a new language is selected from the Language menu, a new view appears in the editor while other things remain equal, including the document that is being edited. Fig. 6 shows the effect of adding Russian to the above example.

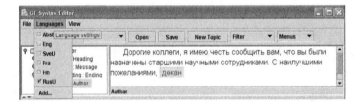

Fig. 6. Now we are able to translate the letter into Russian

The syntax editor itself is meant to be usable by people who do not know GF, but just something of the subject matter and at least one of the target languages. Authoring GF grammars requires expertise on both the subject matter and the target languages, and of course some knowledge of the GF grammar formalism.

A typical GF grammar has an abstract syntax of 1–3 pages of GF code, and concrete syntaxes about the double of that size. The use of resource grammars (Section 3.5) makes concrete syntaxes much shorter and easier to write.

3.1   Abstract Syntax: Simple Example

An abstract syntax gives a structural description of a domain. It can be semantically as detailed and rigorous as a mathematical theory in a Logical Framework. It can also be less detailed, depending on how much semantic control of the document is desired. Asq an example, consider a fragment of the abstract syntax for letters:

```
cat Letter ; Recipient ; Author ; Message ;
    Heading ; Ending ; Sentence ;

fun MkLetter : Heading -> Message -> Ending -> Letter ;
fun DearRec : Recipient -> Heading ;
```

```
fun PlainSent : Sentence -> Message ;
fun ColleagueHe, ColleaguesShe : Recipient ;
```

The grammar has a set of categories `cat` and functions `fun`. The functions are used for building abstract syntax trees, and each tree belongs to a category. When editing proceeds, the system uses the abstract syntax to build a menu of possible actions: for instance, the possible refinements for a metavariable of type C are those functions whose value type is C.

3.2   Concrete Syntax

Concrete syntax maps abstract syntax trees into linguistic objects. The objects can be simply strings, but in general they are records containing inflection tables, agreement features, etc. Each record has a type, which depends on the category of the tree, and of course on the target language. For instance, a part of the English category system for letters is defined as follows:

```
param Num = Sg | Pl ;
param Agr = Ag Num ;

lincat Letter = {s : Str} ;
lincat Recipient, Author = {s : Str ; a : Agr} ;
lincat Message = {s : Agr => Agr => Str} ;
lincat Heading, Ending = {s : Str ; a : Agr} ;
```

Both the author and the recipient have inherent agreement features (number), which are passed from them to the message body, so that right forms of verbs and nouns can be selected there:

```
lin MkLetter head mess end = {s =
      head.s ++ "," ++
      mess.s ! end.a ! head.a ++ "." ++
      end.s} ;
```

Different languages have different parameter systems. French, for instance, has gender in addition to number in the agreement features:

```
param Gen = Masc | Fem ; Num = Sg | Pl ; Agr = Ag Gen Num ;
```

3.3   Semantic Control in Abstract Syntax

The main semantic control in the letter grammar is the structure that is imposed on all letters: it is, for instance, not possible to finish a letter without a heading. This kind of control would be easy to implement even using a context-free grammar or XML. Semantic control of more demanding kind is achieved by using the dependent types of type theory. For instance, the abstract syntax

```
cat Text ; Prop ; Proof (A : Prop) ;
fun ThmWithProof, ThmHideProof : (A : Prop) -> Proof A -> Text ;
```

defines mathematical texts consisting of a proposition and a proof. The type of proofs depends on propositions: the type checker can effectively decide whether a given proof really is a proof of a given theorem. Type checking also helps the author of the proof by only showing menu items that can possibly lead to a correct proof. Proof texts are linearized by to the following rules:

```
lin ThmWithProof A P =
        {s = "Theorem." ++ A.s ++ "Proof." ++ P.s ++ "Q.E.D."} ;
lin ThmHideProof A P =
        {s = "Theorem." ++ A.s ++ "Proof." ++ "Omitted."} ;
```

The latter form omits the proof, but the author is nevertheless obliged to construct the proof in the internal representation.

Mathematical texts with hidden proofs are a special case of proof-carrying documents, where semantic conditions are imposed by using dependent types in abstract syntax (cf. the notion of proof-carrying code [12]). Consider texts describing flight connections:

> To get from Gothenburg to New York, you can first fly SK433 to Copenhagen and then take SK909.

There are three conditions: that SK433 flies from Gothenburg to Copenhagen, that SK909 flies from Copenhagen to New York, and that change in Copenhagen is possible. These conditions are expressed by the following abstract syntax:

```
cat City ; Flight (x,y : City) ;

fun Connection :
        (x,y,z : City) -> (a : Flight x y) -> (b : Flight y z)
                -> Proof (PossibleChange x y z a b) -> Flight x z ;
fun PossibleChange :
        (x,y,z : City) -> Flight x y -> Flight y z -> Prop ;
```

The linearization rule for `Connection` produces texts like the example above, with internal representation that includes the hidden proof. We have left it open how exactly to construct proofs that a change is possible between two flights: this involves a proof that the departure time of the second flight lies within a certain interval from the arrival time of the first flight, the minimum length of the interval depending on the cities involved. In the end, the proof condition reduces to ordinary mathematical concepts.

3.4   Semantic Disambiguation

An important application of semantic control is disambiguation. For instance, the English sentence

> there exists an integer x such that x is even and x is prime

has two French translations,

il existe un entier x tel que x soit pair et que x soit premier
il existe un entier x tel que x soit pair et x est premier

corresponding to the trees

```
Exist Int (\x -> Conj (Even x) (Prime x))
Conj (Exist Int (\x -> Even x)) (Prime x)
```

respectively. Both analyses are possible by context-free parsing, but type checking rejects the latter one because it has an unbound occurrence of x.

Another example of semantic disambiguation is the resolution of pronominal reference. The English sentence

if the function f has a maximum then it reaches it at 0

has two occurrences of it. Yet the sentence is not ambiguous, since it uses the predicate reach, which can only take the function as its first argument and the maximum as its second argument: the dependently typed syntax tree uses a pronominalization function

```
fun Pron : (A : Dom) -> Elem A -> Elem A
```

making the domain and the reference of the pronoun explicit. Linearization rules of Pron into languages like French and German use the domain argument to select the gender of the pronoun, so that, for instance, the German translation of the example sentence uses sie for the first it and es for the second:

wenn die Funktion f ein Maximum hat, dann reicht sie es bei 0

3.5   Application Grammars and Resource Grammars

GF is primarily geared for writing specialized grammars for specialized domains. It is possible to avoid many linguistic problems just by ignoring them. For instance, if the grammar only uses the present tense, large parts of verb conjugation can be ignored. However, always writing such grammars from scratch has several disadvantages. First, it favours solutions that are linguistically ad hoc. Secondly, it produces concrete syntaxes that are not reusable from one application to another. Thirdly, it requires the grammarian simultaneously to think about the domain and about linguistic facts such as inflection, agreement, word order, etc. A solution is to raise the level of abstraction, exploiting the fact that GF is a functional programming language: do not define the concrete syntax as direct mappings from trees to strings, but as mappings from trees to structures in a resource grammar.

A resource grammar is a generic description of a language, aiming at completeness. From the programming point of view, it is like a library module, whose proper use is via type signatures: the user need not know the definitions of module functions, but only their types. This modularity permits a division of labour between programmers with different expertises. In grammar programming, there is typically a domain expert, who knows the abstract syntax and wants to map it into a concrete language, and a linguist, who has written the resource grammar and provided a high-level interface to it.

For instance, the resource grammar may contain linguistic categories, syntactic rules, and (as a limiting case of syntactic rules) lexical entries:

```
cat S ; NP ; Adj ;                  -- sentence, noun phrase, adjective
fun PredAdj : Adj -> NP -> S ; -- "NP is Adj"
fun Condit : S -> S -> S ;      -- "if S then S"
fun adj_even : Adj ;            -- "even"
```

The author of a grammar of arithmetic proofs may have the following abstract syntax with semantically motivated categories and functions:

```
cat Prop ; Nat ;                    -- proposition, natural number
fun If : Prop -> Prop -> Prop ; -- logical implication
fun Ev : Nat -> Prop ;          -- the evenness predicate
```

The concrete syntax that she writes can exploit the resource grammar:

```
lincat Prop = S ; Nat = NP ;
lin If = Condit ;
lin Ev = PredAdj adj_even ;
```

Experience with GF has shown that the abstract interfaces to resource grammars can largely be shared between different languages. Thus a German resource grammar can have the same type signatures as the English one, with the exception of lexical rules. In this case we have

```
lin Ev = PredAdj adj_gerade ;
```

Yet the effects of these rules are language-dependent. German has more agreement and word order variation in the conditional and predication rules. For instance, the syntax tree If (Ev n1) (Od n3) is linearized as follows:

English: if 1 is even then 2 is odd
German: wenn 1 gerade ist, dann ist 2 ungerade

Of course, there are also cases where different linguistic structures must be used in the abstract syntax. For instance, the two-place predicate saying that x misses y is expressed by a two-place verb construction in both English and French, but the roles of subject and object are inverted (x misses y vs. y manque á x):

English: `lin Miss x y = PredVP x (ComplV2 verb_miss y)`
French: `lin Miss x y = PredVP y (ComplV2 verb_manquer x)`

4   Discussion

4.1   Comparison to Other Systems

In computer science, one of the earliest attempt of generating a syntax editor from a language description was the Mentor [2] system at INRIA. Another early example is the Cornell program synthesizer [20], which uses an attribute grammar formalism to describe the language.

The idea of using a strictly formalized language for mathematics to express the abstract syntax of natural language was proposed by Curry [1] and used by Montague [11] in his denotational semantics of English. The followers of Montague, however, usually ignore the abstract syntax and define relations between natural language and logic directly. This makes generation much harder than when using an abstract syntax tree as the primary representation.

The WYSIWYM system [14] by Power and Scott has many similarities with our system. It is also a system for interactive multi-lingual editing. WYSIWYM does not use a mathematical language to express abstract syntax and it seems not to be possible for the user to change the structure of what they call the knowledge base (our abstract syntax).

Processing natural language within restricted domains makes GF related to the KANT translation system [10]. Kant Controlled English (KCE) put constraints on vocabulary, grammar and document structure in order to reduce the amount of ambiguity in the source text in the pre-processing phase. The remaining ambiguities are resolved via interaction with the author in the authoring environment. The only source language in the KANT system is English. KANT does not use any formal semantic representation.

4.2   Future Work

We would like to see the system as a (structured) document editor. This has many implications. The major part of the screen will in the future be devoted to the different documents and not to the various menus. The parts of the document which is not filled in – now indicated by metavariables – will have a meaningful label expressed in the language being presented. The natural action of refining a metavariable by parsing a text from the keyboard is to put the cursor on the metavariable and start typing. In the future it will also be possible to use completions, so when the user enters for instance a tab character the system responds with the longest unique possible continuation of the input together with a list of alternatives. Completion in GF can be controlled both by the application grammar and by statistics of the interaction history.

A grammarian-level user needs an advanced editor for editing grammar. So a natural idea is to extend GF to make it possible to edit the GF formalism itself.

Creating resource grammars is an important part in the development of GF, corresponding to the development of standard libraries for programming languages. The current libraries (end 2002) contain basic morphology, phrase structure, and agreement rules for English, French, German, and Swedish.

GF is generic program capable of using any set of grammars in an. Hardwired grammars, however, permit more light-weight implementations. We use the name gramlets for Java programs implementing such light-weight special-purpose editors. Gramlets can be used in PDAs and as web applets, and they can be automatically compiled from GF grammars.

References

1. H. B. Curry. Some logical aspects of grammatical structure. In Roman Jakobson, editor, *Structure of Language and its Mathematical Aspects: Proceedings of the Twelfth Symposium in Applied Mathematics*, pages 56–68. American Mathematical Society, 1963.
2. V. Donzeau-Gouge, G. Huet, G. Kahn, B. Lang, and J. J. Levy. A structure-oriented program editor: a first step towards computer assisted programming. In *International Computing Symposium (ICS'75)*, 1975.
3. M. Dymetman, V. Lux, and A. Ranta. XML and multilingual document authoring: Convergent trends. In *COLING, Saarbrücken, Germany*, pages 243–249, 2000.
4. R. Hähnle, K. Johannisson, and A. Ranta. An authoring tool for informal and formal requirements specifications. In R.-D. Kutsche and H. Weber, editors, Fundamental Approaches to Software Engineering, volume 2306 of LNCS, pages 233–248. Springer, 2002.
5. T. Hallgren and A. Ranta. An extensible proof text editor. In M. Parigot and A. Voronkov, editors, *LPAR-2000*, volume 1955 of *LNCS/LNAI*, pages 70–84. Springer, 2000.
6. K. Johannisson and A. Ranta. Formal verification of multilingual instructions. In *The Joint Winter Meeting of Computing Science and Computer Engineering*. Chalmers University of Technology, 2001.
7. Z. Luo and R. Pollack. LEGO Proof Development System. Technical report, University of Edinburgh, 1992.
8. L. Magnusson and B. Nordström. The ALF proof editor and its proof engine. In *Types for Proofs and Programs*, LNCS 806, pages 213–237. Springer, 1994.
9. P. Martin-Löf. *Intuitionistic Type Theory*. Bibliopolis, Napoli, 1984.
10. T. Mitamura and E. H. Nyberg. Controlled English for Knowledge-Based MT: Experience with the KANT system. In *TMI*, 1995.
11. R. Montague. *Formal Philosophy*. Yale University Press, New Haven, 1974. Collected papers edited by R. Thomason.
12. G. C. Necula. Proof-Carrying Code. In *Proc. 24th ACM Symposium on Principles of Programming Languages, Paris, France*, pages 106–119. ACM Press, 1997.
13. C. Pollard and I. Sag. *Head-Driven Phrase Structure Grammar*. University of Chicago Press, 1994.
14. R. Power and D. Scott. Multilingual authoring using feedback texts. In *COLING-ACL*, 1998.
15. A. Ranta. GF Homepage, 2002. www.cs.chalmers.se/~aarne/GF/.
16. A. Ranta. Grammatical Framework: A Type-theoretical Grammar Formalism. *The Journal of Functional Programming*, to appear.
17. A. Ranta and R. Cooper. Dialogue systems as proof editors. In *IJCAR/ICoS-3*, Siena, Italy, 2001.
18. S. Shieber. *An Introduction to Unification-Based Approaches to Grammars*. University of Chicago Press, 1986.
19. Coq Development Team. Coq Homepage. http://pauillac.inria.fr/coq/, 1999.
20. T. Teitelbaum and T. Reps. The Cornell Program Synthesizer: a syntax-directed programming environment. *Commun. ACM*, 24(9):563–573, 1981.

QGen – Generation Module for the Register Restricted InBASE System

Michael V. Boldasov[1] and Elena G. Sokolova[2]

[1] Moscow State University (MSU),
Computational Mathematic and Cybernetic department,
Moscow, Russia,
boldasov@nm.ru
[2] Russian Research Institute for Artificial Intelligence (RRIAI),
Moscow, Russia,
sokolova@aha.ru

Abstract. In this paper we present our investigations of constructing of a generation module for the InBASE system - a commercially oriented system for understanding of natural language queries to a Data Base. The initial prototype of the module re-generates the user query from the internal OQL representation into a natural language text presented in the form of extended nominal group. We discuss the main principles and methods of the organization of the generation module and peculiarities of the approaches we use for the knowledge representation as well as at planning and realization phases of generation. The initial prototype demonstrates direct transition from the OQL register specific representation to morphologically marked up structured representation of the query text. Directions of the further investigations are also discussed in the article.

1 Introduction

In this paper we present our investigations of constructing of a generation module for the InBASE system, which were declared in [1]. InBASE system is a natural language (NL) interface to a Data Base (DB) that is intended for commercial purposes[1]. It transforms the user NL query into the SQL query to the DB. After the InBASE system has received the information queried from DB, it presents the result to the user [2]. The system is the improved version of an earlier prototype – the InterBASE, developed in 80th [3].

The process of query understanding realized in the InBASE system represents an original "semantically-oriented" approach organized in terms of register-oriented concepts [5]. Thus, syntactic features of the text of user query are practically not used in the understanding process. The system is tuned on by the adjustment of the dictionary to a specific DB. Another peculiarity of the InBASE system is the separation of Domain Model (DM) from the DB itself [4].

---

[1] http://www.inbase.artint.ru/

A. Gelbukh (Ed.): CICLing 2003, LNCS 2588, pp. 465–476, 2003.
© Springer-Verlag Berlin Heidelberg 2003

The semantically oriented approach makes it possible to realize the real multilinguality of the InBASE system. To date, there are Russian, English and German interfaces that are supported by the same InBASE-analyzer. Multilinguality is the feature that points out the InBASE system from the similar systems that are made for a single language. One of the examples of such systems is MS English Query system that processes English queries[2]. See also the recent investigations made for Spanish in Mexico [6], [7].

To date, the answers to a user query are presented by the InBASE system in a table form as sets of Data, or as a number, if the query contains an operation like "count", "min" and so on, or as a fixed string like "Nothing was found in the DB". These types of answers usually do not satisfy the user. Moreover, the user has no guarantee that his query is understood correctly by the system while cases of misunderstanding really take place. For this purpose we have built a special module QGen that is aimed to extend system's answers to a more friendly form. This module by means of a NL expresses how the query content was formalized by the system and explains what kind of information is represented by the system as a result. QGen is realized as NL generator module. We consider the encapsulation of the generator into the InBASE system as a first step to a more natural "user – InBASE system" communication like, for example, in the START system[3].

In this paper we consider the framework of the QGen module: it's general organization, knowledge representation as well as the content of the two main phases of generation process - planning and realization in a specific NL. We also analyze the linguistic background of the module.

2   Organization of the Generation Module QGen

QGen is encapsulated into the InBASE system in the following way. When the user NL query is being converted by the system into the SQL representation, the system processes the Object Query Language (OQL) representation - Q-query. Q-query is transmitted to the input of the generator module, which re-generates the query from its OQL representation into NL form.

The structure of QGen is presented in Figure 1. The generator is structurally divided into a planning block and a block of realization. The Planning block performs the tasks of strategic and tactical planning. It splits the OQL tree into a sequence of tree segments (structures of further sentences) and transforms each tree segment into a sentence plan. Block of realization receives the sentence plans and applies to them a grammar of a specific NL. As a result sentence plans are converted into the sentence grammatical structures - morphologically marked up structured representations. By applying not complicated flattening algorithm to the constructed trees, we get NL text.

Control structures (resources) contain the rules of tree transformations. They are brought out into text files as separate resources that are interpreted by

---

[2] http://fog.shore.mbari.org/samplesDB/queries/Default.asp

[3] http://www.ai.mit.edu/projects/infolab/ailab.html

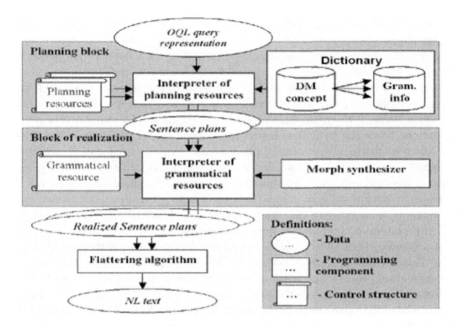

Fig. 1. QGen structure

the appropriate programming components of the QGen module. Such approach ensures an easy adaptation of the system to change of the DB Domain as well as to possible change of the target NL. Every control structure is applied by the Interpreter component to the nodes of tree structures in the following way. Interpreter component traverses the tree top-down and from left to right and applies the set of rules to each of the tree nodes.

The rule, that is applicable to a current node, changes the structure of its subtree, and\or sets some features for the further grammatical realization of the nodes of this subtree. Features are described in the following way: type <operation> value. A Feature is considered a typified string label. It belongs to one of three groups: lexical, morphological, or user defined. Lexical group consists of only one type - lex. Lex feature sets the lexeme of the concept that is associated with the node. Several types form a morphological group. It includes such types as PartOfSpeech, Gender, Number, Case, Person, Tense etc. Types of this group are determined by the NL grammar. All others features belong to the "user defined" group, which is an open to various types, for example, semantic features (SF).

Features restrict realization of the current node. They are pragmatic, semantic, grammatical, morphological and lexical constraints. Features are collected on phase of tactical planning until the tree structure is completely realized. Collecting of the features in the tree nodes is the core idea of the implementation of the QGen module. We distinguish two types of activities in the generation algorithm. They are transformation of the tree structure from the Register specific view (OQL) to the grammatical view, and collecting of the features for the realization in NL.

Every generation phase has its individual sets of the most typical operations of tree transformations. The most typical transformations at the planning phase are structural transformations, while assignments of features are rare, and linear ordering of one level nodes is not used at all. On the contrary, the most typical transformations at the realization phase are assignments of features and ordering operations, while the structural transformations in most cases do not take place. Therefore we distinguish syntax of planning and syntax of realization, changing the emphasis depending on specifics of transformations for the particular generation phase. This allows us to simplify the syntax of control structures and to increase its performance in comparison to similar general-purpose formalisms, for example, a language of the object production - SNOOP, which is used in the InBASE system at the phase of query understanding [8].

Dictionary of the QGen module is also developed as a separate control structure. This resource describes all the concepts of the DM that can be involved in the generation process, and some other NL specific means associated with these concepts. We consider the dictionary as a part of Knowledge base of the generation module. This gives us opportunity to change the NL of the outcoming text independently from the NL of the input user query. If the input query NL and the NL of the re-generated query are different, the InBASE system, extended by the QGen module, can be considered a knowledge based Machine Translation system, which works in the register of NL queries to DB. Such comparison is possible proceeded the "translation" of the query is performed through understanding of the query content.

3   Knowledge Representation

In [1] we have already discussed the structure of knowledge base that is used by QGen module in the InBASE system. Knowledge is divided into two parts: static - the DM, and dynamic - the expressions consisting of the DM concepts. The static part is a DM hierarchy of objects presented as diagram of classes that are associated with the attributes of DB [4]. DM redesigns DB by introducing human specific view to Domain structure in such a way that it releases the process of NL query analysis from the technical aspects of the DB organization. Every DM concept is associated with a set of features that are used by the InBASE system during the understanding process. In [1] we have showed that generator cannot use the dictionary of the InBASE system, that is used for analysis, because the process of analysis is not reverse to generation. Therefore, to solve the generation task we enlarge the DM of the InBASE system by a special Dictionary resource. The dictionary resource gives us ability to set extra features specific to the task of generation. Here is the example of a string of the dictionary resource:

```
['10']     'gender' (number: singular, SF: EssentialQualityOf)
```

The string describes the DM object with ID = '10' that should be lexified as 'gender' and it has two predefined features.

The dynamic part of knowledge representation is presented by Q-queries.Their concepts refer to the objects and attributes of the DM but not to tables of relational DB. Here is an example of Q-query that is expressed in a text form:

```
SELECT count(Employee.Marital state) FROM Employee
WHERE (Employee.Marital state<>'married') AND
(Employee.Sex='f')

OQL user query representation:
    "How many single women work in the company"
```

Q-query uses the syntax of OQL that is very similar to the syntax of SQL. Here we only draw attention to the fact that Q-query has a tree structure - a hierarchy of typified (or named) objects, which is passed to QGen in XML form.

4 Planning

Algorithm of planning is usually divided into phases of strategic and tactical planning. Strategic planner splits the knowledge into a sequence of segments of further sentences that defines the order of narration. At the first step of the QGen development we tackle the problem how to realize the generator of a user query that is expressed only by one sentence. Thus, we do not concern the details of the strategic planning in this paper.

However, sometimes a user query can be expressed in several sentences, i.e. in a text form. Q-query can be considered to be a representation where some "proposition knowledge" is hidden. We can develop it at the planning phase. For example, if we ask about an employee with two children we can use the "existence" predicate: Are there any employees with two children? But to express the information that we need about this employee (for example, we are interested in "age" and "salary") we ought to formulate the next sentence: What are their age and salary? Moreover there are cases when the Q-query can be preferably expressed by several sentences. For example, the query Get the information about cheap cars is interpreted by the system as Everything about autos. The information is arranged by increasing of price.

The tactical planner transforms the domain specific semantic structures, chosen by strategic planner, into structures of further sentences. Besides the structural transformations, according to the directives of the planning resource, generator also adds SFs from the Dictionary to some of nodes of the structure of the future NL sentence. These nodes will be treated by realization block as group nodes. SFs will direct how the group, restricted by the group node, should be realized. To date we use "SocialGroupOf", "LocationOf", "MeasuredParameterOf" semantic SFs and some others.

At the phase of tactical planning we also decide what lexemes should be mapped to the nodes of the structure, so as to realize them as the concepts of the DM. For this purpose tactical generator requests the Dictionary. It is necessary to choose the lexical equivalents to the DM concepts at this phase because the further grammatical realization of these concepts depends on the particular lexical realization of features, chosen at the phase of tactical generation.

Planning resources consist of rules with the following structure[4]:

```
<Node of application>
<Assignments and conditions of application>
    "=>" <actions to transformation >
```

Every rule performs a particular type of transformations of the subtree that is restricted by the node of application[5]. To have the ability to perform the structural transformations, we should name the nodes, which participate in these transformations. For this purpose the Assignments mechanism was developed. Assignment is the naming mechanism for the set of nodes of the substructure restricted by the application node. Using the special expression we pick out a set of nodes interpreted as a list. The further possible conditions of application and actions work with these lists and their elements. Lists are accessed by names that are associated with them. These named lists are called named local variables.

Let us consider an example of assignment that gets data for one of planner actions:

```
#ands =
    #this\And.ForEach(*.Length()=1).ForEach(Compare.Length()=1)
```

At first we consider the right part of assignment expression - the expression that is used to pick out a set of nodes from the structure. According to the syntax of planner rules we mark local variables with ▯#▯sign. Value of #this variable was set by the system as a list of one element - node of application. Expression #this\And organizes the list of all the nodes named And that are related to the nodes stored in #this variable. Then we apply the method-constraint ForEach with argument ▯*.Length()=1▯ to the extracted nodes. This method realizes constraint that every extracted And node should have only one related node (asterisk means "any node"). The next ForEach constraint means that among the nodes, related to #this\And it should be one and only one node named Compare. So, as a result we have a list of And nodes that are related to the focus node #this, that have only one related node and this node is Compare. The result is mapped to the #ands label. So, after this assignment inside the current rule we can refer to the results of this search using name #ands.

Assignments alternate with conditions of application of the rule. If at least one of the conditions is not accomplished, the rule actions are not executed, and the system continues to work with the next rule.

After the calculation of application conditions and assignments, transformation actions are performed. The following actions are possible:

---

[4] Here and further the syntax is written in BNF notation.

[5] Here and further nodes of the tree structure are associated with references to them in the text of rule by the node name and context

- Naming of a node
- Addition of a new node
- Moving of a subtrees
- Removing of a subtrees
- Addition of new features
- Spreading of features across different nodes
- Removing of features

5   Realization in Specific NL

At the realization phase generator applies the grammatical resource of specific NL to the sentence plans, worked out at the planning phase. It realizes all outlined grammatical structures as well as morphological forms of lexemes that are elaborated at the previous phases. Generator treats the tree structure as a recursive structure of one level pattern - groups. Besides the possible extensions of the tree structure, interpreter of grammatical resources calculates the grammatical features for grammatical groups from SFs and spreads the latter ones through the tree structure to the leaves. Grammatical features, collected in leaves, are morphologically realized at this phase.

Grammar resource consists of rules that have the following structure:

```
< Node of application ><rule name><application constrains> "{"
    <body of rule> "}"
```

Node of application sets the node that will be interpreted as the group node for this rule execution. Group node is the node that has all members of the rule related to it.

The rule is applicable if the current node is the application node and if the rule application constraints are satisfied. We distinguish two types of constraints: constraints that prove the existence of a particular node, and constraints that prove the existence of its feature. Application constraints make up a logical expression using basic logical operations such as and, or and not. The system calculates the logical constraints before the rule is applied. If the result is true the rule will be evaluated, otherwise the rule will be skipped.

The Body of rule consists of lines and accomplishes two tasks: ordering the rule members and editing their features. Each line describes one member of the grammatical rule. It has the following structure:

```
[\^][*]"("<member before>")""<member> "("<member after>")" "="
    ("<features>")"
```

The left side of the line, before the sign of equality, orders the rule member among its neighbors. Each of the members of the rule has an identifying name that is unique in the context of a particular group. The right side of the line controls the editing of features of the rule member. We distinguish the following operations upon features:

- Addition of a new feature
- Replacement or addition of a feature
- Moving off a feature

The values of features can be set explicitly, or implicitly by reference to the feature of the same type of another group member. In the latter case we write a name of this group member instead of the value to model agreement between group members.

There are two attributes that can be used in the line definition. They are "main member" (can be set as ⎕*⎕ sign) and "is to be inserted" (can be set as ⎕¬⎕ sign). "Main member" attribute indicates that the there is no node in tree structure related with the group node and that has the same name as the member described in the line of rule's body. This means that described rule member has no node in the tree structure that can be mapped to it. Therefore a new member should be inserted into the tree structure. The "is to be inserted" attribute indicates that the member is the main member of the rule. That means that all morphological features are copied from the group node (node of application) to the main member. There can be several main members in a rule.

6   Linguistic Background

In [9]) the abstract forms of the sources for NL generation systems are considered. They are numeric data, structured objects and logical forms. We also distinguish Register specific and NL specific types of communicated knowledge. In application systems they are often presented in the same DM. Domain specific knowledge is often introduced by the text structure. Language specific knowledge is usually introduced by propositions that are the elements of this structure.

For example, in the AGILE system [10] texts of instructions are organized as the structure of Goal / Method typified blocks of Actions. This structure can be interpreted as following text string: "User needs to do Action1 (for example, to draw a line; this is the Goal); to achieve this user should do Action2 (for example, to start the software system this is the Method how to reach the Action1) and so on.". The shown "Goal / Method" alternation structure is Register specific. Every Action is described close to linguistic semantic frame that is a predicate with several participants also named propositions. When we realize the register specific text structure as a sequence of propositions and express some relations between them, we get a sequence of representations written in the Sentence Planning Language of the AGILE system - SPLs [11]. SPLs are semantic representations since their nodes are presented by meanings - concepts from the Upper Model ontology [12] that is language oriented semantic resource. The most part of the meanings are claimed to be shared by various NLs.

In our knowledge base we deal with OQL tree as a register specific structure. OQL representation has no NL specific elements in its nodes. So, we have two possibilities: to try to get morphological features and linear order directly from the register specific OQL representation or to transform it into NL specific "universal" representation and then to build up generation in the specific NLs. For the initial demonstrator we have chosen the former paradigm.

We interpret OQL Objects, Attributes, Values and some of Operations (such as "count" and "sum") as "Thing" concepts expressed by Nouns. Other operations (such as "min", "max", and "avg") are interpreted as "Qualities" and expressed by Adjectives. The initial demonstrator re-generates the user queries in a standardized NL form - the extended nominal group (NG) form. In contrast to NL expressions that are usually used in the register of the NL queries to DB, the standardized NL form expresses explicitly all the Attributes and Values that are represented in Q-query. For example, to the user query What is the director□ name? QGen generates the extended NG: The name of employee with the position <director>. QGen puts the Values of attributes into the query text in broken brackets in form they were in the OQL expression since they are too diverse for the interpretation in NL for the initial demonstrator.

The extended NG as a query form has the following structure: the focused members begin the query in Russian and English. They are Attributes of the SELECT part of OQL representation. The center of the query structure is the main Object, which is placed in the FROM part. The non-focused members of the re-generated query are the Attributes of the WHERE part. Lexifying the concepts according to the QGen dictionary we also should realize grammatically relations between Attributes and the Object. Moving from the focused - through the Object - to non-focused part of the query structure, we realize two types of relations. The first relation between an Attribute of the SELECT part and the Object is "Attribute-Object" relation. The second relation between the Object and an Attribute of the WHERE part is "Object-Attribute" relation. Considering their realization by a specific NL means we get the following results.

"Attribute-Object" relation can be realized in a single way. It is expressed by Genitive case in Russian, or using "of-" construction in English. Semantics of related concepts has no influence on the choice of its expression in NL. For example, Familija sotrudnika - the name of employee, zarplaty sotrudnikov - salaries of employees, otdely sotrudnikov - departments of employees,and so on.

The "Object-Attribute" relation always depends on semantics of the two related concepts and is realized by different prepositions or cases in Russian and English. In the following examples <.> present concrete Value of the Attribute: Sotrudnik v vozraste <.> let - Employee at the age of <.>, sotrudnik s zarplatoj <.> - employee with the salary <.>, sotrudnik iz otdela <.> - employee from the department <.>.

So, we distinguish various means for realization of the "Object-Attribute" relation depending on semantics of the related concepts. In Dictionary we have ascribed the SFs to the DM concepts that predefine the realization of relation. Here are some SFs we use to date in QGen module:

Name of feature:	Attribute that is extended with this feature:
EssentialQualityOf:	Gender, Color, ...;
MeasuredEssentialParameterOf:	Velocity, Weight, Carrying capacity, ...;
MesuredParameterOf:	Salary, NumberOfDoors (for a car), ...;
SocialGroupOf:	Department, ...;
...	...

The selection of a particular set of SFs depends on the specific means that are used to express the OQL structure in a particular NL. For various languages SFs can vary with more or less degree in granularity.

If one of "Object-Attribute" relations takes place in the OQL expression, at the planning phase the appropriate SF is set to the group node of this relation. At realization phase the group node with the particular SF is realized by one or several rules from the set of rules of the grammatical resource. For example, the SF "SocialGroupOf" is realized in English by the following grammar rule:

```
3 FROM:
[QUERY](defined(FROM, SELECT,WHERE), FROM(SF:SocialGroupOf)) {
    *from = (PartOfspeech: noun)
    ^(select)PREPFROM(from) = (PartOfspeech:prep, lex:'from')
    select =
}
```

But there are cases when we cannot use the form of NG to express relations between the Attributes and the Object. In this case we ought to use a subordinate or participle clause. For example, the "Attribute-Object" relation is sensitive to the topological (cognitive) features in the Talmy style that are peculiar to specific language means [15]. For example, the cognitive constraints on the genitive construction in Russian and on "of-construction" in English are violated when we re-generate some user queries to DB, which describe objects like shops with attributes like customers, town etc. We can generate the customers of the shop ..., but *the town of the shopwould be a wrong expression. The problem is that the genitive construction between two concepts assigns some topological balance between these concepts. The depending member must be "more substantial" than the syntactically governing member in any sense - material (bigger, more stable), and so on, or social, since it is used in speech as a cognitive reference point for the other. To avoid violation of this principle, we ought to insert a predicate, for example, gorod, v kotorom nahoditsja magazin - the town in which the shop is situated.

There are some other motivations for the inclusion of a predicate into the representation. In particular, inclusion of a predicate is always necessary when we want to generate a question form of the query. Question is usually described as a transformation of a propositional declarative form [14]. Predicates have two sources. The first one is the most "general" attribute that implements being and having concepts. In particular, in English the Object is related to the Attribute using the predicate ⟦to have⟧, and an Attribute is related to its Value using the predicate ⟦to be⟧.

```
An employee having the salary 5000
([DM Object] HAVING  [Attr]  [Value])

An employee, whose salary is 5000
([DM Object], whose [Attr] IS [Value])
```

Another source are "trigger" predicates for concepts. For example, if the Attribute concept is typified as the "LocationOf", the Object is situated in it.

7 Conclusion

To date we have developed a working version of initial demonstrator of the QGen generation module. We have tuned the generation module on some particular DM in Russian and English languages. Diverse resources can change the NL of the outcoming text not depending on the NL of the input user query. The further directions of the investigation are:

- Development of strategic block for the planning phase;
- Extension of flexibility of the generator;
- Adaptation of generator module to other tasks of generation, for example to generation of NL answers from the DB results. The simplest possibility is to extend the table form of the answer by a title which is in fact the re-generated query;
- Attempt to realize a more general approach of generation by means of using an intermediate "universal" NL oriented representation between OQL register specific representation and the morphologically marked up structured representation which is the result of tactical planning phase. We suppose that representation in the style of UNL language would be the best choice for the intermediate "universal" NL oriented representation [13] since the nodes of the sentence representations are not meanings, but concepts.

References

1. Boldasov M.V., Sokolova E.G. and Maljkovskij M.G. User query understanding by the InBASE system as a source for Multilingual NL generation module. - in: Text, Speech and Dialogue (P. Sojka, I. Kopecek and K. Pala eds.). - Proceedings of the 5th International conference, TSD 2002, Brno, Czech Republic, September 2002. Springer-Verlag Berlin Heidelberg, Germany, 2002. Pp. 33–40.
2. Sokolova, E.G., Zhigalov, V.A.: InBASE Technology: Constructing Natural Language Interface with Databases. (in Russian) Computational Linguistics and Its Applications International Workshop Proceedings, Vol.2., Dialogue, Aksakovo, (2001) 123–135

3. Trapeznikov S., Dinenberg F., Kuchin S. InterBASE - Natural interface system for popular commercial DBMSs // Proc. Of EWAIC'93. Moscow, September 1993. P. 189–193.
4. Sharoff S., Zhigalov V.: Register-domain Separation as a methodology for development of NL Interfaces to Databases // Human-Computer Interaction - INTER-ACT'99. Angela Sasse and Chris Johnson (eds.) Published by IOS Press, 1999.
5. A. S. Narinjani. Linguistic processors ZAPSIB. Preliminary publication N 199 of Computationa Centre of the Siberian Departement of the USSR Academy of Science. Novosibirsk. 1997. (in Russian)
6. R.A. Pazos R., A. Gelbukh, J.J. Gonzalez B., E. Alarcon R., A. Mendoza M., A. P. Dominguez S. Spanish Natural Language Interface for a Relational Database Querying System. – in: Text, Speech and Dialogue (P. Sojka, I. Kopecek and K. Pala eds.). – Proceedings of the 5th International conference, TSD 2002, Brno, Czech Republic, September 2002. Springer-Verlag Berlin Heidelberg, Germany, 2002. (with Boldasov M.V. and Maljkovskij M.G.) Pp. 123–130.
7. A. Zarate M., R.A. Pazos R., A. Gelbukh, J. Perez O. Natural Language Interface for Web-based Databases. Topics in Robotics, Distance Learning and Intelligent Communication Systems. WSEAS Press, 2002.
8. Sharoff, S., "SNOOP: A System for Development of Linguistic Processors", Proc. of EWAIC'93, Moscow, 1993.
9. McDonald, D.D.; Natural language generation. In: Shapiro, S.C. (Ed) Encyclopedia of artificial intelligence. Wiley, New York,(1987) pp. 642–655
10. Kruijff, G-J., Bateman, J., Dochev, D., Hana, J., Kruijff-Korbayova, I., Skoumalova, H., Sharoff, S., Sokolova, E., Staykova, K., Teich, E.: Multilinguality in a Text Generation System for Three Slavic Languages. Proc. COLING-2000, Luxemburg, (August, 2000)
11. Bateman, J.A.: Enabling technology for multilingal natural language generation: the KPML development environment. Natural Language Engineering, 3 (1), (1997) 15–55
12. Bateman, J.A., R. Henschel, F. Rinaldi. The Generalized Upper Model 2.0, Technical Report, GMD/IPSI, Darmstadt, Germany, 1995. URL: http://www.darmstadt.gmd.de/publish/komet/gen-um/newUM.html
13. Hiroshi Uchida, Meiying Zhu. The universal Networking Language beyond Machine Translation // "International symposium on language in Cyberspace", 26–27 September 2001, Seoul of Korea. 2001.
14. Akmajian and Heny, (1979) An introduction to the principles of transformational syntax, 4th ed. MIT Press, Cambridge
15. Talmy, L. How language structures space // in: H. Pick and L. Acredolo (eds.), Spacial orientation: Theory, research, and application. N.Y.: Plenum Press. 1983. p. 225–282.

Towards Designing Natural Language Interfaces

Svetlana Sheremetyeva

LanA Consulting, Madvigs Alle, 9, 2
DK-1829 Copenhagen, Denmark
lanaconsult@mail.dk

Abstract. The paper addresses issues of designing natural language interfaces that guide users towards expert ways of thinking. It attempts to contribute to an interface methodology with a case study, – the AutoPat interface, – an application for authoring technical documents, such as patent claims. Content and composition support is provided through access to domain models, words and phrases as well as to the application analyzer and generator that provide for natural language responses to user activity.

1 Introduction

The need for processing information and knowledge motivates work in developing different kinds of computer applications. It is therefore imperative to design user-adaptive easy-to-use software interfaces making communication with a computer as natural as possible. A massive collection of papers on human-computer interaction and interface design attempt to bring some structure to the often chaotic interface design process pointing out the difficulty of designing for a complex world. Topics include human limitations, usability principles, screen design, models of the user, task analysis [3], techniques of scenario building and user interviews [9], practical methods of gathering data about users, tasks and environments and how to integrate contextual design into the software development process [1], [4]. It is stressed that there are no minor issues in the field of interface design and even such common topics as error messages, toolbars, tabbed dialogues, icons and responsiveness should be well thought out [2]. To support their recommendations many of the authors conclude with some case studies making it evident that what contributes a lot to the interface design is specificity of application.

In this paper we also try to contribute to an interface methodology with a case study, – an intelligent user-adaptive interface that interacts with the user in a natural language. This interface is a part of AutoPat, an application for document authoring, namely, for authoring patent claims.

Claims are parts of patents that contain crucial information about the invention and are the subject of legal protection. They must be formulated according to a set of precise rules and so as to make patent infringement difficult. Composing a patent claim that meets all legal requirements to its structure is a complex task, even for experts. AutoPat is designed to reduce composition effort, time and costs. It can also be used for training patent attorneys.

A. Gelbukh (Ed.): CICLing 2003, LNCS 2588, pp. 477–489, 2003.
© Springer-Verlag Berlin Heidelberg 2003

AutoPat is a product developed from the experimental patent authoring system described in [8] and [9]. It features a lot of new functionalities and modules, significantly revised and augmented knowledge base (lexicons, grammar rules and linguistic algorithms), and an absolutely new user-adaptive natural language interface. This version of AutoPat is a 32-bit Windows application developed to run in a number of operating environments: Windows 95/98/2000/NT. It covers patents about apparatuses.

In what follows we first give a brief overview of the AutoPat system then concentrate on the design methodology and description of the AutoPat natural language user interface.

2 AutoPat Overview

AutoPat is an NLP application and consists of an interactive technical knowledge elicitation module and fully automatic text generation module. The input to the system is natural language phrases. Apart from automatic generator AutoPat includes morphological and semantico-syntactic analyzers that convert natural language input into a shallow knowledge representation. The two stages of AutoPat are not strictly pipelined. Lexical selection and some other text planning tasks are interleaved with the process of content specification. The latter results in the production of a "draft" claim. This draft, while not yet an English text, is a list of proposition-level structures ("templates") specifying the proposition head and case role values filled by POS-tagged word strings in the form:

> text::={ template){template}*
> template::={predicate-class predicate ((case-role)(case-role}*)
> case-role::= (rank status value)
> value::= {word tag}*

where *predicate-class* is a label of an ontological concept, *predicate* is a string corresponding to a predicate from the system lexicon, *case-roles* are *ranked* according to the frequency of their co- occurrence with each predicate in the training corpus, *status* is a semantic status of a case-role, such as agent, theme, place, instrument, etc., and *value* is a phrase which fills a case-role. *Word* is a word included into a phrase filling a case-role, and tag is a label, which conveys both morphological and semantic information (see section 4).

The AutoPat knowledge base is corpus-based and draws heavily on the sublanguage. It contains AutoPat inherent knowledge and authoring memory (cf. "translation memory"). The inherent knowledge includes analysis and generation grammar, a flexible depth *tagging lexicon* for tagging case-role fillers as mentioned above, and a *deep (information-rich) lexicon* of predicates (heads of predicative phrases describing essential features of an invention) [6]. The user can customize these lexicons through the interface (see section 4). The authoring memory contains lists of terminological units (words and phrases) that were used during user-AutoPat sessions. It is annotated with document(s) it was used in. This supports content specification and terminology consistency. The user through the application interface can easily access the content of authoring memory.

The knowledge supplied by the user is saved in a special file format, which stores both the internal representation of the elicited knowledge and its "human" image on the interface screen . The user can quit the program at any moment of elicitation session so that next time she starts it she can resume her work where she left off. The interface reproduces the selection exactly as it was and it is possible to continue the session without delay.

3 User Interface

3.1 Desiderata for an AutoPat Interface Design

In the AutoPat system the user interface serves the purpose of eliciting technical knowledge about invention from the user. When deciding on particular issues of its development we found out that apart from the problem how to integrate user and task analysis into the design of a user interface, there is also a problem of application and engine analysis. In this framework the term application refers to a class of applications rather than to a specific product. Engine analysis implies the constraints imposed by algorithms and programs (generator in our case) of a computer system. Below we analyze four groups of constraints addressed by our interface.

Application and engine constraints. AutoPat falls into the class of NLP applications, – it concerns generation of patent claim texts. This immediately leads to a number of problems. First of all there is a well-known problem of knowledge bottleneck or coverage. An interface of a natural language application should be designed so as to make it possible and easy for the user to add linguistic knowledge to the system knowledge base.

Second, even with the best available resources, present-day fully automatic NLP systems working in realistic domains do not yield perfect results. There will always be a "hard residue" of language processing problems that can be taken care of only by foregoing the requirement of full automation. AutoPat engine relies on human aid in a) semantico-syntactic analysis of user's input, b) keeping the complexity of the internal meaning representation of a text plan below a certain threshold, c) recognizing references to the same objects, known as coreferences, and d) making decisions about the format of the claim (there are two formats of the claim text, – the first (European) format is the text consisting of two parts divided by the expression "characterized in that", where the novelty features are described in the second part, the second (US) format does not contain this delimiting expression). The user interface should have functionalities to make this process of "helping" the computer as easy as possible.

Task analysis The task is to elicit knowledge about the content of a patent claim to generate a claim text in a legally acceptable format, as shown in Figure 3. If the invention is an apparatus – which is specifically what this version of AutoPat is designed for – the claim should contain the information about such essential features of the invention as, main elements of the invention (obligatory), sub-elements of the main elements (optional), shape and material of some elements (optional), other properties and relations of the elements (obligatory if essential). Other than that the claim text should be such as to prevent infringement. In addition to the main claim a patent may contain the so-called dependent claims in a special format.

User constraints. The interface should meet general user requirements of making the program as easy as possible to use despite its diverse and complex functionality. We put user constraints in three categories.

First, it is necessary to model a professional behavior of a patent expert working with an inventor that is usually an interview.

Second, we should adapt the knowledge elicitation interview to a user profile in terms of proficiency. Users of our system, pursuing our addiction to classifying, can be divided into three groups: trained patent experts, patent officers – beginners and inventors who do not posses legal knowledge about the way patent claims should be created and are far from being technical writers. It is evident that trained experts and other two user groups need different guidance and pace of work. A trained user can be irritated by what is an advantage for a beginner, e.g. by detailed instructions and strict order of authoring steps. This type of constraints is difficult to meet in one mode interface if at all. We addressed the problem by developing two user proficiency adaptive modes, – Verbose and Professional. This is one of the main characteristics of our interface.

Third, we should take into consideration human limitations and desire to automate tedious tasks such as typing, revising texts and making sure terminology is consistent, propagating changes through document [5]. Unavoidable linguistic work dictated by the application analysis should be done so as not to require any linguistic skills. The user also needs content support and control. For that it is desirable to visualize the results of every step of elicitation procedure in the most "human' way. All user-computer communication should be done in the most natural way, i.e. in a natural language. A possibility to redraft or edit text during one or several sessions is also essential. All user constraints listed above are interleavingly addressed by different design functionalities in both modes of the AutoPat interface.

3.2 Interface Overview

Our elicitation technique is a domain-dependent automated mixed-initiative interview. All user-computer communication is done in a natural language (English in our case). The knowledge elicitation scenario consists of the system requesting the user, in English, to supply information about the invention. Using common graphical interface tools (mouse support, dialogue boxes, menus, templates and slide bars) the interface draws the user through a step-by step procedure of describing every essential feature of the invention. It provides content, composition and terminology maintenance support through choices of standing and pull-down menus. These menus supply access to words and phrases required in a claim. Though the user is encouraged to use the AutoPat controlled language given in the menus the user has always a choice to type in active text areas of interface windows. If a word is in a menu it will be automatically completed right after the first characters are typed. In case the word cannot be found in the inherent knowledge of the system the user will be asked to add it through an easy-to-use pop-up entry box (see section 4). Phrases constructed by the user are put in the authoring memory and stay displayed in the "Your terminology" screen area through the end of the session. These and some other lexical units displayed on the screen can be transferred to a new text area on mouse click. All phrases thus transferred can be edited. The interface has an underlying spell checker that is linked to the AutoPat lexicons. This spell checker works in a regular way (i.e. underlines words, which are considered misspelled, suggesting possible corrections). The user can control the content elicited so far in an output window where the immediate results of each quantum of acquisition are displayed. If the content appears incorrect, the user can undo the latest quantum of acquisition and do it again correctly. The interface has two main components, – the background window were the results of elicitation procedure stay displayed through the whole session and a set of pop-up windows corresponding to elicitations steps or providing for lexicon customization. The two modes of the interface, Verbose and Professional, share the background window while the sets of pop-up windows are mainly different. All pop-up windows in both modes can be moved freely around the screen to allow the user to see any part of the background window at any time.

Background Window (Figures 1, 2 and 3). The left pane of this window is headed "Your invention comprises" and displays a graphical representation of the hierarchy of all main elements and sub-elements after the user supplies the knowledge about them into the system. The names of the elements at its nodes can be transferred to any of pop-up windows by simply clicking on them. The right pane is headed "Essential features of your invention". It displays the title of the invention and every essential feature of the invention in the form of a natural language simple sentence that is generated every time the user supplies a quantum of technical knowledge. Visualization of the results of the elicitation procedure is only done to make it possible and convenient for the user to control the results of her session. The simple sentences correspond to statements in the system's internal knowledge representation language that are created from the knowledge elicitation procedures. At the stage of eliciting knowledge about relations of invention elements a new section headed "Your terminology" appears in the bottom of the left pane. Form now on all phrases used in relation descriptions stay displayed and "clickable" there for further reuse.

3.3 Verbose Mode

This mode of the interface is highly recommended for a beginner. It guides a user through a step-by step procedure of describing essential features of invention. The main screen elements of the interface are the background window and Verbose windows that contain detailed instructions, the "Help" button and the "Back" button. A brief description of Verbose windows and functionalities is given below.

Title. Helps the user to select the most appropriate title for the invention. This window contains a title template. The slots of this template contain menus of words and phrases for optional inclusion in the title. To compose the title of an invention the user can either select words from the template slot menus or type them in.

Main Elements. Prompts the user to describe the main elements of the prototype of the invention. This window displays a template of menus similar to that in the *Title* window.

Complex Element. Makes the user specify (by highlighting it in the element tree in the background window) the element whose sub-elements it is necessary to include in the claim. The name of the selected element is transferred to the next window to help the user keep in mind what she is working on.

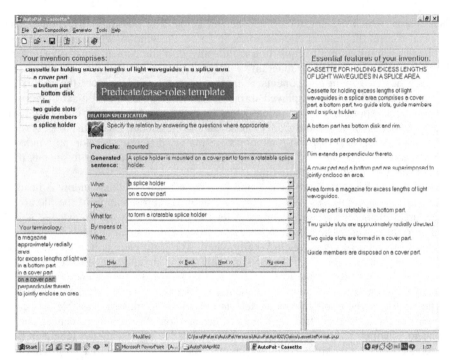

Fig. 1. A screen shot of the AutoPat User interface at the stage of elicitation knowledge about the relation between the elements "splice holder" and "cover part" of the invention. Verbose mode.

Sub-Elements. Prompts the user to describe parts of the element selected at the previous step. This window displays a template of menus similar to that in the *Title* window.

Element with Novel Characteristics. Makes the user specify (highlight in the element tree) the element whose novel properties (that, according to Patent Law, can only be its shape or material) it is necessary to include in the claim. After an element is selected in the tree it appears in the active text area of this window and it is possible to edit it. For example, the user selects, say, the node "four doors" in the element tree and it appears in the text area of the window. The user may now edit it into, say, "one of the doors", and this new phrase will appear in the next window to describe its shape or material.

Shape/Material. Prompts the user to describe novel shapes of materials of the elements specified in the previous window. This window is divided into parts. One part contains two menus of shapes and another displays two menus of materials. This gives the user two ways to describe an element. If the word is selected from the pop-up menus in the "shape" or "material" part of the window AutoPat generates sentences as follows: "An element is in the shape of a circle." If the word is selected from one of the standing menus the user gets the description as follows: "An element is round". The knowledge about shape and material of one element can be elicited in one take by just selecting the words in the shape and material menus. This window has an area where the sentences following the elicitation step are generated (apart from being generated in the background window). This makes it more convenient for the user to control her input.

Relations. Within the procedure the user selects two or more objects in the element tree then specify the relation between them. The initial setup in this window involves two menus, one listing names of relation types (semantic classes) and another listing words (predicates) that can describe these relations. One can start by first selecting a relation type and then, after a semantic class is selected the second menu displays predicates which belong to this class for further selection. By checking a corresponding radio button it is possible to start directly with selecting a predicate among all the predicates included in the AutoPat knowledge base and listed in the predicate menu. In case the selected predicate is polysemantic, i.e. belongs to more than one semantic classes, these classes appear in the semantic class menu and the user is asked to select one of them to specify the meaning of the predicate.

The user can also type in a new predicate if she does not find the word in the menu. In such a case she is guided through a semi-automated and extremely easy procedure of introducing a new word in the underlying predicate dictionary (see section 4). Selecting a predicate constitutes lexical selection, whereupon the system determines the roles played by the highlighted elements.

Relation Specification. Presents the user with a predicate (sentence) template based on knowledge about the case-roles (semantic arguments) of the semantic class underlying the selected dictionary item. The user fills appropriate slots – "What", "Where", "How", and so forth (Fig. 1). (The system records the boundaries of the fillers and their case-role status to be used later for morphological disambiguation, and syntactic analysis and applied to AutoPat's automatic components). To make this easier apart from clickable nodes in the element tree and in phrases in "Your terminology" section every template slot has a pop-up menu of auxiliary phrases from the underlying predicate dictionary entry.

Co-reference. Highlights coreference candidates and asks to mark any elements that are coreferential among them. The coreference candidates are searched by morphosyntactic analyzer and are noun lexemes regardless of their grammatical form.

Main Claim Format-All. Presents a "checkable" menu of all generated sentences-features The user can either check the novel features of the invention to thus have a final claim text containing generic and difference parts with the "characterized in that" expression between them, which is a must according to the European Patent Office, or skip this stage. In the latter case the final claim text will be generated without generic and difference parts in the format accepted by the US Patent Office.

Main Claim Format-Generic and *Main Claim Format-Difference.* Appear only if underlying meaning representation (hidden from the user) of the generic or difference part of the claim built by the generator exceeds a given threshold of complexity. It presents a "checkable" menu of generic/difference sentences-features for the user to check those features of the invention that are closer related. This breaks the corresponding knowledge representation into two parts thus improving the quality of the generator output.

Main Claim Text. Presents the output of the Auto generator, - the main claim text in legally acceptable format, as shown in Figure 2. If necessary the user may edit the text right in this interface window.

The initiative in the Wizard scenario is mixed: the human can use any number of iterations working with windows eliciting elements, shapes, materials or relations but

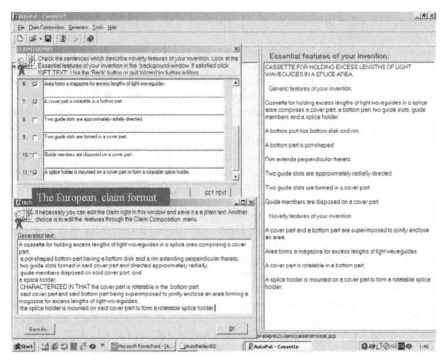

Fig. 2. A screen shot of the AutoPat User interface at the stage of elicitation knowledge about the format of the claim text. A final output of the system, a generated claim text, is shown in the left bottom corner. Verbose mode.

the order in which the user is guided from window to window and, in the case of eliciting coreferences, the order of the presentation of candidates is controlled by the interface.

3.4 Professional Mode

Professional interface mode is designed for a trained user who is instructed by window buttons. The initiative in a Professional scenario is mainly for the human. The content of knowledge elicitation and its output are the same as in Verbose. But Professional allows for more speed and flexibility when authoring a claim, – the user may freely navigate among the stages of claim composition, authoring them in any order. In case of coreferences, for example, the user is presented with a list of coreference candidates and is free to decide whether and which of them to check if at all. The user can also see a generated claim part at any authoring stage. Professional is especially convenient when editing a claim draft but can also be used for composing a claim from scratch. This mode of interface keeps the standing background window while elicitation windows change each other. The difference is that they do not appear after the user fulfills a certain part of the interview as in Verbose but are called through the Main Menu in any order. The setups of changeable windows are mainly different from those of Verbose. They are augmented with extra buttons and functionalities and different menus.

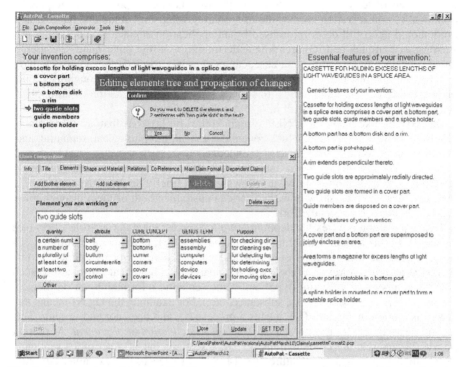

Fig. 3. A screen shot of the AutoPat User interface at the stage of editing a claim draft in the Professional Mode.

For example, the *Elements* window is a merger of the four Verbose windows designed to elicit knowledge about elements and sub-elements. In this window an element tree can easily be restructured; the names of elements can be edited.

All changes done at any stage of authoring propagate through the rest of the draft. Deletion of an element in the element tree automatically deletes all invention features-sentences with this element. Change of an element name in the tree automatically changes its name in all corresponding sentences.

Using this mode of interface it is possible to delete/add/edit any essential feature in a claim draft keeping the rest of the content intact. Pop-up dialogue boxes for dictionary customizing and content support through the menus of words and phrases are provided in the same way as in Verbose.

Professional has two extra windows: *Dependent Claims* and *Dependent Claim Text*. The former appears only if called by the user who wants to compose a dependent claim, it elicits information upon which of other claims the current one depends and lets the user return to feature elicitation pages. The latter presents the text of the main claim and all dependent claims.

4 Lexicon Customization through the Interface

The problem of lexicon customization by the user is very important and requires a great deal of consideration on the side of system developers. On the one hand, a new word should get a full description used by an application engine. This description is often rather complex and requires linguistic training. On the other hand, the user, a patent officer or an inventor in our case, can neither be expected, nor required to have such linguistic skills. If an application forces the user to go through a tough procedure when creating custom dictionaries[1] this alone may ruin the reputation of an application and provoke the user to reject it.

Our system, like many other NLP systems, relies on lexicons that are the essential part of the system knowledge, which covers the lexical, morphological, semantic, and, crucially for our system, the syntactic knowledge.

As was mentioned above, it includes two kinds of lexicons with different descriptions of lexical units. In what follows we first briefly describe the content of these lexicons and then show how the user can customize both of them through the interface without any special effort.

The first lexicon is a flexible depth *tagging lexicon* for tagging case-role fillers (see section 2). In this lexicon lexical units are listed with their class membership that is a morpho-semantic classification of words and phrases. Every word or phrase in this lexicon is assigned a *tag,* – a label, which conveys morphological information (such as POS, number and inflection type) and some semantic information, an ontological concept, (such as object, process, substance, etc.). For example, the tag Nf means that a word is a noun in singular (N), means a process (f), and does not end in *–ing*. This tag will be assigned, for example, to such words as *activation* or *alignment*. At present we use 23 tags that are combinations of 1 to 4 features out of a set of 19 semantic, morphological and syntactic features for 14 parts of speech. For example, currently the feature structure of noun tags is as follows:

Tag[POS[Noun[object[plural, singular]
                  process[-ing, other[plural, singular]
                  substance [plural, singular]
                  other [plural, singular]]]]]]

In the AutoPat interface customization of the tagging lexicon is integrated with the spell checking process. If the user at any stage of the knowledge elicitation procedure types in a word which is not included in the tagging lexicon it is marked as unknown as it would have been marked in any other spell checker with the difference that a pop-up menu which appears on right mouse click in addition to spelling suggestions contains a selection "Add as". If the user knows that the word is spelled correctly, then to add the word to the lexicon she only has to click this selection, which opens

---

[1] In some applications to create a custom dictionary the user has to study instructions running for several pages. When making an entry description the user is not only asked about the part of speech of a new word, which might be easy, but also about. e.g., the declension (if the word is a noun) and (if the word is a verb) the number of objects with which the verb is normally linked in a sentence, what auxiliary verb should be used with it and whether it has a separable prefix, etc. This can be quite frustrating for users other than linguists.

other intuitively understandable[2] selections (see Fig. 4). A terminal selection being clicked, the word is automatically transferred to the tagging lexicon with the corresponding tag and is recognized by the system from now on.

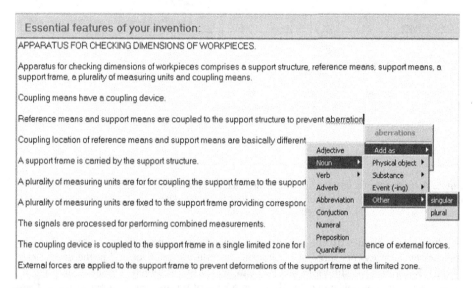

Fig. 4. A fragment of a screen shot of the interface at the moment of adding a new word to the tagging lexicon with the help of pop-up menus integrated with a spell checker. The word "aberration" will be automatically added to the lexicon with the tag Nf (functional noun, singular).

The second lexicon in the AutoPat knowledge base is a *deep (information-rich) lexicon* of predicates (heads of predicative phrases describing essential features of an invention). An organization of a monolingual predicate dictionary is described by the following structure (see [6] for more detail):

major-form The most frequent form of the predicate in which it occurs in patent claims;

other-forms: morphological forms of the verb in which it occurs in patent text

semantics: the verb's semantic class;

case-frame: the verb's case-role frame;

patterns: a list of co-occurrence linearization patterns for the verb's case-role frame.

If the user is not willing to use a predicate from the predicate menu suggested by the system she can always type in a new predicate in the interactive text area of the corresponding window, click the button "Add" and get a pop-up word box (see Fig. 5). This word box is a word template with the following slots: "Relation type" filled by a pull down menu of the semantic classes of predicates, which are presented to the

---

user as types of relations between invention elements (which causes no misunder-standing).

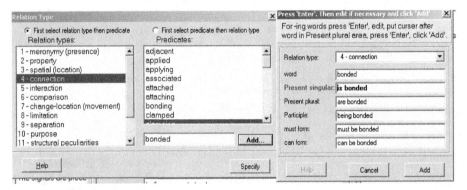

Fig. 5. A fragment of a screen shot of the interface at the moment of adding a new predicate to the predicate lexicon with the help of pop-up wor template. The word "bounded" will be auto-matically added to the knowledge base of the system.

This slot is filled with the selection of the relation type (semantic class) done by the user at the previous stage of elicitation procedure ("connection" in the example in Fig. 5). Relation type shown in this slot can be easily reselected. The next slot "word" contains a predicate as typed by the user at the previous stage. Other slots that are word forms of the new predicate. An underlying morphological generator automati-cally fills out these slots. The user is only supposed to check the fillers and edit them if necessary. Sublanguage restrictions allowed for reducing the number of predicate word forms to just a few.

After user's approval a click on the button "Add" puts a new predicate into the predicate lexicon. The fillers of the word box slots are transferred to "major-form", "other-forms" and "semantics" fields of the new predicate entry. "case-frame" and "pattens" fields of this entry are automatically filled by default depending upon the chosen semantic class. For the example in figure 5, the following entry is created in the AutoPat knowledge base:

bounded

(major-form	"bounded" F
more-forms	(("is bounded" Ss)("are bounded" Sp)("being bounded" Abs))
sem-class	connection
case-frame	((1 subject)(2 destination)(3 manner)(4 purpose)(5 means))
patterns	((1 * 2)(1 3 * 2)(1 * 2 4)(1 * 2 3)(1 * 3)(1 * 4)(1 * 2 5) (1 3 * 2 4)

All the new predicates thus added will further be found in the interface predicate menu and used by the AutoPat engine.

5 Conclusions

We considered the most essential guidelines for designing intelligent user-adapted natural language interfaces. We claim that apart from the well-known problems of user and task analysis designers should also analyze application, engine and user proficiency. Our suggestions are supported by our research and illustrated with a case study: The AutoPat users interface was designed to make the program as easy as possible to use despite its diverse and complex functionality. The AutoPat user interface that can be adjusted to different user profiles and provides detailed and easy-to-use facilities that contribute to the robustness of the system. It automates tedious tasks such as typing, revising texts, propagating changes through document, etc. The interface is tightly interconnected with text processing and can also be used for multilingual generation and machine translation of both patent claims and patent disclosures [6]. It can also be portable to other document authoring.

References

1. Beyer, H., and Holtzblatt, K. Contextual Design: Defining customer-Centered Systems. Morgan Kaufmann: San Francisco, CA. (1998).
2. Bickford, P. Interface Design: The Art of Developing Easy to-Use Software. AP Professional: Boston, MA. (1997).
3. Dix A., Finlay, J., Abowd, G., and Beal, R. Human- Computer Interaction (2nd Edition). Prentice Hall Europe: London. (1998)
4. Hackos, J.T., and Redish, J.C. User and Task Analysis for Interface Design. Wiley: New York. (1998).
5. Paris C. and K. Vander Linden. An Interactive Support Tool for Writing Multilingual Manuals. IEEE Computer. Vol.7. (1996)
6. Sheremetyeva, S. and S.Nirenburg. Interactive MTAs Support For Non-Native Language Authoring. Proceedings of the MT Summit VII, Singapore. (1999).
7. Sheremetyeva S.and S.Nirenburg. Interactive Knowledge Elicitation in a Patent Expert's Workstation. IEEE Computer. Vol.7. (1996)
8. Sheremetyeva, S. and S.Nirenburg. GeneratingPatent Claims. Proceedings of the 8th International Workshop on Natural Language Generation. Herstmonceux, Sussex, UK. (1996).
9. Toth, J., D. Suthers, and A. Weiner. Providing Expert Advice in the Domain on Collaborative Scientific Inquiry. 8th World Conference on Artificial Intelligence in Education (AIED'97), August 20-22. Kobe. (1997)

A Discourse System for Conversational Characters

Ron Zacharski

Computing Research Laboratory
New Mexico State University
Las Cruces, New Mexico U.S.
raz@nmsu.edu

Abstract. This paper describes a discourse system for conversational characters used for interactive stories. This system is part of an environment that allows learners to practice language skills by interacting with the characters, other learners, and native speakers using instant messaging and email. The dialogues are not purely task oriented and, as a result, are difficult to model using traditional AI planners. On the other hand the dialogues must move the story forward and, thus, systems for the meandering dialogues of chatterbots (for example, AliceBot) are not appropriate. Our approach combines two methods. We use the notion of dialogue game or speech act networks [1][2] to model the local coherence of dialogues. The story moves forward from one dialogue game to another by means of a situated activity planner [3].[1]

1 Introduction

This paper describes a discourse system for conversational characters used for language learning. Language learners take part in an adventure story and must use dialogues similar to those found in basal language textbooks to move forward in the adventure. Successful completion of the adventures requires that the students collaborate on various tasks. Students communicate among themselves, advanced students of the language, and with conversational characters using a range of computer-mediated channels including email, instant messaging, audio and video files, and web pages. The conversational characters communicate among one another by structured instant messages. There is no central processor that guides the story; the progression of the story is accomplished by characters pursuing a reactive strategy.

Placing conversational characters in this adventure environment is more pedagogically sound than creating standalone conversational agents. The state of the art is currently not sophisticated enough to create interesting standalone conversational agents that can take part in creative dialogues. However, we can create conversational agents that can take part in highly predictable dialogues. These agents can be extremely useful, particularly for novice and intermediate students. Situating such an agent in this adventure has a number of important advantages. First, the adventure includes interacting with other people (fellow students and experts alike). This provides students with an opportunity to practice language skills in a range of contexts. Conversational characters augment this environment by being tireless

---

[1] I would like to thank Carlos Gomez and Adam Zacharski for their help with this project.

A. Gelbukh (Ed.): CICLing 2003, LNCS 2588, pp. 490–493, 2003.

discourse participants. An example of a dialogue (an instant message exchange) produced by the system is shown in (1):

(1) Maria: *hola, ¿ésta Rachel?*
    Ann: *Sí*
    Maria: *Qué bueno, ¿tienes el telefono de Marta?*
    Ann: *Sí*
    Maria: *¡Qué Bién! ¿Cuál es el número?*
    Ann: *282-8992*
    Maria: *Ok, ¡gracias!*

The implemented prototype system allows three students of Spanish to take part in a magical adventure centered on the famous Mexican polyglot and heroine, La Malinche.

The discourse system for these characters consists of three main components:

- A knowledge store representing the short and long term memory of the conversational character including what the character is currently focusing on. This component is based on file card pragmatics [4], a computational model of a theory of givenness described by Gundel, Hedberg, and Zacharski [5].
- A speech act network described in §2, which represents the coherence of short speech act sequences.
- A situated-activity-based planner described in §3, which determines the actions of the conversational character.

2   Speech Act Networks

As Austin [6], Searle [7], and others have noted, language is not simply a system for conveying thoughts and information. Language is a set of actions that enable people to cooperatively live in the world. These linguistic actions, such as promises, requests, assertions, occur within an implied background of standard practices based on the current context including what is normal in the particular speech community in which the act is situated. Some linguistic actions, like requests and promises, can be initial moves in a conversation and define a simple network of possible continuations For example, if someone makes a request, you can promise, decline, or make a counter-offer; if you then make a promise, the other person can accept or decline that promise; if that person accepts the promise you can report completion or revoke the promise. Any of these acts can be expressed in a number of different ways.

This notion of speech act networks has been used by Carletta [1] to develop agents that describe map routes. In the current system this notion of dialogue games is extended to include the standard 'micro' dialogues that occur in basal language learning textbooks.[2] One motivation for doing so is that the sentences that make up a standard dialogue typically are learned as one unit by the language learner. These speech act networks are modeled by finite state networks.

---

[2] An example of such a micro-dialogue is utterances 3-7 of (1) above.

It is important to distinguish these speech act networks from finite state models of discourse, which are typically used for spoken dialogue systems. In such dialogue systems a large finite state network is used to model the entire conversation. An extremely simplified version of a network for a flight reservation system might look like:

ask origin airport   >   ask destination airport   >   ask departure date   >   etc.

An agent based on this network would simply progress through the set of questions. If the user responded to the initial question *Where will you be flying from?* with *I'd like to fly from El Paso to Houston on December 8th* the system would only extract the information related to the city of origin, ignore the rest, and ask the redundant question *Where will you be flying to?* This problem can be fixed, to an extent, by creating a network with more transitions; however, the size of the network may become problematic. In addition, while this network approach may work for dialogues of simple inquiry (travel, financial, etc.) it will not scale up to model dialogues dealing with complex tasks—for example, the diagnosis and repair of equipment or dialogues dealing with negotiation. Other problems with finite-state dialogue models include difficulties with tasks that involve interdependencies (since backtracking is difficult) and difficulties with verification—asking for verification of each item of information tends to be unnatural and cumbersome.[3] These criticisms do not apply to the use of speech act networks. Speech act networks represent very short exchanges and represent regularities in language use.

3   Situated Action Planner

The most widely recognized theory of dialogue within NLP research uses inferential planning. This method is based on the work of Austin [5] who argued that uttering a sentence is a type of action that is performed by the speaker with the intention of having a specific effect on the addressee. Based on this theory, Cohen and Perrault [9] argued that a standard STRIPS-type AI planner can be used to model dialogue. This notion of plan-based dialogue has been used successfully in a wide range of applications and is still an active area of research. However, Bickmore and Cassell [10], among others, argue that this architecture is not well suited for dynamic, real-time systems such as conversational characters used for interactive, dramatic stories. Instead of STRIP-based planners researchers have used reactive systems (see, for example, [11]) or reactive systems combined with traditional planners (for example, [10]). Our approach uses a situational action planner along with the speech act networks described above. While the prototypical situated action planner has no internal representation and is stateless (see [3]), this system violates these restrictions and has both an internal knowledge store and a sense of state (from the use of the speech act networks described above, and from the knowledge store). The operators of the system resemble those of a traditional planner. Each operator consists of a **situation**, which is a set of propositions that must be in the current utterance and/or knowledge store in order for the situation to be applicable, an **action**, which describes

---

[3] See [8] for a discussion on the limitations of finite state models for spoken dialogue systems.

the action to perform (for example, initiate an instant message exchange with Ann with the content speech-act-network-x), and **result**, which describes changes to the knowledge store. This is similar to the notion of strong autonomy described by Mateas and Stern [11]. An agent based on this notion of strong autonomy chooses its next action based on local perception of its environment plus internal state (knowledge store). At any point, multiple actions may be applicable. For example, the character might choose to continue in an activated speech act network or choose to interrupt that network in favor of pursuing a new action. Choosing among these alternatives is based on a notion of activation similar to that proposed by Maes [13].

4   Conclusion

In this paper I have described an dialogue architecture for conversational characters used for interactive stories. The innovation of the architecture is in its combined use of speech act networks and a situated action planner. We have implemented this architecture in a system that engages three language learners in a Spanish adventure.[4]

References

1. Carletta, J. 1990. Modeling variations in goal-directed dialogue. In Proceedings of the International Conference on Computational Linguistics 13.324–326.
2. Winograd, T. 1988. Where the action is. Byte 13(13).256a–258.
3. Agre, P, and Chapman, D. 1988. What are plans for? MIT AI Memo 1050a.
4. Zacharski, Ron. 1993. A discourse pragmatics model of pitch accent in English. University of Minnesota dissertation.
5. Gundel, Jeanette, Nancy Hedberg, and Ron Zacharski. 1993. Cognitive status and the form of referring expressions in discourse. Language 69.274–307.
6. Austin, J. 1962. How to Do Things with Words. Cambridge, MA: Harvard University Press.
7. Searle, J. 1969. Speech Acts: An Essay in the Philosophy of Language. London: Cambridge University Press.
8. McTear, M. 1998. Modeling spoken dialogues with state transition diagrams. In Proceedings of the Fifth International Conference on Spoken Language Processing (ICSLP-98) 1223–1226.
9. Cohen, P, and Perrault, C. 1979. Elements of a plan-based theory of speech acts, Cognitive Science 3(3):177-212. Reprinted in Readings in Natural Language Processing, ed. By Grosz, B, Jones, K, and Webber, B. 1986. Los Altos, CA: Morgan Kaufmann Publishers.
10. Bickmore, Timothy, and Justine Cassell. 2000. "How about this weather?" Social dialogue with embodied conversational agents. Proceedings of the AAAI Fall Symposium on Socially Intelligent Agents.
11. Jordan, Pamela, Carolyn Rosé, and Kurt VanLehn. 2001. Proceedings of AI in Education. Austin, Texas, May 2001.
12. Mateas, Michael, and Andrew Stern. 2002. A behavior language for story-based believable agents. AAAI Working Notes of Artificial Intelligence and Interactive Entertainment.
13. Maes, Pattie. How to do the right thing. Connection Science Journal 1(3)

---

[4] More detailed information on this work can be found at http://www.zacharski.org/characters.

A Portable Natural Language Interface for Diverse Databases Using Ontologies*

Antonio Zárate[1], Rodolfo Pazos[1], Alexander Gelbukh[2],
and Isabel Padrón[1]

[1] Centro Nacional de Investigación y Desarrollo Tecnológico (CENIDET)
Interior Internado Palmira S/N,
Ap. Postal 5-164, 62490, Cuernavaca, Mor., México
{jazarate,pazos,jipc}@sd-cenidet.com.mx,
[2] Centro de Investigación en Computación, Instituto Politécnico Nacional, Mexico
gelbukh@cic.ipn.mx, www.gelbukh.com

Abstract. The growth of user needs for accessing information resources, the technological advance in this field, and the limitations of graphical and form-based interfaces, motivate the proposal of new solutions and the revision of several others in order to solve one of the main problems in computer applications: human-machine interface. Natural language processing has experienced a new impulse in recent years, and it is proposed as the best solution for the aforementioned problem. The first results of a project for developing a natural language interface to databases are presented, which is an extension of a larger project aimed at developing user interfaces for facilitating access to databases via Internet. In this project the use of ontologies is proposed as a means for making the interface portable to different databases, contributing in this manner to facilitate the configuration task for this type of interfaces, which is one of the main factors that have limited their application. In this paper the conceptual architecture of a natural language interface to databases on the Internet is described as well as the development attained.

1 Introduction

The fast growth of the Internet is creating a society where the demand for storage services, organization, access and analysis of information is constantly increasing. The advent of the Internet has completely changed the research directions in all areas of computer science, especially those related to databases as can be seen in the Asilomar report [5].

The growing need by users without wide knowledge of computers to access data over the Internet has resulted in the development of many types of interfaces, such as QBE (query by example) [42], form-based interfaces, restricted natural languages, etc. These tools, despite all the facility they provide to users, always imply some degree of difficulty when translating what the user would normally express to another person, into a structured form appropriate for the query engine.

---

* This research has been partially funded by COSNET, CONACYT, and RITOS2.

A. Gelbukh (Ed.): CICLing 2003, LNCS 2588, pp. 494–505, 2003.

A solution for the problem of enabling any user to express a data query easily is natural language interfaces to databases (NLIDB's). This topic has attracted interest since the 70's, and has motivated a large series of projects. However, these have not been widely used because of their being considered "exotic" systems, and the complexity and tediousness of their start-up configuration, in order to make the interface work for the first time with a specific database or for using the interface with another database, whose semantics is different from the original.

2 Previous Work of the Authors

The first project developed at the beginning of the last decade by the Distributed Systems Group of CENIDET, Mexico, was the Distributed Database Management System (SiMBaDD) [39]. In recent years, the group has focused on the problems of data access via Internet, with particular interest in interfaces to databases that are friendly enough for the great number of new Internet users, who are usually inexperienced in handling databases. Some examples of projects developed for this purpose are the following:

- A query by example (QBE) tool for databases on the Internet. Its main objective was to develop a tool that enabled inexperienced and casual users to access databases via Internet, in a platform-independent way (which was achieved through its implementation in Java) [32].
- A query by example (QBE) tool for multidatabases on the Internet. This project improved some features of the interface, such as the possibility of processing a query that involves tables in different databases, subquery processing, help windows, and a new three-tier architecture, which is the basis of the current project [21].
- An EzQ query tool for multidatabases on the Internet. The purpose of this project was to improve the human-machine interface, mainly concerning the ease with which inexperienced users can formulate queries that involve *joins*, without the user having to master the complex join concept [6].

These developments have led us to conclude that the next step is the integration of a NLIDB, a point of view shared by several investigators [1], since we consider that we have exhausted the possibilities of other types of database interfaces, either by using formal query languages, like in the project SiMBaDD [39], or using graphic tools for inexperienced users [32, 21, 6]. The current architecture of the QBE tool is shown in Figure 1.

It is well-known that NLIDB's are not the panacea for solving all the problems of human-machine interaction, as shown in a study [37]. However, in the same study it is demonstrated that in the cases when several tables are involved or when the solution is not similar to the examples previously known by the user, NLIDB's prove to be simpler than graphical interfaces or formal query languages.

An experiment carried out using Intellect, concluded that natural language is an effective method for the interaction of casual users with a good knowledge of the database in a restricted environment. The evaluation criteria of such type of interfaces are defined in [1].

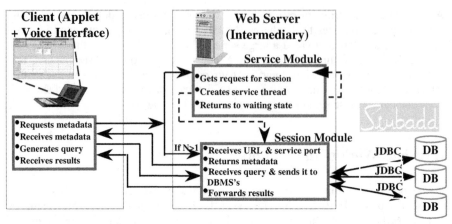

Fig. 1. Architecture of the Query by Example tool

3 Previous Work on NLIDB's and Ontologies

3.1 NLIDB's Projects

There exists in the literature a series of analysis about NLIDB's [1, 36, 41] which describe their evolution over the last four decades. Since our NLIDB is being developed for the Spanish language, we will limit our description to a few of the most important projects related to NLIDB's for Spanish:

- NATLIN (Universidad de las Américas-Puebla, Mexico). This system is a NLI for accessing databases expressed in logic using Sun Prolog (BIMprolog). NATLIN accepts questions for a geographical database domain. A module was added recently for translating into SQL the queries generated by NATLIN [35].
- INTERNAT (Ministry of Industry and Energy, Spain). INTERNAT is based on a translation approach from natural language to a formal language like SQL. It was implemented in C and can interact with dictionaries and other applications based on NLP and menu-based database access systems. INTERNAT was installed at AENA where its operation was validated [27].
- Silvia-NLQ (Universidad Autónoma de Madrid, Spain). The project was aimed at developing a database query system using natural language. The system had a multilingual character (English, German, French, Spanish and Italian) and its final goal was to develop a commercial product (LanguageAccess), which was introduced on the market. The participation of the Universidad Autónoma de Madrid consisted of developing the Spanish grammars for analysis and generation, as well as a dictionary and conceptual models for interpreting certain linguistic subdomains [20].
- GILENA (Universidad de Concepción, Chile). Taking as input several parameters (data dictionary, keywords and grammatical rules), it automatically generates all the source programs for a NLI. This tool was used to implement several interfaces: expert system for failure diagnosis of electric equipment, teaching system of Indian cultures for grammar schools, NLIDB's for products and/or services, and

command shell for Unix in Spanish. The parser was implemented using a nondeterministic augmented transition network [3].

It is worth mentioning that none of the aforementioned NLIDB's was designed for easy porting to databases different from the one for which it was originally developed nor the dictionary and the NLIDB knowledge base were designed for reuse or sharing, which are objectives that are pursued in our project.

3.2 Ontology Projects

Some of the most relevant projects aimed at using ontologies for achieving interoperability among applications are the following:

- Process Interchange Format (PIF). Its purpose is to exchange business process models using different representations. It uses an interlingua with local translators between PIF and local process representations [30].
- Knowledge Sharing Effort (KSE). DARPA (Defense Advanced Research Projects Agency) project aimed at the search of solutions for sharing knowledge among heterogeneous systems [24].
- Knowledge Representation Specification Language (KRSL). Language developed for representing plans and planning information. Its purpose is to provide a common vocabulary for concepts, relationships and common conditions for planning activities. KRSL considers two main aspects: an abstract ontology with the main categories (time, space, agents, actions, and plans) and a set of specialized modular ontologies with alternative concepts and theories common to planning systems (e.g. specific ontologies for time instants, time relationships, etc.) [2].
- Knowledge Interchange Format (KIF). It is a language that intends to represent through ontologies most of the current concepts and distinctions of the most recent languages for knowledge representation. It mainly intends to serve as a bridge between ontologies using proprietary language translators to/from KIF. It is a language based on predicate logic extended for definition of terms, metaknowledge, sets, nonmonotonic reasoning, etc. [19].
- Common Object Request Broker Architecture. Permits to retrieve and invoke operations on objects through a network. It provides a mechanism where objects can issue requests and receive responses transparently. CORBA defines an Interface Definition Language (IDL) that specifies objects and operations for remote/ distributed applications and incorporates informal notions of ontologies [16].
- CYC (project of Microelectronics and Computer Technology Corporation). Its ontology is organized as a microtheories network, where each microtheory captures the knowledge and reasoning needed for a specific domain, such as space, time, causality, or agents. A microtheory can show particular views related to a specific domain, therefore in one domain may coexist several microtheories [16].
- Toronto Virtual Enterprise (TOVE). Intends to develop ontologies for businesses using first order logic and permits to infer answers to common sense questions [15].
- Simple HTML for Ontology Extensions (SHOE). This was the first ontology and Web page tagging developed at the University of Maryland in 1996. SHOE can

define ontologies and tags (which are meaning bearing XML tags), and a knowledge representation language based on HTML. One of its limitations is that it does not permit to define class negation and disjunction [38].

- Ontology Interchange Language (OIL). This language intends to combine Internet models with logic representations and the descriptive structures of ontologic approaches. OIL makes possible to infer conclusions about contents represented in this language [25].
- Resource Description Frame (RDF). It is a model for defining semantic relationships among different URI's. RDF is based on the XML syntax and permits to describe semantically a URI associating to it a set of properties and values. RDF models are constructed as directed graphs specifying triplets (URI, property, value). The metadata specified with RDF are understood by computers, and therefore, can be processed automatically [33].
- DARPA Agent Markup Language (DAML). Consists of a formalism that permits software agents to interact with each other. The DAML language is also an extension of XML and RDF. It provides a large number of constructions for ontology definition and increases semantic information to make it legible and understandable for computers. Ontology definition with DAML provides a new way to face the challenge of large scale integration of services. The proposed extensible interoperability network provides the necessary mediation level to solve the semantic differences among all the value chain participants. It has currently been used for annotating ontologies on the semantic Web [8].
- EuroWordNet. The objective of EuroWordNet is the multilingual extension of the English Word Net for the different languages involved (Italian, Spanish and Dutch). EuroWordNet has been proposed as a standard for the semantic codification of texts, and it is intended to be used as interlingua in multilingual systems for information retrieval and automatic translation [23].

4   Natural Language Query Processing System

The system will be used for the Spanish language spoken in Mexico, and will have additional elements with respect to other similar systems [3, 7, 10, 35]: a better language coverage, much better portability of DBMS and operating system, and transparent access through Internet.

The architecture used previously (Fig. 1) was substantially modified. The three-level client-intermediate-server structure is preserved, but the functionality of each level has been changed. The client functions will be much simpler, which will partially solve the problems of the current QBE interface, at the expense of a more active role of the intermediary level. The new architecture of the natural language query processing system for Web databases is shown in Fig. 2.

At the onset of a session with the interface, the client will present to the user an ontology (that will be stored in a repository), which represents the knowledge stored in the database dictionary. This differs from the QBE interface that shows the database designer's abstractions through tables, which most of the times are difficult to understand by the inexperienced users and also lack a lot of very important semantic information. The presentation of this ontology permits the user to better understand the contents of the database, which facilitates the user to formulate his query.

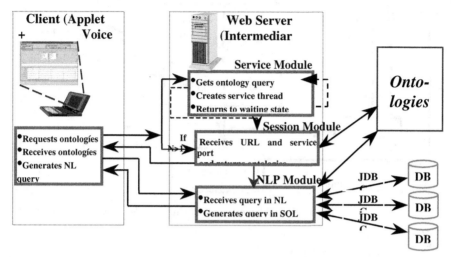

Fig. 2. Proposed system architecture

After receiving the ontology, the user issues a query using a voice interface. The output of this voice interface is received by the client and passed on to the service module of the intermediary, which in turn passes it to the natural language processing module (NLP). The architecture of the NLP module is quite standard, except that the lexicon consists of two parts: a general linguistic ontology based on the approach of the WordNet project [23], and a domain ontology that describes the semantics of the database (Fig. 3).

Upon reception at the NLP module, the natural language query is syntactically and semantically parsed in order to transform it into an internal representation, which in turn is translated into structured query language (SQL). The SQL query is sent back to the session module, which forwards it for evaluation against a database management system (DBMS). The session module forwards the result generated by the DBMS to the final user through the client interface.

Even though, there exist other proposals for separating linguistic and domain knowledge [12, 22], none of those possess a knowledge representation that is reusable, shareable and implemented according to a standard. In contrast, this project proposes the implementation of a lexicon following the outline of the WordNet project [23], which is becoming a de-facto standard, and the development of the domain ontology based on the DARPA Agent Markup Language (DAML) [6], which is backed by DARPA and is being used for tools development and different applications.

An important advantage that we find in DAML is that it can be used to implement both the ontologies and the inference mechanisms that utilize the ontology information. One innovative aspect of our proposal is that the semantic parser will be implemented taking maximum advantage of the possibilities offered by DAML, such as described in [29].

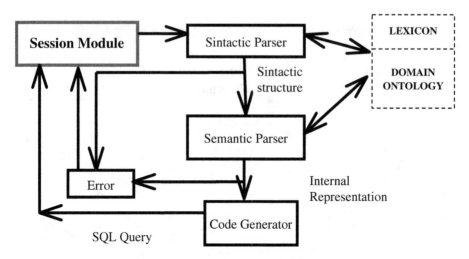

Fig. 3. Natural language processing module

5 Current Progress

Currently eighteen noun categories and seven verb categories have been input to the lexicon, which were coded following the outline of WordNet. Additionally, the lexical parser has been implemented [28], while the syntactic parser is being coded and will use the Spanish grammar developed in a previous work [13]. Table 1 shows an example of the grammar categories that are recognized by the lexical parser.

Table 1. Example of the lexical analysis of a sentence

WORD	CLASSIFICATION
la 'the'	Article, feminine, singular.
peregrina 'pilgrim'	Common noun, feminine, singular.
llevaba 'wore'	Verb llevar, 3rd person, preterit singular, imperfect indicative, first conjugation.
sombrero 'hat'	Common noun, masculine, singular.
negro 'black'	Color adjective, masculine, singular.

The general operation of the lexical analyzer is shown in Fig. 4. The user inputs his question by dictating it to the Dragon Naturally Speaking interface. This software translates the question into text and stores it in a file. The question may contain words that are not useful for the lexical analyzer, and therefore they are eliminated from the question in the text file. The list of irrelevant words was determined through a survey and can be modified as necessary. Examples of this type of words are the following: *quiero* (I want), *dame* (give me), *lístame* (list for me), *muéstrame* (show me), etc.

After the previous filtering, the sentence is passed on to the lexical analyzer, which classifies its words and tags them with syntactical information. Each tag includes all the syntactical categories to which the word belongs.

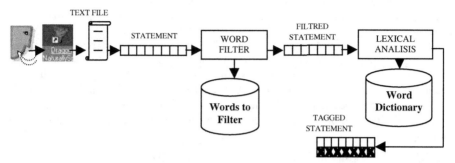

Fig. 4. General operation of the lexical analyzer

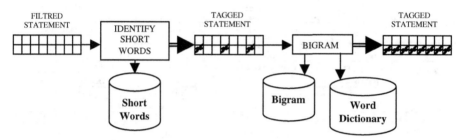

Fig. 5. Internal process of the lexical analyzer

The algorithm that performs the tagging (Fig. 5) consists of two steps. In the first step short words (articles, conjunctions, unions, etc.) are tagged, since they have a small probability of being ambiguous. In the second step, each word following a tagged word is assigned a tag using a Markov grammar [13], which permits to predict with some certainty the syntactic category of a word based on the syntactic category of the preceding word (these two words are also known as bigram). Some examples of the bigrams used are shown in Table 2. This last process is repeated for each remaining untagged word.

Table 2. Fragment of the bigram table

Utterance	Word	Word Tag	Next Word Tag
3	El	A&MS	N&13MS
2	El	A&MS	R&13MS
1	El	A&MS	V&13MS

It is quite possible that some lexical ambiguities arise when using bigrams, since there might exist several alternative categories possible for a word. In order to improve the disambiguation capabilities of the tagging algorithm, it is being expanded to work with trigrams and higher order N-grams. It is important to point out that a working assumption is that the database semantics defined by the ontology will substantially limit the ambiguity possibilities in the query analysis.

The algorithm stops when the entire sentence is completely tagged, then it can be checked by the syntactic parser, so it can be restructured and a syntactic tree can be generated.

The lexicon was implemented using different tables for different word types: nouns, verbs (including the derivations corresponding to all tenses and persons), short words (articles, pronouns, conjunctions, and unions, which are shorter than six characters), adjectives, and adverbs. We chose this implementation instead of lemmatization at execution time, because search time for words in these tables is very fast, considering that today's main memory sizes permits to keep entire tables in main memory.

número	Verbo	presente indicativo primera persona	segunda	tercera	cuarta	quinta	sexta
S	partir	parto		partes	parte	partimos	partís	parten
copretérito indicativo primera persona			segunda	tercera	cuarta	quinta	sexta	
	partía		partías	partía	partíamos	partíais	partían	
pretérito indicativo primera persona			segunda	tercera	cuarta	quinta	sexta	
	partí		partiese	partió	partimos	partisteis	partieron	
futuro indicativo primera persona		segunda	tercera	cuarta	quinta	sexta	
	partiré		partirás	partirá	partiremos	partiréis	partirán	
pospretérito indicativo primera persona		segunda	tercera	cuarta	quinta	sexta	
	partiría		partirías	partiría	partiríamos	partiríais	partirían	
presente subjuntivo primera persona		segunda	tercera	cuarta	quinta	sexta	
	parta		partas	parta	partamos	partáis	partan	
pretérito subjuntivo primera persona		segunda	tercera	cuarta	quinta	sexta	
	partiera o partiese		partieras	partiera	partiéramos	partierais	partieran	
futuro subjuntivo primera persona		segunda	tercera	cuarta	quinta	sexta	
	partiere		partieres	partiere	partiéremos	partiereis	partieren	
presente imperativo segunda persona		tercera	cuarta	quinta	sexta	
	parte		parta	partamos	partid	partan	
infinitivo	gerundio	participio					
partir	partiendo	partido					

Fig. 6. Example of the verb conjugation dictionary

Verb stems were input manually into the verb table (Fig. 6), while the morphological variants of each stem were generated and inserted automatically into the table. Short words and their corresponding tags and bigrams were input manually into the corresponding table. A fragment of this table is shown in Table 3.

Table 3. Fragment of the short words table

Num.	Word	Type	Word Tag	Next Word Tag
1	las 'the'	Article	A&FP	N&&&FP
2	la 'the'	Article	A&FS	N&&&FS
3	el 'the'	Article	A&MS	N&&&MS
4	unas (some)	Indefinite	E&FP	N&&&FP

In order to obtain the noun variants corresponding to number and gender, it was necessary a syllable divider. There exist 15 rules in the Spanish grammar for syllable division [9]. Table 4 shows some of the results obtained.

Table 4. Results of the syllable divider

Word	Syllable Division	Rules
Adscripción	Ads-crip-ción	VCC-CCVC-CDC
Inconsciente	In-cons-cien-te	VC-CVCC-CDC-CV
Costumbre	Cos-tum-bre	CVC-CVC-CCV

Where:
V for vocal,
C for consonant,
D for diphthong.

6 Final Remarks

The importance of developing natural language interfaces is explained by the need to make available computational resources to any user. This means that the language for accessing computers has to be the same as human language, either in written or spoken form.

A study conducted by a group of information system administrators on the usefulness of different applications of natural language interfaces concluded that those used for obtaining information from databases was preferred by users over those for information retrieval and text preparation [37]. This type of interfaces left very far behind other applications such as language translation.

Two aspects of this work are worth mentioning: the use of ontologies which is scarce for Spanish NLIDB's [22] and the portability of NLIDB's over different domains that can be achieved. The first aspect is very important because ontologies are being used for a wide variety of research topics (knowledge management, NLP, etc.). Equally important, the lack of portability together with other NLP problems has resulted in little use and popularization of NLIDB's.

In order to provide portability to our interface an ontology editor is being implemented [10], which will help define ontologies for the database domains. This editor will incorporate some features of other projects such as Protegé-2000 [31] and OntoWeb [26]. Additionally, the ontology design method Methontology [4] will be used for the domain ontology design and construction.

The work on natural language interfaces is necessary because there are more and more people that need access to computer resources, but do not have experience in this nor usually time to acquire it. Also, being Spanish the third language in the world by the number of native speakers (around 390 million), it is very important to develop appropriate tools for this huge market.

References

1. Androutsopoulos I., Ritchie G., Thanisch P.: Natural Language Interfaces to Databases, An Introduction, Department of Artificial Intelligence, University of Edinburg; http://citeseer.nj.nec.com/androutsopoulos95natural.html, 1992.

2. Allen J., Lehrer N.: DRAFT of the DARPA/Rome Laboratory Planning and Scheduling Initiative Knowledge Representation Specification Language (KRSL), Version 2.0.1 Reference Manual. ISX Corporation, June 26, 1992.
   http://www-ksl.stanford.edu/ knowledge-sharing/papers/krsl.tar.Z.

3. Atkinson J.: GILENA (Generador de Interfaces en Lenguaje Natural), M.S. dissertation, Universidad de Concepción, Chile http://www.dai.ed.ac.uk/homes/atkinson/private/gilena, 1991.

4. Blázquez M., Fernández M., García-Pinar J. M., Gómez-Pérez A.: Building Ontologies at the Knowledge Level Using the Ontology Design Environment, Laboratorio de Inteligencia Artificial, Facultad de Informática, Universidad Politécnica de Madrid, mayo de 1997, http://delicias.dia.fi.upm.es/articulos/kaw98/FernandezEtAl97.

5. Bernstein P., Brodie M., Ceri S., DeWitt D., García-Molina H., Gray J., Held J., Ellerstein J., Jagadish H.V., Lesk M., Maier J., Naughton J., Pirahesh H., Stonebraker M., Ullman J.: The Asilomar Report on Database Research, Sept., 1998.

6. Carreón G.: Herramienta para Consultas EzQ para Multibases de Datos en Internet, M.S. dissertation (to be published), Departamento. de Ciencias Computacionales, Centro Nacional de Investigación y Desarrollo Tecnológico, Cuernavaca, Mor.

7. Chay E.: Una Interfaz en Lenguaje Natural en Español para Consultas a Bases de Datos. M.S. dissertation, Monterrey Institute of Technology, Cuernavaca Campus, 1990.

8. DAML, Darpa Agent Markup Language, http://www.daml.org/.

9. Diccionario Básico de Gramática Práctica, ed. Oceano, Barcelona, España 1999.

10. Domínguez A. P.: Implementación de un Analizador Gramatical en Lenguaje Español. M.S. dissertation (to be published), Instituto Tecnológico de Cd. Madero. Jun. 2001.

11. EuroWordNet, supported by the European Union, http://www.hum.uva.nl/~ewn/.

12. Fox, M. S.: "The Tove Project: Toward a Common-Sense Model of the Enterprise." Lecture Notes in Computer Science 604 (1992) 25–43.

13. Galicia S. N.: Análisis Sintáctico Conducido por un Diccionario de Patrones de Manejo Sintáctico para Lenguaje Español, PhD. dissertation, Centro de Investigación en Computación del IPN, Aug. 2001.

14. García M.: Herramienta para la Generación de Ontologías a Partir de un Diccionario de Datos, M.S. dissertation in progress, Departamento de Ciencias Computacionales, Centro Nacional de Investigación y Desarrollo Tecnológico, Sept. 2002.

15. Gruber A.: A Translation Approach to Portable Ontology Specifications, Technical Report KSL 92–71, Knowledge Systems Laboratory, Stanford University, Sept. 1992.

16. Huerta V. O.: Un Método para el Reconocimiento a Bases de Datos en Interrogaciones en Lenguaje Natural, M.S. dissertation, Monterrey Institute of Technology, Cuernavaca Campus., 1989.

17. InBase, Russian Research Institute of Artificial Intelligence, Moscow,
    http:// www.inbase.artint.ru/article/voicnl-eng.asp.

18. Jurafsky D., Martin J.H.: Speech and Language Processing, ISBN 0-13-095069-6, Prentice Hall, 2000.

19. KIF/ontolingua, "Knowledge Interchange Format", http://elies.rediris.es/ elies9/ 5-4.htm.

20. Marcos F., Olmeda C., Martínez J., Guilarte S.: Proyecto Sylvia-NLQ, Laboratorio de Lingüística informática, Universidad Autónoma de Madrid.

21. May A.: Herramienta para Consultas Basadas en Ejemplos (QBE) para Multibases de Datos en Internet, M.S. dissertation, Departamento de Ciencias Computacionales, Centro Nacional de Investigación y Desarrollo Tecnológico, Cuernavaca, Mor., Apr. 2000.

22. Morales E.: Curso de Representación de Conocimiento, Master in Science Faculty, Monterrey Institute of Technology Campus Cuernavaca, 1999,
    http://w3.mor.itesm.mx/ ~rdec/node1.html.

23. Miller G.: Wordnet. Wordnet, a Lexical Database, Cognitive Science Laboratory, Princeton University. http://www.cogsci.princeton.edu/~wn/.

24. Neches R.: The Knowledge Sharing Effort, an Overview, Knowledge Systems Laboratory, Stanford University,
    http://www-ksl.stanford.edu/knowledge-sharing/papers/kse-overview.html.
25. OIL , Ontology Interchange Language, http://www.ontoknowledge.org/oil/.
26. OntoWeb. http://delicias.dia.fi.upm.es/ontoweb/sig-tools/.
27. Palomar M., Moreno L., Molina A.: SISCO, Sistema de Interrogación en Lenguaje Natural a una Base de Datos Geográfica, GPLSI Grupo de Investigación en Procesamiento del Lenguaje y Sistemas de Información, Universidad de Alicante, http://gplsi.dlsi.ua.es/gplsi/menupublicf.htm.
28. Padrón J. I.: Analizador Morfológico-Sintáctico de Oraciones en Lenguaje Español. M.S. thesis in progress, Departamento de Ciencias Computacionales, Centro Nacional de Investigación y Desarrollo Tecnológico, Cuernavaca, Mor., Oct. 2002.
29. Pease A.: Why Use DAML?, Teknowledge on 10 April, 2002,
    http://www.daml.org/ 2002/04/why.html.
30. Process Interchange Format, supported by: ARPA, NSF, Corporate Sponsors of the MIT Center for Coordination Science. http://ccs.mit.edu/pif/.
31. Protégé-2000. http://protege.stanford.edu/index.html.
32. Rasgado F.: Herramienta para Consultas Basadas en Ejemplos (QBE) para una Base de Datos en Internet, M.S. dissertation, Departamento de Ciencias Computacionales, Centro Nacional de Investigación y Desarrollo Tecnológico, Cuernavaca, Mor., Dec. 1999.
33. Resource Description Framework (RDF), World Wide Web Consortium (W3C),
    http://www.w3c.org/RDF/.
34. Reis P., Matias Nuno J.: Edite – A Natural Language Interface to Databases, a New Dimension for an Old Approach. INESC Av. Duque dÁvila 23, 1000 Lisboa, Portugal.
35. Rocher G. : Traducción de Queries en Prolog a SQL, B.S. dissertation. Computer Systems Enginnering Dept, Engeneering Faculty, Universidad de las Américas-Puebla. Sep. 1999.
36. Rojas J., Torres J.: A Survey in Natural Language Databases Interfaces, Proc. of the Eigth. International Congress on Computer Science Research. Instituto Tecnológico de Colima, Colima, México, Nov. 2001, pp. 63–70.
37. Sethi V.: Natural Language Interfaces to Databases: MIS Impact, and a Survey of Their Use and Importance, Graduate School of Business, Univ. of Pittsburgh. Pittsburgh, PA 15260.
38. SHOE, Simple HTML Ontology Extensions, http:// www.cs.umd.edu/ projects/plus/SHOE.
39. SiMBaDD, Sistema Manejador de Bases de Datos Distribuidas, Departamento de Ciencias Computacionales, Centro Nacional de Investigación y Desarrollo Tecnológico, Cuernavaca, Mor., http://www.sd-cenidet.com.mx/simbadd.
40. Validation and Business Applications Group: PASO-PC315 PROJECT, Generator of Natural Language Databases Interfaces, http://www.vai.dia.fi.upm.es/ing/projects/paso.htm.
41. Zárate J.A, Pazos R., Gelbukh A.: Natural Language Interface for Web-based Databases, In Proc: 2nd WSEAS Int. Conf. on Robotics, Distance Learning and Intelligent Communication Systems (ICRODIC 2002),
    http://www.wseas.com/conferences/2002/ skiathos/icrodic/.
42. Zloof M.: Query By Example: a Database Language. IBM Sys. Journal 16. 4 (1977) 137–152.

Time-Domain Structural Analysis of Speech

Kamil Ekštein and Roman Mouček

Dept. of Computer Science and Engineering, Faculty of Applied Sciences,
University of West Bohemia, Univerzitní 22, 306 14 Plzeň, Czech Republic
{kekstein, moucek}@kiv.zcu.cz

Abstract. This paper deals with an auxiliary speech signal parametrisation method based on structural analysis of speech signal in time domain. The method called TIDOSA (TIme-DOmain Structural Analysis) grounds in analysing the "shape" of incoming waveform peaks. The whole input acoustic signal is transformed into a sequence of peak shape class indices. The presented paper summarises the features of TIDOSA-based processing of speech signal, gives an overview of the executory method and the results reached so far (as the research and development is still not finished), and proposes its applications in automatic speech recognition (ASR) field.

1 Introduction

State-of-the-art ASR systems are able to recognise fluent speech and convert it to its orthographic form with accuracy of more than 90%. But such a good performance is usually gained through hard restriction of problem area vocabulary—the recognizer WER[1] usually exceeds 30%. The performance is reliant on a language model which is dependent on the application area again—the above said facts imply that the recognizer performance is determined mostly by training phase, quality and quantity of training data. Some articles (e.g. [1]) signalize that preprocessing and signal parametrisation themselves are not so important in case that powerful and "well-trained" language and semantics modelling is employed. The preparation of the training material is extremely demanding work. It is crucial, too, to estimate which material should be used for recognizer training and such an estimation is empirical only—there is still no technique to define any minimal satisfactory training set. The influence of invalid training data on the recognizer performance encourages search for non-empirical approach in **acoustic-phonetic analysis** methods, which could reduce share of semantics and language modelling on the recognition process and thus lower system sensitivity to training data. The proposed TIDOSA-based parametrisation technique has some properties which indicate its applicability in ASR in the previously discussed way.

---

[1] Word Error Rate; a value used to measure recognizer performance by expressing the number of misrecognized words.

A. Gelbukh (Ed.): CICLing 2003, LNCS 2588, pp. 506–510, 2003.

2   TIDOSA Method Description

An incoming acoustic signal is at first segmented into the so-called "peaks", i.e. into segments bounded by zero points $(f_s(t) = 0)$. Each peak isolated by zero crossing detector is classified into one class out of predefined class set (the classes are discussed later). The given class is represented by a peak shape template (PST) which is in fact an etalon and classification is based on "peak-to-PST" distance evaluation, $\arg\min_i d(Peak, PST_i)$. The distance defined by Euclidian metric is not as distinctive as needed for this task. Lucid and fast method can be used instead: For each peak few simple features are extracted: a) number and positions of local maxima and minima, b) positions of global extremes, c) symmetry characteristics, and d) value with physical meaning of gravity centre. The PST classes are designed in the way that a peak can be classified according to few if-then rules operating over the features and their mutual combinations.

The TIDOSA method core transforms an incoming acoustic signal into a sequence of triplets $\{PST, Amplitude, Duration\}$, where PST is the corresponding PST index, $Amplitude$ is height of the peak, and $Duration$ is length of the peak in samples.

Assessment of $Amplitude$ value is not fully straightforward. The peak maximum is not suitable to be taken as $Amplitude$ value, for the maximum can be influenced by channel distortion, or an electrical problem in the signal path. Maximum of the incoming signal is often an isolated sample or Dirac-like impulse caused by e.g. microphone plug, A/D board, etc. In order to avoid problems resulting from this, the following formula is used to compute the $Amplitude$ value A, $A = 0.5 \cdot (\overline{x(n)} + \max x(n))$, where $x(n)$, $n \in \langle 0, N-1 \rangle$ is the signal segment corresponding to the N-sample long analysed peak.

3   TIDOSA Structural Primitives

Structural primitives for TIDOSA method, i.e. peak etalons, were defined after thorough scanning of 65 digitized speech files. The goal was to figure out how many different "peak shapes" they include. After gaussian convolutive filtering which smoothed temporal course of the signal, it was observed that **all the peaks could be approximated by 8 basic peak shape templates (PST) which thus represent the restricted set of structural primitives.**

The small number of PSTs is reasoned: It is probably not necessary to record superimposed sine waves which are more complex than $y(t) = C_0 \cdot sin(t) + C_1 \cdot sin(3t) + C_2 \cdot sin(5t)$, where $C_n \in \langle 0, 1 \rangle$, because such a sine wave represents signal including formants F_0, F_1 and F_2[2]. The restriction of C_n is also reasoned: The high-frequency resonaces haven't as much energy as base frequency in case of voiced sounds. Unvoiced sounds also do not violate the above presented ideas as they can be modelled as frequency-localised noise and therefore approximated by sine peaks at certain frequency.

---

[2] F_3 and higher formants are not essential for speech intelligibility.

As a result of this analysis, 8 basic peak shape templates (PST)were proposed and designed. Two of them (0 and 7) have a special meaning and are not analytically defined (see hereafter). Analytical functions used to sample the PSTs no. 1 - 6 either for distance-based TIDOSA transformation or for signal reconstruction are listed in the following table:

PST	Function $f(t)$	t range	PST	Function $f(t)$	t range
1	$sin(t)$	$\langle 0, \pi \rangle$	4	$\sqrt[6]{1 - t^6}$	$\langle -1, 1 \rangle$
2	$\frac{1}{2}sin(3t) + sin(t)$♠	$\langle 0, \pi \rangle$	5	$sin(tan(t))$♣	$\langle 0, 0.4 \cdot \pi \rangle$
3	$\frac{1}{2}sin(5t) + \frac{1}{2}sin(3t) + sin(t)$♠	$\langle 0, \pi \rangle$	6	$sin(tan(t))$	$\langle 0, 0.4 \cdot \pi \rangle$

♠ = Normalized, $\max_t f(t) = 1$. ♣ = left-to-right flipped.

The 2 etalons left are PST 0, which represents the signal peaks with amplitude that is lower than a given threshold—simply said silence , and PST 7 representing those peaks which are not long enough to be reliably classified into any of the 1 - 6 PST classes (because in case that the peak is some 10 samples long, resampled PSTs are quite the same and it is impossible to decide which one could "fit" the analysed peak best).

The table below lists frequencies of particular PST occurences (in percents) in the pilot speech signals scanned during the analysis phase:

PST	Description	Freq [%]	PST	Description	Freq [%]
0	silence	39.01	4	"table peak"	1.87
1	sine	2.67	5	left-to-right slope	8.85
2	composed sine	1.84	6	right-to-left slope	13.69
3	composed sine	1.26	7	"short peak" (noise)	30.82

The results were approximately the same for all the pilot speech signal files. This might be accepted as a proof that the preliminary considerations were correct. The signals include about approximately 40% of silence and about 30% of peaks which were classified into PST 7 group—these are all the fricative sounds lying at the very border of Nyquist frequency and therefore being sampled as isolated oscillating samples or peaks with nearly no rise and fall, few (2-5) samples long.

4   Method Application

The primal purpose for developing the TIDOSA-based speech processing was to learn whether temporal structure of speech signal can be used in ASR process. It is evident that time-domain course of speech signal carries important information (see e.g. [2])—some specific speech sounds can be located (by human expert) when observing the raw waveform. It is usually not possible to decide what phoneme is exactly observed, but it can be roughly estimated. For example all the plosive speech sounds like [p], [t], [k], etc. have very significant time-domain waveform courses; TIDOSA was designed to track such significances.

The method—according to its properties described above—is to be utilized in automatic speech recognition in two ways:

1. **Preprocessing**—Ability to "dehumanise" speech signal by suppressing variability introduced by different vocal tract configurations. The result is resynthesised speech signal to be further analysed in ASR system.
2. **Parametrisation**—PST indices sequence could be used as an auxiliary parametrisation method together with some spectral-like one. PST indices sequences are distinctive for various acoustic phenomena (e.g. plosives, occlusives) which are hardly detectable using spectral-like features.

Forasmuch as the method replaces different varying peaks by indices of the best matching PSTs, the speech variability is substantially suppressed. The figures below show two utterances of plosive [t] (in [ta] syllable) by different speakers—original speech signal together with its TIDOSA-based resynthesised projection:

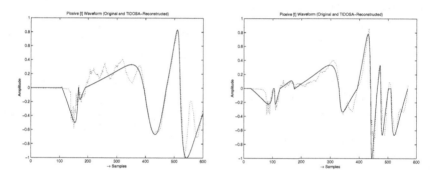

Fig. 1. Speech signal and its TIDOSA-based projection.

The most straightforward way to recognize phones from PST sequences is an application of finite state automaton. The proposed TIDOSA-based phone recognizer should go through TIDOSA sequence and find the occurences of sub-chains that are apriori known, e.g. included in the recognizer vocabulary which is represented by a set of finite state automata detecting the appropriate sequence.

The method cannot operate over the signal alone because it is totally unable to differentiate voiced sounds or vowels—the preferred operation mode is in parallel with another (spectral analysis-like) method as described in [3].

As TIDOSA transformation is principally signal parametrisation method it can be beneficially combined with thoroughly examined, well-known powerful techniques for acoustic-phonetic decoding like e.g. Hidden Markov Models.

The tests carried out so far indicated that the approach is reasonable and well-grounded but the testing and evaluation process is still in progress.

5   Conclusion

All the preliminary tests showed that TIDOSA-based parametrisation, acoustic-phonetic decoding, and speech recognition is either possible and advantageous in case that it is combined with some spectral analysis method. Such a configuration also allows to parallelize the computation so that for example multiprocessor systems can be used to speed up the recognition process.

References

1. Nöth, E., Boros, M., Fischer, J., et al.: *Research Issues for the Next Generation Spoken Dialogue Systems Revisited.* In Proceedings of TDS 2001, pp. 341–348, Springer-Verlag, Berlin Heidelberg New York, 2001. ISBN 3-540-42557-8.
2. Hermansky, H., Sharma, S.: *TRAPS—Classifiers of Temporal Patterns.* In Proceedings of ICSLP '98, Sydney, Australia, November 1998.
3. Ekštein, K.: *SpART I—An Experimental Automatic Speech Recognizer.* In Proceedings of SPECOM 2001, pp. 93–96, Moscow State Linguistic University, Moscow, 2001. ISBN 5-85941-092-1.

Experiments with Linguistic Categories for Language Model Optimization[*]

Arantza Casillas, Amparo Varona, and Ines Torres

Dpt. de Electricidad y Electrónica, Facultad de Ciencias
Universidad del País Vasco (UPV-EHU)
{arantza,amparo,manes}@we.lc.ehu.es

Abstract. In this work we obtain robust category-based language models to be integrated into speech recognition systems. Deductive rules are used to select linguistic categories and to match words with categories. Statistical techniques are then used to build n-gram Language Models based on lexicons that consist of sets of categories. The categorization procedure and the language model evaluation were carried out on a task-oriented Spanish corpus. The cooperation between deductive and inductive approaches has proved efficient in building small, reliable language models for speech understanding purposes.

1 Introduction

Nowadays, Automatic Speech Understanding (ASU) systems require a Language Model (LM) to integrate the syntactic and/or semantic constraints of the language. Thus, ASU systems can allow sequences of words in accordance with the previously defined syntax of the application task, as generated by a Language Model. The most reliable way to integrate LM into an ASU system is to infer statistical models, typically n-grams, from large training corpora. Statistical LMs estimate the a priori probability $P(\Omega)$ of a sequence of words $\Omega \equiv \omega_1 \omega_2 \dots \omega_{|\Omega|}$ being pronounced. Under the n-grams formalism, the estimation of $P(\Omega)$ is based on the estimation of the probability of observing a word given the $n-1$ preceding lexical units, $P(\omega_i/\omega_1 \dots \omega_{n-1})$, for every word ω_i in the lexicon and for every potential n-gram, i.e. combination of n words appearing in the application task.

However, when the size of the lexicon is high, the size of the training corpora needed to obtain well trained statistical LM's is prohibitive. In fact, the lack of training samples for building reliable LM's is an open problem when designing ASU systems for current application tasks such as dialogue systems, speech to speech translation, spontaneous speech processing, etc. The most common solution is to reduce the size of the lexicon by grouping the different words into categories.

---

[*] This research is supported in part by the Spanish Research Agency, project HERMES (TIC2000-0335-C03-03), DIHANA (TIC2002-04103-C03-02) and by the University of the Basque Country (9/UPV 00224.310-13566/2001).

A. Gelbukh (Ed.): CICLing 2003, LNCS 2588, pp. 511–515, 2003.

The aim of this work is to obtain reliable, small, robust Language Models to be integrated into an ASU system. We combine natural language techniques with traditional speech recognition techniques to tackle our objective. Deductive rules are used to define the set of categories and to determine the category of each word. Statistical techniques are then applied to generate category-based LM's.

A task-oriented Spanish corpus is used for category definition and language model generation and evaluation. This corpus, called BDGEO, represents a set of queries to a Spanish geography database. This is a medium-size vocabulary-specific task designed to test integrated systems for Speech Understanding. The lexicon consists of 1,459 words and the training material used for this work includes 82,000 words.

2   Description of Categories

Two sets of categories (or word equivalence classes) are selected and evaluated in the work. We employ the MACO [1] part of speech tagger to determine the set of categories. The MACO toolkit applies deductive techniques to determine the category of each word. In this case, each word belongs to exactly one word class. In general, the number of word classes is smaller than the number of words, so the size of the LM is reduced and it is better trained.

The first set of categories is based on the main classes recognized by the MACO morphological analyzer. From this initial set, three classes are removed since they have no sense in a Speech Understanding framework: abbreviations, dates and punctuation marks. Nevertheless, we need to add the class sentence beginning, required by the statistical language model to independently parse each sentence, i.e. to reset the history of the n-gram model. Table 1 shows the 12 classes that constitute the Reduced Set of Categories (RSC). Table 1 also shows the number of different words that correspond to each category in BDGEO database. This database contains a large number of geographical entities (mount, river, etc.) and proper names (Madrid, Ebro, etc.). Thus, the largest category is Name, accounting for 46% of the lexicon: 669 words. The number of different words in the category Article almost matches the number of different possibilities of a Spanish article.

Table 1. Reduced Set of Categories (RSC) proposed.

category[tag](number)	category[tag](number)	category[tag](number)
Determinant[D00](40)	Adverb[R00](31)	Article[T00](10)
Conjunction[C00](12)	Name[N00](669)	Pronoun[P00](44)
Numeral[M00](47)	Adjective[A00](231)	Interjection[I00](1)
Verb[V00](348)	Preposition[S00](25)	Line begging[S](1)

The second set of categories includes an extended set of the first one. Categories name, pronoun and verb are now expanded to proper name, interrogative pronoun, relative pronoun, auxiliar verb, main verb, etc. We have also taken into account the number of each word (singular (S), plural (P) or common (C)) and its gender (masculine (M), feminine (F) or invariable (I)). Table 2 shows the whole Extended Set of Categories (ESC), including characteristic expansion when considered (TFP: article, feminine, plural; TMS: article masculine, singular, etc.). This table also shows the number of different words of BDGEO vocabulary corresponding to each category. This number is significatively reduced for previous Name and Verb categories.

Table 2. Extended Set of Categories (ESC) proposed. Each cell represents the extension of the corresponding category of Table 1.

tag(number)	tag(number)	tag(number)
DMP(9) DFS(8) DCS(3) DCP(2)	R00(31)	TMP(2) TMS(4) TFS(2) TFP(2)
C00(12)	N00(305) NFS(140) NFP(45) NMS(124) NMP(41) NMN(3) NCS(6) NCP(5)	PCP(5) PCS(9) PFS(5) PMS(7) PT0(2) PCN(7) PFP(3) PMP(4) PRO(2)
[M00](47)	AFS(64) AMS(47) ACS(38) ACP(17) AFP(28) ACN(4) AMP(33)	[I00](1)
VMG(13) VMS0(159) VMSM(13) VMN(33) VMSF(8) VAN(2) VMP0(90) VMPF(11) VMPM(3) VAS0(11) VAP0(5)	[S00](25)	[S](1)

3 Language Model Evaluation

The test set perplexity (PP) is typically used to evaluate the quality of the LM. Perplexity can be interpreted as the (geometric) average branching factor of the language according to the model. It is a function of both the task and the model. The test set Perplexity (PP) is based on the mean log probability that an LM assigns to a test set ω_1^L of size L. It is therefore based exclusively on the probability of words which actually occur in the test as follows:

$$PP = P(\omega_1^{L)})^{-1/L} = e^{-\frac{1}{L}\sum_{i=1}^{L} log(P(\omega_i/\omega_1^{i-1}))} \tag{1}$$

The test set perplexity depends on the size of the lexicon (classically the number of different words in the task). Actually, the highest value of perplexity that could be obtained is the size of the lexicon when all combinations of words are equally probable. Low perplexity values are obtained when high probabilities are assigned to the test set events by the LM being evaluated, i.e., when "good" LM's are obtained.

Several n-gram models, $n = 2, ..., 4$, are obtained using the CMU toolkit [2]. In each case, the proposed set of categories, RSC ($l = 12$ categories in Table 1) and ESC ($l = 52$ categories in Table 2), is considered to build the language model. For comparison purposes, language models based on the lexicon consisting of the whole set of words ($l = 1459$), are also considered. In such cases, No Categorization (NC) is carried out. Table 3 shows the size of each model measured by the number of different n-grams appearing in the training set. Each model is then evaluated in terms of test set perplexity (PP). The whole database is used to train and test models, maintaining training-test set independency by using the well-known leaving-one-out partition procedure. As the three sets of categories lead to very different lexicon sizes (l), the PP cannot be directly compared in these experiments. Thus, a new measure, PP/l, is also included in Table 3.

Table 3. Perplexity (PP) evaluation of n-grams with $n = 2, ..., 4$ for three different lexicons (l): reduced set of categories (RSC) (Table 1), extended set of categories (ESC) (Table 2 sets of categories and no categorization (NC). The number of different n-grams (size) as well as pp/l measure are also provided.

sets of categories		n=2			n=3			n=4		
	lexicon (l)	size	PP	PP/l	size	PP	PP/l	size	PP	PP/l
NC	1459	7971	21.96	0.02	21106	14.99	0.01	36919	14.05	0.01
ESC	52	972	9.48	0.18	5043	6.61	0.13	13439	5.96	0.11
RSC	12	133	5.05	0.42	808	3.94	0.33	2962	4.04	0.34

Table 3 shows important reductions in the size of the model and in PP when linguistic sets of categories are considered. Both measures decrease with the size of the lexicon, leading to smaller, better trained, more efficient Language Models. However, when the number of categories is too small (RSC) the number of words corresponding to each category can be very high (see Table 1), making recognition work more difficult. The aim of an ASU system is to provide the most probable sequence of words according to the acoustic sequence uttered. Therefore, the most probable word in each category has to be selected when the LM is based on categories. This is measured to some extent by PP/l, which expresses a perplexity per lexicon unit. This value is lowest when each category consists of a single word and higher for small sets of categories. Up to a point, it therefore gauges the difficulty if decoding a task sentence. A good agreement between this measure, PP and model size and trainability is represented by the extended set of categories (ESC).

4   Conclusions

The objective of our experiments is to reduce LM complexity to get a set of well trained LM's. Thus, two sets of linguistical categories (or word classes) are evaluated in terms of perplexity. Both sets lead to small, low-perplexity language models that can be trained with reduced training corpora. Experimental comparison carried out in this work enables us to propose the extended set of categories, which includes the number of the word (singular and plural), the gender of the word (masculine and feminine), etc., as an adequate lexicon for building statistical language models for this task. However, these language models need to be integrated into the ASU system to be compared in terms of final word error rates.

References

1. "The MACO Morphological Analyzer." http://www.lsi.upc.es/ nlp
2. "The CMU-Cambridge Statistical Language Modeling toolkit."
   http://svr-www.eng.cam.ac.uk/ prc14/toolkit-documentation.html

Chinese Utterance Segmentation in Spoken Language Translation

Chengqing Zong[1] and Fuji Ren[2]

[1] National Laboratory of Pattern Recognition
Institute of Automation, Chinese Academy of Sciences
Beijing 100080, China
cqzong@nlpr.ia.ac.cn
[2] Department of Information Science and Intelligent Systems,
Faculty of Engineering, The University of Tokushima
2-1, Minamijosanjima, Tokushima, 770-8506, Japan
ren@is.tokushima-u.ac.jp

Abstract. This paper presents an approach to segmenting Chinese utterances for a spoken language translation (SLT) system in which Chinese speech is the source input. We propose this approach as a supplement to the function of sentence boundary detection in speech recognition, in order to identify the boundaries of simple sentences and fixed expressions within the speech recognition results of a Chinese input utterance. In this approach, the plausible boundaries of split units are determined using several methods, including keyword detection, pattern matching, and syntactic analysis. Preliminary experimental results have shown that this approach is helpful in improving the performance of SLT systems.

1 Introduction

In spoken language translation (SLT) systems, an input utterance often includes several simple sentences or relatively independent fixed expressions. However, unlike in written language, there are no special marks to indicate which word is the beginning or the end of a simple sentence. Although some boundaries may be detected by the system's speech recognition module through the analysis of acoustic features, some boundaries may still remain hidden in an utterance. For example, a Chinese speaker may pronounce an utterance as follows: 我来确认一下，您是要带浴缸的单人间，预算在一晚一百美元左右，最好是在闹市区，是吗？ ("Let me confirm. You would like to reserve a single room with a bath. The budget is about one hundred dollars per night. You prefer a downtown location. Is that right?"). In this utterance, there are four simple sentences and one fixed expression, the confirmation question. The potential difficulty of understanding the utterance without punctuation will be easily imagined. To make matters worse, the speech recognition result often contains incorrectly recognized words and noise words. Thus it is clearly quite important in SLT systems to split input utterances into simple units in order to facilitate the job of the translation engine.

A. Gelbukh (Ed.): CICLing 2003, LNCS 2588, pp. 516–525, 2003.

To cope with the problem of boundary detection, many approaches have been proposed over the last decade. Some of these approaches detect boundaries by analyzing the acoustic features of the input utterance, such as its energy contour, the speaking rate, and the fundamental frequency F_0 (Swerts 1997, Wightman 1994). It is true that some of the approaches take into account the linguistic content of the input utterance (Batliner 1996, Stolcke 1996) to some degree. For instance, automatic detection of semantic boundaries based on lexical knowledge as well as acoustic processing has been proposed (Cettolo 1998). However, we believe that none of these approaches have applied sufficient linguistic analysis for reliable sentence boundary detection in speech recognition. We would argue that linguistic analysis on multiple levels, including lexical analysis, syntactic analysis, and semantic analysis, is indispensable. Therefore, we propose a new approach based on linguistic analysis, in order to supplement or enhance this function.

The remainder of this paper will give emphasis on our methods of linguistic analysis in approaching Chinese utterance segmentation. In Section 2, some related work on utterance segmentation is briefly reviewed, and our motivations are presented. Section 3 describes in detail our methods based on multi-level linguistic analysis. Experimental results are presented in Section 4. Finally, Section 5 gives our conclusion.

2 Related Work and Our Motivations

2.1 Related Work

Stolcke et. al. (1998, 1996) proposed an approach to detection of sentence boundaries and disfluency locations in speech transcribed by an automatic recognizer, based on a combination of prosodic cues, modelled by decision trees, and word-based event N-gram language models. In Stolcke's approach, syntactic and semantic analysis were not involved. Ramasway (1998) introduced a trainable system that can automatically identify command boundaries in a conversational natural user interface. Ramasway's system employs the maximum entropy identification model, trained using data in which all of the correct command boundaries have been marked. The linguistic features employed in this method include only words and phrases and their positions relative to the potential command boundaries. However, this method is impractical for segmenting input utterances for an SLT system, since sentences in such systems are generally considerably longer than the commands used in dialogue systems. Cettolo et. al. (1998) used lexical knowledge in his approach to automatic detection of semantic boundaries, but his approach still treats acoustic knowledge as the main basis for detecting semantic boundaries. Kawahara (1996) proposed a novel framework for robust speech understanding, based on a strategy of detection and verification. In this method (Kawahara 1996), the anti-subword model is used, and a key-phrase network is used as the detection unit. Linguistic analysis is performed on a shallow level.

Batliner (1996) proposed a syntactic-prosodic labeling scheme in which two main types of boundaries and certain other special boundaries are labeled for a large VERBMOBIL spontaneous speech corpus. The method only aims at segmentation of these special boundaries. Furse (1998) proposed an input-splitting method for translating spoken language which includes many long or ill-formed expressions. The proposed method splits input into well-balanced translation units based on a semantic distance calculation. However, the method relies heavily on a computational semantic dictionary. Wakita (1997) proposed a robust translation method which locally extracts only reliable utterance segments, but the method does not split input into units globally, and sometimes fails to output any translation result. Zhou (2001) proposed a method of splitting Chinese utterances by using decision trees and pattern matching techniques, but the method lacks robustness when the input utterance is long and ill-formed or when the results from the speech recognizer contain many incorrectly recognized words. Reynar (1997) introduced a maximum entropy approach for identifying sentence boundaries. However, Reynar's approach focused on the boundary identification of English sentences in written language: potential sentence boundaries are identified by scanning the text for sequences of characters separated by white space (tokens) containing one of the symbols !, . or ?. Of course, in spoken language, there are no such specific symbols. Palmer (1994) and Riley (1989) also described methods of identifying sentence boundaries in written text.

Unfortunately, before beginning our work, we found few papers specifically addressing Chinese utterance segmentation.

2.2 Our Motivations

As outlined in Section 1, an utterance segmentation module operates between the speech recognition module and the translation component of a spoken language translation system (Figure 1).

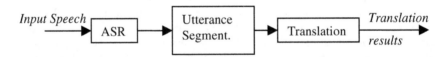

Fig. 1. Location of the utterance segmentation module

In Figure 1, ASR signifies automatic speech recognition. A Chinese input utterance is first recognized by ASR; then the speech recognition result is analysed and possibly split by the utterance segmentation module (USM) before being passed to the translation module. In fact, the input utterance may already have been segmented by the speech recognizer using acoustic feature analysis. Thus in our experimental system an utterance can be split at both the acoustic and the linguistic levels. And so the input to the translation module is usually a simple sentence or a fixed expression, at least in theory. In this SLT design, some analysis work is separated out of the translation module and moved to the segmentation module. Thus the translation module may employ simple direct translation methods, for example using template-based or pattern-based translation engines.

Suppose an input utterance has been transcribed by ASR, and a part of the recognition result is $P = W_1 W_2 \ldots W_n$ (where W_i is a Chinese word and $n \geqslant 1$.). P is possibly separated into k units U_1, U_2, ... U_k ($1 \leq k \leq n$) by USM. A split unit is one of the following expressions:

- A single word
- A fixed expression, such as a greeting phrase in Chinese, "你好 (Hello)".
- A simple sentence
- A clause indicated by certain special prepositions and conjunction words. For example, an input matched with the pattern "因为(because) … , 所以(therefore) … " will be separated into two parts "因为(because)…" and "所以 (therefore) … ".

Each part P is analysed and segmented by USM through the following three steps: (1) splitting using keyword detection; (2) splitting using pattern matching; and (3) splitting using syntactic analysis.

In this approach, a long utterance, especially an utterance containing more than two verbs, is usually split into small units, even if the original utterance is a complete simple sentence. As shown in the following examples,

Example 1. 我预订两个单人间需要多少钱？ (How much does it cost if I reserve two single rooms?)

⇒ 我预订两个单人间 (I reserve two single rooms) ‖

需要多少钱 (How much does it cost ?)

Example 2. 晚上9点以后办理入住手续可以吗？ (May I check in after 9 o'clock in the evening?)

⇒ 晚上9点以后办理入住手续 (Register after 9 o'clock in the evening) ‖

可以吗? (Is it OK?)

The examples show that it is no problem to understand the user's intension even if the utterance is split. This technique relies on the fact that the listener and the speaker both know what they're talking about. That is, they understand the discourse context. By taking advantage of such mutual knowledge, this splitting technique greatly reduces the work of the SLT system's translation component.

3   Segmentation Based on Multi-level Linguistic Analysis

In our methodology, if a string S from ASR is separated into n parts using the method of keyword detection, each part will be further segmented using, in succession, pattern matching methods and methods based on syntactic analysis.

3.1   Splitting by Keyword Detection

In the Chinese language, certain special words always indicate the beginning or the end of a simple sentence. For instance, the Chinese characters '呢(ne)', '吗(ma)' and

'吧(ba)' always indicate the end of a question sentence. Two words '如果(if)' and '的话(a mood word)' often imply that the utterance is a conditional clause. Based on these facts, several special rules have been designed to split an input string. The rules are expressed by the two types of expressions as follows:

$$\#KW_1, KW_2, ..., KW_n \qquad\qquad ... (1)$$

$$\%KW_{11}, KW_{12}, ..., KW_{1m}$$
$$\$KW_{21}, KW_{22}, ..., KW_{2k} \qquad\qquad ... (2)$$

where KW is a keyword, and n, m and k are all integers greater than zero. In formula (1), $KW_1, KW_2, ..., KW_n$ are synonyms, and perform the same role in the utterance. Formula (1) means that if the keyword KW_i ($i \in [1 .. n]$) is present in the analysis input, the input will be split into two parts after the keyword KW_i. In formula (2), $KW_{11}, KW_{12}, ..., KW_{1m}$ and $KW_{21}, KW_{22}, ..., KW_{2k}$ are two sets of synonyms. Any KW_{1i} ($i \in [1 .. m]$) and KW_{2j} ($j \in [1 .. k]$) compose a pair of keywords that collectively determine the boundary of a split unit. KW_{1i} is treated as the starting word and KW_{2j} is treated as the last word of the split unit.

Since the splitting procedure is based only on character comparison and does not involve any lexical analysis, syntactic analysis, or semantic analysis, we say that the splitting is performed at a shallow level. The algorithm is as follows.

Algorithm 1. Segmentation based on keyword detection

Input: a string S_{in} from ASR;
Output: a string S_{out} with boundary marks of split units.

Suppose all keywords given in formula (1) are denoted as a set KS_{single}, and all pairs of keywords given in formula (2) are denoted as a set KS_{pair}.

```
for  ∀K∈KS_single
   {set the boundary mark after the keyword K; }

if S_in is separated into n parts: P_i (i = 1..n){
   for ∀P_i{
       for ∀K_p∈KS_pair {
           set the boundary mark after the second word
           of the keyword pair K_p;
       }
   }
}
Output S_out and return;
```

3.2 Splitting by Pattern Matching

Once an input has been separated into n parts after splitting at the shallow level, each part $P = W_1, W_2, ..., W_m$ (where $m \geqslant 1$, $i \in [1..m]$, and W_i is a Chinese word) will be parsed and tagged with its phrase structure. Each part may be split using the pattern matching method. All patterns are expressed by Chinese words and part-of-speech or phrase symbols. For example,

#太 *AP* 了   ... (3)
#*IJ*   ... (4)

where *AP* indicates an adjective phrase, and *IJ* is the symbol for fixed greeting expressions in Chinese. Pattern (3) signifies that all strings matching the pattern will be treated as a split unit, e.g. 太贵了(It is too expensive.), 太高了(It is too high.). Pattern (4) means that all fixed greeting expressions are treated as split units, e.g. 你好(Hello), 不客气(You are welcome), etc.

For phrase recognition, a partial parser is employed, based on the chart parsing algorithm using a PCFG (Probabilistic Context-Free Grammar). In our system, the goal of the parser is to recognize phrases rather than whole sentences. Although there are large differences between spoken and written Chinese, we think these differences are mainly reflected at the sentence level, e.g., by various orderings of constituents containing redundant words in spoken Chinese expressions. By contrast, spoken and written Chinese follow the same phrase construction patterns. Accordingly, the PCFG rules employed in our system are directly extracted from the Penn Chinese Treebank[1]. All of the rules comply with the condition of $\sum_i P(LHS \rightarrow \alpha_i)=1$. For example:

NN NN $\rightarrow$ NP, 1.00
MSP VP $\rightarrow$ VP, 0.94
MSP VP $\rightarrow$ NP, 0.06

3.3 Splitting by Syntactic Analysis

Splitting on the syntactic level is carried out by recognizing syntactic components and their dependency relations.

Suppose S is a string to be split on the syntactic level. After phrase recognition, $S = H_1 H_2 \dots H_n$, where H_i ($i \in [1..n]$) is a phrase, and n is an integer $\geqslant 1$. As motivated in Section 2.2, when analyzing dependency relations, we treat the verb phrase as the centre of the segment to be analyzed. Notice that we do not treat the *predicate* as the centre of the sentence, as is commonly done. There are two reasons: (1) in SLT systems, an input is often not a complete sentence, and it is frequently difficult to recognize the predicate; and (2) analysis of the dependency relation between a verb phrase and other phrases is relatively simple, as compared with analysis involving predicates, so analysis accuracy is increased.

In our approach, six dependency relations are defined between the verb phrase and other components: agent, quantifier, complement, direct object, indirect object, and adverbial adjunct. There are also six types of verb phrases:

(1) The verb phrase does not take any object, denoted as V_0.
(2) The verb phrase takes only one object at most, denoted as V_1.

---

[1] Refer to Fei Xia, "The Part-of-Speech Tagging Guidelines for the Penn Chinese Treebank (3.0)", http://www.ldc.upenn.edu/ctb/

(3) The verb phrase usually takes two objects, denoted as V_2. One object is the direct object, and the other one is the indirect object.

(4) The verb phrase probably takes a clause as its object, denoted as V_c.

(5) The verb phrase takes a noun as its object, but the noun acts as the agent of another following verb or verb phrase, denoted as V_j. In this case, the noun is called a pivot word. The pivot word's action verb is denoted here as V_p.

(6) The verb is a copula, such as 是(be), denoted as V_{be}.

In the dictionary, each verb is tagged with one of the six types. From V_0 to V_{be}, the level is considered to increase. A higher level type may override a lower-level type. For example, if a verb probably acts as a V_1, but also as a V_2, it will be tagged as V_2 in the dictionary. The type of a verb phrase and its context in an utterance can then be used to identify boundaries in an utterance according to the following algorithm:

Algorithm 2. Segmentation based on syntactic analysis

Input: a part of an input utterance tagged with phrase symbols;
Output: split units of the input.

```
for each phrase XP {
    if XP = V₀
        {the boundary mark (BM) is set after the XP;}
    if XP = V₁
        {the BM is set after XP's object;}
    if XP = V₂ {
        if there is indirect object {
            the BM is set after XP's indirect object;
        }
        else{
            the BM is set after XP's direct object;
        }
    if XP = Vc ‖ XP = Vbe {
        if there is only a noun after the XP {
            the BM is set after the noun;
        }
        else{
            the BM is set after the XP;
        }
    if XP = Vj {
        if there is only a noun after the XP {
            the BM is set after the noun;
        }
        else{
            the BM is set after the Vp's object;
        }
}
```

Figure 2 shows a sample application of the splitting algorithm based on syntactic analysis.

Input: 我预订两个单人间需要多少钱(How much does it cost if I reserve two single rooms?)

Analysis procedure:

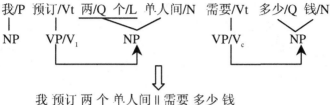

我 预订 两 个 单人间 ‖ 需要 多少 钱
(I reserve two single rooms) ‖ (How much does it cost)

Fig. 2. Sample application of the splitting algorithm based on syntactic analysis

4 Experimental Results

An experimental USM has been developed for a Chinese-to-English SLT system. The Chinese USM is built on 64800 collected utterances in the travel domain. From this corpus, we extracted 18 rules for splitting input on the shallow level, 32 patterns for splitting on the middle level, and 224 PCFG rules for partial parsing. Another 300 long utterances not included in the 64800 utterances are used as the test corpus, which contain 560 simple sentences or clauses, and 210 fixed greeting expressions. Thus each utterance consists of 2.57 split units on the average. The experimental results are shown in Table 1.

Table 1. Experimental Results

RESULTS	FIXED EXPRESSIONS	SIMPLE SENTENCES OR CLAUSES
Output	203	523
Correct	203	411
Correct Rate (%)	100.	78.6
Recall (%)	96.7	73.4

The table shows that the correct rate for the total output can be calculated by the formula: $((203 + 411) / (203 + 523)) \times 100\% = 84.6\%$. The recall rate is $((203 + 411) / (560 + 210)) \times 100\% = 79.7\%$. For the 560 simple sentences and clauses contained in the 300 input utterances, 37 simple sentences or clauses are not successfully separated out, and 112 utterances are split incorrectly. There were three main reasons for erroneous segmentation: (A) incorrect phrase parsing results, (B) incorrect dependency analysis, and (C) lack of semantic consistency checking. Table 2 gives the distribution of the three error types.

Table 2. Error Distribution

RESULT	INCORRECT PARSING RESULTS	INCORRECT DEPENDENCY ANALYSIS	LACK OF SEMANTIC CONSISTENCY CHECKING
Number	71	24	17
Ratio (%)	63.4	21.4	15.2

Clearly, incorrect phrase parsing is the main cause of incorrect utterance segmentation.

5 Conclusion

This paper introduces a new approach to Chinese utterance segmentation for Chinese-to-English SLT systems, based on linguistic analysis. The preliminary results have given us confidence to improve the performance of our SLT system. However, much hard work remains for further research, including the development of robust approaches to phrase boundary recognition, to identification of the field that a verb phrase dominates, to verification of semantic consistency, etc. In the next step, we will focus mainly on the following two points:

- Research on approaches to identifying the semantic boundaries of sentences;
- Combining segmentation methods based on linguistic analysis with statistical methods, including the maximum entropy method, hidden Markov models (HMM), and decision-tree methods.

Acknowledgements. This work is sponsored by the Natural Sciences Foundation of China under grant No.60175012, as well as partly supported by the Education Ministry of Japan under Grant-in-Aid for Scientific Research (14380166, 14022237) and a grant funded by the University of Tokushima, Japan.

The authors are very grateful to Dr. Mark Seligman for his very useful suggestions and his very careful proofreading. The authors also thank the anonymous reviewers for their helpful comments.

References

1. Batliner, A. and R. Kompe *et. al.* (1996) Syntactic-Prosodic Labelling of Large Spontaneous Speech Data-Bases. In *Proceedings of ICSLP*. USA.
2. Cettolo, Mauro and Daniele Falavigna. (1998) Automatic Detection of Semantic Boundaries Based on Acoustic and Lexical Knowledge. In *Proceedings of ICSLP*. pp. 1551–1554.
3. Furuse, Osamu, Setsuo Yamada and Kazuhide Yamamoto. (1998) Splitting Long Ill-formed Input for Robust Spoken-language Translation. In *Proceedings of COLING*, vol. I, pp. 421–427.

4.   Kawahara, Tatsuya, Chin-Hui Lee and Biing-Hwang Juang. (1996) Key-Phrase Detection and Verification for Flexible Speech Understanding. In *Proceedings of ICSLP*, USA.

5.   Nakano, Mikio, Noboru Miyazaki and Jun-ichi Hirasawa *et. al.* (1999) Understanding Unsegmented User Utterances in Real-time Spoken Dialogue Systems. In *Proceedings of ACL.*

6.   Palmer, David D. and Marti A. Hearst. (1994) Adaptive Sentence Boundary Disambiguation. In *Proceedings of the 1994 Conference on Applied Natural Language Processing (ANLP)*. Stuttgart, Germany, October.

7.   Ramasway, Ganesh N. and Jan Kleindienst. (1998) Automatic Identification of Command Boundaries in a Conversational Natural Language User Interface. In *Proceedings of ICSLP*, pp. 401–404.

8.   Reynar, Jeffrey C. and Adwait Ratnaparkhi. (1997) A Maximum Entropy Approach to Identifying Sentence Boundaries. In *Proceedings of the Fifth Conference on Applied Natural Language Processing*. USA. pp.16–19.

9.   Riley, Michael D. (1989) Some applications of tree-based modelling to speech and language. In D*ARPA Speech and Language Technology Workshop*. Cape Cod, Massachusetts. pp. 339–352.

10. Seligman, M. (2000) Nine Issues in Speech Translation. In *Machine Translation*. 15: 149-185.

11. Swerts, M. (1997) Prosodic Features at Discourse Boundaries of Different Strength. *JASA*, 101(1): 514–521.

12. Stolcke, Andreas and Elizabeth Shriberg (1996) Automatic Linguistic Segmentation of Conversational Speech. In *Proceedings of ICSLP*, vol. 2, pp. 1005–1008.

13. Stolcke, Andreas and Elizabeth Shriberg *et. al.* (1998) Automatic Detection of Sentence Boundaries and Disfluencies Based on Recognized Words. In *Proceedings of ICSLP*, pp. 2247–2250.

14. Wakita, Yumi, Jun Kawai *et. al.* (1997) Correct Parts Extraction from Speech Recognition Results Using Semantic Distance Calculation, and Its Application to Speech Translation. In *Proceedings of Spoken Language Translation*. Spain. pp. 24–31.

15. Wightman, C. W. and M. Ostendorf. (1994) Automatic Labelling of Prosodic Patterns. *IEEE Transactions on Speech and Audio Processing*, 2(4): 469–481.

16. Zechner, Klaus and Alex Waibel. (1998) Using Chunk Based Partial Parsing of Spontaneous Speech in Unrestricted Domains for Reducing Word Error Rate in Speech Recognition. In *Proceedings of COLING-ACL'98*, pp. 1453–1459.

17. Zhou, Yun. (2001) Analysis on Spoken Chinese Corpus and Segmentation of Chinese Utterances (*in Chinese*). *Thesis for Master Degree*. Institute of Automation, Chinese Academy of Sciences.

Using Natural Language Processing for Semantic Indexing of Scene-of-Crime Photographs

Horacio Saggion, Katerina Pastra, and Yorick Wilks

Department of Computer Science
University of Sheffield
England – UK
Tel: +44-114-222-1800
Fax: +44-114-222-1810
{saggion,katerina,yorick}@dcs.shef.ac.uk

Abstract. In this paper we present a new approach to the automatic semantic indexing of digital photographs based on the extraction of logic relations from their textual descriptions. The method is based on shallow parsing and propositional analysis of the descriptions using an ontology for the domain of application. We describe the semantic representation formalism, the ontology, and the algorithms involved in the automatic derivation of semantic indexes from texts linked to images. The method has been integrated into the Scene of the Crime Information System, a crime management system for storing, indexing and retrieval of crime information.

1   Introduction

The normal practice in human indexing or cataloguing of photographs is to use a text-based representation of the pictorial record by recourse to either a controlled vocabulary or to "free-text". On the one hand, an index using authoritative sources (e.g., thesauri) will ensure consistency across human indexers, but will make the indexing task difficult due to the size of the keyword list. On the other hand, the use of free-text association, while natural, makes the index representation subjective and error prone. Human indexing and cataloguing of pictorial records continues to be a task undertaken in major institutions (http://lcweb.loc.gov), but the recent development of huge image collections has given rise to content-based (or visually-based) methods in digital libraries in order to overcome the manual-annotation bottleneck [17]. Content-based indexing and retrieval of images is based on features such as colour, texture, and shape. Yet image understanding is not well advanced and is very difficult even in closed domains. Many research projects therefore have explored the use of collateral textual descriptions of the images for automatic tasks such as indexing [13], classifying [12], or understanding [15] of pictorial records.

In this paper we present a new method for deriving semantic relations for the purpose of indexing and retrieval of photographs used to document crime scenes. Crime investigation is a task that relies on both efficient multi-modal

A. Gelbukh (Ed.): CICLing 2003, LNCS 2588, pp. 526–536, 2003.
© Springer-Verlag Berlin Heidelberg 2003

documentation of crime scenes and effective retrieval of the information documented. The current practice in documenting a crime scene involves a Scene Of Crime Officer (SOCO) taking photographs or/and video recording the scene, gathering, packaging and labelling evidence, and then producing an official report of his/her actions. SOCOs create "photo-albums" which include an index page with a description of each photograph or set of photographs [9]. All this documentation procedure is done manually, which results in SOCOs devoting significant time and effort in producing handwritten reports and repeating large chunks of information again and again as they fill in various forms for the same case. On top of this, retrieving available information from past cases, and indicating possible similarities or "patterns" among cases, relies exclusively on the investigators' memory. Our method for semantic indexing of digital photographs using natural language processing techniques has been adopted in the Scene of the Crime Information System, a crime management prototype developed for the SOCIS Project, a 3-year EPSRC funded project undertaken by the University of Sheffield and the University of Surrey, in collaboration with an advisory board consisting of four U.K. police forces[1]. The project aims at the integration of various AI technologies that will change current practices in documenting crime scenes and retrieving case-related information. While research in information retrieval has shown that detailed linguistic analysis is usually unnecessary to improve accuracy for indexing and retrieval; in domains like scene of crime investigation where precision is of great importance, a detailed, semantic analysis of textual descriptions can provide the "pattern-based" search facility and precision required by the end users.

Unlike traditional "bag of words" approaches to photograph indexing, we make use of a meaning representation formalism based on semantic relations, where most of the complexity of the written text is eliminated while its meaning is retained in an elegant and simple way. The triples we extract are of the form: ARG1-RELATION-ARG2 and they are used as indexing terms for the crime scene visual records, where RELATION expresses the relation that stands between two objects, e.g., relative position of the evidence [8]. This is supported by a preliminary user-study on what and how information is conveyed in the image descriptions: an analysis of captions produced by eight SOCOs reveals that the information reported refers mainly to the identification of the object(s) and their relative location in the photo and their relations one with another.

For example, for an image description such as "Showing footwear impression in dust on table" our method generates the following semantic triples:

(1) `footwear impression - Made_Of - dust`

(2) `dust - On - table`

(3) `footwear impression - On - table`

---

[1] South Yorkshire Police, Surrey Police, Kent County Constabulary and Hampshire Constabulary form an advisory board for SOCIS

where On is a semantic relation between two physical objects denoting "where" the evidence was found, in this case the triple `footwear impression-On-table` was inferred from the other two logical relations.

The semantic triples, and their relationships, bear a loose relationship to the semantic templates used as the basis of text representation in [18], although in that earlier work, the RELATION would be instantiated by "action like" verbs and prepositions, whereas in the present work, the instantiated relations are "static" verbs and prepositions. The inference rules set out below are of the general type applied to such triple-representations in [19].

Our approach consists of the application of the following steps in sequence: (i) pre-processing (e.g., tokenisation, POS tagging, named entity recognition and classification, etc.); (ii) parsing and naive semantic interpretation; (iii) inference; (iv) triple extraction. In the rest of this paper, we concentrate on the description of the natural language processing mechanisms and resources involved in the derivation of the triples.

2   Automatic Analysis

Our analyser was developed using GATE components [2] enriched with full syntactic and semantic analysis implemented in Prolog and based on the LaSIE system [7]. The preprocessing consists of a simple tokeniser that identifies words and spaces, a sentence segmenter, a named entity recogniser specially developed for the SOC, a POS tagger, and a morphological analyser. The NE recogniser identifies all the types of named entities that may be mentioned in the captions such as: address, age, conveyance-make, date, drug, gun-type, identifier, location, measurement, money, offence , organisation, person, time. It is a rule-based module developed through intensive corpus analysis and the rules have been implemented in JAPE [2], a regular pattern matching formalism within GATE. Part of speech tagging is done with a transformation-based learning tagger [6]. We have tuned the default lexicon produced by the learning step with our own vocabulary. The lexicon of the domain was obtained from the corpus and appropriate part of speech tags were produced semi-automatically. In addition, the rule set was modified to account for incorrect cases (i.e, uppercase nominals are misinterpreted using the default set of rules). A rule-based lemmatiser is used to produce an affix and root for each noun and verb in the input text. The lemmatiser program is implemented as a set of regular expressions specified in lex and translated into C code.

2.1   Robust Parsing and Semantic Interpretation

We use an implementation of bottom-up chart parsing [4], enriched with semantic rules that construct a naive semantic representation for each sentence in first order logical form. The analysis may be partial if no tree spanning the whole sentence can be constructed. The parser takes as input a context-free phrasal grammar of English enriched with features and values used during syntactic checking and semantic interpretation. The grammar is enriched with a one-rule semantic grammar that is used to construct a semantic representation of the named entities (e.g., a domain specific grammar).

The parser is a particularly accurate in its treatment of noun phrases. The semantic rules produce unary predicates for entities and events (e.g., note(e2), ☐nd(e1), desk(e3)) and binary predicates for properties (e.g., on(e2,e3)). Constants (e.g., e1, e2, e3) are used to represent entity and event identifiers. Predicate names come from the morphological analysis of the tokens (e.g., ☐nd for the token "found"), syntactic logical relations (e.g., lsubj(X,Y) for the logical subject and lobj(X,Y) for logical object), and specific names used for domain modelling (e.g., address(e4), name(e4,☐255 Murder Street☐)for an expression like "255 Murder Street"). The semantic representation produced by the parser is not enough to produce the propositions we need for indexing. On the one hand, a normalisation process is needed to map equivalent constructions into the same standard representation (e.g., "body on ground" and "body lying on the ground" are indeed equivalent); On the other hand, a rule-based reasoning process is used to obtain relations missed during semantic interpretation.

2.2   Domain Modelling

In order to identify how conceptual information is expressed in SOC records, a collection of formal reports produced by SOCOs has been studied. The reports provide, among other things, information on the offence, the scene of the crime, the physical evidence, and the photographs taken to document the scene and its description.

We have collected a corpus consisting of official texts created by police officers and news texts. In particular, the official police data files consist of reports produced at the scene of the crime, photo-indexes, and witness statements written by SOCOs. The files have been collected through field work with police officers. Photo-indexes and SOCO reports contain all the information needed to index the scene of the crime.

Apart from our corpus we have made use of the Police Information Technology Organisation [16] (PITO) Common Data Model which contains words and phrases clustered semantically and hierarchically. We extracted from the model semantic categories of interest for crime investigation applications. This information is used for tuning the linguistic components in our system. We also used OntoCrime, a concept hierarchy whose top node is "entity", a number of object, event and property classes. The object hierarchy consists of a disjunction of classes that denote tangible and intangible objects. Currently, we have fourteen object classes; each with its own subclasses and sub-subclasses down the word level. The event hierarchy contains classes that denote a state or an action. At the moment, we have specified only "criminal events" and "police action" events. Last, the property hierarchy has a number of functional and relational properties/attributes that can be assigned to the object and event classes. Functional properties are single-value e.g 'age', whereas 'colour' is a relational property since an object may have more than one colour. The functional properties are further distinguished as mutable and immutable, according to whether the value of the property can change at some point in time, or it is fixed.

Associated with the ontology there is a dictionary used to map lexical items to their appropriate concept in the hierarchy. The ontology is available in two formats: XI format for linguistic processing and XML format for Query Expansion within the SOCIS prototype. An overview of the XML version of OntoCrime is presented in Figure 1.

```xml
<?xml version="1.0" encoding="UTF-8"?>
<!DOCTYPE Entities SYSTEM "Entities.dtd">
<Entities>
        <!-- 1 -->
        <Entity Name="object">
            <!-- 1.1 -->
            <Entity Name="artifact">
         <!-- 1.1.1 -->
                <Entity Name="conveyance">
....
 <!-- 1.5 -->
        <Entity Name="evidence">
     <Entity Name="impression evidence">
             <Entity Name="impression">
         <Entity Name="dental impression"></Entity>
         <Entity Name="footwear impression"></Entity>
             </Entity>
     <Entity Name="mark">
         <Entity Name="bite mark">
         <Synonym Name="bitemark"/>
         </Entity>
...
 <!-- 2.7 -->
        <Entity Name="semantic event">
                    <Entity Name="Above"></Entity>
            <Entity Name="And"></Entity>
```

Fig. 1. OntoCrime (XML) showing the 'evidence' and 'event' sub-hierarchies.

2.3   Implementation

We have adopted the XI Knowledge Representation Language [3] in order to implement the ontology and the reasoning processes. We have integrated XI into GATE by implementing a Java-Prolog interface. XI provides basic language constructs to specify hierarchical relations needed in OntoCrime. In XI, classes are represented as unary predicates and individuals as atoms. An attribute or property is a binary predicate, the first argument of which is the class/individual the attribute is assigned to and the second being the value of this attribute. The value can be a fixed term or a term that became instantiated in appropriate situations when new knowledge is deduced during reasoning. Below we show how a fragment of Ontocrime is coded in XI:

evidence(X) $\Longrightarrow$ impression_evidence(X) $\vee$ transfer_evidence(X)
transfer_evidence(X) $\Longrightarrow body\_intimate(X) \vee fibre(X)$
criminal_event(X) $\Longrightarrow$ assault(X) $\vee$ criminal_action_with_item(X)
$\vee$criminal_action_with_victim(X)...
assault(X) $\Longrightarrow$ beat(X) $\vee$ bite(X) $\vee$ burn(X) $\vee$ ...
criminal_action_with_victim(X) $\Longrightarrow$ murder(X)

Clauses $A \Longrightarrow B$ are used to specify 'inclusion' relations (all B is an A). Clauses $I \longleftarrow C$ are used to specify 'is a' relations between individuals and classes (I is a C). Operators $\vee$ and & indicate disjunction and conjunction respectively. Properties of individuals and classes are specified through the *props* predicate in the form:

```
props({Class|Individual},[Properties])
```

In addition to the declarative operators, a number of constructs can be used during deduction: $A \Rightarrow B$ is used to verify class inclusion (every B is a A), $A \leftarrow B$ is used to verify if A 'is a' B, and $hasprop(I, P)$ is used to verify if I 'has property' P (also, $nodeprop(I, P)$ can be used to verify properties but only at the instance level). Properties can be attached to individuals or classes conditionally on the actual state of the world. Conditional properties are specified with the "if" operator $(: -)$.

We map the naive semantic representation produced by the parser into the ontology using a dictionary and disambiguation rules. The mapping is robust in the sense that, if a semantic item cannot be mapped into the existing nodes in the ontology, then a new node will be created for it below the "object" or "event" nodes. Our semantic mapping mechanism relies on the use of specific *presupposition* properties that can be defined within the system. Presuppositions are used to complete the partial representation produced by the semantic rules; as an example the following presupposition rule states that in case a preposition "on" (in the semantic representation) is found attached to a "find" event, then a logical relation "On" should be created with the logical object of the "find" event as first argument, and the object of the prepositional phrase as second argument:

```
props(on,[(presupposition(on(Z,Y),['On'(R),argument1(R,X),
argument2(E,Y)]):- Z <- find_event(_),hasprop(Z,lobj(Z,X)))]).
```

This rule is checked whenever the system is trying to map the logical form on(Z,Y) into the ontology; the actual SOCIS extractor rules extract 17 different types of relational triples, some of which denote meta-information:

- ABOVE: e.g. "view of roof above seat..." = view ABOVE seat
- AND: the grouping relation. It is mainly used for inferring other relations that hold for all the entities linked with the AND relation. It covers cases of coordination and enumeration e.g. "bottles, gun and ashtray on...◻ = bottles AND gun, gun AND ashtray
- AROUND: e.g. "tie around right arm" = tie AROUND right arm
- BEHIND: e.g. "view of bottles behind the bar" = bottles BEHIND bar
- BETWEEN: e.g. "photograph of deceased between vehicle and garage wall" = deceased BETWEEN vehicle - garage wall
- DESTINATION: e.g. "view of Mansfield Road heading towards Wales Bar" = Mansfield Road DESTINATION Wales Bar
- IN: for the literal meaning of 'in' (inside) e.g. "blood drops inside the bathroom" = blood drops IN bathroom
- MADE-OF: e.g. "footwear impression in blood" = footwear impression MADE-OF blood
- META-POSITION: e.g. "shot of bar with tables in the foreground" = bar WITH tables, tables META-POSITION foreground
- NEAR: e.g. body NEAR table (denoted via 'near', 'adjacent' etc)
- OF: only for cases when a 'part-of relation' is denoted e.g. rear OF machine
- ON: e.g. "table showing bottles" = bottles ON table
- SOURCE: e.g. "rear garden from Lancing Street " = rear garden SOURCE Lancing Street
- SOURCE-BEHIND: it denotes the viewpoint from which the photograph was taken e.g. "shot of floor from behind the bar" = floor SOURCE-BEHIND bar
- UNDER: e.g. "chair leg found underneath table" = chair leg UNDER table
- WITH: e.g. "bag containing plant leaves" = bag WITH plant leaves
- WITHOUT: it captures negation/absence of something e.g. "table knife with no blood" = table knife WITHOUT blood

As can be seen in the above examples, relation extraction goes beyond the actual presence of prepositions in the captions. The arguments of these relational facts are not necessarily recorded in OntoCrime. Presuppositions rules have been implemented through corpus-based analysis of lexical items that can unambiguously be mapped into these relations.

2.4   Inference and Triples Extraction

After the "explicit" semantics is mapped into the ontology, the following procedure is applied: each semantic relation mapped onto the model is examined in the order it is asserted. For each semantic relation X-Rel-Y, the system checks whether X and Y occur as arguments in other relations and in that case rules that account for transitive and distributive properties of the semantic relations such as AND-distribution, WITH-transitivity, WITH-distribution, etc. are fired to produce new triples.

The WITH-distribution rule is stated as follows:

If X-With-Y & Y-REL-Z **Then** X-REL-Z

So a caption such as "Shows Vauxhall Cavalier X777HET together with pedal cycle in Accident Road" is represented with the triples:

(1) `Vauxhall Cavalier X777HET - With - pedal cycle`

(2) `pedal cycle - In - Accident Road`

(3) `Vauxhall Cavalier X777HET - In - Accident Road`

Our AND-distribution rule over "On" is stated with the following rule:

If X-And-Y & Y-On-Z **Then** X-On-Z

As another example of triple inference, consider the caption presented in section 1 "Showing footwear impression in dust on table": Two explicit relations were found during semantic mapping: "`footwear impression - Made Of - dust`" and "`dust - On - table`" one of our logical rules states the following:

If X-Made Of-Y & Y-On-Z **Then** X-On-Z

thus allowing the inference of the triple: "`footwear impression - On - table`". Rules have a number of exceptions that are used to block inference that would result in incoherent triples. At the end of the process the triples extractor is called to produce a semantic index. Note that the new triples asserted by deduction are not considered in the iterative process, and so the deductive procedure finishes.

The triples extractor produces two different indexes for the text: a "lexical" index, which is a list of all objects mentioned in the caption (i.e., members of the object sub-hierarchy); and a list of all inferred triples $<$ Argument_1, Relation, Argument_2 $>$, where *Relation* is the name of the relation and $Argument_i$ are its arguments. The arguments of the triples and the elements in the lexical index have the form *Class : Object*, where *Class* is the concept on the ontology the entity belongs to, and *Object* is a canonical representation of the object obtained from the morpho-syntactic analysis of the noun phrase or from the named entity identification module. The *Class* is used for ontological expansion during retrieval. The canonical representation of a common noun phrase is of the form $(Adj|Qual) * Head$, where $Head$ is the head of the noun phase and Adj and $Qual$ are adjectives and nominal qualifiers syntactically attached to the head. For example, the noun phrase "the left rear bedroom" is represented as premises : left rear bedroom and the named entity "23 Penistone Rd." is represented as address : 23 Penistone Rd.

3 A Retrieval Mechanism

Our retrieval mechanism is based on a preliminary observation of a user-study showing that, when looking for photographic evidence in past cases, the SOCOs will submit caption-like queries looking specifically for objects in specific relations to each other. Given a natural language user query, SOCIS extracts triples in the way described in the previous sections. For each triple $<$

Class_1:Arg_1, Relation, Class_2:Arg_2 > in the user query and < Class_3:Arg_3, Relation, Class_4:Arg_4 > in the index, a similarity score is computed. Two triples are considered similar in the following cases: (i) if $Arg\_1 = Arg\_3$ and $Arg\_2 = Arg\_4$ then score=1; (ii) if $Class\_1 = Class\_3$ and $Class\_2 = Class\_4$ then score=0.75; (iii) if $Arg\_1 = Arg\_3$ or $Arg\_2 = Arg\_4$ then score=0.5; (iv) if $Class\_1 = Class\_3$ or $Class\_2 = Class\_4$ then score=0.25; for each image the similarity scores are summed-up in order to obtain its final relevance measure. These weights implement a preference for identical triples without discarding "conceptually" close triples ("knife on table" and "blade on kitchen table" are considered similar but not identical). The images with relevance scores that are non null are presented in quantitative relevance order. When no triples can be extracted from the user query, a search for either the entities (score=1) or the class (score=0.5) they belong to is performed in the "lexical" index.

4   Related Work

The use of conceptual structures as a means to capture the essential content of a text has a long history in Artificial Intelligence [18,14,1] and debate continues on what the inventory of semantic primitives used to capture meaning should be [20]. For SOCIS, we have attempted a pragmatic, corpus-based approach, where the set of primitives emerge from the data. Extraction of relations has been attempted in the MINDNET project [10] in order to construct a lexical knowledge base containing meaningful relations (e.g., wheel-Part-Car) going beyond simple co-occurrence statistics. Some of the relations covered by MINDNET are indeed present in OntoCrime but most of them have not been observed in our corpus. MARIE [5] uses a domain lexicon and a type hierarchy to represent both queries and captions in a logical form and then matches these representations instead of mere keywords; the logical forms are case grammar constructs structured in a slot-assertion notation. Our approach is similar in the use of an ontology for the domain and in the fact that transformations are applied to the "superficial" forms produced by the parser to obtain a semantic representation, but we differ in that our method does not extract full logical forms from the semantic representation, but a finite set of possible relations. In PICTION [15], a NLP module is used to obtain semantic constraints on the entities mentioned in the caption (usually persons) using rules attached to lexical items providing spatial constraints (e.g., "left", "above", etc.), locative constraints (e.g., "between") or contextual constraints (e.g, syntactic relations). The semantic constraints are mainly used to guide an image understanding system in locating people in newspaper photographs, while in SOCIS we use the representation for semantic indexing and posterior search. The ANVIL system [11] parses captions in order to extract dependency relations (e.g., head-modifier) that are recursively compared with dependency relations produced from user queries. Unlike SOCIS, in ANVIL no logical form is produced nor any inference to enrich the indexes.

5   Conclusions and Future Work

We have developed a new approach to photo indexing based on the extraction of relational triples from their captions. The triples are a means to capture the meaning of captions (the objects and their relations) in an elegant and simple way. The formalism and the algorithm for semantic analysis have been developed through corpus analysis, the implementation relies on existing components adapted for the purpose of the SOCIS system. The method is now undergoing formal testing using a new set of captions from police sources.

Our indexing mechanism based on the extraction of semantic triples was successfully integrated into the SOCIS prototype and is undergoing intensive testing by professional users, and we are now implementing the retrieval mechanism. But, the current interface allows the user to browse the indexes to search for photographic evidence and to use the ontology for query expansion.

Acknowledgements. We are grateful to the Surrey-SOCIS research team: Khurshid Ahmad, Bodgan Vrusias, Mariam Tariq, and Chris Handy. We would like to thank Andrew Hawley from South Yorkshire Police, for helping us to understand Scene of Crime procedures and for allowing us access to SOC documentation. This Research is being funded by EPSRC grant RA002260.

References

1. R. Alterman. A Dictionary Based on Concept Coherence. *Artificial Intelligence*, 25:153–186, 1985.
2. H. Cunningham, D. Maynard, K. Bontcheva, and V. Tablan. GATE: A framework and graphical development environment for robust NLP tools and applications. In *Proceedings of the 40th Anniversary Meeting of the Association for Computational Linguistics*, 2002.
3. R. Gaizauskas and K. Humphreys. XI: A Simple Prolog-based Language for Cross-Classification and Inhetotance. In *Proceedings of the 7th International Conference in Artificial Intelligence: Methodology, Systems, Applications*, pages 86–95, Sozopol, Bulgaria, 1996.
4. G. Gazdar and C. Mellish. *Natural Language Processing in Prolog*. Addison-Wesley, Reading, MA, 1989.
5. E. Guglielmo and N. Rowe. Natural language retrieval of images based on descriptive captions. *ACM Transactions on Information Systems*, 14(3):237–267, 1996.
6. M. Hepple. Independence and commitment: Assumptions for rapid training and execution of rule-based POS taggers. In *Proceedings of the 38th Annual Meeting of the Association for Computational Linguistics (ACL-2000)*, Hong Kong, October 2000.
7. K. Humphreys, R. Gaizauskas, and H. Cunningham. LaSIE Technical Specifications. Technical report, Department of Computer Science, University of Sheffield, 2000.
8. R. May. *Criminal Evidence*. Sweet and Maxwell Pbl., 1999.
9. K. Pastra, H. Saggion, and Y. Wilks. Socis: Scene of crime information system. Technical Report CS-01-19, University of Sheffield, 2001.

10. S. Richardson, W. Dollan, and L. Vanderwende. Mindnet: acquiring and structur-
    ing semantic information from text. In *Proceedings of COLING*, 1998.
11. T. Rose, D. Elworthy, A. Kotcheff, and A. Clare. ANVIL: a System for Retrieval
    of Captioned Images using NLP Techniques. In *Proceedings of Challenge of Image
    Retrieval*, Brighton, UK, 2000.
12. C. Sable and V. Hatzivassiloglou. Text-based approaches for the categorization of
    images. In *Proceedings of ECDL*, 1999.
13. H. Saggion, H. Cunningham, K. Bontcheva, D. Maynard, C. Ursu, O. Hamza,
    and Y. Wilks. Access to Multimedia Information through Multisource and Mul-
    tilanguage Information Extraction. In *7th Workshop on Applications of Natural
    Language to Information Systems (NLDB 2002)*, Stockholm, Sweden, 2002.
14. R. Schank and R. Abelson. *Scripts, Plans, Goals and Understanding.* Lawrence
    Erlbaum Associates, Publishers, 1977.
15. R.K. Srihari. Automatic Indexing and Content-Based Retrieval of Captioned Im-
    ages. *Computer*, 28(9):49–56, September 1995.
16. Police Information Technology Organisation Data Standards Team. Common data
    model v8.1. CD Version 1.1 - PITO, 1999.
17. R. Veltkamp and M. Tanase. Content-based image retrieval systems: a survey.
    Technical Report UU-CS-2000-34, Utrecht University, 2000.
18. Y. Wilks. A Preferential, Pattern-Seeking, Semantics for Natural Language Infer-
    ence. *Artificial Intelligence*, 6:53–74, 1975.
19. Y. Wilks. Making Preferences More Active . *Artificial Intelligence*, 11:197–223,
    1978.
20. Y. Wilks, L. Guthrie, and B. Slator. *Electric Words.* The MIT Press, Cambridge,
    MA, 1996.

Natural Language in Information Retrieval

Elżbieta Dura

Lexware Labs, Göteborg, Sweden
elzbieta@lexwarelabs.com

Abstract. It seems the time is ripe for the two to meet: NLP has grown out of prototypes and IR is having hard time trying to improve precision. Two examples of possible approaches are considered below. Lexware is a lexicon-based system for text analysis of Swedish applied in an information retrieval task. NLIR is an information retrieval system using intensive natural language processing to provide index terms on a higher level of abstraction than stems.

1 Not Much Natural Language in Information Retrieval So Far

Problems of finding the right data in a big data collection had been addressed long before NLP and are still addressed without NLP. The two fields hardly meet: "There is (...) an inherent granularity mismatch between the statistical techniques used in information retrieval and the linguistic techniques used in natural language processing." [8]. The results obtained in attempts of using NLP in information retrieval were so poor that the title of an article describing yet another test in 2000 is meant to surprise: "Linguistic Knowledge Can Improve Information Retrieval" [1]. The tenet of SMART seems to be still generally valid in IR: "good information retrieval techniques are more powerful than linguistic knowledge" [2].

When NLP-track was introduced in TREC in the nineties, several experiments proved that language resources can actually help. The gain in recall and precision is not negligible even if far from a dramatic breakthrough. For instance, adding simple collocations to the list of available terms could improve precision by 10%. [2] More advanced NLP techniques remain too expensive for large-scale applications: "the use of full-scale syntactic analysis is severely pushing the limits of practicality of an information retrieval system because of the increased demand for computing power and storage." [6].

2 NLIR – A Natural Language Information Retrieval

NLIR and Lexware are examples of projects which pursue improvement in IR by incorporation of NLP, each in a different way. The conviction behind the Natural Language Information Retrieval system – NLIR, is that "robust NLP techniques can help to derive better representation of text documents for indexing and search purposes than any simple word and string-based methods commonly used in statistical

A. Gelbukh (Ed.): CICLing 2003, LNCS 2588, pp. 537–540, 2003.

full-text retrieval." [6] The system is organized into a "stream model". Each stream provides an index representing a document in one special aspect. Various streams have been tried and reported in TREC, from 1995 on. Streams are obtained from different NLP methods which are run in parallel on a document. Contribution of each stream is optimised during merging the results of all streams.

All kinds of NLP methods are tested in NLIR. In TREC-5 a Head-Modifier Pairs Stream involves truly intensive natural language processing: part of speech tagging, stemming supported with a dictionary, sentence analysis with Tagged Text Parser, extraction of head-modifier pairs from the parse trees, corpus-based disambiguation of long noun phrases. Abstract index terms are obtained from the stream, in which paraphrases like *information retrieval, retrieval of information, retrieve more information,* etc can be linked together. In TREC-7 the streams are yet more sophisticated, e.g. a functional dependency grammar parser is used, which allows linking yet more paraphrases, e.g. *flowers grow wild* and *wild flowers.* The conclusions are positive but cautious: "(…) it became clear that exploiting the full potential of linguistic processing is harder than originally anticipated." [7] The results prove also that it is actually not worth the effort because the complex streams turn out to be the less effective than a simple Stems Stream, i.e. content words.

The approach of NLIR is a traditional statistical IR backbone with NLP support in recognition of various text items, which in turn is supposed to provide index terms on a higher level of abstraction than stems. The approach of Lexware is almost opposite: an NLP backbone plus support from statistics in assigning weights to abstract index terms. These are constituted primarily by lexemes.

3   Rich Resources and Shallow Analysis in Lexware

Lexicon and the concept of lexeme are central in Lexware approach. This means that word forms are associated with content from the beginning, which in its turn opens up for adding content information dependent on a specific task. In the information retrieval task described below Lexware performance is boosted by integration of its lexicon with a thesaurus specifically developed for the domain of the documents to be retrieved.

Text-analysis is shallow and it is not demanding in terms of computing power and storage. [3] The strength of the system is its rich lexicon and the possibility to expand the lexicon with external information without negative impact on access times. [4] Lexware has about 80 000 lexical items represented with features and relations of their forms and senses. Complex items are represented in terms of components. Kernel vocabulary items are separated, which is important when weights are calculated - occurrences of kernel items are less relevant than occurrences of more specific items.

4 Lexware Applied in Indexing of Swedish Parliamentary Debates

"Djupindexering" is the Swedish name of an application which assigns keywords to documents of Swedish parliamentary debates. Keywords are chosen from a thesaurus of about 4000 terms specially created for parliamentary debates. Each document is assigned from 2 to 10 keywords that best represent its content. The indexing is performed manually at the moment. The task for automatic indexing is the same as for human indexer: choose such terms for keywords that not only are representative of the subject of the document but also have proper level of specificity. For instance, when a document takes up university education the term *university education* and not *education* should be picked from the thesaurus.

The task is performed by Lexware as follows. In the preprocessing phase lexemes are identified in thesaurus terms. A document is analyzed in order to establish its index terms. Both thesaurus terms and lexemes are identified in text occurrences. Independent occurrences of components of complex thesaurus terms are also recorded if semantically heavy. Relevance weights of index terms in a document can be very precisely calculated thanks to the possibility of taking into consideration thesaurus relations. For instance, if a term occurs in a document together with its parent term or with majority of its children its weight can be increased.

Lexware does not use parallel sources like in NLIR but it operates on index terms of high level of abstraction from the beginning. When relevance of an index term of a document is to be decided Lexware can invoke all information present in its lexicon besides corpus statistics.

5 Evaluation

The Swedish parliament library – Riksdagsbiblioteket, designed and conducted tests of software in order to determine whether manual indexing of the parliament documents could be supplemented or even substituted by automatic indexing. Software from Connexor, Lingsoft, Kungliga Tekniska Högskola and LexWare Labs participated in the tests. The evaluation was based on a comparison of keywords assigned manually and automatically by the tested programs. The overlap in keywords assigned manually by two different indexers was only 34%, which is not astonishing given a high detail level of the thesaurus. Lexware proved to obtain the best F-value (2*precision*recall) / (precision + recall)): 36%, Kungliga Tekniska Högskola 32%, Connexor 22%, Lingsoft 19%.

Recent tests of the fully developed Lexware application for indexing of parliament documents proves to have surprisingly high coverage with full precision. Lexware automatic indexing was compared with manual indexing for 1400 documents from Riksdagsbiblioteket. 64.61% of keywords from Lexware are the same as those assigned manually, 22.99% are closely related in the thesaurus to those assigned manually. Thus 87.60% of keywords selected from the thesaurus are relevant. 9.84% of Lexware keywords not found among manually provided keywords are significant proper names. Only 2.56% of keywords are really different from the ones chosen in manual indexing. These require manual inspection in order to determine whether they are different but relevant or different and irrelevant.

6   Conclusions

Natural language processing may not be of assistance in all information retrieval applications but there are clear cases in which it leads to better results. For instance, NLIR tests show that query building clearly gains from NLP. Lexware indexing system based on a thesaurus performs very well: it is both fast and precise. Considering the fine results of Lexware Djupindexering it seems that the limitation to a specific language is not a major drawback.

The reluctance of IR people is not astonishing at all. They equate NLP with costly syntactic analysis which helps them very little if at all. Language resources rather than NLP techniques proved so far to have some impact on effectiveness in document retrieval. The Meaning-Text Theory advocating enormous size lexicons and multitude of paraphrasing rules in a description of any natural language may be the proper inspiration for natural language processing in information retrieval tasks. Now that language resources are built for many languages, it is not necessary that information retrieval should be limited to methods which do not involve comprehensive knowledge of a specific language. As a matter of fact, it is hard to see how precision can be hoped to improve otherwise.

References

1. Bookman, L.A., Green, S., Houston, A., Kuhns, R.J., Martin, P. and Woods, W.A. 2000. http://research.sun.com/techrep/1999/abstract-83.html Linguistic Knowledge can Improve Information Retrieval. Proceedings of ANLP-2000, Seattle, WA, May 1–3, 2000.
2. Buckley, C., Singhal, M., Mitra, M. 1997. Using Query Zoning and Correlation within SMART: TREC-5 Report. Online at: http://trec.nist.gov/pubs/trec5/t5_proceedings.html
3. Dura, E. 1998. Parsing Words. Data linguistica 19. Göteborg: Göteborgs universitet.
4. Dura, E. 2000. Lexicon-based Information Extraction with Lexware. In: PALC99 Proceedings.
5. Strzalkowski, T., Lin, F. J. Wang, J., Guthrie, L., Leistensnider, J. Wilding, J., Karlgren, J., Straszheim, T., Perez-Carballo, J. 1997 Natural Language Information Retrieval: TREC-5 Report. Online at: http://trec.nist.gov/pubs/trec5/t5_proceedings.html
6. Strzalkowski, T., Stein, G., Bowden Wise, G., Perez-Carballo, J., Tapanainen, P., Jarvinen, T., Voutilainen, A., Karlgren, J.1999. Natural Language Information Retrieval: TREC-7 Report. Online at: http://trec.nist.gov/pubs/trec7/t7_proceedings.html
7. Strzalkowski, T., Perez-Carballo, J., Karlgren, J., Hulth, A., Tapanainen, P., T. Lahtinen, T. 2000. Natural Language Information Retrieval: TREC-8 Report. Online at: http://trec.nist.gov/pubs/trec8/t8_proceedings.html
8. Survey of the State of the Art in Human Language Technology. 1996. Cole, R.A, Mariani J., Uszkoreit, H., Zaenen, A., Zue, V. (eds.). Online at: http://cslu.cse.ogi.edu/HLTsurvey/ch7node4.html

Natural Language System for Terminological Information Retrieval

Gerardo Sierra[1] and John McNaught[2]

[1] Engineering Institute, UNAM, Ciudad Universitaria, Apdo. Postal 70-472,
Mexico 04510, D.F., Mexico.
gsm@pumas.iingen.unam.mx
[2] Department of Computation, UMIST, PO Box 88, Manchester M60 1QD, UK.
John.McNaught@umist.ac.uk

Abstract. The purpose of any information retrieval (IR) system in response to a query is to provide the user with the data that satisfy his information need. In order to design a user friendly onomasiological system (one to find a word from a description of a concept), we firstly must consider the searching process, i.e. query and matching. This paper is organised in two broad parts. The first part situates the general methodology for IR in relation to the particular problem of onomasiological searching. The second part discusses an experiment in onomasiological searching carried out on dictionaries to validate design principles for an onomasiological search system.

1   Introduction

Users often need dictionaries to look for a word that has escaped their memory although they remember and can describe the concept [1], [2]. Any dictionary used in this way, where lookup is not by the headword but by concept, is an onomasiological dictionary [3]. Such a dictionary can be considered an information retrieval system, as it provides the user with the data that satisfy his information need.

Calzolari [4] suggests the use of dictionaries as full-text databases for practical terminological searching. In full-text databases, attributes used to identify a set of terminological data include the headword of a dictionary entry, meanings or definitions, as well as examples, etymological and encyclopaedic information. Today, most dictionaries available on CD-ROM allow the user some kind of onomasiological search, using standard IR techniques, however these do not lead to good results especially for technical and scientific terms. We thus investigate a novel method for overcoming the main problems facing onomasiological search for term forms: how to match up a user description of a concept with relevant term forms, and how to narrow the search towards the term form required (as opposed to returning a large set of potentially relevant term forms as found by a traditional IR approach). This method involves constructing semantic paradigms by processing pairs of definitions for the same senses taken from different dictionaries, and is found to have advantages over standard IR approaches such as simple query expansion or reference to a thesaurus.

A. Gelbukh (Ed.): CICLing 2003, LNCS 2588, pp. 541–552, 2003.

2   Main Issues of IR

2.1   Database Structure

Records in full-text databases contain unprocessed text that, in basic search mode, is processed to find any clue words of the query. However, these may not be present: the concept the user has in mind may be there, but differently characterised. Thus, significant material may be missed.

An efficient way to increase the search speed for a particular piece of data is to construct an inverted index: only a search of the index is required to identify the data that satisfy the query. A further increase in search efficiency may be gained by using an index of indexes, hierarchically co-ordinated, resulting in various databases, each with its own index. For example, in an inverted file scheme for onomasiological search, each dictionary entry might be represented by a collection of index paradigms (first, inner index), and similarly the paradigms may be assigned to one or more keywords (second, outer index). When the user inputs the description of a concept, the system matches it in the database of indexed keywords in order to differentiate, among words entered by the user, relevant words from non-relevant or functional words. After the relevant words of the concept are identified as keywords, the system identifies the paradigms that match with those keywords, then from the paradigms can index into the entries themselves. Each entry will be typically indexed by one or more paradigms.

2.2   Searching

The use of natural-language queries has been developed in IR systems in order to give greater flexibility in searching to the user. Natural language searching seems more "natural", since the user can input without syntax restrictions, sentences, paragraphs, phrases, a set of keywords, or a combination of the above.

A natural language system does not necessarily "understand" the user's input, since it may, for example, just extract those words which are not in a stop list and connect them by the usual Boolean operators. However, the Boolean *NOT* has a different interpretation in natural language searching. For example, the input "not rain" means the lack of rain, while the Boolean *NOT* yields wrongly the value 1 when there is not the term "rain". The success of natural language retrieval relies on the automatic manipulation of the keywords, and on the online expansion of queries, together with ranking and matching processes, all further discussed below.

2.3   Expanded Searching

A successful onomasiological search relies upon the clue words used in the query to describe the concept that the user is looking for. Since the user often does not employ precisely the same terminology as the indexed keywords or stored full-text database, the retrieved words may be far from the concept desired. As a result, it has been found advantageous to expand the original query with closely related keywords [5].

Formalising a concept with the exact clue words is sometimes a heavy task for the user, but searching can become harder if the user has also to identify clusters of related keywords, particularly when the query is expressed in natural language. The systematisation of this task has been hence placed on the system. Moreover, clusters can be provided in the search session in order to allow the user to select the best ones, or alternatively they can be automatically used by the system.

There are two main techniques used by IR systems to expand the original query and improve retrieval effectiveness. The best known approach is to assign all related morphological variants or inflected forms to the same word. Thus, every keyword is automatically reduced to a *stem* or *lemma*. For inverted files, this technique allows compression of the database file and expansion of the initial query keywords. As a result of stemming the words of the query, the original keywords are mapped to the file of index stems, and the system will retrieve the items corresponding to the stem. In addition to the user's own knowledge of expressing the same concept in alternative ways, a relational thesaurus brings related words together and thereby helps to stimulate his memory. In order to help the user focus on the search, it is appropriate that the system produces and manages semantic paradigms transparently, without any intervention by the user.

Therefore, the success of an onomasiological dictionary relies on the accurate identification of the semantic paradigms. To achieve this, we adopted an algorithm designed to construct semantic paradigms by aligning definitions from two general dictionaries [6]. The method relies on the assumption that two lexicographers use different words to describe the same concept. The alignment matches the words of two definitions and shows the correspondence between words that can replace each other in a definition without producing any major change in meaning. The difference in words used between two or more definitions enables paradigms to be inferred by merging the dictionary definitions into a single database and then using the alignment technique.

2.4   Ranking

The performance of an IR system is often evaluated on a comparison between the number of retrieved or unretrieved items, and the number of relevant or non-relevant items. This evaluation fails to take into account two observations. First, the amount of retrieved material is usually large, and second, simple systems retrieve either an unordered set that is presented randomly to the user, or in the best case in simple alphabetical order. Cooper [7] introduced the concept of *ranking* to evaluate the efficiency of IR systems. Today, ordering according to relevance is seen as essential, particularly when the user expects few hits, as in the case of onomasiological searching. Ranking is used here to mean the capability of the system to discard irrelevant words for relevant ones and present sequentially these relevant ones in order of importance. In the best case, the system should present just one word, the one expected by the user.

2.5   Scoring

Scoring is the relevance value given to each retrieved item after the ranking algorithm is applied. It gives positive numbers so that ranks with numerically higher scores are retrieved in preference to those with lower scores. After ranking, the outcome is a retrieved list of items ranked according to their designated scores, with those likeliest to be relevant to the search query being shown at the top of the list. It could be displayed in a continuous list, with limited size, or a set of short lists by levels up to N scores. In the latter case, a level can represent just one term. When there is a bag of retrieved items, all with the same weight, the most accessible way to present them is sorted alphabetically.

Table 1. Hypothetical queries

Keywords	Query	Keywords	Query
3	device for measuring atmosphere	6	meteorological device for measuring atmospheric pressure and predicting
4	device for measuring atmospheric pressure	7	meteorological device for measuring atmospheric pressure and predicting changes
5	meteorological device for measuring atmospheric pressure	8	meteorological device for measuring atmospheric pressure and predicting changes in weather

3   Experiments

The preceding sections have described the bases for information retrieval in general, and some topics in particular for an onomasiological search. We now discuss some principles to be applied later in the design of the search system. According to Wilks *et al* [8], an onomasiological search may be carried out on a dictionary, as a full-text database, through a Boolean combination of keywords. This assumption allows us to avoid the construction of an inverted file, which requires us to determine the keywords associated with each concept. We assume a need for finding a combination of unweighted keywords wherever they occur within the definitions of dictionary entries that will lead us to our target word. The word we are looking for, let us further assume, is "barometer".

Two general language dictionaries were used, both available in machine-readable form: the Collins English Dictionary [9] and the Oxford English Dictionary on CD-ROM [10].

3.1   Query

Although the user may enter any kind of query, we assume here a natural language query describing the concept, rather than an enumeration of related words, in order to allow logical discussion.

Table 2. Intuitive paradigms

meteorological	device	measuring	Atmospheric
meteorol	device*	measur*	*atmosphere*
aerolog	instrument*	determin*	Air
climatol	*meter	indicat*	Gas
weather	apparatus	*record*	Gases
	machine*	*show*	
	tool	test	
	implement	testing	
	utensil*	weigh*	
		estimat	
		graduat	
		gauge	
		assess	
		scale	

pressure	predicting	changes	Weather
pressur	*predict*	*chang*	*weather*
Weight	*forecast*	*variation*	*climate*
force	*foresee*	*vary*	*air
	estimat	*varie*	
	foresight	*alteration*	
	*predetermin	*deviation*	
		difference	
		move*	

3.1.1   Hypothetical Queries

Five queries were constructed, representing increasingly specific concepts (three to eight keywords: Table 1). Terminologically speaking, the five-keyword query often contains the necessary and sufficient elements to represent a concept [11]. Conversely, queries with fewer keywords tend to be incomplete descriptions, while more keywords give insignificant properties of the concept. Our experiment shows output behaviour in relation to an increase in the number of keywords.

3.1.2   Paradigms

Each clue word of the query is replaced by a cluster composed of all the members of the paradigms wherever the clue word appears. These members are then used as keywords to search in the definitions. The keywords for the eight paradigms (table 2) were determined with the aid of a thesaurus and selected by intuition (i.e., common sense and knowledge of English) to assess the results. Similarly, the lemmatisation of keywords was carried out manually in an indicative manner.

The keywords "weather" and "estimate" belong to two paradigms. Most of the clue words would appear in several paradigms. Every member of a paradigm has a weight equal to one, independent of the query. For example, for the query "measuring instrument", "instrument" belongs to N paradigms; in each of these, "instrument" will have the same weight as the other keywords in that paradigm, such as "tool" or "utensil." A query is expressed by the knowledge the user has about a concept, while definitions contain lexicographic knowledge. Comparison of definitions from different sources shows they use different words. Compare these definitions for "alkalimeter":

> *An apparatus for determining the concentration of alkalis in solution (CED)*
> *An instrument for ascertaining the amount of alkali in a solution (OED2)*

Because of this likely difference in terminology, the use of a paradigm is essential to achieve good retrieval. In order to avoid high recall and increase precision, the construction of paradigm members must be carried out with care.

3.2   Searching

Because of the extension of the original query to a large set of keywords with the paradigms, an automatic Boolean combination of keywords and paradigms is applied. Since the Boolean *AND* combines the items containing all the keywords, the result is *concentrated*. Conversely, the result is *extended* when the Boolean *OR* selects those items containing any of the keywords.

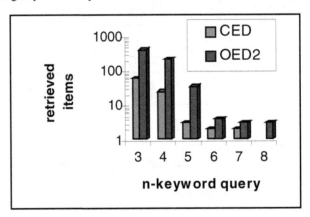

Fig. 1. Retrieved items in a concentrated search

3.2.1   Concentrated Search

According to [5], concentrated search is the most typically adopted Boolean search. Words occurring within the same paradigm are automatically combined by the logical connective *OR* while those appearing in separate paradigms are combined by the operator *AND*. Therefore, an entry should only be retrieved if its definition contains at least one word from each of the paradigms. Concentrated search automatically ranks the output according to the number of keywords in the query. The more keywords a query contains, the smaller the number of possible results that will be retrieved (see fig. 1).

OED2 yields results for all our queries, but the target word is successfully retrieved with queries up to five keywords. Conversely, CED does not yield any word with an eight-keyword query, but any other query retrieves the target word.

3.2.2 Extended Search
In extended search, an entry is retrieved if its definition contains at least one word from any paradigm. Both words occurring within the same paradigm and those appearing in separate paradigms are automatically combined by the logical connective *OR*. At the paradigmatic level, the Boolean operator is strictly used, i.e., the score is 1 if any member of the paradigm matches, and 0 if no members of the paradigm match. At the syntagmatic level, a sum of paradigmatic scores is applied. The final score for the retrieved entries ranges from 1 to N, where N is the number of paradigms related to the query. Unlike concentrated search, extended search will yield a larger output if the number of paradigms increases in a query. Furthermore, the output will increase substantially if either a keyword appears in different paradigms or the size of the paradigm is bigger (fig. 2 for CED).

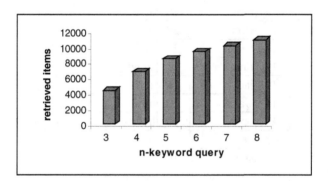

Fig. 2. Retrieved items in an extended search in CED

3.2.3   Remarks on Searching
Neither concentrated nor extended search are efficient by themselves. Concentrated search homes in on the target word by adding clue words, but just up to a certain level because after this the retrieval is unsuccessful. Conversely, the list of words increases directly in relation to the clue words in extended search. Therefore, ranking of the list is essential.

3.3   Ranking

The retrieved results appear in alphabetical order. Concentrated search retrieves items that contain just N paradigms, so that it is possible to rank by keywords. Extended search retrieves any of N paradigms, so that ranking by the number of paradigms is essential. Since both searches are applied to the whole entry, without differentiation among senses, we can apply proximity matching as a filter for ranking.

Table 3. Top words ranked by keywords

Rank	any keyword		different keywords	
	word	score	word	score
1	air	437	air	20
2	pressure	197	pressure	19
3	wind	84	gauge, gage	17
4	gauge, gage	79	wind	16
5	electric	36	centre, center	14
6	stand	31	electric	14
7	iso-	26	sea	14
8	give	26	stand	14
9	turn	24	give	13
10	storm	24	heat	13
11	beat	24	rain	13
12	rain	22	snow	13
13	jack	21	sun	13
14	wave	20	turn	13
15	open	20	hydro-	12
16	heat	20	iso-	12
17	sun	19	wave	12
18	barometer	19	barometer	11

3.3.1   Ranking by Keywords

Since concentrated search groups items, given a specific number n of paradigms, it may be useful to rank by keywords when the number of retrieved words is large. Take the following sense for "gauge" as an example:

"(of a *pressure measur*ement) *measur*ed on a *pressure gauge* that registers zero at *atmospher*ic *pressure*; above or below *atmospher*ic *pressur*e: 5 bar *gauge.*"

It is possible to count: The total keywords (italicised here) appearing in a definition = 10 items. The total of different keywords disregarding the paradigm = 4 items. When a keyword belongs to different paradigms, it will be counted as many times as it occurs in the paradigms. For example, since "weather" appears in two paradigms (meteorological and weather, see table 2), the definition "able to *chang*e or be *changed*; fickle: *change*able *weather*" counts 3 items = 2 for weather + 1 for change (from the changes paradigm of table 2).

Table 3 shows a comparison of the top items retrieved before the target word is itself found, and ranked by the above two criteria, for a five-keyword query in OED2.

The high score for top words ranked by the total of keywords gives a clue to the multiple senses for those entries in OED2. The difference between both criteria is trivial in relation to the position for almost all the words. There are 35 retrieved entries and the target word appears in position 18 after both ranking criteria are applied. Thus, we conclude that the result is not satisfactory.

3.3.2   Ranking by Paradigms

Ranking by paradigms is applied in extended search, in a similar way to the quorum function [12]. Given a query associated with N paradigms, a word has a hit for each paradigm occurring in the entry and a score equal to the sum of the hits. Finally, the output ranks scores in decreasing order. The first level corresponds to the highest score, which could be•N. The second level corresponds to the next lower score and in this way consecutively up to the lowest level which corresponds to a score of one. For an eight-keyword query, the number of results at each level decreases exponentially in relation to the upper level (fig. 3). The lowest level corresponds to the retrieved items which contain only one paradigm, and it is too high. Conversely, for the top level, the definitions which contain the N paradigms number just a few.

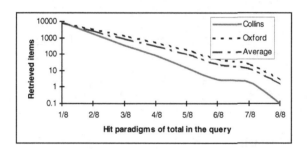

Fig. 3. Retrieved items ranked by paradigms for an eight-keyword query

A comparison of the top levels among OED2 and CED for extended search ranked by paradigms appears in table 4. The words that appear in the table correspond to the headwords in each dictionary. Each level, separated by horizontal lines, consists of a set of words with a common score, and the level with the highest score is presented first, so that this is the first level ranking by paradigms in decreasing score order. The list of words within each level is presented in alphabetical order.

The top level by this criterion corresponds to the top level of the concentrated search. In the first level, CED presents the target word beside another word related to the query with a score of seven, corresponding to the concentrated search for a seven-keyword query. Levels below the top one do not correspond exactly, because a concentrated search looks for N-1 specific paradigms, while by this criterion we look for any N-1 paradigms.

Table 4. Top words ranked by keywords

OED2		CED	
Word	**score**	**Word**	**Score**
Give	8	barometer	7
Open	8	gauge	7
Storm	8	break	6
Air	7	clear	6
Balance	7	uncertain	6
Barometer	7	aneroid barometer	5
Beat	7	drag	5
Break	7	float	5
center, center	7	fly	5
drop-	7	lift	5
fall	7	line	5
Gauge, gage	7	record	5
...		show	5
Stand	7	statoscope	5
Stress	7	storm	5
Summer	7	tumbler	5
Sun	7	weatherglass	5
thunder	7	whip	5
Weather	7	wind	5
wind	7	windage	5

3.3.3   Proximity Match

Since each entry has one or more senses, there are two ways to retrieve entries when searching for words in definitions. The first is to search for the word in all senses of the entry, while the other is to look just for words for every sense. The proximity criterion is applied for search by senses, rather than the distance between words, because of the likely diversity of queries. In fact, the user may not enter a definition of a concept, but a sentence with several non-relevant words among other relevant ones. Retrieval effectiveness improves substantially with an extended search by senses. In table 5, the first level corresponds only to the target word, while the second level presents words closely related to the query. The scoring difference between first and second level is seven to five, i.e., two paradigms. This means the degree of confidence is higher when the target word is the word appearing at the first level.

3.3.4   Remarks on Ranking

Two ranking criteria by keywords have been considered, but neither improves the concentrated search. Conversely, ranking by paradigms substantially improves the extended search, and this criterion is refined when proximity match is applied. Although proximity match improves retrieval, a user can input two or more senses, thinking that in this way he gives a better idea of the word he is looking for.

Table 5. Top words ranked by proximity matching in OED2 and CED

OED2		CED	
word	score	word	score
barometer	7	barometer	7
anemoscope	5	aneroid barometer	5
baby-house	5	barogram	5
baroscope	5	show	5
hydrometer	5	statoscope	5
pressure	5		
statoscope	5		
weather-glass	5		

4   Conclusion

In this paper, the description of the methodology for terminological IR has been covered, followed by a discussion of a design for an onomasiological search system. Whatever the type of database structure used in the design, it is clear that it is necessary to expand the query by reference to paradigms, both morphological and semantic. An experiment was conducted on dictionary definitions as a full text database, using some intuitive paradigms. We observed that general language dictionaries provide enough information for onomasiological search. In the case of such a concept-oriented search, it is not easy to assign weights to keywords or paradigms, because this means the user should choose them, while the fact remains that the user can choose keywords with low weight and then retrieve irrelevant terms. Our experiment demonstrated how the use of unweighted keywords and paradigms yields successful retrieval, thus we have firm evidence allowing us to reject any kind of weighting. It should be emphasised that the user query is expressed in natural language. Then the search procedure will analyse the words introduced by the user, identify their paradigms, connect them with Boolean operators, search (extended search and search by senses) either in the indexed or full text database, rank the retrieved words and finally provide to the user an ordered list of words representing potentially relevant concepts.

References

1. McArthur, T.: Living Words: Language, Lexicography and the Knowledge Revolution. University of Exeter Press, Exeter (1999)
2. Riggs, F.W.: Terminology and Lexicography: Their Complementarity. Int. J. Lexicography 2(2) (1989) 89–110
3. Sierra, G.: The Onomasiological Dictionary: A Gap in Lexicography. Proc. Ninth EURALEX International Congress. Universität Stuttgart, Stuttgart (2000) 223–235
4. Calzolari, N.: The Dictionary and the Thesaurus can be Combined. In: Evens, M.W. (ed.): Relational Models of the Lexicon: Representing Knowledge in Semantic Networks. CUP, Cambridge (1988) 75–96
5. Fox, E.A.: Improved Retrieval Using a Relational Thesaurus for Automatic Expansion of Extended Boolean Logic Queries. In: Evens, M.W. (ed.): Relational Models of the Lexicon: Representing Knowledge in Semantic Networks. CUP, Cambridge (1988) 199–210
6. Sierra, G., McNaught, J.: Extracting Semantic Clusters from MRDs for an Onomasiological Search Dictionary. Int. J. Lexicography 13(4) (2000) 264–286
7. Cooper, W.S.: Expected Search Length: A Single Measure of Retrieval Effectiveness Based on the Weak Ordering Action of Retrieval Systems. American Documentation 9 (1968) 30–41
8. Wilks, Y.A., Slator, B.M., Guthrie, L.M.: Electric Words: Dictionaries, Computers, and Meanings. ACL–MIT Press, Cambridge MA (1996)
9. CED: Collins English Dictionary. HarperCollinsPublishers, Glasgow (1994)
10. OED2: Oxford English Dictionary. OUP, Oxford (1994)
11. Ndi Kimbi, A.: The Conceptual Structure of Terminological Definitions and their Linguistic Realisation. PhD Thesis. University of Manchester. Manchester (1994)
12. Cleverdon, C.: Optimizing Convenient Online Access to Bibliographic Databases. Information Services and Use 4(1–2) (1984) 37–47

Query Expansion Based on Thesaurus Relations: Evaluation over Internet

Luiz Augusto Sangoi Pizzato and Vera Lúcia Strube de Lima

Pontifícia Universidade Católica do Rio Grande do Sul
Faculdade de Informática
Programa de Pós-Graduação em Ciência da Computação
Av. Ipiranga, 6681 - Prédio 16 - Partenon
90619-900 Porto Alegre - RS - Brazil
{pizzato,vera}@inf.pucrs.br

Abstract. In this work we present a heuristic for query expansion and its evaluation with information retrieval over the Internet. We obtained the precision and recall measures for the top-50 documents from 13 different queries. For those we had good results on estimated recall and F-measure values indicating that query expansion is a reasonable technique when few documents are retrieved.

1 Introduction

Today's web search engines provide users with features like Boolean search and full-text indexes. Boolean queries give the searcher a chance to say precisely what he wants. For instance, a query could say: "give me all documents that contain these words, and do not have these other words in it". Full-text index gives the search engines the ability to find a document by any word that appears in the document body.

Evaluating a web search engine is quite a difficult task. Hoenkamp & Van Vugt [4] tried to judge the importance of precision and recall measures in information retrieval (IR) over the Internet, by observing a group of people on a set of search tasks. Precision refers to the amount of relevant documents retrieved over a set of documents retrieved, while recall informs how many relevant documents where retrieved over all relevant documents. The conclusions obtained by Hoenkamp & Van Vugt were, that precision is the primary factor influencing user satisfaction, while recall had virtually no importance on the user behavior or satisfaction.

The recall measure can be obtained in a small collection of documents, with exhaustive search by a human specialist. In a very large corpus, the task of finding all existent relevant documents for a specific query is very difficult, perhaps impossible. The Internet corpus, beyond its size, is a very dynamic corpus, documents can easily be published, modified and unpublished over the Internet. The recall measure can only be estimated in an environment like the Internet, and

A. Gelbukh (Ed.): CICLing 2003, LNCS 2588, pp. 553–556, 2003.

the estimation can only be done over the documents previously indexed by the search engine. We cannot assure 100% Internet cover by a search engine, nor even 100% updated information of the documents content.

If precision of the top retrieved document drives users satisfaction, ranking is probably the most important feature in a web search engine. Ranking values are normally computed by the similarity of a query with its documents and from the pages importance in the Internet. Query expansion is a technique that web searchers use to restrict or expand the group of retrieved document in a way to find the correct documents. In this paper we present an automatic approach for query expansion that uses different thesauri in a unified way. Our query expansion method is useful for searching small document collections as demonstrated by a previous work [7]. The query expansion technique is also known as query enrichment [2].

In this paper we show the result obtained with our query expansion technique over the Internet. In the second section, we describe the heuristic used for query expansion. After, in the third section, we show the differences between the IR results obtained by the original queries and the expanded ones. Finally, we draw conclusions from this work.

2   Query Expansion Heuristic

The proposed query expansion heuristic uses different thesauri defined according to a standard XML definition. For this evaluation we used 4 different thesauri combined as if it were only one large thesaurus. Three of them were manually constructed and focus mainly on controlling vocabulary of keywords on library indexing. These thesauri were offered by the libraries of the Brazilian Federal Senate, USP University, and PUCRS University. The used corpus-based thesaurus was constructed automatically by syntactic similarity measure described by Grefenstette [3], and adapted to Brazilian Portuguese by Gasperin [1].

Robin & Ramalho [8] show that synonym expansion gives better results than hyponym expansion. We assume that some word relations could give better IR result than others. For that, our technique for generating an expanded query gives different weights for different relation.

Tudhope et al. [9] instigate ways of using associative relations (RT relations in ISO 2788 [5]) in IR. Tudhope et al. show that an associative relation that links two terms in the same top concept tree, can be semantically closer than a relation between different terms in different trees. In our work we propose to give a value to terms according to their distance from the terms of an original query.

In our technique a term is closer to another term if these values are bigger. Since every relation had a weight inside the interval $(0, 1]$, a distance between two terms is the product of every relation in a path between one term to another. Once the interval of the relation weight is $(0, 1]$, the more distant two terms are, the more this value is closer to zero.

The measured semantic distance is related to a path between two terms. But, the query expansion is related to all terms in the original query. We needed a value that shows the semantic distance of a term with all query. This value is attached to all the related terms, and it is calculated as the sum of all the individual semantic distance between a term and every term in an original query. Once the semantic distance measure of a term and all query terms, are bigger than a certain value, the term is added to the expanded query. Details, and a formalization of the query expansion method used can be found in [7] and in [6].

3   Expansion over the Internet

We have executed some tests using a tool that implements the heuristic presented in section 2 over the Internet. We use the AltaVista search engine at www.altavista.com We had chosen AltaVista because it implements a good Boolean search, and it can treat queries bigger than 10 words.

We formulated 13 queries, and for every query we retrieved the top 50 documents published in Brazilian Portuguese. We expanded those queries and retrieved the documents over the same condition of the original queries.

We analyzed the first 50 document retrieved for both original and expanded queries. We made a set of all relevant documents for every search done. It was measured the precision of each search and the recall obtained. Precision was calculated by dividing the number of relevant documents retrieved over the number of document retrieved (50 or less, when there were less than 50 documents retrieved). Recall was measured using the number of relevant documents retrieved over the number of documents in the union set of relevant documents in the original and expanded queries.

We had obtained a decrease of precision and recall when using the expanded query. The average precision decrease while using the expanded query was 19,14%, and 8,30% for the recall measure. The average measures are shown in table 1. In our previous work [7], we had shown that over a small and static corpus, our query expansion obtained good results. The precision over the corpus used had decreased but the recall obtained was much increased.

Since in this study we use top n documents for measuring recall, the recall measure are partial over the whole Internet search. Due to the Internet size and its dynamic nature, obtaining a true recall measure is an impossible task. Nevertheless we try to estimate the whole search recall, by assuming a constant precision rate and using the estimate number of relevant documents while estimating the recall rate. The total number of relevant document is the total number of documents obtained by the expanded query, since all documents retrieved by the original query are in the set of documents retrieved by the expanded one. The recall of the top-50 documents was used to estimate a number of relevant documents over the Internet.

By roughly estimating the recall measure for both types of queries, we conclude that for all documents retrieved we get a much larger recall rate in the expanded query. Table 1 show the average estimated recall numbers. We calculated the F-measure (the harmonic mean) for both top-50 and estimated recall and precision. The result, see table 1, shows that our query expansion technique

Table 1. Average results

Query Type	Precision	Top-50 Recall	Est. Recall	Top-50 F-Measure	Est. F-Measure
Original	0,5912	0,8596	0,1700	0,7005	0,3648
Expanded	0,5458	0,7215	0,4348	0,6215	0,6099
	(-19,14%)	(-8,30%)	(+155,7%)	(-11,28%)	(+67,88%)

had degraded IR results, but when estimating a total IR, the result for query expansion increased 67,88%.

4   Concluding Remarks

This paper focus on using the query expansion technique proposed in [7] over the Internet, which is a very large, heterogeneous and dynamic corpus. This paper had shown that this query expansion technique degrades precision which, according to Hoenkamp & Van Vugt in [4], degrades user's satisfaction. But when considering the standard measures for IR evaluation (precision, recall and F-measure) and estimating its values for the whole Internet search, we get a lower precision with a larger recall, which gives us a better F-measure. The number of documents retrieved where 41,62% larger for query expansion, which shows that our query expansion technique could be used on the Internet when few documents are retrieved. The higher recall is very important when few documents are retrieved, but the user is not happy to analyse all documents when the IR gives hundreds or thousands of them.

References

1. C. V. Gasperin. Extração automática de relações semânticas a partir de relações sintáticas. Master's thesis, PPGCC, FACIN, PUCRS, Novembro 2001.
2. A. Gelbukh. Lazy query enrichment: A simple method of indexing large specialized document bases. In *11th International Conference and Workshop on Database and Expert Systems Applications*, Greenwich, September 2000. Springer-Verlag.
3. G. Grefenstette. *Explorations in automatic thesaurus discovery*. Kluwer Academic Publishers, EUA, 1994.
4. E. Hoenkamp and H. V. Vugt. The influence of recall feedback in information retrieval on user satisfaction and user behavior. In *23rd Annual Conference of the Cognitive Science Society*, pages 423–428, 2001.
5. International Organization for Standardization, Geneva. *ISO 2788: Guidelines for the establishment and development of monolingual thesauri*, 2nd edition, 1986.
6. L. A. S. Pizzato. Estrutura multitesauro para recuperação de informações. Master's thesis, PPGCC, FACIN, PUCRS, Janeiro 2003.
7. L. A. S. Pizzato and V. L. Strube de Lima. Desenvolvimento e avaliação de uma estrutura multitesauro para a recuperação de informações. In *XXVIII Latin-American Conference on Informatics (CLEI 2002)*, Montevidéo, Uruguay, 2002.
8. J. Robin and F. S. Ramalho. Empirically evaluating WordNet-based query expansion in a web search engine setting. In *IR'2001*, Oulu, Finland, Setembro 2001.
9. D. Tudhope, H. Alani, and C. Jones. Augmenting thesaurus relationships: Possibilities for retrieval. *Journal of Digital Information*, 1(8), Fevereiro 2001.

Suggesting Named Entities for Information Access

Enrique Amigó, Anselmo Peñas, Julio Gonzalo, and Felisa Verdejo

Dpto. Lenguajes y Sistemas Informáticos, UNED
{enrique,anselmo,julio,felisa}@lsi.uned.es

Abstract. In interactive searching environments, robust linguistic techniques can provide sophisticated search assistance with a reasonable tolerance to errors, because users can easily select relevant items and dismiss the noisy bits. The general idea is that the combination of Language Engineering and Information Retrieval techniques can be used to *suggest* complex terms or relevant pieces of information to the user, facilitating query formulation and refinement when the information need is not completely defined a priori or when the user is not familiar with the contents and/or the terminology used in the collection. In this paper, we describe an interactive search engine that suggests Named Entities extracted automatically from the collection, and related to the initial query terms, helping users to filter and structure relevant information according to the persons, locations or other entities involved.

1 Introduction

Current Internet search engines are quite efficient at finding information, but there are still a number of (common) search scenarios where users are not properly supported:

- *The requested information is available only in a foreign language.* Even if the user is able to read documents in some foreign language(s) (*passive vocabulary*) he might not be able to formulate adequate queries in such language(s) (*active vocabulary*), or he might just ignore in which language he will find the information he is seeking for.
- *The user is not aware of the appropriate wording for the search.* The missing piece here is a better knowledge of the document collection and the specialized terminology in the domain of the search.
- *The user need is vague or not completely defined.* Search engines are good at solving precise information needs, such as "Where can I buy soja milk online in the New York area?". But for more vague requests navigation and browsing of documents is also necessary for refining, tuning and accomplishing the information need [4].
- *The user aim is to compile or summarize pieces of information around a topic.* This kind of searching needs lots of queries and users don't receive any kind of help to cover the main concepts or entities around the topic. In a traditional Information Retrieval setting, the system retrieves a set of relevant documents, and the user has to analyse their contents and extracts the relevant information without assistance.

A. Gelbukh (Ed.): CICLing 2003, LNCS 2588, pp. 557–561, 2003.

These challenges motivate further research on interactive search engines using NLP techniques and wide lexical resources as *CrossLexica* [2] or *EuroWordNet* [8]. TREC experiences on interactive Information Retrieval failed to establish quantitatively the benefits of interactive assistance in a classical Information Retrieval task (Interactive Track Reports of TREC/3-9[1]) but positive results are now being obtained when fuzzy information needs are considered, and when the search task is cross-lingual (the document collection is written in a language unknown to the searcher) [6], [5]. The *Website Term Browser (WTB)* [6], [7] is an interactive multilingual searching facility that provides, besides documents, a set of terminological expressions (mainly phrases) related to the query as an alternative way to access information. Such expressions match and refine the user needs according to the contents and the terminology in the collection. This approach, based on the automatic extraction, retrieval and browsing of terminology from the collection, was showed to be helpful for users to access information when compared to the use of Google's document ranking.

Beyond phrase suggestion, linguistic techniques permit further kinds of processing in order to improve searching facilities and overcome the limitations mentioned above. The hypothesis underlying our approach is that, within an interactive framework, robust linguistic techniques provide rich information without compromising precision, because such information is offered as suggestions where the user will make his final choices.

In this paper, we describe an interactive search engine that, along this general philosophy, suggests Named Entities which are related to the initial query terms, helping users to filter and structure relevant information according to the persons, locations or entities involved. In a hypothetical searching task where the user has to collect and summarize bits and pieces of relevant information around a topic, this kind of information may help not only finding the appropriate documents, but also finding and structuring the relevant information scattered along them.

The Named Entities are automatically extracted from the document collection using linguistic processing software. This approach has been implemented in the first Hermes[2] project prototype. The following sections describe the parts of the system aimed to extract, select and suggest Named Entities, as well as the kind of interaction that this feature introduces to help users in the searching process.

2   Linguistic Processing of the Document Collection

The *Hermes* prototype applies NLP techniques to lemmatize documents and extract Named Entities before they are used to index the collection. The document collection currently consists of 15,000 news in Spanish (the final collection will be ten times larger and will contain also documents in English, Catalan and Basque languages). This collection has been lemmatized and POS tagged with MACO and Relax [3]. The Named Entities (NE) have been recognized and classified with an NLP package developed by the Technical University of Catalonia [1] in two steps:

---

[1] http://trec.nist.gov

[2] This work has been supported by HERMES project under a grant (TIC2000-0335-C03-01) from the Spanish Government. http://terral.lsi.uned.es/hermes

1. Named Entity Recognition (NER), consisting of detecting the pieces of text that correspond to names of entities.
2. Named Entity Classification (NEC), consisting of deciding whether each detected NE refers to a person, a location, an organization, etc.

3   Search Process

Figure 1 shows the *Hermes prototype* interface. Results of the querying and retrieval process are shown in four separate areas:

1. A ranking of classified Named Entities (Person, Organization, Location and Miscellaneous, on the left area) that are salient in the collection and probably relevant to the user's query.
2. A ranking of documents (right) classified by date, subject or category (document metadata fields).
3. An area where a refined query is built interactively (central part of the interface) according to the available named entities and the documents being found at each refining step.
4. An area to view individual documents (bottom part of the interface).

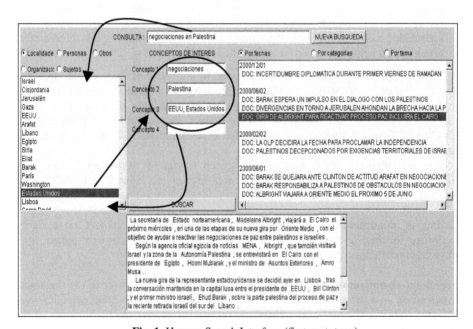

Fig. 1. Hermes Search Interface (first prototype)

All this information is presented to the user, who may browse the ranking of entities, refine the query or directly click on a document to view its content. The complete search process follows four steps:

Initial querying. The user introduces some initial filtering words or a natural language expression. From this first query the system determines the subset of documents that will be explored. Then the system performs a local analysis over the document subset in order to extract relevant information. *Figure 1* shows that user has written *"Palestina"* as a query, expressing a quite vague information need.

Query refinement. The system automatically identifies and classifies the entities present in the document subset, obtaining statistics of their presence both in the subset and in the whole collection. Entities are then shown to the user, ranked and organized in a hierarchy according to:

- *Type of Entity*, i.e., Location, Person, Organization or Miscellaneous. Note that the automatic classification of Named Entities highly depends on world knowledge and context. As we don't apply deep semantic processing there can be some errors in the classification, but they are easily detected by users. For example, *Figure 1* shows that "Arafat" has been classified as a location in some of its occurrences. However, there are texts in which "Arafat" has been correctly classified as person, so it will also appear under the Person hierarchy.
- Salience of the entities weighted according to their presence (document frequency) in the pre-selected documents.
- Subsumed entities. For presentation purposes, a group of entities containing a sub-entity are presented as subsumed by the most frequent sub-phrase in the collection. For example, both *"president Bill Clinton"* and *"Bill Clinton"* are subsumed as instances of *"Clinton"* in the hierarchy. This hierarchical organization helps browsing the space of entities.

From the space of named entities suggested by the system, the user can drag and drop his choices into the query refinement area. Names can be dropped over a new field, implying a new search entity, or can be dropped over a pre-selected name, implying a synonymy for search purposes. *Figure 1* shows that the user has selected both "EEUU" and "Estados Unidos" (United States) and has dropped them into the same concept field.

The new query is submitted to the search engine as a boolean expression, producing changes both in the document area and in the Named Entities area, as illustrated by the flow arrows in *Figure 1*.

Listing of documents. Documents can be listed by date, subject or category according to their metadata. These metadata were automatically assigned in a previous classification process.

Document visualization. A selected document is shown to the user in the document visualization area, where there is an alternative feedback facility: users can click over a Named Entity in the text of the visualization area, producing the highlighting of the documents in the list that contain the selected entity.

4   Conclusions

The system described in this paper follows an interactive browse/searching paradigm to help users stating and refining their information needs. For this task, the Hermes first prototype uses automatically recognized and classified Named Entities. An initial user query determines the context of documents in which salient entities are selected automatically and presented for user selection. Entities become very significant to locate relevant pieces of information and to reduce the space of documents to be explored. This approach complements the traditional ranking of documents being helpful when users have vague or broad information needs.

Our immediate work includes incorporating multilingual aspects to the search process, scaling the system to deal with larger document sets, and designing a methodology to establish quantitative and qualitative parameters to evaluate the utility of Named Entities in interactive information access applications.

References

1. Arévalo, M. Carreras X. Màrquez L. Martí M. A. Padró L. and Simón M. J. A Proposal for wide-coverage Spanish Named Entity Recognition. *Revista de la Sociedad Española de Procesamiento del Lenguaje Natural.* 2002; 1(3):1–15.
2. Bolshakov, I. A. anf Gelbukh A. A very large database of collocations and semantic links. Mokrane Bouzeghoub Et Al. (Eds.)   Natural Language Processing and Information Systems. Lecture Notes in Computer Science. Springer-Verlag. 2001; 1959:103–114.
3. Carmona, J. Cervell S. Màrquez L. Martí M. A. Padró L. Placer R. Rodríguez H. Taulé M. and Turmo J. An environment for morphosyntactic processing of unrestricted Spanish text. *Proceedings of LREC'98.* 1998.
4. Hearst, M. Next generation web search: setting our sites. *IEEE Data Engineering Bulleting, Issue on Next Generation Web Search*, Luis Gravano (Ed.). 2000.
5. López-Ostenero, F. Gonzalo J. Peñas A. and Verdejo F. Interactive Cross-Language Searching: phrases are better than terms for query formulation and refinement. Evaluation of Cross-Language Information Retrieval Systems, Springer-Verlag LNCS Series, to appear.
6. Peñas, A. Gonzalo J. and Verdejo F. Cross-Language Information Access through Phrase Browsing. Applications of Natural Language to Information Systems, Proceedings of 6th International Workshop NLDB 2001, Madrid, Lecture Notes in Informatics (LNI), Series of the German Informatics Society (GI-Edition). 2001; P-3:121–130.
7. Peñas, A. Verdejo F. and Gonzalo J. Terminology Retrieval: towards a synergy between thesaurus and free text searching. Proceedings of VIII Iberoamerican Conference on Artificial Intelligence, IBERAMIA 2002. Springer-Verlag Lecture Notes in Computer Science. 2002.
8. Vossen, P. Introduction to EuroWordNet. Computers and the Humanities, Special Issue on EuroWordNet. 1998.

Probabilistic Word Vector and Similarity Based on Dictionaries

Satoshi Suzuki

NTT Communication Science Laboratories
NTT, Japan
satoshi@cslab.kecl.ntt.co.jp

Abstract. We propose a new method for computing the probabilistic vector expression of words based on dictionaries. This method provides a well-founded procedure based on stochastic process whose applicability is clear. The proposed method exploits the relationship between headwords and their explanatory notes in dictionaries. An explanatory note is a set of other words, each of which is expanded by its own explanatory note. This expansion is repeatedly applied, but even explanatory notes expanded infinitely can be computed under a simple assumption. The vector expression we obtain is a semantic expansion of the explanatory notes of words. We explain how to acquire the vector expression from these expanded explanatory notes. We also demonstrate a word similarity computation based on a Japanese dictionary and evaluate it in comparison with a known system based on $TF \cdot IDF$. The results show the effectiveness and applicability of this probabilistic vector expression.

1 Introduction

Word frequency vectors for information retrieval (IR) are generally calculated with Term Frequency · Inverse Document Frequency ($TF \cdot IDF$) or simple normalization. While these methods are certainly useful and effective in some applications, they are heuristic and do not seem to be firmly grounded in a principle that explains why these methods are selected or why they work well. Papineni, for example, showed that IDF is optimal for document self-retrieval with respect to a generalized Kullback-Leibler distance [1]. However, this argument does not take into account the co-occurrence of words and, therefore, cannot be applied to $TF \cdot IDF$. Such uncertainty regarding $TF \cdot IDF$ may often cause confusion when it is applied to particular applications, for example, not knowing whether these word frequency vectors can be reasonably added up or multiplied. To avoid such confusion, we investigate a new well-grounded method for computing word frequency vectors that can be used instead of $TF \cdot IDF$ or simple normalization.

Recently, learning methods based on stochastic processes have become popular in the field of computational learning theories because of their simple descriptions and logically founded procedures. As for IR, some probabilistic methods have also been proposed lately. Hofmann, for example, suggested Probabilistic Latent Semantic Indexing (PLSI), which provides an alternative method that

A. Gelbukh (Ed.): CICLing 2003, LNCS 2588, pp. 562–572, 2003.

can be written as a matrix product resembling the singular-value decomposition underlying Latent Semantic Indexing (LSI) [2]. Using a probabilistic description makes it easy to understand what each process does and how the processes are applied. Hence, we also try to apply a stochastic process to the computation of word frequency vectors from dictionaries to establish a well-grounded method.

The method we propose constructs probabilistic vectors by expanding the semantics of words that are given as explanatory notes in dictionaries. The explanatory notes may not sufficiently describe the general meaning of the words, but each explanatory note consists of words that are further explained by their own explanatory notes. Such semantic expansion can be repeatedly applied to assemble many large explanatory notes. We can therefore expect them to provide a more general description of word semantics.

A way of dealing with these large explanatory notes expanded infinitely will be described in the next section. We explain how to deal with headwords and their explanatory notes in dictionaries and produce a word frequency vector based on a stochastic process.

To check the effectiveness of the proposed vector expression, we examined an application for measuring word similarity that is also based on a stochastic process. Our definition of word similarity and our computational method is detailed in Section 3. Results of computational experiments with a Japanese dictionary are also reported in that section.

2   Probabilistic Word Vector

2.1   Basic Idea

Dictionaries are composed of sets consisting of a headword and a related explanatory note. However, the explanatory note does not always explain the headword sufficiently. Therefore, we investigated a method of realizing ideal explanatory notes from the original notes. This approach is based on the following assumption (see Figure 1).

A headword is explained by its explanatory note, and the words in the explanatory note are also explained by their own explanatory notes. Consequently, hierarchical explanations may continue infinitely. As a result, a headword obtains many large explanatory notes, each of which has a different depth of hierarchy. Here, we assume that the ideal explanatory note is a probabilistic combination of these large explanatory notes, whose ratios become smaller according to the hierarchical depth. This assumption makes it possible to calculate the ideal explanatory note even if the hierarchical explanatory note at infinity cannot be computed.

2.2   Methods

Here, we describe how to compute ideal explanatory notes from dictionaries. First, we explain the notation of word frequency in explanatory notes. Explanatory notes are expressed as a set of probabilistic word frequencies.

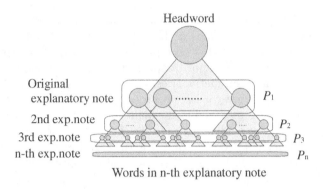

Headword

Original explanatory note

2nd exp.note

3rd exp.note

n-th exp.note

P_1

P_2

P_3

P_n

Words in n-th explanatory note

Fig. 1. Model of semantic expansion

We write the relationship between headword w_i and word w_j in the form $P(w_j^{(1)}|w_i)$, where $w_j^{(1)}$ means word w_j in the original (first) explanatory note. This means that $P(w_j^{(1)}|w_i)$ is the probability that word w_j appears in the explanatory note of headword w_i. The probabilities over all headwords can be formulated as a square matrix:

$$A = \begin{bmatrix} P\left(w_1^{(1)}|w_1\right) & P\left(w_1^{(1)}|w_2\right) & \cdots & P\left(w_1^{(1)}|w_m\right) \\ P\left(w_2^{(1)}|w_1\right) & & \ddots & \\ \vdots & & & \ddots \\ P\left(w_m^{(1)}|w_1\right) & & & P\left(w_m^{(1)}|w_m\right) \end{bmatrix}, \tag{1}$$

where m is the number of headwords in the dictionaries. Each element $P(w_j^{(1)}|w_i)$ is equal to the probabilistic frequency of w_j in the explanatory note of w_i, i.e.,

$$P(w_j^{(1)}|w_i) = \frac{N(w_j^{(1)})}{\sum_{all\ k} N(w_k^{(1)})}, \tag{2}$$

where $N(w_j^{(1)}), N(w_k^{(1)})$ is the frequency of the word in the explanatory note of w_i. Column vectors of probability matrix A are the original word frequency vectors.

Next, we try to obtain a secondary explanatory note that is a probabilistic combination of the original explanatory notes. All words in the original explanatory note are regarded as headwords, and their explanatory notes are probabilistically combined into a secondary explanatory note. The probability of word w_j in the secondary explanatory note of headword w_i is expressed in a formula:

$$P(w_j^{(2)}|w_i) = \sum_{all\ k} P(w_j^{(2)}|w_k^{(1)})P(w_k^{(1)}|w_i), \tag{3}$$

Headwords

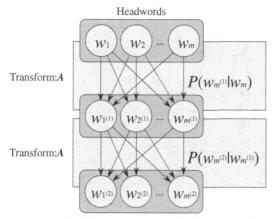

Words in secondary explanatory notes

Fig. 2. Model of secondary explanatory notes

where $w_k^{(1)}$ is a word in the explanatory note of w_i. Formula (3) over all words can be written as a formula of matrix A: A^2.

Figure 2 shows a model of secondary explanatory notes. All paths from a headword on the top layer to a word on the bottom layer pass through one of the words on the second layer. Formula (3) shows all of these paths, and matrix A expresses the relationship between the neighboring two layers.

Generally, we can formulate probability $P(w_j^{(n)}|w_i)$ as follows, where $w_j^{(n)}$ is a word in the nth explanatory note of headword w_i:

$$P(w_j^{(n)}|w_i) = \tag{4}$$

$$\sum_{all\ k_{n-1}} \sum_{all\ k_{n-2}} \cdots \sum_{all\ k_1} P(w_j^{(n)}|w_{k_{n-1}}^{(n-1)}) P(w_{k_{n-1}}^{(n-1)}|w_{k_{n-2}}^{(n-2)}) \cdots P(w_{k_1}^{(1)}|w_i).$$

Formula (4) over all words can also be written as a formula of matrix A: A^n.

Now, we probabilistically combine all the explanatory notes from the first to infinity. That is, we compute the following formula:

$$C = P_1 A + P_2 A^2 + \cdots + P_n A^n + \cdots, \tag{5}$$

where $P_1, P_2, \cdots, P_n, \cdots$ are probabilities of selecting the models of the hierarchical explanatory note.

Figure 3 shows a model of the ideal explanatory notes. This model illustrates the probabilistic combinations of all hierarchical explanatory notes as expressed by formula (5).

Generally, it is extremely difficult to calculate C exactly. However, when the probability P_n becomes smaller at a certain rate according to n, C can be formulated as

$$C = b(aA + a^2 A^2 + \cdots + a^n A^n + \cdots), \tag{6}$$

where a, b are parameters that satisfy the following:

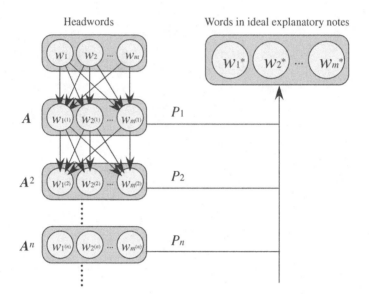

Headwords

Words in ideal explanatory notes

Fig. 3. Model of ideal explanatory notes

$$0 < a < 1, \tag{7}$$

$$P_n = ba^n, \tag{8}$$

$$\sum_{n=1}^{\infty} P_n = 1. \tag{9}$$

We can obtain b as a formula of a from the infinite series given by these equations:

$$b = \frac{1-a}{a}. \tag{10}$$

Consequently, we can transform formula (6) into an equation:

$$(I - aA)C = (1 - a)A. \tag{11}$$

If matrix $(I - aA)$ is non-singular, we can directly compute matrix C by the following formula:

$$C = (1 - a)A(I - aA)^{-1}. \tag{12}$$

Alternatively, we could use a numerical solution of linear equations of the ith column vector v_i of C:

$$(I - aA)v_i = (1 - a)A_i, \tag{13}$$

where A_i is the ith column vector of A. Otherwise, we could estimate v_i with some learning methods in formula (13). In any case, vector v_i can be computed.

The (j, i) element of matrix C is $P(w_j^*|w_i)$, which indicates the probability that word w_j appears in the ideal explanatory note of headword w_i. We can therefore regard the ith column vector of matrix C as a probabilistic frequency vector of word w_i.

2.3   Computation of Word Vectors

We next describe simulation results based on the method presented above. We used a Japanese dictionary in the simulation [3]. As preprocessing, general nouns and verbal nouns[1] were listed as headwords, and example sentences in their explanatory notes were as far as possible excluded. ChaSen [4] was used as a morphological analyzer. The total number of headwords was 44,050, and the average number of words in an original explanatory note was about seven.

First, probability matrix A was calculated with formula (2), which is a 44,050-dimensional square matrix.

Second, all column vectors of matrix C were estimated by a learning method that minimizes squared errors to solve equation (13), where parameter a was set at 0.9. After the learning, we excluded words where the learning did not converge or where the learning error was bigger than a certain threshold. The result provided us with 43,616 headwords and their probabilistic frequency vectors. The average number of non-zero elements of the column vectors was around 25,000. This means that more than half of all the headwords are used in each ideal explanatory note.

Table 1 shows examples of the probabilistic frequency vectors.[2] Probabilistic frequencies in the original and ideal explanatory notes are listed in the table with regard to two headwords. These values are elements of probabilistic frequency vectors, and all of the elements of each column vector naturally add up to 1. We can roughly say that the probabilistic frequency in an ideal explanatory note is large according to the probabilistic frequency in the original explanatory note, aside from the headword itself.

3   Word Similarity

To evaluate the probabilistic word vector, we tried to compute word similarity. First, we define the similarity of words and explore a method for computing it, which is based on a stochastic process.

3.1   Definition and Method

We define the similarity of words as the probability that a headword is estimated from the ideal explanatory note of another headword. This similarity expresses how closely a headword represents the ideal explanatory note of another headword. Therefore, the similarity of all headwords to a certain headword can be described as a probability vector.

---

[1] Some nouns work as verbs with a post-positional auxiliary verb "suru" in Japanese. For example, "denwa"(telephone) + "suru" means 'make a phone call'.

[2] See the next section for a detailed explanation of word similarity.

The probability that headword w_i represents a word w_j in an ideal explanatory note is formulated as follows:

$$P(w_i|w_j^*) = \frac{P(w_j^*|w_i)P(w_i)}{\sum_{all\ k} P(w_j^*|w_k)P(w_k)}, \tag{14}$$

where $P(w_i)$ is the a priori probability of w_i. Note that $P(w_i|w_j^*)$ is the probability of a headword estimated from an ideal explanatory note, not of a word in the next hierarchy of the explanatory note. We cannot calculate $P(w_i|w_j^*)$ directly but can use the (i, j) element of the probabilistic frequency matrix C as $P(w_i^*|w_j)$ in formula (14).

The similarity of headword w_i from headword w_j is obtained by processing all the words in the ideal explanatory note of w_j, i.e.,

$$P(w_i|w_j) = \sum_{all\ k} P(w_i|w_k^*)P(w_k^*|w_j)$$
$$= \sum_{all\ k} \frac{P(w_k^*|w_i)P(w_i)P(w_k^*|w_j)}{\sum_{all\ l} P(w_k^*|w_l)P(w_l)}. \tag{15}$$

3.2   Simulation

To compute formula (15), we applied the results of the probabilistic frequency vector obtained in Section 2.3. $P(w_k^*|w_i)$ in the formula is the kth element of the probabilistic word vector of w_i. By contrast, the values of another unknown parameter, a priori probability $P(w_i)$, are not yet given. $P(w_i)$ means the probability of word w_i appearing without a precondition. Here, it should be remembered that all headwords appear once in a dictionary. Hence, we can assume the a priori probabilities of all headwords to be equal, giving the following formula:

$$P(w_i|w_j) = \sum_{all\ k} \frac{P(w_k^*|w_i)P(w_k^*|w_j)}{\sum_{all\ l} P(w_k^*|w_l)}. \tag{16}$$

The results of the computation with formula (16) are also shown in Table 1. Compared with the probabilistic frequency result, shown on the left hand in the table, common words such as "標準 (standard)" or "人物 (person)" have relatively low values. By contrast, words that are semantically close but do not appear in the explanatory notes have high values, e.g., "レベルアップ (raise level)" or "ガード (guard)".

3.3   Evaluation

We evaluated our results by comparing them with those of the system proposed by Kasahara et al. [5]. This system vectorizes original explanatory notes in a dictionary using $TF \cdot IDF$ and measures word similarity in terms of the inner product of those vectors. A feature of this system is that the vectors produced by $TF \cdot IDF$ are manually tuned to accord with human feelings.

Table 1. Examples of probabilistic word vector and similarity.

レベル (level)				
Words	Probabilistic frequency		Word similarity	
in explanatory note	Original exp.	Ideal exp.	Similarity	Order
水準儀 (leveling instrument)	0.1	0.012765	0.005534	1
レベル (level)	0.1	0.012487	0.005037	2
レベルアップ (raise level)	0	0	0.003480	3
平準 (make level)	0	0	0.001155	4
水準 (level)	0.2	0.025732	0.000914	5
精度 (precision)	0	0.002002	0.000791	6
儀 (affair)	0	0.000002	0.000754	7
準 (semi-)	0	0.000001	0.000684	8
准 (semi-)	0	0.000001	0.000684	8
別儀 (distinguish)	0	0	0.000617	10
級 (degree)	0.1	0.011949	0.000273	25
トップ (top)	0.1	0.011806	0.000197	47
標準 (standard)	0.2	0.026058	0.000092	166
程度 (grade)	0.1	0.019590	0.000085	187
段階 (echelon)	0.1	0.014523	0.000070	277
⋮				

ボディーガード (bodyguard)				
Words	Probabilistic frequency		Word similarity	
in explanatory note	Original exp.	Ideal exp.	Similarity	Order
ボディーガード (bodyguard)	0	0.024390	0.025666	1
ガード (guard)	0	0	0.004786	2
身辺 (one's affair)	0.25	0.047686	0.003050	3
警衛 (guard)	0	0	0.002760	4
親衛 (guard the king)	0	0.000010	0.002464	5
用心棒 (bodyguard)	0.25	0.026339	0.002308	6
エスコート (escort)	0	0	0.002254	7
座右の銘 (familiar proverb)	0	0	0.001947	8
警護 (guard)	0	0.000192	0.001810	9
護衛 (guard)	0.25	0.033887	0.001569	10
人物 (person)	0.25	0.026765	0.000090	224
⋮				

For comparison with our results, we used psychological data from questionnaires on word similarities [6]. In the psychological experiment, 77 subjects were asked if the stimulus words were synonyms of the headwords or not. Stimulus words that gained more than 50% agreement from the other subjects were regarded as true synonyms.

We analyzed the population of the order of each true synonym in the computed similarity. Associative words were also examined in the same manner. Figure 4 shows the difference between our method and the tuned system. It illustrates the ratio of accumulated true synonyms (A) and true associative words (B) plotted over the order of similarity. In both cases, the plotted values of the proposed method are almost always larger than those of the tuned system,

(A)

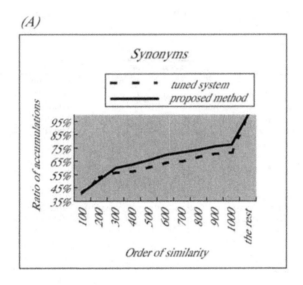

(B)

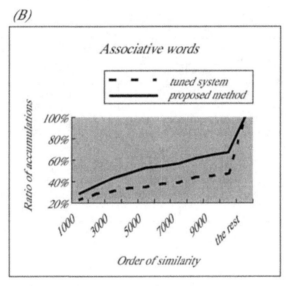

Fig. 4. Comparison of proposed method and tuned system.

which means that these true words appear earlier in the order of similarity in our results than in that of the tuned system. As for associative words, the effectiveness is more significant. However, these are not accurate comparisons because the tuned system contains words other than nouns, e.g., verbs and adjectives. Nevertheless, we can easily expect our method to have almost the same results as the simulation results, even with words other than nouns, because common or frequently used words such as verbs have a low similarity in our method as shown in Table 1.

4   Discussion

As mentioned at the beginning of this paper, we know that the $TF \cdot IDF$ method is useful and works well. However, it does not provide us with a well-grounded comprehension. By contrast, due to the stochastic process, it is quite clear what the proposed method computes, and why the procedure is necessary. This clarity is required when we are confused as to how to apply frequency vectors. For example, if we assume that an application contains the process $(A + A^T)$, is it possible to compute this reasonably? Here, A is a word-by-word square matrix such as that used in our simulation. $TF \cdot IDF$ gives us no idea whether it is possible to add A and A^T. However, in terms of the stochastic process, it is clear that adding $P(w_i|w_j)$ and $P(w_j|w_i)$ does not make sense. Of course, a matrix based on $TF \cdot IDF$ need not abide by the rules of a stochastic process. However, the meanings of the matrix elements are still the same. It is easy to understand this idea if we assume a document-by-word matrix instead of a word-by-word matrix.

In our simulation of word similarity, the probability $P(w_i|w_j)$ was given by formula (16). This process resembles a calculation of the inner product of $TF \cdot IDF$ vectors when headwords are regarded as document indices. This is because, in this case, the denominator adds up word frequencies over all documents, and the numerator is the word frequency in a document. A widely used document similarity method computes the inner product of $TF \cdot IDF$ vectors, i.e., $\sum (TF)^2 \cdot (IDF)^2$. On the other hand, our method nearly computes $\sum (TF)^2 \cdot IDF$ as follows:

$$
\begin{aligned}
P(w_i|w_j) &= \sum_{all\ k} \frac{P(w_k^*|w_i)P(w_k^*|w_j)}{\sum_{all\ l} P(w_k^*|w_l)} \\
&= \sum_{all\ k} \frac{P(w_k^*|w_i)}{\sqrt{\sum_{all\ l} P(w_k^*|w_l)}} \frac{P(w_k^*|w_j)}{\sqrt{\sum_{all\ l} P(w_k^*|w_l)}} \\
&\simeq \frac{TF}{\sqrt{DF}} \frac{TF}{\sqrt{DF}}.
\end{aligned}
$$

As described above, our method clarifies how we can use the method for other applications. From this point of view, the proposed method is significantly different from $TF \cdot IDF$, although these two processes work similarly in some ways. As for the word similarity, we may be able to undertake some further work to evaluate its accuracy, but the simulation results clearly show the effectiveness of the probabilistic frequency vectors.

5   Conclusions

We proposed a probabilistic method for computing word frequency vectors based on dictionaries. This method is significant in its well-founded procedure. A stochastic process clearly shows how to employ this method for certain applications. As an example of such applications, we demonstrated the computation of word similarity. The results show the effectiveness of our approach.

The key feature of our method is the semantic expansion of dictionaries. However, the dictionaries themselves may influence this expansion. To avoid such an influence, we may need to use as many dictionaries as possible or investigate a way of applying corpora to our procedure.

References

1. Papineni, K.: Why Inverse Document Frequency? NAACL, Pittsburg, (2001)
2. Hofmann, T.: Probabilistic Latent Semantic Indexing. 22nd Intl. Conf. on Research and Development in Information Retrieval (SIGIR). (1999) 50–57
3. Kindaichi, H., Ikeda, Y.: Gakken Japanese Dictionary, 2nd Ed. Gakushu-kenkyu-sha. (1988)
4. Matsumoto, Y. et al.: Morphological Analysis System ChaSen version 2.2.1 Manual. http://chasen.aist-nara.ac.jp/. (2000)
5. Kasahara, K., Matsuzawa, K. Ishikawa, T.: A Method for Judgement of Semantic Similarity between Daily-used Words by Using Machine Readable Dictionaries. Information Processing Society of Japan. *38* (1997) 1272–1283
6. Kasahara, K., Inago, N., Kanasugi, Y., Nagamori, C., Kato, T.: Analysis of Word Relationship. 9th Workshop on Linguistic Engineering, Japanese Society for Artificial Intelligence (JSAI). (2001) 17–27

Web Document Indexing and Retrieval

Byurhan Hyusein[1] and Ahmed Patel[1]

Computer Networks and Distributed Systems Research Group,
Department of Computer Science,
University College Dublin,
Belfield, Dublin 4,
Ireland
{bhyusein, apatel}@cnds.ucd.ie

Abstract. Web Document Indexing is an important part of every Search Engine (SE). Indexing quality has an overwhelming effect on retrieval effectiveness. A document index is a set of terms which show the contents (topic) of the document and helps in distinguishing a given document from other documents in the collection of documents. Small index size can lead to poor results and may miss some relevant items. Large index size allows retrieval of many useful documents along with a significant number of irrelevant ones and decreases the search speed and effectiveness of the searched item. Though the problem has been studied for many years there is still no algorithm to find the optimal index size and sets of index terms. This paper shows how different attributes of the web document (namely *Title*, *Anchor* and *Emphasize*) contribute to the average precision in the process of search. The experiments are done on the WT10g collection of a 1.69-million page corpus.

1 Introduction

The process of term selection for indexing in Web (text) retrieval systems is known as feature selection. The frequency of word occurrences in an article furnishes a useful measurement of word significance [1]. Salton [2]proposed a common feature selection method based on the number of occurrences of particular terms in the documents. The feature selection algorithms usually perform three steps to select the term for indexing:

- apply a stemming and stop-word algorithm, i.e. extracting the root of each word and removing the common words (terms) (example and, or, etc.) from the text of the document,
- compute the term frequency for all remaining terms in each document,
- select N terms with high term frequency from each document as index vector.

Another method involves inverse document frequency idf in the feature selection process. The weight of a term T_j in a document D_i is given by $w_{ij} = tf_{ij}idf$, where tf_{ij} is the term frequency of T_j in D_i. Again N terms with the highest weights in all the documents are chosen as features. This method has the

A. Gelbukh (Ed.): CICLing 2003, LNCS 2588, pp. 573–579, 2003.

disadvantage that it may extract those features with relatively low document frequency because the lower document frequency will give a higher weight of the feature. Wong and Fu [3] proposed an algorithm which involves coverage of the features (terms). Coverage of a feature (term) T_i is the percentage of documents in the collection containing this feature. They observe that because the above methods choose only the best N terms, there is no guarantee that these terms cover a high percentage of the documents. So if the coverage is too low, there will be many documents represented by a feature vector with zero weight in all entries. They propose the following feature selection algorithm:

- randomly select a subset of documents with size M from the collection of documents,
- extract the set of words that appear at least once in the documents,
- remove stop words and apply stemming algorithm,
- count the document frequency of the words which are extracted after applying stop-word and stemming,
- set *lower* = k and *upper* = k,
- select all words with document frequency in the range from *lower* to *upper*,
- check if the coverage of these words is larger than pre-defined threshold. If so, stop. If not, set *lower* = *lower* − 1 and *upper* = *upper* + 1 and go to the previous step.

The weakness of this method is that it depends on the number of documents and the documents which are randomly selected. A better indexing scheme would not depend on the coverage of the terms and document frequency in the collection. In the next section we examine some indexing schemes used in the most popular search engines in the Web. Much of the discussion in the next Section closely follows those in [5].

2   Related Works

The indexing scheme mainly depends on the type of search which the engine supports. Full text indexing is required when the engine supports search by phrase. This kind of indexing is used by search engines such as Alta Vista, Excite, HotBot, InfoSeek Guide, OpenText etc. It can generate large indexes and consequently requires powerful computers for search. To increase search speed HotBot and InfoSeek Guide's indexes are distributed across several computers, which enables the search engine to process the queries in parallel. Depending on the type of indexing, search engines use different weighting and ranking algorithms. So InfoSeek for example ranks its output, calculating the RSV (retrieval status value) by giving more weight to documents that contain the query terms at the beginning of the document. Others give more weight to the words in the Title tag etc.

To minimize the index size, some other search engines, for example Lycos and Worldwide Web Worm (WWWW), use the meta tags in the web documents. So Lycos indexes the terms which appear in titles, headings, and subheadings of

HTML documents as the first few lines of the beginning of the document. Because some of the documents include too many terms in these parts of the documents, if the number of index terms exceeds 100, then only the 100 most-weighted terms are taken. Lycos uses a $tf.idf$ weighting scheme, but terms which appear in the title and/or in the beginning of the document are given more weight.

Worldwide Web Worm uses a slightly different technique which indexes the titles, anchor text and URLs of HTML documents. Title, anchor text, and URL names alone cannot represent document content. Moreover, it has been estimated that 20 percent of the HTML documents on the Web have no title. In the next section we examine the different indexing schemes and report the results obtained.

3   Web Documents Indexing Scheme

Our aim is to create an indexing scheme which extracts the valuable terms of the documents and minimizes the index size without decreasing the quality of the retrieved result with respect to precision and recall. As we mentioned in the above section, title, anchor text, and URL names alone cannot represent document content. This kind of indexing automatically would lead to poor retrieved results and this is proved by our experiments. On the other hand, if the index includes all terms which appear in the document, the index size can be very big and consequently search processing would be very slow.

We decide to construct an index using the document's whole content, but giving special meaning to the following document attributes:

- title text (the text, which appears in <TITLE> </TITLE>),
- anchor text (the text, which appears in <A </A>),
- emphasized text (in our case emphasized include only <I> </I> and <EM> </EM> tags of the HTML documents),
- and all words with frequency equal or greater than two, which appears in the whole HTML document.

In addition to Worldwide Web Worm indexing scheme we included emphasized text and all words with frequency equal or greater than two which appears in the whole HTML document. Emphasized text was included because it conveys more meaning than just the words themselves. There is a difference between "Mars is known as the red planet" and "Mars is known as the red planet". In the second case, the word red contains more information than just the color of the planet. Indexing the words with frequency equal or greater than two, which appears in the HTML documents contributes for the index size and ensures (but does not guarantee) that the index will not have zero size.

More information about HTML can be found on the official Web site of World Wide Web consortium (http://www.w3.org/).

We denote these sets as follows:

- TITLE — the set of terms, which appears in <TITLE> </TITLE>,

- ANCHOR — the set of terms, which appears in <A </A>,
- EMPHASIZED — the set of terms, which appears in <I> </I> and <EM> </EM>,
- ALL — the plain text of the HTML document.

Then our indexing algorithm has the following steps.

- Create the sets TITLE, ANCHOR, EMPHASIZED and ALL for the HTML document,
- Remove all the common terms from TITLE, ANCHOR, EMPHASIZED and ALL (stop-word),
- Apply a stemming algorithm to TITLE, ANCHOR, EMPHASIZED and ALL,
- For each term in ALL calculate the term frequency,
- Create index of all terms from TITLE, ANCHOR, and EMPHASIZED plus all terms from ALL with frequency greater than one.

Our research aimed to study whether the parts indexed contribute to the average precision, and if so, how they contribute to the average precision of the retrieved results.

4   Experiments and Results

We performed experiments on a 10 gigabyte Web Task, i.e. using WT10g collection of 1.69-million pages. All runs use only the title part of TREC-9 queries 451-500. Stop word lists of 595 English, 172 German and 352 Spanish words were used. Porter's [4] stemming algorithm was applied to both documents and queries. Consider the following sets:

- All — all words, which appear in the document (its include all tags) (ALL);
- AllG1 — all words in the document with frequency greater than 1, i.e. all words from ALL with frequency greater than 1;
- T — title texts of the HTML document (i.e. the set TITLE);
- A — anchor texts of the HTML document (i.e. the set ANCHOR);
- E — emphasized text of the HTML document (i.e. the set EMHASIZED).

We performed experiments using the following indexing schemes: All, AllG1, AllG1_T, AllG1_A, AllG1_E, AllG1_T_A, AllG1_T_E, AllG1_A_E, AllG1_T_A_E, T, A, E, T_A, T_E, A_E, and T_A_E. Using the above notation, it may be seen, that for example AllG1_T_A_E means that the index includes all words in the document with term frequency greater than 1 (i.e. all words from ALL with frequency greater than 1), plus all words which appear in the TITLE, ANCHOR and EMPHASIZED sets (without repetition).

Table 1 shows the average index size using different indexing schemes (the index size depends on the collection). In the experiments we used a new weighting scheme, which gave very good results:

$$2.5 - \frac{1}{1 + \log(tf)} , \tag{1}$$

where tf is the term frequency of a particular term, which appears in a given document. In contrast to other indexing schemes, we applied this weighting algorithm to each indexed part of the document, that is the value of the weight for given term in the document depends on the frequency of this term in the whole document's text.

All terms in the query were equally weighted by one. Inner product is used as a similarity function in all experiments. The results are evaluated using the trec_eval package written by Chris Buckley of Sabir Research (available at ftp://ftp.cs.cornell.edu/pub/smart/). Table 2 shows the results obtained.

Table 1. Average index size for different types of indexing sorted in order of decreasing index size

Type of indexing	Average index size
All	132.548
AllG1_T_A_E	60.590
AllG1_A_E	59.845
AllG1_T_A	57.735
AllG1_A	56.989
AllG1_T_E	47.749
AllG1_E	46.982
AllG1_T	44.270
AllG1	43.503
T_A_E	30.016
A_E	27.599
T_A	25.463
A	22.852
T_E	9.633
E	6.283
T	3.714

In Table 2, P@10 means the precision computed after 10 documents have been retrieved. Each document precision average is computed by summing the precisions at P@10 and dividing by the number of topics (50). R-Precision is the precision after R documents have been retrieved, where R is the number of relevant documents for the topic. The average R-Precision for a run is computed by taking the mean of the R-Precisions of the individual topics in the run. The reader can find the experimental results of TREC-9 participants on http://trec.nist.gov/pubs/trec9/appendices/A/web/ and compare them with the results obtained using our indexing and weighting schemes. More detail about the algorithms for indexing and weighting schemes and the retrieval algorithms

Table 2. Results obtained using different indexing schemes. Results are sorted in order of decreasing average precision

Indexing scheme	Num. of docs	Ave. prec.	P@10	R-precision
All	1223	0.1673	0.2000	0.1895
AllG1_A_E	1005	0.1419	0.1940	0.1765
AllG1_T_A_E	1007	0.1419	0.1940	0.1765
AllG1_T_A	997	0.1413	0.1940	0.1742
AllG1_A	998	0.1412	0.1940	0.1742
AllG1_T_E	977	0.1391	0.1940	0.1718
AllG1_E	975	0.1390	0.1940	0.1718
AllG1_T	965	0.1388	0.1940	0.1699
AllG1	963	0.1387	0.1940	0.1703
E	419	0.0514	0.1100	0.0830
A_E	405	0.0514	0.1100	0.0830
A	351	0.0501	0.1200	0.0818
T_A_E	437	0.0407	0.0920	0.0687
T_A	391	0.0393	0.0960	0.0657
T_E	243	0.0372	0.0760	0.0533
T	206	0.0244	0.0600	0.0447

used by the Ninth Text REtrieval Conference (TREC-9) participants can be find on http://trec.nist.gov/pubs/trec9/t9_proceedings.html.

5   Conclusions

As we expected, the results shows that full indexing of the text leads to large average index size (132.548 terms in our case) giving high precision. On the other hand, indexing only the title, anchor and emphasized text produces small indexes, but leads to very poor results. Indexing words with frequency greater than one contributes to the precision of the retrieved results. The results show that the words belonging to the attribute title, which have frequency 1 in the attribute, All do not contribute to the average precision and they can be omitted in the process of indexing. So indexing scheme AllG1_T_A_E gives us the same precision as AllG1_T_A_E. This is confirmed by the results achieved by AllG1_T and AllG1 schemes, where the difference between the average precision is 0.0001 and the difference in the index size is 0.77 terms.

Approximately half of the index size of AllG1_T_A_E belongs to T_A_E (30.754 terms of 60.590, i.e. 22.852 to anchor text, 3.714 to title, and 6.283 to emphasized text), but the difference in the achieved average precision is quite big, respectively 0.1419 and 0.0407. So indexing only some attributes leads to very poor results.

The results show that there is a big difference between average index size of the AllG1_T_A_E scheme and AllG1 (16.342 terms) and a difference of only

0.0032 in achieved average precision. We believe that this is because the WT10g collection is created with the ultimate aim of testing different weighting and ranking algorithms, which use link analysis, and therefore it contains too much anchor text (average 22.852 terms per page).

We chose this collection because of the large number of documents which it contains. We believe that omitting title, anchor and emphasized text and indexing only the terms with frequency greater than one would lead to poor results in other collections of documents, where the documents contain terms with low frequency, which would lead to documents with index size zero and that the optimal weighting scheme is AllG1_T_A_E. Sometimes the document's index can increase too much depending on its size, term frequency and other attributes discussed above. In this case only the terms occurring in title, anchor, emphasized text, and terms with high terms frequency, can be taken as index terms.

6   Future Works

Currently we are developing a more complex indexer which will allow us to index any attribute of the web and pdf documents. This will help us to investigate: (a) in more detail how the different parts of the documents contribute to the average precision in the process of search; (b) will allow users to perform more flexible search for documents using different attributes (such as abstract, author, etc.) of the text.

References

1. Luhn, H. P.: The automatic creation of literature abstracts. IBM Journal of Research and Development, Vol. 2. (1958) 159–165.
2. Salton, G.: Automatic Text Processing: The Transformation, Analysis and Retrieval of Information by Computer. Addison-Wesley (1989).
3. Wong, W., Fu, A. W.: Incremental Document Clustering for Web Page Classification. In: 2000 International Conference on Information Society in the 21st Century: Emerging Technologies and New Challenges (IS2000), Aizu-Wakamatsu City, Fukushima, Japan, November 5-8 (2000); available at
    http://www.cse.cuhk.edu.hk/ kdd/web_mine/WPClustering/paper.ps.gz.
4. Porter, M. F.: An algorithm for suffix stripping. Program, Vol 14, No. 3, July (1980) 130–137.
5. Gudivada, V., Raghavan V., Grosky W., Kasanagottu R.: Information retrieval on the WWW. IEEE Internet Computing, Vol 1, No. 5, Sep-Oct (1997) 58–69.

Event Sentence Extraction in Korean Newspapers

Bo-Hyun Yun[1], Tae-Hyun Kim, Yi-Gyu Hwang, Pal-Jin Lee[2],
and Seung-Shik Kang[3]

[1] Human Information Processing Dept., ETRI,
161, Gajeong-Dong Yuseong-Gu, Daejeon, 305-350, Korea
{ybh, heemang, yghwang }@etri.re.kr
[2] Computer Science Dept., Chodang University
Muan, Chonnam, 534-701, Korea
pjlee@chodang.ac.kr
[3] School of Computer Science, Kookmin University
861-1 Chungnung-dong, Songbuk-gu, Seoul, 136-702, Korea
sskang@kookmin.ac.kr

Abstract. Information extraction is to extract information about the main events in the text. This paper presents an event sentence extraction method in Korean newspapers for information extraction. Event sentences contain meaningful information such as the agent, the time and the place of an event. To extract these sentences, we acquire various features such as verbs, nouns, noun phrases, 3Ws, and their weights. And then, the system computes weights of sentences and extracts event sentences by our extraction algorithm. The experimental result shows the average precision of 86.1%.

1 Introduction

Information extraction (IE) is the process of analyzing natural language text and extracting specific information such as entities, relations or events [1]. Especially, the ultimate purpose of IE is to extract information about the main events in the text. 'Event' can be defined as 'something (non-trivial) happening in a certain place and a certain time'. That is, event is some information that attracts users' interests, but this cannot be specified as a formal action or a formal situation. Namely, there is no generalized event that can be applied to all cases. In this reason, most of IE studies have usually focused on some narrow subject domain, and extracted event information related with it.

Previous IE works can be classified into two methods: one is made up of four tasks such as named entities, template elements, template relations, and scenario templates [1]; and the other is composed of two phases such as key part extraction and pattern recognition [2, 3, 4]. However, both of them must construct domain knowledge or domain specific patterns requiring a lot of human effort.

In this paper, we will propose an event sentence extraction system which can reduce the cost of constructing domain knowledge and patterns. This system automati-

A. Gelbukh (Ed.): CICLing 2003, LNCS 2588, pp. 580–583, 2003.
© Springer-Verlag Berlin Heidelberg 2003

cally learns domain knowledge from a document set related with some specific domain. By using this knowledge, we extract event sentences containing the subject, object, time, or location, etc. Extracted sentences can be used for information extraction and utilized as domain knowledge.

2 Event Sentence Extraction

In this paper, we define three types of features which can be used in the event sentence extraction as follows:

Verb: This represents action, condition, or experience leading topics of a specific domain. To obtain this kind of feature, we extract verbs tagged like 'PV' and 'NC+XSV'.

Noun and noun phrase: This will be used to reflect domain dependent information. In the cases of nouns tagged like 'NC', 'PERSON', 'LOCATION', 'ORGANIZATION', etc., we extract their lexicons as noun features. And the other cases, nouns tagged like 'NN', 'PERCENT', 'DATE', 'TIME', 'QUANTITY', etc., we extract their tags themselves, because these kinds of nouns has low frequencies. After extracting of noun features, we generate noun phrases by combining adjacent noun features.

3W(Who, When, Where): This is useful in order to take the subject, object, time, and location related with an event. Each of named entities tagged like 'PERSON' and 'ORGANIZATION', 'DATE' and 'TIME', and 'LOCATION' is respectively assigned to 'Who', 'When', and 'Where' feature.

To extract event sentences, this system takes two phases such as domain knowledge learning phase and sentence extraction phase. Both of them use language processor to get POS and named entity tags from the input documents. In the first phase, given a document set as an input, the system extracts features mentioned in chapter 2 and the weights of features by the following equations.

$$w_i = \left(tf_i \times \left(\log \frac{D}{df_i} + 1 \right) \right) \Big/ w_{\max} \qquad (1)$$

$$w_{ij} = (w_i + w_j)/2 \qquad (2)$$

The equation (1) is used to calculate weights of the verb features and the noun features. The equation (2) is utilized to calculate the noun phrase weights. Here, tf_i and df_i are the term frequency and the document frequency of the feature i. D is the document number of the training document set and $w_{\max}$ means the maximum weight. After calculating the weight, the system chooses features of high weights and stores them into the domain knowledge base. Each type of features is stored respectively.

In the sentence extraction phase, this system extracts event sentences by using the domain knowledge and the event extraction algorithm. First, sentence extractor extracts features in each sentence of the text and then combines them with the domain knowledge such as weights, frequencies, and sentence identifier lists. Moreover, it collects information of the 3W features in each sentence such as $C_{i,who}$, $C_{i,when}$, and $C_{i,where}$. These represent the number of the 'Who', 'When', and 'Where' features in the i-th sentence. After the sentence analysis, the i-th sentence weight (W_i) is calculated by the equation (3). $Co\_vn_{i,j}$ is the average weight of the noun features that co-occurred with the j-th verb in this sentence. $Co\_vp_{i,j}$ is the average weight of the noun phrases features that co-occurred with the j-th verb in this sentence. $C_{i,verb}$ is the number of verbs in this sentence. W_{v_j} is the weight of the j-th verb.

$$W_i = \sum_{j=1}^{C_{i,verb}} \left(W_{v_j} \times \left(\alpha \cdot Co\_vn_{i,j} + \beta \cdot Co\_vp_{i,j} \right) \right) \Big/ C_{i,verb} \qquad (3)$$

As mentioned before, each sentence of the input text is processed and then the information will be used to extract event sentences by using the algorithm, as shown in Fig. 1. To achieve the best performance, we tested various combinations of the features. Among 19 combinations, $C_{i,when} \wedge C_{i,where} \wedge W_i$ showed the best. Thus, we adopted it and adjusted the sentence weight thresholds(θ_k).

```
FOR all Sententces IN this Document
    IF (C_{i,when} ∧ C_{i,where} ∧ (W_i > θ_1))  THEN SELECT_SENT;
FOR all Remained_Sentences IN this Document
    SELECT max_weight SENT;
    IF ((W_i > θ_2) ∨ ((selected < θ_3) ∧ (W_i > θ_4)))  THEN
        SELECT_SENT;
END FOR
```

Fig. 1. Event Sentence Extraction algorithm

3   Experiment Results

The empirical evaluation is done on three test sets: 'Airplane crash', 'Traffic accidents', and 'Disaster'. In each test set, 20 of them are used for training and all of them are used for testing. Each of them has 40 documents. Human experts assigned five-level score (0-4) to each sentence; they gave weakly related sentences with the domain events the score 0 and the most strongly related sentences the score 4. In Table 1, "Baseline" is the method of extracting sentences by using the POS features such as noun, NP, verb and "Weighting" means the extraction method by the equation (3). "3W" is the method of extracting sentences by using the features who, when, where.

"Proposed method" means the method combining "Weighting" and "3W" by the algorithm of Fig. 1.

We derive the measure of precision, shown in the equation (4) for the evaluation. Here, n_i represents the number of selected sentences with the score i. In the results, we can see that the average precision is 86.1% and the features such as verb, who, when, where is very important in event sentence extraction.

$$P = \left(\sum_{i=0}^{4} 0.25i \times n_i \right) \bigg/ \sum_{j=0}^{4} n_j \tag{4}$$

Table 1. Precision of Each Domain

Method	Baseline	Weighting	3W	Proposed Method
Airplane crash	0.664	0.756	0.698	0.815
Traffic accidents	0.694	0.774	0.888	0.919
Disaster	0.617	0.779	0.776	0.850
Average Precision	0.658	0.770	0.787	0.861

4 Conclusion

In this paper, we proposed event sentence extraction system appropriate to Korean. We used various features such as verbs, nouns, noun phrases, and 3Ws. The system automatically trained domain knowledge with a document set and then extracted event sentences by using the knowledge and the event sentence extraction algorithm. Experiment results shows that our event extraction system can extract meaningful event sentences for IE.

References

1. Ralph Grishman, "Information Extraction: Techniques and Challenges", *In Proceedings of the Seventh Message Understanding Conference (MUC-7)*, Columbia, MD, April 1998.
2. Eduard Hovy and Daniel Marcu, "Automated Text Summarization" *Pre-conference Tutorial of the COLING/ACL'98, Université de Montréal Montréal/Canada*, August 1998.
3. Dong-Hyun Jang, "A Study of Automatic Text Summarization using a Sentence Clustering Method", Ph D. diss. Chungnam National University, Taejon, Korea, 2002.
4. J. Kupiec, J. Pedersen, and F. Chen, "A Trainable Document Summarizer," *Proceedings of the 18th Annual International ACM SIGIR Conference on R&D in IR*, 1995.

Searching for Significant Word Associations in Text Documents Using Genetic Algorithms

Jan Žižka[1], Michal Šrédl[1], and Aleš Bourek[2]

[1] Faculty of Informatics, Department of Information Technologies
Masaryk University, Botanická 68a, 602 00 Brno, Czech Republic
{zizka,sredl}@informatics.muni.cz
[2] Faculty of Medicine, Department of Biophysics
Masaryk University, Joštova 10, 662 43 Brno, Czech Republic
bourek@med.muni.cz

Abstract. This paper describes some experiments that used Genetic Algorithms (GAs) for looking for important word associations (phrases) in unstructured text documents obtained from the Internet in the area of a specialized medicine. GAs can evolve sets of word associations with assigned significance weights from the document categorization point of view (here two classes: relevant and irrelevant documents). The categorization was similarly reliable like the naïve Bayes method using just individual words; in addition, in this case GAs provided phrases consisting of one, two, or three words. The selected phrases were quite meaningful from the human point of view.

1 Introduction

The classification of generally unstructured text documents is an important task also for physicians, who need to automatically categorize electronic text documents (mostly obtained from various resources in the Internet via different search engines) into several classes—usually between relevant and irrelevant articles, reports, abstracts, etc. Many experiments revealed that using methods based on occurrences of individual words in the documents (e.g., the naïve Bayes algorithm [2], [4]) generally worked very well. However, another problem is what is actually really significant for the categorization in addition to the individual word frequencies, and what could be used as, e.g., key-words for weighty characterizations of the documents or for the Internet searching engines. One possibility is to automatically look for significant word associations (phrases). In our case, we were interested—in addition to individual words—in two- and three-word associations typical for relevant and irrelevant unstructured text documents. The described method, applied to the automatic searching for the phrases, used Genetic Algorithms (GAs) in Machine Learning, see e.g. [1]. For the training process, GAs used real medical text documents obtained from the Internet (e.g., the MEDLINE resource, and others)—actually the same data which were used in [6] and [5] for experiments with topically very similar documents in one very particular medical area, specialized gynecology.

A. Gelbukh (Ed.): CICLing 2003, LNCS 2588, pp. 584–587, 2003.
© Springer-Verlag Berlin Heidelberg 2003

2   The Application of GAs to the Searching Process

The research work started with 639 medical individual unstructured text documents (each of them having very different numbers of words—from tens to
hundreds) that were used for creating a basic dictionary of distinct words. The
dictionary was reduced from the original 12,631 words (by cutting out selected
irrelevant words—prepositions, definite/indefinite articles, and so like, and by using an English lemmatizer) to the fundamental 2,593 words. This subset served
as a dictionary of possible key-words which could be associated by couples or
triplets (e.g., genetic and algorithms can create a specific couple genetic algorithms). Then, every two and three adjacent remaining words (1th,2nd; 2nd,3rd;
3rd, 4th; ...; 1th,2nd,3rd; 2nd,3rd,4th; ...) represented a potential association as
being significant for relevant or irrelevant documents. The reason for this rep-
resentation was that a computer normally does not understand meanings of
words, so many associations were, of course, meaningless from the human point
of view. Altogether, there were 11,091 phrases having one word (2,593 phrases),
two words (5,651 phrases), or three words (2,847 phrases).

The goal of GAs was to find a vector of weights of the phrases to reveal
which phrases were—more or less—important for relevant documents and which
for irrelevant ones. The chromosomes were generated using the phrases and their
weights w_i, $-10.0 \leq w_i \leq +10.0$, $i = 1, \ldots, 11,091$. Thus, each chromosome consisted of 11,091 weights (genes), initialized randomly in the zeroth generation.
For the correct categorization of a document, the sum of weights of its specific
words and word associations played the decisive role. The population size was
300, the number of generations was 500. So, each individual in the population was
set up from certain weights of all the possible phrases, and the best chromosome
within a population assigned weights to phrases from the best classification accuracy point of view. After a chromosome decryption, a set of phrases with their
importance was available. The process of grading up looked for chromosomes
set up from certain phrases which would be able to categorize the documents
between the relevant and irrelevant class (the original classification was done
by a human physician). For the crossover operator, the algorithm selected chromosomes using the roulette-wheel method, and the probability of the crossover
for an individual was 0.9. The mutation (taken from a Gaussian distribution
around the original value) was randomly applied to each chromosome for 1% of
its genes. The best individual within each generation was copied unchanged to
the next generation. A publicly accessible library of genetic algorithms [3] was
used for the implementation[1].

3   The Results of Experiments

For the experiments of looking for a set of important word-associations to categorize the text documents, 40 text documents from 639 ones were used as the

---

[1] The software for this work used the GAlib genetic algorithm package, written by
Matthew Wall at the Massachusetts Institute of Technology.

testing examples and 599 as the training examples. The evolution of chromosomes used a cross-validation method for testing to find the best chromosome,
i.e., the best vector of weights associated with phrases. The average categoriza-

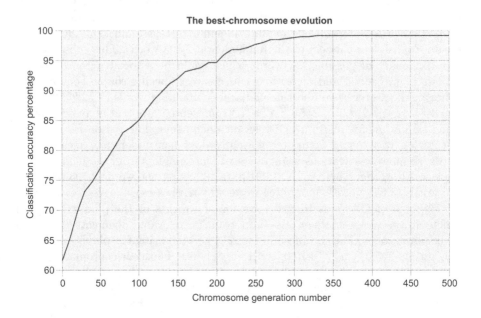

Fig. 1. The best classification-chromosome evolution on the training data.

tion accuracy for the testing documents (not used for the training process) was
75% which was quite similar to the results (using exactly the same data) of the
naïve Bayes algorithm published in [6]; however, significant word associations
were found here as the contribution of the method described above, and as the
main goal. The experiments revealed that omitting any word from the remaining
basic set of 2,593 words always decreased the classification accuracy of any of
the tested text documents. Therefore, each word—either individual or as a part
of a phrase—was somehow important. As expected, some words or phrases were
found to be far more significant than others from the specific classification point
of view—which, of course, depends on a human user.

Among the results, an interesting fact sometimes appeared: some frequent
phrases were not very much significant, e.g. a phrase have been, which was on
the fourth place among very frequent phrases, shifted down to the 98th position
as a significant association from the total 11,091 phrases. Also, many phrases
with high weights were expected as being significant. These phrases[2] were of-

---

[2] The shown examples of some resulting (and here emphasized) words have rather
distorted forms provided by an English lemmatizer.

ten just one-word phrases, like improv (words as improve, improvement, etc.), effct, surgeri, rheumatologi, diagnosi, neoplasm, ... , but many times two- or three-word phrases (e.g., depress discord, manag program, med contract, testi cure, beneΠt analysi, review tutori aim, orl head neck, beneΠt harm cost, ...). The opposite side of the scale, i.e., less important significant words, really included more common words (letter, train, infant, glucos, child, educ, letter aim, correspond Πgur achiev, computer remind system, link between intervent, ...). The similar situation was with phrases for irrelevant documents. Of course, the same set of the text documents could have different classification for different users, so different phrases would be found.

4   Conclusions

Genetic algorithms can be used for looking for word associations, which are important, e.g., for the classification of text documents. As a result, GAs provided a set of one-, two-, and three-word phrases significant for relevant and irrelevant documents, therefore supporting the automatic filtering of large amounts of unstructured text documents, as well as automatically discovering important word associations. The results are based on using a set of training examples classified into two classes (relevant and irrelevant) by a human expert in the field of his area and from his specific point of view, so the word associations also are specific from his point of view.

More experiments should be done to discover a relation between the frequency of words in documents (which supports tools based on other classification methods) and weights of found phrases for possible combinations to improve the categorization and filtering.

References

1. Goldberg, D. E. (1989): Genetic Algorithms in Search, Optimization, and Machine Learning. Addison-Wesley Pub. Co.
2. Lewis, D. D. (1998): Naïve (Bayes) at Forty: The Independence Assumption in Information Retrieval. In: *Proceedings of the 10th European Conference on Machine Learning ECML'98*. Springer Verlag, Berlin Heidelberg New York, pp. 4–15.
3. Library of genetic algorithms in C++: `http://lancet.mit.edu/ga/`
4. McCallum, A. and Nigam, K. (1998): A Comparison of Event Models for Naïve Bayes Text Classification. In: *Proceedings of the AAAI-98 Workshop on Learning for Text Categorization*. ICML/AAAI-98, Madison, Wisconsin, July 26–27.
5. Žižka, J., Bourek, A. (2002): Automated Selection of Interesting Medical Text Documents. In: *Proceedings of the Fifth International Conference Text, Speech, and Dialogue TSD-2002*. Springer Verlag, Berlin Heidelberg New York, LNAI 2448, pp. 99–106.
6. Žižka, J., Bourek, A. (2002): Automated Selection of Interesting Medical Text Documents by the TEA Text Analyzer. In: A. Gelbukh (Ed.) *Computational Linguistics and Intelligent Text Processing*, Lecture Notes in Computer Science, N 2276, Springer-Verlag, Berlin, Heidelberg, New York, 2002, pp. 402–404.

Cascaded Feature Selection in SVMs Text Categorization

Takeshi Masuyama and Hiroshi Nakagawa

Information Technology Center
The University of Tokyo
7-3-1 Hongo, Bunkyo, Tokyo, 113-0033, Japan
{tak,nakagawa}@r.dl.itc.u-tokyo.ac.jp
http://www.r.dl.itc.u-tokyo.ac.jp/{~tak,~nakagawa}/

Abstract. This paper investigates the effect of a cascaded feature selection (CFS) in SVMs text categorization. Unlike existing feature selections, our method (CFS) has two advantages. One can make use of the characteristic of each feature (word). Another is that unnecessary test documents for a category, which should be categorized into a negative set, can be removed in the first step. Compared with the method which does not apply CFS, our method achieved good performance especially about the categories which contain a small number of training documents.

1 Introduction

The World Wide Web continues to grow at an amazing speed. As the available online documents increase, the inability of users to assimilate and profitably utilize such large numbers of documents becomes more and more apparent. In this paper, we focus on the demand for high-precision systems in real-world applications [4]. When using a search engine, for instance, users can only afford to read the top few documents retrieved for a query, and therefore a search engine with high precision returns would be preferred to one with a high recall but low precision. Similarly, when a classifier is used to help users to decide the categories relevant to a document, again only a few candidate categories can be read by the users. Published papers in the text categorization domain have mainly focused on optimizing performance in the range where precision and recall are balanced (where the break-even point or F_1 is optimized), and do not focus on precision-recall trade-off [4].

In this paper, we propose a cascaded feature selection (CFS) using Support Vector Machines (SVMs). SVMs are a machine learning method for solving two-class pattern recognition problems and have been shown to yield good generalization performance on a wide variety of classification problems that require large-scale input space, such as handwritten character recognition, face detection, and text categorization.

SVMs learn from the training set to find a decision surface (classifier) in the vector space of documents that 'best' separates the documents into two

A. Gelbukh (Ed.): CICLing 2003, LNCS 2588, pp. 588–591, 2003.

classes (i.e. relevant and non-relevant). Although SVMs are a binary classifier, we used 'One-against-the-Rest' version of SVMs to treat a multi-class (multi-label) problem. This approach constructs k classifiers, one for each class. The kth classifier constructs a hyperplane between class k and the k-1 other classes.

2   Our Approach

While many feature selection strategies, such as information gain, mutual information, and χ^2 statistic, have been applied to SVMs text categorization so far, we propose a cascaded feature selection (CFS) using linear SVMs.

CFS has two steps which SVMs classify test documents either into a positive or a negative set (Step 1), and then SVMs again classify the test documents categorized into the positive set in Step 1 either into a positive or a negative set (Step 2). Since we focused on Part-Of-Speech (POS) information, the difference between Step 1 and Step 2 is that all types of parts of speech (ALL) are used in Step 1 and only nouns (NOUN) are used in Step 2.

Taira et al. report that the best feature set (POS) greatly differs from category to category [2]. Therefore we can expect high precision, if we select suitable POSs in each step.

3   Experiments

3.1   Data and Preprocessing

We used the Reuters-21578 corpus (the ApteMod version, 90 categories) for evaluating our method. We obtained the training set of 7,769 documents and the test set of 3,019 documents. The average number of categories assigned to a document was 1.3, and the most categories assigned to a document were 15.

All documents were tagged using Brill's POS tagger. From the tagged documents, we obtained two sets, one consisting only of noun (NOUN), and the other composed of all types of parts of speech (ALL). We added synonyms (NOUN) of WordNet 1.7 in both steps[1]. We extracted only 300 words for each category, which are handled by a threshold for high mutual information (MI)[2]. We also used the word frequency (i.e. the word occurrence) in a document as an attribute-value for each feature.

Reuters-21578 has a skewed category distribution. The most common category has 2,877 training documents, but 82% of categories have less than 100 documents, and 33% of the categories have less than 10 documents. Takamura et al. (2001) report that when training documents are few in number, SVMs often fail to produce a good result, although several efforts against this problem have been made [3].

---

[1] After tagging, stemming, and stop word removal, the training set contained 38,958 distinct words (ALL) and 26,686 distinct words (NOUN).

[2] We selected the words using five-fold cross validation [1], [5].

3.2   Results and Discussion

We evaluated our method using precision (Pr), recall (Re), and $F_1(Pr, Re) = \frac{2PrRe}{Pr+Re}$. In our experiments, we paid attention to the following points: 1) whether precision increased, 2) whether precision was higher than recall, 3) whether F_1 value was constant or increased, after applying CFS.

Table 1 shows the comparison of our method (CFS) and NON-CFS method[3]. In Table 1, the column 'POS' represents the part-of-speech we applied, while the columns 'Pr', 'Re', and 'F_1' represent precision, recall, and F_1 value. As shown in Table 1, we find that the precision of our method is 2.1% higher than the precision of NON-CFS method, keeping F_1 value constant. This improvement was mainly achieved by the categories which contain a small number of training documents. We show this in Table 2.

Table 1. The comparison of our method (CFS) and NON-CFS method (CFS/NON-CFS)

POS	$Pr(\%)$	$Re(\%)$	$F_1(\%)$
NOUN	92.4/90.3	73.4/74.7	81.8/81.8

Table 2 shows the top 5 categories which precisions increased. In Table 2, the column 'Category(Tr)' represents a category name (Category) and the number of documents assigned to the category (Tr). As shown in Table 2, we find that precisions of the categories which contain the small number of training documents increased dramatically. We also find that F_1 values of these categories increased significantly. For example, the category 'heat' represents the validation of our method clearly, since precision increased and was higher than recall increasing F_1 value after applying CFS. Precisions increased in 75.0% categories which contain more than 100 documents and also increased in 22.9% categories which contain less than 100 documents. Furthermore, F_1 values were constant or increased in 76.6% categories.

Table 3 shows the results of the existing methods which were tested on the Reuters-21578. Yang et al. (1999) chose 10,000 words which were handled by a threshold for high χ^2 statistic, and used TF-IDF as an attribute-value for each feature [5]. Their precision and recall were 91.3% and 81.2%, respectively. Fukumoto et al. (2001) used synonyms and their hypernymy relations of WordNet 1.6 for representing documents. They extracted only nouns, treating the word frequency in a document as an attribute-value for each feature [1]. Their precision and recall were 83.3% and 89.9%, respectively.

---

[3] We treated only 300 words (NOUN) for each category using MI threshold. The attribute-value was assigned as the word frequency in a document.

Table 2. The top 5 categories which precisions increased (CFS/NON-CFS)

Category(Tr)	$Pr(\%)$	$Re(\%)$	$F_1(\%)$
housing(16)	100/50.0	50.0/50.0	66.6/50.0
soy-meal(13)	100/50.0	23.0/23.0	37.5/31.7
yen(45)	100/50.0	7.1/7.1	13.3/12.5
heat(14)	100/57.1	60.0/80.0	75.0/66.6
hog(16)	100/66.6	33.3/33.3	50.0/44.4

Table 3. Comparison to Previous Results

Method	$Pr(\%)$	$Re(\%)$
Yang et al.(1999)	91.3	81.2
Fukumoto et al.(2001)	83.3	89.9
our method	92.4	73.4

4   Summary and Future Work

We focused on the demand for high-precision systems and proposed a cascaded feature selection (CFS) using linear SVMs. Compared with NON-CFS method, we showed the validation of our method, especially about the categories which contain a small number of training documents.

While we validated our method for the Reuters-21578 corpus, we have to apply CFS to other corpora such as Reuters Corpus Volume I (RCV1) and Japanese corpus.

Although we applied CFS to all categories, we have to consider automatic variable CFS for each category.

References

1. Fukumoto, F. and Suzuki, Y.: Learning Lexical Representation for Text Categorization. *Proceedings of the NAACL'01 Workshop on Wordnet and Other Lexical Resources: Applications, Extensions and Customizations*, pp.156–161 (2001).
2. Taira, H. and Haruno, M.: Feature Selection in SVM Text Categorization. *Proceedings of the 16th National Conference on Artificial Intelligence (AAAI'99)*, pp.480–486 (1999).
3. Takamura, H. and Matsumoto, Y.: Feature Space Restructuring for SVMs with Application to Text Categorization. *Proceedings of the 2001 Conference on Empirical Methods in Natural Language Processing (EMNLP'01)*, pp.51–57 (2001).
4. Yang, Y.: A Study on Thresholding Strategies for Text Categorization. *Proceedings of the 24th Annual International ACM SIGIR Conference on Research and Development in Information Retrieval (SIGIR'01)*, pp.137–145 (2001).
5. Yang, Y. and Liu, X.: A re-examination of text categorization methods. *Proceedings of the 22nd Annual International ACM SIGIR Conference on Research and Development in Information Retrieval (SIGIR'99)*, pp.42–49 (1999).

A Study on Feature Weighting in Chinese Text Categorization[*]

Xue Dejun and Sun Maosong

National Key Laboratory of Intelligent Technology and Systems
Department of Computer Science and Technology, Tsinghua University
Beijing, China 100084
xdj00@mails.tsinghua.edu.cn, lkc-dcs@mail.tsinghua.edu.cn

Abstract. In Text Categorization (TC) based on Vector Space Model, feature weighting and feature selection are major problems and difficulties. This paper proposes two methods of weighting features by combining the relevant influential factors together. A TC system for Chinese texts is designed in terms of character bigrams as features. Experiments on a document collection of 71,674 texts show that the F1 metric of categorization performance of the system is 85.9%, which is about 5% higher than that of the well-known TF*IDF weighting scheme. Moreover, a multi-step feature selection process is exploited to reduce the dimension of the feature space effectively in the system.

1 Introduction

Text Categorization (TC) is to automatically assign natural language texts with thematic categories from a predefined category set [1]. With the population of Internet and electronic publications, TC has been studied extensively in the last decade, and a growing number of statistical classification methods and machine learning techniques have been applied to solving this challenging task, including Bayesian classifier [3],[4],[5], neural network classifier [6], nearest neighbor classifier [7], decision rule classifier [8], centroid-based classifier [9], Rocchio classifier [10], support vector machine [11], classifier committees [12],[13], hierarchical classification [14], etc. Originally, these efforts target at the English language. In recent years, some works of TC for Chinese are reported [17],[18],[19],[21].

In TC, Vector Space Model (VSM) is often adopted to index texts [2]. In the model, a text is abstracted as a weighted feature vector. All potential features usually form a very high dimensional feature space, so feature selection is needed by selecting the top significant features according to their weights almost without sacrificing the categorization performance. Weighting features in feature vectors as well as in feature space is thus a key problem in TC.

Term Frequency (TF, *tf*) and Document Frequency (DF, *df*) serve as the simplest criteria for weighting features, mainly used in feature selection [1]. It is assumed that

---

[*] This research is supported by National 973 Project of China under grant No.G1998030507 and Foundation for the University Talent Teacher by the Ministry of Education of China.

A. Gelbukh (Ed.): CICLing 2003, LNCS 2588, pp. 592–601, 2003.

rare features are either non-informative or noisy. As most features have low *tf/df* in the original space, feature selection with the criteria can scale the space dramatically. But they fail to treat the features with high *tf/df* which contribute nothing to category prediction. And, many informative features with low-medium *tf/df* may be eliminated as the threshold increases.

Term Frequency * Inverse Document Frequency (TF*IDF) is widely used to evaluate features in Information Retrieval [1],[2]. The frequent features distributing evenly in the document space and the rare features will gain small weight with it. By introducing a simplified version of information gain (IG') into TF*IDF, Lu et al. [20] proposed a method of TF*IDF*IG' to reduce dimension and weight features for feature vector. The experimental results on a corpus (6,518 documents) shown that it does not improve the categorization performance considerably compared with the standard TF*IDF.

Yang et al. [15] systematically compared the performance of DF, Chi-square (CHI), Information Gain (IG), Mutual Information (MI), and Term Strength (TS) in feature selection. The experiments on Reuters-22173 (13,272 documents) and OHSUMED (3,981 documents) claimed that CHI and IG are most effective.

There is no explicit word boundary, like spacing in English, in Chinese texts, and practical word segmentation system is still not available to date, N-Gram character string is therefore considered as an alternative of index unit. Nie et al. [22],[23] reported that, in Chinese information retrieval, the average retrieval precision of using character bigrams as features (39.21%) is fractionally better than using words (longest-matching segmentation algorithm) as features (39.04%). Using N-Gram character strings as features can achieve satisfactory categorization performance [24].

By analyzing the influential factors of weighting features under the framework of VSM, we further propose two formulae, i.e. TF*IDF*IG and TF*EXP*IG, and design an automated TC system for Chinese texts based on the features of character bigrams. In the system, we adopt a multi-step feature selection process with different criteria to reduce the dimension of the feature space. Large-scale experiments indicate that our methods considerably improve the categorization performance.

The remainder of this paper is organized as follows. In section 2, we analyze the influential factors of weighting features through an example. In order to combine the factors, we come up with our methods to evaluate features in feature vector. In section 3, we experiment the methods in a TC system for Chinese on a large-scale corpus, and discuss the experimental results. Some conclusions appear in section 4.

2   Feature Weighting

2.1   The Related Formulae

For convenience of discussion, we list the related formulae here, and claim that all feature weights should be normalized to eliminate the impact of document size. In the formulae below, we omit this process.

TF*IDF Weighting. There are several variants of the standard TF*IDF. We adopt formula 1 which shows good performance in our experiments.

$$w(t_k,c_j) = TF(t_k,c_j) \times IDF(t_k) = \log(tf_{kj}+1.0) \times \log(N/df_k) \,. \qquad (1)$$

where tf_{kj} is the frequency of feature t_k occurring in documents which belong to category c_j, df_k is the document frequency of t_k, and N is the total number of training documents.

IG Weighting.

$$w(t_k) = -\sum_{j=1}^{M} P_d(c_j)\log P_d(c_j) + P_d(t_k)\sum_{j=1}^{M} P_d(c_j \mid t_k)\log P_d(c_j \mid t_k) \qquad (2)$$

$$+ P_d(\overline{t_k})\sum_{j=1}^{M} P_d(c_j \mid \overline{t_k})\log P_d(c_j \mid \overline{t_k}) \,.$$

In the formula, $P_d(c_j)$ is the number of documents involved in category c_j over the total number of documents in the document collection, $P_d(t_k)$ is the number of documents containing feature t_k over the total number of documents, $P(c_j \mid t_k)$ is the number of documents of category c_j which contain t_k over the number of documents containing t_k.

TF*IDF*IG' Weighting. The original form in [20] is as formula 3.

$$w(t_k,c_j) = tf_{kj} \times \log(N/df_k + 0.01) \times IG'_k \,. \qquad (3)$$

$$IG'_k = -\sum_{l=1}^{M} \left(P(c_l) \times \log P(c_l)\right) + \sum_{l=1}^{M} \left(P(c_l \mid t_k) \times \log P(c_l \mid t_k)\right)$$

$$P(c_j) = tf_j \Big/ \sum_{l=1}^{M} tf_l \,, \quad tf_j = \sum_{k=1}^{S} tf_{kj} \,, \quad P(c_l \mid t_k) = tf_{kl}/tf_k \,.$$

where IG'_k is a simplified version of IG, M is the size of the predefined category set, s is the total number of features.

Replacing TF*IDF of formula 3 with that of formula 1, we get formula 4 (We will refer TF*IDF*IG' to formula 4 throughout the paper):

$$w(t_k,c_j) = TF(t_k,c_j) \times IDF(t_k) \times IG'_k = \log(tf_{kj}+1.0) \times \log(N/df_k) \times IG'_k \,. \qquad (4)$$

CHI Weighting.

$$w(t_k, c_j) = \frac{N\left[P_d(t_k, c_j) \times P_d(\overline{t_k}, \overline{c_j}) - P_d(t_k, \overline{c_j}) \times P_d(\overline{t_k}, c_j)\right]^2}{P_d(t_k) \times P_d(c_j) \times P_d(\overline{t_k}) \times P_d(\overline{c_j})} .$$

(5)

$$w(t_k) = \max_{j=1}^{M}\left\{w(t_k, c_j)\right\}.$$

(6)

As for the probabilities involved, please refer to formula 2.

Correlation Coefficient.

$$\rho_{XY} = \frac{Cov(X, Y)}{\sigma_X \cdot \sigma_Y} .$$

(7)

where X, Y are random variables, $Cov(X, Y)$ is their covariance, and σ_X, σ_Y are their standard deviations respectively.

2.2   The Influential Factors of Weighting Features

In TC based on VSM, there are two phases where features need to be weighted: one is to reduce feature dimension, another is to represent feature vectors for documents/categories.

In order to study the influential factors of weighting features, we design an example in the context of TC. Supposed that there are 2 categories $\{c_1, c_2\}$, each of which contains 3 documents $\{d_{j1}, d_{j2}, d_{j3}\}$, and there are 10 distinct features $\{w_1\text{-}w_{10}\}$ appearing in the document collection. The feature-document matrix is shown in the upper part of Table 1. The task is to select a feature subset from the feature space (10 features) and create a proper feature vector for each category. With these two feature vectors, the category of any free document can be predicted.

In Table 1, tfs and dfs of features $w_8\text{-}w_{10}$ are very small, indicating that $w_8\text{-}w_{10}$ are likely to be noisy. Though w_7 has high tf and may possess some degree of capability in document discrimination, it is non-informative for category prediction due to its even tf/df distribution over c_1 and c_2. Feature w_6 occurs only in some documents of c_2 with a high tf, so its occurrence in a document provides an evidence of assigning the document to category c_2. Features w_1 and w_3 have almost equivalent tf and df, but their df distributions over category space are meaningful. The most documents involving w_3 appear in c_1, so w_3 is better than w_1 for category prediction. Features w_4 and w_5 have high tfs and occur mostly in c_2, so they should be powerful for categorization. However, w_5 should get a higher weight than w_4, because the latter has higher df. Features w_2, w_3 and w_5 should have same categorization capability for their almost similar properties in all aspects. With these analyses, we can reduce the original feature space to $\{w_1\text{-}w_6\}$.

Now, upon the features $\{w_1\text{-}w_6\}$, we can create feature vectors for c_1 and c_2, and measure the features in the vectors. From Table 1 we can see, in the feature vector of

c_1, features w_2 and w_3 should have high weights for their strong categorization capabilities and high tf in c_1. Although w_4 and w_5 are individually more powerful for category prediction than w_1, in the feature vector for c_1, w_1 should weight more for its high tf in c_1 than w_4 and w_5. Similarly, we can discuss the feature vector for c_2.

Table 1. An Example of TC

	w_1	w_2	w_3	w_4	w_5	w_6	w_7	w_8	w_9	w_{10}
d_{11}	10	12	2						1	
d_{12}		5	10	1			10	1		1
d_{13}	10	8	10	2	3		10			
d_{21}	2		1	20	10		10			
d_{22}		5		12	5	5	10			
d_{23}	2			10	20	20				1
tf	24	30	23	45	38	25	40	1	1	2
df	4	4	4	5	4	2	4	1	1	2
IDF	0	0	0	0	0	0	0	0	0	0
	.2	.2	.2	.1	.2	.5	.2	.8	.8	.5
TF*ID	0	0	0	0	0	0	0	0	0	0
F	.2	.3	.2	.1	.3	.7	.3	.2	.2	.2
μ	12	15	11.5	22.5	19	12.5	20	0.5	0.5	1
σ	11.3	14.1	14.8	27.6	22.6	17.7	0	0.7	0.7	0
σ/μ	0.9	0.9	1.3	1.2	1.2	1.4	0	1.4	1.4	0
CHI	0	3	3	1.2	3	3	0	1.2	1.2	0
IG'	0	0	0	0	0	0.2	0	0.1	0.1	0
IG	0	0.1	0.1	0.1	0.1	0.1	0	0.1	0.1	0

In sum, the influential factors of weighting features in TC include: (1) tf; (2) df; (3) the distribution of tf over category space; (4) the distribution of df over category space; (5) relative tf in a document/category.

In order to measure these factors, we introduce several statistics shown in the lower part of table 1. TF*IDF statistic combines tf and df distribution over the document space, but it does not depict df distribution over category space. For example, w_7 has a high TF*IDF value, but it is weak for categorization. On the contrary, σ/μ statistic describes feature distribution in the category space very well (σ and μ are the standard deviation and mean of a feature over category space), but it is weak to depict feature distribution in the document space. For example, σ/μ can discriminate w_1 and w_3, but can not discriminate w_1 and w_2. Statistics CHI, IG and IG' are criteria to measure the categorization capability of features individually in the feature space. From the example, we can see that CHI is the best of the three, and IG' is the worst.

2.3   Our Methods of Weighting Features

According to the analyses in the above section, we proposed two methods of weighting features for representing feature vectors: TF*IDF*IG, TF*EXP*IG:

$$w(t_k, c_j) = TF(t_k, c_j) \times IDF(t_k) \times IG(t_k) \ . \tag{8}$$

$$w(t_k, c_j) = TF(t_k, c_j) \times EXP(t_k) \times IG(t_k) \ . \tag{9}$$

where TF, IDF and IG refer to section 2.1, $EXP(t_k)$ equals to $e^{h \times \frac{\sigma_k}{\mu_k}}$, σ_k, μ_k are the standard deviation and mean of feature t_k, and h is a constant which is used to adjust the proportion of the statistic in the weight and determined by experiments. By introducing information gain into TF*IDF, formula 8 combines all the five influential factors mentioned in section 2.2 into a single function. In formula 9, we further introduce σ and μ to emphasize the distribution of a feature in the category space. Here, the non-linear transformation on statistic σ/μ intends to amplify its changes.

3 Experiments

In order to validate the new methods, we design a TC system for Chinese texts, and experiment with a large-scale document collection. We use Chinese character bigrams as features.

3.1 Training and Test Set

We adopt the categorization system of Encyclopedia of China as predefined category set which comprises 55 categories. According to the categorization system, we build up a document collection consisting of 71,674 texts with about 74 million Chinese characters. Each text is manually assigned a category label. The number of documents in the categories is quite different, ranging from 399 (Solid Earth Physics Category) to 3,374 (Biology Category). The average number of documents in a category is 1303. The average length of documents is 921 Chinese characters. We divide the document collection into two parts: 64,533 texts for training and 7,141 texts for test in proportion of 9:1.

3.2 The Multi-step Dimension Reduction

Because the number of extracted character bigrams is huge (about 1.75 million unique brigrams are derived from the training set in our experiments), we carry through a three-step feature selection process to reduce the dimension of the feature space. First, we simply use *tf* threshold at 10 to eliminate the rare features (the number of unique features reduced from about 1.75 millions to about 0.41 million, or, 76.4% of original features are removed at this step). Second, we use *df* threshold at 10 to further terminate 2.8% of the original feature space (see Section 3.4 for detailed discussion). These two steps focus on terminating noisy features and avoiding over-fitting, removing in total 79.2% features from the original feature space. At last, CHI is applied to reduce dimension, keeping the maximum 70,000 features as the feature set.

3.3 The Centroid-Based Classifier

In the TC system, we adopt centroid-based classifier which is a kind of profile-based classifier, because of its simplification and fast speed. After bigram extraction and dimension reduction, we build *tf* vectors for documents, then sum up *tf* vectors in each category to get the *tf* vector of the category, and further weight the features based on the summed *tf* vectors of categories with certain criterion, such as formula 8 or 9, to create weighted feature vectors for categories. The resulting feature vectors are considered as the centroids of the categories, as shown below:

$$V_j = \left(w_{1j}, w_{2j}, ..., w_{sj} \right) . \tag{10}$$

where w_{kj} is the weight of feature t_k in feature vector V_j, s is the total number of features.

Then, classifier f can be set up:

$$f = \arg\max_{j=1}^{M} \left(V_j \bullet d \right) . \tag{11}$$

where d is the feature vector of a free document.

For a category, classification performance is measured in terms of precision (Pr) and recall (Re). For the whole category set, we adopt F1 metric with micro-averaging of individual Pr and Re.

3.4 Experimental Results

Fig. 1 illustrates the changes of the number of retained features with the increasing of the *df* threshold at the second step of dimension reduction. Fig. 2 shows the categorization performance of four methods of interest when setting different *df* thresholds at the second step. As can be seen, if the *df* threshold is above 10, the number of features eliminated will increase very fast, and the categorization performance drops down significantly. It indicates that in the feature space, most of features are low frequent, and many of them are informative for category prediction. Therefore we set the *df* thresholds at 10.

Fig. 3 reveals that with enough features, the two methods we proposed can improve the categorization performance considerably, i.e., about 2% better than TF*IDF*IG', and 5% better than TF*IDF. As the number of retained features decreases, the performances of all the tested methods converge to the same. It indicates that if the feature set is too small, it can not properly represent documents and categories. Upon the small feature set, we achieve neither satisfactory categorization performances nor differences among the methods.

Among the six methods in Fig. 3, TF*EXP and TF*IG are tested as components of other methods. According to categorization performance, the methods can be classified to three groups: Group 1 (G1) includes TF*EXP*IG and TF*IDF*IG with the best performance; Group two (G2) includes TF*IDF*IG' and TF*IG with the moderate performance; Group 3 (G3) includes TF*IDF and TF*EXP with the worst performances. Introducing IG into two methods in G3 can improve the performance about 5%, signaling that IG is significant for categorization. The categorization performances of TF*EXP*IG and TF*IDF*IG in G1 are about 2% higher than TF*IG in G2 in the best case, suggesting that EXP and IDF can contribute a lot to categorization as well. The performance of EXP is about 0.8% higher than IDF (but the constant h needs to be adjusted in experiments. Here, h is regulated from 0.35 to 0.2 with the decline of the number of features). TF*IDF*IG gains a better performance than TF*IDF*IG', meanwhile the performances of TF*IG and TF*IDF*IG' are very close, implying that IG is more powerful for categorization than IG'.

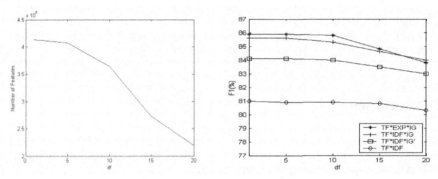

Fig. 1. Dimension Reduction with *df* Thresholds   **Fig. 2.** The Categorization Performance with Different *df* Thresholds in Feature Selection

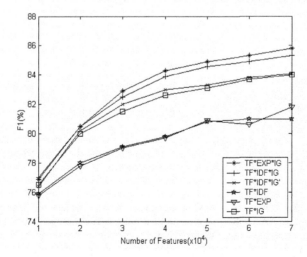

Fig. 3. Categorization Performance with Different Methods of Weighting Features

As the influential factors of weighting features are not independent of each other, and every statistic introduced does not usually describe a single factor exclusively, we calculate the correlation coefficients among the statistics with formula 7. The results are given in Table 2: TF is negatively correlated with other 4 basic statistics. IDF and EXP have a positive correlation coefficient 0.69. It is amazing that the correlation coefficient between IDF and IG reaches 0.91, and even surprisingly, the correlation coefficient between IG and IG' is near 1.0.

Table 2. Correlation Coefficients of Statistics

	TF	IDF	EXP	IG	IG'	TF*EXP	TF*IDF
TF	1	-0.97	-0.62	-0.86	-0.86	-0.49	0.52
IDF	-0.97	1	0.69	0.91	0.91	0.60	-0.40
EXP	-0.62	0.69	1	0.76	0.76	0.88	-0.27
IG	-0.86	0.91	0.76	1	1	0.81	-0.27
IG'	-0.86	0.91	0.76	1	1	0.81	-0.28
TF*EXP	-0.49	0.60	0.88	0.81	0.81	1	0.08
TF*IDF	0.52	-0.40	-0.27	-0.27	0.73	0.08	1

4   Conclusion

This paper propose two formulae, i.e. TF*IDF*IG and TF*EXP*IG for feature weighting in TC, after analyzing the relevant influential factors under the framework of VSM. Experiments on large-scale document collection show that these two formulae outperform TF*IDF. An automated TC system for Chinese texts is also conducted based on Chinese character bigrams, and a multi-step feature selection process is exploited to reduce the dimension of the feature space in the system.

References

1. Fabrizio Sebastiani: Machine Learning in Automated Text Categorization. ACM Computing Surveys, Vol. 34(1). ACM Press New York (2002) 1–47.
2. Salton, G., McGill, M.: Introduction to Modern Information Retrieval. McGraw-Hill Book Company, New York (1983).
3. Lewis, D.D.: Naïve Bayes at Forty: The Independence Assumption in Information Retrieval. In Proceedings of 10th European Conference on Machine Learning (1998) 4–15.
4. Domingos, P., Pazzani, M.: Beyond Independence: Conditions for the Optimality of the Simple Bayesian Classifier. In Proceedings of 13rd International Conference on Machine Learning (1996) 105–112.
5. McCallum, A., Nigam, K.: A Comparison of Event Models for Naïve Bayes Text Classification. In AAAI-98 Workshop on Learning for Text Categorization (1998) 41–48.
6. Wiener, E., Pedersen, J.O., Weigend, A.S.: A Neural Network Approach to Topic Spotting. In Proceedings of 4th Annual Symposium on Document Analysis and Information Retrieval (1995) 317–332.

7. Yang, Y.M.: Expert Network: Effective and Efficient Learning from Human Decisions in Text Categorization and Retrieval. In Proceedings of 17th Annual International ACM SIGIR Conference on Research and Development in Information Retrieval (1994) 11–21.
8. Apte, C., Damerau, F., Weiss, S.M.: Automated Learning of Decision Rules for Text Categorization. ACM Transactions on Information Retrieval, Vol. 12(3). ACM Press New York (1994) 233–251.
9. Theeramunkong T., Lertnattee V.: Improving Centroid-Based Text Classification Using Term-Distribution-Based Weighting System and Clustering. In Proceedings of International Symposium on Communications and Information Technology (2001) 33–36.
10. Joachims, T.: A Probabilistic Analysis of the Rocchio Algorithm with TFIDF for Text Categorization. In Proceedings of 14th of International Conference on Machine Learning (1997) 143–151.
11. Joachims, T: Text Categorization with Support Vector Machines: Learnging with Many Relevant Features. In Proceedings of 10th European Conference on Machine Learning (1998) 137–142.
12. Quinlan, J.: Bagging, Boosting, and C4.5. In Proceedings of 13th National Conference on Artificial Intelligence, AAAI Press/ MIT Press (1996) 163–175.
13. Schapire, R.E., Singer, Y.: BoosTexter: A Boosting-Based System for Text Categorization. Machine Learning, Vol. 39(2/3), (2000) 135–168.
14. Theeramunkong, T., Lertnattee, V.: Multi-Dimensional Text Classification. In Proceedings of 19th International Conference on Computational Linguistics (2002) 1002–1008.
15. Yang Y.M., Pedersen, P.O.: A Comparative Study on Feature Selection in Text Categorization. In Proceedings of 14th International Conference on Machine Learning (1997) 412–420.
16. Ng, H.T., Goh, W.B., Low, K.L.: Feature Selection, Perceptron Learning, and a Usability Case Study for Text Categorization. In Proceedings of 20th Annual International ACM SIGIR Conference on Research and Development in Information Retrieval (1997) 67–73.
17. Xie, C.F., Li, X.: A Sequence-Based Automatic Text Classification Algorithm. Journal of Software, Vol. 13(4), (2002) 783–789.
18. Xue, D.J., Sun, M.S.: An Automated Text Categorization System for Chinese Based on the Multinomial Bayesian Model. In Proceedings of Digital Library – IT Opportunities and Challenges in the New Millennium (2002) 131–140.
19. Huang, X.J., Wu, L.D., Hiroyuki, I., Xu, G.W.: Language Independent Text Categorization. Journal of Chinese Information Processing, Vol. 14(6), (2000) 1–7.
20. Lu, S., Li, X.L., Bai, S., Wang, S.: An Improved Approach to Weighting Terms in Text. Journal of Chinese Information Processing, Vol. 14(6), (2000) 8–13.
21. Gong, X.J., Liu, S.H., Shi, Z.Z.: An Incremental Bayes Classification Model. Chinese J. Computers, Vol. 25(6), (2002) 645–650.
22. Nie, J.Y., Brisebois, M., Ren, X.B.: On Chinese Word Segmentation and Word-based Text Retrieval. In Proceedings of International Conference on Chinese Computing (1996) 405–412.
23. Nie, J.Y., Ren, F.J.: Chinese Information Retrieval: Using Characters or Words? Information Processing and Management Vol. 35, (1999) 443–462.
24. Zhou, S.G., Guan, J.H.: Chinese Documents Classification Based on N-Grams. In Proceedings of 3rd Annual Conference on Intelligent Text Processing and Computational Linguistics (2002) 405–414.

Experimental Study on Representing Units in Chinese Text Categorization

Li Baoli, Chen Yuzhong, Bai Xiaojing, and Yu Shiwen

Institute of Computational Linguistics,
Department of Computer Science and Technology,
Peking University, Beijing, P.R. China, 100871
{libl, degai, baixj, yusw}@pku.edu.cn

Abstract. This paper is a comparative study on representing units in Chinese text categorization. Several kinds of representing units, including byte 3-gram, Chinese character, Chinese word, and Chinese word with part of speech tag, were investigated. Empirical evidence shows that when the size of training data is large enough, representations of higher-level or with larger feature spaces result in better performance than those of lower level or with smaller feature spaces, whereas when the training data is limited the conclusion may be the reverse. In general, representations of higher-level or with larger feature spaces need more training data to reach the best performance. But, as to a specific representation, the size of training data and the categorization performance are not always positively correlated.

1 Introduction

With the emergence of WWW, more and more electronic documents are available. To detect, extract, and summarize information effectively and efficiently from such a huge text collection, many new technologies have been and have to be created and developed. Text categorization is among these technologies. As the first step of exploring huge text data, automatic text categorization aims at assigning one or more pre-defined category tags to free text documents [1]. In the past years, many machine learning techniques have been applied to text categorization, including decision trees, Naïve Bayes, neural networks, K-nearest neighbor, support vector machine, and so on.

Obviously, text that is already stored in machine-readable form (e.g. HTML, PDF) is not suitable for most learning algorithms. It has to be transformed into some appropriate representation. Such a representation of text has a crucial influence on how well the learning algorithm can generalize. It should capture as much information as possible from the source text and can be easily managed by computer.

In text categorization, vector space model (VSM) is frequently used for text representation. That is, each document is represented as a vector of weighted feature counts. The representing unit or feature can be a character, a word, a phrase, even a sentence or a whole document. Choosing appropriate representing unit is the first step of feature selection.

A. Gelbukh (Ed.): CICLing 2003, LNCS 2588, pp. 602–614, 2003.

In this paper, we will try to find if there is a more effective representation in Chinese text categorization. Character based and word based Chinese text categorization were both widely used in the literature, e.g. [2] [3]. But other representations such as n-grams were rarely studied. Marc Damashek reported in [4] that n-grams are effective for document retrieval, sorting and categorization in English and Japanese. Moreover, comparative study on different representations in Chinese text categorization has not been found, whereas several efforts have been made to investigate the relationship between feature selection and Chinese information retrieval [5] [6]. Text categorization and information retrieval focus on different goals in feature selection, although the former is usually regarded as a subfield of the latter. In Text Categorization, the ability of distinguishing different categories is focused on, whereas in Information Retrieval, the representativeness for a document is the greatest concern.

Some special difficulties should be considered in Chinese text categorization. Unlike English, there is no explicit space between Chinese words in a running text. So, word segmentation, which turns a Chinese character string to a sequence of words, usually has to be done as the first step for a Chinese processing system. In addition, there are several different Chinese character encoding systems widely used in Chinese community, e.g. GB2312 and BIG5. Chinese web pages encoded differently co-exist on the WWW. However, till now there is no such a Chinese word segmentation and POS tagging system that can smoothly deal with all different encoding systems.

In this paper we present the empirical evidence for the influence of text representation on Chinese text categorization. We try to seek answers to the following questions:

- What are the strengths and the weaknesses of different Chinese text representations?
- To what extent can Chinese word segmentation and part of speech tagging modules affect the performance of a categorization system?

In section 2, we introduce the text representation issue in automatic categorization. Then we briefly explain the kernel algorithm used in our experiments. Experimental data, methods, and results are presented in section 4, followed by some discussion.

2 Text Representation in Automatic Categorization

Text representation has a crucial influence on how well an automatic categorization system works. Ideally, to get better performance, it should capture as much semantic and contextual information as possible from the source text and can be easily managed by computer. Obviously, the text itself (e.g. HTML, XML, DOC, PDF) is not suitable for computer processing. It has to be transformed into some appropriate representation. Different approaches to representing text for classification recognize or ignore semantic information and contextual dependencies to varying extents. They can be structured according to the level on which they analyze the text [7]:

(1) *Sub-Word Level*: decomposition of words and their morphology;

n-Gram is the most popular representation at this level. This representation has the potential for dealing with multilingual texts. And it is robust against some spelling errors. As to Chinese, one character is usually represented by two or more bytes. Thus, we can regard a Chinese sentence as a sequence of bytes and get n-grams from this representation.

(2) *Word Level*: words and lexical information;

In many cases, words are meaningful units of little ambiguity even out of a context. The word-based representations have been found very effective in text classification. Only the frequency of a word in a document is recorded, while the logical structure and the layout of the document and the word order are ignored. This representation is commonly called the bag-of-words approach. And it appears to be a good compromise between expressiveness and complexity.

Chinese character can also be seen as a representation at word level. As we know, Chinese character is ideograph. Most characters are words by themselves. They can be combined to form another word. In a sense, words consisting of two or more characters can be regarded as compound words. Therefore, it is understandable why character based methods could obtain desirable performance in Chinese text categorization. Because there is no need for word segmentation, character based method has much advantage in time complexity. Furthermore, this method can easily process texts with different encoding systems.

(3) *Syntactic Level*: phrases and syntactic information;

With efficient parsing tools available, some researches have been done using syntactic structure information. Noun phrases are the most commonly used structure.

In a sense, the part of speech of words in running texts could be regarded as one kind of syntactic information.

(4) *Semantic Level*: the meaning of text;

(5) *Pragmatic Level*: the meaning of text with respect to context and situation (e.g. dialog structure);

Generally, the higher the level, the more details the representation captures about the text. However, along with greater details comes an increased complexity in producing such representations automatically. For example, producing semantic representations requires substantial knowledge about the domain of interest and can only be solved approximately with state-of-the-art methods. Due to higher cost and low performance, representations recognizing the pragmatic structure of text have not been explored yet.

Different representations have different sizes of potential feature space. There are about 6,700 Chinese characters in GB2312 encoding system, whereas tens of thousand words will be included in a lexicon.

In our experiments, we compared four kinds of text representation method, including byte 3-gram, Chinese character, Chinese word, and Chinese word with part of speech tag. They belong to different representation levels.

At sub-word level, we just selected byte 3-gram to evaluate. In fact, Chinese character representation can be regarded as a special representation of byte 2-gram, which eliminates unreasonable 2 byte combinations. Higher n-grams, such as 4-gram, are not experimented with because feature spaces of these representations are too huge and we do not have enough data to justify the conclusion, if any.

In addition, to study how different word segmentation and part of speech tagging modules affect the performance of automatic categorization, two different lexical analysis modules were tested. One is based on simple forward maximum matching algorithm, and the other is developed by us in the past years and proved more effective than the former one.

3 Naïve Bayes Classifier

In our experiments, we use the Naïve Bayes algorithm to compare different representing units, because it is one of the most efficient algorithms in time cost [8].

The idea of the naïve bayes classifier is to use a probabilistic model of text to estimate $P(c|d)$, the probability that a document d is in class c. This approach assumes that the text data is generated by a parametric model, and uses training data to calculate Bayes-optimal estimates of the model parameters. Then, it classifies new test documents using Bayes' rule (equation 2) to calculate the posterior probability that a class would have generated the test document in question. The class that achieves the highest score is regarded as the class of the test document (equation 1).

$$c = \arg\max_{c'} P(c'|d).$$ (1)

$$P(c_j|d_i) = \frac{P(c_j)P(d_i|c_j)}{P(d_i)}.$$ (2)

In equation 2, $P(d\ i)$ is a constant while j varies. Therefore, $P(c\ j)P(d\ i|c\ j)$ is the only effective part for classification. $P(c\ j)$ can be estimated by equation 3, which means the proportion of documents tagged as category $c\ j$ in the training collection. D stands for training collection. $|D|$ is the number of documents in entire training corpus.

$$P(c_j) = \frac{\sum_{i=1}^{|D|} P(c_j|d_i)}{|D|}.$$ (3)

$$P(d_i|c_j) = P(|d_i|)|d_i|! \prod_{t=1}^{|F|} \frac{P(f_t|c_j)^{N_{it}}}{N_{it}!}.$$ (4)

$$P(f_t|c_j) = \frac{1 + \sum_{i=1}^{|D|} N_{it} P(c_j|d_i)}{|F| + \sum_{s=1}^{|F|} \sum_{i=1}^{|D|} N_{is} P(c_j|d_i)}.$$ (5)

$P(d\ i|c\ j)$ can be estimated by equation 4 and 5. In our implementation, we adopted multinomial model, which in contrast to the multi-variate Bernoulli event model captures word frequency information in documents. F is the set of features. $|F|$ is the number of features in F. $f\ t$ is the t-th feature in F. $N\ it$ is defined as the count of the number of times feature $f\ t$ occurs in document $d\ i$.

4 Experiments and Results

4.1 Corpus for Training and Testing

We designed a web site directory for Chinese search engine (http://e.pku.edu.cn), which includes 12 top-categories, and about 1,006 sub-categories. To train and test our system, we manually extracted typical web pages for each class. This was done by tens of selected graduate students with related background. Some search engines such as Google were utilized in extracting typical web pages. Roughly, 20 web pages were collected for each sub-category. We totally got 20,283 web pages. By removing the incomplete web pages and web pages encoded not in GB2312[1], we obtained a corpus containing 19,892 Chinese web pages and 278M bytes. Table 1 lists the 12 top-categories and their distributions in the corpus.

In the following experiments, the collected corpus was evenly divided into 10 parts at random.

Table 1. 12 top-categories and their distributions in the corpus

No.	Category	Number	Percentage
1	Humanities and Arts	764	3.84
2	News and Media	449	2.26
3	Business and Economy	1642	8.25
4	Entertainment	2637	13.26
5	Computer and Internet	1412	7.10
6	Education	448	2.45
7	Region and Organization	1343	6.75
8	Science	2683	13.49
9	Government and Politics	493	2.48
10	Social Science	2763	13.89
11	Health	3180	15.99
12	Society and Culture	2038	10.25

4.2 Word Segmentation and Part of Speech Tagging

Unlike English, Chinese words are not explicitly delimited by white space. Therefore, word segmentation is usually the first step for Chinese processing. In our experiments, we tested two different Chinese word segmentation modules. One is based on forward maximum matching and named FMM. The other is rule and statistic based and named SEGTAG. These two modules share the same basic lexicon (about 79,000 entries) and part of speech tagging module, whereas SEGTAG module utilizes some extra lexicons. The two modules were used in the form of dynamic link library (DLL).

---

[1] Because the tested word segmentation and POS tagging modules can not deal with Chinese texts in other encoding systems, we only conducted our experiments with Chinese texts encoded in GB2312.

We evaluated these two modules on a large public available annotated corpus (People's Daily Corpus)[2], which contains about 1,140,000 Chinese words. The evaluation metrics used in [5] were adopted in our research.

$$p = \frac{N_3}{N_2} . \tag{6}$$

$$r = \frac{N_3}{N_1} . \tag{7}$$

$$F_1(p,r) = \frac{2 \times r \times p}{r + p} . \tag{8}$$

Let S be the original segmented corpus, U be the unsegmented corpus, and S' be the resulted corpus by a word segmentation system. The precision, recall and $F\,1$ measure are defined as equation 6, 7, and 8, respectively. Where $N\,1$ denotes the number of words in S, $N\,2$ denotes the number of words in the estimated segmentation S', and $N\,3$ the number of words correctly recovered.

Table 2 gives the empirical results of these two modules on the People's Daily corpus.

Table 2. Performance of two word segmentation and POS tagging modules

Module	Recall in Word Segmentation	Precision in Word Segmentation	$F\,1$ measure in Word Segmentation	Precision in POS tagging
FMM	90.13%	84.31%	87.12%	87.44%
SEGTAG	95.11%	94.59%	94.85%	89.10%

4.3 Scoring Text Categorization

For evaluating the effectiveness of category assignments by classifiers to documents, the standard precision, recall, and $F\,1$ measure are often used. Precision is defined to be the ratio of correct assignments by the system divided by the total number of the system's assignments. Recall is the ratio of correct assignments by the system divided by the total number of correct assignments. The $F\,1$ measure combines precision (p) and recall (r) with an equal weight as equation 8.

These scores can be computed for the binary decisions on each individual category first and then be averaged over categories. Or, they can be computed globally over all the $n*m$ binary decisions where n is the number of total test documents, and m the number of categories in consideration. The former way is called macro-averaging and the latter called micro-averaging. It is understood that the micro-averaging scores (recall, precision, and $F\,1$) tend to be dominated by the classifier's performance on

---

[2] This corpus can be obtained from http://icl.pku.edu.cn/Introduction/corpustagging.htm.

common categories, and that the macro-averaging scores are more influenced by the performance on rare categories.

4.4 Experiments and Results

We experimented with six different representing units, i.e. byte 3-gram, Chinese character, word from FMM module, word with POS tag from FMM module, word from SEGTAG module, and word with POS tag from SEGTAG module. In the feature selection phase of the experiments, we removed features that occurred only once[3].

In addition to varying representing units, we also examined the relationship between performance in text categorization and the proportion of data used for training. For example, in the 1:9 Chinese character experiments, we randomly selected one of the ten sub-corpora as training data, and the others for testing. Each experiment was conducted three times using different sub-corpora. The overall performance was calculated by averaging three experiments.

Figure 1 illustrates the micro-averaging $F\ 1$ scores with different representing units while the ratio of the number of documents used for training to the number of documents for testing varies. Figure 2 illustrates the macro-averaging $F\ 1$ scores.

In experiments based on Chinese character, micro- and macro-averaging $F\ 1$ scores reach the highest when the ratio of the number of documents used for training to the number of documents for test is 1:9. After that, the scores slightly decrease while the ratio increases. When using word derived from FMM module as the representing unit, the scores steadily increase until the highest points arrive at the ratio of 4:6. Then the scores begin to decrease. The $F\ 1$ scores show the similar trends while using the other four representations. It can be found that the higher the representing level or the larger the feature space of a representation, the larger the size of training data for achieving the best performance. As to a specific representation, the size of training data and the categorization performance are not always positively correlated. After the size of training data exceeds a threshold, more data will lead to a reduction in performance.

It should be noted that byte 3-gram achieves surprisingly high performance when training data is enough. Its scores are higher than those of word from FMM module. The macro-averaging $F\ 1$ scores of byte 3-gram are even closer to those of word from SEGTAG module. It is out of our expectation. We try to give some explanations here. Obviously, byte 3-gram can capture some contextual information. In the mean time, it does not loss the ability of carrying semantic information. A byte-3-gram contains a complete Chinese character. In fact, most Chinese words consist of one or two characters. And the average Chinese word length in running texts is about 1.83 characters [9], which is close to the length of a byte 3-gram. Moreover, the specific encoding system for Chinese characters may also contribute to the final results. About 3008 Chinese characters in GB2312 are encoded according to their components, which carry some important semantic information. For example, two characters beginning

---

[3] According to [10], document frequency is a simple but effective means for feature selection in Information Retrieval as information gain and Chi-Square test.

with a component "鱼" may be given two adjacent codes in GB2312, and their meanings are usually related to *Fish*.

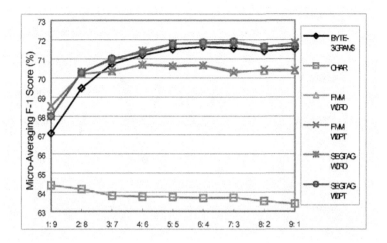

Fig. 1. Micro-Averaging *F 1* scores with different representing units while the proportion of data used for training varies

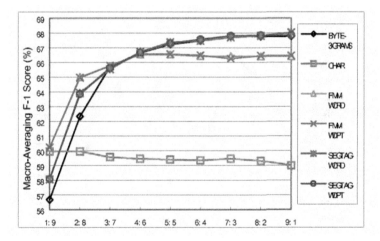

Fig. 2. Macro-Averaging *F 1* scores with different representing unit while the proportion of data used for training varies

When the size of training data is small, representations of lower level or with smaller feature space may obtain higher performance, e.g. in figure 2 the representation based on Chinese character achieves higher score than the representation based on word from SEGTAG module at the point 1:9. However, when the size of training data is large enough, the advantage of representations of higher level or with larger feature space appears, e.g. in the same figure the representation based on word from

SEGTAG module achieves higher score than the representation based on Chinese character at point 9:1.

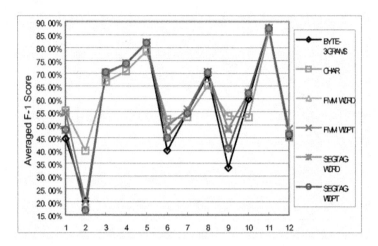

Fig. 3. Results of experiment 1(1:9), which takes one of the ten sub-corpora as training data, and leaves the rest nine as test data

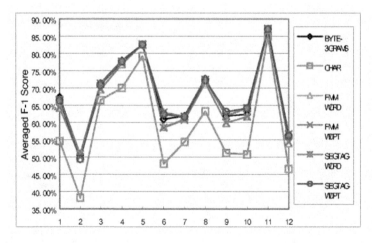

Fig. 4. Results of experiment 9(9:1), which takes nine of the ten sub-corpora as training data, and leaves the rest one as test data

In our experiments, the representation based on Chinese word with part of speech tag is slightly superior to the representation based only on Chinese word, although at some points (e.g., point 7:3 in figure 2, FMM-WORD vs. FMM-WDPT) the former achieves lower score than the latter. This suggests that part of speech tags contribute few to text categorization performance. But it should be noticed that we used a small POS tag set which contains only about 40 tags.

Figure 3 and 4 illustrate the *F 1* scores of each top-category with two different proportions of training data, i.e. 1:9 and 9:1 respectively.

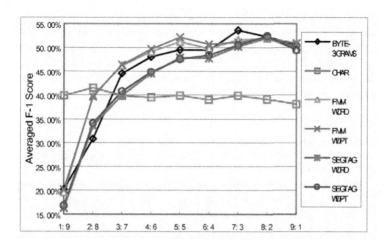

Fig. 5. Results of category 2 (*News & Media*)

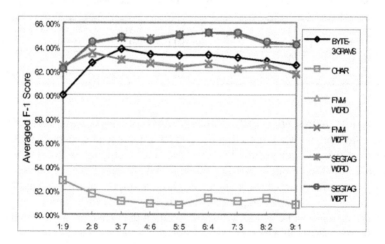

Fig. 6. Results of category 10 (*Social Science*)

The documents of health category (No. 11) are correctly classified with the highest accuracy, whereas the documents of news & media category (No. 2) are very difficult to recognize. Maybe the phenomenon is not strange, because these two categorizes are the most and the least common categories respectively in our corpus. However, it is not predeterminate that categories with larger training data will result in better performance than categories with smaller training data. For example, category 10 (Social Science) is not more detectable than category 5 (Computer & Internet) in all experiments. Some categories, e.g. social science and society & culture, fall into confusable clusters.

Figure 5 and 6 show results of category 2 and 10 respectively. In figure 5, representing units from FMM module demonstrate better performance than representing units from SEGTAG module on average and in most cases. One reason may be that a weak word segmenter accidentally breaks compound words into smaller constituents [6] and these smaller constituents make important features overt rather than lose key semantic information. Another reason may be that FMM module is accidentally more suitable to deal with documents on news & media in the corpus than SEGTAG module, although the latter achieves better performance than the former in experiments on People's Daily corpus.

Table 3. Top 10 features when using Chinese character and Chinese word from SEGTAG module respectively as the representing unit. They were derived from the entire corpus according to their TFIDF weights

SEGTAG-WORD	经济	社会	制度	管理	企业	理论	问题	政治	法律	政策
CHAR	政	济	义	策	社	思	企	民	革	争

Table 4. Time costs of different representations (*Unit: second*) in experiment 1(1:9)[4]

Time \ Representation	BYTE-3GRAM	CHAR	FMM-WORD	FMM-WDPT	SEGTAG-WORD	SEGTAG-WDPT
Training	270	40	317	320	517	523
Running	1100	310	1500	1500	2400	2400

In figure 6, representing units from SEGTAG module achieve much better performance than others when detecting documents about social science, which is one of the most confusable categories. For example, the averaging performance of using word from SEGTAG module is over 13% higher than that of using Chinese character. Chinese word other than Chinese character plays an important role in classifying confusable categories, because bigger constituents like words or technical terms usually carry more detailed and exact semantic information than smaller ones, which could be easily observed from table 3.

Table 4 shows time costs of different representations in experiment 1(1:9). Using Chinese character as the representing unit has obvious advantage over other options.

5   Discussion

It is interesting to compare the results of our experiments with those of related researches on information retrieval although there are some differences between Infor-

---

[4] The experiments were done under Windows 2000, P-IV 1.5G CPU, and 256M memories.

mation retrieval and text categorization. Palmer and Burger [5] observed that accurate segmentation tends to improve retrieval performance. But, Peng Fuchun et al. [6] found that the relationship between segmentation and retrieval performance is in fact nonmonotonic and at around 70% word segmentation accuracy an over-segmentation phenomenon begins to occur which leads to a reduction in information retrieval performance.

In our experiments, the relationship between Chinese word segmentation accuracy and text categorization performance is not monotonic. But we have not found similar observation to [6] in text categorization. In fact, the size and the characteristic of training data and test data play an important role in the overall system performance. When the size of training data is small, poor word segmentation accuracy may result in better performance (refer to figure 1 and 2). However, when the size of training data is large enough, the advantage of good word segmentation accuracy appears. On the other hand, evaluation on different data sets may be another factor affecting the investigation of the relationship between Chinese word segmentation accuracy and text categorization performance. That is, a system with poor word segmentation accuracy, which is evaluated on one data set, may achieve better performance when dealing with another different data set.

Table 5. Comparison between different representations

Aspect \ Representation	BYTE-3GRAM	CHAR	FMM-WORD	FMM-WDPT	SEGTAG-WORD	SEGTAG-WDPT
Performance	better	poor	better	better	better	better
Cost	high	lower	higher	higher	higher	higher
Algorithm	simpler	simpler	simple	complicated	complicated	complicated
Extra Resource	none	none	Word list	lexicon, rules	lexicon, rules	lexicon, rules
Multilingual or multi-encoding	easier	easy	difficult	difficult	difficult	difficult

Table 5 summarizes the strengths and the weaknesses of different representing units that we have experimented with. In general, representing units derived from word segmentation and POS tagging result in better performance. We got the highest performance when using a good module for word segmentation and POS tagging. But, obtaining such representing units usually need more complicated processing and pays out higher costs of time and space than getting Chinese character or byte 3-gram. Moreover, when dealing with documents in different encoding systems, we have to do some extra work for the systems using these representations, such as reconstructing lexicon, rewriting some rules, even rebuilding systems. On the contrary, algorithms for recognizing Chinese character and byte 3-gram are very simple. They could be easily used for processing documents written in different Chinese encoding systems. Using byte 3-gram as representation unit demonstrates quite good performance in our experiments. It promotes our further investigation on n-grams with different n values and at different levels (e.g. sub-word, word, phrase, and so on.) as representing units in the future. The performance of systems using Chinese character is poor in general (when the size of training data is large enough), although their time and space costs are lower than those of systems using other representing units. In one word, there is no unique best representation. When choosing the appropriate representing unit, we have to consider several factors carefully according to the practical applications.

Acknowledgements. Many thanks to Mr. Feng Shicong for providing the corpus. And we gratefully acknowledge comments from two anonymous reviewers. This research was funded by National Natural Science Foundation of China (69973005 and 60173005) and 985 Projects of Peking University.

References

1. Christopher D. Manning, Hinrich Schutze: Foundations of Statistical Natural Language Processing. MIT Press (1999)
2. Wang Mengyun, Cao Suqing: The System for Automatic Text Categorization Based on Chinese Character Vector. Journal of Informatics (in Chinese), 19:6 (2000) 644–649
3. Pang Jianfeng, et al.: Research and Implementation of Text Categorization System Based on VSM. Journal of Research on Computer Application (in Chinese), 9 (2001) 23–26
4. Marc Damashek: Gauging Similarity with n-Grams: Language-Independent Categorization of Text. Science, 267:10(1995) 843–848
5. Palmer D., Burger J.: Chinese Word Segmentation and Information Retrieval. In AAAI Symposium Cross-Language Text and Speech Retrieval (1997)
6. Peng Fuchun, et al.: Investigating the Relationship between Word Segmentation Performance and Retrieval Performance in Chinese IR. In the Proceedings of the 19th International Conference on Computational Linguistics (2002)
7. Joachims T.: Learning to Classify Text Using SVM: Methods, Theory and Algorithms. Kluwer Academic Publishers (2002)
8. Li Baoli, et al.: A Comparative Study on Automatic Categorization Methods for Chinese Search Engine. In the Proceedings of the Eighth Joint International Computer Conference (2002) 117–120
9. Liu Yuan, et al.: Segmentation Standard for Modern Chinese Information Processing and Automatic Segmentation Methodology. Tsinghua University Press (1994)
10. Yang Y., Pedersen J.O.: A Comparative Study on Feature Selection in Text Categorization. In the Proceedings of Fourteenth International Conference on Machine Learning (1997) 412–420

Partitional Clustering Experiments with News Documents

Arantza Casillas[1], Mayte González de Lena[2], and Raquel Martínez[2]

[1] Dpt. de Electricidad y Electrónica, Facultad de Ciencias
Universidad del País Vasco
arantza@we.lc.ehu.es
[2] Escuela Superior de CC. Experimentales y Tecnología
Universidad Rey Juan Carlos
{mt.gonzalez,r.martinez}@escet.urjc.es

Abstract. We have carried out experiments in clustering a news corpus. In these experiments we have used two partitional methods varying two different parameters of the clustering tool. In addition, we have worked with the whole document (news) and with representative parts of the document. We have obtained good results working with a representative part of the document. The experiments have been carried out with news in Spanish and Basque in order to compare the results in both languages.

1 Introduction

The document clustering deals with the problem of identifying sets of thematically related documents. Document clustering has been investigated for using in a number of different areas: information retrieval, browsing collections of documents, etc; and a number of techniques have been used [3]. We are investigating the use of clustering techniques for addressing the linking of news documents and we are working in two languages: Spanish and Basque. We have employed partitional methods in our experiments. With partitional methods the clusters generated contain objects that agree with a strong pattern. For example, their contents include some shared words or terms; in each cluster there are objects (news) that share a subset of the dimension space. In this paper we present the results of the experiments that we have carried out with two different news corpus, one in Spanish and the other in Basque. In the next Section we briefly describe the documents; Section 3 describe the used clustering tool, the type of parameters and the experiments; in Section 4 we present the results; finally, section 5 summarizes the conclusions drawn from the work carried out.

2 Documents Description

In the project we are involved [4], we are working with a corpus of categorized news. The categories are the Industry Standard IPTC Subject Codes [2]. We have selected for the experiments the sport category in order to test the clustering

A. Gelbukh (Ed.): CICLing 2003, LNCS 2588, pp. 615–618, 2003.

of news of the same category. We have selected 37 news of 6 different sports; in Spanish there are: football 16, baseball 2, swimming 2, athletics 6, cycling 7, and skiing 4; in Basque: football 4, cycling 7, pelota 16, swimming 2, athletics 6, and handball 2. The news corpus in Spanish and Basque are not parallel or comparable. The news selection has been random among news of the first days of the 2000 year. The documents have been preprocess in order to work with the lemmas instead of inflected forms. In addition, the words of a stoplist used in Information Retrieval (with articles, determines, ...) have been eliminated of the Spanish documents.

3   Experiment Description

The tool we have selected for experimenting is CLUTO [1]. In addition to the different classes of clustering algorithms, criterion functions and similarity functions, CLUTO can operate on very large datasets with respect to the number of objects (documents) as well as the number of dimensions.In these experiments we have varied 3 different parameters that control how the tool computes the solution: the method, the similarity function, and the clustering criterion function.

- We have used two methods: RB and RBR. In RB method the k clustering solution is computed by performing $k - 1$ repeated bisections. In each step, the cluster that is selected for further partitioning is that one whose bisection will optimize the value of the overall clustering criterion function the most. The RBR method is similar to the previous one, but at the end the overall solution is globally optimized.
- Two similarity function have been used: COS and CORR. These functions determine how the similarity between objects will be calculated. COS represents the cosine function, and CORR the correlation coefficient.
- We have used three clustering criterion functions: I1, I2, H2. The I2 and H2 functions are told to lead generally to very good clustering solutions (see formulas in [1]).

In order to determine if working with the whole document leads to better results than working with a representative part of the document, we have experimented: (1) with the whole document, (2) only with the title and the first paragraph, and finally (3) with the title and the first paragraph but increasing the weight of the title words. This aspect can be very important in reducing the computational cost of the clustering when a large corpus of news must be clustered.

4   Results

We carried out a manual clustering in order to test the experiments results. The manual clustering consisted of grouping the documents by sport category (football, cycling, ...). This manual clustering is used by the clustering tool in order to compute the quality of the clustering solution using external quality measures. The tool computes this quality in terms of entropy and purity (see formulas in [6]). Small entropy values and large purity values indicate good clustering solution.

The results of the experiments can be seen in Table 1 and Table 2. Each table reflects the three best results in connection with entropy and purity showing the parameters that have been used. In addition, we propose the coherence metric in order to show other quality metric of the clustering solution. We consider that a cluster is coherent if it has at least two clearly related objects (news). The percentage of coherence is the percentage of coherent clusters in the solution.

Table 1. Results of the three best combinations of Spanish document clustering

Num. clusters & Part of docu.	Method	Similarity Function	Criterion Function	Entropy	Purity	% Coherence
10 cl. & The whole document	RBR	COS	I2	0.256	0.784	100
	RB	COS	I2	0.320	0.730	100
	RB	COS	H2	0.335	0.703	90
10 cl. & Title, First paragraph	RB	COS	I2	0.292	0.703	80
	RB	CORR	H2	0.298	0.703	80
	RBR	CORR	H2	0.298	0.703	80
10 cl. & First parag. weighted title	RB	COS	H2	0.292	0.676	70
	RBR	COS	I2	0.342	0.676	90
	RB	COS	I1	0.347	0.703	90
6 cl. & The whole document	RB	COS	I2	0.456	0.622	100
	RB	COS	H2	0.460	0.649	100
	RBR	COS	I2	0.461	0.622	100
6 cl. & Title, First paragraph	RB	COS	H2	0.401	0.676	100
	RB	COS	I2	0.463	0.595	100
	RBR	COS	I2	0.466	0.622	100
6 cl. & First parag. weighted title	RB	COS	I1	0.445	0.649	100
	RBR	COS	I1	0.445	0.649	100
	RB	COS	I2	0.476	0.595	100

Working with a number of clusters equal than the number of different sports the news belong to, that is 6, the best results are obtained taken into account only the title and the first paragraph of each news. However, if the number of cluster increases, the best results correspond to the whole document. The best clustering solutions have been obtained in most of the tests with the I2 or H2 clustering criterion functions. With regard to the others parameters, there are appreciable differences among both groups of news. Whereas in Spanish the RB method is the best in most of the cases, in Basque the best is the RBR method. With regard to the similarity function, the cosine function (COS) leads to better results with the Spanish news, whereas the correlation coefficient (CORR) works better in half of the Basque ones.

5   Conclusions

The best clustering solutions have been obtained with different parameters (method and similarity function) in both groups of news. Each type of document and language will require experimentation in order to determine the best

A. Casillas, M. González de Lena, and R. Martínez

Table 2. Results of the three best combinations of Basque document clustering

Num. clusters & Part of docu.	Method	Similarity Function	Criterion Function	Entropy	Purity	% Coherence
10 cl. & The whole document	RBR	CORR	I2	0.293	0.730	80
	RBR	CORR	I1	0.303	0.730	100
	RB	CORR	I2	0.323	0.676	70
10 cl. & Title, First paragraph	RBR	CORR	H2	0.306	0.730	100
	RBR	COS	H2	0.340	0.703	90
	RB	COS	I2	0.347	0.676	100
10 cl. & First parag. double title	RB	COS	H2	0.368	0.676	100
	RBR	COS	I1	0.376	0.649	70
	RB	COS	I1	0.376	0.649	70
6 cl. & The whole document	RBR	COS	I2	0.513	0.595	100
	RBR	CORR	I2	0.514	0.595	100
	RB	CORR	H2	0.529	0.541	100
6 cl. & Title, First paragraph	RBR	COS	H2	0.446	0.622	100
	RB	COS	H2	0.448	0.649	100
	RBR	COS	I2	0.479	0.541	100
6 cl. & First parag. double title	RBR	CORR	I2	0.495	0.595	100
	RBR	CORR	H2	0.525	0.568	100
	RB	CORR	I2	0.528	0.595	100

combination of parameters. When reducing the computational cost is a critical criteria in a particular clustering task, our experiments show that working with the title and the first paragraph of the news leads to good enough results in entropy in some cases. However, in other domain this conclusion could be uncertain. With regard to the number of clusters, the more clusters there are the entropy metric improves, but the coherence decreases in some cases, so working with the whole document is required in order to obtain better results.

Acknowledgments. This research is being supported by the Spanish Research Agency, project HERMES (TIC2000-0335-C03-03).

References

1. "CLUTO. A Clustering Toolkit. Release 2.1". http://www-users.cs.umn.edu-/karypis/cluto.
2. Industry Standard IPTC Subject Codes. http://www.sipausa.com/iptcsubject-codes.htm.
3. A. Gelbukh, G. Sidorov, A. Guzman-Arenas. "Use of a weighted topic hierarchy for text retrieval and classification." *Text, Speech and Dialogue. Proc. TSD-99. Lecture Notes in Artificial Intelligence, No. 1692, Springer,* 130–135, 1999.
4. "Project HERMES (Hemerotecas Electrónicas: Recuperación Multilingue y Extracción Semántica)" of the Spanish Research Agency, (TIC2000-0335-C03-03). http://terral.ieec.uned.es/hermes/.
5. Y. Zhao and G. Karypis. "Evaluation of hierarchical clustering algorithms for document data sets". *CIKM,* 2002.
6. Y. Zhao and G. Karypis. "Criterion functions for document clustering: Experiments and analysis". http://cs.umn.edu/karypis/publications.

Fast Clustering Algorithm for Information Organization*

Kwangcheol Shin and Sangyong Han

Dept. of Computer Science and Engineering, Chung-Ang Univ.,
221 Huksuk-Dong, DongJak-Ku, Seoul, 156-756, Korea
kcshin@archi.cse.cau.ac.kr hansy@cau.ac.kr

Abstract. This study deals with information organization for more efficient Internet document search and browsing results. As the appropriate algorithm for this purpose, this study proposes the heuristic algorithm, which functions similarly with the star clustering algorithm but performs a more efficient time complexity of $O(kn),(k<<n)$ instead of $O(n^2)$ found in the star clustering algorithm. The proposed heuristic algorithm applies the cosine similarity and sets vectors composed of the most non-zero elements as the initial standard value. The algorithm is purported to execute the clustering procedure based on the concept vector and produce clusters for information organization in $O(kn)$ period of time. In order to see how fast the proposed algorithm is in producing clusters for organizing information, the algorithm is tested on TIME and CLASSIC3 in comparison with the star clustering algorithm.

1 Introduction

The document clustering method was first developed to organize the database text and visualize it before the searching process is operated. Then recently, the method is applied in studies to cluster the search result documents and automatically refine them in order to make the search more efficient. Organizing document groups can be helpful for the user in browsing after classifying the related document group from the non-related document group and also reduce the search range when the user has input a query. It is also convenient to scan through the texts of the document groups since the search results provided by the search engine are organized.

The most recent study on information organization deals with star clustering [1]. The star clustering algorithm presents the information system by applying the undirected, weighted similarity graph $G=(V,E,\omega)$ and forms a dense subgraph $G'=(V,E_\rho)$ based on G in order to organize the information. Compared to the formerly used average link or single link algorithm, the star clustering algorithm scored higher in the recall-precision measurement and is also capable of automatically determining the appropriate number of clusters when the user has not input a specific digit. However,

---

* This research is supported by the ITRI of Chung-Ang University.

A. Gelbukh (Ed.): CICLing 2003, LNCS 2588, pp. 619–622, 2003.

in order to form the similarity graph, which is required for executing the algorithm, the required time amount is $O(n^2$, n is the number of documents). But the time period $O(n^2)$ is too much time wasting when one has a massive amount of document groups to process or search on real time.

The current study therefore suggests a new algorithm which retains the benefits of the star clustering algorithm but only requires $O(kn),(k<<n)$ amount of time in organizing the information.

This study is organized in the following format. First, section 2 will describe the newly proposed algorithm. Section 3 shall compare the test results of the two algorithms.

2   New Clustering Algorithm That Supports the Dense Area Search

The key idea of the suggested algorithm is as follows. The concept vector [2] is used to find the dense area. Let's say a single cluster contains a single document vector. Then the cluster's concept vector would be the normalized value of the document vector. But if the cluster is to contain another document vector, then the normalized value of the mean vector [2] of the two document vectors is the concept vector. Its concept vector can represent the cluster. Due to this fact, it is more efficient to use the concept vector when measuring the similarity between the cluster and documents. Accordingly if one could perceive the concept vector among the related document vectors gathered together in a certain area, then binding the vectors with high similarity with the concept vector could produce a very refined cluster.

The following algorithm is suggested based on this idea.

First, among the document vectors amounting up to n, the ones with the most elements excluding *zero* are selected to form a cluster.

Cst_t *($1 \le t \le k$, k is the number of clusters)= {V_i ($1 \le i \le n$): V_i has the largest number of non-zero elements in documents set}* .

The reason for selecting the document vectors with the most elements excluding *zero* is because such vectors contain many words and so could have more connections to other document vectors. By selecting such vectors one can find the dense area more quickly.

When a cluster is formed, the concept vector of the cluster Cst_t is set and the similarities between the concept vector and the rest of the documents are measured. The document vectors that show a similarity higher than a certain level are added to the cluster and the concept vector is renewed after each document vector is added. Then the next document vector's similarity is measured with the new concept vector.

if Sim($C(Cst_t)$, V_j) $> \rho$($1 \le j \le n$, ρ is the threshold value),
    then $V_j \in Cst_t$ and recalculate $C(Cst_t)$; $C(Cst_t)$ means the concept vector of Cst_t .

Once a cluster has been produced, the document vectors that are contained in the cluster are excluded from the document group. (If the documents are not excluded, the same document can appear in several different clusters. Since the test results did not show much difference under the two conditions, the present study executed the tests excluding the existing documents.) Then the rest of the document vectors go through the process described above repeatedly for k number of times to form clusters in the dense area. Table 1 shows the operation of the suggested algorithm.

Table 1. The Suggested Clustering Algorithm

1. Convert the documents in the document group into vectors of L2 norm.
2. Set the document vector with the most non-zero elements as the core and form a cluster. $Cst_t=\{V_i\,(1\leq i\leq n) : V_i \text{ has the largest number of non-zero elements in documents set}\}$.
3. Measure the similarity between the concept vector of the cluster and the documents included in the document group. Add the documents that show similarities over a certain level to the cluster and renew the mean vector and concept vector of the cluster. $\quad$ if $Sim(\,C(Cst_t)\,,V_j\,)>\rho(1\leq j\leq n,\,\rho$ is the threshold value), $\quad\quad$ then $V_j\in\,Cst_t$ and recalculate $C(Cst_t)$.
4. Exclude the documents that were included in the cluster by step 3, from the document group.
5. Repeat the step 2 to step 4 for k times.

3 Test Results

Test was executed on the data sets of TIME and CLASSIC3 (ftp://ftp. cs.cornell.edu/pub/smart/) in order to verify the efficiency of the proposed algorithm. The TIME dataset is composed of 423 documents extracted from the TIME magazine, and CLASSIC3 of 3893 documents extracted from the well-known document data groups MEDLINE, CISI and CRANFIELD.

First the data is vectorized. Here, stopwords and words of low frequency below 0.2% and high frequency above 15% are removed. As a result, 7704 words in TIME and 4262 in CLASSIC3 remained to form 7704 dimensions and 4262 dimensions respectively. Then the **txn** scheme is used to produce document vectors.

The results from applying the star clustering algorithm and the newly suggested algorithm on the vectorized document groups are as shown in Table 2 and Table 3. The clusters indicated in the table are listed in order starting from the one containing the most data. The top five and eight clusters are indicated in the tables. The coherence [2], which evaluates the quality of clustering, was measured and average coherence value is shown in the table. The ρ indicated on top of each table indicates the threshold value used in operating the algorithm. The ρ parameter has an impact on the number of data contained in the clusters, and the number of data should be almost equal to compare two algorithms fair. So a little different ρ value are used for each algorithm. The k is used to determine the number of clusters to form by the suggested algorithm. For TIME k is 15 and for CLASSIC3 k is 60. Also the results did not improve by increasing k. This is because the clusters with the most non-zero elements are processed first as the standard value so the clusters formed later relatively have fewer elements.

As observed in the test results shown in Tables 2 and Table 3, while the two algorithms did not differ much concerning the number of data searched and the total and average coherence, the newly suggested algorithm operated much faster. The gap between operating speeds of the two algorithms becomes larger along with the increase of documents to be processed.

Table 2. The Result over TIME dataset [ρ=0.44(star), 0.48(proposed)]

	Star			Proposed		
	Number of	Coherence		Number of	Coherence	
	Data	Total	Average	Data	Total	Average
Cluster 1	25	15.225	0.609	25	15.225	0.609
Cluster 2	20	13.660	0.683	18	12.492	0.694
Cluster 3	16	10.576	0.661	16	10.384	0.649
Cluster 4	13	8.788	0.676	13	8.892	0.684
Cluster 5	8	5.192	0.649	7	5.187	0.741
Sum	82	48.249		79	46.993	
Average			0.656			0.675
Run Time	4.89 seconds			0.47 seconds		

Table 3. The Result over CLASSIC3 dataset [ρ=0.44(star), 0.47(proposed)]

	Star			Proposed		
	Number of	Coherence		Number of	Coherence	
	Data	Total	Average	Data	Total	Average
Cluster 1	69	43.109	0.624	66	38.534	0.583
Cluster 2	49	31.614	0.645	51	30.815	0.604
Cluster 3	34	21.407	0.629	36	20.768	0.576
Cluster 4	27	17.424	0.645	30	18.447	0.659
Cluster 5	27	18.447	0.683	26	15.695	0.603
Cluster 6	23	15.982	0.694	20	12.217	0.610
Cluster 7	21	13.267	0.631	19	13.187	0.694
Cluster 8	19	12.020	0.632	17	11.480	0.675
Sum	269	161.250		265	149.663	
Average			0.647			0.625
Run Time	113.55 seconds			3.18 seconds		

References

1. Aslam, J., Pelekhov, K., and Rus, D.: Information Organization Algorithms. In Proceedings of the International Conference on Advances in Infrastructure for Electronic Business, Science, and Education on the Internet.(2000)
2. Dhillon I. S. and Modha, D. S.: Concept Decomposition for Large Sparse Text Data using Clustering. Technical Report RJ 10147(9502), IBM Almaden Research Center (1999)

Automatic Text Summarization of Scientific Articles Based on Classification of Extract's Population

Maher Jaoua and Abdelmajid Ben Hamadou

Faculté des Sciences Economiques et de Gestion de Sfax
Laboratoire LARIS B.P. 1088- 3018 Sfax – Tunisie
{Maher.Jaoua, Abdelmajid.BenHamadou}@fsegs.rnu.tn

Abstract. We propose in this paper a summarization method that creates indicative summaries from scientific papers. Unlike conventional methods that extract important sentences, our method considers the extract as the minimal unit for extraction and uses two steps: the generation and the classification. The first step combines text sentences to produce a population of extracts. The second step evaluates each extract using global criteria in order to select the best one. In this case, the criteria are defined according to the whole extract rather than sentences. We have developed a prototype of the summarization system for French language called ExtraGen that implements a genetic algorithm simulating the mechanism of generation and classification.

1 Introduction

With the rapid growth of online information, it has become necessary to provide improved tools to find the real information according to the user interest. Actually, conventional search engines are unable to give the user the relevant documents according to his query. For example, there are 2340 documents matched to the query "automatic summarization" submitted to Google engine. So there is a great need of *any* kind of document abstraction mechanism to help user in their information search. Consequently, summarization has become one of the hottest topics in the last decades, and some summarization technologies are rapidly gaining deployment in real world situations.

Since their beginning [1] researches done about document extraction were emphasizing on the evaluation of the sentence's importance in order to integrate these sentences into the extract that summarizes the key ideas of the document. Improved extraction of the most appropriate sentences from a source text would seem to be a matter of incremental tuning. Unfortunately, however, a collection of extracted sentences often shows a marked lack of coherence due to the rupture of the text discourse.

Considering these points, the method, proposed in this paper, evokes a new insight of the extraction process by adopting a methodology based on the extract as a unit of classification. The method proposes a generation of a population of extracts that are evaluated and classified in order to choose the best extract according to specific criteria.

A. Gelbukh (Ed.): CICLing 2003, LNCS 2588, pp. 623–634, 2003.
© Springer-Verlag Berlin Heidelberg 2003

The organization of this paper is as follows: In the next section, we briefly present related work. Section 3 exposes the bases of our approach followed by the discussion of our interest in the extract as a whole, rather than its constituents. In section 4, we describe the architecture of ExtraGen system and we present in section 5 the evaluation of our system. Finally, we discuss the perspectives of our approach while focusing on the considered extension.

2   Related Works on Document Summarization

We can classify recent works on automatic summarization into three main classes:

2.1   The Statistical Methods

These methods concern lexical and statistical features of the textual substance of the electronic documents. The majority of these methods are based on the assignment of a weight (a score) to each sentence of the document. This weight depends on the sentence position or its abundance in keywords. As a result, researchers tended to concentrate their efforts on the clues including:

- The position of a sentence within the document or the paragraph [2],
- The presence of cue words and expressions such as "important", "definitely", "in particular" (all positive), and "unclear", "perhaps", "for example" (all negative) [2],
- The presence of indicator constructs such as "The purpose of this research is" and "Our investigation has shown that" [3],
- The number of semantic links between a sentence and its neighbors [4],[5],
- The presence of words that appear in title or subtitles [2], or in the bibliography [6].

Other researches, [7] exploited the techniques of information retrieval in order to calculate the sentence weight, or by using heuristics [8], or stochastic measure developed on a corpus of documents [9].

2.2   The Discourse Methods

These methods are based on the discourse analysis. They intend to determine a set of labels according to the semantic features of the sentence. These labels, such as the thematic enunciation, causality and definition are determined thanks to surface indicators and interconnection words that bind sentences together. The importance of a sentence is deduced from the importance of its "semantic" labels, e.g.[10].

Other works exploit the representation of the speech of the original text in order to take out rhetorical structure to determine the intra-sentence [11] and inter-sentence [12] relations. For example, the system proposed by Teufel is interested in the identification of argumentative units such as background, topic, related work, purpose, solution, result and conclusion.

2.3 Template Extraction Methods

An alternative approach, making use of techniques from artificial intelligence, entails performing a detailed semantic analysis of a source text, and so constructing a semantic representation of the meaning of the document. Those methods are based on pragmatic knowledge and use predefined extracts depending on the original text.

These generic extracts, generally answer specifics corpora [13], which penalizes their generalizations. Unfortunately, the knowledge base required for a system of this kind is of necessity large and complicated, and is moreover specific to the domain of application.

The system proposed by Mckeown summarizes a series of news articles on the same event [13]. It uses summarization operators, identified through empirical analysis of a corpus of news summaries, to group together templates from the output. In the same context, the method proposed by Strzalkowski [14] generates extracts of news by using the Discourse Macro Structure (DMS). His approach falls into the observation that certain types of text conform to a set of style and organization constraints. In this case, extraction is based on DMS template filling, such as background and event templates.

3   Characteristics of the Proposed Method

The method, proposed in this paper, evokes a new insight of the extraction process. It consists in adopting a methodology based on the generation of a population of extracts that are evaluated and classified in order to choose the best extract according to specific criteria.

This new vision of the extraction process, which can be characterized as a systemic insight, operates on the extract on its totality and not on its independent parts (i.e, sentences). Therefore, we can consider the problem of extraction as an optimization one where the optimal extract is chosen among a set of extracts formed by the conjunction of sentences of the original document. We propose to generate a population of extracts that are compared with each other and classified in order to produce the best extract. We define the best extract as the set of sentences maximizing the quality of information and containing the essential concepts, while reducing incoherence and redundancies.

To determine the criteria used to compare the extracts we performed a corpora study. Our corpus is composed from 121 articles presented in the field of a natural language processing. These documents are collected from major conferences (Like TALN, ACM) and associated workshops to make variability in our corpus. These papers, initially in PDF Format are translated to Ms-Word with Acrobat Distiller, then in Html Format with MsWord.

We analysed the corpus articles according to their statistical, logical, linguistic and discourse structure and we collected human judgment about relation between human summaries and extract performed by judges (3 judges). The results of this study are resumed in the following points:

- There is only 20.35% of agreement between author summaries and extract generated by judges
- Indicative extracts performed by judges contains a keywords that appears in title, subtitle…
- The middle number of extract sentence is 7, (about 150 words)
- 86% of extract discourses structure respect a global schema that is composed by the following thematic labels {topic, Background, related work, purpose, method, solution, evaluation, conclusions, perspectives}.

This study allows us to define some criteria used in the classification of extracts in this research:

- **The extract's length:** the sum of the length of sentences composing the extract must be close to a value fixed by the user.
- **The coverage of informative words:** this criterion permits the elimination the redundant sentences. Indeed, if two sentences deal with the same concepts, only one will be chosen in the extract. The probability to choose other sentences dealing with other concepts will be higher avoiding all redundancy.
- **The weight of sentences:** the choice of the extract depends on the middleweight of the extracts of sentences. This criterion permits to choose the extract having the best weights.
- **The discourse texture of extracts:** The coherence of the extract can be evaluated according to the discourse schema of extract.
- **The cohesion between sentences:** A first level of cohesion of extract sentences can be detected by analysing conjunction words.

4 Design of ExtraGen System

We have implemented a prototype system named ExtraGen (EXTRAction using GENitic algorithm). Extraction in ExtraGen is performed by generation and classification of extract's population. The latter process is achieved thanks to the aggregation of statistics and rhetorical criteria evoked above. The implementation of these different criteria requires a preliminary module, which constitutes the first module of the ExtraGen system. The second and the third module are interested in the statistical and rhetorical feature of sentences. The last module implements generation and classification of extracts. In the following, we expose these modules implemented in ExtraGen system (see Fig. 1).

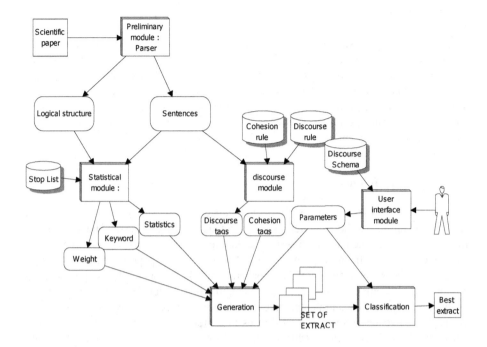

Fig. 1. ExtraGen architecture

- Preliminary module: this module is composed of a parser that identifies the logical structure of the document based on the different tags that it contains (case of HTML tags). The second step performed by the parser is to decompose text on sentences. So, it determines the length of each sentence as well as the length of the whole text.

- Statistical module: it produces lists of word frequency and lemma frequency by using n-gramm similarity.

- Discourse module: this module labels each sentence of the document by a set of rhetorical and cohesion tags. It uses a set of rhetorical rules that deduct the label from the combination of key-phrases in the sentences. To determine cohesion, this module uses a set of rule that explores conjunction word that appears in the beginning of each sentence.

- User Interfaces module : it accepts parameters that determine extract length and discourse schema recommended by user.

- Generation and classification module: this module allows to generate and to classify a population of extracts. This module is implemented by using a genetic algorithm that simulates generation and classification. The classification is performed by a function that aggregates statistical and rhetorical indicators determined from the two previous modules.

4.1 Statistical Module

This module is composed of two sub-modules: the first calculates the words frequency in the document, whereas the second focuses on the sentences weight. The first sub-module calculates the number of occurrences of each word of the document (except stop list words). The second sub-module computes the weight of the keywords of the document according to the hierarchy of the logical structure elements where keywords are extracted from besides; it calculates the weight of each sentence by adding key-word weights that it contains.

4.2 Discourse Module

This module identifies discourse labels of sentences. These labels allow us to assign a semantic meaning to the sentence. The concatenation of discourse labels of extract forms the extract schema, which will be compared with discourse schema base. This base is constructed from corpora of abstracts of scientific papers written in French. Discourse labels determined by our corpora are: Background, theme presentation, related work, method presentation, problem, method, solution, experience, results, evaluation, conclusions and perspectives. Each label is identified by a set of rules that verify the existence of specific key-phrases in sentences. For example, when the sentences begin with "cet article" (this article) and we find the verb "présente" "present", we can conclude that the rhetorical label of this phrase is "Topic".

From our corpora we determine 52 rules that uses 532 key-phrases. We have also determined 12 schema extracts that cover 86.3% of extracts performed by human judges. Figure 2 represents the first and the second schema that occurs frequently:

In the other part, the discourse module uses a cohesion rules that determine which sentences causes a cohesion rupture by analysing conjunction word. For example, if the term "because" appears in the beginning if the sentences, this module mark this sentences.

4.3 Generation and Classification Module

We have already highlighted the problem of extraction and how it can be considered as optimizations one. The problem consists to choose the best solution from a set of potential solution formed from the conjunction of sentences of the document. In this case, the objective function maximizes criteria of extract selection already enumerated. Among methods of resolution of optimization problems, we are interested in the genetic algorithms [15].

Genetic Algorithms are powerful general-purpose optimization tools, which model the principles of evolution. They operate on a population of coded solutions which are selected according to their quality, then used as the basis for a new generation of solutions found by combining (crossover) or altering (mutating) every individual (in our case, a solution is an extract that formed by the concatenation of some sentences).

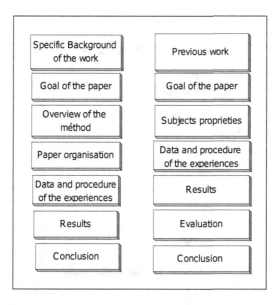

Fig. 2. Two examples of discourse schema

A genetic algorithm starts by generating, randomly, a set of extracts (the initial population: in our system there is 10 initial solutions). (see fig. 3). Each solution is coded using an array that contains number of sentences that compose the extract

After applying genetic operator with a random value, we obtain a number of intermediary solutions. The classification of this population is based on several layers by using statistical and discourse indicator. Nondominated extracts (in sense of the pareto) get a certain dummy fitness value and then are removed from the population [SRI 93]. The process is repeated until the entire population has been classified.

We notify that Extract E_i is dominated Extract E_j (in sense of the pareto) if all feature $f_x i$ of the extract E_i are greater or equal to the same feature $f_x j$ of the extract E_j and there is at least one x that $f_x i$ is greater then the same feature $f_x j$.

Criteria used in the process of classification are:

- **Length indicator:** this indicator noted ω_1 is calculated as the following:

$$\text{if } 0.9 \times L \leq L_{ex} \leq 1.1 \times L \text{ then } \omega_1 = 1$$

$$\text{if } L_{ex} \leq 0.9 \times L \text{ then } \omega_1 = \frac{L_{ex}}{L}$$

$$\text{if } L_{ex} \geq 1.1 \times L \text{ then } \omega_1 = \frac{L}{L_{ex}}$$

where L_{ex} is the length of the generated extract,
L: extract length desired by the user;
m : number of sentences in the extract.

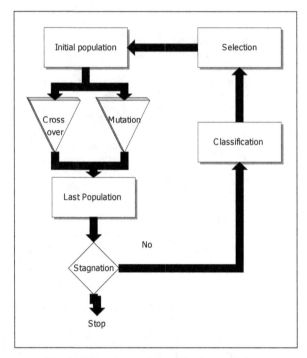

Fig. 3. Generation and classification module

- **Keyword Coverage indicator:** This criterion, designed by ω_2, permits to generate extracts without redundancy. If two sentences deal with the same concepts, only one is chosen. The indicator of this criterion is calculated as follows:

$$\omega_2 = \frac{\sum M_{ext}}{\sum M_{doc}}$$

M_{ext} : number of Keyword founded in extract

M_{doc} : number of Keyword founded in documents

- **Weight of sentences indicator(ω_3):** We consider the weight of sentences as an indicator of their semantic importance. So, the extract must contain sentences with consistent information.

$$\omega_3 = \frac{\sum P_{ext}}{Max(P_{pop})}$$

P_{ext} : sentence weight in extract.

P_{pop} : maximal weight of extract in a population.

The division is used to normalize the result of the indicator.

- **Discourse similarity indicator:** This coefficient designed by ω_4 is determined by discourse module as the maximal coefficient calculated by matching the schema extract and each of the 12 predefined schema. This indicator is calculated as follows:

$$\omega_4 = 2 \times \frac{A}{B+C}$$

where A is the number of present labels in the schema of the extract and present in the compared schema in the base. B design the number of labels of the extract schema and C design the number of labels in the compared schema.

- **Cohesion indicator:** This coefficient designed by ω_5 is determined by discourse module and calculate the rate of sentence that presents a rupture of cohesion. This indicator is calculated as follows:

$$\omega_5 = \frac{A}{B}$$

where A is the number of sentences in the extract that presents a cohesion rupture and the antecedent sentences does not appears in the extract. B design the number of sentence in the evaluated extract.

5 Evaluation

Evaluation is very important and necessary for automatic summarization, because it permits to compare results and methods. As a consequence, there are many evaluation conferences that were organized around standard corpora (like MUC, TIPSTER, DUC) to directly assess developed systems and methods. In these conferences, the only language used for corpora, is English, so work for French, Spanish or Arabic language cannot be considered (Japanese is an exception with TSC evaluation conference).

The main difficult problem for evaluation is to define a set of summaries as a gold standard [12]. There is, also the problem of contextual factor that must be considered in the evaluation. For the first problem there are many attempts to build manual [12], automatic [17] or semiautomatic [18] corpora for summarization. The challenge solution for the second problem consists to build several corpora for each combination of factors. These corpora must be considered characteristic of the abstract, interest user, etc.

Due to these limitations, we used a baseline method that considers a gold extract formed by sentences in the document that matches author summaries. We define 4 relations as the following:

- Direct sentence match: minor modifications between sentence in summaries and the text source

- Direct join: when two or three sentences from the document cover one sentence from summaries
- Incomplete sentence match: when one sentence from summaries cover one sentence from text source
- Incomplete join match: when one sentence from summaries cover two or three sentence from document.

We use as inputs 111 papers in French language, selected from different proceedings published in international conferences related to computer sciences. In this intrinsic evaluation, we chose 5 experts to determine document sentences that match author summaries we consider the best extract, the non-dominated extract generated in the last generation. After, we compare recall and precision indicator performed by the extract of our system, Micrsoft Autosummarizer, and Copernic summarize. We repeat the experiences for several length and we calculate the recall and precision indicator:

$$\text{Recall} = \frac{\text{hits}}{\text{hits} + \text{misses}}$$

$$\text{Precision} = \frac{\text{hits}}{\text{hits} + \text{mistakes}}$$

where *hits*: sentences identified by the optimal extract and referenced by the baseline extract; *mistakes*: sentences identified by the optimal extract but not exist in the baseline extract; *misses*: Sentences selected by the baseline extract but not identified by the optimal extracts.

Table 1. Average recall and precision for ExtraGen, MS-Autosummarize and Copernic summarizer.

Extract Length	System	Average Recall	Average Precision
5 %	ExtraGen	23.21%	17.21%
	MS-Autosummarizer	14.82%	09.12%
	Copernic summarizer	17.85%	11.78%
10 %	ExtraGen	30.21%	24.81%
	MS-Autosummarizer	17.08%	10.54%
	Copernic summarizer	20.31%	12.15%
15%	ExtraGen	38.51%	26.94%
	MS-Autosummarizer	20.27%	13.75%
	Copernic summarizer	22.15%	14.91%
20 %	ExtraGen	43.38%	29.06%
	MS-Autosummarizer	21.08%	16.00%
	Copernic summarizer	24.48%	16.33%

The result of this evaluation shows that for all rate reduction our system obtains the best value of the recall and precision. This result can be explained by the weakness of using a greedy method (case of MS-Autosummarizer and Copernic summarizer) to construct extracts.

6 Conclusion

In this paper, we have presented a method of extraction based on the generation and classification of a set of extracts produced from the text. For this purpose, we have developed a genetic algorithm that simulates the two mechanisms of generation and classification.

This method opens a new perspective concerning filtering and automatic extraction. Currently, we have tried to search new criteria of classification of extracts and we look for extending our systems to summarize a multiple documents.

References

1. Luhn, H.P.: The Automatic creation of literature Abstracts. In: IBM J.R & D2-2 (1958) 156–165
2. Edmundson, H.P. : New methods in automatic extracting. In: Newspaper of ACM tea, 16-2 (1969) 264–85
3. Paice, C.D., and Al.: The identification of important concepts in highly structures technical papers. In: proceeding of sixteenth annual international ACM SIGIR Conference, ACM PRESS (1993) 69–78
4. Boguraev, B., Kennedy, C.: Salience-based Content Characterization of Text Documents. In: Proceedings of the Workshop on Intelligent Scalable Text Summarization. ACL/EACL Conference Madrid Spain (1997) 2–9
5. Gerard, S., Allan, J., Singhal, A.: Automatic text decomposition and structuring. In: Information Procssing & Management, 32(2) (1996) 127–138.
6. Kan, M.Y., Klavans, J., McKeown, K.: Using the Annotated Bibliography as a Resource for Indicative Summarization. In: Proc LREC 2002 Las Palmas Spain (2002)
7. Goldstein, J., Kantrowitz, M., Mittal, V., Carbonell, J.(1999).: Summarizing text Documents: sentence selection and evaluation metrics. In: proceeding of SIGIR'99 (1999)
8. Kupiec, J., and Al.: A trainable document summarizer. In: SIGIR 95 Sattle Wa, USA, (1995)
9. Conroy, J., Leary, D.P.O.: Text Summarization via Hidden Markov Models and Pivoted QR Matrix Decomposition. Technical Report, Dept.Comp.Sci. CS-TR-221. Univ. Maryland (2001)
10. Minel, J.L., et Al. : Seraphin, système pour l'extraction automatique d'énoncés importants. dans : les actes du colloque IA 95- Quinzièmes journées internationales de génie linguistiques Montpellier France (1995)
11. Marcu, D.: Discourse-based summarization in duc-200. In: Proceedings of the Document Understanding ,Conference DUC'01 (2001)
12. Teufel, S., Moens, M.: Sentence Extraction as a Classification Task. In: Proceedings of the Workshop on Intelligent Scalable Summarization ACL/EACL Conference Madrid Spain (1997) 58–65
13. Mckeown, R.K., and Al.: Generating summaries of multiple news Articles. In: proceeding of the Seventeenth Annual International ACM/SIGIR Washington (1995) 74–82

14. Strzalkowski, T., Wand, J., Wise, B.: A robust practical text summarization. In: AAAI 98 Spring Symposium on Intelligent Text Summarization (1998) 26–33
15. Holland, J.H. and Al.: Classified systems and genetic algorithms. In: revue Artificial Intelligence N°40 (1989) 235–282
16. Srivinas, N., Deb, K.: Multiobjective optimization using nondominated sorting in genetic Algorithms. Technical report, Department of Mechanical Engineering, Institute of Technology India (1993)
17. Marcu, D.: The automatic construction of large-scale corpora for summarization research. In: The 22nd International ACM SIGIR Conference on Research and Development in Information Retrieval (SIGIR'99). Berkeley, CA, (1999) 137–144
18. Orasan, C.: Building annotated resources for automatic text summarisation. In: Proceedings of LREC-2002. Las Palmas, Spain 2002.

Positive Grammar Checking: A Finite State Approach

Sylvana Sofkova Hashemi, Robin Cooper, and Robert Andersson

Department of Linguistics
Göteborg University
Box 200, SE-405 30 Göteborg, Sweden
{sylvana,cooper,robert}@ling.gu.se

Abstract. This paper reports on the development of a finite state system for finding grammar errors without actually specifying the error. A corpus of Swedish text written by children served as the data. Errors are more frequent and the distribution of the error types is different than for adult writers. Our approach (following Karttunen et al. [9]) for finding errors involves developing automata that represent two "positive" grammars with varying degree of detail and then subtracting the detailed one from the general one. The difference between the automata corresponds to a grammar for errors. We use a robust parsing strategy which first identifies the lexical head of a phrase together with the lexical string which precedes it beginning at the left margin of the phrase. The technique shows good coverage results for agreement and verb selection phenomena. In future, we aim to include also the detection of agreement between subject and predicative complements, word order phenomena and missing sentence boundaries.

1 Introduction

Research and development of grammar checking techniques has been carried out since the 1980's, mainly for English and also for other languages, e.g. French [6], Dutch [15], Czech [11], Spanish and Greek [4]. In the case of Swedish, the development of grammar checkers started not until the later half of the 1990's with several independent projects, one of them resulting in the first product release in November 1998 - Grammatifix [2,3], now part of the Swedish Microsoft Office 2000. Our approach differs from the other Swedish projects in that the grammatical errors are found without direct description of the erroneous patterns. The detection process involves light parsing and subtraction of transducers representing "positive" grammars at different accuracy levels. The difference between the automata corresponds to a grammar for the errors to be found. Karttunen et al. [9] use this technique to find instances of invalid dates and our work is an attempt to apply their approach to a larger domain.

The rest of this paper includes a short description of the child data, followed by the system architecture with separate subsections on each module. Then follows evaluation of the system and comparison with the other Swedish systems.

A. Gelbukh (Ed.): CICLing 2003, LNCS 2588, pp. 635–646, 2003.
© Springer-Verlag Berlin Heidelberg 2003

2   The Child Data

The analyses of writing problems is based on a small corpus of 29 812 words (3 373 word types), composed of computer written and hand written essays written by children between 9 and 13 years of age. In general, the text structure of the compositions reveals clearly the influence of spoken language and performance difficulties in spelling, segmentation of words, the use of capitals and punctuation, with fairly wide variation both by individual and age. In total, 260 instances of grammatical errors were found in 134 narratives. The most recurrent grammar problem concerns the omission of finite verb inflection (38.8% of all errors), i.e. when the main finite verb in a clause lacks the appropriate present or past tense endings:

(1) På natten   *vakna   jag av   att brandlarmet tjöt.
     in the-night **wake [untensed]** I   from that fire-alarm   howled
     – In the night I woke up from that the fire-alarm went off.

The correct form of the verb vakna 'stop' should be in the past tense, i.e. vaknade 'stopped'. This type of error arises from the fact that the writing is highly influenced by spoken language. In spoken Swedish regular weak verbs in the past tense often lack the appropriate ending and the spoken form then coincides with the infinitive (and for some verbs also imperative) form of the verb.

Other frequent grammar problems are: extra or missing words (25.4%), here the preposition i 'in' is missing:

(2) Gunnar var på semester *_ norge   och åkte skidor.
     Gunnar was on vacation _ Norway and went skis
     – Gunnar was on vacation in Norway and skied.

word choice errors (10%), here the verb att vara lika 'to be alike' requires the particle till 'to' in combination with the noun phrase sättet 'the-manner' and not på 'on' as the writer uses:

(3) vi var   väldigt **lika** *på sättet
     we were very   **like on the-manner**
     – We were very alike in the manners.

errors in noun phrase agreement (5.8%), here the correct form of the noun phrase requires the noun to be definite as in den närmsta handduken 'the nearest towel':

(4) jag tar **den**   **närmsta**   *handduk   och slänger den i
     I   take **the [def]** **nearest [def]** **towel [indef]** and throw it   in
     vasken
     the sink
     – I take the nearest towel and throw it into the sink.

errors in verb chains (2.7%), here the auxiliary verb should be followed by an infinitive, ska bli 'will become', but in this case the present tense is used:

(5) Men kom ihåg att   det inte **ska** *blir   någon riktig brand.
     but   remember that it   not **will becomes[pres]** some real   fire
     – But remember that there will not be a real fire.

Other grammar errors occurred less than ten times in the whole corpus, including reference errors, agreement between subject and predicative complement, specificity in nouns, pronoun form, errors in infinitive phrases, word order.

Punctuation problems are also included in the analyses. In general, the use of punctuation varies from no usage at all (mostly among the youngest children) to rather sparse marking. In the following example the boundary between the first and second sentence is not marked.:

(6) nasse blev   arg   han gick och la sig   med dom andra syskonen.
     nasse became angry he   went and lay himself with the other siblings
     – Nasse got angry. He went and lay down with the other siblings.

The omission of end of sentence marking is quite obvious problem, corresponding to 35% of all sentences that lack marking of a sentence boundary. But the most frequent punctuation problem concerns the omission of commas, left out in 81% of clauses.

The finite verb problem, verb form in verb chains and infinitive phrases and agreement problems in noun phrase are the four types of errors detected by the current system.

3   System Architecture

The framework for detection of grammar errors is built as a network of finite state transducers compiled from regular expressions including operators defined in the Xerox Finite State Tool (XFST) [10]. Each automaton in the network composes with the result of previous application and in principle all the automata can be composed into a single transducer.

There are in general two types of transducers in use: one that annotates text in order to select certain segments and one that redefines or refines earlier decisions. Annotations of any kind are handled by transducers defined as Ωnite state markers that add reserved symbols into text and mark out syntactical segments, grammar errors, or other patterns aimed at selections. Finite state Ωlters are used for refinement and/or revision of earlier decisions.

The system runs under UNIX in a simple emacs environment used for testing and development of finite state grammars. The environment shows the results of an XFST-process run on the current emacs buffer in a separate buffer. An XFST-mode allows for menus to be used and recompile files in the system.

The current system of sequenced finite state transducers is divided in four main modules: the dictionary lookup, the grammar, the parser and the error Ωnder.

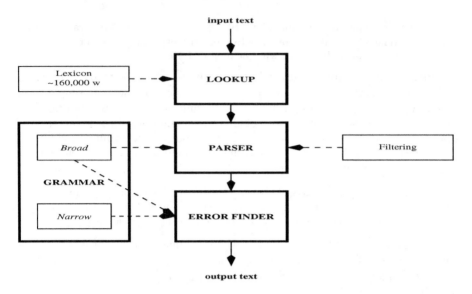

Fig. 1. The system architecture

3.1   The Lexicon Lookup

The lexicon of around 160, 000 word forms, is built as a finite state transducer, using the Xerox tool Finite State Lexicon Compiler [8]. The lexicon is composed from two resources, the SveLex project under the direction of Daniel Ridings, LexiLogik AB, and the Lexin project [13]. It takes a string and maps inflected surface form to a tag containing part-of-speech and feature information, e. g. applying the transducer to the string kvinna 'woman' will return [nn utr sin ind nom]. The morphosyntactic tags follow directly the relevant string or token. More than one tag can be attached to a string, since no contextual information is taken into account. The morphosyntactic information in the tags is further used in the grammars of the system. The set of tags follows the Stockholm Umeå Corpus-project conventions [7], including 23 category classes and 29 feature classes, that was extended with 3 additional categories. Below is an example of lookup on the example sentence in (5):

(7)   Men[kn] kom[qmvb prt akt][vb prt akt] ihåg[ab][pl] att[sn][ie]det[pn neu sin def sub/obj][dt neu sin def] inte[ab] ska[vb prs akt][mvb prs akt] blir[vb prs akt] någon[dt utr sin ind][pn utr sin ind sub/obj] riktig[jj pos utr sin ind nom]brand[nn utr sin ind nom]

3.2   The Grammar

The grammar module includes two grammar sets with (positive) rules reflecting the grammatical structure of Swedish, differing in the level of detail. The broad grammar is especially designed to handle text with ungrammaticalities and the linguistic descriptions are less accurate accepting both valid and invalid patterns. The narrow grammar is fine and accurate and accepts only the grammatical segments. For example, the regular expression in (8) belongs to the broad grammar set and recognizes potential verb clusters (VC) (both grammatical and ungrammatical) as a pattern consisting of a sequence of two or three verbs in combination with (zero or more) adverbs (Adv*).

(8) **define VC   [Verb Adv* Verb (Verb)];**

This automaton accepts all the verb cluster examples in (9), including the ungrammatical instance (9c) (marked by an asterix '*'), where a finite verb follows a (finite) auxiliary verb.

(9)
   a. *kan inte springa* 'can not run'
   b. *skulle ha sprungit* 'would have run [sup]'
   c. **ska blir* 'will be [pres]'

Corresponding rules in the narrow grammar set represented by the regular expressions in (10) take into account the internal structure of a verb cluster and define the grammar of modal auxiliary verbs (Mod) followed by (zero or more) adverb(s) (Adv*), and either a verb in infinitive form (VerbInf) as in (10a), or a temporal verb in infinitive (PerfInf) and a verb in supine form (VerbSup), as in (10b). These rules thus accept only the grammatical segments in (9) and will not include example (9c). The actual grammar of grammatical verb clusters is a little bit more complex.

(10)
   a. **define VC1   [Mod Adv* VerbInf];**
   b. **define VC2   [Mod Adv* PerfInf VerbSup];**

3.3   Parsing and Ambiguity Resolution

The various kinds of constituents are marked out in a text using a lexical-prefix-first method, i.e. parsing first from left margin of a phrase to the head and then extending the phrase by adding on complements. The actual parsing (based on the broad grammar definitions) is incremental in a similar fashion as the methods described in [1], where the output from one layer serves as input to the next, building on the segments. The system recognizes the head phrases in certain order in the first phase (verbal head, prepositional head, adjective phrase) and then applies the second phase in the reverse order and extends the phrases with complements (noun phrase, prepositional phrase, verb phrase).

Reordering rules used in parsing allows us to resolve certain ambiguities. For example, marking verbal heads before noun phrases will prefer a verb phrase interpretation of a string over a noun phrase interpretation and avoid merging constituents of verbal heads into noun phrases and yielding noun phrases with too-wide range.

For instance, marking first the sentence in (11) for noun phrases will interpret the pronoun De 'they' as a determiner and the verb såg 'saw', that is exactly as in English homonymous with the noun 'saw', as a noun and merges these two constituents to a noun phrase as shown in (12). De såg will subsequently be marked as ungrammatical, since a number feature mismatch occurs between the plural De 'they' and singular såg 'saw'.

(11) De   såg   ledsna ut
      They   looked sad   out – They seemed sad.

(12) <np>De såg </np> <np>ledsna </np> ut .

Composing the marking transducers by first marking the verbal head and then the noun phrase will instead yield the more correct parse. Although the alternative of the verb being parsed as verbal head or a noun remains, the pronoun is now marked correctly as a separate noun phrase and not merged together with the main verb into a noun phrase:

(13) <np> De </np> <vpHead> <np> såg </np> </vpHead> <np> ledsna </np> ut .

At this stage, the output may be further refined and/or revised by application of filtering transducers. Earlier parsing decisions depending on lexical ambiguity are resolved (e.g. adjectives parsed as verbs) and phrases extended (e.g. with postnominal modifiers). Other structural ambiguities, such as verb coordinations or clausal modifiers on nouns, are also taken care of.

3.4   Error Detection

The error finder is a separate module in the system which means that the grammar and parser could potentially be used directly in a different application. The nets of this module correspond to the difference between the two grammars, broad and narrow.

By subtracting the narrow grammar from the broad grammar we create machines that will find ungrammatical phrases in a text. For example, the regular expression in (14) identifies verb clusters that violate the narrow grammar of modal verb clusters (VC1 or VC2, defined in (10)) by subtracting these rules from the more general (overgenerating) rule in the broad grammar (VC, defined in (8)) within the boundaries of a verb cluster ('<vc>', '</vc>'), that have been previously marked out in the parsing stage.

(14)   `define VCerror     [ "<vc>" [VC - [VC1 | VC2]] "</vc>" ];`

By application of a marking transducer in (15), the found error segment is annotated directly in the text as in example (16).

(15) `define markVCerror [VCerror -> "<Error verb after Vaux>" ...`
      `"</Error>"];`

(16) Men   <vp><vpHead>kom   ihåg </vpHead></vp>att <np>det </np><vp> <vpHead>inte <**Error verb after Vaux**><vc> ska blir </vc> </**Error**> </vpHead><np>någon <ap>riktig </ap>brand </np></vp>

4   The System Performance

The implemented error detector cannot at present be considerred as a fully developed grammar checking tool, but still even with its restricted lexicon and small grammar the results are promising. So far the technique was used to detect agreement errors in noun phrases, selection of finite and non-finite verb forms in main and subordinate clauses and infinitival complements. The implementation proceeded in two steps. In the first phase we devoted all effort to detection of the grammar errors, working mostly with the errors and not paying much attention to the text as a whole. The second phase involved blocking of the resultant false alarms found in the first stage.

In Table 1 we show the final results of error detection in the training corpus of Child Data. There were altogether 14 agreement errors in noun phrase, 102 errors in the form of finite verb, 7 errors in the verbform after an auxiliary verb (Vaux) and 4 errors in verbs after infinitive marker (IM).

Table 1. Error detection in Child Data: correct alarms (C), false alarms (F), missed errors (M), recall (R), precision (P)

ERROR TYPE	NO. ERRORS	C	F	M	R	P
Agreement in NP	14	14	15	0	100%	48%
Finite verb form	102	93	94	9	91%	50%
Verb form after Vaux	7	6	32	1	86%	16%
Verb form after IM	4	4	4	0	100%	50%
TOTAL	127	117	145	10	92%	45%

The error detection of the system is quite high with a recall rate of 92% on text that the system was designed to handle. Only ten errors were not detected, nine of them in the finite verb form and one in the verb form after an auxiliary verb. The precision rate of 45% is not that satisfactory, but comparable with the other Swedish grammar checking tools that report precision rates on adult texts between 53% and 77%. The recall values are between 35% and 83%.

There are in general two kinds of false alarms that occur: either due to the ambiguity of constituents or the "wideness" of the parse, i.e. too many constituents are included when applying the longest-match strategy. The following example shows an ambiguous parse:

(17)   Linda, brukade ofta   vara   i   stallet.
        Linda used   often to be in the-stable
        – Linda used to be often in the stable.

(18)   **\<Error finite verb>** \<vp>\<vpHead>\<np> **Linda** \</np>
        \</vpHead>\</vp> **\</Error>**, \<vp>\<vpHead> \<vc>brukade ofta
        \<np>vara\</np> \</vc> \</vpHead> \<pp>\<ppHead>i\</ppHead>
        \<np>stallet\</np>\</pp> \</vp>.

Here 'Linda' is a proper noun and parsed as a noun phrase, but it also is a (non-finite) verb in infinitive ('to wrap') and will then be marked as a verb phrase. Then the error finder marks this phrase as a finite verb error, due to the violation of this constraint in the narrow grammar that does not allow any non-finite verbs without the presence of a preceding (finite) auxiliary verb or infinitival marker att 'to'.

Some of the effects of the longest-match strategy can be blocked in the parsing stage, as mentioned above, but some remain as in the following example:

(19)   till vilket man kunde ringa ...
       to which one could call
       – to which one could call ...

(20)   <pp><ppHead>till   </ppHead><Error   gender><np>vilket
       man </np></Error>   </pp><vp><vpHead>kunde   <np>ringa
       </np></vpHead></vp>

Here the pronoun vilket 'which' in neuter gender is merged together with the noun man 'man' in common gender to a noun phrase, causing a gender missmatch.

There are also cases where other types of errors are recognized by the detector as side-effects of the error detection. Some split words and misspellings were recognized and diagnosed as agreement errors. For instance in the example (21) the noun ögonblick 'moment' is split and the ögon 'eyes' does not agree in number with the preceding singular determiner and adjective.

(21)
       a. För ett kort ögon blick   trodde jag ...
           for a   short eye   blinking thought I ...
           – For a short moment I thought ...
       b. För <Error number> ett kort ögon </Error> blick trodde jag ...

Others as errors in verbal group. In the example (22) fot 'foot' in the split word fotsteg 'footsteps' is interpreted as a noun and is homonymous with the (finite) verb steg 'stepped' and causes an error marking in the verb form after an infinitival verb.

(22)
       a. Jag hör fot steg från trappa
           I   hear foot steps from stairs
           – I hear footsteps from the stairs.
       b. Jag <Error verb after Vaux> hör fot steg </Error> från trappa

Further, sentence boundaries that are not marked out can be detected. The diagnosis is always connected to the verbal group, where verbs over sentence boundaries are merged together. Mostly it is a question of more than one finite verb in a row as in the example below:

(23)
       a. I hålet   som pojken hade hittat fanns en mullvad.
           in the-hole that the boy had   found was   a   mole
           – in the hole the boy had found was a mole.
       b. I hålet som pojken <Error verb after Vaux> hade hittat fanns
           </Error> en mullvad.

Here the verb cluster boundary is too wide, including both a verb cluster and a finite verb belonging to the next clause.

Preliminary results on arbitrary text also show some promising results. In Table 2 we show the system evaluation on a small literal text of 1 070 words (after updating the lexicon with words necessary to the text). We found 16 noun phrase agreement errors, 4 errors in the form of finite verb and 1 error in the verbform after an auxiliary verb in the text. The error detector found all the verb form errors and most of the agreement errors, ending in a recall value of 81%. False alarms occurred also only in the agreement errors, resulting in an overall precision of 85%.

Table 2. Error detection in Other Text: correct alarms (C), false alarms (F), missed errors (M), recall (R), precision (P)

ERROR TYPE	No. ERRORS	C	F	M	R	P
Agreement in NP	16	12	3	4	75%	80%
Finite verb form	4	4	0	0	100%	100%
Verb form after Vaux	1	1	0	0	100%	100%
TOTAL	21	17	3	4	81%	85%

5   Test with Other Tools

Three other Swedish grammar checkers: one commercial Grammati☐x [2], and two prototypes Granska [5] and Scarrie [12], have been tested on the child data. Here we give the results of detection for the error types implemented in this system (Tables 3, 4 and 5).

These tools are designed to detect errors in text different from the nature of the child data and thus not surprisingly the accuracy rates are in overall low. The total recall rate for these error types is between 10% and 19% and precision varies between 13% to 39%. Errors in noun phrases seem to be better covered than verb errors.

In the case of Grammati☐x (Table 3), errors in verbs are not covered at all. Half of the noun phrase errors were identified and only five errors in the finite verb form. Many false alarms result in a precision rate below 50%.

Granska (Table 4) included all four error types and detected at most half of the errors for three of these types. Only seven instances of errors in finite verb form were identified. The number of false alarms varies among error types.

Errors in verb form after infinitive marker were not detected by Scarrie (Table 5). Errors in noun phrase were the best detected type. The tool performed best of all three systems in the overall detection of errors with a recall rate of 19%. On the other hand, many false alarms occurred (154) and the precision rate of 13% was the lowest.

Agreement errors in noun phrases is the error type best covered by these tools. All three managed to detect at least half of them. Errors in the finite verb form obtained the worse results. Granska performed best and detected at least half of the errors in three error types with an overall precision of 39%.

The detection performance of these three tools on child data is in general half that good in comparison to our detector and the fact that the error type with worst coverage (finite verbs) is the one most frequent among children indicates clearly the need for specialized grammar checking tools for children. The overall precision rate of all the tools including our system lies below 50%.

Table 3. Grammatifix error detection in Child Data: correct alarms (C), false alarms (F), missed errors (M), recall (R), precision (P)

ERROR TYPE	No. ERRORS	C	F	M	R	P
Agreement in NP	14	7	20	7	50%	26%
Finite verb form	102	5	6	97	5%	45%
Verb form after Vaux	7					
Verb form after IM	4					
TOTAL		127	12	26	104	10%	32%

Table 4. Granska's error detection in Child Data: correct alarms (C), false alarms (F), missed errors (M), recall (R), precision (P)

ERROR TYPE	No. ERRORS	C	F	M	R	P
Agreement in NP	14	7	25	7	50%	22%
Finite verb form	102	7	1	95	7%	88%
Verb form after Vaux	7	4	5	3	57%	44%
Verb form after IM	4	2	0	2	50%	100%
TOTAL		127	20	31	107	16%	39%

Table 5. Scarrie's error detection in Child Data: correct alarms (C), false alarms (F), missed errors (M), recall (R), precision (P)

ERROR TYPE	No. ERRORS	C	F	M	R	P
Agreement in NP	14	8	133	6	57%	6%
Finite verb form	102	15	13	87	15%	54%
Verb form after Vaux	7	1	7	6	14%	13%
Verb form after IM	4	0	1	4	0%	0%
TOTAL		127	24	154	103	19%	13%

These three tools were also tested on the small literal text, that reflects more the text type these tools are designed for. The results given in Tables 6 – 8 show that all three tools had difficulties to detect the verb form errors, whereas most of the errors in noun phrase agreement were found. This means that the overal coverage of the systems is slightly lower than for our detector (see Table 2) lying between 52% and 62%.

Table 6. Grammatifix error detection in Other Text: correct alarms (C), false alarms (F), missed errors (M), recall (R), precision (P)

Error type	No. Errors	C	F	M	R	P
Agreement in NP	16	12	0	4	75%	100%
Finite verb form	4	1	0	3	25%	100%
Verb form after Vaux	1	0	0	1	0%	0%
Total	21	13	0	8	62%	100%

Table 7. Granska's error detection in Other Text: correct alarms (C), false alarms (F), missed errors (M), recall (R), precision (P)

Error type	No. Errors	C	F	M	R	P
Agreement in NP	16	12	0	4	75%	100%
Finite verb form	4	0	1	4	0%	0%
Verb form after Vaux	1	1	0	0	100%	100%
Total	21	13	1	8	62%	93%

Table 8. Scarrie's error detection in Other Text: correct alarms (C), false alarms (F), missed errors (M), recall (R), precision (P)

Error type	No. Errors	C	F	M	R	P
Agreement in NP	16	10	4	6	63%	71%
Finite verb form	4	1	0	3	25%	100%
Verb form after Vaux	1	0	0	1	0%	
Total	21	11	4	10	52%	73%

6 Conclusion

The simple finite state technique of subtraction presented in this paper, has the advantage that the grammars one needs to write to find errors are always positive grammars rather than grammars written to find specific errors. Thus, covering the valid rules of language means that the rule sets remain quite small and practically no prediction of errors is necessary.

The approach aimed further at minimal information loss in order to be able to handle text containing errors. The degree of ambiguity is maximal at the lexical level, where we choose to attach all lexical tags to strings. At higher levels, structural ambiguity is treated by parsing order, grammar extension and some other heuristics. There is an essential problem of ambiguity resolution on complement decisions that remains to be solved. Sequences of words grammatical in one context and ungrammatical in another are treated the same. The system overinterprets and gives rise to false alarms, mostly due the application of longest-match, but more seriously information indicating an error may be filtered out by erroneous segmentation and errors overlooked. A 'higher' mechanism is needed in order to solve these problems that takes into consideration the complement distribution and solves these structural dependencies.

The linguistic accuracy of the system is comparable to other Swedish grammar checking tools, that actually performed worse on the child data. The low performance of the Swedish tools on child data motivates clearly the need for adaptation of grammar checking techniques to children. The other tools obtained in general much lower recall values and although the error type of particular error was defined, the systems had difficulties to identify the errors, probably due problems to handle such a disrupted structure with many adjoined sentences and high error frequency.

Further, the robustness and modularity of this system makes it possible to perform both error detection and diagnostics and that the grammars can be reused for other applications that do not necessarily have anything to do with error detection, e. g. for educational purposes, speech recognition, and for other users such as dyslectics, aphasics, deaf and foreign speakers.

References

1. Ait-Mohtar, Salah and Chanod, Jean-Pierre (1997) *Incremental Finite-State Parsing*, In ANLP'97, Washington, pp. 72–79.
2. Arppe, Antti (2000) Developing a Grammar Checker for Swedish. *The 12th Nordic Conference of Computational Linguistics*, 1999.
3. Birn, Juhani (2000) Detecting Grammar Errors with Lingsoft's Swedish Grammar Checker. *The 12th Nordic Conference of Computational Linguistics*, 1999.
4. Bustamente, Flora Ramírez and León, Fernando Sánchez (1996) GramCheck: A Grammar and Style Checker. In the *16th International Conference on Computational Linguistics*, Copenhagen pp. 175–181.
5. Carlberger, Johan and Domeij, Rickard and Kann, Viggo and Knutsson Ola (2000) *A Swedish Grammar Checker*. Association for Computational Linguistics.
6. Chanod, Jean-Pierre (1996) A Broad-Coverage French Grammar Checker: Some Underlying Principles. In the *Sixth International Conference on Symbolic and Logical Computing*, Dakota State University Madison, South Dakota.
7. Ejerhed, E. and Källgren, G. and Wennstedt, O. and Åström, M. (1992) *The Linguistic Annotation System of the Stockholm-Umeå Corpus Project*. Report 33. University of Umeå, Department of Linguistics.
8. Karttunen, Lauri (1993) *Finite State Lexicon Compiler*. Technical Report ISTL-NLTT-1993-04-02, Xerox Palo Alto Research Center, Palo Alto, California.
9. Karttunen, Lauri, Chanod, Jean-Pierre, Grefenstette, Gregory and Schiller, Anne (1996) Regular Expressions for Language Engineering, In *Natural Language Engineering* 2 (4) 305–328.
10. Karttunen, Lauri and Gaál, Tamás and Kempe, André (1997) *Xerox Finite-State Tool*. Xerox Research Centre Europe, Grenoble, Maylan, France.
11. Kirschner, Zdenek (1994) CZECKER - a Maquette Grammar-Checker for Czech. In *The Prague Bulletin of Mathematical Linguistics 62*, Praha: Universita Karlova.
12. Sågvall Hein, Anna (1998) A Chart-Based Framework for Grammar Checking: Initial Studies. *The 11th Nordic Conference of Computational Linguistics*, 1998.
13. Skolverket (1992) *LEXIN: språklexikon för invandrare*. Nordsteds Förlag.
14. Tapanainen, Pasi (1997) Applying a Finite State Intersection Grammar. In Roche, Emmanuel and Schabes, Yves (eds.) *Finite State Language Processing*, MIT Press.
15. Vosse, Theodorus Gregorius (1994) *The Word Connection. Grammar-based Spelling Error Correction in Dutch*. Enschede: Neslia Paniculata.

Author Index

Lecture Notes in Computer Science

For information about Vols. 1–2493

please contact your bookseller or Springer-Verlag